MW01056878

The Fairchild Books DICTIONARY of INTERIOR DESIGN

The Fairchild Books DICTIONARY of INTERIOR DESIGN

4th Edition

MARK HINCHMAN

FAIRCHILD BOOKS
NEW YORK • LONDON • OXFORD • NEW DELHI • SYDNEY

FAIRCHILD BOOKS
Bloomsbury Publishing Inc
1385 Broadway, New York, NY 10018, USA
50 Bedford Square, London, WC1B 3DP, UK
29 Earlsfort Terrace, Dublin 2, Ireland

BLOOMSBURY, FAIRCHILD BOOKS and the Fairchild Books logo are trademarks of Bloomsbury Publishing Plc

First edition published 1983
Second edition published 2006
Third edition published 2014
This edition published 2022

Cover design by Louise Dugdale
Cover image: Living Coral color of the Year 2019. Leather texture © Shutterstock.

Library of Congress Cataloging-in-Publication Data
Names: Hinchman, Mark, author.
Title: The Fairchild Books dictionary of interior design / Mark Hinchman.
Description: Fourth edition. | New York : Fairchild Books, 2022. | Includes bibliographical references. |
Identifiers: LCCN 2020057276 | ISBN 9781501366710 (hardback) | ISBN 9781501365263 (paperback) | ISBN 9781501365164 (pdf)
Subjects: LCSH: Interior decoration–Dictionaries. | Decoration and ornament–Dictionaries. | Design services–Dictionaries.
Classification: LCC NK1165 .P4 2022 | DDC 747–dc23
LC record available at https://lccn.loc.gov/2020057276

ISBN: HB: 978-1-5013-6671-0

Typeset by Integra Software Services Pvt. Ltd.
Printed and bound in the United States of America

To find out more about our authors and books visit www.fairchildbooks.com and sign up for our newsletter.

contents

Icons next to some terms indicate that they are archival (∞, or infinity).

preface and acknowledgments

IN 2019, FAIRCHILD BOOKS decided to update all three of their dictionaries of the arts, and I was asked to attend to the 4th edition of *The Dictionary of Interior Design*. The bulk of the work for the present text occurred in the spring of 2020 during the global shutdown. It was an interesting time to be working on a general text about interior design. Many contemporary design topics, from new workplace design to home offices, took on new relevance as many offices lay empty for months, and families had to reconfigure their living quarters overnight to accommodate multiple people working, video conferencing, and children studying remotely. I am grateful that this publication was the major task I grappled with during this time. While I had plenty of time, my frazzled attention span was perfectly attuned to attending to the minutiae of definitions and biographical entries, with their demands for historical and technical precision. I was writing this from a location in America's heartland, Lincoln, Nebraska, and had numerous video conference calls with the editors in the New York/New Jersey area whose living and working circumstances were very different.

Martin Pegler (1923-2020) died shortly before the start of the pandemic. He wrote the initial *Dictionary of Interior Design* and had put it in my care for the 2014 third edition. Pegler specialized in store planning and visual merchandising, and the book he wrote covered those areas particularly well and had a sustained focus in residential design, with attention to European heritage, particularly of England and France. His first publications came before the time of computers and the internet. This, the fourth edition, is the second edition of the dictionary in the 21st century and continues the project which was started in 2014, which is to emphasize the commercial realm, and to attend to contemporary subjects such as new technologies, smart materials, the production process, digital fabrication, sustainability, wellness, and inclusive environments.

The worldwide shutdown of many commercial sectors brought renewed attention to the topics of remote working, telecommuting, proxemics, and hot desks. As we go to press, it is clear that the 21st-century interior environment has changed drastically and many of these changes are here to stay. More people work remotely, fewer people are physically present in offices, and many communications previously done in person now occur virtually. How construction sites operate has changed, and the healthcare, hospitality, and academic sectors of design have all faced unprecedented space planning challenges. The imperative for the design industry to look at all its practices in order to better safeguard the environment has never been more clear.

The Fairchild Books Dictionary of Interior Design covers history as well as the current condition. It is a comprehensive reference book of terms that relate to interior design and related fields. As it presents the vocabulary that is important to the interior design field, it makes a statement about what the discipline is now, what it has been, and where it is headed. The dictionary covers interior design and architecture and addresses multiple aspects of the industry, including structural and decorative features of interiors and their furnishings, technology, business practices, green design, and universal design. These topics are addressed through new vocabulary words for this edition that include *coworking*, *free address*, *lossy*, *prototyping*, and *raster image*. Interior design practitioners, students, academics, producers, and merchandisers—in other words, all consumers of interior design services and products—will find this a handy and richly illustrated reference. There is focus on commercial interiors, wellness, institutional, and hospitality facilities, as well as residential interiors. The global turn of the 21st century has made clear that it is important to continue to expand coverage of non-Western cultures. The design fields have been making strides in being more inclusive and that is represented in the terms of this edition. We have also added fifty new line drawings that are in addition to the over 700 existing images for terms old and new.

Debts incurred for this long-term project are many. At the University of Nebraska, the Undergraduate Creative Activities & Research Experience (UCARE) funded the highly capable research assistant Caroline Goertz, who assisted on tasks small and large. The research compiled by my colleague Kendra Locklear Ordia for our studio on greening the urban interior proved invaluable in revealing new design terms and understanding the concepts behind them. My thanks to the interior design program director Lindsey Ellsworth-Bahe for her support and, as always, the University of Nebraska Libraries, particularly the indefatigable Interlibrary Loan. At Fairchild Books, Acquisitions Editor Emily Samulski shepherded in the project, and once it was rolling, Art Development Editor Edie Weinberg and Editorial Assistant Jenna Lefkowitz have been indispensable with their attention to detail and the big picture.

The Publisher wishes to gratefully acknowledge and thank the editorial team involved in the publication of this book:

Senior Acquisitions Editor: Emily Samulski
Development Editor/Assistant Editor: Jenna Lefkowitz
Art Development Editor: Edie Weinberg
In-House Designer: Louise Dugdale
Production Manager: Ken Bruce
Project Manager: Deborah Maloney

The Publisher would also like to thank Graphic World for providing new illustrations for this edition.

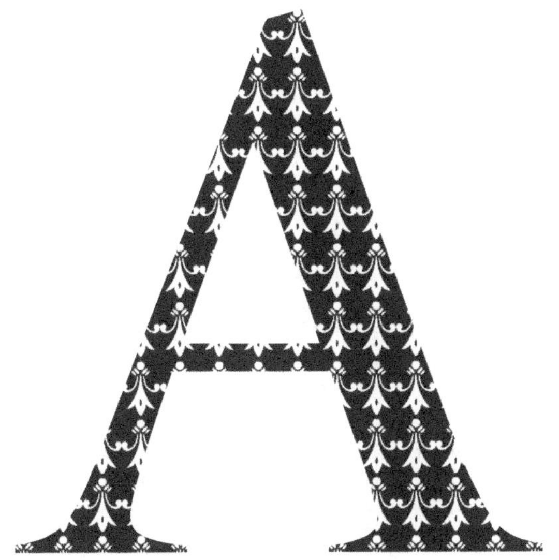

Aalto stool Simple stool designed by ALVAR AALTO in the early 1930s. Originally made of birch, its seat is a round disc of banded wood with three legs made of solid wood that has been sliced (kerfed), bent, and glued to the seat. Inexpensive copies are made of plywood. See *Designers and Architects.*

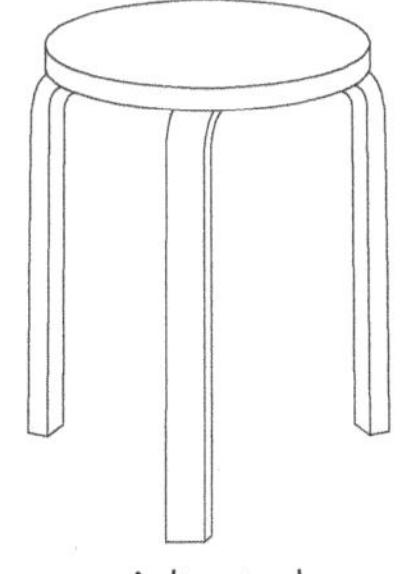

Aalto stool

abaca The technical name for manila hemp, a hard fiber prized for its tensile strength. Uses: woven matting, carpeting, wall covering, and for making rope. See *Table 2.*

abachi A wood. See AYOUS.

∞abacus The slab or pillow that forms the top of the capital of a column. In Greek Ionic, Roman Doric, and Tuscan classical orders, it may be square with a molded lower edge. In other orders, it may have concave sides with chamfered edges. The Gothic abacus is round or octagonal.

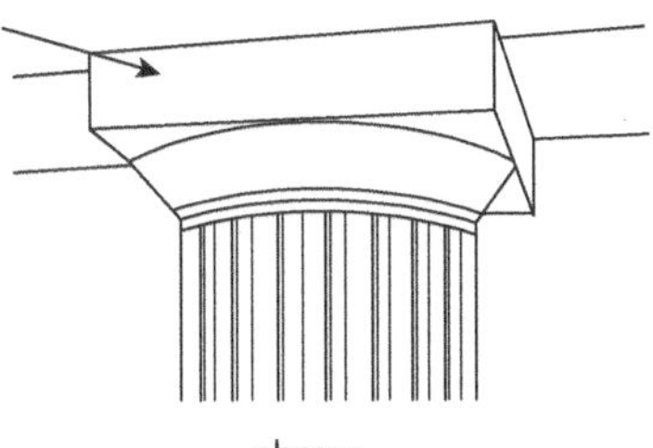

abacus

abattant (French) A drop-lid, or fall front, as in SECRÉTAIRE À ABATTANT, a drop-leaf secretary.

abbey A Christian monastery or convent.

ablutions fountain Water source outside of a mosque for ritual cleansing.

aboudikrou An African wood that resembles mahogany and SAPELE.

abrasion resistance The degree to which a fabric or floor covering resists wearing out from rubbing or applied friction.

absorption chiller Air-conditioning device that uses heat instead of mechanical energy, which reduces operating costs by using very little electricity but lowers the coefficient of performance.

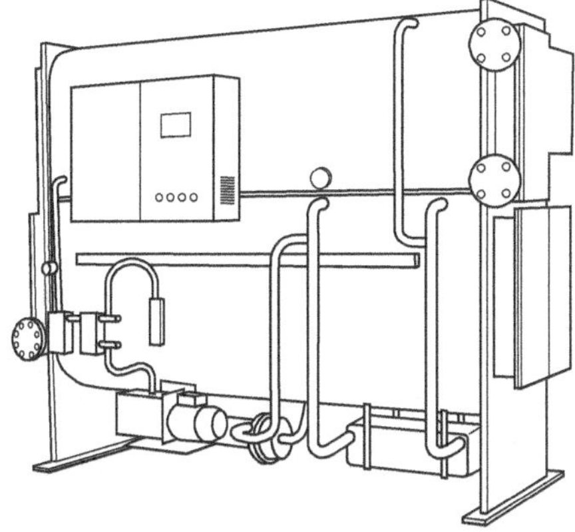

absorption chiller

abstract art An art form in which the artistic values reside in forms and colors rather than representational or recognizable objects.

abstract expressionism Art movement that explores the subconscious through rapid renderings of shapes and the free use of color. The English version is known as "action painting."

acacia A figured wood that varies from light brown to shades of red and green, found in Asia, Australia, and America. Similar to the American locust, it was used as veneer in French and English furniture-making in the 18th century. See BLACKWOOD.

acajou (French) See MAHOGANY.

acajou moé A fine-quality mahogany with wavelike markings and small dark spots in the grain, popular in the late Louis XVI period for tables and commodes.

acanthus (akanthos) leaf A carved or painted ornament that resembles the foliage of a plant native to Greece and Rome. A classical motif, it appears in the Gothic art, Renaissance, and neoclassical periods. The leaf appears in Corinthian and Composite capitals. The Greek design has pointed edges, while the Roman version is round and broad. In Byzantine and Romanesque decoration, the form is less delicate. In the Renaissance, the acanthus-and-tendril motif reaches its highest degree of refinement.

acanthus (akanthos) leaf

Acapulco chair Iconic 1950s Mexican lounge chair inspired by Mayan woven hammocks and made by an unknown designer; now made in multiple materials, colors, and forms.

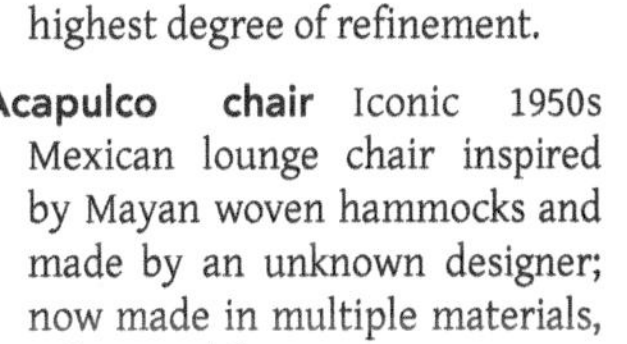

accent color A sharp, intense secondary color used for contrast and to add excitement to a palette.

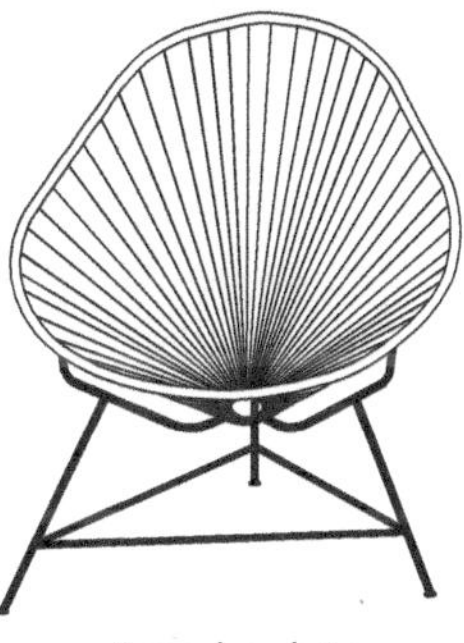

Acapulco chair

accent lighting A type of lighting that creates an emphasis or focus used to highlight a painting, objet d'art, sculpture, or architectural feature.

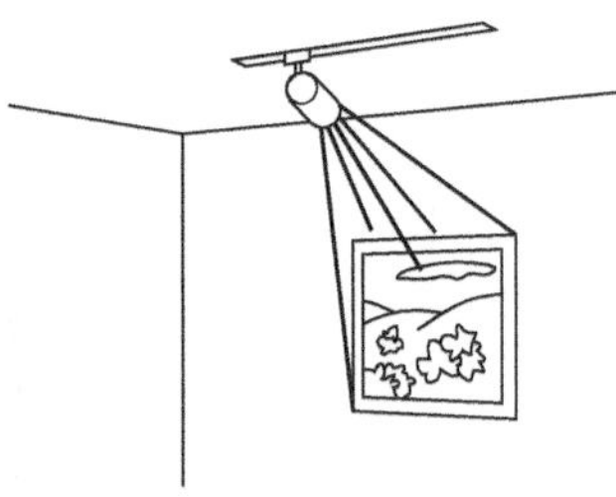

accent lighting

accent scheme A color palette built on a related, contrasting, or achromatic scheme. It may involve introducing an accent color or a neutral color to offset an established scheme and make it less predictable; or introducing a hue in a monochromatic scheme; or adding a small amount of a complement to an analogous or a monochromatic scheme.

accessible design Design that is in compliance with the Americans with Disabilities Act (ADA). Also called BARRIER-FREE DESIGN.

accessories The small items necessary to aesthetically complete a room, often with accents to the general color scheme. Ashtrays, vases, plants, lamps, books, pillows, pictures, and sculptures are typical accessories.

accotoir (French) The wood stile that extends from the frame of the chair seat upward to support the chair's arm. See ARM STUMP.

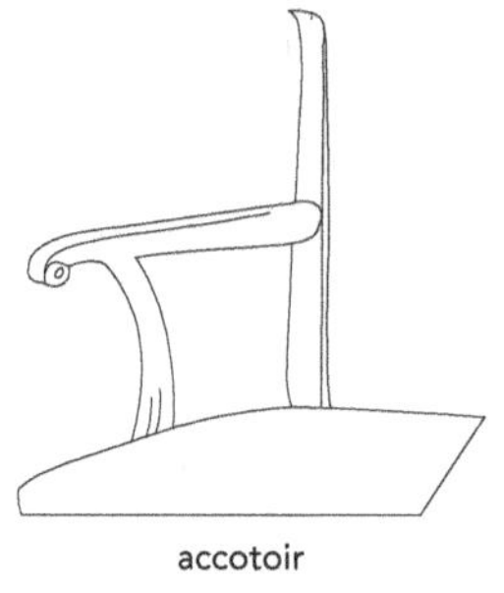

accotoir

acetate A generic name for a cellulose fiber. Textile fibers, yarns, threads, and fabrics made from these fibers are also called acetate. The fabric drapes and dyes well but has limited abrasion resistance and strength. See *Table 2.*

acetylation A chemical reaction that changes cellulose linters (cotton) into cellulose acetate. This reaction improves the heat and rot resistance of the fiber yet does not adversely affect the other desirable properties of cotton.

achech A fantasy animal, half lion and half bird, in ancient Egyptian art. See HIERACOSPHINX.

acorn A wood turning that resembles the fruit of the oak tree, used as a finial, drop pendant, or furniture foot in Jacobean furniture of the early 17th century in England.

acorn

acorn chair A 17th-century Jacobean oak chair with acorn-shaped pendants decorating the cross-rail of the back.

acoustical panels Panels made of sound-absorbing materials, covered in fabrics or vinyls, and used as dividers or sound deadeners. They may be equipped with "feet" to stand independently, applied directly to hard wall surfaces, or suspended from the ceiling.

acoustical tiles Rectangular panels, usually 12 inches by 12 inches (300 mm × 300 mm), made of pulped wood, fiberglass, compressed Styrofoam pellets, or mixtures of these materials. Used for quieting sounds in a room. Perforated tiles provide greater sound absorption. In areas where greater sound control is required, acoustical tiles may cover the walls as well.

acoustics The science of sound and sound reception, including the implementing of sound, the reinforcement of sound, and the controlling or reduction of sound transmission. See ACOUSTICAL PANELS and ACOUSTICAL TILES.

Acrilan A trademark for acrylic fiber composed of 85 percent or more acrylonitrile, a liquid derivative of natural gas and air. Acrilan fibers have stability, strength, and a luxurious wool-like feel. Acrilan fabrics hold a pressed crease and have characteristics similar to those of Orion carpets. Also used as a carpeting fiber.

∞acrolith A classic Greek statue with a wooden body, often sheathed in gold, and with heads, legs, and arms carved of marble.

∞acroteria (Greek, plural. ***acroterion,*** singular) Summit or extremity. In classical architecture, the flat pedestals at the apex and the lowest ends of a pediment. Used to hold carved ornaments or statues. The term is sometimes applied to the ornament itself, which resembles a stylized palmette leaf. In furniture, acroteria refers to the end blocks of the pediment top or to the central block in a broken pediment which might hold an urn, vase, or finial. See AKROTER.

acroteria

acrylics Synthetic polymer fibers made of natural materials: coal, air, water, limestone, petroleum, and natural gases. The fibers are strong and durable and resist sunlight and changing weather conditions. Also chosen for their insulating qualities, acrylic fibers result in soft, bulky, wool-like fabrics and carpets. See *Table 2* and *Table 3.*

Act of Parliament clock A mid-18th- to early-19th-century English hanging timepiece with a short trunk and a large wooden dial, without a glass cover, usually painted black and accented with gold numerals. The trunk design varied: oblong and paneled, bulbous, or fiddle-shaped. The overall measurement varied from 3 feet, 9 inches to 5 feet tall.

actuator The part of a device or machine that converts energy into motion. From 18th-century mechanical furniture to CNC routers, many objects need to create motion in order to operate. To power the motion, there are three primary sources of energy: electric, hydraulic, and pneumatic. This feature is present in analog manufacturing, digital fabrication, and robotics.

acuity Amount of electricity needed.

Adamesque English neoclassical design that resembles the work of the ADAM BROTHERS.

additive manufacturing (AM) The process that makes 3D printing possible. It was a transformative event in industrial production, as factory assembly started to move from analog to digital and from human to robot. This technical advancement was made possible with the widespread adoption of CAD. As the process unfolds, AM deposits material, layer on layer, in a precise way to create a desired object.

Adelphi (Greek) The trademark name of the Adam brothers of England, in the latter part of the 18th century. See ADAM BROTHERS.

admixtures Water-repellent or coloring agents added to mortar. Also any additives that speed up or retard the setting time.

adobe (Spanish) Sun-dried brick. Also the clay used to make sun-dried brick. A building material in Mexico, Central America, and the Southwest U.S.

∞aecicrames The heads or skulls of rams used as decorative elements in classic Greek and Roman sculpture.

∞aedicule (Latin, *aedicula*) A small temple. A niche into which a statue was placed. A pediment, resting on two columns, usually enframed the opening.

aedicule

aesthetic finish A surface effect that improves the appearance or hand of the fabric.

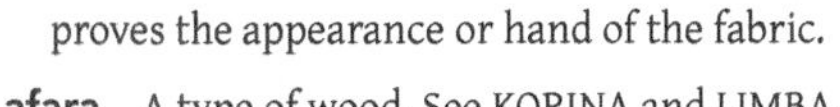

afara A type of wood. See KORINA and LIMBA.

agate ware Originally an 18th-century pottery produced by Wedgwood and others in England. The finish resembled agate or quartz.

Age of Mahogany The period of interior and furniture design in England lasting from approximately 1710 to 1765. Designers and clients favored the red-hued wood; many Georgian and Chippendale pieces were made of mahogany.

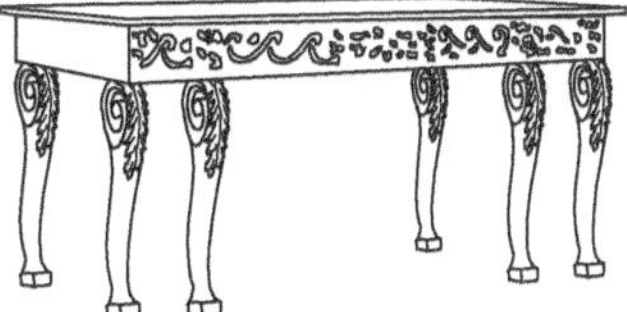

Age of Mahogany console

Age of Oak The period of the English Renaissance (*c.* 1500–1660) when the durable wood was prominently used for furniture, interior paneling, wainscoting, and so on. It encompasses the Tudor, Elizabethan, Jacobean, and Cromwellian periods.

Age of Oak bed

Age of Revivals The 19th century was largely a time of revivals of past styles for architecture, interiors, art, and decorative arts. The Classic, Renaissance, Rococo, Gothic, Egyptian, and Turkish revivals followed and overlapped one another. See VICTORIAN.

Age of Satinwood The elegant period in England from about 1765 to 1800, when cabinetmakers and designers favored this light, delicate-toned wood for furniture. The Adam brothers used it extensively, as did Hepplewhite, Shearer, and Sheraton. See SATINWOOD.

Age of Walnut The Restoration, Stuart, William and Mary, and Queen Anne periods in England, which ran from about 1660 to 1714. Walnut was the dominant material for furniture and interiors.

Age of Walnut secretary

aggregate A type of stone manufactured in combination with other substances, such as resin and epoxy.

agile working An approach to 21st-century economic activity, summed up as "anytime, anyplace, anywhere." This affects how designers work, how construction projects are managed, and how workplaces are designed. In this flexible occupational mindset, work is an activity, not a place, where a group of processes are rendered possible with connectivity. Technology is leveraged to enhanced communication, and spatial boundaries are bypassed to avoid constraints and achieve maximum adaptability. There is a high amount of collaboration and limited formal control.

agrifiber Fibrous material made from recovered agricultural waste that is used to create biocomposite agriboard, a lightweight, strong, and environmentally friendly alternative for building materials.

aigrette (French) Egret, a beautifully plumed bird. Also a decorative feather or plume.

air brick A manufactured masonry unit perforated with holes, allowing air to enter and pass through a wall.

Airfoam Goodyear's trademark name for rubber, foam, and latex material used for cushions and padding.

aisle (Latin, *alae*, wings) A passageway usually giving access to seats. See ALAE.

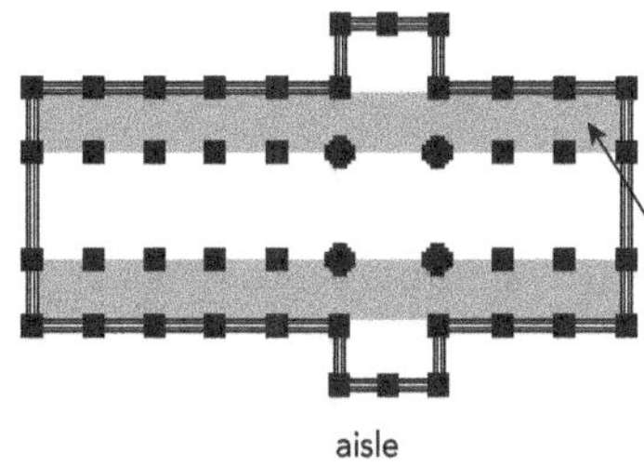

aisle

ajouré A design produced by piercing holes in a set pattern in ceramics, wood, metal, etc. Also used in parchment lampshades, the pierced design has a brilliant, jewel-like effect when the lamp is lit. See PIERCED WORK.

∞akanthos See ACANTHUS LEAF.

akari lamps Folding ricepaper Japanese lanterns of varied shape and size. Many exciting lanterns were designed by ISAMU NOGUCHI in the mid 1950s, based on traditional designs but adapted to modern use. See *Designers and Architects.*

akari lamp

ako See CHEN CHEN.

∞akroter An ornamental finish for the apex of a gable. On Greek and Roman structures, the akroter, which decorated the top angle of the pediment, was usually a variation of the palmette ornament, although griffins, figures, and other sculptured devices were also used. See ACROTERIA.

akume A wood. See BUBINGA.

alabaster A fine-textured, compact, marble-like mineral, a variety of sulfate of lime or gypsum (milky white or semitranslucent), used for ornaments and sculpture.

∞alae (Latin, wings) Recesses opening out from the central atrium in a classic Roman house. See ATRIUM.

"A" lamp An incandescent lamp used in residential settings. Typical wattages are 25W, 40W, 60W, 75W, 100W, and 150W.

Alcazar A magnificent walled residence built in Seville, Spain, in the middle of the 14th century, noteworthy for its blend of Gothic and Moresque, or Islamic, motifs.

alcove A recess in a room, or a small room attached to a larger one, often to accommodate a bed, piano, etc. Also a niche for a statue or a seat. Originally a Spanish concept: a private area separated from the main room by an ESTRADE or row of columns.

alcove cupboard An 18th-century English corner cupboard, often part of the paneling of the room. See ENCOIGNURE and QUOIN.

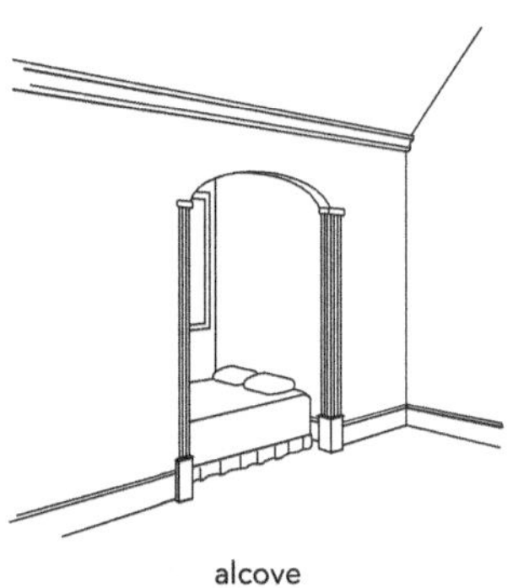
alcove

alder An American hardwood that has a maple-like figure but can be stained to imitate mahogany or walnut. Because of its strength, it is ideal for plywood cores. In 18th-century England, the wood was used for country or provincial furniture. See *Table 5.*

Alençon lace A decorative fabric with a solid design outlined in cord on a sheer net ground.

Alençon lace

Alhambra A citadel and palace, a masterpiece of 13th-century Spanish-Moslem art, near Granada in Spain, begun in 1248 and enlarged in 1279 and 1306. Much of the decoration is in the tile and stamped plaster with exquisite geometric patterns, intricate arabesques, and Arabic characters. For the unusual ceiling treatment in the *Hall of the Abencerrages,* see STALACTITE. See also MORESQUE.

Alhambra

Alhambra vases Tall, amphora-shaped containers of luster earthenware done in the Hispano-Moresque style, made in Valencia in the 11th century, usually decorated with arabesques and Arabic inscriptions.

alkyd paint Paints containing a synthetic resin used as the vehicle for the paint pigment. Alkyd paints can be thinned with turpentine or mineral spirits, and they have replaced oil paints to a large extent.

allegory A symbolic representation, such as the sun for Louis XIV, a dolphin for the Dauphin, or a fearless leader represented as an eagle or a lion.

allegory

alloy A new metal created from a mixture of two or more metals. An alloy has the characteristics of the original metals but also has new qualities. See BRONZE.

∞almery Originally a cupboard set into the thickness of a wall of a medieval structure. Later, a cupboard that contained the portion of food set aside for servants and pensioners. See AMBRY.

almon A Philippine wood used for veneer. Its color varies from tan to a soft reddish tone, and it usually has an interrupted stripe figure. Almon is sometimes sold as white lauan.

almond A two-pointed, oval-shaped pendant of cut glass or crystal used to embellish a chandelier.

alpaca A hard, shiny-surfaced fabric made of wool from a llama-like animal found in the mountains of Chile and Peru. Its wool is long, fine, and usually dark. The cloth may be woven completely of the alpaca wool or mixed with sheep wool, cotton, or silk. See *Table 2.*

altarpiece A decorative feature, such as a screen or painting, that appears above the back of the altar in a church.

aluminum A light, strong, silvery blue metal that resists oxidation and tarnishing. As hard as zinc, it is malleable, can be made into threadlike wires, and is a good heat conductor. Used for furniture frames and outdoor furniture.

altarpiece

AM Acronym for ADDITIVE MANUFACTURING.

amaranth A wine-red or dark violet mahogany wood of Central and South America, especially Brazil and the Guianas. Its brilliant, exotic coloring is prone to fade when exposed to light. A hard, strong wood also called violet wood, purpleheart, and bois violet, it was popular during the latter part of the 18th century in France for veneer and MARQUETRY.

ambience (French) The overall effect of an interior; its "look" or the general atmosphere. The effect created by the combination of color, line, form, textures, lighting, decorative items, and accessories.

ambience lighting or ambient lighting Atmospheric lighting using soft lights with shadows to create an effect rather than for better visibility. See INDIRECT LIGHTING and SECONDARY LIGHTING.

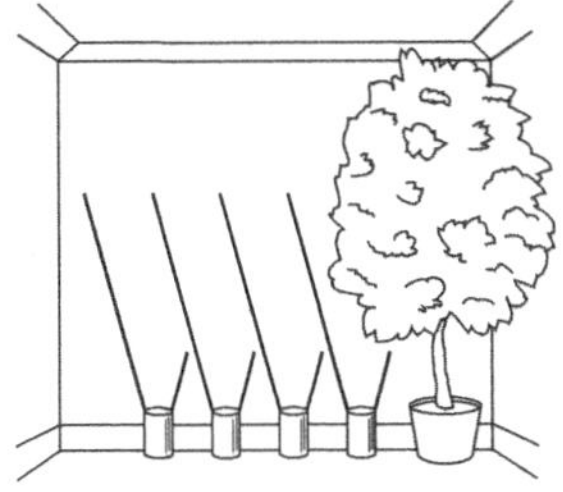

ambience lighting

amboyna A rich golden brown to orange wood, mottled and marked with a "bird's-eye" figure. Adam and Hepplewhite used the wood as a veneer in the second half of the 18th century.

∞ambry (Latin) Chest or cupboard. In ecclesiastic work, the ambry or aumbry was a small cupboard that held the sacred vessels, books, and altar linens. Also called almery.

ambry

ambulantes (French) Small, portable serving tables, such as tea tables. This type of furniture became popular in the Louis XV period in France. See RAFRAÎCHISSOIR or SERVANTE and SERVITEUR FIDÈLE.

ambulatory A walking area. It particularly refers to the circulation around an apse in a church or cloister. The ambulatory is indicated on the plan for the Chartres Cathedral in France. Often curved.

ambulatory

American Chippendale The furniture American craftsmen made in the colonies in the mid-to-late 18th century, based on Queen Anne and Georgian designs as well as those in THOMAS CHIPPENDALE books. Many of these pieces were produced in Philadelphia, Pennsylvania, and are sometimes called Philadelphia Chippendale. See *Designers and Architects.*

American Eagle Period The early part of the Federal Period in America, immediately after the Revolutionary War (late 18th, early 19th century), when the bird was a popular motif on mirrors, the bases of couches, and other furniture. The eagle also appeared on finials, standards, and the exteriors of public buildings. See FEDERAL PERIOD.

American Empire The style of furnishing and design popular in the United States from about 1820 to 1840. The French Empire style and the later Sheraton designs were interpreted in crotch-grain mahogany veneers, cherrywood, curly maple, and maple. Duncan PHYFE was the leading designer of the period, and acanthus leaves, pineapples, cornucopias, and stencil gilding were important decorative motifs and techniques. See BUTCHER FURNITURE. See *Designers and Architects.*

American Empire mirror See CONSTITUTION MIRROR.

American Queen Anne furniture See AMERICAN CHIPPENDALE.

Americans with Disabilities Act (ADA) Legislation that went into effect in 1990 and is maintained by the Department of Justice. The act mandates that public spaces be accessible to all individuals regardless of their physical abilities.

amilan A Japanese synthetic fiber of the nylon type. See NYLON.

amorino (Italian, little love) A small cupid or cherub used as a carved or painted decoration in the Italian Renaissance period, as well as in Louis XV ornament. The Adam brothers used the motif in wall-panel designs and ceiling decorations. These elements were often painted by such artists as Pergolesi and Zucchi.

amphitheater or amphitheatre An oval or circular structure with seats and steplike ledges rising above and behind each other and surrounding a central open space, stage, or arena.

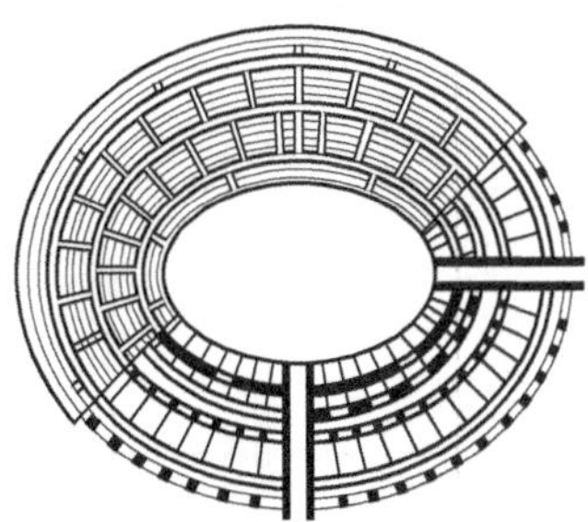

amphitheater or amphitheatre

amphora A large, two-handled earthenware vase of ancient Greece, with a narrow neck and an ovoid body. It is often praised for its beautiful proportions.

anaglyph A type of relief sculpture or ornament with more depth than a bas-relief but less depth than a high relief.

anaglypha A metal urn, vase, or vessel with raised or relief ornamentation.

anaglypha

∞**anaglypta** (Greek, raised ornament) Raised ornaments were made in gesso and plaster compounds. They are now produced in many materials and are available in paintable wallpapers. The three-dimensional pieces are applied to walls and ceilings to simulate a carved, bas-relief effect. See CARTON-PIERRE.

anaglypta

analogous colors Colors that are next to each other on the color wheel; for example, orange, red-orange, and red are analogous to each another; and yellow, green-yellow, and green are analogous to each other.

anchor bolt A long metal device used for reinforcing cornices and pinnacles to ensure greater stability.

ancona (Italian) A group of pictures, or one major painting, formally arranged. Also a recess or niche architecturally framed and used as the setting for a sculpture.

ancones The brackets used on either side of a door or opening capped with a cornice, serving to support the cornice. See CONSOLE.

ancona

ancones

andirons (French, chenets) A pair of upright metal supports with a transverse rod that holds logs for burning on an open hearth. Also called fire dogs.

∞**andron** The area of a Greek house reserved for men.

∞**androsphinx** In Egyptian art, a lion with a human head like that of the great sphinx at Giza. See also CRIOSPHINX and SPHINX.

androsphinx

angel bed An 18th-century French sleeping platform with a canopy that extends partially over the bed. There are no front pillars, back pillars, or brackets that support the canopy. Only the headboard's posts support the canopy, and the side draperies continue down to the floor and are pulled back at either side. See LIT D'ANGE.

angle iron A metal bar that forms a right angle or L shape. Usually made of rolled, mild steel.

Anglo-Japanese A style of furniture and decorative arts created by English designers who were inspired by Japan; related to JAPONISME.

Anglophile One who is enamored of all things English. Anglophile designers are especially interested in 18th-century English furniture, such as QUEEN ANNE, and 19th-century ARTS AND CRAFTS pieces.

angora A yarn made from the fleece of the angora sheep, used in weaving mohair. See ALPACA and MOHAIR. See also *Table 2.*

aniline dyes Any dyes chemically obtained from aniline or other coal-tar derivatives.

animal couchant foot A furniture leg or support that resembles an animal lying down. Found in ancient Egyptian, Greek, and Roman furniture and successfully revived in the early 19th century.

ankh An Egyptian symbol for life and prosperity.

ankh

annealing A method of slowly cooling off heated glass or metal to decrease its brittleness.

annulet A ring. One of the fillets around the lower part of the Greek Doric capital. Also a band of molding around a Norman column, or the ring of molding joining a group of column shafts in Gothic architecture.

anodized aluminum The lightweight metal that has been coated to give it a sheen and a smooth feel. See ANODIZING.

anodizing The process of coating metal with a hard, protective oxide film by means of an electrochemical treatment.

∞**anta** A projecting pier (like a pilaster) placed behind a column at the end of a side wall of a Greek temple. The base and capital differ from those of the column. "Anta" may also refer to the short wall that partially or wholly encloses the side of a portico. Columns between the antae are "in antis."

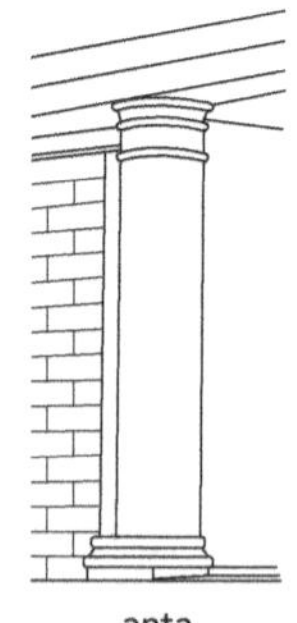

anta

∞antefix An upright, conventionalized, fanlike ornament that resembles a spreading leaf. It was originally used in ancient Greek and Roman decoration to conceal the end of a roof tile.

antefix

antepagmenta Molded jambs on either side of an opening or door. The over-door and lintel moldings are called the "supercilia."

∞anthemion (Greek, flower) A classical Greek and Roman decoration; a conventionalized honeysuckle, flower, or leaf ornament that radiates from a single point. Used to enhance CYMA RECTA moldings, it was a popular motif during the French Empire period in the early 19th century.

antepagmenta

anthemion

antimacassar A small textile, often lace, used to prevent parts of upholstered furniture from being soiled by the macassar hair dressing (an oil) that Victorian men favored. A mid-19th-century favorite, it became a symbol of gentility and elegance. Matching doilies protected the arm rests.

antique A collectible piece of furniture or other object that comes from a previous period. Usually 100 years old or older.

antique finish A surface technique used to give a material an aged look; an artificially created patina. A darker shade of paint or stain may be applied over a lighter tone and then rubbed off, or a lighter tone may be used over darker wood. Wood can be "antiqued" by artificial weathering, distressing, and gouging.

Antron A trademark name for a nylon fiber originally created by DuPont that is tough, is abrasion-resistant, and has built-in static control. Used to loom carpets of various textures and patterns.

ao dai Usually means the traditional national dress of Vietnam, particularly when worn by women, but can also refer to the textile from which it is made, when used for interior applications.

∞apophyge (Greek, flying off) The slight concave curve or sweep at the top and bottom of the shaft of a column. It does not appear in the Greek Doric column.

appartement de parade (French) The room of a home that is meant to be seen. A reception room, used for public purposes.

applewood An American fruitwood used for provincial furniture. See *Table 5.*

applied molding A geometric-shaped embellishment applied to the face of furniture to create a paneled effect. Also called Jacobean ornament, it was popular in the late-17th-century English cabinet and cupboard designs.

appliqué (1) (French) A wall bracket, sconce, or candelabrum on a wall. See GIRANDOLE and SCONCE. (2) (French) A shape cut out and sewn or pasted onto the surface of another material, as in a decorative trim.

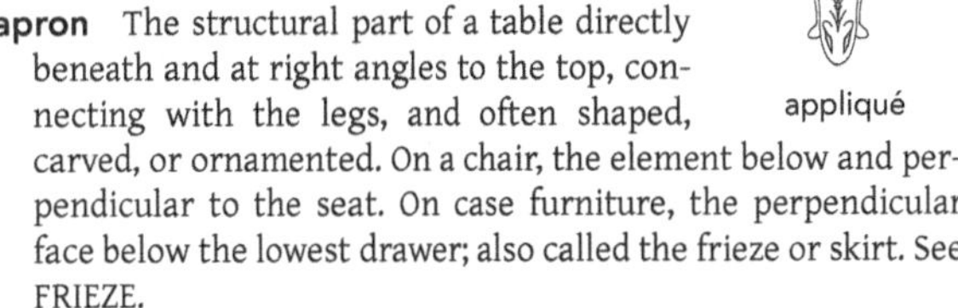

appliqué

apron The structural part of a table directly beneath and at right angles to the top, connecting with the legs, and often shaped, carved, or ornamented. On a chair, the element below and perpendicular to the seat. On case furniture, the perpendicular face below the lowest drawer; also called the frieze or skirt. See FRIEZE.

apse The semicircular or angular extension at the east end of a Christian church. It is typical of basilica plan churches. See NAVE and TRANSEPT.

apron

apse

aquatint A form of intaglio etching that produces tones and renders a transparent effect similar to watercolor. It was first used by the artist Paul Sand, but Goya is considered the greatest aquatinter. See ENGRAVING.

aqueduct A Roman elevated channel (often arcaded) for transporting water, relying on gravity. Engineered for pure function, the structure's aesthetics were admired as well.

arabesque (Arabian) The complex ornamental designs used by the Moors, whose religious beliefs eschewed the representation of animal forms. The designs were based on plant growth fancifully intertwined with lines and geometric patterns. In Greek, Roman, and Renaissance art, arabesques appear in carvings, paintings, and inlay work, where plant and animal forms are combined in intertwining vertical patterns. Islamic arabesques are mostly geometric and nonrepresentational.

arbor A framework, sometimes latticed, used as a support for vines. See TRELLISWORK.

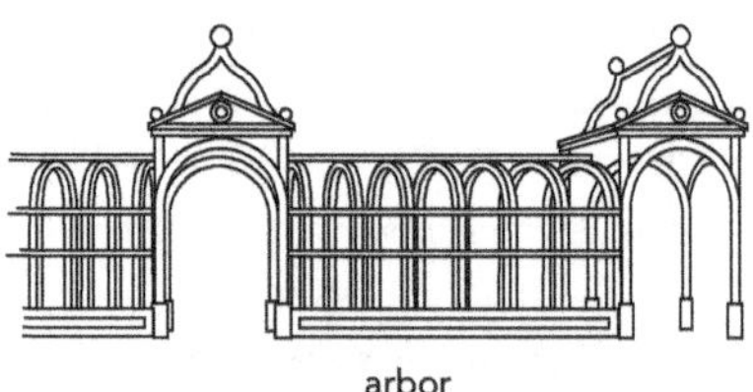
arbor

arbraum A red ocher material used to color mahogany.

arca (Spanish) A storage chest of the early Renaissance period.

arcade A series of adjoining arches with their supporting columns or piers.

arcade arcaded panel

arcaded back A furniture vertical element with a series of arches between the top rail and the seat. It is a compositional strategy more commonly associated with buildings that nonetheless is found on some pieces of furniture. A Louis XVI motif, Sheraton in England favored it in his late-18th-century designs.

arcaded panel A popular motif in early English Renaissance woodwork. The field or face of a piece of furniture is ornamented with small piers that support arches. Also used on chests in the French Renaissance.

arch A curved structural device that spans an opening. It may span the space between two walls, columns, or piers; it can be flattened, ornamental, or structural. The inner face of the element is the "intrados," and the exterior face is the "extrados." It also appears on furniture. See INTRADOS, EXTRADOS, and KEYSTONE.

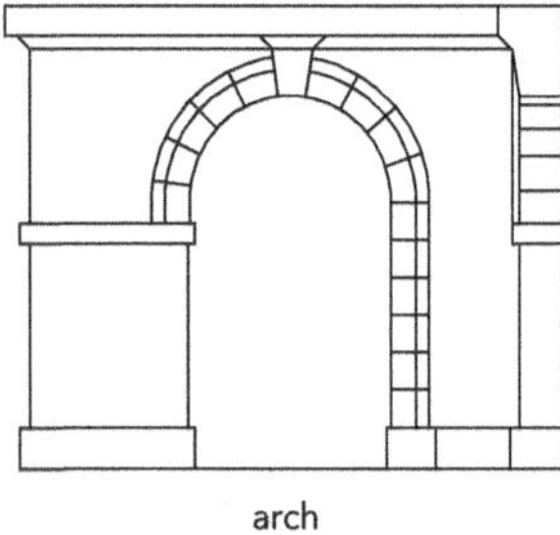
arch

arch brick The wedge-shaped construction units that constitute the structural device when it is made of multiple parts. See VOUSSOIR.

∞**archebane-couchette** (French) A 16th-century Renaissance furnishing that is a combined coffre and bench. The slight upward projections of the sides can form armrests or a headrest. See COFFRE.

arched molding A simple, undecorated half-round convex embellishment.

arched stretcher An arc-shaped or hooped connection between the legs of tables, chairs, or case furniture in the English Restoration period. It was introduced into England from Spain, where it was popular in the 17th century. See RISING STRETCHERS.

arched stretcher

architect (Greek, master builder) The designer, detailer, and often the engineer of buildings and other structures.

Architects' period Term for the furniture and decoration of 18th-century England, dominated by architects: Christopher Wren, James Gibbs, William Kent, Isaac Ware, and the Adam brothers. Their work featured architectural motifs and concepts, including classical detailing.

architect's table A combination DRAWING TABLE and desk with an adjustable lid that lifts up to make an inclined work surface. An 18th-century English innovation.

architect's table

architectural lighting Built-in fixtures considered essential parts of a design; e.g., an illumination plan that includes fixtures set into the ceiling in chosen positions. In contrast to freestanding movable fixtures.

architectural terra-cotta Machine-extruded or hand-molded, hard-burned clay building blocks, usually larger than bricks. May be plain, decorated, glazed, or unglazed.

architecture The art and science of designing and building edifices for human use. John Ruskin defined it as "the art which so disposes and adorns the edifices raised by man—that the sight of them contributes to his mental health, power and pleasure." John Ruskin. *The Seven Lamps of Architecture.* London: Dover, 1989 [orig. 1849].

architrave In architecture, the lintel; in the classical entablature, the lowest of three main divisions. The architrave supports the frieze, rests directly on the column, and spans the space between columns. A molding around a door may be called an architrave molding.

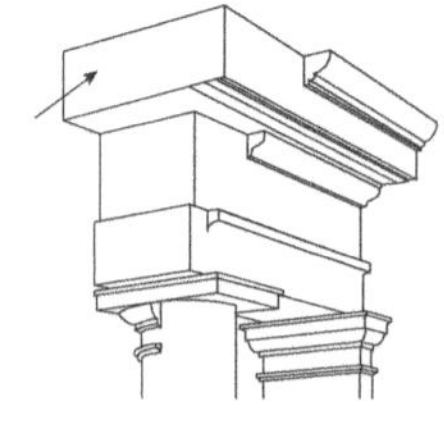
architrave

archivolt The ornamentation or moldings, or both, on the face of an arch. An architrave molding applied to an arch. See ARCHITRAVE.

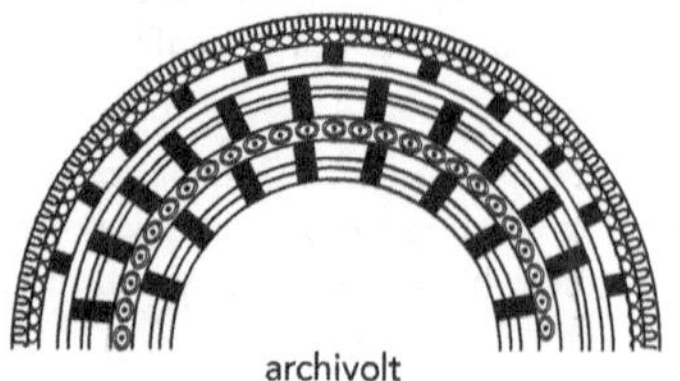
archivolt

arch lamp A floor or table light fixture with the light source (the lamp or bulb) a distance away from the base; i.e., the bulb and its housing are cantilevered, being at the far end of an arc that is connected to a weighted base.

arch rib The projecting band on the edge of the circular structural device in a ceiling or vaulting. They appear in a series in a barrel vault.

structure with arch rib

arch rib roof A 19th-century CAST-IRON girder construction technique. The protruding elements distribute the roof thrusts downward.

arcuate Arched or archlike. See ARCH.

arcuated architecture Architectural style or buildings that emphasize the arch, including Roman, Romanesque, Gothic, and Renaissance, for example.

Ardabil rug Originally a Caucasian design with geometric figures, the traditional designs have either a single, central medallion surrounded by characteristic figures or a central design of three diamonds. The background is usually ivory or a combination of strong, vivid colors in which red, green, blue, and salmon are predominant.

ardish An East Indian form of decoration. Bits of colored glass embedded in the ceiling or wall plaster create a sparkling effect.

area rug A floor covering, sometimes rectangular, used to highlight one section or area of a room. Usually patterned, more decorative, and more highly colored than wall-to-wall broadloom.

area wall A brick or stone partition surrounding a designated space. Also, the vertical element around basement windows below grade.

arena A theater configuration in which the audience is on all sides of the performance area. Also called "in the round." Commonly used for sporting events.

argamasse A West African form of WHITEWASH. A light plaster coating made of sand, water, calcium in the form of seashells, and pulverized brick material.

Argand lamp A light fixture invented by the Swiss chemist Aimé Argand in 1783. The device had a round wick with provisions for introducing air around the outside of the wick. This increased the draft and produced a brighter flame.

arkwright A late Gothic term for cabinetmakers and their products, which were usually more like carpentry and joinery than fine cabinetry.

∞**armarium** A bookcase or cupboard near the entrance to a church in the CLOISTER of a monastery.

armchair A seat with rests or upper-body appendage supports as distinguished from an armless side or pull-up chair. Armchairs entered popular use in the late 17th century. See CACQUETEUSE.

armoire (French) A large, movable clothes wardrobe or closet, originally used to store armor. See GARDEROBE.

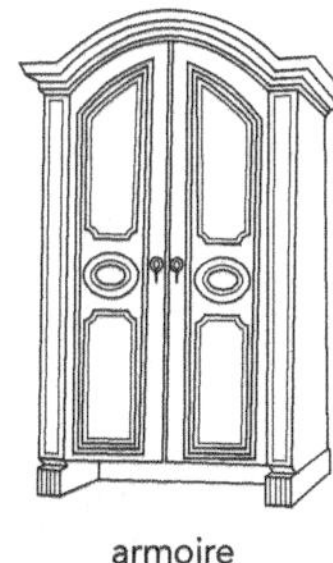

armoire

armoire à deux corps (French) A Renaissance cupboard having two parts. The lower part, originally only a supporting base, functioned as a larger cupboard, with a smaller cupboard set on top. The French equivalent of the English highboy. See BEAUFAIT.

arm pads Partial upholstery on the wooden horizontals of a chair, which serve as cushioned places of repose. See (French) MANCHETTES.

arm stump The vertical element, above the seat, that supports the front part of a chair arm. It may be a turned, carved, or shaped piece of wood. See ACCOTOIR.

armure A raised satin (nonreversible) pattern on a fabric with a rep background. The pattern usually consists of small, isolated, conventional motifs that form an allover design. Originally a fabric woven with a small interlaced design of chain armor, used during the Crusades in the 11th and 12th centuries.

Arnel A trademark name for cellulose acetate yarns and fibers, originally produced by the Celanese Corporation. It drapes well, is soft in hand, is colorfast, and holds its shape.

arras A Gothic tapestry used as a wall hanging, typically with figures as part of a design that incorporated precious metals. They were produced in Arras, France, in the 14th and 15th centuries.

arras

arris In architecture and interiors, the sharp edge produced by two surfaces forming an angle less than 90°. The sharp edge between two adjoining concave flutings of a column shaft.

arrow A slender shaft with a triangular pointed tip at one end and a feathered end at the back, used as a decorative motif in the Classical Revival periods, including the Louis XVI, Directoire, Empire, and Biedermeier.

arrow back Name given to chairs with three or more ARROW SPINDLES in back. Seen in the work of Sheraton, American Federal designers, and in some WINDSOR CHAIRS.

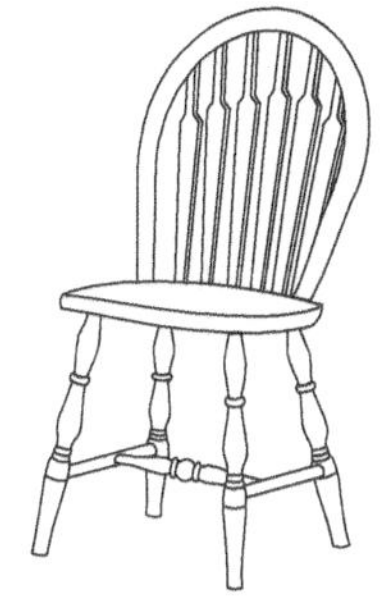

arrow spindle chair

arrow spindle A decorative flattened vertical with a tip that resembles the pointy weapons shot with a bow; used in the chairbacks of Sheraton, American Federal designers, and in some WINDSOR CHAIRS to support the top rail.

Art Deco A decorative style that started in France in 1925 and featured luxurious materials and rectilinear forms. Pieces were often made by hand, and the designs made stylized references to classicism and Egyptian works. The versions that spread around the world in the 1930s increasingly took inspiration from streamlined forms of the transportation industry. See ART MODERNE.

arte povera (poor man's art) (Italian) An 18th-century form of decorating furniture similar to the French DÉCOUPAGE. Engraved prints were hand-colored and applied to wooden furniture in imitation of painted court furniture.

artesonado Moorish woodwork or joinery, usually made of Spanish cedar. The wood used for paneling, ceilings, and doors was mostly left in its natural state but was painted or gilded.

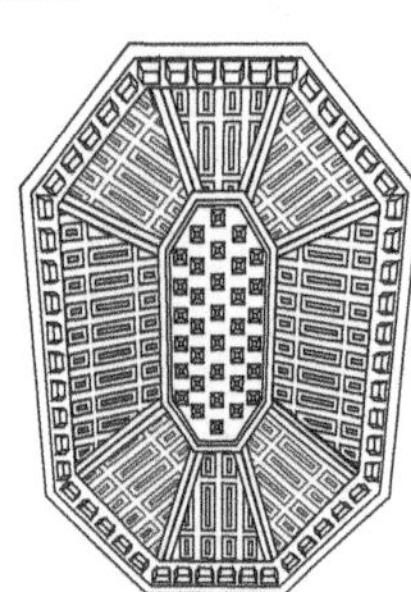
artesonado

artifact An object made by human efforts, such as a carving, a vessel, an ornament, or a tool. A designed object in contrast to a natural one.

artisan A skilled worker in an industrial art, e.g., cabinetmaker or weaver.

Art Moderne A decorative style in furniture and decoration from the 1930s–1950s that relied less on historical forms and more on shapes inspired by industrial production. A decorative strand of Modernism.

Art Nouveau The "new art" that started in Belgium and France in the 1890s and was a reaction against Victorian historicism. It was a style of decoration that used patterns of twisting plant forms based on nature and was strongly influenced by Japanese and Gothic art forms. Aubrey Beardsley, Victor Horta, Louis Comfort Tiffany, and Hector Guimard were important players. The trend quickly spread throughout Europe and eventually the world, although its creative forces were largely spent by 1910.

Art Nouveau cabinet

Arts and Crafts movement The works and principles of a group of late-19th-century artists in England emphasizing the design of everyday objects based on preindustrial methods and artistic collaboration. A reaction against the industrial revolution and Victorian eclecticism, its followers made no distinction between high art and craftwork. See PRE-RAPHAELITE BROTHERHOOD. See MORRIS, WILLIAM; and WEBB, PHILIP in *Designers and Architects.*

Arundel marbles A collection of Greek and Roman statues and fragments that belonged to the Earl of Arundel in England during the reign of Charles I (first half of the 17th century).

∞Asbestall A trademark name for fire-resistant fabrics woven of asbestos and nylon yarns.

asbestos A nonmetallic mineral fiber that is non-combustible but carcinogenic. Woven with other yarns and materials, the addition of the fibrous mineral results in flameproof materials.

∞asbestos cement A fire-resistant material made of Portland cement and non-combustible fibers; its use is now banned.

Asceticism The practice of rigorous self-denial for religious purposes; associated with restraint and simplicity in design.

ash A handsomely figured blond wood with a pleasing texture. It takes dark stains well and is hard and difficult to work. See *Table 5.*

ash, English A native wood of the British Isles sometimes called olive burl. It has an unusual lateral grain known as fiddleback or ram's horn. It was used for country-made or provincial furniture in the 18th century. See OLIVE WOOD.

ashlar Finished, or hewn, large pieces of stone used for exterior walls.

ashram A religious retreat or community, often for spiritual instruction. Typically located in a natural setting.

aspen An American wood of the poplar family, light-colored and silky-textured with light brown stripes. The crotch cut is extremely decorative. A soft, easy-to-work-with wood that tools well and has a natural sheen. Similar to European white POPLAR.

asphalt tile A synthetic floor covering material, nonporous, easy to maintain, fire-resistant, and fade-resistant. It can be ruined by oil, paint, grease, and organic solvents; a grease-proof asphalt tile is available. Affected by extreme temperature changes, it becomes soft under extreme heat and brittle under extreme cold. It can be laid on wood or concrete floors, and it comes in a multitude of colors and patterns, in assorted sizes of squares or strips, and varies in thickness from 1/8 inch to 3/8 inch (3.175 mm–9.525 mm).

aspidistra stand A late-19th-century plant base, usually a tripod made of bamboo, three to four feet in height (91 cm–122 cm), and reinforced near the bottom with stretchers. The open top of the small table sported a flowerpot, often with the popular Asian flowering plant.

Assyrian The art form of an ancient civilization contemporary with ancient Egypt (*c.* 1275–538 B.C.E.). The winged bull, the lion, and the eagle are typical motifs. The first true arch was developed here. Glazed tile and bricks were used in building because stones were scarce. Not to be confused with the modern nation of Syria. See BABYLONIA and MESOPOTAMIA.

Assyrian relief

aster carving A decorative relief of three flowers on the central panel of Connecticut chests made in the 17th and 18th centuries. Crafted sunflowers that project from their background also appeared.

astragal In architecture, a small torus molding that is semicircular in section. When decorated with beads or olive or laurel berries, it is called a barquette, chaplet, or bed molding. In furniture, it is the small convex molding used on the edge of an overlapping door of a cabinet, chest, secretary, etc. to keep dust out. See TORUS.

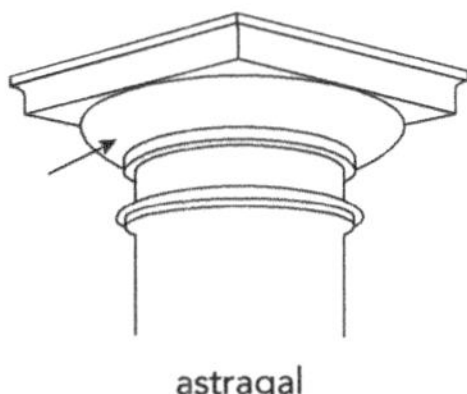
astragal

astrakhan cloth A heavy-pile fabric with curled loops that simulates the caracul lambskin fur. Originally associated with the Russian city on the Volga River.

astral lamp An early-19th-century oil light fixture with the burner set on a swinging tubular arm positioned lower than the fuel reservoir. Made of brass, cast-iron, silver plate, or china and sometimes adorned with prisms. They were usually equipped with an Argand burner. See ARGAND LAMP.

asymmetrical The opposite of symmetrical. Unequal. Not evenly proportioned or balanced. Asymmetry was a favorite decorative line device of the Rococo and Art Nouveau periods.

atelier (French) A studio or workshop, usually of a designer, artist, or artisan.

athénienne (French) A small tripod table of the Louis XVI and Empire periods. Sometimes used as a basin stand.

atlantes Full- or half-relief male figures used in place of columns to support an entablature or in place of furniture legs to support chests, tabletops, etc. The atlantes are male versions of the caryatids although less common; they were popular in the Renaissance. See CARYATIDS.

atlantes

atrium In classical Roman and contemporary architecture, a central room or courtyard of a home, with a central opening in the roof, either open to the sky or glazed.

attic base A scotia (concave) molding between two torus (convex) moldings used as the support for a column in Greek, Roman Doric, and Corinthian orders.

attic base

attic style The pure, elegant classicism associated with the city at the heart of ancient Greece, Athens.

aubergine (French, eggplant) A deep purplish color.

Aubusson A rug with no pile, woven like a tapestry, and usually with French floral and scroll design motifs. The name originally referred to the famous tapestry factory in central France, dating back to the 15th century.

auditorium A hall, enclosure, or theater, usually equipped with seats. A meeting place or an area for presentations that depend on sightlines and acoustics.

aureole (Latin, gold) A circular, elliptic, or quadrangular halo around a Christ figure, Madonna, or saint, depicted in art.

aureole

Austrian drape A shirred fabric treatment for windows that gives the effect of vertical rows of swags from top to bottom. The bottom edge then makes a horizontal band of semicircular scallops. It sometimes works on a pulley cord like a Roman shade, with the textile bands drawn up in a series of poufs. See AUSTRIAN SHADE CLOTH.

Austrian shade cloth A crinkled, woven, striped cotton fabric produced by weaving alternating groups of slack and tight warp ends. May be made of silk, cotton, or synthetic fibers and used for window coverings.

autogenic Describes structures that offer an alternative vision for the future of the built environment; related to the next generation of surface materials and building membranes in an era of sophisticated computational control.

avant-garde Culturally progressive, vanguard.

aventurine lacquer A finish that imitates the color and sparkling quality of the mineral, usually hues of blue and green. Used during the 18th century in France for lining drawers in small chests or cabinets.

avodire An African blond wood with strong, dark brown vertical streaking and a medium-hard texture, with a pronounced mottled figure and a lustrous quality that makes it a popular veneer and modern cabinet wood.

awning windows Wide horizontal panels of glass, in frames, set one over the other inside the overall frame of the opening. Each panel is hinged onto the frame and opens outward, with the lower end projecting beyond the building line. Permits air and ventilation and protects from rain or snow.

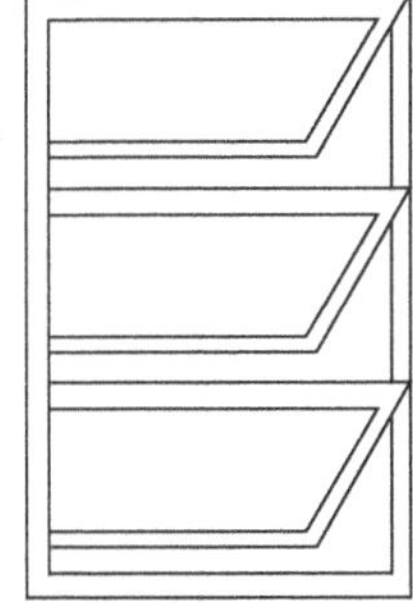
awning windows

Axminster A type of carpet. Originally a rug woven in the parish town in the county of Devon in England in the mid 18th century, where Turkish carpets were imitated on special looms that made possible an almost unlimited number of colors, designs, and patterns. The carpet is tightly woven, the pile is usually cut, and the back of the weave is heavily ribbed.

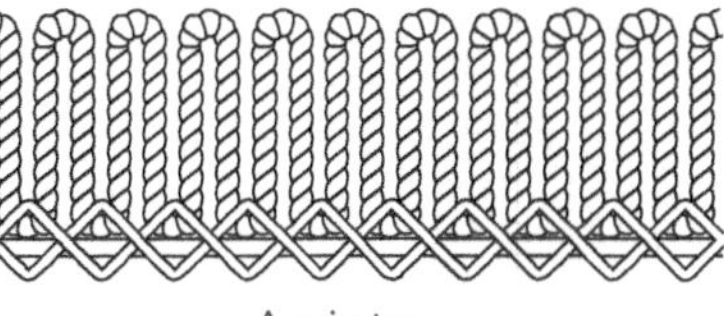
Axminster

axonometric projection A three-dimensional, accurately scaled representation of an architectural space. It uses the floor plan, turned on a 30/60- or 45-degree angle, as a base. Vertical lines are then projected and horizontal lines measured to create a precisely dimensioned image. Because there is no diminution based on distance, sometimes the drawings appear distorted.

ayacahuite A satiny pinewood of Mexico and Central America with a small, fine grain, used for furniture, and often given a painted or lacquered finish.

ayous A west African coast wood, creamy white to pale yellow, similar to primavera. In veneers, can resemble mahogany. The wood is soft and lightweight and has an even texture. Also called ABACHI.

ayurvedic Ancient Hindu science of health and medicine, whose principles are applied to sustainable design.

azulejos Spanish or Portuguese wall tiles decorated with scenes of sports or bullfights, usually done in blue on white. These tiles were used in the late Gothic period to cover walls in place of tapestries.

Babylonia The center of the ancient Mesopotamian Empire, which reached its cultural peak circa 1800 B.C.E. It had a renaissance under Assyrian rule (1275–538 B.C.E.), and the stepped ziggurats were a major architectural accomplishment. See ZIGGURAT.

baccarat Originally a French card game. The name of a fine crystal used for chandeliers, sconces, and for table service.

bachelor chest Storage unit consisting of drawers, usually 20 inches to 36 inches wide (50–90 cm) by 30 inches to 36 inches tall (75–90 cm), either traditional or contemporary in style. Often used in pairs, and sometimes in place of sofa tables.

back arch A concealed curved structural element that carries the inner part of a wall, whereas a lintel carries the exterior facing material.

back-cut veneer Flitch from a log sliced in a manner similar to half-round slicing. The result is a striped figure, with the sapwood included on the edges. See HALF-ROUND SLICING VENEER.

back filling In wall construction, the rough masonry behind the facing material, or the material which takes up the space within the extrados of an arch. Brickwork used between studs in a frame building. Also called brick nogging.

back post A rear upright of a chair that is a continuation of a rear leg. A top rail usually connects two posts and may have a splat between them.

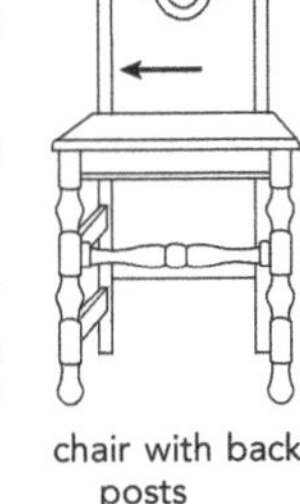

chair with back posts

back stool An upholstered chair without arms, or a seat with an upright back. This term describes the simple seats of the 15th and 16th centuries.

backup The masonry wall behind the exterior facing.

∞**bacon cupboard** A late-17th-century English storage unit for holding cured pork, usually the back of a settle, which had an ornamented drawer under the seat.

bagheera A fine uncut pile velvet with a rough, crush-resistant finish.

bag table A small 18th- and early-19th-century work surface, usually distinguished by the cloth pouch under one or two drawers. Popular in England and America. See also POUCH TABLE.

bahut (1) A large-footed chest of the Middle Ages, used to hold tapestries, cushions, etc. It eventually evolved into a high cabinet. (2) A leather envelope used to protect a chest in transit. See CASSONE.

baigneuse (French) A tub-like upholstered daybed introduced during the French Empire period. The back piece sloped down and turned to form the sides; thus the arms or sides angled from the back down to the front of the seat. Similar to a MÉRIDIENNE. See also GRECIAN SOFA and RÉCAMIER.

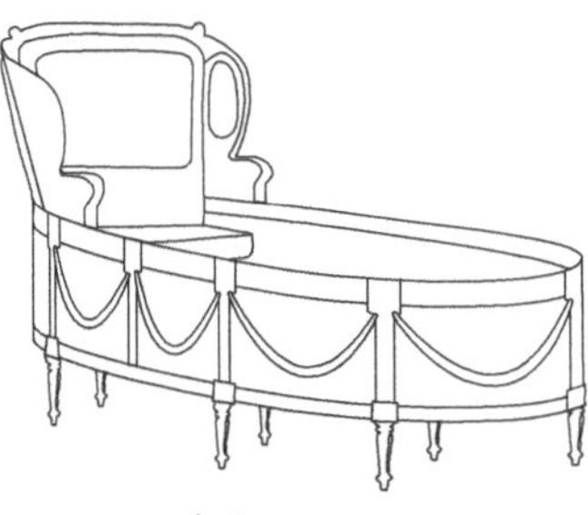

baigneuse

bail handle A drawer pull which hangs downward in a reversed arch or half-moon. Brass drop handles were introduced in the William and Mary period in England.

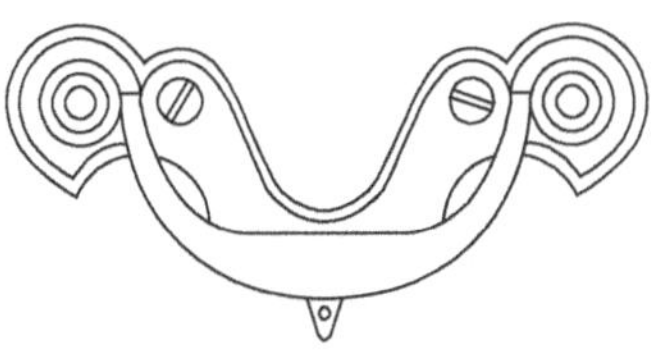

bail handle

baize A wool fabric similar to felt, originally from Baza, Spain. Made of wool or cotton, it is a plain, loosely woven fabric with soft twist filling yarns. The longish nap is sometimes frizzed on one side. It found great acceptance as a cover, for card table inserts, and for lining drawers and case furniture.

baked finish A painted or varnished applied surface that has been baked at a temperature of over 150°F, which made the coating tough and durable.

Bakelite A trademark name for vinyl resins manufactured by Union Carbide Corporation. A group of thermoplastic resins and plastics used for moldings, extrusions, castings, and adhesives. Popular at one time as a tabletop material.

baku A lightweight, very fine, dull-finished straw fabric.

balcony A platform projecting out from a wall of a building, usually surrounded by a balustrade. Also, the upper section of an auditorium, a shelflike projection over the ground floor of the hall.

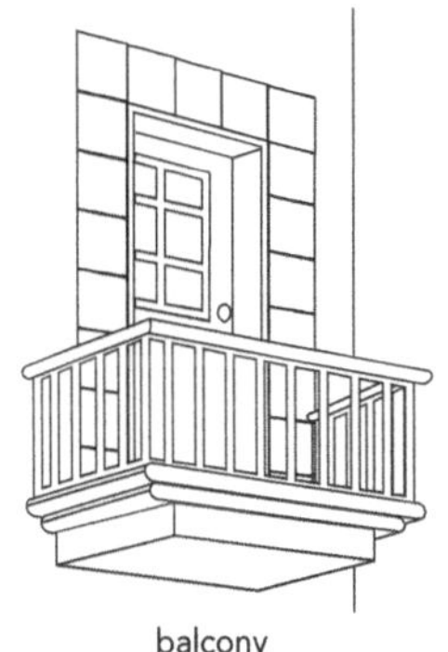

balcony

baldachino, baldachin, baldaquin A canopy resting on columns, used over altars, thrones, or beds in Italian Renaissance buildings. Originally described as a fine, embroidered cloth of gold and silk used as a portable shield over shrines and statues in processions. See CANOPY.

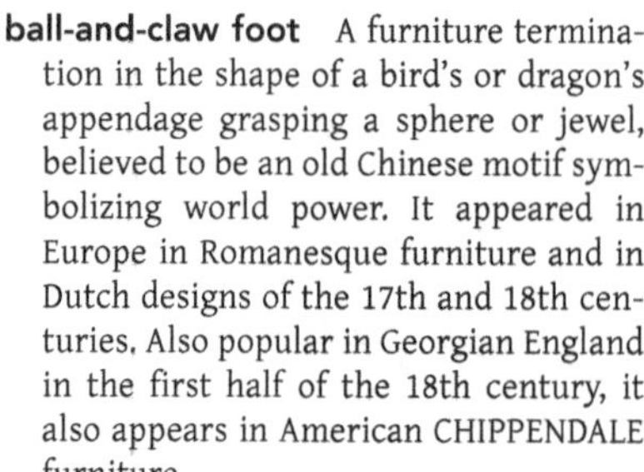

baldachino

baldaquin bed (French) A canopy or tester sleeper. A late-18th-century French or English canopy or CROWN BED. The fabric canopy was attached to the wall, rather than supported by bedposts extending from the four corners of the frame.

baline A plain, woven, coarse fabric used for stiffening and for underwork in upholstery.

ball-and-claw foot A furniture termination in the shape of a bird's or dragon's appendage grasping a sphere or jewel, believed to be an old Chinese motif symbolizing world power. It appeared in Europe in Romanesque furniture and in Dutch designs of the 17th and 18th centuries. Also popular in Georgian England in the first half of the 18th century, it also appears in American CHIPPENDALE furniture.

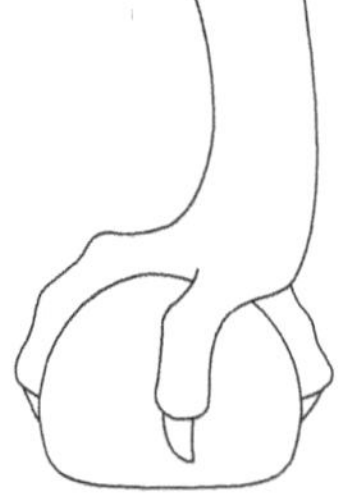

ball-and-claw foot

ball and ring A 17th-century turning used for furniture legs and decorations, consisting of a series of spherical turnings separated by flattened discs.

ball-and-steeple finial A wood turning popular in 18th-century American furniture. The lowest element of the termination was a sphere surmounted by a series of rings of graduated sizes, which resulted in a tapered peak.

ballast A vital part of gas discharge lamps. Linear and compact fluorescents and HID lamps all require a ballast. It is a key part of a fluorescent light that starts a lamp and keeps it in operation. There are two ballast types: electric and magnetic. Starting times range from instant to fast, and a ballast factor is a multiplier that indicates how much light the lamp will emit.

ball flower A carved Gothic ornament, circular in shape, with a three-lobed or petal effect in the center. Often a carved enrichment in the convex part of a molding. Popular during the latter part of the 13th and most of the 14th centuries.

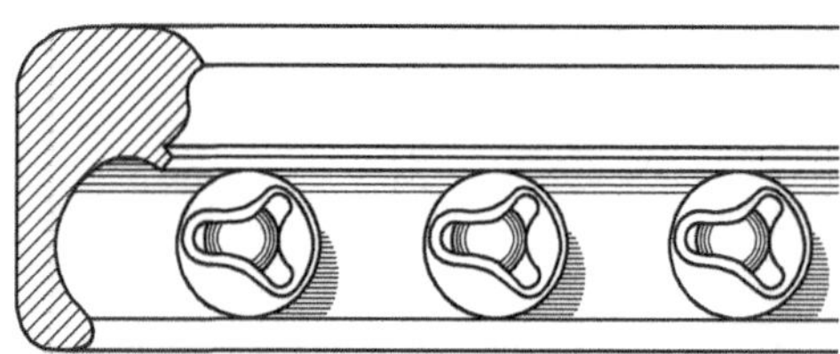

ball flower

ball foot A turned furniture support of a spherical or nearly spherical shape with a narrow disc-like pad at its base. Used extensively in 17th-century Flemish and English furniture. Similar to a BUN FOOT or FLEMISH FOOT.

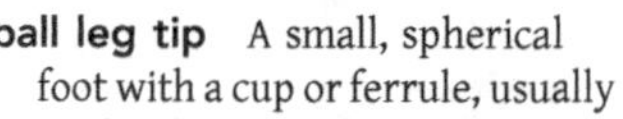

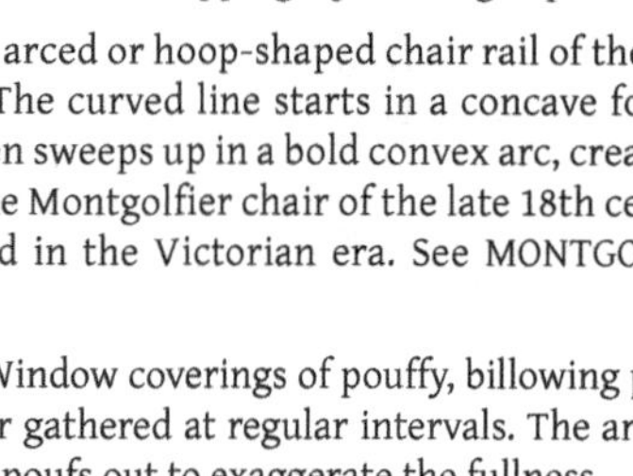

console with ball feet

ball leg tip A small, spherical foot with a cup or ferrule, usually made of brass. It fits over the end of a chair or table support.

balloon A globelike element topping a pillar or gatepost.

balloon back The arced or hoop-shaped chair rail of the Hepplewhite period. The curved line starts in a concave form at the seat frame then sweeps up in a bold convex arc, creating a loop. Similar to the Montgolfier chair of the late 18th century in France. Revived in the Victorian era. See MONTGOLFIER CHAIR.

balloon curtains Window coverings of pouffy, billowing panels of fabric shirred or gathered at regular intervals. The area between the gathers poufs out to exaggerate the fullness.

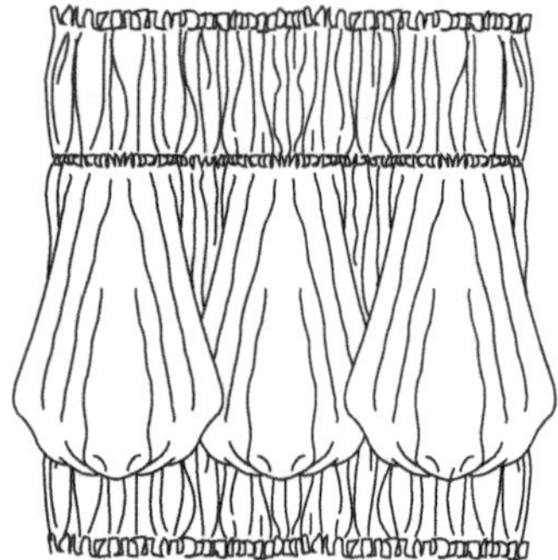

balloon curtains

balloon shade Window covering composed of a textile that forms billowy poufs when raised.

ballroom chair A small-scaled armless seat popular in the late 19th and early 20th centuries. These typically had an arcaded back filled with delicate spindles, and had turned wooden legs. They were often finished in a gold color, with an applied red velvetseat.

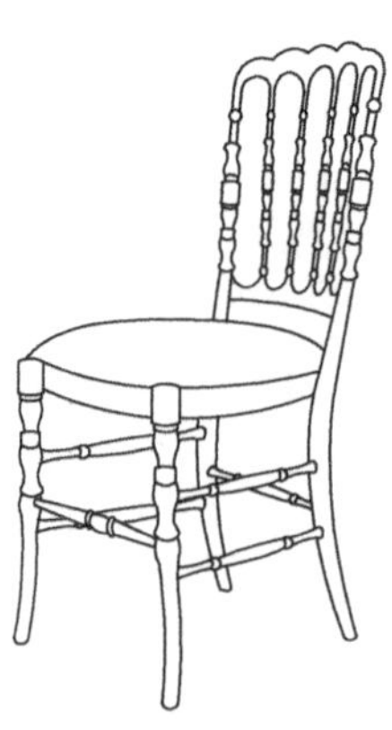

ballroom chair

ball turning See KNOB TURNING.

baluster A turned spindle column that supports a railing and is part of a balustrade. A baluster may also serve as a stretcher between chair legs or as part of a chair back. Commonly an elongated urn or vase shape. Split or half balusters were a favorite applied ornament in English Restoration furniture. Also called a BANISTER.

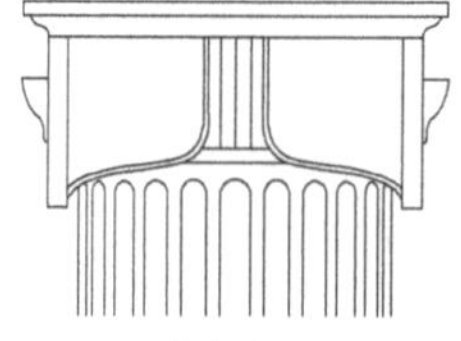

baluster

balustra A dense South African hardwood of a light tobacco-brown color.

balustrade A continuous ornamental railing of stone, wood, or metal. It consists of a series of balusters topped with a rail and serves as a decorated enclosure for balconies, terraces, and stairways. Also used as a decorative motif in 18th-century furniture designed by English architects.

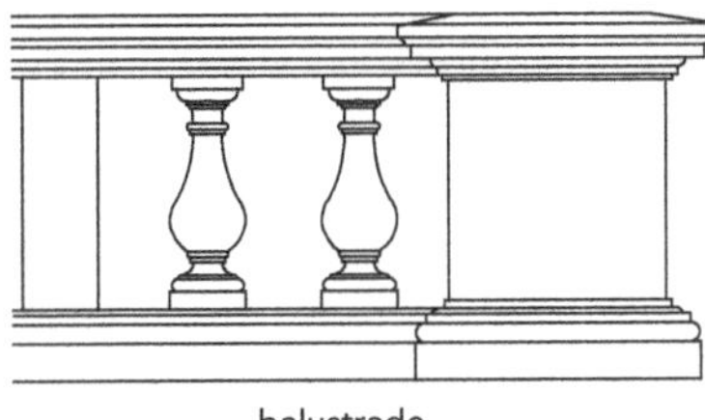
balustrade

bamboo A woody tropical plant used for furniture and ornament that is biologically a grass. Its distinctive nodular look became popular in Europe in the 17th and 18th centuries as part of the Chinese influence on European design. Reproduced as a wood turning in Europe and English colonies. See BAMBOO-TURNED CHAIR.

bamboo shade Rolldown window protector made of thin strips or slats of the tropical wood. May be left in a natural yellowish finish, treated to resemble malacca, or stained or lacquered.

bamboo-turned Wood lathe-work that simulates the nodular or jointed look of natural bamboo, favored in the late 18th and early 19th centuries for furniture.

bamboo-turned chair A seat, usually made of maple or other light hardwoods, and often gilded or painted a light, fanciful color. The turnings resemble a stylized version of the natural material. This style developed from the SPOOL FURNITURE of the mid 19th century.

bancone A 15th- or 16th-century Italian writing table that consisted of a flat writing surface over two paneled drawers and a recessed section. The entire piece rested on stretcher-connected pairs of legs called "running feet." See RUNNER FOOT.

banded column A vertical support that has a lower drum of a larger diameter than the shaft itself. This bottom drum may be more richly decorated than the rest of the shaft. Popular in the French Renaissance period.

banderole A Renaissance decoration consisting of a carved or painted ribbon-like motif. An inscription often filled the flat part of the ribbon. See RIBBON BACK and RIBBAND BACK.

banded column

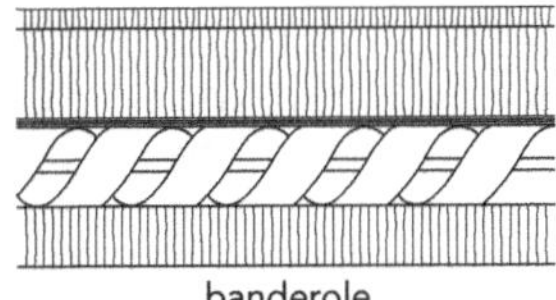
banderole

ban-dew A process devised by the Joseph Bancroft & Sons Company to render fabrics mildew resistant.

banding A narrow strip of veneer used as a border or edging on tabletops, drawer fronts, etc. Usually made of a contrasting inlay, it was popular in 18th-century furniture. See CROSSBANDING.

band sawn (adj.) A serpentine shaping, achieved by a high-speed, thin-banded saw.

bandy-legged A colonial American term for bowlegged or cabriole-legged furniture in the early 18th century. See CABRIOLE CHAIR and CABRIOLE LEG.

bandy-legged

banister In furniture, usually the split, turned splats that make up a banister-back chair of the late 17th century. See BALUSTER.

banister-back chair A late-17th-century English or American seat with split, turned spindles or flat bars for the uprights of the chair vertical support. A more elegant and polished variation of this type of chair rest was popular in the Hepplewhite period (later 18th century). See BAR BACK.

banjo clock A 19th-century wall-mounted timepiece that resembles, in contour, an inverted version of the musical instrument. See BAROMETER CASES.

bank A long Gothic bench. See BANQUETTE.

Bank of England chair A 19th-century English Regency seat, similar to a tub chair in that the arms start at the front post and sweep around the back in a continuous rising curve. The legs are usually cabriole, and the front edge of the seat is serpentine in form.

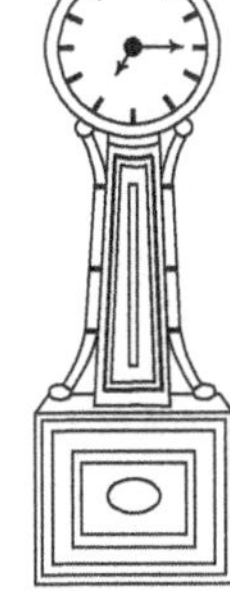
banjo clock

banner screen An adjustable vertical panel that stands in front of a fireplace and protects objects and people from airborne embers. In the mid 18th century, it became a popular accessory, and the shield was often made of tapestry or needlework. Also called a "pole screen" because the vertical element moved up and down a pole. Some of the protection devices were made of carved mahogany in cheval form. See CHEVAL SCREEN.

banquette (French) An upholstered bench.

bantam work A Dutch and English lacquer technique of the late 17th century. The design was etched into a black ground. Originated in Bantam, Dutch Java, now Indonesia.

baptistery A room or building, usually round or octagonal, used for the rite of baptism.

bar back Hepplewhite's term to describe the carved and shaped upright verticals that curve to fit the shield of an open shield-back chair or sofa. A bar-backed sofa contained three or four of the ovoid elements. See BANISTER-BACK CHAIR.

baptistery

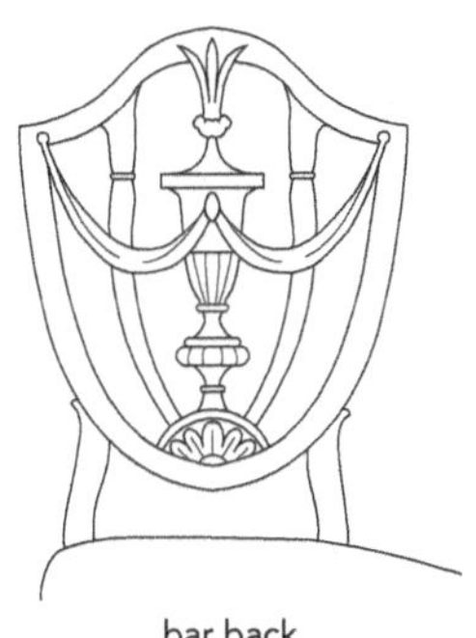
bar back

barber's chair An 18th-century English corner or writing seat. A headrest was sometimes perched over the semicircular top rail. Sometimes the headrest was a continuous broad splat that extended up from the seat frame and was supported by the arms. See TRIANGLE SEAT.

Barbizon School A group of mid-19th-century landscape painters who portrayed romanticized scenes of peasant life and the countryside. Included were Jean-François Millet, Theodore Rousseau, and Narcisse Diaz de la Peña.

bar cart A mobile table and cabinet for storing and serving liquor, similar to a tea cart.

Barcelona chair (1) A 17th- and 18th-century ladder-back chair in Spain. The top cross-slat was enlarged and elaborately carved, with carved rosettes and chiseled grooves. (2) The 20th-century design by Lilly Reich and Mies van der Rohe: the front legs curve up and back to become part of the back, while the rear legs sweep forward to support the seat. The side view is a graceful X shape. The seat and back are tufted leather pillows.

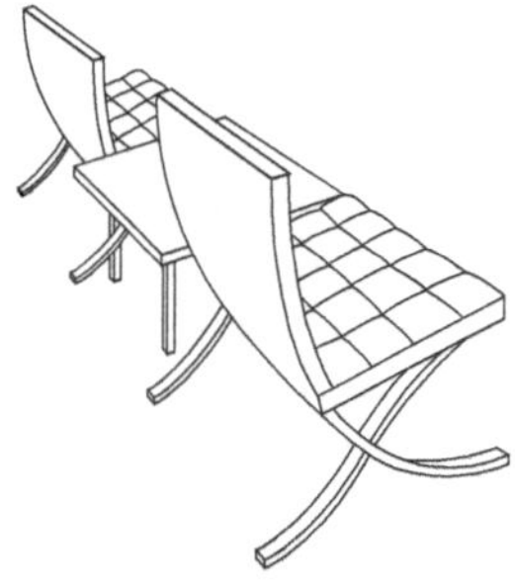

Barcelona chair

Barclite A trademark name for the rigid fiberglass panels made by the Barclite Corporation of America. The panels are translucent and patterned with embedded fabrics, foliage, etc. Depending upon their gauge, the panels can be rigid enough for a variety of uses: room dividers, sliding doors, cabinet inserts, dropped ceilings, and skylights.

barefaced tenon A shaped piece used in the joinery of furniture and cabinets. The tenon usually has two angled edges or "shoulders." A barefaced tenon has only one shoulder.

barefaced tongue joint In furniture and cabinet joinery, a protrusion that is flush on one side of a board and set into a grooved piece of wood. Also called a GROOVE-AND-RABBET JOINT.

barège (French) A sheer, gauzelike fabric made of wool combined with cotton, silk, and other fibers.

bar foot See RUNNER FOOT.

bariatric Healthcare sector focusing on obesity that requires redesign of furniture, patient rooms, and equipment. See LUXE DEPTH.

∞barjier or barjeer Hepplewhite's term for an armchair or *bergère*. See BERGÈRE.

barley-sugar turning Spiral lathe-work that resembles a twisted rope, frequently used in the mid-and-late 17th century for furniture legs and stretchers.

Barocco (Portuguese and Spanish) A large irregular-shaped pearl whose name was given to a style characterized by complex curves.

barometer cases In the 18th century, usually elegant mahogany storage units banded with satinwood or boxwood and topped with a broken or swan's neck pediment. A circular mirror in a reeded frame often surmounted the dial. The banjo type was formed by a wide circular dial topped by a bulbous upper part. Adam and Chippendale designed many beautiful examples of this popular accessory.

Baroque (French, curious, odd, or strange). The period in architecture, painting, and sculpture in the 17th and 18th centuries created an overwhelming and direct appeal to the senses of the beholder. A blend of illusionism, light, color, and movement, it was a new approach to classic art. It was characterized by large-scale, bold details, sweeping curves, and a wealth of ornament. It was a period of religious emotionalism.

Baroque plan

Baroque armchair

Baroque armchair A seat with a back (in profile) that cants away from the seated person at the top. It has arm rests, straight legs, and curved STRETCHERS.

barquette molding A small semicircular decorative band composed of beads or olive berries. See also ASTRAGAL.

barquette molding

barred door A closure with wood or metal fretwork in a glass cabinet, secretary, or bookcase. Because of the high cost of glass, the small precious pieces were set into the intricate, cutout, lacy wood framework. See also FRETWORK.

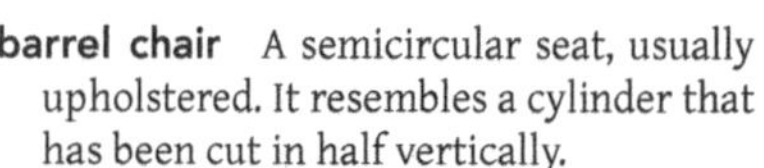

barrel chair A semicircular seat, usually upholstered. It resembles a cylinder that has been cut in half vertically.

barrel-shaped seat See GARDEN SEAT.

barrel vault A semicircular ceiling shape supported by parallel walls that can span long distances. It is the result of an arch extruded in a horizontal direction.

barrel chair

barrier-free design See ACCESSIBLE DESIGN.

bartizan Small castle-like turrets that protrude from a wall. Their initial purpose was for defense.

bar tracery Late Gothic fretwork in which the stone, wood, or metal was cut into rectangular units and arranged in a variety of geometric patterns. See TRACERY.

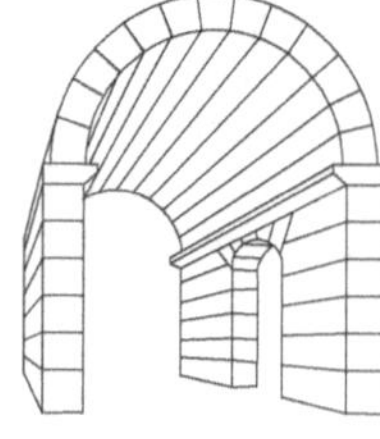

barrel vault

basalt A dark green or brown stone with columnar strata used in Egyptian statues. A favored material during the European Empire period because of its Egyptian association and its rich, strong coloring.

basalt ware A black porcelain pottery Josiah Wedgwood developed in 18th-century England.

base The series of moldings at the bottom of a column shaft that helps to distribute the weight. In sculpture, the base is any block or molding at the bottom of a piece. In case furniture, the lowest supporting part that rests on the ground.

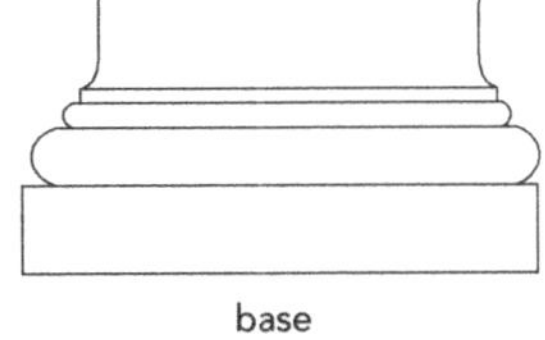
base

baseboard The horizontal piece of milled lumber placed at the bottom of the wall and resting directly on the floor, usually trimmed with moldings.

basement In classical and Renaissance architecture, a story below the main level of a building, not necessarily below ground level. In contemporary usage, a story partially or entirely below ground level.

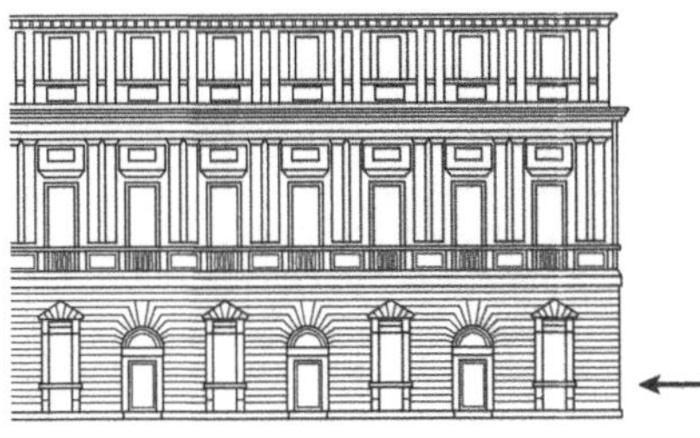
basement

base rail Wood trim at the bottom edge of a seat and above the legs of a chair or sofa. Also, the wood trim at the bottom edge of a dresser, chest, or other case piece; it lies directly above the legs or flush with the floor.

base wood The basic construction material or carcass of a piece of furniture, which is veneered with a more costly or more beautifully grained flitch. Oak and beech are often used in European furniture, whereas native softwoods are used in the United States. Also called CARCASE or CARCASS.

basilica (1) A large central space designed as a Roman hall of justice or commercial exchange, with rows of columns, and galleries with upper columns that supported the roof. (2) Early Christian church with a high nave, clerestory, side aisles, and a semicircular apse.

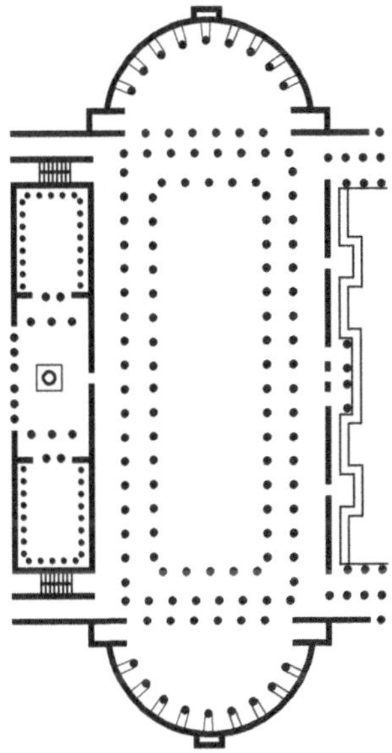
Roman basilica

basin stand Small Chippendale and Hepplewhite 18th-century surface-creating units designed to support a container for water.

basket stand A late-18th-century two-tiered work table. Galleries composed of small turnings or spindles surrounded the tiers, and the unit rested on a tripod base. Similar to a canterbury and a dumbwaiter.

basketweave (1) A textile woven with large similar-sized warps and wefts. The weft crosses over alternate warp threads, creating an effect like a woven reed container. Used to make homespun and monk's cloth. (2) An inlay technique that simulates an interwoven quality.

basketweave

bas-relief (French, low-profile figuration) A form of sculpture in which the design is raised slightly from the background.

bas-relief

bass (1) The lower part of a 17th-century English or French bed. (2) The fabric treatment that covers the span between bedstead and floor, today called the dust ruffle.

∞**basset table** A Queen Anne gaming surface for playing the popular five-handed card game.

basswood A lightweight, light-colored material used extensively for core stock and crossbanding in plywood panels. It does not warp readily and is moderately strong. In the northern United States and Canada, the material is related to the European linden.

bast fibers Filaments obtained from plants such as jute, flax, and ramie. The stalks are retted (steeped in water to cause a weakening) and decorticated (the hard outer covering is removed). See *Table 2.*

bat In masonry, a part of a brick. A half bat is half of a brick.

∞Batavia The historical Dutch name for Jakarta, Indonesia, which is an important location for textiles because of early global trade.

batik A Javanese process of resist-dyeing on cotton or silk. The design is waxed on the cloth, and the cloth is then dyed. The waxed areas resist the stain, and the pattern appears in the background color of the fabric. The process can be repeated several times. Streaks are obtained when the stain crawls through cracks in the wax. Machine printing can imitate the process.

batik

batiste (French) A sheer, fine fabric, usually made of cotton, with a lengthwise striation. May also be made of wool or silk, where it resembles mull and is called *batiste de soie*. Can be made of rayon and decorated with woven stripes and jacquard florals.

bat's wing brasses An early American hardware design that resembles a conventionalized silhouette of the flying mammal's outstretched wings. Used on handle plates and ESCUTCHEONS.

batten A long piece of sawed wood used for flooring, wainscoting, or as an upright for lathing. It is usually fastened to one or more boards as a cleat.

batter The inclination of the face of a wall.

batting Carded cotton prepared in sheets or rolls and used for stuffing, lining, or padding for quilts and upholstered pieces.

Bauhaus An influential school of architecture, art, and design in Weimar and, later, at Dessau, Germany. During its short life (1919 to 1933), the school declared that art and crafts were inseparable and that craftsmanship was the driving force of design. Its leaders opposed ornament and historicism and felt passionately that design could solve social inequities. Famous associates included Marianne Brandt, Marcel Breuer, Walter Gropius, Johannes Itten, Wassily Kandinsky, Paul Klee, László Moholy Nagy, Lilly Reich, and Gunta Stölzl.

bay (1) The space between columns or supports, or the compartment in a structure, that is separated from the rest of the building by an arch, buttress, or vaulting. A bay is also called a severy. (2) An organizational division of a façade of a building, interior, or piece of furniture.

bay

bayadére (1) A fabric of strongly contrasting multicolored horizontal stripes, originally the garment worn by female dancers in India. (2) *La Bayadère* is a famous Russian ballet about a temple dancer who wears the garment.

Bayeux Tapestry A famous French Romanesque embroidered wall hanging, 213 feet long (65 m), that commemorates the victory of the Normans in England.

bay window A three-sided opening that projects outward from the perpendicular wall surface of a building.

baywood A material with fine markings, lighter in color and softer than Cuban or Spanish mahogany. A desirable source for veneer. Also called Honduras mahogany

beach cloth An imitation linen crash made of a lightweight cotton warp and mohair (or cotton) filling. Often used for draperies in informal rooms.

bead A small cylindrical molding carved to resemble a continuous string of pearls or spheres. An ASTRAGAL.

bead and butt A panel that is set flush with the stiles and rails that make up the framework of the wall or paneled surface. The spherical molding emphasizes the edges of the panel that hits the stiles.

bead and reel A decorative half-round molding with alternating circular and elongated oval shapes.

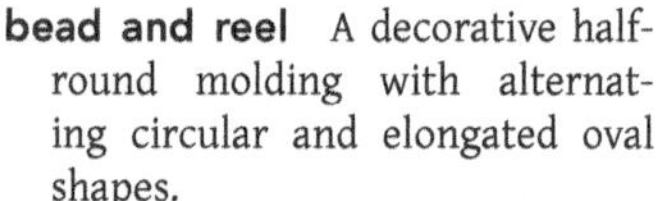

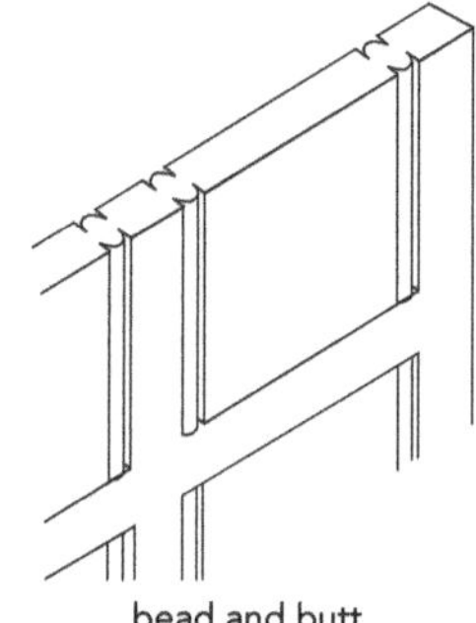
bead and butt

bead curtains Individual strings of perforated spheres (glass, wood, plastic, ceramic, bamboo, etc.) hung together to form a drape over a window, opening, or arch. May serve as a semitransparent room divider. Originally an Eastern or Near Eastern device, then taken up by hippies in the 1960s.

bead flush A small, almost circular applied molding that runs completely around the four sides of a panel.

beak head A Norman decorative molding. The carving on this early Gothic enrichment resembles a stylized bird's crown and rostrum.

beam A long piece of timber or metal set horizontally or at a slant that supports a roof or ceiling.

beamed ceiling Upper interior surface of a room in which the exposed or encased supports are part of the decorative scheme.

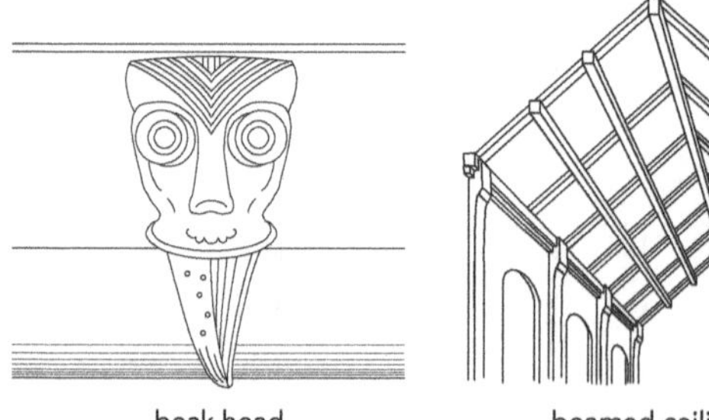
beak head　　beamed ceiling

bearer strip See BEARING RAIL.

bearing partition An interior wall of one story or less in height that supports a load set on it from above, in addition to supporting its own weight.

bearing rail The horizontal carrying member for a drawer in a table, chest or cabinet. Also called a bearer strip.

bearing wall A partition that supports a vertical load in addition to its own weight.

bear's-paw foot A decorative furniture termination used by French and English designers in the late 17th and early 18th centuries. It is a carved representation of a furry animal foot, sometimes grasping a ball.

beast mode A trend in several industries that springs from a can-do attitude, centered on skill and determination. The look draws from punk, Goth, and heavy metal, although it is more refined and technological. It made inroads into design, and its influence is found in gyms, video arcades, salons, retail, and other commercial sectors. The *Transformer* movies, and related games, are seminal events for weekend warriors. In their rejection of refinement, theirs is an irreverent mash-up of Holly Hunt and Optimus Prime.

Beau Brummel An early-19th-century Englishman's dressing table with adjustable mirrors, drawers, shelves, and candlestands, named after a famous dandy during the time of George IV.

∞**beaufait** (French) The original spelling of buffet. See BUFFET.

beaufait

Beauvais An art factory that specialized in textiles and tapestries, in France during Louis XIV's reign. François Boucher, during the period of Louis XV, designed many tapestries for the Beauvais looms, including the "Story of Psyche." Toward the end of the 18th century, the factory started to produce pile rugs. The most popular motifs were love scenes and pastorals in soft pastels. See CANAPÉ and CAUSEUSE.

Beaux-Arts Literally, the fine arts painting, sculpture, and architecture; refers to the Parisian school ÉCOLE DES BEAUX-ARTS; a pre-modern design method that was eclectic, urban, and complex; symmetry was important as was the plan as the generator of design.

bed chair An early-18th-century Dutch innovation. An armed seat with a back that let down and a hidden leg that unfolded to support the lowered back. The legs and the lowered arms came together to stabilize the center. The front rail was hinged so that the entire seat and back unit could come over and down. Often made of nut wood or maple inlaid with tulipwood and styled with bandy (cabriole) legs and Dutch feet. See also CHAIR BED.

bedding (1) (adj.) Describes types of textiles; for example, "bedding quilt," signifying the quilt's destination and context of use. (2) (noun) Furniture for sleeping on, and its linens.

bed frame A rectangular wooden skeleton that supports the spring and mattress; the box with an opening in the center may rest on casters, or it may be bolted to a headboard. See HARVARD FRAME and HOLLYWOOD BED.

bedford cord A strong, durable rib-weave fabric with raised lengthwise lines produced by warpwise stuffing threads. May be made of wool, silk, cotton, rayon, or a combination of these fabrics. Used for upholstery and similar to piqué. Originally woven in New Bedford, Massachusetts.

bed molding A small framing device, or series of ornamentations, placed under a projection, as under the corona of a cornice.

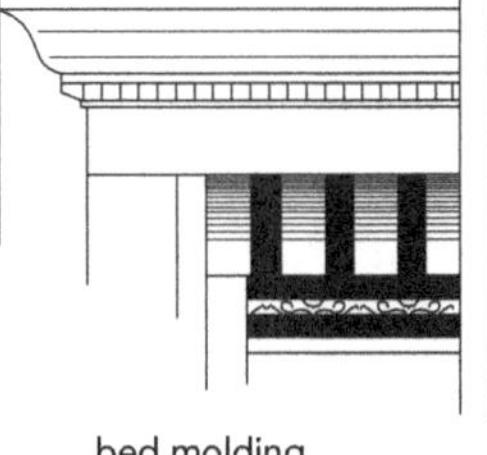
bed molding

bed rails Strips, usually of wood, that connect the headboard to the footboard and keep them in a vertical position. Combined with the slats, which are set at right angles to the rails, they support the box spring and mattress.

bedrest A pillow that has a back and arms. Sometimes called a husband.

bedside cupboard A small 18th-century storage unit that usually contained a chamber pot. Also called a pot cupboard.

bedspread A fabric covering for the top and sides of a bed. Can be made from a variety of fabrics and comes in various styles: for example, a coverlet with dust ruffles, a fitted top, or a loose throw that falls to the floor at the sides.

bedstead The frame or piece of furniture for sleeping, without the mattress or bedding. The supporting framework of a mattress.

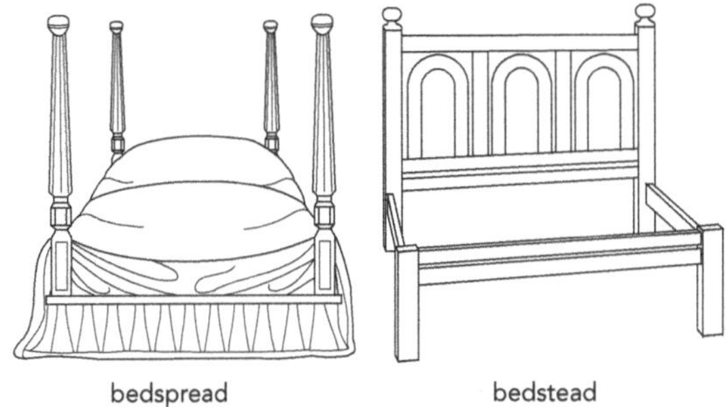
bedspread bedstead

bed steps An 18th-century English and American device for getting in and out of high sleeping platforms. The risers and treds were often incorporated into other pieces of furniture, sometimes with a chamber pot.

∞**bedstock** The supporting framework of certain 16th-century sleeping devices in England and continental Europe. The front posts or pillars that supported the wood tester or canopy stood free, and the bedstock supported the bedding. Similar to the current bed frame.

bee The personal emblem of Napoleon. Along with laurel wreaths, the letter N, stars, and eagles, it was a popular motif of the French Empire period (1804–1814). The resemblance between the bee and the Bourbon fleur-de-lis made it possible to convert the Bourbon symbol into the Napoleonic symbol. In Rome, the insect is a symbol of the alliterative Barberini family.

beech A tough, strong, pale, straight-grained wood that resembles birch and maple. Though used for furniture and flooring in the 17th and 18th centuries, it is mainly used today for furniture frames, rocker supports, and bent chairbacks. The European variety is similar to the American but is easier to season and work. See *Table 5.*

bel étage (French) The main story of a building, usually containing salons and reception rooms. Most often the first story above the ground level. See PIANO NOBILE.

bell (of a capital) The body of the crowning member of a column between the necking and the abacus, whose shape resembles that of an inverted hollow sonorous object.

∞**bell and trumpet** See BELL TURNING.

bella rosa A moderately hard and heavy, pink to yellowish beige wood grown in the Philippines and Malaysia. The graining is usually straight.

belleek A fine, ivory-colored china produced in Ireland, highly translucent with an iridescent quality to the glaze. Frequently used for small decorative items and tea sets.

bellflower ornament A popular 18th-century carved motif used to enrich furniture and interiors. Based on conventionalized blossoms or catkins, the ornament was used in a continuous chain or swag, as well as in graduated sizes as a pendant. See HUSK ORNAMENT.

bellows A blowing device that creates a blast of air when contracted or collapsed and serves as a fireplace accessory. The pointed objects are often highly painted, carved, or otherwise embellished.

bell seat A Queen Anne chair with a rounded front, popular in early-18th-century England.

bell turning A conventionalized lathe-work motif popular during the William and Mary period (late 17th century). Used for furniture legs and pedestal supports.

below-grade (adj.) Area or items set lower than the street level or ground level. May be only a foot or two below, or as much as one or more stories underneath the ground level.

belvedere (Italian, beautiful view) (1) In Italian Renaissance architecture, the uppermost story of a building open on several sides to allow for viewing the countryside and to let in cooling breezes. (2) A lantern atop a building can also be called a belvedere. (3) A famous part of the Vatican with a roof pavilion.

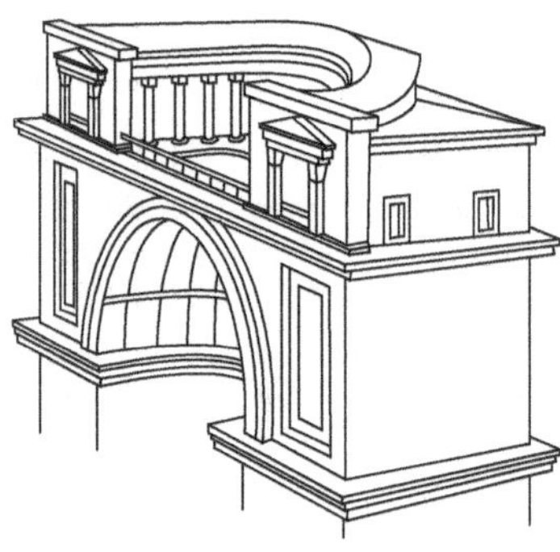
belvedere

Bemberg A trademark name for rayon thread and yarns made by the American Bemberg Company, using a cuprammonium process.

bench A long stool or rectangular seating device, backless or with a low back.

benching Space-planning strategy for commercial space in which off-site workers, when in the office, sit at a long, continuous, undifferentiated work surface. Typically with little storage or privacy. This alternative to a traditional office results in a smaller real estate footprint. Paradoxically, sitting on a bench is not a required part of the configuration.

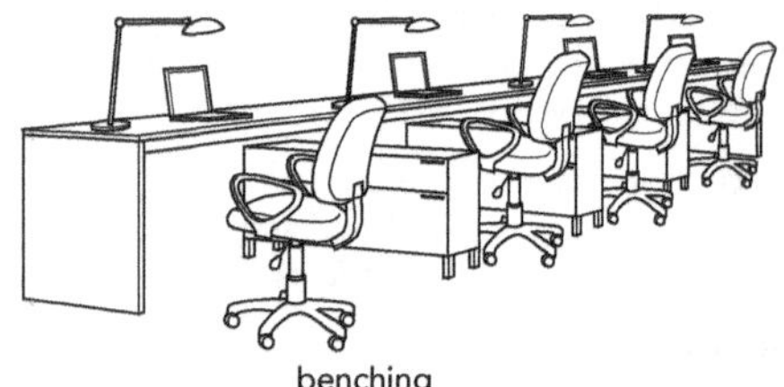
benching

bench table See SETTLE.

benday Dots created by commercial printing processes that are used to express shading. A method of adding tone to a printed image by imposing a field of dots or other patterns at a stage in the photographic reproduction process. Benday dots appear in comics and in the work of artist Roy Lichtenstein. See ZIP-A-TONE.

∞**bended back chair** A seat whose vertical support swoops in the shape of a bowl-shaped cutlery item, sometimes with continuous arms. Often mistakenly given to a Hogarth chair because of its vase-shaped splat. See FIDDLEBACK CHAIR and SPOON-BACK CHAIR.

bengaline A heavy faille fabric with a fine weave and crosswise ribs. It may be woven of silk, rayon, or wool warp yarns, with worsted or cotton fillings (weft).

benge An African wood of rich brown with tan or darker brown markings, with a hard texture and strong contrasting figure.

bento box or bento Compartmentalized sushi container that has inspired Japanese interior designers because of its organization and compactness.

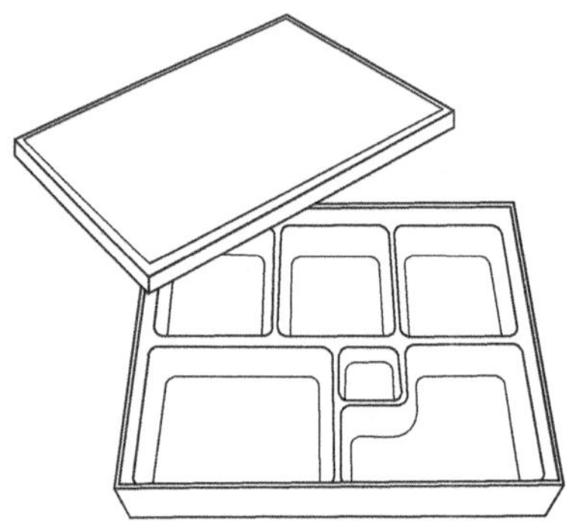
bento box

bentwood furniture Furniture made of wood softened by steaming and then molded into curved forms. The term often describes the furniture made by Michael Thonet of Austria, beginning in 1857. Modern contour pieces by Eames and Aalto are created in a similar fashion.

bentwood rocker A chair made by Thonet in the late 19th century that moves backwards and forwards on two curved rails. The rails were initially rectilinear, and then steamed or soaked, then contorted to form the desired sinuous shape. The back and seat are caned.

Berber (1) Originally, the name for both the North African ethnic groups and their simple, geometric hand-knotted rugs, made of undyed, natural, pure wool yarns. (2) Today, a coarse, heavy-textured carpet or rug in natural wool or synthetic yarns having the look of undyed wool and a heavy, pebbly surface.

bergère (French) A mostly upholstered low armchair, usually with exposed wood frame and enclosed sides. The upholstered arms are shorter than the length of the seat, and a soft loose pillow rests on a fabric-covered seat. Introduced in the Louis XV period and popular in the Louis XVI period. Also called BARJIER, BARJEER, or BURJAIR.

∞**bergerie** A popular 18th-century rural scenic design in France and England. These designs idealized rural life, depicting elegant farmers and gentle shepherdesses in pastoral landscapes that often featured water mills and meandering cows.

Paintings and the popular *toile de Jouy* prints featured these bucolic compositions that have little in common with actual rural life. See TOILE DE JOUY.

bespoke (adj.) Describes a commercial transaction that predates manufacturing, in which individuals directly commissioned handmade furniture and other items. Also indicates pieces which are not standard but individually customized to meet particular client needs.

bevel The edge of a flat surface that has been cut on an angle. See CANTED and CHAMFER.

beveled glass Transparent, non-crystalline solid material whose edges are canted, made by grinding and polishing the perimeter of the vitreous sheet at an angle. Used in mirrors, doors, leaded-glass windows, and other decorative applications.

bibelots (French) Trinkets or knickknacks. Small art objects such as miniature paintings, sculptures, snuffboxes, etc. created for personal use or as decorations. See OBJET D'ART.

Bible box A 17th-century carved container that contained a family copy of the Christian scriptures. Later made with a hinged sloping lid, which when closed served as a reading stand or desk. The interior sometimes featured compartments and small shelves.

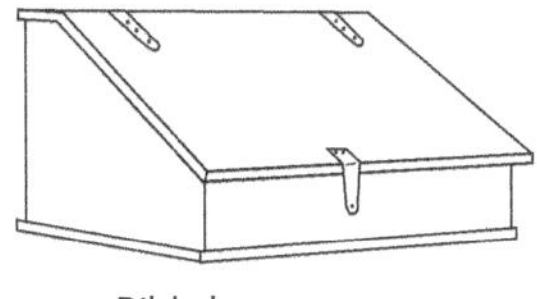
Bible box

∞Bible chair English seat dating from 1600 to 1650 in which the seat frame lifted up so that the Christian scriptures could be stored below. Otherwise, similar to a simple wooden seat. See CHANCEL CHAIR and WAINSCOT CHAIR.

bibliothèque (French) (1) A large bookcase or book press. (2) The location of a book collection or library.

bidet (French) A plumbing device. A washing unit or a container for a basin, often associated with personal hygiene.

Biedermeier (German) An early-19th-century furniture and decoration style (1815–1848). A simplified version of neoclassicism but rendered "homey" and "bourgeois" with painted details in black and gold that simulate carving. The furniture was made of fruitwoods and mahogany and was characterized by arches, pediments, columns, lyres, plumes, and wreaths. The name of the style is derived from "Papa Biedermeier," a comic symbol of middle-class contentment. Biedermeier pieces were also made in Austria, northern Italy, Denmark, and Poland.

∞Bilbao mirror A late-18th-century reflecting device, often with a frame of marble, or marble and wood, and a pair of slender columns. The name derives from the Basque city in northern Spain.

billet A type of Norman ornament that consisted of short cylinders and blocks. In 18th-century furniture, inlaid banding was used for decoration around cabinet drawers and doors.

BIM Acronym for BUILDING INFORMATION MODELING.

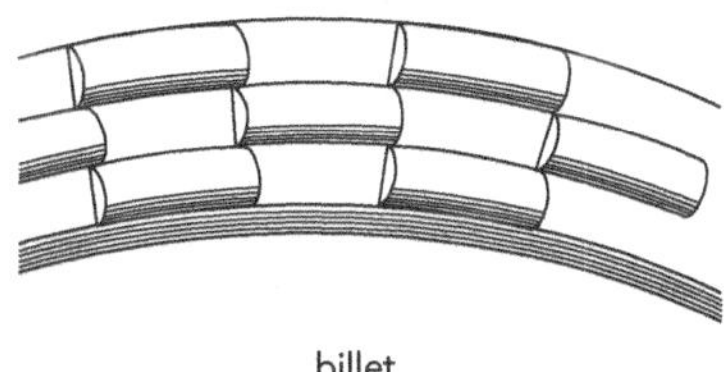
billet

bioclimactic A design approach focused on the weather of a region considered in the long term, initially Southeast Asia. Dating to the 1970s, this was a clarion call for ecologically responsible architecture, particularly in high-rises. In this mindset, buildings should respond to climate and utilize passive lighting and circulation systems. Early adapters include Ken Yeang and Geoffrey Bawa, who encouraged a move beyond technology and to include nature in the construction and daily life of buildings, collectively termed eco-architecture.

biodesign A field of study, and a discipline, a distinct sector of healthcare concerned with improving human wellness, sustainability, and security (as related to the previous two). Harnessing the design rules of the planet and the building blocks of nature, the medical/engineering/industrial design hybrid respects nature as a designer. Among their interests are reducing reliance on fossil fuels, concern for the future of healthcare, and multidisciplinary innovation.

biodiversity A concern with the extinction of species, and a simultaneous celebration of the richness of the biosphere. A decline in the number of species resulted in calls for conservation, promotion of sustainability, and respect for natural resources. The opposite of a mono-culture. The variety of life and its genetic diversity in a habitat or ecosystem is to be preserved for future solutions. New materials, ways of designing, and medicinal cures will come from the diverse gene pool.

bioluminescence The production of light by a living organism. Lanternfish, algae, fireflies, squid, and jellyfish are some of the flora and fauna that produce light. The name of the phenomena lends itself to a design sector trying to replicate the natural processes in order to create ecological friendly products, such as glowing refugee blankets, and off-the-grid camping equipment.

biomimicry A design approach that finds inspiration in nature for functional and aesthetic purposes.

biombo A Mexican screen based on Japanese prototypes. Originally during the Baroque period.

biomorphic A nonrepresentational form or pattern that resembles a living organism in shape or appearance.

biophilia (1) An innate love for the natural world. (2) A design approach with strong ties to nature, not for pure aesthetic reasons but from a belief that nature designs well and human activity should follow suit.

biosphere (1) A particular habitat or ecosystem. The natural biosphere is the result of atmosphere + lithosphere + hydrosphere. The totality of a realm or region that supports biological life. (2) An artificial biosphere is an attempt to replicate the qualities of the biosphere in a man-made artificially created environment, with a focus on self-sustaining processes of viability of the enclosed ecosystem.

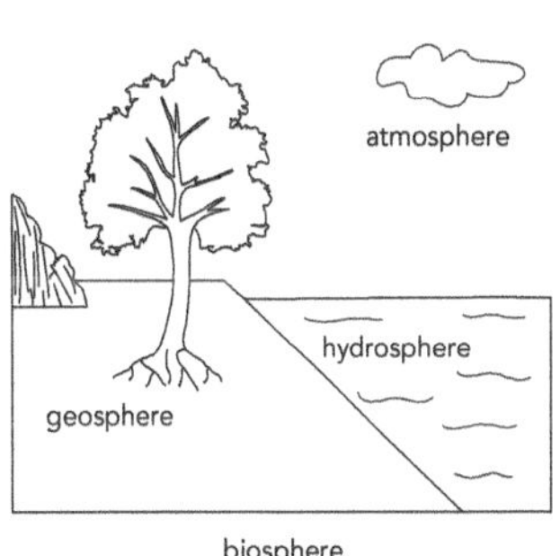

biosphere

birch A light brown, fine-grained American wood. Strong and hard, it can take a natural finish or be stained to simulate mahogany, walnut, satinwood, and other expensive woods. Used for doors, trims, and floors as well as furniture. In quartered or flat-sliced veneer, it is possible to create a curly figure. The European variety is less available than its American cousin. See *Table 5.*

∞birdcage clock A late-17th-century English openwork timepiece made of brass with exposed pendulum and weights.

birdcage support In early American furniture, the double-block construction that resembled the outline of an aviary and made it possible for a tilt-top table to rotate and tilt. In other styles such as 18th-century English, the piece is made of turned colonnettes.

bird's beak (1) In Greek classic architecture, a supporting molding that resembled the downward curve of the flying vertebrate's upper mandible. (2) In furniture, a round V-cut on molding corners.

bird's eye A figure on wood that resembles small avian globular organs, caused by cutting on a tangent through the indentations that sometimes appear on the annual rings of the log. Often noted on maple wood.

bird's-eye perspective Aerial view of an interior or of architecture that enables the designer to present a panoramic view.

biscuit tufting A method of tying back upholstery and padding to create plump, square tufts on chairbacks and seats. Buttons are usually sewn back taut in a regular square or diamond pattern. The excess padding is forced into the center of each square or diamond, making a small "pillow."

bisected vault An arch or curved ceiling structure with one impost only; the crown abuts the opposite wall. It resembles one quarter of a cylinder or half of a barrel vault.

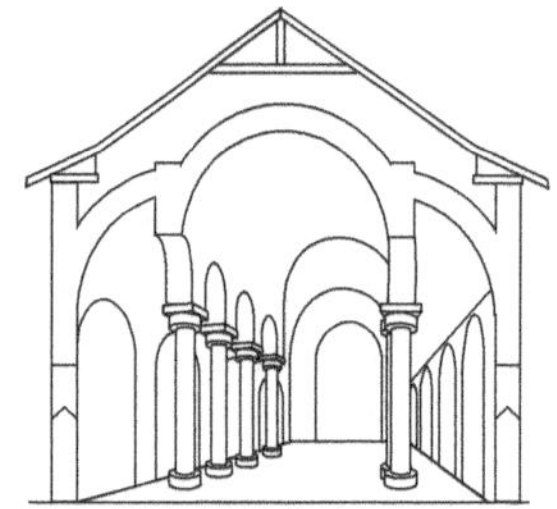
bisected vault

bisque Pottery that has been fired once and has no glaze or a very thin one. Dull in color, tan or red terra-cotta, depending upon the clay. Also refers to white, unglazed porcelain figurines and groups, made at Sèvres in France in the late 18th century. Also called BISCUIT.

bistro table A small surface unit, 28 inches to 30 inches in diameter or less (71–76 cm), atop a slender upright pedestal that ends in a weighted base. The top may be marble, metal, or plastic laminate. Common in French cafés.

∞Blackamoor A decorative statue of an African, often in an elaborate costume. A popular motif during the Italian Renaissance, it was revived in the Victorian period. Today it is considered offensive.

black gum See TUPELO.

∞blackline An outdated method of making architectural copies that was considered an improvement over blueprints because dark figures showed clearly on a white background. Predates CAD. See BLUEPRINT and CAD.

blackwood (1) A material similar to acacia and native to Australia and Tasmania. (2) Hardwood painted or stained to look like ebony, used by John Belter in his American Victorian furniture. See ACACIA.

blackwork A technique of embroidery of the English Tudor period (16th century) in which patterns were picked out in black and silver thread; these designs inspired many printed linings and wallpapers. Such embroidery became popular at the end of the Elizabethan reign, circa 1603.

blanc de plomb (French) White lead, used in paint for interior paneling and furniture. Some Louis XV furniture ordered for the Petit Trianon was originally white, but dust and time grayed the furniture down to gris Trianon, a soft gray color.

blanket chest A 17th- and 18th-century American space-containing piece with a lidded top and one or two drawers below. The lowboy, the highboy, and the chest of drawers eventually replaced such units. See CONNECTICUT CHEST and HADLEY CHEST.

bleaching The process that removes natural and artificial impurities in fabrics to achieve a pure white for even dyeing or printing. The results vary with the fiber content of the fabric. The process occurs by exposure to air, light, or chlorine. Open-textured woods can be chemically brought to lighter tones. Blond walnut and mahogany are results of the process. See *Table 4.*

bleeding The running off or blending together of excess dye from a dyed fabric during washing. In printing wallpaper and fabrics, the color or pigment spreads out beyond the actual printed designs, usually into the SELVAGE.

blend A mixture of different fibers in the same yarn or fabric.

blind A shade or screen device used over a window to control light and air. The device works on either a roller or a pull cord, as in a Roman or Austrian shade. May be made of various fabrics or may be made of wood, metal, or plastic slats, as in Venetian blinds or Boston blinds. See ROMAN SHADE.

blind arcade A decorative, non-structural series of arches applied to a wall surface with no actual opening.

blind arcade

blind header In masonry, a course of brick work perpendicular to the wall but configured so that the length of brick is within the wall.

blind stitching In upholstery, a method of sewing in a particular area of a sofa or chair that is eventually covered and becomes impossible to reach. The hidden area is sewn first from the back, then the flap is put into place and finished off by sewing or tacking from the front.

blister A wood-grain effect produced by the uneven contour of the annual ring growth. It presents a bumpy figure, also called a "quilted figure." This figuration often appears in maple, cedar, poplar, and mahogany.

block flooring See PARQUET.

block foot A cube-shaped support, usually used with a square, untapered leg. When tapered, it is called a spade, taper, or therm foot. See MARLBOROUGH LEG.

bed with block feet

blockfront A furniture elevation divided into three vertical panels side by side; the center panel is concave or recessed between two convex or advancing side panels. Especially associated with John Goddard and the Newport School of 18th-century American chests, secretaries, and highboys. Also called a tub front. See BREAKFRONT.

block print Fabric printed by hand, using carved wooden bricks or plates. The dye is rolled over the raised pattern on the form, which is then pressed down, under pressure, on the fabric. If a two-color design is desired, separate shapes are used. This technique also produced early wallpapers and gilded leather tapestries.

blond woods Light beige-toned natural materials such as primavera, avodire, aspen, holly, birch, and bleached mahogany and walnut. Also refers to natural materials clouded with a white pigment or open grains filled in with white pigment.

∞blueprint An outdated method of creating copies in which a positive print of white lines contrasts with a blue paper (ferroprussiate) background. The negative is a translucent drawing, usually of building or engineering details or plans.

blunt arrow leg The support of an 18th-century American Windsor chair, which ends in a ball-like tip. It resembles a used and therefore worn flying weapon.

boasting The rough shaping of stone by a carver or sculptor before the finished sculptural or architectural details are accomplished.

boat bed (1) A sleeping device placed in an alcove with one long side showing. (2) A low, massive piece popular in the French Empire and Restoration periods and in American furniture contemporary with these periods. It is similar to the gondola or sleigh bed, boat-shaped, and often made in light-colored woods with contrasting wood marquetry. Often raised on a massive, step-like base.

boat-shaped table A modern conference and dining surface. The long sides are shaped like parentheses (they bow out gently in the center and taper in toward the short ends). The two short ends are straight. The shape is a long oval with a flattened top and bottom.

boatswain's chair A seat similar to a captain's chair but smaller and with half-arms. Sometimes spelled "bosun's chair."

bobbinet A sheer, mesh-like curtain fabric.

bobbin turning Legs and stretchers made on a lathe with spindle-like swellings. This style was popular in the early 17th century. In the late-18th-century Windsor chair, this type of turning was sometimes used for stretchers.

bobeche A socket with a wide rim for a candle or an electric bulb. Originally used to catch wax drippings, today it is used as a decorative top to a candlestick or as a device on which to hook prisms and crystals.

bobote A tropical hardwood.

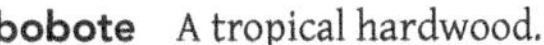

chair with bobbin turning

body In pottery, the clay or other material from which a piece of pottery or porcelain is manufactured. The glaze is applied later.

bodying in A process of wood finishing, in which the recesses of a wood's coarse grains are filled in, resulting in an even finish.

∞boffet or boffet chair A three-legged, triangular, Scandinavian seat that was produced until the end of the 16th century. They were made of turnings and had carved ornaments.

bog oak A natural wood that has been preserved in muddy peat ground to affect its color. Used for banding, paneling, and ornaments.

bois de bout (French) Wood cut across the grain, thus appearing darker.

bois de fil (French) See FIL DE BOIS.

bois (or boise) de rose (French) A yellowish wood with reddish striped markings. The wood turns blond as it ages. See TULIP WOOD.

bois de violette (French) Also called BOIS DE VIOLET and amaranth. See KINGWOOD.

boiserie (French) The carved woodwork and paneling of 17th- and 18th-century French interiors, often painted and picked out in gilt.

Bokhara rug See TURKOMAN RUGS.

bolection moldings A series of rounded embellishments that project far beyond the panel or wall to which they are applied. Such a panel projects from the wall surface, as opposed to a sunk panel. See PANEL, BOLECTION, and PANEL, SUNK.

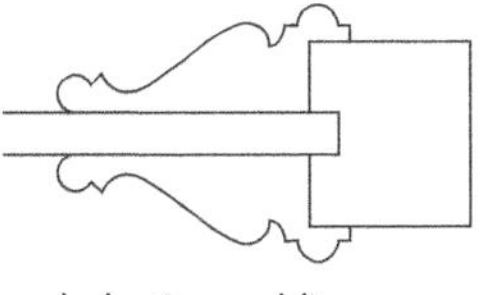

bolection moldings

bolster A long, usually cylindrical, stuffed pillow or cushion. Also an oversized pillow or back rest, which may be wedge-shaped or rectangular.

bolster

bolster arm A 19th-century term for a fat, rounded or cylindrical upholstered horizontal support on a chair or sofa that resembles the cylindrical stuffed pillow.

Bombay furniture Furniture manufactured in India after the fall of the Mogul Empire in 1740. A conglomeration of French and Portuguese styles and forms, the pieces are overlaid with elaborate and minute Indian carving. English and Dutch influences also appear.

bombé (French) (1) (adj.) Convex, arched, or humpbacked. A flowing curve; a surface that swells outward and then recedes. The line appears in commodes and chests at the end of the Louis XIV and Régence periods in France and reaches its height during the Louis XV or Rococo period. Bombé cabinets and drawer furniture also appear in the Venetian Rococo and Chippendale's French style. (2) (noun) A commode.

bonader An 18th-century Swedish or Swedish-American wall hanging depicting rural subjects, painted on paper or canvas.

bond An arrangement of bricks, masonry, concrete blocks, etc., in which the vertical joints are staggered. The pattern can be emphasized by using different colored finishing bricks. See CHECKERBOARD BOND; COMMON BOND; ENGLISH BOND; ENGLISH CROSS-BOND; FLEMISH BOND; RUNNING BOND; and STRETCHER BOND.

bond course The layer of bricks that overlaps the bricks below.

bonded fabric A nonwoven textile made up of a mass of fibers glued, cemented, fused, or otherwise bonded together. Similar to FELT.

bone china Vitrified ceramic material first produced in England in 1800. Originally manufactured with oxen bones that were pulverized into ash and added to the kaolin.

bonheur du jour A small upright lady's desk with a cabinet top and drawers, in which the desk area was usually covered with a let-down front. A small cupboard or bookshelf was often at the rear. A popular design of the Louis XVI period.

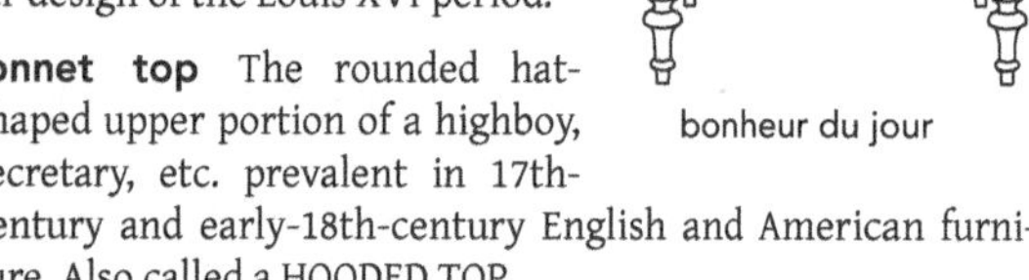

bonheur du jour

∞bonnet top The rounded hat-shaped upper portion of a highboy, secretary, etc. prevalent in 17th-century and early-18th-century English and American furniture. Also called a HOODED TOP.

bonnet top

bookcase In the late 17th and early 18th centuries, the storage unit resembled a typical china cabinet. In the mid-and-late 18th century, the space-containing device took on a new importance, and usually was made in two parts: a glazed door section on top of a closed cupboard. The area below had additional shelves or drawers. The top sometimes served as a writing desk.

bookcase

book-match veneering A method of joining thin sheets of wood in which pairs of adjacent slices, as they are cut from the log, are opened up like pages. Every other sheet of the material is turned over, as with pages in a bound volume, so that the back edge of one meets the front edge of the adjacent panel. This produces a mirror image of the grain pattern.

book table A rectangular, circular, or hexagonal pedestal with either exposed shelves on all sides or doors to cover the shelves. An 18th-century innovation similar to the POLE TABLE or POTE TABLE.

Boolean A system of algebraic notations, or logic, with two possible values, true and false, that is the basis of computing and hence many electronics. Named for George Boole. The data type with its two functions is the basis for algorithms, coding, internet searches, and increasingly sophisticated computer modeling, especially of complex curvilinear objects, including furniture, interiors, and architecture.

booty Items seized during warfare for commemoration, a classical and neoclassical motif.

borax A slang expression for cheap, commercial furniture, usually poorly constructed, badly styled, and poorly finished.

border A continuous running motif or ornament used for edging a design, fabric, or panel.

borne A round or oval type of seating with an upholstered upright or rail in the center that serves as a back, surrounded by a tufted circular seat. Popular in public areas during the VICTORIAN period. Also called a sociable.

boss The projecting ornament placed at the intersections of moldings or beams. Angel heads, flowers, foliage, and animal heads are common motifs. In Gothic architecture, often a hanging, ornamental pendant at the meeting of ribs in vaults. On furniture, the element is a small oval or semicircular applied ornament found in 17th- and 18th-century English and colonial designs. See CUL-DE-LAMPE.

borne   boss

bosse An African wood used for large veneers. A uniform pink-brown color with a mottled, satiny texture, also called African cedar and cedar mahogany. The material emits a cedar-like aroma when cut. See PIQUA.

bossona A hard Brazilian wood with black and brown streaks on a red-brown background. See GONÇALO ALVES.

Boston rocker A motion chair that is purposely non-static. The chair is built on curved supports,

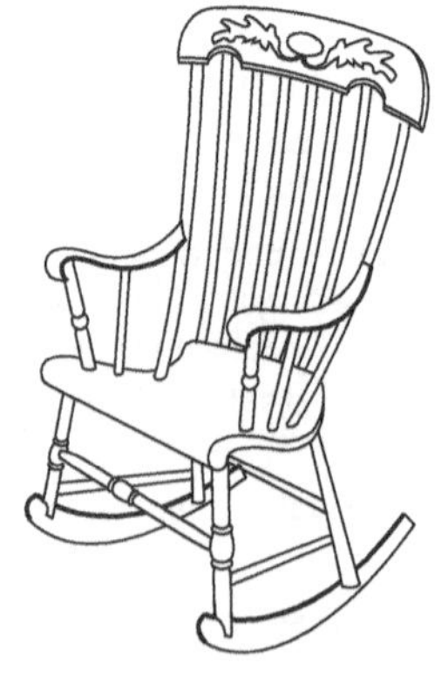

Boston rocker

and the wooden seat curves upward in the rear and dips down in front. The chair is often spindle backed and ornamented with a painted design on the wide top rail. An early-19th-century American design.

bottle-end glazing (1) Style of glass in cabinet doors in the 18th century that resembled vessel bottoms leaded together. (2) A bull's eye effect in a circular glass disk. See CROWN GLASS.

bottle turning Dutch lathe-work that resembles a glass storage vessel and appears in William and Mary furniture in late-17th-century England.

bouchon A cork pad covered with BAIZE on one side and leather on the other. In the 18th century, it served as a removable cover over the marble top of a BOUILLOTTE TABLE. The bouchon filled the space between the actual tabletop and the surrounding brass gallery, thus creating a level surface.

bouclé (French, buckled or crinkled) A plain or twill weave with small, regularly spaced loops and flat, irregular surfaces produced by twisted yarns. Made of wool, rayon, silk, cotton, or linen, the texture is well suited for contemporary furniture upholstery.

boudoir (French *bouder,* to pout) A woman's private apartment or room. Also the nucleus of the court social life in the period of Louis XV; guests were received and entertained in these feminine retreats, which were lavishly decorated and furnished.

boudoir chair A small-scaled seat, usually fully upholstered, for a woman's bedroom or dressing room. May be of any style or period, but often French Rococo.

∞bouillotte A foot warmer used in the 18th century.

∞bouillotte lamp A late-18th-century candlestick-like fixture, often a three- or four-armed candlestick set into a brass galleried base. A shallow shade, covered and protected the candle flames. A decorative brass handle finial above the shade made it portable. Originally associated with the small galleried tables they were set upon. See BOUILLOTTE TABLE.

∞bouillotte shade A shallow, drum-shaped light diffuser used for a lamp or candlestick. Sometimes made of decorated metal (tôle). See BOUILLOTTE LAMP and TÔLE.

∞bouillotte table An 18th-century French small, circular gaming surface, with a brass or bronze gallery edge. The piece usually had two small drawers as well as a pair of candle slides set into the apron, below the marble top. Originally used for playing *bouillotte,* a card game. See BOUCHON.

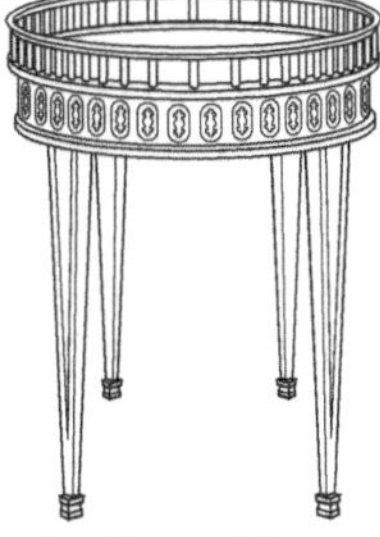

bouillotte table

Boulle work The inlay technique of ANDRÉ-CHARLES BOULLE, using ebony, tortoiseshell, silver, brass, ivory, and other precious materials. A sheet of metal (usually brass) and a sheet of tortoiseshell were glued together, and the design was cut out of both. The pieces of brass which dropped out could then be set into the tortoiseshell, resulting in première partie; or the shell could fill in the brass sheet, contrepartie. Associated with the Louis XIV and Régence periods. See *Designers and Architects.*

Bourbon period The classical part of the French Renaissance, dating from 1589 to 1730. It encompasses the reigns of Henry IV, Louis XIII, Louis XIV, and the Régence.

bow back An 18th-century Windsor chair with a hooped or curved vertical support continuing in its sweep to the arms or chair seat.

∞bowfat An 18th-century American term for a buffet. See BUFFET.

bow front A convex or "swell" shape, typical of mid- and late-18th-century chests, commodes, sideboards, etc.

bow front

bow top The uppermost rail of a chair with an unbroken curve between the uprights.

bow window A large projecting curved or semicircular glazed opening. See BAY WINDOW.

bow window

box bed A sleeping platform with bedding enclosed on three sides, or sometimes a device that folds up against the wall. In the French Gothic period, the open side was draped or shuttered to provide privacy and keep out drafts. See BUILT-IN FURNITURE and LIT CLOS.

box chair A sturdy four-legged seat with four stretchers, sometimes continuous, that are close to the ground and that connect the legs.

box match A veneering pattern similar to the diamond match but angled to create a series of consecutive squares radiating out from the center.

box pleating A technique in which fabric is folded back on itself and then folded back again in the opposite direction, creating a partially hidden panel of fabric. Similar to a LINENFOLD motif.

box seat Dining room seat cushion in which the welt on top emphasizes its rectangular shape.

box set A three-walled stage design, with one long wall upstage and two side walls.

box settle A chest with a hinged lid that, when closed, serves as a seat. This piece was popular in the early English Renaissance (Tudor and Elizabethan periods) and also in 17th- and 18th-century American Provincial furniture. See also CASSAPANCA.

box spring A sleeping unit made of spiral steel coils encased in a rectangular-like frame. A layer of cotton felt, hair, rubberized hair, or foam is placed over the coiled metal and tightly covered with ticking. Usually used in conjunction with a mattress.

box stool A simple Renaissance seating unit consisting of an enclosed rectangle made from boards with a flat hinged top that functioned as the seat.

box stretcher A square or rectangular reinforcement at the furniture base, created by four stretchers between the legs of a table, chair, or cabinet. Makes the piece very sturdy.

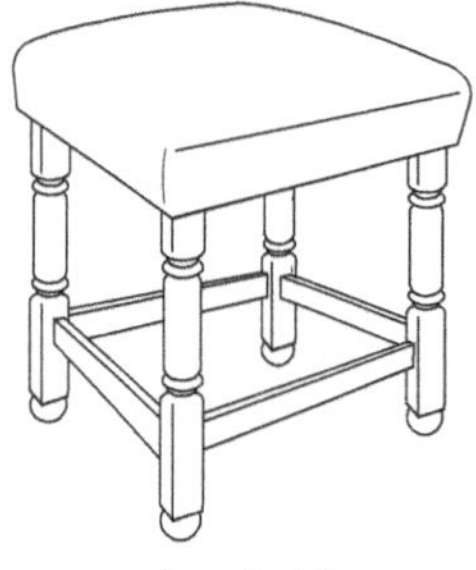
box stretcher

boxwood A dense, light-colored, grained West Indian wood used almost entirely for inlays and small decorative articles. During the 16th century, it was used as an inlay wood on walnut and oak, and in the late 18th century for edge work on satinwood pieces.

BPE Acronym for BUILDING PERFORMANCE EVALUATION.

brace (1) The part of a piece of furniture that provides added strength or rigidity. Stretchers on the legs of a piece of furniture are braces. (2) In construction, an angled reinforcement that transmits the weight from one part of a structure to another. It is often a piece of wood angled between two major timbers to keep them in place and to preserve the angle they create.

∞**braced back** A Windsor chair in which the top rail is reinforced by two spindles projecting up from an extension behind the seat to the chair rail. Also called a fiddle-braced back.

bracket (1) In furniture, a shaped support between the leg and the seat of a chair or between the leg and the top of a table. (2) A bracket is also a decorative wall-hung shelf and a sconce or wall fixture. (3) In architecture, a supporting element that projects from a wall or pier at a right angle and helps to carry the weight of a beam or other architectural member.

bracket candlestick A sconce or appliqué. A decorative wall-hung unit with a wax taper projecting forward.

bracket

bracket clock A small timepiece designed to sit on a projecting wall-hung bracket; a shelf timepiece rather than one that is wall-hung.

bracket cornice (1) An ornamental entablature whose vertical loads are counteracted by a series of angled supports. (2) An interior wooden version of a corbel table. See CORBEL and CORBEL TABLE.

bracket foot In cabinetry, a popular furniture leg in 18th-century English and American designs, with a straight corner edge and a curved inner edge. In English furniture, the termination is usually wider than it is high. Also called CONSOLE LEG.

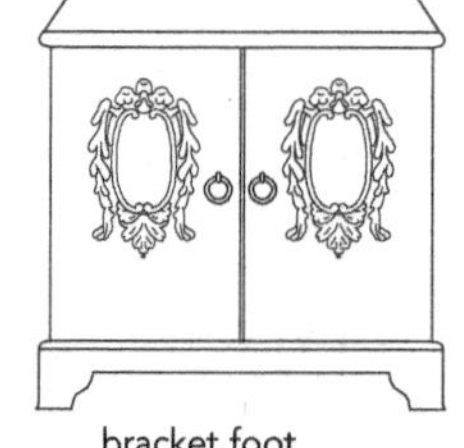
bracket foot

brad A small, thin nail with little or no head and less than one inch in length, often used for finishing work.

Braganza toe See SPANISH SCROLL FOOT.

braid A narrow strip made by intertwining several strands of silk, cotton, or other fabric. Uses: trimming, binding, or finishing edge.

braided rug Provincial floor covering, oval or round in shape, made of strips of fabric twisted into a thick coil. The coil is laid flat and stitched together, usually in the traditional oval shape. Braided floor coverings are associated with early American interiors. See RAG RUG.

braid

branding A commercial sector related to advertising and marketing. The holistic activity of promoting a person, group, company, or product. The branding is not synonymous with the product but is the value of the name independent of the physical product. This approach concerns not bricks-and-mortar assets but, in the commercial sphere, values, identity, and reputation. Interior design, in terms of branding, does not reflect a pre-existing corporate value but is a constituent part of creating and communicating commercial value.

brass An alloy of one part zinc and three to seven parts copper.

brass, antiqued The alloy given an aged look through oxidation. Can also be artificially produced.

brass, polished The alloy given a bright mirror-like finish.

brasses Hardware or decorative handles, escutcheons, hinges, etc. made of the copper/zinc alloy.

brattishing A cresting in an ornamented or pierced parapet. A decorative leaf design used as a cresting device on the top of English Tudor screens or paneling. Also called Tudor flower. See CRESTING.

brazier (1) A pan on legs, which held hot embers and was used for heating during the 19th century. Also called a brasero or brasera. (2) Someone who works with brass.

Brazilwood A reddish-colored wood similar to mahogany.

breakfront A case piece of furniture in which the forward elevation is formed of two or more planes; the central portion is either advanced or recessed from the two ends. Particularly describes bookcases, cabinets, and secretaries made in 18th-century England and its colonies. See also BLOCK FRONT.

breakfront

breeze brick Standard-sized building unit made of coke breeze concrete instead of baked clay. The addition of coke breeze renders the unit less dense. Unlike clay units it is possible to drive a nail or screw into breeze brick.

Brewster chair An early New England seat with turned spindles and a rush seat. Named after Elder Brewster. The seat usually has a double row of vertical spindles on the back. Resembles Provincial Jacobean furniture and is similar to the CARVER CHAIR, which also incorporates horizontal rails on the back.

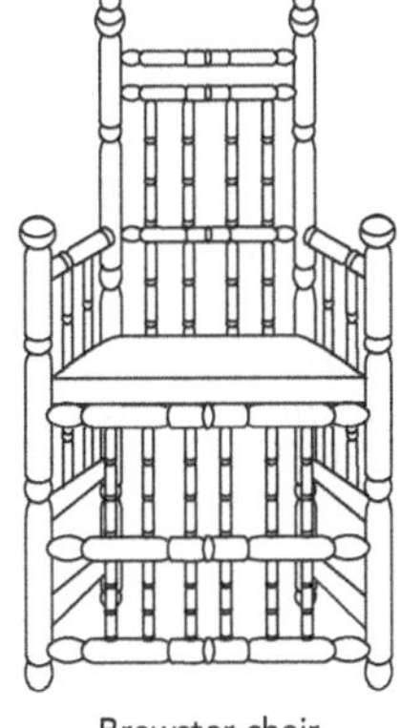
Brewster chair

bric-à-brac Small items collected and displayed for ornamental or antiquarian purposes.

brick A hardened rectangular block of clay, sun-dried or dried and baked in a kiln. The blocks are a common building material and can be stacked in a variety of designs to create wall and floor patterns. Patterns are also reproduced in paper, embossed paper, plastic, vinyl, etc. The standard brick size is 8¾ inches by 4¼ inches by either 2⅝ inches or 2⅞ inches. Some common types of brick: blue or engineering, fletton, glazed, London stock, and sand lime. See *Table 3*.

brick, adobe Large clay blocks of varying sizes that are roughly molded and sun-dried.

brick, arch See VOUSSOIR.

brick, building Also called a common brick. Not specially textured or surfaced.

brick, clinker An extremely hard, burned construction unit.

brick, common See BRICK, BUILDING.

brick, economy A building unit that measures 4 inches by 4 inches by 8 inches, with one COURSE laid every 4 inches. See COURSE.

brick, engineered A clay building unit that measures 3⅕ inches by 4 inches by 8 inches, with five COURSES laid in every 16 inches.

brick, facing Specially treated, colored, or textured building blocks used for exterior or decorative facing.

brick, fire A ceramic building block that resists high temperatures.

brick, gauged A specially dimensioned block such as an ARCH BRICK or VOUSSOIR.

brick, Norman A block that measures 2⅔ inches by 4 inches by 12 inches with three COURSES laid to every 8 inches.

brick, Roman A building unit that measures 2 inches by 4 inches by 12 inches, with two COURSES laid in every 4 inches. The Roman unit is sometimes made up to 16 inches long.

brick, salmon A soft, under-burned, pinkish building material. Also called a chuff brick or place brick.

bridal chest A storage unit meant to hold a betrothed woman's household linens. Also called a MARRIAGE CHEST or HOPE CHEST. See CASSONE and CONNECTICUT CHEST.

brightness The quality of producing or reflecting light; luminance. It is an attribute of light sources, devices which emit light, and a measure of the intensity of the light produced. A means to measure the perceived intensity of light of a light-emitting object such as a diode. Such an object produces candelas, while the impact of light on the eye is measured as luminous flux.

brise-soleil (French) A porous FAÇADE screen that lets in air and casts the building in shadow.

British Colonial Describes the style of Georgian-like furniture, interiors, and architecture of the 18th century developed by members of the English colonial administration in the Americas, Asia, West Indies, India, and parts of Africa. It resembled the styles that were popular in England at that time, but interpreted by indigenous craftsmen in native woods using local motifs.

broadcloth A lustrous cotton textile with a tight, plain weave and a crosswise rib. Can also be woven of wool, rayon, or silk.

broadloom A seamless carpet woven in widths of 6 feet or more, usually 9, 12, 15, or 18 feet wide; the length is indeterminate. Made in a variety of textures, weaves, colors, and fibers.

brocade (Low Latin, embroider or stitch) Originally a fabric of silk, satin, or velvet, variegated with gold and silver or raised and enriched with flowers, foliage, and other ornaments. The fabric resembles embroidery and is woven on a jacquard loom. The threads do not appear on the surface but are carried across the width on the reverse side. Favored for drapery and upholstery in period and traditional rooms.

brocade carpet A fabric in which the pattern is formed by heavy twisted yarn tufts on a ground of straight fiber yarns. An engraved appearance results, although the yarns are often the same color.

brocatelle (1) A heavy fabric that resembles damask, in which the pattern appears to be embossed or raised. The pattern is usually a silk weave against a twill background. A textile from the highlands, it was originally an imitation of Italian tooled leather. (2) Also, a calcareous stone or marble having a yellow ground, flecked with white, gray, and red.

brocatelle violette The most French of all marbles. A stone or marble with a purplish undertone, usually richly grained and patterned.

broché A silk or satin ground fabric similar to brocade, with small raised floral designs made to resemble embroidery. Threads that are not used in the surface design are carried only across the width of the design on the reverse side, rather than across the entire reverse side as in brocade.

broken arch A curved or elliptical structural device that is not completed or joined at its apex. The open center section is sometimes filled with a decorative device such as an urn or finial. See also GOOSENECK PEDIMENT and SWAN NECK PEDIMENT.

broken front Similar to a block front or breakfront, a piece of furniture in which the elevation is made up of different planes. The center section may project beyond the side sections. See BLOCK FRONT and BREAKFRONT.

broken pediment An architectural element frequently used in 18th-century English furniture on top cabinets, bookcases, curio cabinets, corner cabinets, highboys, etc. The raking cornices are interrupted at their apex; the resulting open central area is often filled with a decorative device such as an urn, finial, shell, etc.

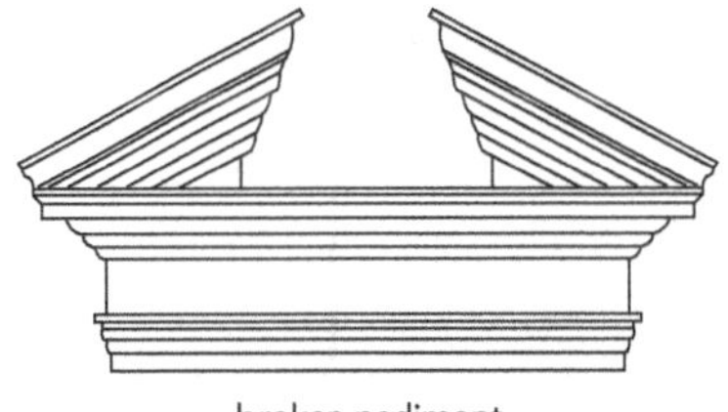
broken pediment

bronze A compound metal consisting mainly of copper and tin, originally used for sculpture in ancient Greece and Rome as well as in China and Africa. As bronze ages and reacts with chemicals, it takes on a greenish tint and matte surface called a patina. A patina can also be chemically induced. See also PATINA.

bronze d'ameublement Furniture mounts made of the copper/tin alloy, including handles, escutcheons, drawer pulls, etc.

bronze doré Gilded bronze. See ORMOLU or ORMOULU.

bronze furniture Metal furnishings used by the ancient Greeks and Romans. The designs were light and open since the material was so strong. In the late Renaissance and Empire periods, the alloy was again popular for tables, bases, etc., as well as for mounts, hardware, and trim. See BRONZE DORÉ and ORMOLU or ORMOULU.

brouillon (French) A rough draft or design at an interim stage, which is noted for its confusing mixture of elements.

Brussels carpet An uncut wool loop-pile fabric woven on the Wilton loom, with a cotton back. It is also called a "round wire" floor covering. Distinguished by its long pile and unusual wearing qualities.

Brutalism (French, *beton brut*, raw concrete) A strain of Modernism that emphasizes not detailed perfection but materiality, especially that of concrete. Related to the art brut movement.

bubinga An African wood with a beautiful, purple, closely striped grain, on a pale to red-brown ground. The figure is either narrow broken stripes or mottled. Also called AKUME.

bucket armchair A Regency seat, similar to the spoon-back chair. The arms rise in a scroll from the middle of the side rails of the seat, then form a continuous curve to create the top rail. Caning often fills in the space below the rounded back.

buckram A stiffly finished, heavily sized, plain-weave fabric, used as a stiffening for valances.

∞**bucranium** A decorative sculptured ox skull that sometimes appeared on the friezes of Roman structures.

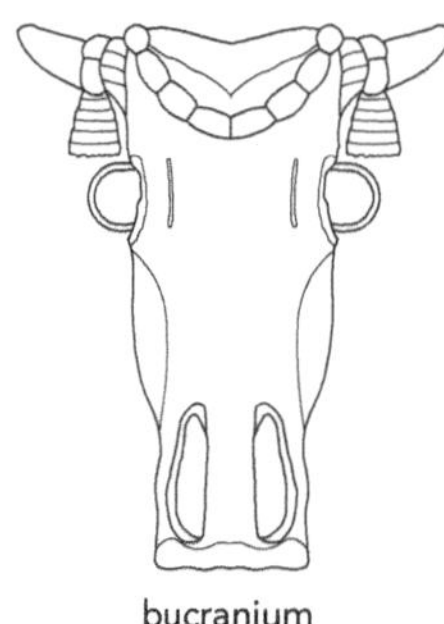
bucranium

Buen Retiro See CAPO DI MONTE.

buffet A cupboard or sideboard. A side table, sometimes with cupboards or shelves. Early Renaissance examples resembled medieval cupboards and were supported on bases. The entire piece was usually decorated with columns, medallions, and arabesques. See CRÉDENCE and DESSERTE.

∞**buhl work** The English term for BOULLE WORK, André-Charles Boulle's inlay technique using brass and tortoiseshell.

building board Also called plasterboard. Made from repulped paper, shredded wood, gypsum, and other plaster composition and then sandwiched between sheets of kraft paper. Usually placed on lathing strips to create partitions, walls, or ceilings. The panels are usually 4 feet by 8 feet (122 cm by 244 cm).

building information modeling (BIM) The process of digitally managing a structure, starting during its construction, and sharing knowledge at all phases between designers, contractors, subcontractors, and clients.

building performance evaluation (BPE) The inspection of a structure one or two years after its first use. The goal is to improve design practice and measure the success of the design by evaluating occupant performance and satisfaction.

built-in furniture Elements typically of carpentry, such as cabinets, seats, beds, or chests, that are constructed as an integral part of the interior architecture. The practice dates from the earliest interiors. In contemporary use, these pieces are constructed into the actual wall or into a false wall, designed with the aim of economizing floor space.

built-in furniture

bulbous form A heavy, melon-like wood turning that was popular for furniture supports and bases during the early Renaissance in Flanders, Belgium; Holland; England; France; and Italy.

bullion A type of fringe made of thick cord wrapped in gold or silver thread.

bullnose edge A deep, almost half-round form at the perimeter of the surface of wood furniture. A thick slab of marble used as a tabletop or desktop having an exposed, rounded termination that approximates 180 degrees.

bull's eye (French, *oeil de bouef*) (1) A circular or oval window. (2) A circular distortion in the center of a disk of crown glass. See CROWN GLASS.

bull's-eye mirror A round reflective surface, often with a convex or concave glass set in an ornamental frame. A GIRANDOLE.

bundle A unit of wallpaper, usually delivered in single, double, or triple rolls.

bun foot A furniture support resembling a flattened ball, used on Flemish, late French Renaissance, and late-17th-century English furniture. See also FLEMISH FOOT.

bunk bed Two sleeping units set one directly over the other, separated by vertical frames or uprights in the four corners. Each unit has its own spring and mattress. A built-in ladder or steps provide access to the upper unit. Also called a DOUBLE-DECKER BED.

bunk bed

bureau (1) Originally, the fabric used to cover a table that served as a writing surface. (2) A desk or writing table with pigeonhole compartments. According to Sheraton, in late-18th-century England, "a common desk with drawers." (3) In the 19th and 20th centuries in America, a chest of drawers used in a bedroom, or a part of a bedroom suite.

bureau à cylindre (French) A rolltop desk, also called a BUREAU À RIDEAU.

∞bureau à pente (French) A folding, slant-lid desk.

bureau à rideau (French) A rolltop desk. See BUREAU À CYLINDRE.

∞bureau bookcase A desk with a cabinet over the writing surface, according to Chippendale, in 18th-century England.

bureau bookcase

bureau commode A Louis XIV large writing table with drawers.

bureau en dos d'âne A Louis XV drop-leaf desk that took its name from its contour; the desk top resembled the back of an ass. The unit stood on tall cabriole legs with a slant-fronted unit on top. The slanted front dropped down to become a horizontal writing surface.

bureau plat A flat writing table or desk. See TABLE DESK.

bureau table A kneehole table designed by Goddard of Newport, Rhode Island, in the late 18th century.

∞Burgomaster chair See ROUNDABOUT CHAIR.

Burgundian A provincial French Renaissance furniture style of the Rhone Valley. Classical in its use of architectural elements, it was noteworthy for its massive construction and high-relief carving. A two-tiered cupboard, cabinet à deux corps, with carved human or allegorical figures, is typical of the style. Hugues Sambin of Dijon, France, was an architect associated with the style. In 1570, he published a book of engraved ornaments, architectural details, etc. See CABINET À DEUX CORPS and *Designers and Architects.*

burl A growth in the bole or root of a tree. The wartlike protuberance, which is sliced to obtain veneer wood, contains dark pith centers and underdeveloped buds that produce a pitted "little eye" or "knotted effect" on the surface. The growth often appears in walnut trees. See CARPATHIAN ELM BURL.

burlap A plain weave of cotton, jute, or hemp that is coarse and loosely woven. Used to cover springs in upholstered furniture and also as webbing. In informal, contemporary settings, it can be used for draperies, bedspreads, etc.

burling (verb) A final checking and finishing in broadloom production. Long tufts may be clipped or hidden, and sunken tufts may be straightened out.

burnt-out or etched-out fabric A textile in which patterns are produced by chemically burning out one of the two types of yarns used in making the fabric. This technique is used in the production of brocaded velvet.

burnt work Line designs drawn on wood with a heated metal instrument, or shading achieved by applying hot sand.

∞buro table An early-18th-century American term for a bureau on legs, usually with drawers.

burr A veneer made from transverse slices of the gnarled roots of the walnut tree, popular in England from the mid 17th century to the beginning of the 18th century. See BURL.

bust A painting or sculpture of a human head and shoulders, sometimes including the chest or breast. It may be used as a freestanding piece of art, incorporated into an architectural niche, set on a pedestal, or used as a finial in a broken pediment.

butcher furniture (1) The heavy, architectural furniture produced by DUNCAN PHYFE after 1825. (2) The massive scrolled furniture that was characteristic of the Second or Late Empire in France. See SECOND EMPIRE or LATE EMPIRE.

butler finish A distinctive surface luster produced on silver by mechanical buffing with abrasives. The traditional butler finish was originally achieved by hand rubbing.

butler's tray table

butler's tray table A small surface and stand with hinged sides that lift up to form the edges of a removable carrier. Cutout sections in the hinged flaps make it possible to lift up the entire device and move it about as one might carry a large platter.

butterfly A popular Asian motif that became associated with the SECOND EMPIRE period in France (1848–1870). Many of the symbols of the first Empire period were revived under Louis Napoleon Bonaparte, but the colorful winged insect replaced the honey-gathering and punitive bee. The polymorphic member of the lepidoptera order was better suited to the romantic and naturalistic tendencies of the period.

butterfly table

butterfly table A colonial American drop-leaf surface on legs with broad bracket like a wing that supports the raised leaf.

butterfly wedge A double V-shaped fastener that holds adjoining boards together. The V's connect at their points to form a shape reminiscent of the insect's wings in gliding position.

butternut An American wood also known as white walnut. The wood resembles black walnut in fine graining, carvability, polishability, etc. but is lighter in color, hard, and durable. The annual rings form a beautiful figured pattern.

butt hinge A simple movable connection with two leaves. When the piece of hardware is attached to a door and a vertical frame, the pin joint is visible.

butt joint The simplest and cheapest type of connection, but one that will not take much strain. One piece of wood is set perpendicular and at right angles to another (the pieces touching each other) and then glued, nailed, or screwed together.

butt match Veneer arrangement similar to BOOK-MATCH VENEERING but joined end-to-end in a continuous strip. Also called end match.

buttress A mass of masonry on the exterior of a building set at an angle to the wall that it strengthens or supports; a separation of structure from space-defining elements.

buttwood veneer In wood grains, the section of the tree toward the root where the trunk fibers swing out and produce, in cross-section, a crinkly texture in addition to the long grain. Also called a stump grain.

Byzantine (adj.) Related to the Byzantine Empire, centered at Constantinople from 476 until 1453. The name is derived from the original town of Byzantium, which the Emperor Constantine renamed Constantinople. Byzantine designs were composed of Roman forms overlaid with Near Eastern motifs. A dome on pendentives, the rounded arch, and mosaics play an important part. Some Byzantine motifs still appear in Russian and south European decoration.

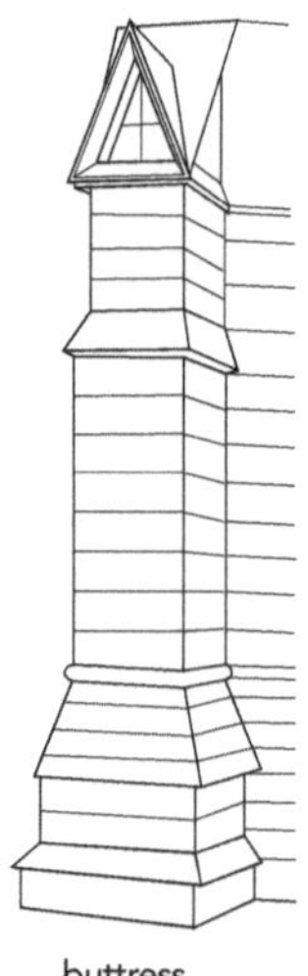

buttress

Byzantine decoration

cabbage rose A flamboyant, overblown floral motif popular in the Victorian era for carpets, wallpapers, and fabrics. Often combined with lovers' bowknots, doves, and cherubs.

∞cabinet (French, closet or receptacle) A unit of case furniture with shelves and doors, or a wooden or metal housing to contain an object, such as a television or radio.

cabinet

cabinet à deux corps A late-16th-century Renaissance case piece consisting of one cupboard or cabinet set upon a second and usually larger one. Often carved and ornamented with classic motifs, and with caryatid supports at the corners of the lower unit.

cabinet bed See MURPHY BED.

cabinet secrétaire A desk with a storage unit set above the writing surface. The storage part may have glass, metal, grill, or wood-paneled doors. It was a popular innovation of the 18th century in France and England.

cabinet secrétaire

cabinet vitrine A storage unit with glass doors, essentially a display case, first popularized in the late 17th and early 18th centuries, when porcelain from China was rare and precious and collections of Chinese articles were worthy of display.

cabinetwork Furniture and finished interior woodwork, in contrast to construction work or rough carpentry.

cable A twisted-rope motif often used as a molding enrichment in Norman and Romanesque architecture. Still used today for wood moldings, frames, and carved furniture embellishments.

cable fluting A semi-rounded molding worked into the hollowed-out channels of a column. The cords usually rise about one-third of the way up the shaft. The Romans originally used this detail in the classical period, and it was also popular in the Renaissance period in France and Italy. Also called cannellation.

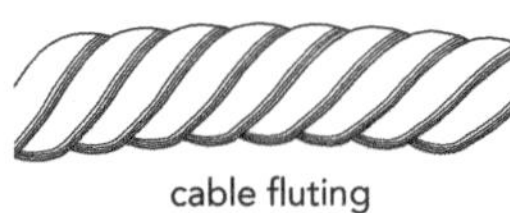

cable fluting

cable system A type of ceiling lighting system consisting of flush-mounted or suspended conductors with attached light fixtures that may be movable. The conductors provide power and may also support the fixtures. The track may curve. See also TRACK LIGHTING.

cabochon (French, hobnail) (1) A round or oval, convex, polished stone. (2) A concave or convex shape used as a carved enrichment on furniture, sometimes surrounded by leaf carvings. Found in ROCOCO furniture and decoration.

cabriole chair (French, *cabriolet*) A small seat with an upholstered back made in the mid 18th century in England during Chippendale's French period. (The name does not refer to the cabriole leg.) See CABRIOLET and FRENCH CHAIR.

cabriole leg (French, to leap or caper) A conventionalized furniture support with knee, ankle, and foot adapted in wood as a furniture support. Greatly favored by designers in the late 17th and 18th centuries for French, English, Flemish, and Italian furniture. The leg curves outward toward the knee and then in and downward to the ankle, making an S shape. In the Queen Anne period, a shell often adorned the knee. The cabriole leg reached the height of refinement during the Louis XV period and is considered a typical Rococo feature. It also appears on some Chinese pieces.

cabriole leg

cabriolet (French) (1) A small Louis XV chair with a concave back. In the Louis XVI period, the name was applied to a chair with an oval, hollowed-out back. A ribbon and bow often decorated the top of the frame as though the chair back were a frame ready to be hung. (2) Also a two-wheeled, one-horse carriage. See CABRIOLE CHAIR.

cache-pot A vessel made of china, wood, or porcelain, used as a container or to hold flowers.

∞cacqueteuse (chaise de femme) An early French Renaissance conversational chair with a high, narrow back and curved arms. The front of the chair seat was wider than the back and sometimes arranged to turn on a pivot. An early French Renaissance design, it was introduced into England in the 16th century and served as a prototype for the smaller-scaled fauteuils of the 18th century. Also called a caqueteuse. See also CAQUETOIRE.

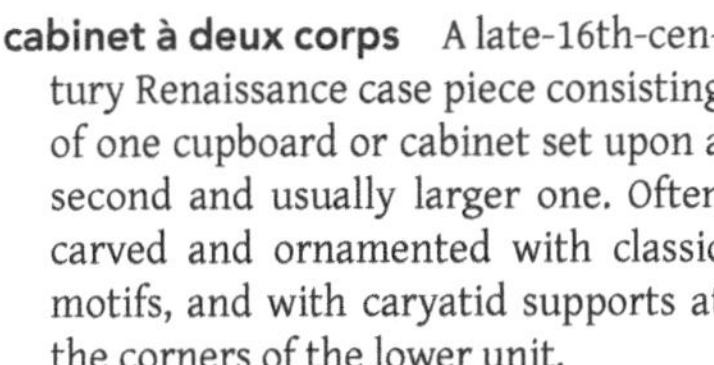

cacqueteuse

CAD Acronym for COMPUTER-AIDED DESIGN.

∞caduceus A wand or staff, entwined by two serpents and surmounted by a pair of wings. In the classical period, this was the symbol for the Greek god Mercury. The motif also appears in carvings and paintings of the Louis XVI period. Today, it is the symbol of the medical profession.

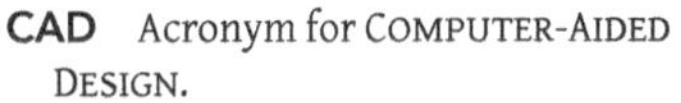

caen stone A limestone from Normandy used in medieval English architecture.

café curtains Short window coverings, usually with a scalloped top. The top points of the scallops are hooked, clipped, or slipped over a rod, usually decorative, sometimes by means of sewn-on fabric loops. Often used in pairs, one set below the other, resulting in an informal window treatment.

caffoy A rich 18th-century fabric of silk and cotton used for hangings and draperies in state rooms.

caissons Sunken panels in a ceiling or dome, also called coffers or lacunaria. The oldest examples are found in Greek and Roman architecture. Simulated in wood in English Renaissance interiors, and interpreted in plaster composition or gesso by the Adam brothers in mid-18th-century England. This ceiling, arch, or dome enrichment is also found in French and Italian Renaissance structures, especially in domed buildings. See COFFERED PANEL and COFFRE.

calamander A wood from Sri Lanka used for banding and veneering in 18th-century furniture. See COROMANDEL and MACASSAR ebony.

∞calathos (1) The basket- or bell-shaped element that supports the acanthi of the Corinthian capital. (2) Also the name of the basket-like element on the head of a caryatid figure. See CARYATIDS.

calcimine A painting mixture often used on ceilings and as a whitewash. It is a cold-water mixture of whiting, glue, and coloring.

caldarium The room equipped with hot water in a Roman bath.

calendering A finishing process for fabrics (and paper) that produces a flat, smooth, glazelike finish when the material is passed between hollow, heated cylinders.

calico A plain-weave, printed cotton fabric originally produced in Kolkata (Calcutta), India, similar to PERCALE.

calligraphy (1) The art of free rhythmic handwriting. (2) The brushstrokes used for Chinese, Japanese, or Arabic written characters. (3) In painting, free and loose brushwork suggesting letters.

camber The slight convexing or bellying on the lower surface of a beam or other element to accommodate the optical illusion that the beam appears to sag in the center. Also used on horizontal furniture supports. See ENTASIS.

cambric A soft, white, loosely woven cotton or linen fabric originally from Cambrai, France. The true linen version is sheer; coarser versions serve as linings.

came The soft metal strip used as the divider between adjacent pieces of glass in a stained or leaded-glass window.

camelback A chair or sofa back with a serpentine curved top rail. A late Chippendale or Hepplewhite piece.

came

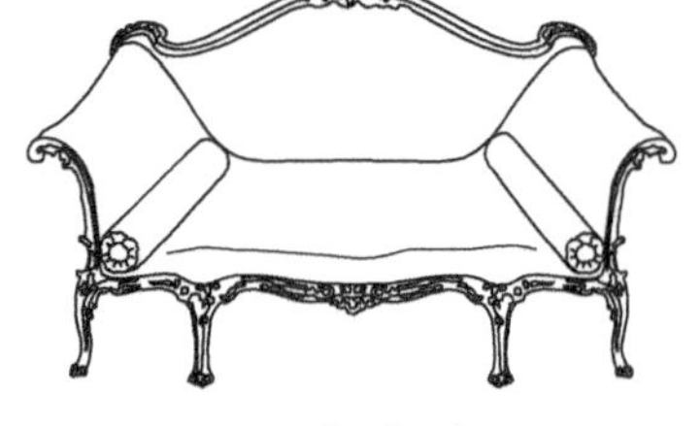

camelback sofa

camelback sofa An upholstered seating unit in the mid 18th century in which a serpentine line rises from the rollover arms to a high point in the middle of the back, reminiscent of the single-humped dromedary; common in the Georgian periods.

camel hair The wool-like under-hair of the hardy work animal from the desert. Natural color varies from light tan to brownish black. Soft and lustrous, it may be combined with sheep's wool. The yarn is sometimes used for Oriental rugs. See *Table 2.*

cameo A low-relief carving. A striated stone or shell carved in relief. Ideally the artist skillfully uses the natural striations for contrasting elements of the representation. Used for decoration on late-18th-century English furniture and in jewelry.

cameo back An oval-framed chair support with an upholstered oval insert, popular in the Louis XVI, Adam brothers, and Sheraton styles. The cameo-back chair is similar to the Louis XV cabriolet and to Hepplewhite's chair. See LE MÉDAILLON and OVAL BACK.

camera (Italian, room) An arcaded or vaulted roof, or a room with a vaulted roof.

∞camlet A rich fabric made of camel's hair. Made in France in the 14th century from hair, wool, and silk. Also used and manufactured in England in the 17th and 18th centuries.

camp Part of an office design in which workers who usually work outside of the office can check email and do other simple tasks. Camp provides a moderate amount of visual privacy. Locations are often shared among workers. The related terms pack and unpack indicate the arrival and departure of the worker.

campagnola (Italian, provincial furniture) Furniture made in outlying districts in a simple, unsophisticated manner.

campaign chest Originally a portable storage unit with drawers used by officers on military outings. The units were reinforced with metal edges and corners to withstand rough traveling conditions. Today, this is a "bachelor chest," often lacquered and embellished with metal corner strips, corner pieces, and pronounced hardware. Usually sits flush on the floor.

camp bedstead See FIELD BED.

∞Campeachy chair A rocking seat made of logwood, also called blood-wood, grown in Campeachy, Mexico. The sloped back is upholstered in leather and finished with nailbead trim. Thomas Jefferson's Campeachy chair at Monticello dates back to 1819.

canapé Originally, a 17th-century small, two-seater couch covered with a canopy. The canopy was later removed, but the name still applied to a small sofa. See BEAUVAIS.

canapé à corbeille (French, *corbeille,* wide basket) A kidney-shaped sofa. The ends curve in so that the sofa takes on the appearance of a wide-topped basket.

candela The SI (International System of Units) unit of measurement of luminous intensity. One candela represents the luminous intensity from a source focused in a specific direction on a solid angle called the steradian.

candelabrum A branched, highly ornamental candlestick, lampstand, or hanging lighting unit or chandelier. See CHANDELIER.

candle board A small shelf under the writing surface of a desk, which slides out and holds a wax taper. An 18th-century English furniture device, also called a candle slide.

candlepower The intensity of a light source measured in candelas.

candle slide See CANDLE BOARD.

candlestand A light table used for lights, vases, and other small ornaments, usually associated with tripod furniture. Made in the early Georgian period and continued in use through the 18th century.

candlestick A socketed receptacle for tapers made of metal, wood, china, or pottery. It can be a simple tube with an opening at one end to receive the wax taper and a flattened base at the other to sit securely on a flat surface, or it can be elaborately decorated.

candlestand

candlewick fabric Textile with a chenille effect created by making heavy-pile yarn (candlewick) loops on unbleached muslin bed sheeting. The cut loops simulate the fuzzy effect of a chenille yarn. Used for draperies and bedspreads.

C and S curve A swirling, delicate, and asymmetrical curvilinear design typical of the Rococo style and named for the letterforms it simulates.

cane (Latin, reed) The stems of certain palms, grasses, or plants, such as bamboo and rattan, which are plaited or woven into a mesh that is yielding and comfortable to sit on or lean back against. Used as a decorative and elegant seating and chairback material in the Louis XIV, XV, and XVI periods in France and in the 17th and 18th centuries in England and Holland.

caned-back chair A popular seat named for the material of its vertical support, of the latter part of the 18th century. An intricately woven pattern of rattan was set into a round or oval frame, which usually had an inlaid wood center. The stems appear to radiate out from the center medallion.

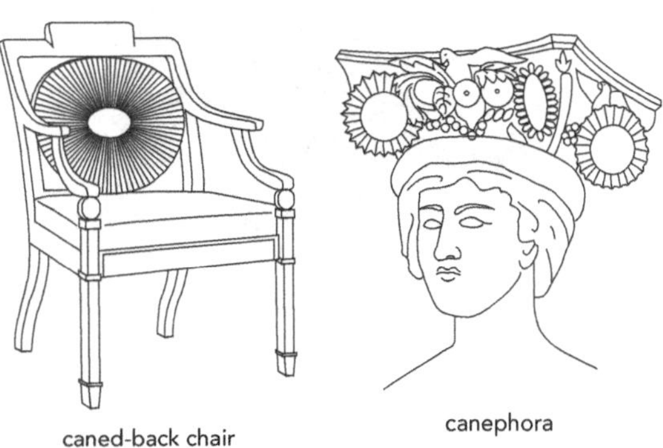
caned-back chair

canephora

∞canephora A sculptured female C-shaped figure with a basket on her head. Originally used as a classical structural decoration like a caryatid. Used as an ornamental support for furniture and shelves in the French and Italian Renaissance. (See CARYATIDS and ATLANTES.)

cannellation See FLUTING.

canopic (adj.) Describes objects from three areas of the ancient world. In Egypt, relating to the preservation of body parts in jars in preparation for burial. In Greece, it refers to objects or events associated with the burial location of Menelaus' boat captain. In Rome, it refers to statues and other items related to one area of Hadrian's Villa.

canopy (Greek, a net to keep out gnats) A covering, usually of drapery, over a piece of furniture. See CANAPÉ and TESTER.

canopy bed A sleeping device with a fabric roof. Four posts often support the covering, one at each corner of the bed, or it hangs from the ceiling. See ANGEL BED, FOUR-POSTER BEDSTEAD, and TENT BED.

canopy bed

canopy chair A late-15th-, early-16th-century stately seat with a broad back that angles upward over the seat to form a projecting covering. The design was usually heavily enriched with carved ornament. It was the probable forerunner of the smaller, wider, and more intimate 17th-century canapé. See CHAYER À DORSERET.

canted Slanted or sloped; angled, beveled, or chamfered. Usually applies to large elements such as the angles of a half-octagonal bow window. See BEVEL and CHAMFER.

canterbury An ornamental stand having compartments for papers, books, envelopes, etc. A portable magazine rack of the 18th century. It was probably originally designed to carry trays, plates, and cutlery and to serve as an auxiliary piece for tea service or dining.

cantilever A rigid member extending well beyond its vertical support. One end extends out free and unsupported. Originally, the term referred to brackets of stone, wood, or metal that projected out from a building (corbels) and supported shelves, cornices, balconies, or eaves, as seen in Gothic and early Renaissance structures. FRANK LLOYD WRIGHT favored this structural device. See *Designers and Architects.*

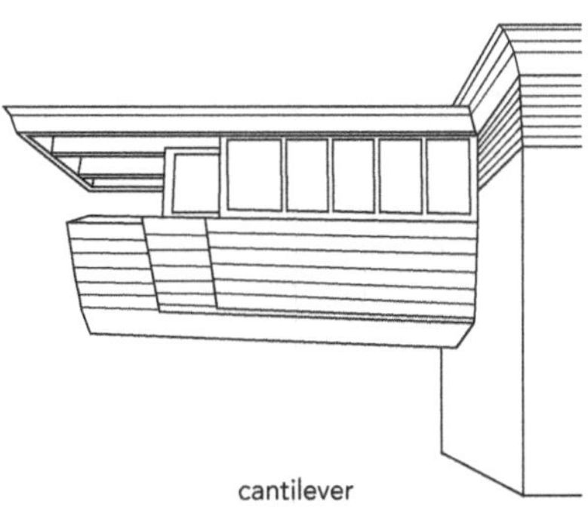
cantilever

Canton china A blue-and-white ceramic ware exported from the port of Guangzhou (Canton), China, from the 17th century to the present day. Popular in America and Britain.

cantoned piers Vertical architectural elements decorated with pilasters or columns at the corners or other exposed faces. A classical form of decoration that appeared in Renaissance architecture.

∞cantonnière (French) A valance, especially the elaborate valance arrangements on French beds of state in the 16th and 17th centuries. See LAMBREQUIN, PELMET, and VALANCE.

canvas (1) A heavy cotton or linen fabric with an even weave. May be bleached or unbleached. (2) A stiff open-weave

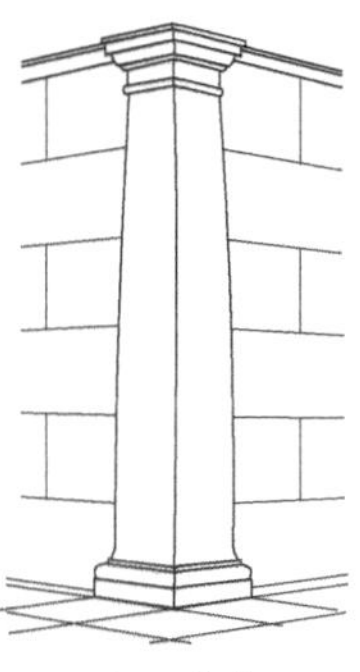
cantoned piers

material used for needlework. (3) A firm, closely woven fabric used as the paint surface in oil painting.

capital The head of a column or pillar. The ensemble is placed directly over the shaft and immediately under the entablature. Structurally, it distributes the load to the shaft. Each of the classical architectural orders has its own type. Columns and capitals appear as decoration and for supports on many styles of furniture. See COMPOSITE ORDER, CORINTHIAN ORDER, DORIC ORDER, ETRUSCAN ORDER, and IONIC ORDER.

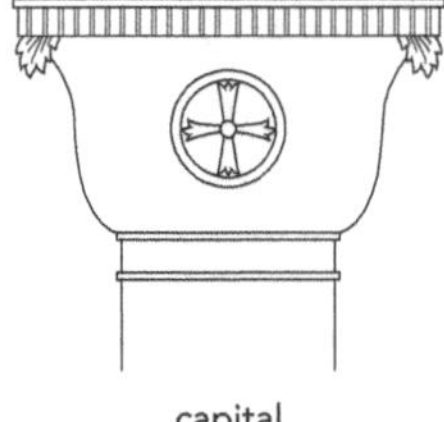

capital

Capo di Monte A Spanish porcelain factory founded by King Charles III in 1743. In 1760, the plant moved to Buen Retiro, near Madrid, Spain, and thus the porcelain is also called Buen Retiro. Figures and groupings of soft paste were made in Rococo patterns and vivid colors. Large plaques and wall brackets of Capo di Monte decorated palaces in Madrid and Aranjuez. See also BUEN RETIRO.

capomo See SATINE RUBANNE.

caprolan Nylon fibers that have a high abrasion resistance. Used in upholstery fabrics and as a carpet fiber.

captain's bed A single bunk-type sleeping platform with a series of drawers below the wooden surface that supports the mattress. An adaptation of the built-in captain's bunk aboard a ship.

captain's chair A sturdy, all-wood, provincial-style seat with a rounded back and curved arms, both supported by tiny spindles. The seat is shaped, and the legs are wood turnings joined to each other by means of turned stretchers. Favored by 19th-century sailors aboard ship. See MATE'S CHAIR.

captain's chest A sturdy, straight-lined storage unit made of wood, usually oak, with recessed pulls and hardware, used on 19th-century sailing vessels.

∞caqueteuse See CACQUETEUSE.

∞caquetoire A small, light, four-legged conversation chair of the mid French Renaissance. The back of the seat is narrower than the front, and the arms curve inward from the front to the chair back. See CACQUETEUSE.

carbon footprint The amount of carbon dioxide (CO_2) and other harmful compounds emitted by a person, company, or activity (building a building, taking a flight, packaging and transporting a construction material) due to the consumption of fossil fuels. A measure of the negative effects of commercial design activity. Carbon offsetting is one counterbalance. It is one of the principal metrics in certifying a construction job as LEED certified and acknowledges the considerable damage done to the environment by past construction methods.

carcase or carcass The base wood framework of a piece of furniture without veneering, carving, ornament, or finish. Usually refers to case furniture. The skeleton of an upholstered piece of furniture is called a frame. See BASE WOOD and CORE.

card cut A Chinese-style fretwork or latticework design. The pattern is carved in low relief rather than pierced or sliced.

card table A small folding horizontal surface used for gaming. These originated in the 17th century and were especially popular in the William and Mary and Queen Anne periods. Early versions had depressions at the four corners of the surface to hold candles and often four additional wells or "guinea holes" for holding the money used during gaming. Green baize covered the gaming surface. See also DISHED and MECHANICAL CARD TABLE.

carlton table A writing surface on legs with a raised back and sides, fitted with pigeonholes, small drawers, and fittings for pens and inkwells. The desk made its appearance at the end of the 18th century in England and was made of mahogany or satinwood with inlay trim. Sheraton referred to it as a "ladies' drawing and writing table."

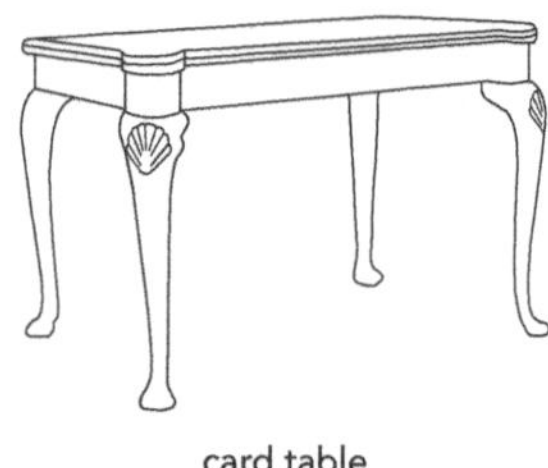

card table

Carolean period The era in English furniture and interior design that spanned the years 1660–1688, during the reigns of Charles II and James II of England. Also referred to as Restoration, Late Stuart, or part of the long Jacobean period.

Carolingian The period in architecture and art in Western Europe from about the 7th to the 10th centuries, roughly the dynasties before, of, and immediately after Charlemagne.

Carpathian elm burl A decorative, light brown to brick red veneer wood with darker brown veins and figurations, often combined with walnut as a decorative accent. Found in Europe's Carpathian Mountains.

carpet In the 16th and 17th centuries, a woven table covering. Since the late 17th century, a floor covering. See TAPET and *Table 1.*

carpet

carpet cushion See CARPET PADDING.

carpet padding The undersurface placed between the floor and a rug. Provides additional softness underfoot, protects the floor covering, insulates against heat loss, and adds sound absorption. The heavier the padding, the higher the price point. When made of polyurethane, it is nonallergenic, mold resistant, durable, and good for heat insulation and sound absorption. Produced in thicknesses of ¼ inch to ½ inch (6 mm–13 mm). Also made of sponge rubber. Alternate terms include foundation; CUSHION; LINING; padding; and UNDERLAYMENT.

carpet tiles Carpet squares precut into definite modules (24 inches by 24 inches) (50 cm by 50 cm) and laid, like tiles, directly onto a hard floor. May be produced with a sponge-like backing for comfort and resiliency. Their major advantage, especially in areas with heavy traffic and in contract design, is that soiled or worn areas can be easily replaced. Especially effective in open-office planning.

carreau (French, square) (1) A square tile or brick. (2) A loose, stuffed cushion used on chairs and settles before upholstery, as known today, came into use. (3) A squab cushion. See also SQUAB.

carrel A bay or study nook separated from the rest of a library or other units by an architectural screen or flanking bookcases.

carriage or carriage piece The supporting member for steps in stairway construction.

∞**carrousel** A triple-arched construction designed by CHARLES PERCIER and PIERRE FRANÇOIS LÉONARD FONTAINE in the early 19th century that was inspired by the Arch of Septimus Severus in Rome. See *Designers and Architects.*

cartel (clock) A hanging wall-mounted timepiece. In the Louis XV and Louis XVI periods, it was highly ornate in design and made of gilded bronze (see ORMOLU). See also RÉGULATEUR or REGULATOR.

cartonnier A decorative 18th-century pasteboard box, usually ornamented, for holding papers.

∞**carton-pierre** A Robert Adam, mid-18th-century English technique of carved ornamentation using a gesso-like composition applied to the surface of wood, panels, and ceilings. See also ANAGLYPTA, COMPO, COMPOSITION ORNAMENT, and GESSO.

cartoon (Italian *cartone*, big sheet of paper) A full-sized drawing for a painting, worked out in detail, and ready to be transferred to a wall, canvas, or panel. A preliminary step in the preparation for a fresco or tapestry.

cartouche (1) A sculptured ornament in the form of an unrolled scroll, often appearing on cornices. The element frequently serves as a field for inscriptions and as an ornamental block in the cornices of house interiors. (2) A conventionalized shield, oval, or ornate frame that appears in other materials and media, such as engravings.

cartouche back The upholstered vertical support of a side chair or fauteuil that is ovoid.

carved rug A floor covering on which pile cut at different levels creates the pattern, making lights and shadows. A sculptured look may also result by eliminating some tufts or pulling some pile yarns tightly back. See *Table 1.*

∞**Carver chair** An early American wood-turned seat with rush caning. A straight, square-looking seat named for a possession of Governor John Carver of New Plymouth in colonial America. The rear legs continued upward to form the uprights of the back. A single row of vertical and horizontal spindles was set between the uprights. Mushroom-shaped turnings usually acted as finials on the uprights. Related to the Brewster chair. See BANISTER-BACK CHAIR and BREWSTER CHAIR.

carving A sculptured, incised, gouged, or appliquéd three-dimensional decoration or ornament.

caryatids Sculptured female figures used in place of columns or pilasters to support entablatures; decorative figures used as supporting members of a design. They appear in classical architecture and decoration and again in the Renaissance and Empire periods. The male version of the caryatid is the atlante. See CANEPHORA. Caryatids support the roof of the famous "Porch of the Maidens" in the Erechtheum. See also ATLANTES.

casbah A rectilinear, but not gridded, older section of a city in North Africa and the Middle East, often with a market that sells carpets and other textiles.

caryatids

cascade See JABOT.

case clock A timepiece contained in a wooden housing.

case goods or case piece Furniture designed to contain or store objects: chests, cabinets, desks, bookcases, drawer units, etc. These are volume-creating pieces. Also called architectural furniture.

case goods or case piece

casein paint A finish for interior use, in a phosphoprotein solution instead of the usual drying oils. It is prepared by mixing with water. The hiding property of the paint comes from lime, powdered chalk, and kaolin.

casement A frame for glass that forms a window or part of one.

casement cloth A lightweight, usually sheer, drapery textile used as a curtain fabric. Made of a variety of fibers: silk, cotton, rayon, mohair, nylon, or a mixture of these.

casement window A side-hinged opening that swings in and out, rather than one that is pushed up and down.

casework Built-in furniture, or furniture that attaches to walls, whether prefabricated or custom built. See BUILT-IN FURNITURE.

cashmere A soft wool textile or yarn made from Indian goat hair. See *Table 2.*

cashmere work From the province of Kashmir in India, a "mirror mosaic" form of decoration in Indian furniture of the 18th and early 19th centuries. Small pieces of mirror were inlaid into the carved geometric patterns of a panel or surface.

casing The wood or metal framework around a window, set into the construction of the wall.

casket A box or miniature chest, usually lavishly ornamented and made of wood, ivory, and precious metals. A container for trinkets, jewels, etc.

cassapanca (Italian *cassone*, chest; and *banca*, bench) A mid-Renaissance Italian long, wooden, hinged-top chest with wooden arms and a back. It functioned as both a bench and a chest. A prototype of the box settle. See BOX SETTLE.

cassolet or cassolete A small box, made in a variety of shapes, for holding or burning perfumes. The term also applies to a covered urn-shaped vase, sometimes with a top that reverses to become a candle holder.

cassone An Italian decorated, hinge-topped chest that was a material manifestation of a marriage and usually held the bride's household linens. This 14th- to 16th-century chest was richly decorated, carved with gilt moldings, and often had painted front and back panels that measured 4 feet to 6 feet long and about 18 inches in height. See CASSAPANCA, CHEST, and MARRIAGE CHEST.

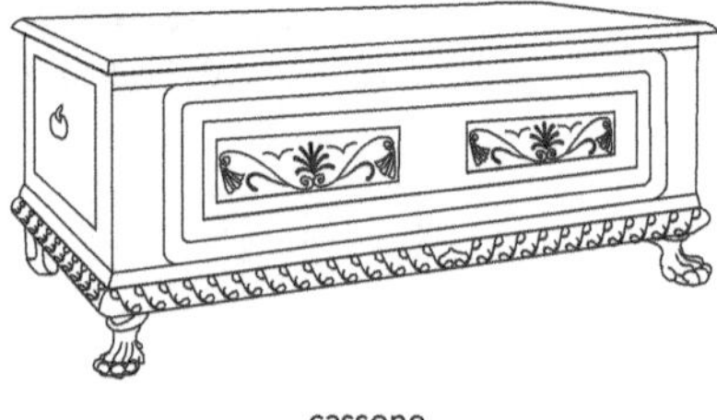

cassone

cast A reproduction of a piece of sculpture, often made of plaster of Paris.

cast aluminum The ductile metal and element that has been shaped by standing in molds. Furniture produced from the process looks like cast-iron, but it is lighter and rust-resistant.

casters or castors Small wheels on swivels that are applied to legs or bases of furniture to make them movable.

cast-iron The malleable element which contains 3.5 percent carbon was first made commercially by the Darby family in England in the early 18th century. They smelted ore with coke instead of charcoal. In about 1750, using coal, they turned out pig iron of a quality they could forge into bars, and mass production became possible. Columns of the material appear in 1780 as structural elements. During the 19th century, it was an important building material.

catenary Chainlike. A swag or festoon. See FRUIT FESTOON and SWAG.

catenary arch The curve formed by a cord or chain of uniform density hanging freely between two points of suspension. Structural or decorative.

∞cathedra An ancient Roman chair with a curved back used primarily by women. Resembles the Greek klismos chair, but heavier in its proportions. See KLISMOS.

cathedral A bishop's church, usually the principal church in a diocese.

cathedral ceiling A high-pitched overhead closure in a modern home. The living room in a ranch or split-level house is sometimes enhanced by an extra-high roof line whose interior surfaces are often embellished with beams.

cathedral glass A rolled vitreous material with one surface textured to obscure transparency. May be tinted, and comes in many patterns.

cathode ray tube (CRT)

cathode ray tube (CRT) The largest component in early computer monitors that predated flat screens. Work space design included deep work surfaces that accommodated computer keyboards and CRT monitors, which are still found in some offices and work areas. A common solution was to place the monitor in the corner of a two-sided work surface at a right angle with its corresponding increased depth.

∞catkin A decorative 18th-century motif such as the bellflower or husk ornament, usually used as a pendant, or as a chain of stylized and graduated bell-shaped flowers. See BELLFLOWER ORNAMENT and HUSK ORNAMENT.

Caucasian rugs Hand-knotted floor coverings made of undyed wool yarns, with a dense, thick pile. Originated with the nomadic people of northern Iran. Some of the characteristic geometric patterns commonly used are the swastika, the cross, and the eight-pointed star, as well as linear figures and animals. The favored colors are vivid reds, blues, greens, bright yellow, and sometimes black. Some of the most popular designs are Kabistan, Kazak, Karabagh, and Shirvan.

∞caulicoli The stalks that support the volutes on a classic Corinthian capital. See VOLUTE.

causeuse A wide armchair, or a small sofa with open sides. The back and seat were often covered with BEAUVAIS tapestry in the 17th and 18th centuries. Similar to a LOVE SEAT, MARQUISE CHAIR, or SETTEE. See BEAUVAIS.

cavetto A quarter-round, concave molding. In late-17th-century English furniture, the molding was often veneered crosswise. See COVE.

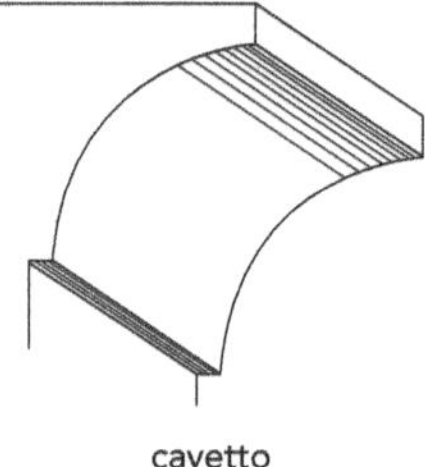

cavetto

cavity wall Also called a hollow wall. Two brick vertical surfaces that are spaced 2 or 3 inches apart and connected to each other with metal ties or bonding bricks.

cedar A fragrant, fine-grained wood used for chests and lining closets. The Persian variety is an eastern hardwood used for building. A favorite wood of the Egyptians and ancient Romans. See *Table 5*.

cedar, red Not a decorative wood, it is used mainly for shingles and as a lining material. See *Table 5*.

cedar chest A long, low storage unit, either lined with the aromatic wood or made entirely of it. Used for the storage of linens, blankets, and woolens; often referred to as a hope chest. See CASSONE.

ceiling paper Wall covering used specifically on the underside of floors and roofs when blank stock is too thin to hide defects.

celadon (1) A light-grayish sea-green color. (2) Also, pottery or Chinese porcelain of this color.

Celanese Textiles originally produced by the Celanese Corporation of America.

Celaperm A previously trademarked name for solution-dyed acetate yarns.

celature A method of decorating metal surfaces by embossing or cutting into the metal.

cella The central enclosed chamber of a Greek temple.

cellar (1) In medieval architecture, a storage room above ground level. (2) In contemporary usage, an underground or below-grade storage area.

cellarette (1) A portable or movable cabinet or liquor chest with a place for bottles, glasses, etc. (2) Also, the drawer of a sideboard fitted with divisions to hold bottles, often lined with lead. See SARCOPHAGUS.

cellulose An insoluble starchlike matter taken from plants, used as a basis for many synthetic materials. See *Table 2.*

Celtic cross Medieval Irish version of the Christian symbol with a long vertical piece and short horizontal arms. At the intersection, a circle represents the pagan sun.

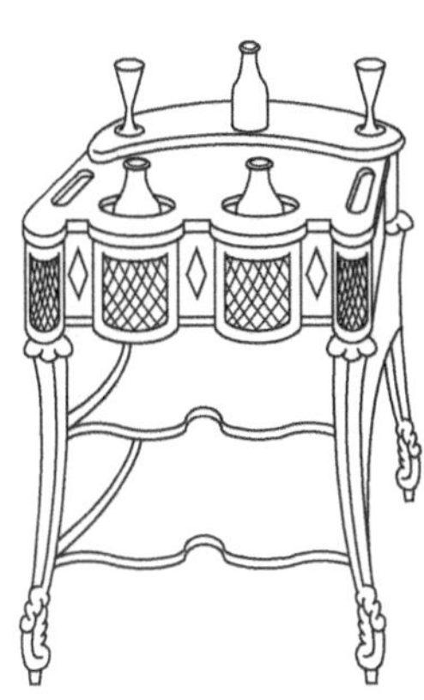

cellarette

Celtic cross

cement A natural or artificial lime compound that is burnt and ground and used to make a mortar to bond bricks, stones, etc. See *Table 3.*

cement block A building unit of cast blocks, usually 8 inches by 8 inches by 16 inches (20 cm × 20 cm × 40 cm).

cementitious (adj.) Describes an element by focusing on its materiality, for example cementitious panels. Having the qualities of cement.

cement mortar A mixture of cement, sand, and water used for binding bricks, stones, etc.

centaur A figure with the torso of a human male, and the lower body and legs of a horse. It appeared in ancient Greek mythology and reappeared in Renaissance and later periods.

center or centering In masonry, a temporary timber framework upon which the masonry of an arch, or a reinforced masonry lintel, is supported until it becomes rigid and self-supporting.

center match Two flitches (veneer pieces) or log slices butted in the middle of a single veneered panel.

centaur

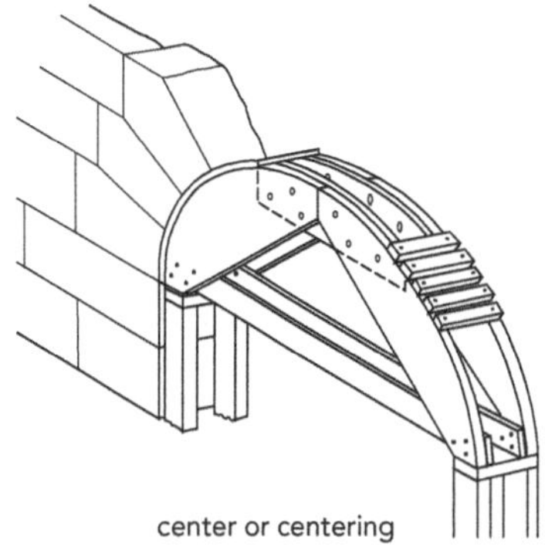

center or centering

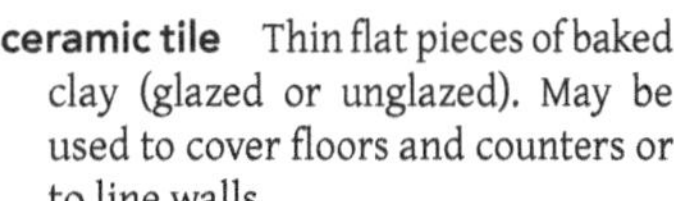

center ottoman See BORNE and CONFIDANTE.

ceramic Any product of baked clay, such as porcelain, pottery, tile, or earthenware.

ceramic color glaze An opaque glaze obtained by spraying a clay tile, brick, or object with a compound of metallic oxides, chemicals, and clays, then heating it in an oven at a high temperature. The glossy surface fuses with the clay object.

ceramic tile Thin flat pieces of baked clay (glazed or unglazed). May be used to cover floors and counters or to line walls.

ceramic

ceramic veneer An architectural terra-cotta plate with large face dimensions but less than 2 inches (5 cm) thick. An oversized tile applied to a brick, stone, or rough concrete surface as a facing material.

certosina (Italian) An inlay of marble, ivory, or blond woods on a darker background. It has an eastern character, as it is generally set into small geometric patterns. The name derives from the Carthusian monks who excelled in inlay work. See INLAY, INTARSIA or TARSIA, and INTARSIO.

chabudai (1) A sunken Japanese dining area with table close to ground level and recessed seating. (2) A short-legged table found in traditional Japanese homes; the ensemble may include ZABUTON or TATAMI in lieu of chairs. The four legs of a chabudai collapse for removal and storage.

Chac-Mool Pre-Columbian or Mesoamerican statue depicting a human figure lying down on his or her back with a tray or bowl resting on the stomach. A popular item in Southwestern-style interiors.

Chac-Mool

chaffeuse A low, fireside chair of the early French Renaissance. Originally the seat was so low that the knees of a seated person were higher than the lap. Nursing mothers used it when cradling children between their knees and body. Also spelled *chauffeuse.*

∞chaiere or chaire (French Gothic) A throne-like, wood-carved chair. See CHAIRE.

chair (Old French, *chaiere*) A seat with a back for one person. Chair parts can include feet, legs, stretchers, brackets, apron, a seat frame, rails, arms, splat, and top rail.

chair and a half An 18th-century English seat with overly generous proportions. The seat usually had wings or cheeks, and the seat proper was smaller than a love seat but larger than a regular upholstered chair. It is similar to the French MARQUISE in proportions and was also known as a DRUNKARD'S CHAIR.

chairback headboard Refers to an open vertical panel at the head of a bedstead that resembles the back or backs of a dining room chair.

chair bed A seat or settee with a draw-out arrangement that converts the seat into a device suitable for sleeping. An 18th-century English innovation. See BED CHAIR.

∞chaire (French) An early Renaissance choir stall. It resembles a chest (or box-like seat) with a tall, heavily carved back. The arms were also carved. In the Gothic period, it was also called a *chayère*, and its throne-like proportions made it the special seat for the lord or head of a family.

∞chaire à haut dossier A 16th-century French Renaissance high-back chair, usually ornately carved and covered in leather or tapestry.

chair rail The top molding of a dado, also called a DADO CAP. Usually placed about 30 inches (75 cm–80 cm) off the ground, and the wall area below the molding is called the DADO. The wood strip originally protected the plaster wall from being damaged by the top rail of chairs.

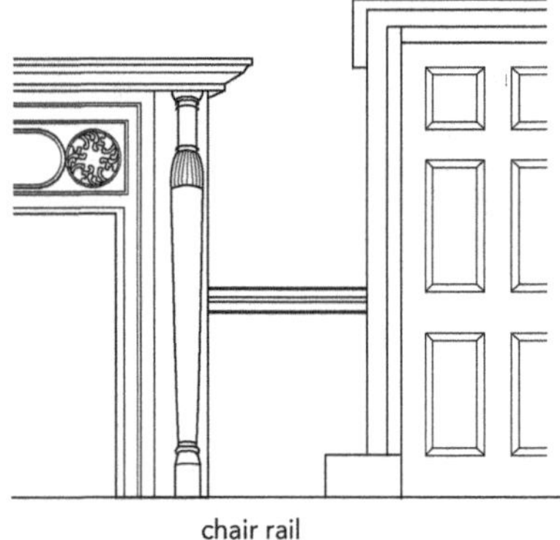

chair rail

chair table A seat that converts into a useable surface when the hinged back drops to a horizontal position. See TABLE CHAIR.

chaise (French) Side chair.

∞chaise à accoudoir See COCKFIGHT CHAIR and FUMEUSE.

chaise à bras A Renaissance armchair.

∞chaise à capucine A low slipper chair. The name is probably derived from the Capuchin nuns, who might have used this type of chair.

chaise à porteurs (French) A sedan chair. Originally an enclosed, covered chair that seated one person and was suspended between two poles that porters carried. Present-day variations are hooded and winged chairs that simulate the enclosure. See PALANQUIN and SEDAN CHAIR.

chaise brisée (1) A CHAISE LONGUE in two parts, one of which is the footrest. (2) Also, a folding chair.

chaise longue A long chair for reclining or stretching out. It is upholstered, with a continuous, elongated seat supported by extra legs. See DUCHESSE.

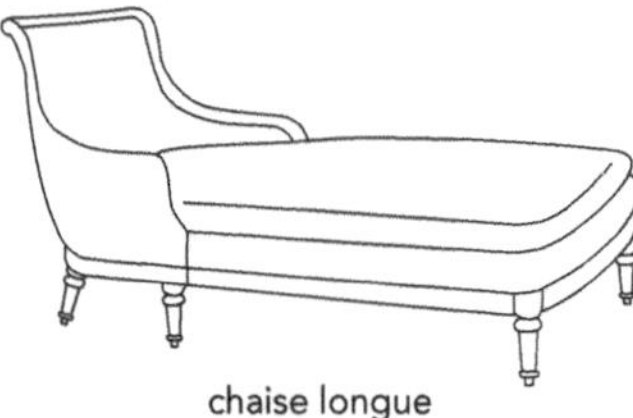

chaise longue

chaise percée (1) A chair with an opening cut in the seat, which is over a chamber pot. Originally, a movable toilet styled like a throne or an imposing arm chair in keeping with the current vogue of the period (Louis XIV, XV, or XVI). (2) Today, a chair to cover an existing toilet fixture. See COMMODE.

chalice A cup or goblet used in church ceremonies and often made of precious metals beautifully ornamented and jeweled.

challis A soft fabric woven of wool, silk, rayon, or cotton. Usually has a small allover design but may be solid color.

∞chamber horse An 18th-century English exercising mechanism Thomas Sheraton designed with a bellows-like affair made up of several wooden boards separated by coils and covered with leather equipped with vents. This bellows was set on a wood base with arms and a front step. The individual sat on the bellows-pillow, held onto the arms, and bounced up and down.

chamfer The edge of a corner that is beveled or angled off. A splayed effect. See BEVEL and CANTED.

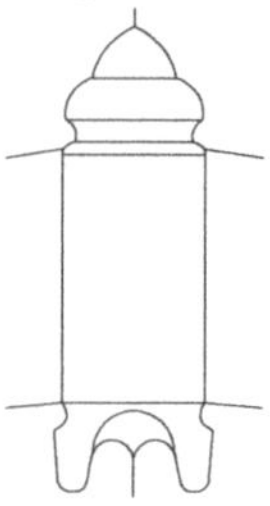

champlevé A type of enamelware in which a pattern is grooved out in a metal base and colored enamels fill the grooves. The thin raised lines that separate the enamel color are similar to the cloisons in CLOISONNÉ.

chancel chair English Jacobean seat whose seat proper concealed a bible storage compartment. See BIBLE CHAIR and WAINSCOT CHAIR.

chamfer

chandelier A hanging lighting fixture. A pendant unit with branches to hold candles or lights, often decorated with prisms and crystals. Introduced into England by the French émigrés of 1685. See CANDELABRUM.

chandelier

channel back Type of upholstered rear support for chair or sofa with rows of vertical tufting.

channels (1) Long, shallow, concave grooves that run vertically up and down the shaft of a column. A narrow edge called a fillet separates one channel from another. See FILLET and FLUTING. (2) Also a form of rolled steel.

Chantilly lace A bobbin lace with a delicate ground. A cordonnet of thick silky threads outlines the design. See VALENCIENNES LACE.

chaplet A small torus molding with a bead or berry decoration. See ASTRAGAL.

chaplet

charcoal Twigs of charred willow, mainly used for preliminary drawings on a canvas or wall. Can be readily erased.

Charles of London sofa A heavily upholstered, 20th-century piece, with flat, massive, low armrests, barely rising above the T cushions that are set next to them. The Charles of London chair, also a 20th-century innovation, has the same massive look. An early overstuffed sofa.

Charles X period From 1824 to 1830; part of the French Restoration. Furniture and architecture from this period is characterized by a mixture of Louis XVI, late Empire, and Rococo and Renaissance detailing.

charmeuse (1) A soft, silken luster produced on fine cotton-warp sateens by MERCERIZING and SCHREINERIZING. (2) Also a satin weave fabric (of cotton, silk, or rayon) with a matte back and a semilustrous face.

chase A long, recessed area in masonry, brickwork, or concrete left to accommodate service pipes.

chasing A method of ornamenting on any metal surface. A pattern is produced by embossing or cutting away parts of the metal. A burin or graver may also be used in this technique. Chasing with a burin is done on MARQUETRY, on metal mounts for furniture, or on Boulle metal inlays. Chasing, as a form of metal enrichment, reached its peak during the 18th century in France. See EMBOSSED and REPOUSSÉ.

chatbot A product that is the result of natural language processing moving into the digital world and commercial interiors. It is a combination of natural and synthetic speech and is found on phones, websites, and robots. These conversational agents, an amalgam of robot and human, are making inroads into multiple design sectors, including customer service, and wayfinding locales, such as welcome, reception, registration, and information desks. The expanded use of chatbots has the potential to dramatically reconfigure how airports, stores, and hotels are designed.

château A large French country house.

chattri or chhatri A stone parasol or finial that crowns a STUPA.

chayer à dorseret Late-14th- and early-15th-century Gothic canopied chair, usually carved of oak or chestnut, elaborately gilded, and highlighted with color. The chayer (or *chaire*) was massive and throne-like. Tapestry lined the back of the chair. See CANOPY CHAIR.

∞**checker** (1) Originally the office of one of the heads of a monastery. The office usually had a tabletop whose pattern was formed with rows of squares of alternating light and dark; on this surface accounts were reckoned. (2) An abbreviated form of the word *exchequer.* See also CHEQUER.

checkerboard bond In masonry, a pattern in which only headers are laid one directly over the other in vertical lines. A purely ornamental arrangement, as it does not structurally stabilize the ensemble. See BOND.

checkerboard match Veneer or wood panels set so that the stripe figure is vertical in one panel and horizontal in the next. The alternating pattern is then repeated.

check In cabinetry, a small crack that sometimes appears in lumber that has not been dried evenly. The defects appear perpendicular to the annual rings and radiate out from the heart of the trunk.

cheek (1) The side pieces of a DORMER WINDOW. (2) Also the side post of a gate or door.

cheek pieces The wings, or fins, of the tall easy chairs designed in 18th-century England, designed to keep drafts away from the person seated. See DRAFT CHAIR, GRANDFATHER CHAIR, and WING CHAIR.

chef d'oeuvre (French) (1) A masterpiece. (2) Also the name of a miniature piece of furniture made by a journeyman as a test of his level of accomplishment and readiness to be considered a master craftsman.

chen chen A pale, light, soft North African wood with color ranging from whitish to pale gray. Works well and has a characteristic stripe pattern. Also called ako and quen quen.

chenets (French) Andirons, or fire dogs. See ANDIRONS.

chenille (French, caterpillar) A woven yarn that has a pile protruding all around at right angles to the body thread. Used for embroidery, fringes, and tassels. Also fabrics woven from the yarns, having a plushlike surface. Can be made of cotton, silk, rayon, etc.

chenille carpet A thick, soft, cut pile fabric woven on two looms, the weft loom and the chenille loom. Woven in any design, coloring, type, or surface yarn. May be made in any shape or size, up to 30 feet (9 m) wide and seamless.

chequer (1) One of the squares in a chequered (or checkered) pattern. (2) An inlay design.

cherrywood A light reddish to dark reddish grained material that resembles mahogany and darkens with age. Used for small carved articles and French and American 18th-century Provincial furniture. Popular for inlays and marquetry. The figure varies from plain to a rich mottle. Black cherrywood is found in the Appalachians. French cherry is found in France and England. Wild cherry is found in England, Europe, and arid Asia Minor. See *Table 5.*

cherub See AMORINO.

cherub head A popular decorative motif that appears in Renaissance church or secular architecture and as furniture decoration. See TÊTES D'ANGES.

chess table A tabletop with a checkered pattern either painted or inlaid. In medieval Europe, checkerboards decorated the tops of some chests.

chest Originally, a container or box with a hinged lid, broader than its height. Drawers were added in the mid 17th century.

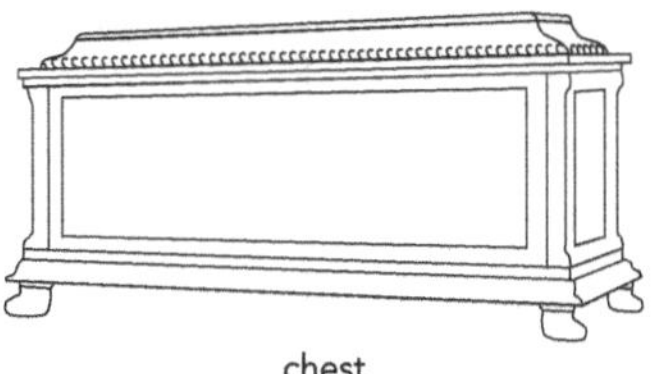

chest

Ornate versions of these storage items in the Medieval period were architectural in concept and decoration.

chesterfield An overstuffed, heavily upholstered sofa. Usually a large piece of buttoned furniture with a continuous back and scrolled, rollover arms of the same height. Thought to be named by Philip Stanhope, the 4th Earl of Chesterfield.

chest of drawers A box or storage unit with multiple rectangular units that can be retracted horizontally.

chest of drawers

chest on chest A storage unit with two parts, with one set of larger drawers and one set of smaller drawers. Also called a DOUBLE CHEST.

chestnut A soft wood with coarse grain. It resembles oak and can be used as is when a quartered effect is not desired. Unsuitable for fine details because the grain is coarse and has marked annual rings. Certain cuts in late-18th-century England imitated satinwood. WORMY CHESTNUT is desirable because of its unique discoloration.

cheval glass or mirror Literally, a "horse mirror"; a reflective device suspended between HORSES. A full-length surface which throws back and does not absorb light; decoratively mounted so as to swing in a frame and large enough to reflect the length of the human figure. A French innovation introduced into England in the late 17th century. In 18th-century England, a table model was introduced. Also called a swing glass.

cheval screen A fire protection device that stands on two bracketed feet. See BANNER SCREEN.

cheveret An 18th-century English table with an oblong top and drawers with slender legs joined at the bottom by a shelf.

chevet (French) (1) The head of a bed. (2) Also a bolster or pillow, or a night table. (3) In a church, the rear of the structure opposite the entry, consisting of the choir and ambulatory, as viewed from the exterior.

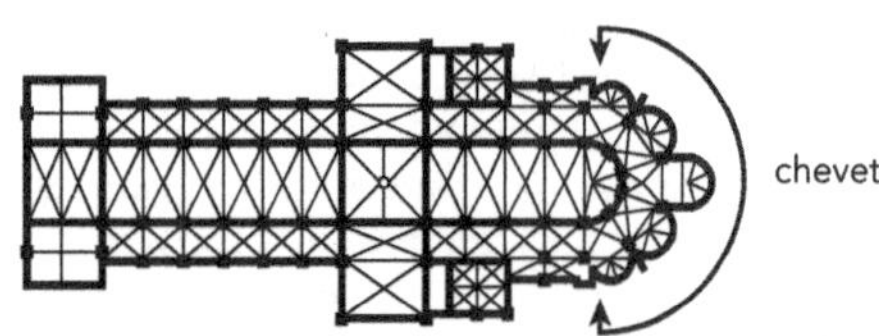
chevet

cheviot A loosely woven, rough-napped woolen cloth originally made from the wool of the sheep in the Cheviot Hills of Scotland.

chevron (French, rafter) In ornament, a zigzag design or molding. A continuous band of V's, frequently used in Norman and Gothic ornament and also in the 17th century, as an inlay motif.

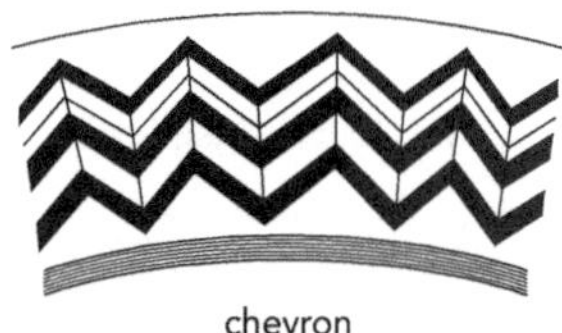
chevron

chiaroscuro (Italian, light-dark) The balance of light and shadow in a picture. The Italian painter Caravaggio is considered the master of the technique. See GRISAILLE.

Chicago School The late-19th-century group of architects and engineers who pioneered the skyscraper and indirectly gave rise to the open plan.

chiffon (1) (noun) A sheer, gauzelike silk fabric. (2) (adj.) A term used to describe the light, soft finish of a fabric such as chiffon velvet.

chiffonier Originally, a unit for collecting and containing assorted odds and ends. In the period of Louis XV, it refers to a tall chest with five drawers. In 19th-century England, the term applies to a sideboard with two doors below, enclosing shelves. Sometimes there were shelves at the back and top of the sideboard to hold ornaments, decorative serving pieces, etc.

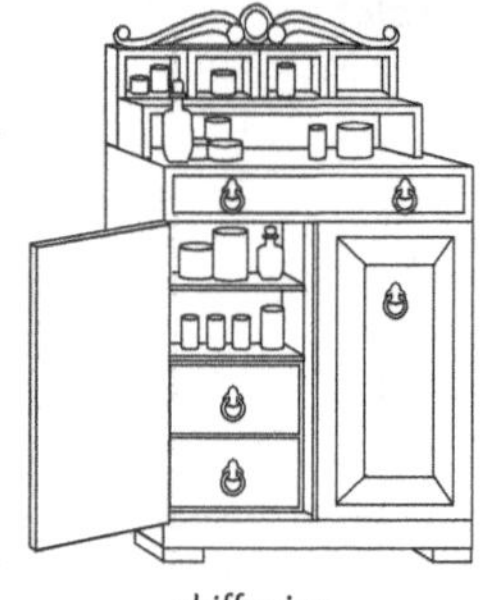
chiffonier

chiffonnière A sewing table, with a three-sided gallery on top, drawers, and a shelf at the bottom, which was enclosed and held balls of wool. A Louis XV innovation.

chifforobe A forerunner of what is now called an armoire. A piece of bedroom furniture that combines hanging space with drawers in a single unit. Part chiffonier (drawer unit) and part wardrobe (closet unit), thus the name *chifforobe.*

chimera A mythical dragon-like animal or a composite, part-human, part-animal, used in decoration. Appears in legs or furniture supports in the Renaissance, Empire, and later-19th-century designs.

chimera

chimney breast The projecting stone or brickwork above a fireplace that houses the flue.

chimneypiece (1) The ornamental structure surrounding the fireplace opening and the breast above it. (2) A projecting hood, sometimes called the mantel.

china (1) The European name given to porcelains imported from Asia. (2) A hard, translucent porcelain with a large percentage of bone ash. See also HARD PASTE and KAOLIN.

chimneypiece
china closet or cabinet

china closet or cabinet A display unit, usually with glass sides and front, used for exhibiting porcelain collections. A popular piece of furniture in the late 17th and early 18th centuries when internationally ceramics from China and other parts of Asia were considered rare and precious and were avidly collected.

china silk A sheer, plain-weave soft lustrous fabric made from fibers produced by silkworms that is nearly transparent. It may include rayon fibers.

Chinese bracket foot or Chinese foot A bracket-type leg termination with a reverse S-shaped curve (see CYMA RECTA) on the face of the bracket. Also called an OGEE BRACKET FOOT.

Chinese Chippendale A period in Chippendale's work, in the mid 18th century, that was influenced by chinoiserie, Chinese motifs, and the work of SIR WILLIAM CHAMBERS. See *Designers and Architects.* See CHINOISERIE, FRETWORK, and LACQUER WORK.

Chinese Chippendale

Chinese key design A continuous geometric border design, similar to the Greek key design or meander. Used by Chippendale in fretwork and openwork grille doors.

Chinese room A room decorated "à la chinoise," with imported furniture or adaptations such as those Chippendale produced. The walls were covered with European-made Chinese wallpaper or "India" or "Japan" paper or handpainted paper murals from China, India, or Japan. Many of these wallpapers were produced in England, modeled after Chinese originals. This was a limited although influential craze in 18th-century Austria, England, and Germany. See CHINESE WALLPAPER and CHINOISERIE.

Chinese rugs Floor coverings from the populous East Asian country differ from others made in Asia in their plainer background, narrower border, and central medallion. Popular background colors are blue and cream; soft yellow, cream, apricot, and gold are preferred top colors. These soft pastels are used to render clouds, dragons, waves, peonies, and other floral motifs. See ORIENTAL RUG.

Chinese wallpaper A treatment for vertical surfaces introduced in Europe in the 17th century as "India" or "Japan" paper. Sold in sets of twenty-five rolls, 12 feet long and 4 feet wide (3.6 m × 1.2 m). There was a studied dissimilarity from panel to panel. In the 18th century, chinoiserie reached the peak of its popularity. Favorite motifs included trees, flowers, birds, and butterflies. Some contemporary occidental figures are portrayed wandering through pseudo-oriental scenes. James Minikin produced wallpapers of the type.

chinoiserie The European taste for Chinese-style or Chinese-like decorative motifs: gay, picturesque, imaginative occidental versions of Asian designs. Particularly popular in the Louis XV period in France and the 18th-century English and German styles. See HUET, CHRISTOPHE in *Designers and Architects.* See CHINESE CHIPPENDALE and VENETIAN CHINOISERIE.

chintz (Hindi, spotted) A fine cotton cloth with a printed design, usually glazed or calendered. The design can be printed by blocks, copper plates, screens, or rollers. The unglazed version is called CRETONNE.

chip carving A simple, low-relief form of ornamentation on Romanesque furniture, early-17th-century English furniture, and 18th- and early 19th-century American furniture. The work was accomplished with flat chisels, semicircular gouges, and hammers.

chipping In wood finishing, a defect that develops when a dried film of finishing material separates as flakes from the surface underneath.

choir The area of the church fitted for the singers; more broadly, the enclosed space for all those engaged in an ecclesiastic ceremony.

chroma or chrome The degree of intensity, brilliance, or saturation of a spectrum color. Yellow is in the center of the spectrum and is the most brilliant, but it is the palest chroma because it has the least saturation. Blue is the darkest, and has the greatest saturation. Red has a medium chroma.

chrome-plated Covered with a thin layer of chromium deposited by electrolysis to give the underlying metal a shiny appearance and make it corrosion-resistant.

Chromespun A trademark name for solution-dyed acetate fibers. Used in carpet and upholstery fabrics.

chryselephantine (adj.) Made of ivory and gold. Certain Greek statues were assembled so that the exposed body, face, and hands were made of ivory, and the clothing or drapery was made of gold.

churrigueresque The bold and massive Spanish Baroque style of the 17th century. The period was mainly influenced by the architect JOSÉ DE CHURRIGUERA. The Baroque period in Spain ran concurrently with the Rococo period and continued through the mid 18th century. The exuberant color and extravagant ornamentation in this period affected Spanish colonies in the Americas. See *Designers and Architects.*

chute (French, fall or tumble) Decorative bronze plates that fitted over the exposed angles and on the legs of wood furniture pieces, to protect and reinforce the fragile areas. These functional enrichments appear in 18th- and 19th-century French furniture. Sometimes finished as ORMOLU or as BRONZE DORÉ. See also SABOTS.

ciel de lit (French) A bed TESTER or CANOPY.

cincture The broad fillet below the concave molding (CONGA) located at the bottom of the shaft of a classic-order column. See FILLET.

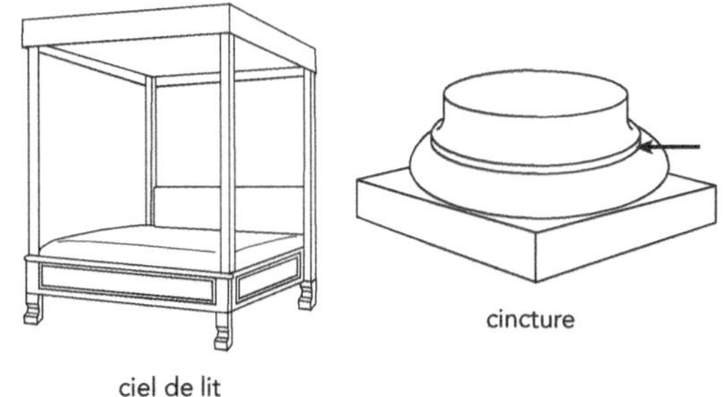

cincture

ciel de lit

cinder block A hollow building unit made of concrete.

cinetectural (adj.) Describes spaces or designs that have qualities associated with films and film sets.

cinquecento The 16th century or 1500s.

cinquefoil (1) A five-leaf clover shape. (2) A common motif in Gothic tracery.

cinquefoil

cirage A monochromatic painting in yellow.

circassian walnut A highly figured veneer wood that is produced from twisted, gnarled, and warped trees grown in the dry Black Sea area of Europe.

circular economy A financial system of wealth and resources that concerns goods and services from a different perspective: it seeks to replace the current extractive cycle in which a construction project takes and reconfigures resources and in the process produces vast quantities of waste. A circular economy will eliminate waste, maximize efficiency, and use building materials efficiently. It separates economic activity from consumption of resources and production and seeks to regenerate natural systems by keeping products and materials in use.

cire perdue (French, lost wax) A method of casting in which a figure is modeled in wax and then coated with hard clay. The figure is heated, the melted wax runs out through holes left in the clay, and molten metal is poured into the clay shell. Final details are worked directly on the casting.

ciseleur A chiseler; a craftsman who ornaments bronze and other metals by chiseling; one who does chasing. Applied to finishers of metal mounts and chutes for 18th-century furniture.

giselé velvet A raised, cut fabric with a pile, typical of Renaissance fabrics of Genoa, Italy. The pattern was raised against a flattened background.

cistern In furniture, a wine cooler, sarcophagus, or cellarette of the latter part of the 18th century. Most often used to keep bottles on ice but sometimes used for washing up. See CELLARETTE, SARCOPHAGUS, and WINE COOLER.

cistern

citronnier (French, lemon tree) A pale, honey-colored wood popular for furniture at the end of the 18th century.

cladding The use of masonry, metal, ceramic, glass, wood, solid-surfacing, and laminate materials as a wall finish.

clapboard house The typical 17th-century New England dwelling. The treatment was originally used as a protection for half-timbered houses in late Gothic and early Renaissance England and was brought over to the New World. The Parson Capen House, Topsfield, Massachusetts (1683), is an example. See CLAPBOARD WALL.

clapboard wall An exterior wall facing made up of horizontal, overlapping planks. A weatherboarded wall.

clap table An early-18th-century English pier or console table that had a pier looking glass set over it.

classic Of high quality, outstanding or exemplary; something with an antique source or established degree of excellence. An early foundational era of excellence of any culture.

classical (1) Referring to the architecture, sculpture, arts, and literary arts of the ancient Greeks and Romans. (2) The 18th- and 19th-century architecture and arts based on Greek and Roman elements, usually called NEOCLASSICISM.

Classical Revival The early-19th-century architectural trend in Europe that stressed the revival of classic forms and motifs. Classic prototypes were reexamined, which supplied inspiration for new structures. Greek columns and porticoes were frequently used. Examples of the Classic Revival are the Royal Exchange in London, the Palais de Justice in Paris, and the Court Theater in Berlin.

clavated Club-shaped. A type of turning used for furniture legs and stretchers in early Renaissance Spanish furniture.

clavecin See CLAVICHORD and PIANOFORTE.

∞clavicembalo A predecessor of the pianoforte that resembled a dulcimer with an attached keyboard.

clavichord A 17th-century forerunner of the piano. A stringed instrument used in England during the Carolean, William and Mary, and Queen Anne periods.

clay mortar mix A finely ground earth-based material added to the binding paste between bricks or other building units.

clear ceramic glaze A translucent vitreous oxide coating for fired clayware. See CERAMIC COLOR GLAZE.

clearcole A priming or sizing solution made of white lead ground in water with glue. Used in the United Kingdom.

cleat A wood strip fastened on a wood surface as a means of joining two adjacent surfaces or a method of reinforcing the join. Can prevent warping. See BUTTERFLY WEDGE.

clef pendante (French, boss) A hanging or projecting ornamental pendant. See BOSS.

clerestory A window or strip of windows placed near the top of a wall, originally above an adjacent roof, especially in Christian churches although not limited to religious structures.

cloche A glass dome fitted over a wood base, usually to protect artificial flowers, a clock, or an objet d'art from dust or harm.

cloisonné A type of enamelware in which delicate metal partition filaments hold and separate colored enamels in a pattern. The individual metal partitions are called cloisons.

cloisonné

cloister A covered walk connecting a church to other buildings in a monastery.

cloister

close chair or close stool An enclosed box used as a seat with a removable chamber pot, in use before the toilet or water closet. Sheraton describes his design (1793) as "made to have the appearance of a small commode, standing upon legs; when it is used the seat part presses down to a proper height by the hand, and afterward it rises by means of lead weights, hung to the seat."

closed plan An interior with constructed walls and dividers that separate areas into distinct sections or rooms for particular activities. See OPEN PLANNING.

closer The last tile or brick in a COURSE.

closure A cut or trimmed brick, usually ¼ or ¾ of a brick. It is used at corners to obtain proper bonding.

cloud A metaphor for the virtual location of data storage, which has the result of reducing the amount of filing cabinets necessary in traditional workplace design and increasing the amount of space needed for data processors. It is mentioned in discussions of online collaborative work, remote working, accessing product information, and new ways of managing the construction process.

clothespress A chest of drawers, sometimes with a cupboard set above it. The cupboard or cabinet has shelves to hold clothes.

cloven foot Decorative base of a Louis XIV furniture leg. It resembles a deer's cleft hoof. See PIED DE BICHE.

CLT Acronym for CROSS-LAMINATED TIMBER

club chair A large, roomy, upholstered seat. It may or may not be skirted, and the type of arms vary with period or style, from high to low, from thick to thin, from all-upholstered to partially upholstered. An oversized BERGÈRE.

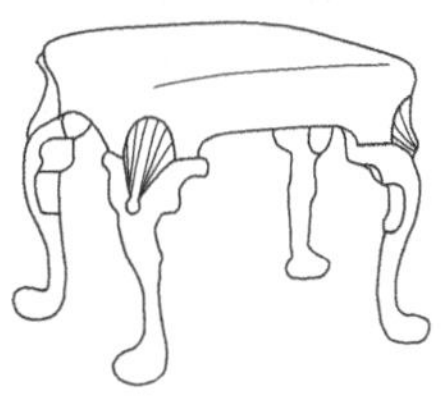
club foot

club foot A flat, round, pad ending for a cabriole leg, used frequently on early-18th-century English furniture. See DUTCH FOOT, PAD FOOT, and SPOON FOOT.

Cluny lace See VALENCIENNES LACE.

clustered column leg A furniture support made up of several grouped or engaged turnings that suggest classical structural elements. Used by WILLIAM INCE in mid-18th-century England. See *Designers and Architects.*

clustered columns Several vertical structural elements placed together or having overlapping shafts, which form a single support. A Gothic architectural motif.

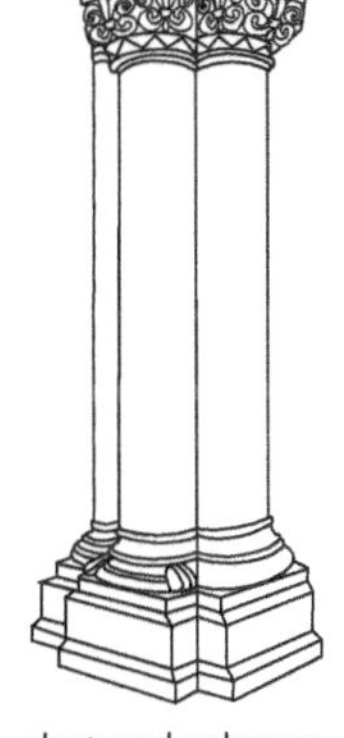
clustered columns

CMYK A term of digital printing, on paper or textile, of color. The process is a means of color management and uses as its base cyan, magenta, yellow, and key (black). It is a subtractive process. The base "color" of paper is white, and the ink subtracts all the other colors from white light in order to create the desired color. Used for textiles, wallpapers, and other printed graphic materials.

CNC Acronym for a COMPUTER NUMERIC CONTROL.

CNC router The digital cutting device that is the mainstay of the 21st-century carpentry shop. Working with coordinates, a computer controls the process through a CAD-based operation. Using computer numerical control, it cuts a number of materials including woods, metals, plastic, and model foam. The computer-controlled cutting machine works on X and Y axes, with shallow Z-axis movement. It processes less dense materials than a CNC miller.

coal scuttle A box or bucket used as a receptacle for the household fuel made from carbonized plant matter. Sometimes made of brass and ornamented. See PIPKIN.

coated glass A one-way mirror; a vitreous pane on one side and a reflective surface on the other, so that vision through the transparent sheet is possible in one direction only.

coat of arms (1) Originally a lightweight garment, usually embroidered or decorated with heraldic emblems and worn over armor. (2) In recent terminology, the heraldic emblems of a family or institution.

cobbler's bench A shoemaker's combination seat and work surface, with holders and compartments for pegs, etc. Usually made of pine in colonial America. Reproductions and adaptations are used as cocktail tables in American Provincial or colonial rooms.

cockade A ribbon rosette or badge popular in the French Revolution. It was in use in the French Directoire period as a decorative element.

cock beading or molding A small convex or half-round projecting embellishment used around the edges of drawers. See SINGLE ARCH MOLDING.

cockfight chair A saddle-like seat with a small shelf as the top rail of the back. The user straddles the device facing backwards. The top rail, usually padded, functioned as an armrest. Used for reading, writing, and viewing sports events (such as blood sports). An 18th-century English favorite. See also FUMEUSE, PONTEUSE, STRADDLE CHAIR, VOYELLE, and VOYEUSE.

cockleshell Also called the escallop or shell ornament. It was used as a carved decorative feature on furniture knees, crestings, and pendants of chairs and other furniture pieces in early-18th-century English, Georgian, Louis XIV, and Louis XV period designs. See also ROCOCO and SCALLOP SHELL.

coco bolo A fine, dark brown wood with a purplish cast and uniform grain. It takes a polished finish. Found in Central America and used for modern furniture and fancy cabinetwork.

coco wood A hard and brittle wood with purplish-brown stripes on a medium dark ground. It is native to India.

coextrusion A part of manufacturing, forcing out two or more materials simultaneously, for example aluminum and polymer, for a multilayered end product.

coffee table A low horizontal surface, usually placed in front of a sofa, and used to hold ashtrays, magazines, and refreshments. In the 18th century, similar tables were designed as tea tables to hold tea service, cups, saucers, etc. Although its initial use was different, the Chinese KANG resembles the coffee table.

coffer See COFFRE and COFFERED PANEL.

coffered panel A sunken element in the ceiling of a vault or dome or in the underside of a protruding cornice, usually ornamented and decorated.

coffered panel

coffin stool A small, oak, four-legged seat with stretchers, usually left undecorated. It may have been used to elevate corpse receptacles awaiting interment.

coffre or coffer A chest or strongbox used for holding valuables. It also served for seating and an occasional sleeping unit in modest Gothic interiors.

coffret A small chest or coffer, often on its own stand or table.

cogging A form of joinery with the pieces of wood crossing each other at right angles. The lower member is grooved out so that a projection fits into a slot on the underside of the upper member.

cognac chair A 20th-century molded fiberglass version of the TUB CHAIR or BARREL CHAIR, except it is placed on a pedestal base. It was designed by EERO AARNIO of Finland and resembles, in profile, the classic brandy glass. The outer form is fiberglass, and the interior is upholstered. See *Designers and Architects.*

Cogswell chair A 20th-century seat with a fully upholstered back and a low generous platform. The sides are not enclosed. The arm stump rises from the platform and carries an overstuffed arm pad.

coiffeuse (French) A hairdressing table or make-up table of the Louis XV and Louis XVI periods. See also POUDREUSE and TABLE À COIFFER.

coign See QUOIN.

coir Fiber retrieved from the husk of coconuts. Used in the pile layer of track-off mats. See *Table 2.*

collage (French, gluing) A picture or ornament built up with pieces of paper, cloth, and other materials that are fastened to a canvas or other surface. See MONTAGE.

collar An ASTRAGAL, or molding that forms a band or ring around a furniture element such as a table or chair leg.

colonial (adj.) (1) Related to a colony or colonies. (2) In the United States, of or related to the thirteen original British colonies. (3) Colonial style often indicates a simplified version in contrast to a more complex original, or a hybrid between the indigenous and imported cultures.

colonial American period The era in American art and architecture from 1620 up to the Revolution. The period of early settlement in America, it blends English, French, and Dutch influences with indigenous provincial interpretations. Also colonial revivals, especially in the 19th century.

colonnade A row of columns supporting a single ENTABLATURE. An architectural treatment for a passageway or corridor.

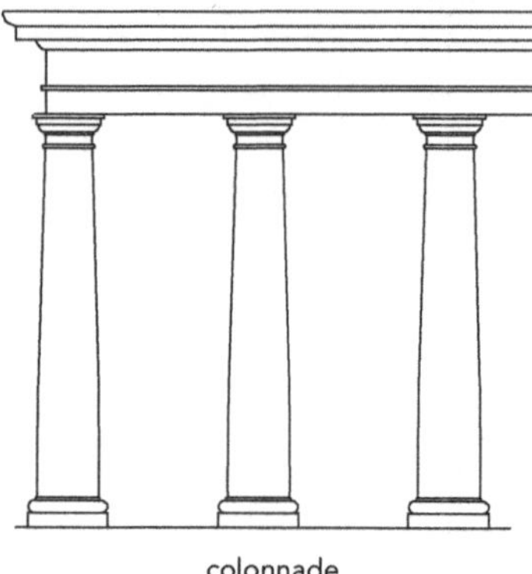

colonnade

colonnette (1) A miniature column used in architecture. A group or cluster of the elements is sometimes used as a support for a pedestal table. (2) A furniture decoration. A classical motif, and a favorite of the Renaissance period.

color block A trend of solid colors, often in combination, for striking effect, in fashion and interior design. Chromatic strategies include a saturated color paired with a neutral (yellow and gray), unexpected color combinations (olive green and teal), different shades of the same color (red and maroon), or opposites on the color wheel (tangerine and kiwi). A reaction against traditional color theory that involves no concern with matching or traditional color combos. Dates to approximately 2010; can also be monochromatic.

colorbond A trademark name for an oil-in-water resin pigment dyeing technique. It makes cotton, viscose rayon, acetate, nylon, and other synthetics or blends colorfast to sunlight, washing, and dry-cleaning gases.

colorfast (adj.) Describes the ability of a fabric to retain its pigment when subjected to normal light, gases, and laundering. Little or no noticeable change of shade should take place, though it is impossible to produce an absolutely colorfast fabric.

color temperature The degree of warmth or coolness of a light source; measured in degrees kelvin (K) in the International System of Units (SI). Also referred to as chromaticity.

colorways The various pigment or dye schemes in which a commercial pattern or design is available. The colorways of a particular design is the number of different color arrangements printed on paper, screened on fabric, etc.

colossal order An architectural composition dominated by a column that is higher than one story; Michelangelo's Campidoglio palaces are an example. Henry Ives Cobb's City and

colossal order

Country Building, Chicago, has columns the equivalent height of six stories.

colossus A very large statue.

column An upright member that is taller than it is thick and serves as a support for something resting on its top. In architecture, a shaft set on a base, topped with a capital, and which supports an entablature. The structural elements are distinguished by the name of the style or period of architecture to which they belong.

comb back A Windsor chair vertical support in which the central group of spindles extends above the curved back proper and is topped with an additional rail (the cresting rail). The top unit is thusly named because it resembles high, Spanish hair accessories. Also called a three-back Windsor chair.

combed yarns Strands spun after the longer cotton fibers are separated and straightened to make them as parallel as possible. Yarn treated in this fashion produces a smooth, lustrous fabric, as fewer fiber ends project from the fabric surface.

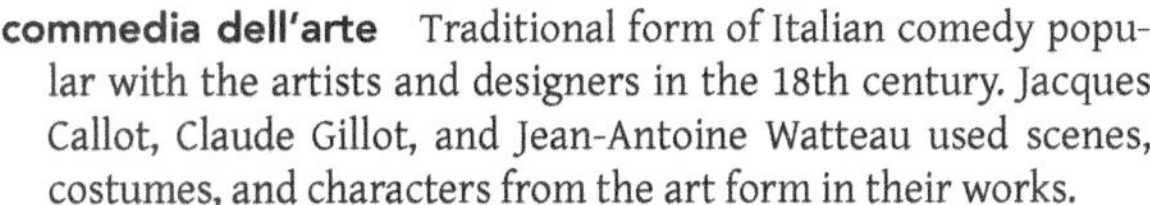

column

commedia dell'arte Traditional form of Italian comedy popular with the artists and designers in the 18th century. Jacques Callot, Claude Gillot, and Jean-Antoine Watteau used scenes, costumes, and characters from the art form in their works.

commesso (Italian) A geometric type of mosaic work used in Italy during the Middle Ages.

commode (1) A low chest of drawers. In the Louis XIV period, "bureau commode" described a table with drawers. In the Regency and the Louis XV periods, the item was bombé in shape. Finer pieces showed no dividing rail or strip between the upper and lower drawers; with two or three ranges. (2) Also a night stand or bedside chest. (3) A latrine or toilet. See CHAISE PERCÉE and COMMODE CHAIR. See CRESSENT, CHARLES, in *Designers and Architects.*

commode

commode chair A throne-like seat construction used to camouflage a toilet bowl. A 20th-century conceit. See CHAISE PERCÉE.

commode desserte A French 18th-century sideboard with a center cabinet area and open shelves on either side.

commode en tombeaux An early Louis XV chest, usually designed with two small drawers on top, and two full-width drawers below. The units were heavy in appearance, and the lowest drawer was inches off the floor, resting on short legs. *Tombeau* is French for tombstone, and the designs were massive, squat, and robust.

commode step The curved bottom tread of a stairway.

common bond In masonry, several courses of stretcher bricks with the sixth or eighth course made up of headers only. This provides transverse strength to the ensemble, as the headers tie back into the other face of the wall. See BOND and COURSE.

common rafters The structural elements that support the roofing of a building. They slope from the top of a wall to the ridge or apex of a pitched roof.

Commonwealth The period in England from 1649 to 1660 in which England, Ireland, and Scotland were part of a confederation under the Lord Protector, Oliver Cromwell. A puritanical period of chasteness, with severe forms. The subject of Bellini's opera *I Puritani.*

communications raceway A channel at the bottom of some open-planning panels or acoustical panels for offices, through which telephone, communications, and electrical wires may be pulled to bring outlets to the machines out on the floor and away from walls and columns. See ACOUSTICAL PANELS and OPEN PLANNING.

companion chair Three curved, upholstered seats joined together at one point so that they appear to radiate from a central junction. Each seat accommodated two people. These were popular in the 19th century. Similar to a three-part TÊTE-À-TÊTE or SIAMOISE.

compass seat An early-18th-century term for a round chair. Also referred to as a PINCUSHION CHAIR.

complementary colors Each of the primary colors (red, yellow, and blue) has its complement, which is produced by mixing the other two. Yellow and blue make green, and green is red's complement. Violet complements yellow; orange complements blue.

compo A plaster or papier-mâché material molded or applied to a ceiling, panel, frame, or piece of furniture to create bas-relief enrichment. See CARTON-PIERRE, COMPOSITION ORNAMENT, and GESSO.

composite order A variation of the Corinthian architectural category. The Roman capital resembles an Ionic volute placed above rows of Corinthian acanthus leaves.

composition ornament An embellishment made of plaster or plaster-like material. The material is cast in a mold and then applied to a surface to make a bas-relief decoration that resembles carving. The material and resulting ornament are also called gesso and yeseria. See ANAGLYPTA, CARTON-PIERRE, COMPO, GESSO, PAPIER-MÂCHÉ, PARGE WORK, and YESERIA.

compradoric (adj.) (1) Semi-foreign. Originates from the *comprador* or *compradore* in China, who was a local resident and translator for European businesses. (2) Can also be used to describe similar conditions globally. (3) Can refer to culturally hybrid objects such as English or Portuguese colonial furniture.

computation Field of computer-based activity that includes initial designing, creation of working drawings, and eventual fabrication based on sophisticated software.

computer-aided design (CAD) Computer software used for drafting, printing, and constructing designs. Many types exist, and they are becoming increasingly complex in their capabilities. There is a progression from 2-D to 3-D capabilities and from simpler shapes to highly involved geometries. The data files contain more and more information, such as inventory numbers and materials.

computer numeric control (CNC) An automated machine system that uses computer technology, such as computer-aided design, for production or fabrication. The intention is no longer to produce drawings that instruct human agents how to build; the digital files are integral to the construction process.

computer numeric control (CNC) milling machine A piece of shop equipment that uses CAD/CAM cutter paths to cut into blocks. Handles larger pieces and denser materials than a router.

com-yards A unit of measurement that specifies the quantity of fabric needed to upholster a particular piece of furniture.

concave A sunken or caved-in, curved line or surface. The reverse of a convex line or surface.

concha A shell motif in Spanish or Latin American art, interiors, and furniture. See also SCALLOPING.

concrete A construction material made of cement, sand, and crushed stone, tile, or brick, mixed with water. See *Table 3*.

concha

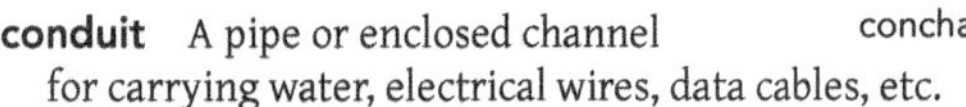

conduit A pipe or enclosed channel for carrying water, electrical wires, data cables, etc.

confessional (1) An 18th-century large, upholstered French wing chair. (2) Also a small enclosure in which a priest hears a confession.

confidante Three seats attached in a single unit. The two end seats are smaller, angled, and separated from the prominent center section by arms. The divisions make it respectable for people to sit close to each other and therefore also promotes intimate whisperings.

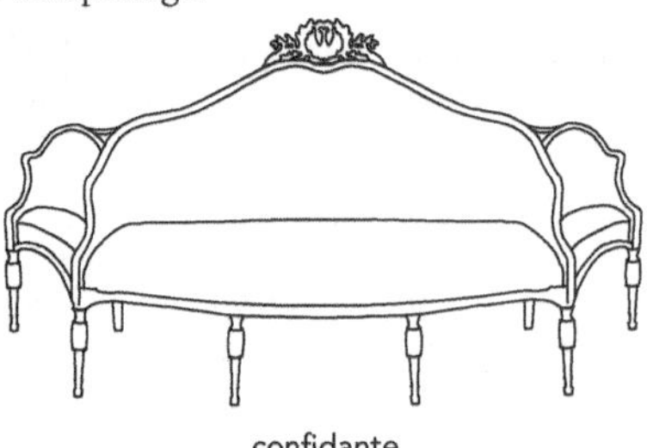

confidante

∞confortable An early French Renaissance all-upholstered chair. A forerunner of the BERGÈRE.

conge A concave molding similar to a CAVETTO but tangent to a plane surface. The ASTRAGAL under the bell of a capital consists of bead, fillet, and congé moldings. See CINCTURE.

congé

Connecticut chest An early American storage unit that stands on four short legs and has two rows of double drawers. It was frequently painted black, decorated with split spindles, and sometimes ornamented with three carved panels (see ASTER CARVING). The volume-creating devices were often made of oak, with pine tops, backs, and bottoms. See BLANKET CHEST and HADLEY CHEST.

connoisseur (French, to be acquainted with) A person knowledgeable in a specific subject matter related to design, specifically antiques and other objects.

connoisseurship A method of identifying an object's provenance and maker based on an encyclopedic knowledge of details. Based on the work of Italian art critic Giovanni Morelli.

conoidal vault See FAN VAULTING.

conservatory A greenhouse. Usually a glassed-in room in which plants and trees grow, often with a glass ceiling. Also called a *jardin d'hiver* or *Wintergarten*. A late-19th-century favorite.

conservatory

consignment Selling products where the original owner retains ownership of the goods and the seller typically makes a small profit, as in a furniture resale shop.

console (French, bracket) (1) A bracket, usually in an S-scroll or curve, used to support a cornice or shelf. In furniture, it is more decorative than functional. (2) A console table, which is actually a shelf supported against a wall by a bracket, a leg, or a pair of legs.

console

console leg In late-18th-century furniture, a scroll leg that is bracket-shaped. Also called a BRACKET FOOT.

console mirror A mirror that is set over a console or pier table and frequently framed with GIRANDOLES.

console servante A serving table with a marble top and a shelf below, of the Louis XVI period. Similar to the CONSOLE DESSERTE and COMMODE DESSERTE.

console table A shelflike table attached to a wall and either supported by a receding front leg or legs or set on an S-shaped curved or caryatid-type bracket. Originally popular in 18th-century France and England in foyers and entries. Also called a PIER TABLE.

console mirror

console table

constitution mirror A late-18th-, early-19th-century rectangular Sheraton gilded frame with a reflecting pane, with a row of balls under the cornice and a painted upper panel. In the 19th century, the painting often featured the frigate *Constitution* of the War of 1812. See TABERNACLE MIRROR.

constructability A long-term pre-construction analysis, in order to avoid do-overs.

construction The assembling of component parts into an integral unit.

contador A Portuguese version of the cabinet on a stand in the Baroque period.

contemporary (1) The current, present-day, style of decoration or furniture, often erroneously related to modernism. *Contemporary* is opposed to *traditional,* which refers to a conventional past period or an antique style. (2) Also, existing in the same historical time period; for example, a style that is contemporary with Marie Antoinette.

continuous filament yarn An unbroken or uncut fiber that is indefinitely long.

contour chair Any molded, shaped, or upholstered seat that conforms to the shape of the human body. Many modern pieces are so designed in plywood, Plexiglass, aluminum, etc. See EAMES, CHARLES; Eames, RAY; and SAARINEN, EERO in *Designers and Architects.*

contract administration Management and oversight of all the services for a project, including schedules, costs, contracts, specifications, liaising and monitoring legal agreements, and ensuring compliance with codes and regulations.

contract design The interior configuration and furnishing of non-residential areas: offices, reception spaces, hospitals, healthcare facilities, schools, libraries, restaurants, theaters, hotels, etc. Interior design based on commercial requirements. Contract design often involves quantity purchasing.

contract documents All the legal documents for services among the parties, including working drawings, specifications, instructions, and other legal papers, replete with text and image.

contract furniture Furniture designed for heavy use by many people in non-residential interiors and in public areas. Must be strong enough to withstand exposure to wear and tear over extended periods.

contrasting color scheme An arrangement of colors derived by focusing on the differences among the selection of hues. Hues at a distance from one another on the color wheel. It is considered more dynamic and active than a related color scheme.

contrepartie or contre Boulle A form of French veneer work in which the brass forms the groundwork. The tortoiseshell is set into it and is the less prominent material. The reverse form of the usual Boulle work, or *première partie.* See BOULLE, ANDRÉ-CHARLES *in Designers and Architects.* See also BOULLE WORK and PREMIÈRE PARTIE.

conventionalization The simplifying or exaggerating of natural forms to make them reproducible in other materials.

conversation chair A comfortable seat that is not as low or deep as a chaise longue. Over time, a variety of chairs have been thusly described: the CAQUETEUSE in the 16th century, the ROUNDABOUT CHAIR or COCKFIGHT CHAIR in the 18th century, and the S-shaped VIS-À-VIS or DOS-À-DOS of the 19th century.

conversation piece An oddity or unique piece of decoration in a room that may cause comment and become the subject of a lively discussion.

conversation pit In contemporary interiors, a sunken area in a living room or family room that is surrounded by an architectural ledge, usually covered with upholstery or pillows. The riser to the floor level, above the ledge, serves as the backrest for those seated in the depression. The unit may be rectangular, oval, or circular, but the conversationalists face one another. The masterpiece of the genre is found in the Eero Saarinen and Alexander Girard collaboration the Miller House.

convertible sofa A multiple-seating unit that unfolds into a bed. When folded, it resembles a seating unit, such as a love seat, complete with cushions; people sit on top of the folded mattress. Used in small areas for sitting during the day and sleeping at night. Also called a sleeper, SLEEPER SOFA, or SOFA BED.

convex A swelling or outgoing curved line or surface, as opposed to a concave line or surface.

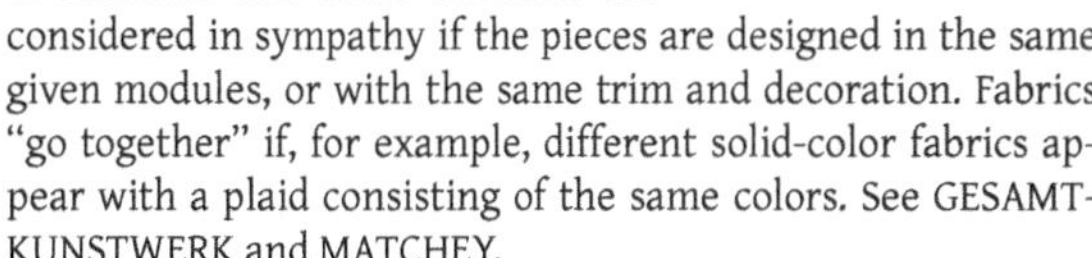

convex

convolute A scroll or paper-roll shape.

coordinated Designed or arranged to be harmonious together. A collection of furniture and other elements are considered in sympathy if the pieces are designed in the same given modules, or with the same trim and decoration. Fabrics "go together" if, for example, different solid-color fabrics appear with a plaid consisting of the same colors. See GESAMTKUNSTWERK and MATCHEY.

cope A method of joining two molded strips at an angle. Instead of the pieces being mitered, one piece fits over the top of the other.

coping Flat stone or other material applied as the cap for a freestanding wall.

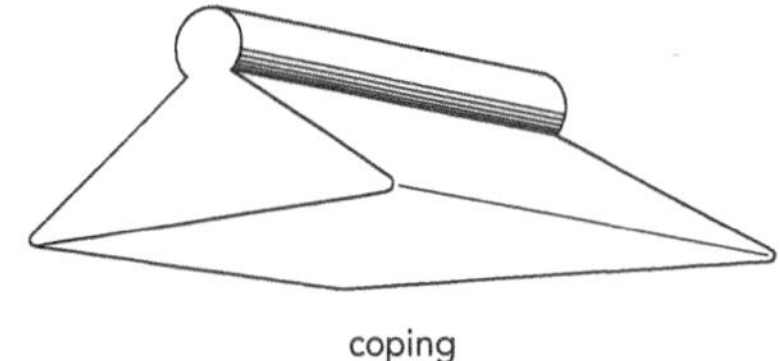

coping

Coptic Referring to the Copts, a Christian group in Egypt and Ethiopia. From the 4th through the 7th centuries A.D., their work included representational portraits and basilica-shaped churches.

Coptic cloth A small-patterned, plain-woven, cotton upholstery fabric that usually has a provincial or rustic appearance.

Coptic textile A linen fabric woven and designed in Egypt by Coptic 1 sect (4th to 7th centuries A.D.).

coquillage A French Rococo shell-like pattern used with birds, flowers, masks, and other carved ornaments to decorate mirrors, frames, clocks, etc. It appears in Chippendale's French-style furniture.

corbeil or corbeille (French, *corbeille,* basket) A sculptured or carved representation of a basket of fruit or flowers.

corbel In architecture, a bracket or shoulder set in a wall to carry a beam. The device was also adapted for use on interiors and on furniture and was popular in Renaissance designs. See BRACKET and CONSOLE.

corbeled arch (1) A span of stonework constructed by advancing the successive courses from either side until the top ones nearly meet. A capstone is set in the center to close the gap. (2) Also, a false arch. It is considered an intermediary step in the development of a rounded Roman arch.

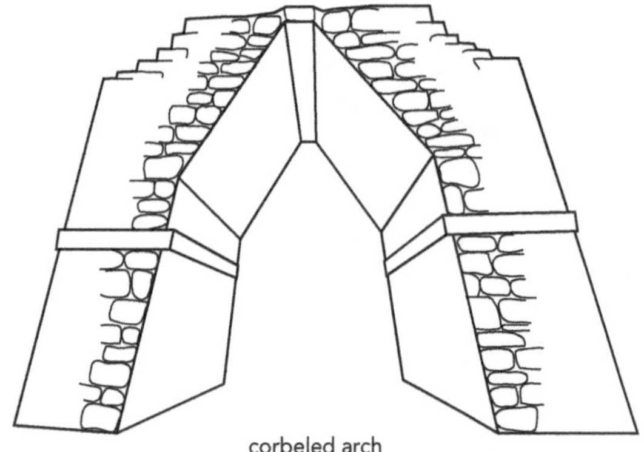
corbeled arch

corbel table A slab of stone or masonry supported by a row of brackets.

cordonnett Lace in which the pattern is outlined in cord. Also called reembroidered lace.

cordovan leather The decorated animal hides made in the technique and style begun in Cordova, Spain, during the Middle Ages. The animal skins were often stamped, carved, or embossed with gilt arabesques and Moorish patterns.

cordovan tapestry See GUADAMICIL.

corduroy (French, king's cord) A cotton or rayon cut pile fabric with ridges or cords in the pile that run lengthwise, giving a ridged, velvety quality.

core (1) In cabinetry, the structural wooden body of a piece of furniture. Usually it has a veneer finish. (See CARCASE.) (2) The central body of plywood that has crossed layers of veneer or other wood applied to either of its surfaces. This internal layer, or core, is usually made of a porous wood.

∞corinthianesque (adj.) A design similar to, but not identical to, the classical Corinthian order.

Corinthian order The most slender and elaborate of the classic architectural groups. The Romans made the height of the column equal to ten times the diameter of the shaft. Rows of acanthus leaves and four volutes enrich the capital.

Corinthian order

cork tiles Pressed plant-based material baked into a solid, homogeneous block and cut into rectangular sheets. The squares may serve as flooring or wall surfacing. It is a resilient material. When reinforced with resin, the waxed variety is less porous than natural cork and requires less maintenance. The material will stain, and because of its softness it will indent or pit. The material from the periderm of plants can be laminated with vinyl or impregnated with vinyl resins.

Corlon A trademark name for sheet vinyl flooring with a hydrocord back, made by Armstrong. Usually comes in 6-foot widths (183 cm) and can be used on grade and below-grade subfloors. Available in a variety of colors, patterns, and textures.

corner block (1) In carpentry, a square piece of wood used to form a junction, as between the sides and head strip of a door. (2) In cabinetry, a triangular block used as a brace in joining legs to seat rails.

corner cupboard A triangular cabinet or chest originally designed by architects as an integral part of a room. In the 18th century it became a mobile piece of furniture. See ENCOIGNURE and QUOIN.

corner stiles The vertical members in a paneled piece of furniture found at the extremes or edges of the elevation.

corner table A square or triangular work surface used at the intersection of two walls between a pair of sofas or chairs set at a right angle to each other. The surface-creating piece fills in the space that is left. A corner table may be from any period, design, or material.

cornice (1) The projecting top portion of a classical entablature consisting of bed FASCIA and crown moldings. In the Renaissance, it was used on walls directly below the ceiling, without the FRIEZE or ARCHITRAVE. (2) A decorative cap applied to a drapery arrangement. Usually made of wood with molding trim, it may be carved or covered with fabric. Similar to a VALANCE, LAMBREQUIN, or PELMET (PALMETTE). In the mid 18th century, it was called a WINDOW MANTEL.

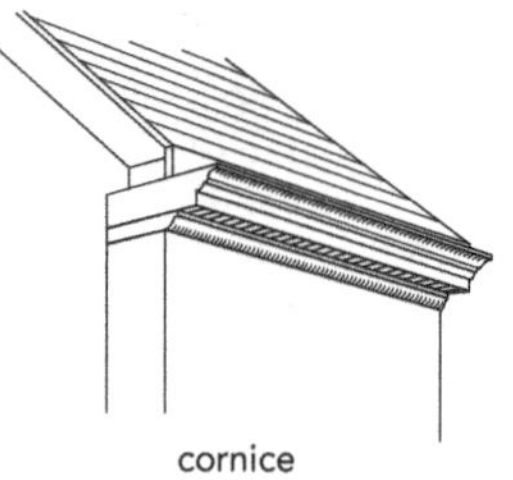
cornice

∞cornish See CORNICE.

cornucopia The twisting, spiraling horn of plenty of mythology, often represented with fruits and flowers pouring forth. As a decorative motif, it was popular in the Renaissance, Empire, and Victorian periods. Arms and legs of sofas were sometimes cornucopia-shaped in 19th-century furniture, particularly in the English Regency and American Empire periods.

corolitic (adj.) Describes something decorated with sculptured branches of foliage.

coromandel A hard, dark brown wood with black stripes. It resembles black rosewood and was used for banding and veneering in late-18th-century furniture. Also called coromandel ebony, CALAMANDER, and MACASSAR ebony.

coromandel lacquer A finishing technique originally from the Henan province in central China, greatly admired and used in the Louis XV period for finishing commodes and cabinets. The background was a reddish-black, which turned brown with age. The finish was thick and applied in successive layers, so designs could be incised in it. Panels were decorated with figures, houses, landscapes, etc. See COROMANDEL SCREEN.

coromandel screen A Chinese lacquered panel often decorated with an allover pattern in low relief or executed with a landscape design. The East India Company originally introduced them into Europe in the mid 17th century. The finest were first made in Beijing and Suzhou, China.

coronize (verb) A trademarked process for applying a heat-treated finish to fiberglass cloth. This sets the weave of the fabric and releases strains in the glass yarns. The finish gives the fiberglass a firm hand, and it drapes better. The Owens Corning Fiberglas Corporation developed the process.

correlated group Matching suite pieces that can be grouped to form sets that allow a choice of configurations in a room. An example is bedroom furniture with a variety of desks, chests, and bookcases.

Cor-Ten A type of weathering steel, and part of a group of steel alloys developed to obviate the need for painting. Cor-Ten develops a layer of rust that prevents further rust from occurring when it is outdoors.

cortile (Italian) An inner court surrounded by an arcade.

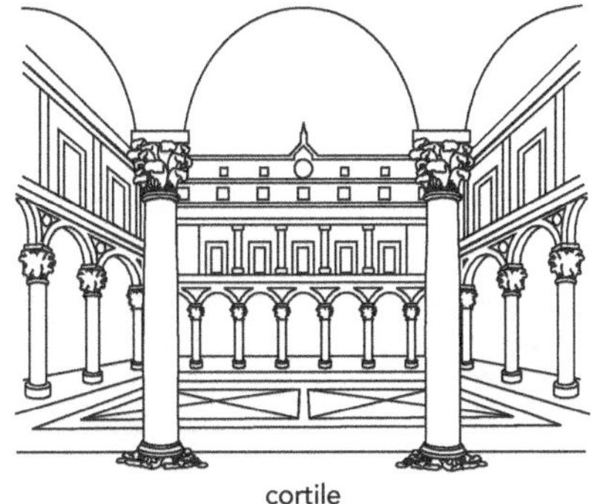

cortile

cosmati The marble and mosaic workers of Rome, from the 12th to the 14th century. They created pavements, tombs, pulpits, etc. in marble with inlays of mosaic, gilding, colored stones, and glass. By the 14th century, these workers, many of whom were from the same family, also produced sculpture.

cosmati work Generic term for work in colored stone. See COSMATI.

cosy corner An upholstered sofa or couch that fit into the corner of a room, forming a complete right angle. It usually had an upholstered and tufted back and was a popular piece in the late 19th century. It was similar to the corner ottoman and was sometimes the main furnishing of a Turkish corner. See TURKISH CORNER.

cottage furniture Mid-19th-century, mass-produced Victorian furniture. Inexpensive pieces made of pine, and painted and decorated in a colonial or provincial style. The DRY SINK is an example.

cottage orné (French) A pseudo-rustic middle-class dwelling fashionable in the 18th century.

cottage piano An upright musical instrument of the 18th and early 19th centuries. It usually had a fretwork panel in front of and above the keyboard. A pleated silk curtain hung behind the fretwork.

cottage-set curtain A two-tier set of drapery usually made of a sheer or semi-sheer fabric. The lower tier may be pleated or shirred and extends across the width of the window. The upper tier is usually ruffled along the edges and is pulled back to either side of the window, allowing an open center area.

cotton The plant that produces the versatile natural fluffy fiber. The fiber when used alone makes a popular fabric, and it also blends well with other fibers. It combines with rayon, dacron, and Fortisan as well as with wool, and it lends its good characteristics to other fibers in a mixture. See *Table 2* and *Table 3*.

couch A lounge chair used for resting, with supports and cushions at one or both ends but no back. A French innovation of the early 17th century, it later developed into a daybed. In 18th-century America, the multiple-seating unit was synonymous with the daybed. Today, in common usage, a couch is mistakenly confused with a sofa or settee.

count of cloth The number of threads per inch. The lengthwise yarns are called ends, and the crosswise yarns are called picks. The density of a fabric may be given in the number of ends and the number of picks.

∞counter Boulle See CONTREPARTIE.

counterfloor A sub-layer under a main floor, made of battens laid on the supporting joists.

counterlathing A layer of thin flat strips of wood laid at right angles and on top of a first layer of similar strips, producing a latticed effect.

counterpane The top layer of multiple bed linens. A quilt, usually the exposed one placed on top of a bed. The pattern is raised, or quilted. A bedspread.

countersink A depression made in a piece of wood so that the head of a screw inserted into it is either flush with the wood or just below its top surface. See CUP.

country Chippendale A mid-18th-century provincial version of the Chippendale chairs in English colonies. Often made of pine and painted, these were simplified but skillfully made.

country French A heavier, sturdier, simplified version of the Rococo style. Usually made of solid wood, often with caning, and sometimes painted. See FRENCH PROVINCIAL.

country-made (adj.) Describes furniture or cabinets made by rural cabinetmakers or those outside of major centers of manufacturing. The term usually implies less refined workmanship and simplified design.

coupled columns Vertical structural elements or shafts grouped in pairs. In classical orders, they are usually spaced half of a diameter (of the column shaft) apart.

coupled columns

course A horizontal row of stones, bricks, tiles, etc. that can be arranged in decorative patterns. A module of masonry.

wall with multiple courses

court cupboard (French *court*, short) A low storage unit mounted on legs, or a double version, usually heavily carved and massive. It was originally designed to hold plates, utensils, and goblets. In the Tudor period, it was a buffet and related to the Italian and French crédence.

court cupboard

court furniture Formal, elegant, traditional pieces, including chairs, storage units, and tables, much of which were originally designed for the European nobility.

∞courting chair An upholstered double seat or settee, popular in the Louis XIV period. In the Queen Anne style, the design had an open back and looked as though two chairbacks had been joined together with a common seat. A forerunner of the LOVE SEAT.

courting chair

courting mirror A small 18th- to 19th-century reflective device with a simple wood frame with insets of small pieces of glass. The pieces of glass were often painted or decorated. It may originally have been a gift presented by a swain to the young lady he was courting.

cove (1) A quarter-circle, concave, downward curve from the ceiling to wall. (2) Also, a large concave molding used in a cornice or under the eaves of a roof. See CAVETTO.

cove base See SKIRTING.

cove lighting A form of indirect lighting. The lighting source in the room or area is concealed from below by a recess, or projecting cornice, and the light is directed to a reflecting surface.

coved ceiling A finished roof interior into which the supporting walls flow in a curve, rather than meeting at a right angle. A curved joining of walls and ceiling.

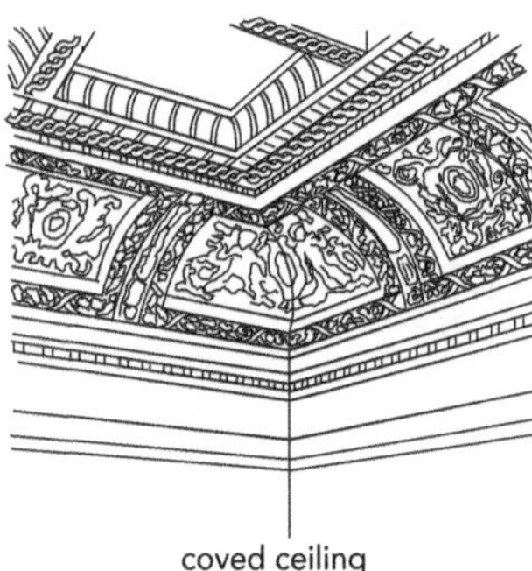

coved ceiling

coved cupboard An early American space-containing piece with a hoodlike projection on top.

coved skirting An applied circular-shaped strip that covers the joint of the wall and the floor. Wooden, rubber, asphalt, and vinyl coves have replaced flat floorboards. Also called a cove base, or SKIRTING.

co-working An economic activity of numerous occupations and the places of work. An economic model for the workplace in which a flexible, collaborative, technologically connected space serves freelance workers and entrepreneurs, for a fee. The environments can be furnished space for rent or can cater to specified sectors, such as bio-engineering. Multiple features appeal to a diverse workforce, including coffee bars, lactation rooms, and heads-down areas. These inspirational locales foster collaboration and are technologically advanced, including fast internet.

cracking The development of defects in the finish of a piece. An advanced stage of checking or crazing, where breaks in the decorative finish are deep enough to expose the underlying surface. See CHECK and CRAZE.

crackle glaze A fine web of lines on the surface of a ceramic piece. The ware is cooled quickly after firing to create this effect.

cradle A baby's bed usually set on a swinging device or on curved rocker supports.

∞cramoisy A crimson-colored cloth used in medieval and Renaissance England.

cramp A thin piece of metal with both ends turned back at right angles, used to bind together blocks of masonry or timber.

craquelure The network of fine cracks on the surface of an old painting. It may be caused by shrinkages and by movement of paint film or varnish.

crash Cotton, jute, or linen fabric having coarse, uneven yarns and a rough texture. May be hand-blocked or printed. Used for draperies.

craze A small crack, or patterns of cracks, in a ceramic object.

∞crédence A serving table and sideboard of the French Gothic period that may have evolved from a church piece. It was a chest mounted on a stand, a display cabinet for plates, or for preparing and carving meats. See BUFFET and DESSERTE.

credenza (1) The Italian form of the CRÉDENCE. (2) In commercial settings, a work surface with storage behind a person seated at a desk.

Creil–Montereau A French ceramic that imitated English creamware. Made in Creil and in Montereau, two towns in northern France that had factories known for producing the popular decorative plates with detailed painted scenes and decoration.

crémaillère (French) A swinging crane on a fireplace hearth.

cremo An Italian marble with a creamy white ground and a network of golden veins.

crenellated (adj.) Describes repeated square indentations on the top of a wall.

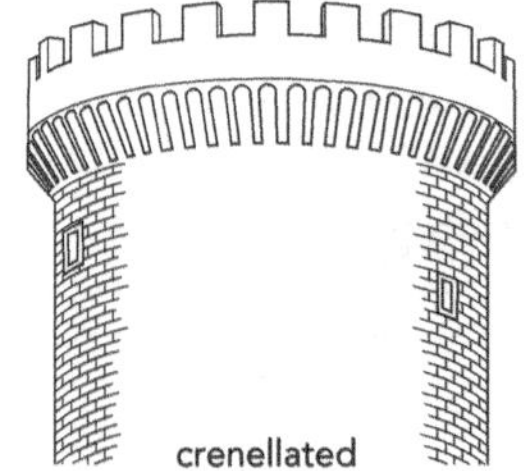

crenellated

crêpe A large group of fabrics characterized by a crinkled surface, which is obtained by various methods: hard twisting of the yarns, chemical treatment, embossing, or using a certain weave. The textured textile can be made of natural or synthetic fibers.

crêpe de chine (French) A fine, lightweight, plain-weave silk fabric.

∞crepidoma The stepped platform of a classical temple.

crescent stretcher An arched or hooped stabilizer, sometimes used between the legs of 18th-century furniture. A reinforcing element on American Windsor chairs. See CRINOLINE STRETCHER.

Creslan An acrylic fiber similar to Orlon and Acrilan. A soft, bulky fiber with a wool-like hand.

cresting Elaborate carving on the top rail of a chair back or settee, often centered on the top rail. The crown-and-cherubs was a favorite English Restoration motif. See BRATTISHING.

crest rail The uppermost or top horizontal element of a chair back. In the 16th and 17th centuries, this element was elaborately shaped and carved.

cretonne An unglazed chintz, made of cotton or linen, and printed with larger designs than usual for chintz. A common fabric for slip covers.

crewelwork Embroidery done with loosely twisted worsted yarn and a large-eyed needle on unbleached cotton or linen. Crewelwork was a popular fabric decoration in 16th- and 17th-century England. In the Jacobean period, often used in winding floral designs such as the East Indian "tree-of-life" motif.

crib An infant's bed with enclosed sides, usually raised off the ground on tall legs.

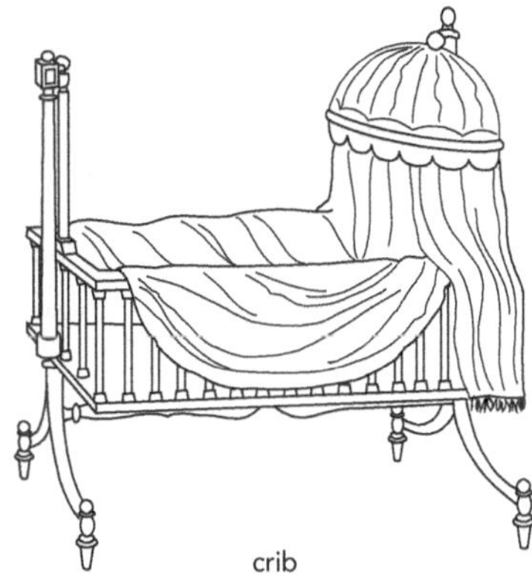

crib

cricket An archaic name for a low wooden footstool. An English and early American design.

cricket table A small, three-legged table of the English Jacobean period with a round or polygonal top. A triangular frame with high stretchers between the legs supported the top.

∞**crinoline stretcher** A common device of Chippendale's Windsor chairs. The connector is concave, and it separates and reinforces the two front legs. Two short arms extend from the back legs to support the device. See CRESCENT STRETCHER.

criosphinx An ancient Egyptian carved representation of an animal with a lion's body and a ram's head. See ANDROSPHINX and SPHINX.

criss-cross curtains See PRISCILLA CURTAIN

∞**criteria matrix** A technique for condensing and formatting many of the programming requirements of an interior design project, including square footage needs and adjacencies, when developing preliminary design schematics.

crocket A projecting carved ornament used on the side of pinnacles and spires. The ornament is often bud- or leaf-shaped and appears in Gothic art and architecture. In 19th-century English Gothic revival furniture, this motif was sometimes carved on architecturally inspired cabinets, bookcases, and throne-like chairs.

crocket

crocking The tendency of excess dye to rub off a printed or dyed fabric. It is most apt to happen in deep-colored pile or napped fabrics.

Cromwellian chair A severe unadorned seat of the English COMMONWEALTH PERIOD (1649–1660). It usually had knob or bobbin turnings, a low back, a leather seat and back, and nailhead trim.

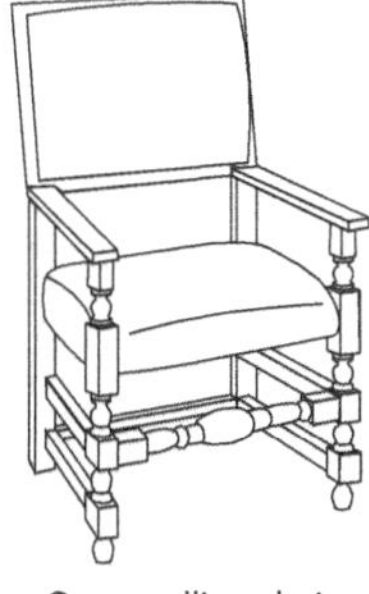

Cromwellian chair

Cromwellian period See COMMONWEALTH PERIOD.

croquet chair A mid- to late-19th-century woven wicker or rattan barrel seat. The base resembles an inverted woven basket. The arms and back make a continuous line that encircles the seated person. The back and seat are equipped with button-tufted upholstery. See PEACOCK CHAIR.

croquis A preliminary sketch or rough draft.

crossbanding A narrow strip of wood veneer used as a frame or border design on a panel, door, tabletop, etc. The grain of the veneer wood of the strip is at right angles to the grain of the panel itself. See BANDING.

cross-fire A vivid, mottled effect across the grain of some mahoganies, walnuts, and satinwoods that creates a striking pattern. The effect created is an uneven, corrugated, transverse pattern that appears as highlights.

cross-grain A wood or fabric with the growth pattern running diagonally.

cross-hatching A pattern created by the intersection of two or more series of parallel lines.

cross-laminated timber (CLT) Glued laminated timber, also called Glulam, a structural wood product composed of several layers of dimensioned natural materials adhered together.

cross-rail or member A horizontal element that joins two verticals or two sides. In a chair back, the connecting element between the back posts.

cross-section A view of an object with an imaginary cut through it, representing a side view with the constructional elements, projections, and recesses from the straight elevation.

cross-stretchers See SALTIRE and X-SHAPED STRETCHERS.

cross-vault A roof or ceiling formed by two spherical segments intersecting at right angles.

crotch The part of the tree from which the limbs and branches develop. It produces a highly figured V-grain of a decorative character.

crotch veneer A thin sheet of wood cut at the branch-intersect area of the tree, used for veneer. The graining is featherlike in appearance, or curly in effect, and always decorative.

crowd sourcing A method of obtaining products and materials in which a coordinator uses outside sources and integrates them with inside sources; this activity combines human resources that are in house with those that are out of house. The outsourcing of tasks that had traditionally been performed by an employee or hired contractor is sometimes arranged through an open call for contractors.

crown (1) The top point of an arch. (2) A decorative motif. The crown is the symbol of royalty, and it appears in carved, painted, and embroidered form.

∞**crown bed** A simple canopy sleeping device of the late 18th and early 19th centuries. The canopy is suspended over the

crown

sleeping platform or extends out partially over it. See BALDAQUIN BED.

crown glass An early form of window material made with a blowpipe. The vitreous material is formed as a flat dish with a button or bull's eye center. See BULL'S EYE.

crown molding The topmost decorative strip, particularly the FILLETS and cymas placed above the FASCIA in a classical cornice.

crow's bill A Gothic architectural enrichment in trim that looks like a BIRD'S BEAK.

crypt A hidden underground passage, or an underground level in a church that contains chapels and sometimes tombs.

crystal A clear, transparent quartz that resembles ice. It is usually cut and faceted to sparkle and reflect light. The material is often imitated in glass.

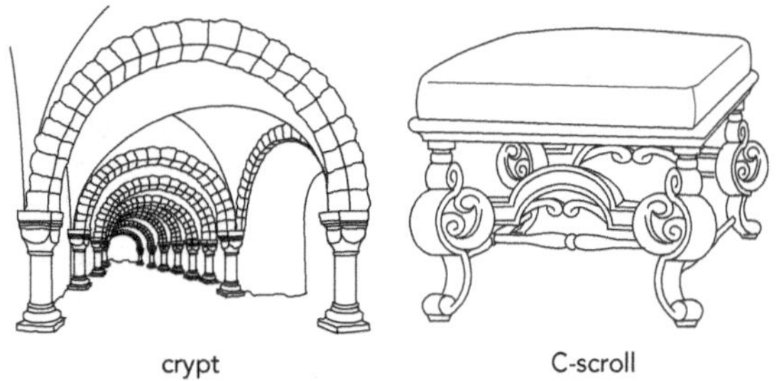
crypt C-scroll

C-scroll An ornamental motif painted, applied, or carved that resembles the letter or various combinations of the letter C. The curved lines may be inverted, touching back to back, top to bottom, or set askew of each other. Found in Spanish and French Gothic furniture. Used extensively in the Baroque, Rococo, Queen Anne, and Chippendale periods.

cube foot See BLOCK FOOT.

cubiculum A bedroom in an ancient Roman house.

Cubism A period of art and design that emphasized the analysis of forms and their relationships to each other and to the surrounding space. Several views of the object were often superimposed on one another, expressing the idea of the object rather than a single view. The movement was the precursor of abstract art, and Picasso, Braque, and Le Corbusier were among its major proponents.

cul-de-lampe A pendant, either of wood, metal, or stone, used as a bracket for a light fixture. These brackets were highly decorated with carving or painting.

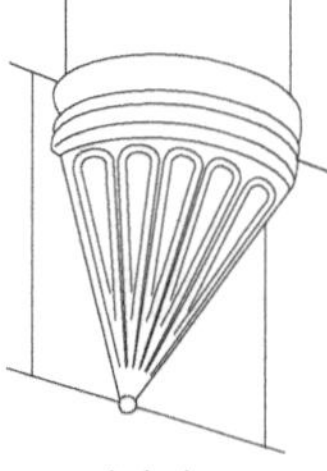
cul-de-lampe

cuneiform (1) Wedge-shaped. (2) The wedge-shaped characters the Assyrians and Babylonians used in writing on clay.

cup A metal sheath for the head of a screw in countersunk work. See COUNTERSINK.

cup-and-cover turning A popular Elizabethan and Jacobean turning used for furniture supports. It resembles a vessel topped with a lid or an inverted saucer.

cupboard A storage cabinet with doors. It may be raised up on high legs or be set low. The cabinet may have drawers or another cabinet below.

cupboard

cup caster A brass vessel with a roller below it that fits on the bottom of a furniture leg.

cupid's bow (1) A Chippendale-style top rail of a chair back that is shaped like the propulsion part of the archaic weapon, with compound curves and spiral volutes on the ends. (2) The motif was also used in the Louis XV and Louis XVI periods.

cupola A domed roof set on a circular base.

cupola

cuprama A cuprammonium-type rayon fiber produced in Germany. It has a wool-like hand, resists soiling, and dyes darker than regular rayon.

cup-turned leg The prominent vessel-like feature in a turning popular in the late 17th and early 18th centuries. It was developed from a Portuguese bulb shape and was also known as the bell and-trumpet leg. In England, the motif is characteristic of the William and Mary style. See BELL TURNING.

curing Process of treating with dry heat to set finishes or pigments.

curio cabinet A type of space-containing furniture piece used to display accessories. Dates from the Victorian era. See also WHATNOT.

curl The markings or figures in a wood. The appearance of the grain of certain woods when they are sliced against the grain.

curled hair The hardened protein shafts of animals used as a filler, with stuffing, in upholstered pieces under the muslin and the upholstery fabric, to add resiliency. Horsehair is more desirable than hog or cattle hair.

curon A multicellular plastic material, with a fine sponge-like appearance, and produced in many colors. The synthetic material may be used for wall or ceiling installations and will serve as an insulating or acoustical material.

∞curricule chair A late-18th-century to early-19th-century seat with a semicircular back and splayed legs that, according to Sheraton, resembles an open carriage of the period.

curtail step The bottom tred of a flight of stairs that has a curved end extending partially around the newel post.

curtain A movable covering of lightweight fabric for windows, doors, or alcoves. It was originally used to screen beds and bed areas.

curtain

curtain wall In contemporary architecture, a large swath of façade made from glass and metal, rendered possible by advances in the metal and plastics industries in overcoming problems of waterproofing, insulation, expansion, and contraction. Lever House, in New York City, 1952, has an early, dynamic example: the principal elevations are made of green glass and aluminum. The wall does not carry any compressive forces and symbolically announces the separation of structure from space-defining elements.

curule bench (1) A seating unit that, when viewed frontally, has curved supports. (2) The seat upon which senior magistrates, masters of the house, consuls, and praetors were entitled to rest.

∞**curule chair** A 17th-century seat in which the arm supports, back rails, and legs are semicircular in shape. The general appearance is an X created by the two intersecting S curves or one C resting on an inverted C. Leather strips serve as the back rest and the seat. The design is based on a classic Roman prototype, the sella curulis of the Roman magistrate. Another version of the curule chair became popular in the early 19th century. Similar to the 20th-century director's chair. See DANTE CHAIR.

curule chair

∞**curule legs** The X-shaped supports that were used on classical Greek and Roman folding stools. They became popular again in the Renaissance period and continued in favor up through the Regency and French Empire periods. See CURULE CHAIR.

curvilinear (adj.) Created within sinuous or arced lines. Some Gothic tracery was curvilinear in concept. A serpentine line quality was prevalent during the Rococo and Art Nouveau periods.

cushion (1) A shaped, flexible bag of fabric or leather, filled with feathers or other materials. The poufy objects are added to an upholstered platform and back for softness and comfort. A pillow. (2) Another term for carpet padding.

cushion frieze A Renaissance convex or cushion-shaped frieze. Sometimes used on cabinets of the late 17th and early 18th centuries.

cusp The pointed ending of a trefoil or quatrefoil in Gothic architecture. The meeting points are the pendants between the arcs. See QUATREFOIL and TREFOIL.

cusped arch A curved structural device with lobed motifs (trefoil or quatrefoil) on its inner face.

cusped arch

cutout borders Wallpaper designs usually applied below the ceiling line or molding and used as a dado decoration, or around doors, windows, arches, etc. Designs are often architectural motifs combined with swags, garlands of flowers, fruits, etc. The lower edge of the design is cut out to conform to the outline of the artwork. When the paper is applied, it appears as part of the wall. Also called a scalloped border.

cut pile Fabric woven with an extra set of warp or filler yarns. These threads form the extruding loop, which is later sheared. Velvet and plush are two examples. See *Table 1.*

cutting A swatch or clipping of a piece of carpet or fabric. A small representation or sample of a larger whole.

cyclopean masonry An elemental type of construction with large, irregular blocks of stone.

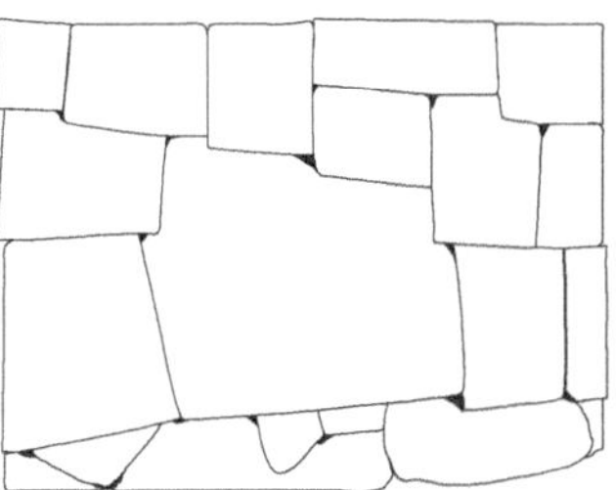
Cyclopean masonry

cylinder front A quarter-round front of a desk or secretary mounted so that it can be pivoted.

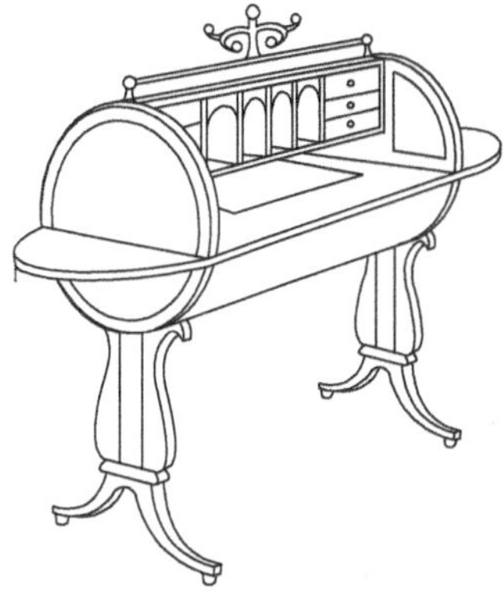
cylinder front

cylinder top A curved and movable cover to a bureau or desk. It differs from the TAMBOUR top in that it does not roll up on itself.

cyma curve An S-shaped sinuous line.

cyma recta An S-shaped line that starts and ends in a horizontal plane. An OGEE molding.

cyma reversa An S-shaped line that starts and ends in a vertical plane.

∞**cymatium** A curved molding that forms the uppermost member of a cornice.

cypress A light brown wood, adapted to all types of finishes. Generally free from warping and twisting, it is too weak for structural timber or flooring. In the Tudor period, it was used for storage chests. "Pecky cypress" is popular today for paneling and wall finishes. See CYPRESS CHEST and *Table 5.*

cypress chest Early Renaissance storage unit made to hold tapestries, robes, and other fabrics. The aromatic wood was used because it repels moths. The storage item was a forerunner of contemporary cedar chests.

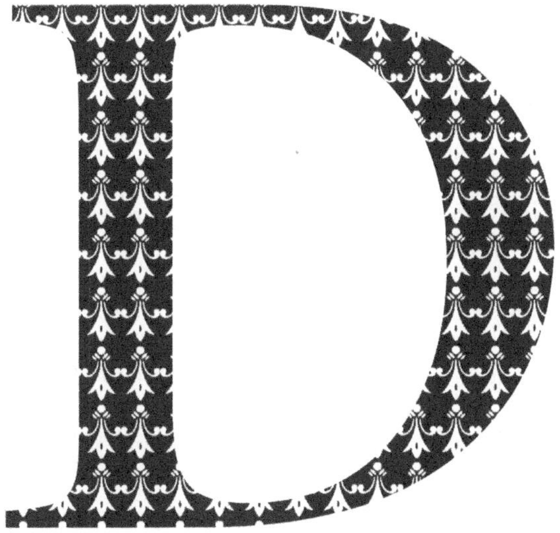

Dacron A trademark name for a polyester fiber obtained from a polymer with 85 percent or more ethylene glycol and terephthalic acid. A crisp, resilient fiber manufactured by DuPont, the synthetic material combines well with cotton, linen, and wool.

Dada (French, hobbyhorse) An art movement in which the artists emphasized shocking effects rather than literal understanding (1915–1922). Marcel Duchamp was a leading figure of the nihilistic art movement; a predecessor of surrealism.

dado The lower portion of a wall, when treated differently or separated from the rest of the wall by a molding strip or other material transition. In classical design, the element had a base, shaft, and cap molding and was often paneled or ornamented. See WAINSCOT.

dado

dado cap The crown or cap molding of the lowest field of a wall in classical detailing. Also called a CHAIR RAIL.

dado joint A joining technique for supporting shelving or drawer bottoms in vertical units. The edge of the vertical piece of wood fits into a groove in the horizontal piece, and this stiffens or reinforces the vertical member. Also called a RABBET JOINT.

Dagobert chair (archaic) A famous 7th-century folding seat, originally made of gilt bronze, and supposedly built by St. Eloi. The Abbot Suger, the patron of Gothic architecture, added the back and arms in the 12th century. One of the few pieces of furniture remaining from this period.

Dagobert chair

daguerreotype An early photographic process Louis Daguerre invented in 1839. It resulted in a faint image that had to be viewed from an angle for clarity.

dairy farmer (slang) A CAD renderer who creates an unnecessary amount of detail for impressive visual effects. Derived from the phrase "milking it for all it's worth."

dais A low, raised platform usually located at the end or side of a room, for example at a wedding banquet or in an English Great Hall.

dalburgia An Indian wood used for carved decorative elements such as boxes and gong stands.

dallage (French) A pavement or floor of stone, marble, or tile.

Damascus work A type of metal inlay work in patterns or arabesques. The design is incised in metal and then inlaid with other metals or wires that are cut to fit.

damask A firm, glossy, patterned fabric with a jacquard weave. Marco Polo introduced the fabric to Europe, and it became named for the Syrian city of Damascus. The resulting fabric is similar to brocade but flatter and reversible, and it may be a one- or two-color design. On the face side, the pattern is matte, whereas on the reverse side the pattern changes in color or may appear shiny. Originally made of silk, it is now woven in cotton, rayon, linen, silk, wool, or a combination of these fibers.

damassé (French) See DAMASK.

∞Dan Day chair A form of the Windsor chair produced in Suffolk in the early 19th century and named for its maker. Norwegian copies of this chair exist, with slight variations on the design of the underframe.

Danish modern See SCANDINAVIAN MODERN.

Dante chair An X-shaped seat of the Italian Renaissance, usually carved and upholstered in leather. The X curved up from the floor and became the arms. Variations appeared in English, French, Spanish, and Teutonic early Renaissance furniture. See CURULE CHAIR and DIRECTOR'S CHAIR.

∞Dantesca chair See DANTE CHAIR.

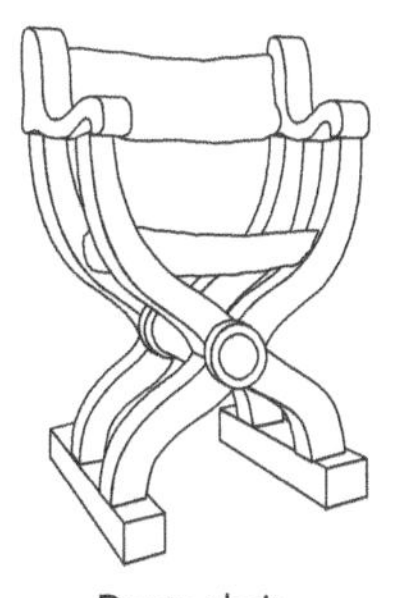

Dante chair

Darby and Joan chair

∞Darby and Joan chair A mid-18th-century English seat with a double or triple chair back and a wide pad to accommodate several persons. A settee named for characters in the 1735 poem, "The Joys of Love Never Forgot."

darnick An 18th-century coarse damask.

dauphine A matte-finish silk fabric popular in the late Louis XVI period.

davenport (1) An early-19th-century small kneehole desk with a lift-top writing slope and drawers at the side, named after a Captain Davenport. (2) In contemporary usage, an overstuffed upholstered sofa, named after the original manufacturer, A. H. Davenport and Company of Boston.

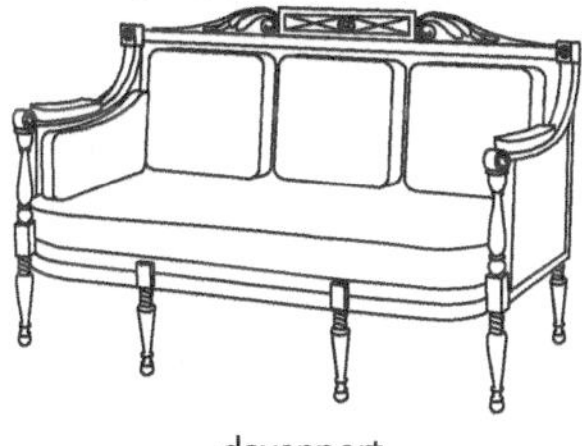

davenport

∞davenport bed A sofa that converts into a sleeping platform.

daybed A resting platform, or narrow couch, usually placed lengthwise along a wall. May have head and foot boards of equal height, or none at all. The item was introduced as a seating unit in the 17th century. It is related to chaise longues and couches. See also STUDIO COUCH.

deaccession The process by which a curator culls items from a collection.

deacon's bench Long wooden sitting device that originated in early New England churches. It had arms and a back, usually with spindles.

dead hung (adj.) Describes theater rigging that is immovable after its installation for a particular production; a stationary prop.

deal (1) In the United States, southern yellow pine. (2) In England, Scotch fir is called yellow deal. (3) In Canada, deal refers to northern soft pine. (4) Also, pine wood cut into planks and the furniture made from these planks. (5) Used for the carcasses of veneered furniture.

decalcomania A form of decoration based on a transfer technique. Designs are printed on thin paper in reverse, then transferred onto a piece of furniture or accessory. An inexpensive method of creating decoration.

decanter (French, to pour from one vessel to another) A crystal, glass, or metal container that holds wine or other liquids. A serving piece.

decanter

deception bed (1) A concealed or partially concealed unit in 18th-century American cabinetwork. (2) A sleeping device that converts from a chest, chair, or table.

deck The cabinet, open or closed, with a grill or glass covering, that is set on top of a buffet or credenza to make a hutch or breakfront for use in a dining area. See BUFFET, CREDENZA, HUTCH, and BREAKFRONT.

deck chair A folding wood-frame seat with a canvas seat and back.

deckle edge A rippled, irregular perimeter with a torn appearance, usually associated with handmade paper.

declutter A systematic approach to what previously was the effort to keep one's home neat and tidy. This is occurring within a context of capitalism and consumerism. The activity first focuses on reducing the quantity of objects in a home and is related to broader societal issues including hoarding, overconsumption, and a throwaway economy. The method involves assessing the totality of one's possessions and then removing excess items from a space. The global phenomenon resulted in consultants and celebrity experts.

deconstruction or deconstructivism An architectural movement from the late 1980s through the 1990s, which existed in tandem with a method of literary interpretation of the same name. The movement is related to post-structuralism in the desire to expose and undermine cultural assumptions. It frequently refers to popular culture, technology, and common materials, and it seeks to reveal structure and the building process. Deconstruction could sometimes be illogical and paradoxical and had formal similarities to Russian constructivism.

décor The mode of decoration of an interior or of a theater stage. Often implies a "fashion trend" and may suggest something gay, whimsical, fanciful, and changeable.

Decorated period The English Gothic architecture of the 14th century, noted for geometric and flowing tracery, enlarged clerestories, and star-shaped vaulting. Also known by several other names: Geometrical period, Curvilinear period, Middle Pointed period, Edwardian period, or Later Plantagenet period.

Decorated Queen Anne period The English furniture style prevalent from about 1710 to 1730, also called Early Georgian. A continuation of the Queen Anne era, it features cabriole legs, claw-and-ball feet, and shaped splats that are more ornate than those of the previous era.

decorative drapes Window coverings that do not move. They are hung with an opening in the center and are fixed on the sides.

découpage An art form created by cutting and pasting down assorted materials in new patterns and arrangements. It became popular in the 18th century as the "poor man's" method of embellishing wood furniture. The technique is also employed to decorate boxes, screens, trays, etc. Découpage is similar to ARTE POVERA, COLLAGE, and MONTAGE.

delamination A defect resulting from separation of laminated plastic from core stock, or of piles in plywood, because the adhesive has failed.

Delft Brilliant blue, heavily glazed pottery and ceramic tiles produced in the Dutch city, featuring brilliant blue designs on a white field. The rich designs are either scenic or provincial patterns. Used to face fireplaces and to decorate walls and floors.

demidome A half sphere topping cupboards, bookcases, and other architectural furniture of the early and mid 18th century. Often interpreted as a shell-shaped niche in Georgian furniture and interiors.

demilune (1) A half of a circle or half-round plan. (2) A semicircular commode, console, or sideboard. See DOE'S FOOT LEG for a Hepplewhite demilune table.

demi-patera A rosette of a half circle or oval, a decoration often found in 18th-century pier tables, consoles, or demilune commodes. See DEMILUNE.

∞demoiselle (French) See WIG STAND.

∞demoiselle à atourner (French) A Gothic wig stand that also served as a dressing table. It was usually a round tabletop on a shaft base, with a carved wooden head placed in the center to hold the wig. See WIG STAND.

den (1) Formerly, a small, comfortable room equipped for the man of the house. (2) A retreat or informal library. It may serve as a small family room or guest room.

denier The size or number of filaments of silk or man-made fibers in a yarn or thread. The higher the denier, the coarser and heavier the yarn.

denim A firm, heavy twill-weave cotton fabric originally called serge de Nîmes; hence the name. The filler yarns are usually white with colored warp yarns, and they give the fabric its whitish cast.

dentil One of a series of small projecting rectangular blocks in a cornice. It appears in Ionic and Corinthian cornices and was also used as a furniture and interior detail.

dentil course A series of the projecting blocks in a row.

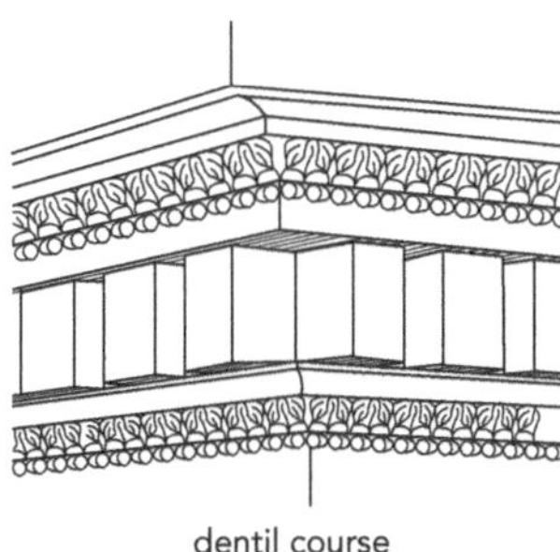
dentil course

∞Derbyshire chair A provincial Jacobean seat. The straight upright ends have inward scrolls on top, and the top rail and cross-rail are arch-shaped.

design thinking Cognitive process that combines quantitative analysis with intuition and an understanding of aesthetics. The goal of the method is to reach a practical and creative resolution of a problem or issue. Promoters of this process endeavor to join empathy, rationality, and artistic creativity in order to meet user needs and create a successful business model.

desk A writing surface, with or without storage. See BUREAU, CYLINDER TOP, DROP-LID, ESCRITOIRE, KNEEHOLE DESK, PEDESTAL DESK, SCRITOIRE, SCRUTOIRE, SECRÉTAIRE, and SECRETARY.

désordoné corrigé A disorganized person who has achieved organization; these people often become the clients of closet organizers and other design consultants.

desornamentado (Spanish, without ornament) A severe style of architecture and decoration that the Spanish Renaissance architect Juan de Herrera developed under Phillip II in the mid 16th century. An example of his work is the Escorial near Madrid.

desserte A small serving table or sideboard with one or more under shelves, similar to a DUMB-WAITER. It appears in the Louis XVI period. See BUFFET and CRÉDENCE.

desserte

De Stijl A Dutch magazine published from 1917 to 1928 that fostered a group of architects, artists, and poets, including Piet Mondrian and Theo Van Doesburg, and the movement they created. Their works emphasized primary colors, geometric shapes, and bold typefaces. De Stijl came to have a great influence on the Bauhaus movement, as well as on German commercial art, posters, packages, etc. See BAUHAUS.

determinism The concept that events or designs in a given context are bound by causality; that a state (of an object or event) is largely the result of prior conditions.

deu-darn A two-tiered TRI-DARN, or a court cupboard without the dresser.

Deutscher Werkbund A German association of architects and designers who promoted functionalism; a harbinger of the BAUHAUS, whose members were committed to bridging the gap between the arts and manufacturing.

dhurries Flat, lightly woven wool carpets from India with traditional geometric or stylized animal designs.

diamond-match veneer Four pieces of straight-grained wood flitches that are cut diagonally and joined to meet in a central geometric shape. Increasingly larger shapes emanate from the central point.

diamond ornament A favorite late Tudor ornament used to enrich carved chest fronts, bedsteads, cabinets, etc. See LOZENGE.

diaper pattern An allover or repeating decoration without limits, applied as a decoration to a plain surface. Often the area is latticed and floral, or geometric designs are set into boxes. Used on walls, wallpapers, cabinet enrichments, etc.

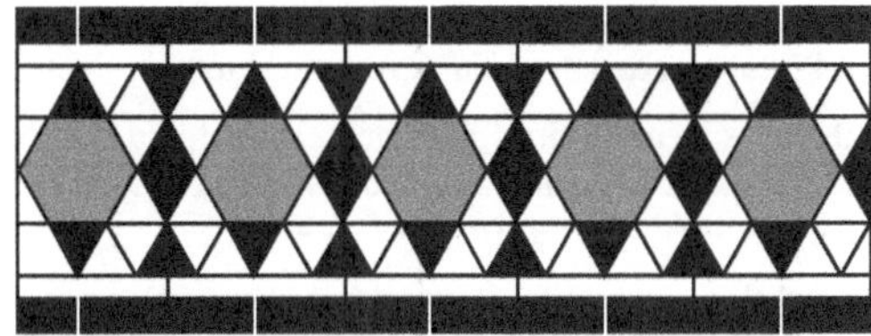
diaper pattern

die (1) The space between the cap and base of a pedestal. (2) A rectangular block on top of a furniture leg. See PATERA.

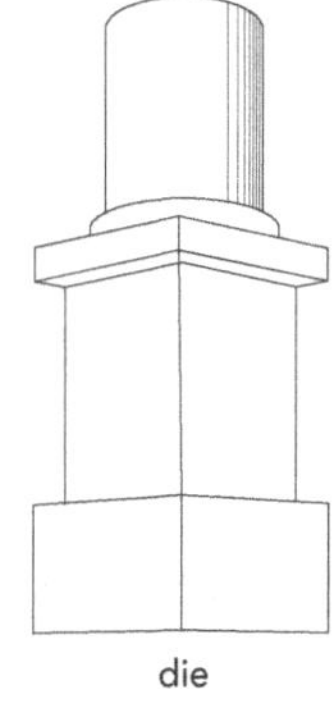
die

diffuser or diffusing shield A baffle or screen set over a source of illumination to soften and disperse the light and to cut down on glare.

dimensional stability The ability of a material to retain its shape.

dimetric A technical drawing term that refers to a projection or perspective with geometric axes, two at the same scale and scalable, one at another scale and distorted, that creates a desired three-dimensional effect.

dimity A double- or multiple-thread, sheer cotton fabric usually woven in a corded, striped, or checkered pattern. Used for bedspreads and curtains.

dimmer A mechanism for varying the intensity of light in a given area by reducing the amount of electric current allowed to pass through the wires. The resistance dimmer is the only type that works on direct current (DC). Several types of dimmers work on alternating current (AC): autotransformer, electronic resistance, electronic amplifier, and magnetic amplifier. Dimmers can reduce both the amount of heat generated and the amount of power consumed.

∞dinanderie A 15th-century metal alloy of copper, tin, and lead; a forerunner of pewter. Used to make ornamental figures in Dinant, Belgium. Also called bell metal.

dinette table A small informal surface for eating, usually used in kitchens, kitchenettes, foyers, or otherwise restricted eating areas. Seldom intended to accommodate more than four people but may be designed to open up to seat more.

diorite A dark-colored, hard stone used in Egyptian and Assyrian sculpture.

dip seat

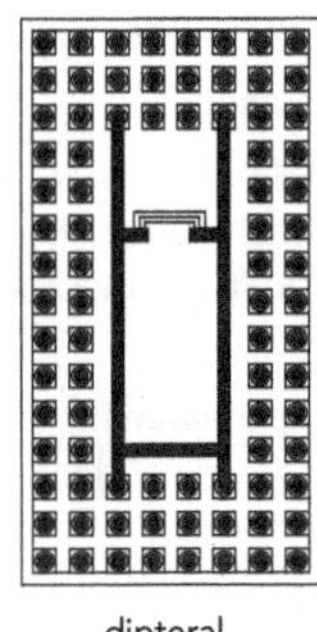
dipteral

dip seat A chair pad that is lower in the center than at the sides. It is curved (concave) to accommodate the body of the sitter. See DROPPED OR DIPPED SEAT and SCOOP SEAT.

dipteral Surrounded by a double row of columns.

diptych A two-panel, hinged screen, either painted or carved. It may be made of wood, metal, or ivory. A broad category of two-dimensional art with two similarly sized parts.

direct lighting A technique in which illumination strikes its primary target first before illuminating secondary objects.

Directoire period See DIRECTORY PERIOD and FRENCH DIRECTOIRE PERIOD.

director's chair

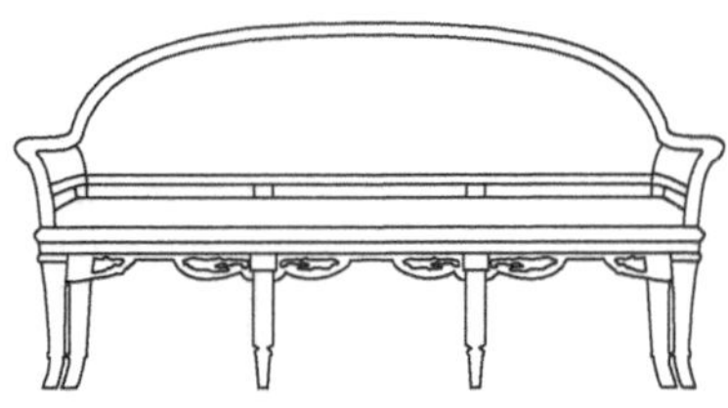
Directory period furniture

director's chair A scissors-folding wood armchair with a canvas sling seat and back, so named because of its use by those who create movies; a 20th-century X-FRAME CHAIR.

Directory period A French neoclassical style dating from 1789 to 1804. Antique Greek and Roman decorations found greater favor in the period and were superimposed on the already classical lines of the Louis XVI style. Related to the Directory (1795–1799), the democratic political system that followed the French Revolution. The Directory period preceded the EMPIRE PERIOD. See also FRENCH DIRECTOIRE PERIOD.

dished (adj.) Describes the sunken areas in the top surface of card tables, used to hold money or candles. A dished-top table has a raised edge or rim that makes the entire table surface appear to be sunken.

disk foot A small, flattened ball or pad on a cabriole leg in the Queen Anne style.

disk turning Flat, circular turnings used to ornament furniture.

dispossession The process of getting rid of excess items; a solution for HOARDING. See also DEACCESSION.

distant colors Colors that appear to recede, creating a spacious effect. Light, airy, cool, open colors: blues, aquas, violets.

distemper An art medium: opaque water color paints, similar to tempera, consisting of pigments, water, and egg-white, size, or egg-yolk emulsion.

distressed (adj.) Describes old pieces of wood furniture that show small scratches or holes, resulting from age and use. In new furniture, these holes and scratches may be deliberately simulated in paint or spatter ("fly-specked") or artificially created signs of wear.

divan (1) A long armless and backless upholstered settee. (2) Originally, a Turkish or Persian court or council, or a room where such gatherings took place. (3) In current usage, a sofa. See BENCH.

diverter A piece of plumbing equipment which directs water to a specific device (and thereby prevents both being used simultaneously), such as two shower heads, a bathtub and a shower, or a sink faucet with a spray and faucet.

diwan An Islamic reception chamber with raised platforms for seating, furnished with carpets and cushions and otherwise not relying on freestanding furniture.

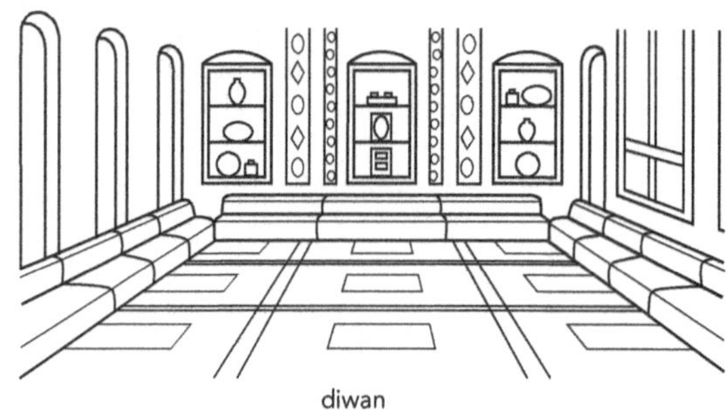
diwan

DIY Acronym for DO-IT-YOURSELF

dobby weave A cloth with a small geometric woven pattern. A special attachment is required on the loom to weave in this manner.

document box or drawer A small vertical compartment in 18th-century English and American secretaries and cabinet desks. Usually ornamented with colonnettes, it is found on either side of the central compartment in the interior.

doe's foot leg

doe's foot leg An elongated, five-lobed support typical of the Louis XV period. It originally terminated in a deer's cleft hoof.

dog grate A fireplace accessory. A movable metal lattice basket that holds and elevates logs or charcoal, allowing air to circulate.

doglegged staircase A circulation element in which the outer string of the upper flight of stairs lies vertically above that of the lower flight.

dog's tooth A form of ornamentation used in early English Gothic architecture that resembles a row of teeth.

do-it-yourself (DIY) A reinvigorated trend in home improvement, large and small, which is the result of a conflation of economic and cultural events, including big box hardware stores and their seminars, home decorating TV shows, instructional videos, and blogs and other social media. In many design areas, including garden, crafts, and multiple aspects within the sphere of interiors, from plumbing repair to tiling, projects are presented for the determined amateur.

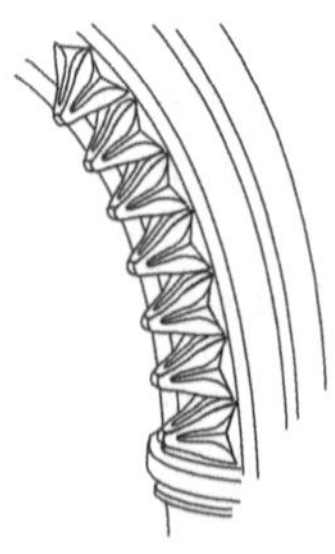
dog's tooth

dolmen A MEGALITHIC structure consisting of two upright, undressed stones that support a horizontal capstone.

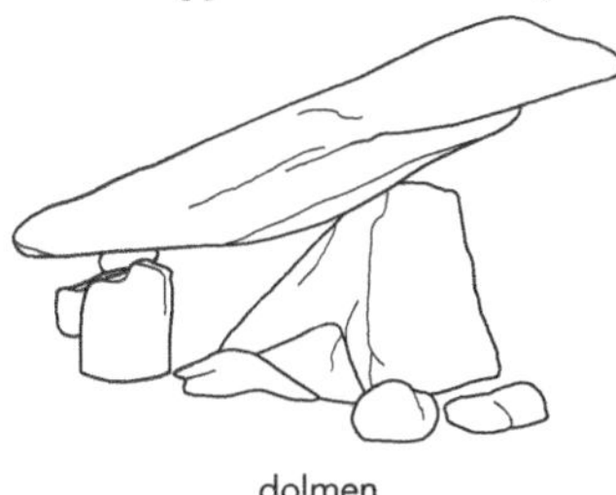

dolmen

dolphin (1) A mid-16th-century decoration and symbol for the Dauphin, the eldest son of the king of France, playing off of the fact that in French the word for the heir apparent of the king is the same word as denotes the swimming mammal. (2) Also the symbol for love and swiftness, the motif reappears in the Louis XVI period.

dome bed An 18th-century canopied sleeping device with a spherical tester. Heavily draped and swagged, also called a Polish bed.

domed top See HOODED TOP.

domestic Manufactured or grown in the country where the label is applied; domestic products in the United States are produced in the United States.

domestic oriental rug See SHEEN RUGS.

domino papers Marbleized squares of wallpaper, originally produced in Italy (late 16th and early 17th centuries).

∞**dominotiers** (French) Producers of domino papers in France in the late 16th century.

domus (Latin) (1) An ancient Roman house for a wealthy or middle-class family. (2) *Domus* is also an Italian design magazine.

doratura (Italian) Gilding.

doreur (French) A person who gilds or applies a gilt finish to wood, metal, etc.

Doric order The oldest and simplest of the Greek classic orders of architecture. The shaft of a Greek Doric column has no base and sits directly on the PLINTH. In the Roman version, the column is eight times the diameter of the shaft, and the entablature is two diameters high. See CLASSIC.

dormer window A projecting upright element of fenestration that breaks the surface of a sloping roof.

dormeuse A type of CHAISE LONGUE resembling an upholstered DECK CHAIR.

dorure (French) Gilding.

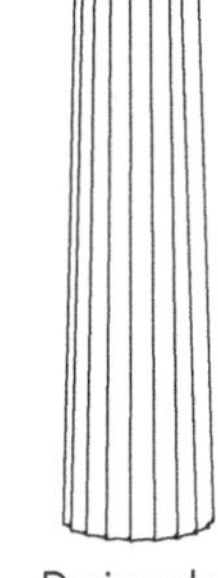

Doric order

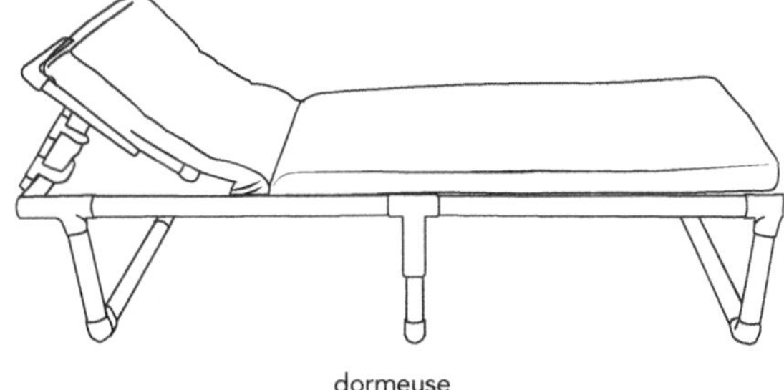

dormeuse

dos-à-dos (French, back to back) A seating device that consists of two attached seats facing in opposite directions. See CONVERSATION CHAIR, SIAMOISE, TÊTE-À-TÊTE, and VIS-À-VIS.

dosser (archaic) A medieval or Gothic fabric hanging. It was hung behind thrones or on walls behind benches.

dossier (French, chair back or SPLAT) (1) A 16th-century French armchair or FAUTEUIL. (2) Also a high-backed, canopied, wooden bench built into the wainscot of an English Gothic building. Usually made to hold four, it also served as a seat for dining. (3) In French interiors, the headboard or footboard of a bed.

dossier plat (French, flat back) Describes the back of a chair.

dotted swiss A crisp cotton, usually sheer, which is woven, embroidered, or printed with tiny, regularly spaced dots. It is a plain-weave fabric.

double-acting hinge A special movable piece of hardware that allows a door to swing 180° on its jamb.

double bed A standard-size double bed is usually 53 inches wide by 75 inches long (137 cm × 187 cm). There are longer versions.

double chest A storage unit on storage unit. The lower storage unit is wider and deeper, and the second set of drawers is set on top of it. See CHEST ON CHEST.

double-decker bed Two single beds, one over the other, with four uprights holding the upper bed aloft. See BUNK BED.

double-hung sash A standard window made up of two sliding framed glass sections; one is lowered from the top, and the other is raised from the bottom. Pulleys and weights control the raising and lowering.

double stretcher Flemish bond In masonry, two bricks used lengthwise alternate with a single header in a course. The header in the next course is centered over the joint between the long sides of the two bricks. See BOND, FLEMISH BOND, and FLEMISH CROSS-BOND.

doublet In ornamentation, a pair of the same design.

double up A term used in relation to new household creation, which is of concern to those who study housing and urban development. It is a feature of inequality and times of economic stress. This 21st-century family structure can involve adult children who move back into parental housing or two related or unrelated adults who share a single household. Often an outcome of housing instability and homelessness.

Douglas fir A handsome, curly, grained wood that resembles white pine or soft pine, used extensively for plywood or laminated sheets. The material takes a natural or stained finish and is inexpensive.

douppioni or duppion (1) Silk fibers that are reeled from two silkworms that have spun a single cocoon. The yarns thus produced are rough and slubby such as those found in shantung or pongee fabrics. (2) Also, fabric made from such fibers. (3) Also, rayon or acetate fibers of an uneven texture.

dovetail In cabinetry, a type of joint that connects the front and sides of a drawer. Wedge-shaped projections on one piece of wood interlock with alternating grooves in the other piece to produce a tight, secure joint.

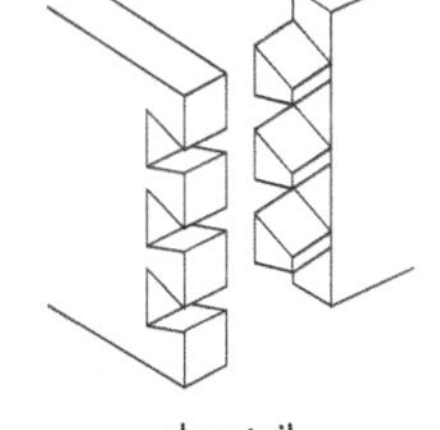

dovetail

dowel A headless wooden peg or metal pin to hold two pieces of wood together. Used in joints to prevent slipping and also to join the side rails or stretchers of chair legs.

dower chest See CASSONE, CONNECTICUT CHEST, and HOPE CHEST.

down Soft, fluffy feathers from young birds or from under the ordinary feathers of older birds or fowls. Used for stuffing pillows, cushions, duvets, and chair upholstery. See EIDERDOWN.

downlights Standard fixtures installed on the ceiling or wall to cast pools of light below. Originally, incandescent lights, sometimes referred to as "cans."

draft (1) A line drawing, often geometrically or mechanically projected, of a proposed structure or design. A preliminary sketch or drawing. (2) A smooth strip on the face of a stone made by one line of following strokes with a chisel. When stones are left with a rough face but the edges are made smooth, the edges are drafted edges.

dragging A paint-texturizing technique in which pulling a dry brush over a wet glaze produces subtle stripes that reveal a base color. The process can imitate fabric.

dragon's claw foot An 18th-century furniture leg end that was a carved representation of a dragon's scaly claws, often grasping a ball or pearl. See BALL-AND-CLAW FOOT.

dragon's head An Asian motif, often found on heavily carved furniture. The dragon is also the symbol of Wales, and the dragon's head appears as an ornamental carved motif on English TUDOR and JACOBEAN chests.

dragon's claw foot

dragon's head

∞drake foot An 18th-century English furniture support with three toes, which resembles the contracted appendage of a male duck.

drape The way a fabric hangs or falls. The ability of a fabric naturally to shape well when pleated, shirred, or pinched.

drapery

drapery (1) Fabric hangings on either side of a window, or covering a window or door, or an entire wall of windows. The fabric may be shirred, pleated, or pinched and may be made of natural or man-made fibers. Swags, jabots, lambrequins, and cornices can enhance regular vertically falling drapery. (2) Also the fabric treatment on 16th-, 17th-, and 18th-century beds.

draft (or draught) chair (archaic) An 18th-century upholstered wing chair with or without closed sides, which was constructed to protect one from drafts, similar to a PORTER CHAIR.

draught chair

draw curtain A drapery that may be drawn along a traverse rod or rail by means of cords and pulleys.

∞drawing book chair back A popular design for a chair back that American cabinetmakers widely copied from Thomas Sheraton's *The Cabinet-Maker and Upholsterer's Drawing Book* (London: T. Bensley, 1793).

drawing room An abbreviation for the term *withdrawing room.* A comfortable spare room to which people withdrew after dinner. In contemporary usage, a living room.

drawing table A late-18th-century worktable designed by Sheraton for artists or designers. The top of the device rises on a double horse and is adjustable so that the artist may either stand or sit to work. A small flap draws out of the top to hold a model for a still life. The sliders at each end hold drawing instruments and lamps. See ARCHITECT'S TABLE.

drawn work An openwork textile pattern or design created by drawing or pulling out either filling or warp threads.

draw runner A supporting device for the drop-lid surface of a secretary or desk, a small strip of wood inserted into a slot immediately below the surface to be supported.

draw table A three-leaved, refectory-like surface, for work or eating, in which the two end leaves rest under the center one. When these two end pieces are extracted from under the large central table surface, the center leaf falls down into the opening thus created, and the two end leaves constitute a large, continuous flush surface with the central leaf. The forerunner of the telescope dining table. Also called a DRAW LEAF TABLE.

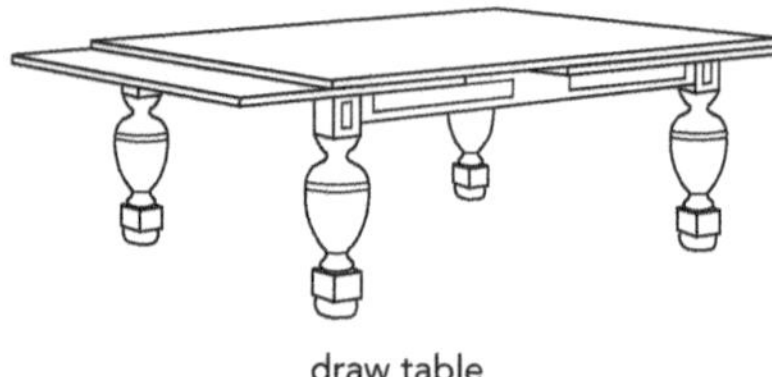

draw table

dress (verb) To smooth or finish the surface of stones, or to plane the surface of wood.

dresser (1) Originally a sideboard or buffet with storage space for plates and other utensils, or a cabinet with drawers, shelves, or both. (2) In contemporary usage, a long chest of drawers about 36 inches tall and 6 feet long or longer (90 cm × 183 cm); usually part of a bedroom suite.

dressing mirror A small standing portable reflective device, or a mirror on a stand, sometimes with drawers, that was set on a table, low chest, or cabinet and used as an adjunct to preparing oneself regarding costume, hair, and make-up. Also called a toilet mirror.

dressing room (1) A small room or area with a closet and drawer space, usually adjacent to a bedroom. It sometimes includes a dressing table and mirror arrangement. (2) Similar, in a theater or other performance space.

dressing table A kneehole worksurface with large and small drawers surrounding the central knee area. A mirror is usually attached to the horizontal surface. Its present form derives from a 19th-century version of a KNEEHOLE DESK. For an earlier type of dressing table, see POUDREUSE.

∞dressoir de salle à manger (French, dining room dresser or buffet) A 16th-century large dresser-top cupboard unit, such as a French Renaissance piece from the period of François I. See BUFFET, CRÉDENCE, DRESSER, and WELSH DRESSER.

drill A denim-like, heavy twill fabric that is rough and durable.

dromos A long passageway leading to an ancient underground chamber.

drop (1) The length of fabric that falls from the top of a bed to the floor. (2) In theater, a textile that hangs on the farthest upstage wall of the stage. The drop is painted muslin, showing scenery such as a landscape, an urban area, or an architectural setting.

drop handle A pendant-like piece of hardware that functions as a drawer pull.

drop-leaf table See FLAP TABLE.

drop-lid The top or front of a desk that is hinged to cover an inner compartment of drawers, boxes, pigeonholes, etc. When the front is lowered, the outer surface of the desk front makes a flat or slightly sloped writing surface. See SLOPE-FRONT DESK.

drop ornament A carved, shaped, or pierced embellishment that extends below the underframe of a chair or cabinet but does not extend across the entire width of the underframe. When it does extend across the entire length, it is an APRON, FRONT, or SKIRT.

dropped ceiling An interior roof line partially or completely lowered from its original height to a lower and more intimate height. Often the false ceiling hides pipes and ductwork. A hung or suspended horizontal plane. See HUNG CEILING.

dropped or dipped seat A seat with a concave surface between the two side rails. A depressed center area in a chair seat. Also called a SCOOP SEAT or DIP SEAT.

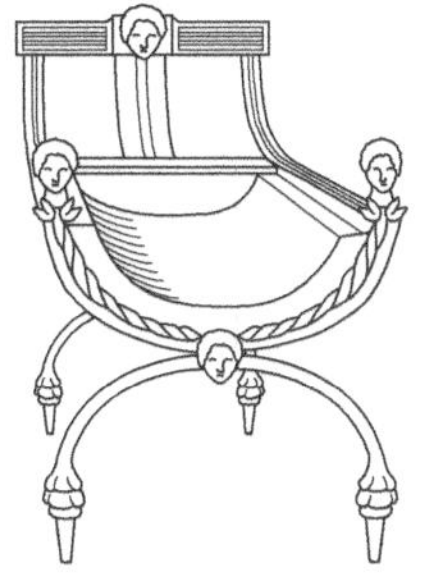
dropped or dipped seat

drugget See NUMDAH.

drum table A round surface-producing unit with a deep apron, sometimes made with drawers set in around the apron. The piece of furniture presents a squat appearance, like the musical instrument.

∞**drunkard's chair** A Queen Anne period vogue that lasted through the 18th century. The seats were up to 33 inches wide (84 cm) and allowed one person to sprawl comfortably or two to nestle closely. Also called a lover's chair. In current usage, sometimes referred to as a CHAIR AND A HALF.

dry cleaning A process for laundering fabrics that are not conventionally washable. Carbon tetrachloride mineral spirits are used to remove dirt and stains.

drypoint engraving The simplest type of etching technique, which consists of drawing with a hard steel pencil on a metal plate. The burr that results from scratching the surface gives the line its ability to catch the ink; it prints with a depth that adds sharpness to the design. A limited number of impressions can be made from a plate. A form of INTAGLIO ENGRAVING.

dry sink A 19th-century low kitchen cabinet made to hold a pitcher and washbasin on the top surface, with closed cabinet space below. Usually made of pine, with a slate or marble piece supporting surface.

drywall Manufactured plaster product used in interior construction. It is the most commonly used wall material because it is lightweight and durable. See GYPSUM BOARD.

dual bed See HOLLYWOOD BED.

duchess A once-popular curtain fabric with an appliqué design.

duchesse A CHAISE LONGUE in one piece.

duchesse bed A canopy sleeping platform without posts. The tester is attached to the wall above the headboard, and it extends forward over the frame. The draperies from the tester are pulled back to either side and usually extend to the floor. Originally an 18th-century French design.

duchesse bed

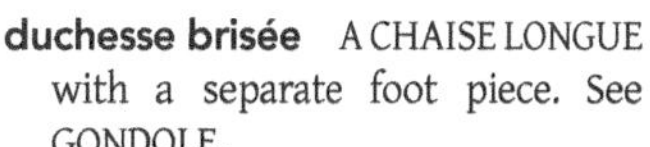

duchesse brisée A CHAISE LONGUE with a separate foot piece. See GONDOLE.

duchesse lace See VALENCIENNES LACE.

duck A tightly woven cotton or linen fabric with a plain or rib weave, similar to canvas. Its stripes may be woven in or painted or printed on one side.

duck foot A webbed furniture termination of the late 17th to early 18th centuries, found in Flemish and English furniture, that resembles the appendage of a waterfowl.

dumbwaiter A three-tiered, tripod, circular table, dating from the 18th century. In the Victorian period, the device was a lift for bringing up food from the basement kitchen to the dining room. See RAFRAÎCHISSOIR.

dummy board figures Flat, oil-painted trompe l'oeil human figures. They are often life-sized. Also called picture-board dummies. See FIRESIDE FIGURES.

∞**duppion** See DOUPPIONI.

dust bottom or dust board A thin wood separator between drawers to keep out airborne particulates that enter through open spaces.

dust ruffle A shirred, pleated, or tailored fabric piece that extends from under the mattress of a bed down to the floor. It covers the legs of the bed frame and ideally forms a barrier to keep airborne particulates from getting under the bed. Examples are seen from the Elizabethan period to the present.

Dutch door A hinged panel horizontally divided into an upper and lower section. Each section is independently hinged, and either or both can be opened.

Dutch dresser A hutch cabinet. A two-section unit with a closed cupboard or drawer unit below and open shelves above. See WELSH DRESSER.

Dutch foot A pad foot or spoon foot on a cabriole furniture leg, especially popular in late-17th-century and early-18th-century furniture. See PAD FOOT and SPOON FOOT.

Dutch leg A wooden, turned furniture support consisting of rounded forms spaced with flattened oval discs. It usually ends in a squared-off form and rests on a flat, oval foot.

Dutch settle A wooden bench with arms and a hinged tabletop surface that, when vertical, serves as the back. When flipped down, the element becomes a table.

duvet (French) A down comforter with a removable cover.

duvet cover Envelope-style enclosure for down bedding that minimizes the need for cleaning. Sometimes called sheet casings.

∞**dwarf wall** (1) An outdated term for a partition that does not extend up to the ceiling. (2) Also an interior wall between the top ceiling level and the finished roof.

dyeing A process for coloring yarns or fabrics with either natural or synthetic pigments. Applied pigments differ in their ability to resist sun fading, laundering, perspiration, etc. See COLORFAST and YARN-DYED.

dymaxion A term created by the designer-inventor Buckminster Fuller for industrial designs that give maximum performance at maximum economy.

Dynel A synthetic fiber made from acrylonitrile and vinyl chloride. Originally made by Union Carbide Corporation. The fiber is characterized by resilience, strength, and resistance to chemicals. Dynel fibers are used in upholstery, drapery, and carpeting.

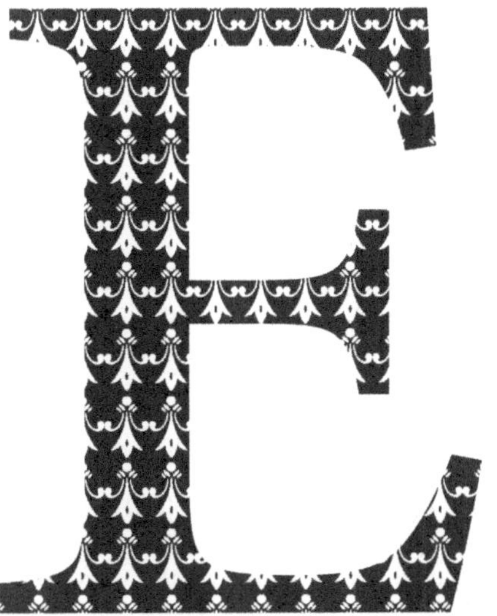

eagle A decorative motif from ancient times to the present day, favored by Persians, Assyrians, and Egyptians. The Greeks considered the flying raptor the companion of Zeus, and the Romans used the imposing bird as a military standard. Napoleon and the Empire used the bird of prey as a motif on furniture, on fabrics, in carvings, and in paintings. When the American Revolution took the bald eagle as its emblem, it appeared on furniture, mirrors, fabrics, and buildings.

eagle

Eames chair A new concept of separating a chair's back and seat from its supporting frame. An inexpensive, armless seat made of molded plywood and a metal frame. The design has been widely copied, especially in academic settings. See EAMES, CHARLES, and EAMES, RAY, in *Designers and Architects.*

Eames chair

Early American (adj.) Refers to the art, architecture, and furniture from about 1650 to about 1720. The designs of the 17th and 18th centuries were based on the English Jacobean, Carolean, and William and Mary periods; they are executed simply and provincially using native woods. Dutch influences were strong in New York.

Early English period The earliest Gothic architecture on the British Isles, dating from 1189 to 1307. This period is also known as the Lancet, First Pointed, or Early Plantagenet period. The architecture is marked by tall lancet openings, projecting buttresses, pinnacles, and steep-pitched roofs.

earpiece A scroll or volute springing from the knee of a cabriole leg and ending in the underframing of the furniture piece. Especially popular in 18th-century English and French furniture.

ears (1) In architecture, horizontal moldings or cornices over doors or windows that overlap the uprights of the door or window frame. They were used as a cornice decoration in the 18th century in England and America. (2) In chairs, the extended parts of the top rail beyond the upright supports of the back, seen in the Chinese yoke-back chair.

earthenware Pottery made of coarse clay. Heavy, soft, porous, and opaque such as a common red flowerpot. May be glazed.

easy chair A roomy, comfortable, upholstered seat made for relaxation. It may be of any style or period, and the design is based on the bergère and the wing chair.

easy chair

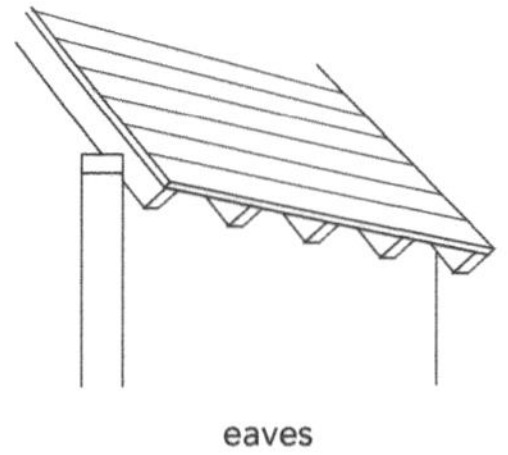

eaves

eaves The lowest part of a roof that overhangs the top of a wall, especially the underside of that part.

EBD Acronym for EVIDENCE-BASED DESIGN.

ébéniste (French) A furniture maker or wood worker at the top of a hierarchical system. In the early French Renaissance (15th and 16th centuries), the cabinetmakers who worked on fine pieces were called ébénistes and were considered superior to carpenters or sawyers. MAÎTRE ÉBÉNISTE was the official title of the king's cabinetmakers.

ebony A tropical, hard, dense, heavy brown-black wood with a fine grain, popular in France during the Louis XIV period and again in the Empire period and in the mid 19th century. True ebony comes from Sri Lanka, and black ebony is found in northern India and the Himalayas. See *Table 5.*

ebony, gaboon An African rusty brown-black wood that is expensive and available only in relatively small pieces. It is mainly used for veneering, musical instruments, and inlay work. See EBONY, MACASSAR.

ebony, macassar A hard, dense wood, with an intense, black-brown stripe on a reddish ground. It takes a brilliant polish and is usually figured in contrasting stripes. Also called COROMANDEL.

∞**echinus** (1) An oval-shaped molding. It is part of a classical capital, located between the shaft and the abacus. (2) In furniture, an ornamental motif called the EGG AND DART, egg and tongue, or egg and anchor that is carved on the ovolo molding of furniture.

echinus

eclecticism The borrowing and combining of art forms and motifs from multiple past periods and adapting them to contemporary uses. The Victorian 19th century was an era of eclecticism; older patterns and styles were borrowed and adapted to form new mechanized processes.

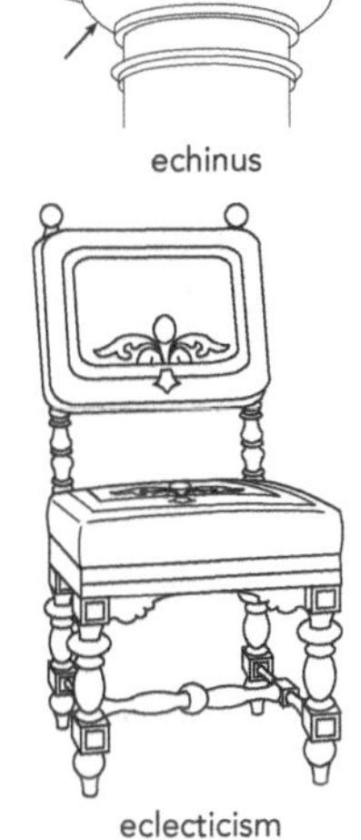

eclecticism

École des Beaux-Arts The leading French art school of the 19th and early 20th centuries. The design process of its adherents emphasized composition and elaborate architectural programs, and the resulting historicist projects relied on strong axes and a studied interplay of symmetry and asymmetry. Adherents of the school designed in many historicist styles. There was an emphasis on carefully configured plans as a principal generator of design concepts.

ecoresin A synthetic material made, in part, from recycled materials. When mixed with water in the correct proportions, it forms a fluid mass that can be poured into molds. This can result in an object of high relief, including peaks and valleys. The substance can be used for a variety of forms, including models, statues, vases, and furniture.

écran (1) A fire screen, or a small screen set on a table to shield one from the firelight. (2) A small shade on a candlestick.

écran à cheval A frame with a sliding panel, used as a fire screen. See BANNER SCREEN, CHEVAL SCREEN, and HORSE SCREEN.

écran à coulisse (French) A CHEVAL SCREEN or FIRE SCREEN.

écran à éclisse (French) See POLE SCREEN.

edge virtualization A wireless technology of interconnectivity that is the antithesis of a traditional network. The uncabled system represents a shift from physical to virtual networking (cabled workstations) and cloud-based systems. Its contrast is core virtualization. As a fundamental 5G enabler, it should produce efficiencies and instant data. Autonomous cars, phones as processors, and smart cities and homes will negatively affect the need for wired and cabled furniture systems. This affects how designers work, their client interactions, and the offices they design.

Edwardian period See DECORATED PERIOD.

egg and dart A molding decoration that resembles a continuous string of ovoid forms separated by arrowhead points. Egg-and-tongue and egg-and-anchor moldings are almost identical. See ECHINUS.

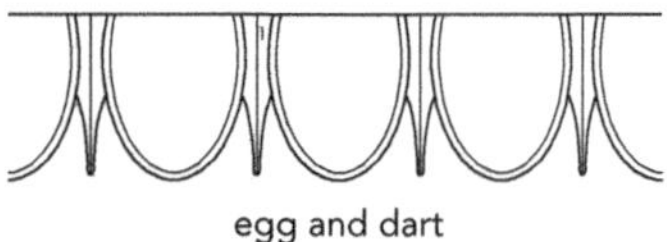

egg and dart

egg crate A metal or plastic unit that resembles a cardboard separator for the foodstuff; used to diffuse ceiling light, usually over fluorescent light strips. The individual cells are often made of a reflective material.

eggshell finish A semi-flat paint with a soft, dull, low luster.

églomisé An art form in which the painting is done on the reverse side of glass and often embellished with gold leaf.

égouitoir A piece of French provincial furniture with open rack shelves for drying or storing dishes.

Egypt The land of the Pharaohs and one of the earliest civilizations. Its art and architecture preceded classical Greece and Rome. From the Egyptians came motifs including the sphinx, the lotus column, the lion's paw, the palmetto leaf, mother-of-pearl inlays, and veneer work. Designed objects included cross-legged chairs with leather seats, tables, stools, and elaborate sarcophagi. Napoleon helped make Egyptiana an important part of the early-19th-century Empire style.

Egypt

eiderdown The soft, fluffy feathers obtained from large sea ducks, used for luxurious stuffing of pillows, cushions, and bolsters.

eight-legged table An 18th-century English form of the gateleg dining surface, usually made of mahogany. See GATELEG TABLE and THOUSAND-LEG TABLE.

elbow chair A seat with arms on which a seated person may rest his or her weary appendages.

electric light A type of illumination that includes incandescent, fluorescent, neon, high-intensity discharge, and LED (light-emitting diode). Also called artificial light.

electric raceway See POWER RACEWAY.

electroplating An electrical process for covering one base metal with a thin layer of a more expensive material.

elevation A drawing of a flat, two-dimensional vertical view of a room or building, usually to scale, to show the relative sizes of architectural and decorative details. A vertical section cut in front of the element to be represented. See FAÇADE.

elevation

ell See THREE-QUARTER WIDTH.

electrochromic (adj.) Describes the ability of some materials or assemblies to reversibly change color when an electrical charge is applied.

Elizabethan era One of the great epochs of world history, from 1558 to 1603. This was a transitional design era combining MEDIEVAL forms, a profusion of decoration, and the beginnings of the English RENAISSANCE.

elm A strong, tough wood that looks good when stained and polished. It is a light, brownish red with dark-brown ring marks and a strong figure. The northern elm has a finer, more uniform texture than the southern elm.

emaki or emakimono (Japanese) Traditional, horizontal, paper or silk hand scrolls with illustrated narratives.

emaki or emakimono

émaux de niellure (French) An enameling process in which lines are cut into the metal and filled with enamel. See NIELLO.

emblem A decorative symbol or device used in heraldry. It appears in carvings, embroideries, and painted panels. Examples are Napoleon's bee and François I's salamander.

embossed Decorated with a raised design produced on a surface by hammering, stamping, or molding. See CHASING and REPOUSSÉ.

embossing In fabrics, a process for pressing a design onto a fabric by passing the fabric through hot engraved rollers. See CUT PILE.

embroidery The art of decorating a fabric with a raised design or pattern worked out with a needle and thread, either by hand or machine. May be done in one or more colors, and a great variety of stitches or combinations of stitches may be employed.

embossing

embroidery

emissivity The ability of a surface to transfer energy by radiation; mitigating factors include temperature, angle of emission, and wavelength. The material property is related to light transmission and solar control.

empaistic (adj.) Sculpture or structural elements made of, or covered with, sheet metal that has been hammered in decorative patterns. A forerunner of BOULLE WORK.

Empire bed A neoclassical sleeping platform of the early 19th century. Low and often set against a wall or in an alcove, with only one long side exposed. Curved, sweeping ends form the headboard and footboard. Similar to the boat bed, it was a forerunner of the American sleigh bed.

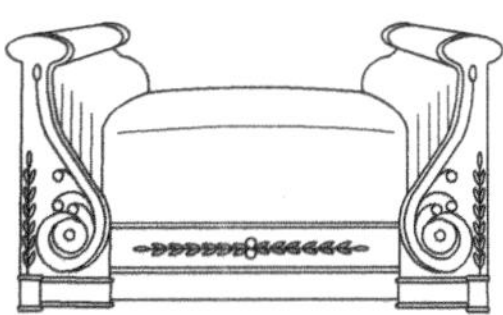
Empire bed

Empire drape A simple, classic hanging fabric treatment. The fabric is caught at the top hem at equidistant points, and the valleys, formed between these points, fall freely. A formal pattern is created of fairly rigid verticals from the caught points to the floor, alternating with poufy billows. Popular in the early 19th century.

Empire period In Napoleonic France, and the classical revival style of 1804 to 1820. Objects combined the grandeur of Rome with Greek and Egyptian motifs. Furniture pieces are massive, architectural, and trimmed in bronze on rosewood and ebony. CHARLES PERCIER and PIERRE FONTAINE were the preeminent interior designers. In England, Thomas Hope and Thomas Sheraton became its leading proponents. In America, Duncan Phyfe created a celebrated body of work.

∞**empreintes veloutées** (French) Flocked prints or wallpaper.

enamel (1) A colored glaze that decorates metal or ceramics. After firing it becomes hard and permanent. After a preliminary glaze, it is applied to pottery or porcelain. The piece is then fired again to fuse the layer to the original glaze. (2) Also a generic name for a paint with a hard, shiny surface. See *Table 4.*

∞**encarpus** A fruit or flower festoon that enhances flat surfaces. It was employed extensively in the Italian Renaissance and in the Louis XV and Louis XVI periods.

en charrette (French, on the cart) (1) Last-minute work. Derived from the practice of 19th-century artists working on their paintings as they were being carted to the ÉCOLE DES BEAUX-ARTS. (2) Also, a competition finished within a prescribed short period of time, for example twelve hours.

enclosing wall An exterior, nonbearing partition in skeletal frame construction that is anchored to columns, piers, or floors but not necessarily built between columns or piers as a curtain wall. See CURTAIN WALL.

encoignure A corner cabinet or table, often built in as part of the architecture of the room.

encrusting The application of gold or platinum over an etched surface.

end table A small surface-producing unit placed at the end of a sofa, settee, or couch or at the side of a chair to hold a lamp, ashtray, etc. See SIDE TABLE.

∞**endive marquetry** A Queen Anne style of fine flowing-line veneer work similar to seaweed marquetry. The flowing lines resemble the leaves of the endive plant. See SEAWEED MARQUETRY.

end table

ends The lengthwise yarns in cloth. See COUNT OF CLOTH and WARP.

enfilade (French) A set or suite of rooms on a visual and circulatory axis. Also describes a low provincial buffet with four or more doors.

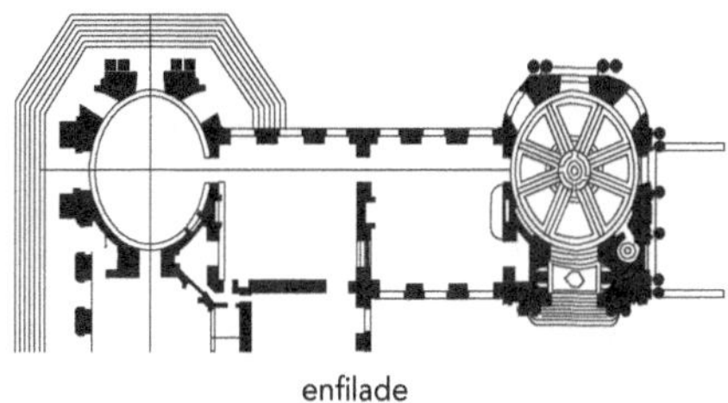
enfilade

engaged column A vertical structural element, partially attached to a wall and projecting from it ⅓ to ¾ of the extent of its diameter. See PILASTER.

engawa A traditional Japanese veranda or terrace surrounding a house.

English bond In masonry, bricks laid in alternate courses of headers and stretchers (the header is the end of the brick, and the stretcher is the side of the brick). The headers are centered on the stretchers, which lie in horizontal lines. See BOND and ENGLISH CROSS-BOND.

English cross-bond A masonry method similar to English bond in that it consists of alternate courses of headers and stretchers. Instead of the stretchers lying one directly above the other in alternate courses, they break joints evenly in the successive stretcher courses. See BOND and ENGLISH BOND.

engaged column

engraving A generic term describing various methods of multiplying prints. In general, a design is cut in a hard material such as copper, steel, or wood. The artist may incise the design or may remove the areas around it. The design is inked, and impressions are taken for multiple strikes. Engraving techniques include: WOODCUT, LINOCUT OR LINOLEUM CUT, LINE

ENGRAVING, DRYPOINT, ETCHING, MEZZOTINT, AQUATINT, and INTAGLIO.

en ressaut Engaged to a wall or projecting from it.

enrichment A painted or carved repeated design on moldings, such as the GUILLOCHE, EGG AND DART, HONEYSUCKLE, and CHEVRON.

ensemble A set of matching furniture pieces, popular in the BAROQUE period and afterward, up to the present day.

ensemblier (French) One who groups objects and materials together for aesthetic appeal.

en suite (1) Part of a set. (2) A tourist hotel in which the rooms feature individual lavatories. See SETS.

entablature In architecture, the upper portion of a classic order, which consists of three parts: an architrave, a frieze, and a cornice. The entablature rests on the column. See ARCHITRAVE, CLASSIC, and CORNICE.

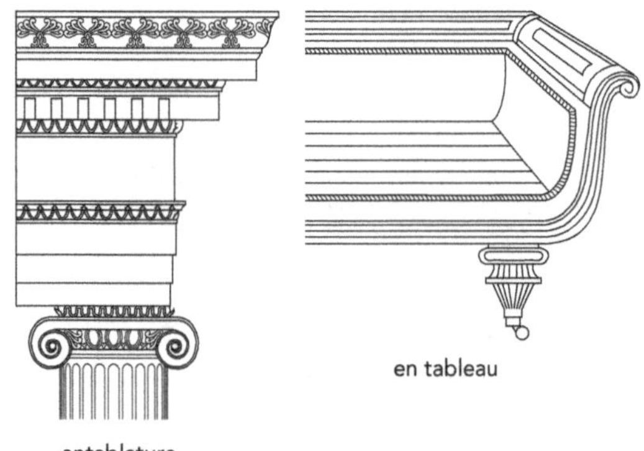

entablature

en tableau

en tableau An upholstery technique of the late 18th century. A sharp ridge, outlined in gimp, braid, or cord, defined the straight lines of the sofa or chair.

∞en taille d'épargne (French) Champlevé enamel. See CHAMPLEVÉ.

entasis A slight curve on the shaft of a column that creates an optical illusion and makes a column appear straight. Paradoxically, the swelling makes the column appear straight. See CAMBER.

entertainment center The wall unit or cabinetry designed to hold a large-screen television and other components constituting a home theater.

∞entrelac A Louis XVI decorative, carved, interlacing motif that is similar to a GUILLOCHE.

entresol (French) A mezzanine. A low story over the ground floor, or a low story between two high stories.

entasis

envelope table A square work surface with four flaps or hinged sections that, when flipped back, increase the workable horizontal area. A late-18th-century design, common in the French Directoire period. Often used for card table designs, it is similar to the triangular HANDKERCHIEF TABLE.

∞épergne (French) An ornamental stand with a dish on top. May have candelabra branches extending out from the stand, below the dish, or a trumpet-like container rising above. The bell-like opening functions as a flower container.

epistyle A horizontal beam that spans the space between two columns or piers or between a column or pier and a wall. Also called an ARCHITRAVE.

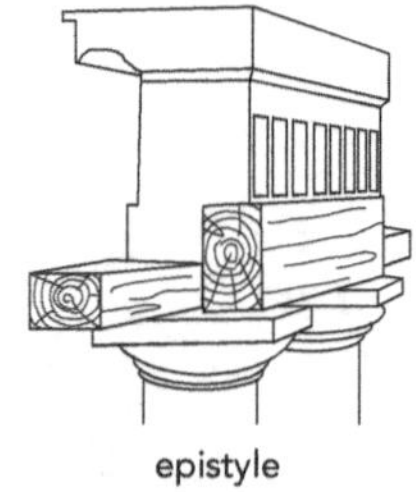

epistyle

epoxy A strong adhesive or sealant available in kit form. Also available as a liquid resin that must be catalyzed to become effective as a coating or cement. Used in molding, casting, and laminating and as a means of encapsulating other materials. This class of resins are thermosetting and are widely used in reinforced plastics because they adhere well to glass fibers.

ergonomic design Making aesthetic and functional decisions based on the needs of humans in relation to machines or mechanical devices. As biotechnology, it takes into consideration the psychological and physiological problems inherent in the performance of specific tasks using a mechanism. An increasingly important approach to the planning of offices and workspaces.

ergonomics The study of equipment design and human dimensions and how interaction with products affects human performance, health, and user comfort.

∞escabeau See ESCABELLE.

∞escabelle An early French Renaissance stool or chair supported on trestles, similar to the Italian sgabello. See SGABELLE.

escritoire (French) A small desk with drawers and compartments. A SECRETARY.

escutcheon (1) A shield with a heraldic device. (2) In hardware, a protective plate, sometimes decorated, for the area surrounding a keyhole, knob, pull, or doorknob.

escabelle

escutcheon #1

escutcheon #2

∞espagnolette A terminal ornament popular in 16th- and 17th-century French furniture. It is a female bust used as part of a support, or the ending of a volute. In the French Régence period, it is a female head with a tall, stiff lace collar or ruff that gives a generally Spanish flavor. The ornate head was a popular decorative motif for wood carvings and bronze mounts.

espalier (1) A wood latticework on which fruit trees or ornamental shrubs are trained to assume decorative patterns. The branches are tied to grow in a set direction and follow a preconceived design. (2) The trained, stylized trees are also referred to as espalier.

∞estagnie A French provincial, open, hanging shelf unit used to hold pewter utensils. The piece sometimes had a drawer under the shelves.

estrade (1) The French version of the Spanish estrado, or drawing room. It originally meant a location for a couch or bed in an alcove, which was a feature in 17th-century Spanish architecture. See ALCOVE. (2) Also, an elevated part of a floor or room; a platform is placed at one end.

Estron A trademark name for a natural, uncolored acetate fiber produced by the Eastman Company. A heavydenier yarn, especially designed for home-furnishing uses.

étagère Hanging or standing open shelves. A light, elegant unit for displaying books, bric-à-brac, etc. A WHATNOT unit.

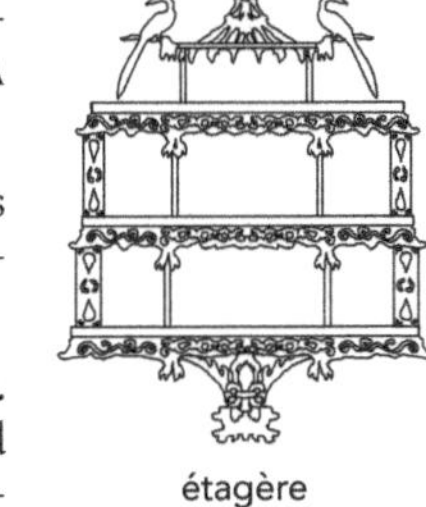
étagère

etched glass Sandblasted vitreous material that has a milky, opaque quality. Also called frosted glass.

etching A form of intaglio engraving. A resinous ground impervious to acid covers a copper plate, and the artist then draws on this surface with a needle or stylus. The plate is bathed in acid, which bites into the scratched lines, engraving the design. The design is inked and impressions are taken. The 17th century was a noteworthy period in the production of this type of reproduction.

Etruscan order Also called the Tuscan order. A Roman variation of the simple Doric order, although with a base. A heavy, massive column, seven diameters high. See DORIC ORDER.

étui (French) Box or container.

eucalyptus See WALNUT, ORIENTAL.

éventail (French) Fan.

even wash A soft plane of light from track, wall-washers, or other light fixtures.

evidence-based design (EBD) The use of research to inform the decision-making process. In healthcare design, EBD involves gathering information from multiple fields to improve building, user, and patient outcomes. Interiors specialists using EBD conduct both qualitative and quantitative research on commercial and residential spaces to achieve optimal solutions. In contrast to an instinctual decision-making process.

∞evolute A continuous wave, or Vitruvian scroll. A classical motif used in the 18th century as a decoration on bands, cornices, friezes, etc. See VITRUVIAN SCROLL.

exedra (1) A public room in a Pompeiian or Roman home. (2) A semicircular or rectangular recess for seating or other use. (3) An apse or niche in a church.

exedra

expanded vinyl A stretch upholstery fabric made of a plastic derivative with an elastic knit backing. Its capacity to stretch and shape against curved contours makes it ideal for covering irregular shapes.

Expressionism The works of art and literature in which reality is represented in a distorted way to express an inner vision, a transformation of nature, rather than an imitation of it. Influential during the opening decades of the 20th century.

extension table A work or dining surface that separates in the center, and extends outward in both directions. Leaves are then added in the open space, creating a longer horizontal expanse.

extrados The outer curve or boundary of the obverse of an arch. See INTRADOS.

eye The center of an Ionic volute.

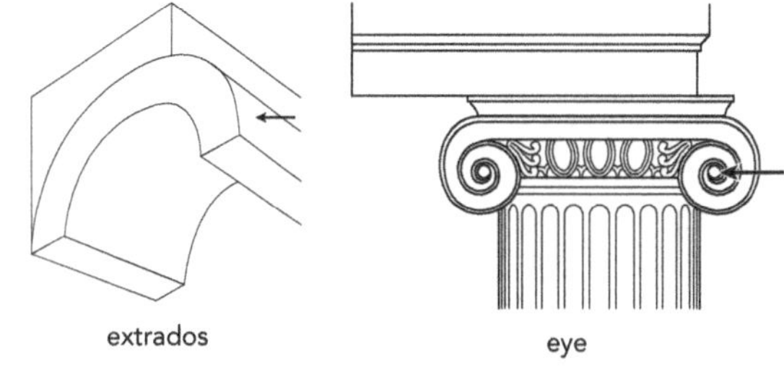
extrados eye

Fabrilite A vinyl-coated fabric and sheeting originally manufactured by DuPont, used as an upholstery material and as a durable wall covering.

façade (1) The front or vertical face of a structure; the main view. See also ELEVATION. (2) The front of an architecturally designed piece of furniture.

façade

façade d'honneur (French) The principal face of a building. See POSTERN.

facciata (Italian) Façade or front. See FAÇADE.

face (1) The exposed surface of a wall or structure. (2) Technically, the top side of a fabric.

face brick Units of construction material that have been selected for their better color and texture to be used to cover, or surface, exposed walls or fireplaces. Cheaper bricks or baser materials are used behind the face brick.

faced wall Constructed partition in which the facing and backing bond together to work as a single unit under the common load.

face fibers Strands used in the surface, or pile, of a carpet, rug, or broadloom.

facet A flat surface.

facettes (French) The flat projections between the flutes of a column.

Fachwerk (German) Timber-frame construction, similar to English TUDOR.

facia The flat, vertical face in the architrave of an entablature. See FASCIA.

facility manager (FM) A professional who is active in the interdisciplinary field concerned with the coordination and maintenance of commercial space. This includes providing infrastructure and designing work areas for corporations, government, and academic settings.

facing The finishing material that is applied to the façade of a building or wall. May be stone, brick, stucco, wood, etc.

façonné (French, fancy weave) A jacquard type of fabric made of silk or rayon. A brocaded velvet.

faïence (French, pottery) (1) Terra-cotta. A rural glazed pottery originally made at Faenza, Italy. (2) A glazed biscuit ware. Used as a facing for buildings or walls in the form of tiles or blocks. Also used as a flooring material. See TERRA-COTTA.

faille A soft, slightly glossy silk, rayon, or cotton fabric in a rib weave. The filler yarns are heavier than the warp yarns; thus they cause a flat cross-grain rib or cord.

∞faldistorium A late Italian Renaissance curule chair made of wrought iron and brass, with a leather or velvet seat. See CURULE CHAIR.

∞faldstool A folding or portable Gothic seat.

∞famille noire, famille verte, famille jaune, famille rose (French) Names for Chinese pottery having a background of a certain color. Literally black family, green family, yellow family, rose family, etc.

∞fanback chair A seat or settee with a motif similar to the semicircular cooling device, either upright or reversed, on the back. Originally an 18th-century French design.

∞fancy chair A Sheraton-designed small-scaled, elegant armless seat. A late-18th-century favorite.

fan design A semicircular ornament that takes its shape from the semicircular cooling device; used in late-18th-century furniture in England and English colonies.

fanlight A window set above a door or entranceway. In Georgian buildings, the opening is semicircular in shape, and bars radiating from the center separate the panes in a radial arrangement.

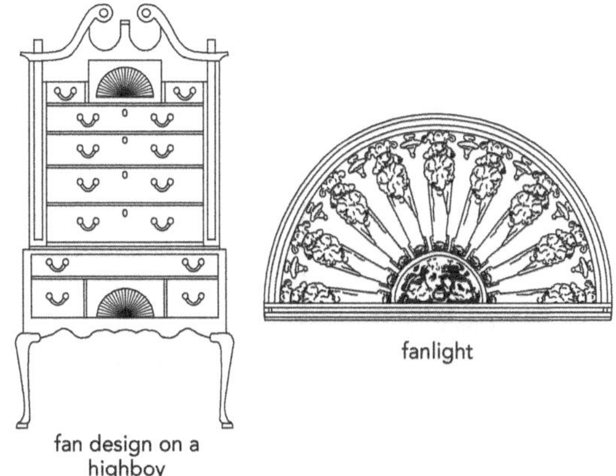
fan design on a highboy

fanlight

fan vaulting A collection of ribs springing from a point and spreading out in a radial configuration, specific to the PERPENDICULAR STYLE in Gothic architecture. Also called palm vaulting.

farthingale chair An armless seat with a box stretcher and turned legs and uprights. The lack of arms accommodated the voluminous skirts (farthingales) of Elizabethan costume.

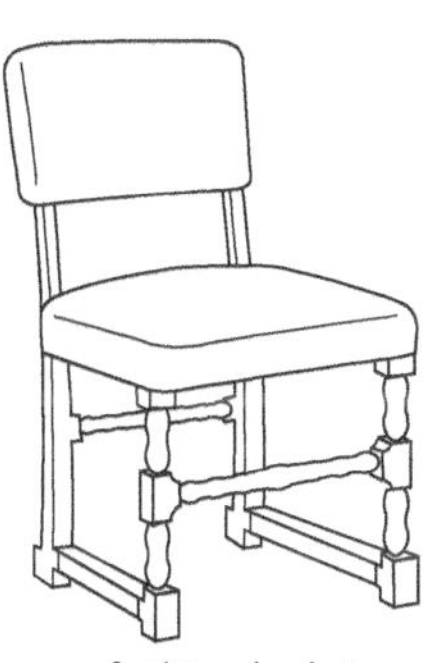
farthingale chair

fasces A Roman symbol of power consisting of a bundle of rods enclosing an axe. It reappeared in the 20th century as a symbol of the Italian Fascists.

fascia (1) The projecting crown molding of a cornice. A molding with a mostly flat vertical plane in section. (2) Any vertical nonstructural outer surface of a façade detail. Also spelled FACIA.

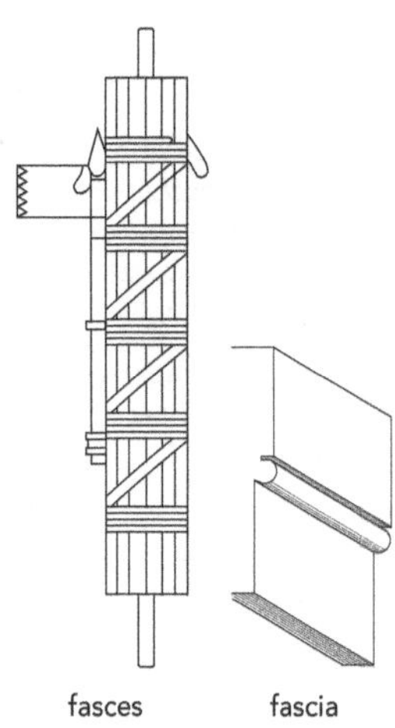

fasces fascia

faudesteuil A Romanesque bench or seating stool with curved, X-shaped supports. This type of stool usually had a leather sling for a seat, and the piece was collapsible. In the Gothic period, the legs were fixed, and the chair did not fold. See PLIANT.

faudesteuil

faun A creature from classical myth, half-man, half-goat. A decorative element in the French and Italian Renaissance periods that reappeared in the neoclassical era.

fauteuil (French, armchair) An upholstered chair with open sides, usually with upholstered arm or elbow pads. Popularized in the Louis XIV period; the arms originally extended directly over the front legs. In the Régence and Louis XV periods, the arms receded to a position further back, and the legs were shortened. Early Renaissance armchairs were not upholstered. See CAQUETOIRE.

fauteuil

fauteuil à châssis Armchair constructed by a French method devised in the Louis XIV period. (The same method was used for sofa construction.) A secondary wood framework was covered with fabric, then slipped into the prime wood frame of the piece of furniture. This technique made changes of upholstery relatively simple; the upholsterer merely inserted a new framed upholstered seat or back into the ornate carved frame. See SLIP SEAT.

fauteuil de bureau A desk chair of the Régence and Louis XV periods. It usually had one leg centered in the front, one centered in the back, and one at either side. The curved sloping back was caned or upholstered in leather. Similar to the 18th-century English ROUNDABOUT CHAIR.

Fauve movement (French, wild beast) An early-20th-century art development led mostly by two-dimensional artists who used bright, strong colors, flat patterns, and wild distortions. Henri Matisse, Maurice de Vlamenck, and Georges Rouault were among this artistic group.

faux finishing Fake renderings of various natural materials (e.g., wood, stone, and gems) or surface patinas (e.g., old painted plaster or distressed finishes). For example, faux bois mimics wood, and faux marbre mimics marble.

faux rose A French rosewood or Madagascar rosewood. A richly hued pinkish-brown wood with striped markings.

faux satine An amber to golden-brown cypress crotch wood that grows mostly in the southeastern United States. A soft, oily wood, it is easy to work and is used as a veneer and for paneling. Similar in appearance to SATINWOOD.

favrile A late-19th-century iridescent glass made by LOUIS COMFORT TIFFANY. Made in a variety of delicate and decorative patterns, many classified as Art Nouveau. See *Designers and Architects.*

feather bed A thick mattress pad filled with avian plumage for warmth and comfort.

feathered edge A chamfered or beveled effect in which the perimeter of a board is thinner than the board's thickness. A thinned-off termination of a piece of wood.

feathering Tracery, in the Gothic style, formed by an arrangement of cusps and foils. Also called foliation. See CUSP and FOIL.

Federal period American era of architecture, art, furniture, and decoration from about 1790 to 1820. A classical period greatly influenced by the ADAM BROTHERS, GEORGE HEPPLEWHITE, THOMAS SHERATON, and the English Regency. DUNCAN PHYFE was the leading American furniture designer. See AMERICAN EAGLE PERIOD. See *Designers and Architects.*

felt A material made by matting and interlocking, under heat and pressure, of woolen and other fibers. It has no weave or pattern.

felt base rug An inexpensive floor covering material that has an enameled design printed and sometimes an embossed pattern pressed on the base material. Similar to linoleum but not as durable; the wearing surface does not extend through to the backing.

fender A low metal guard made of iron or brass, used to protect the rug or floor from flying embers and sparks from the fire. A hearth or fireplace accessory.

fender

fenestration The window and door arrangement of a building in its entirety, and the relative proportions of the openings in the façade.

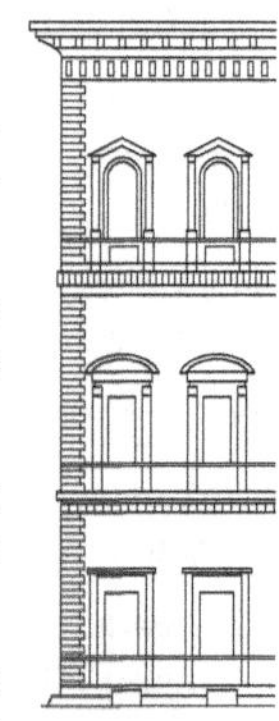

fenestration

fenêtre à battants (French) A pair of door-like windows that extend from ceiling to floor. See FRENCH WINDOWS.

Feraghan rugs Persian-style floor coverings that usually have a deep blue background and a rich overall pattern of small stylized flowers in rows.

∞**Ferronerie velvet** An antique Venetian pile textile with a delicate pattern similar to wrought iron.

ferrule (French *virole,* formerly *verrel,* metal ring) (1) A metal ring that holds an object and is fixed to the end of another object. (2) In current usage, a metal cup (usually of brass) placed on the bottom of a wood furniture leg for protection and as a reinforcement. (3) Also the metal section of a paintbrush that connects the hairs or bristles to the wood stem.

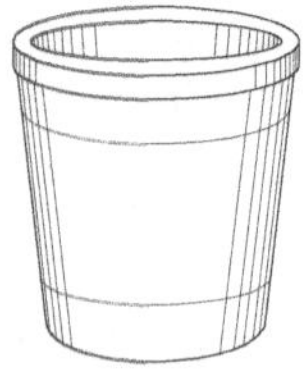

ferrule

Festina lente A classical adage meaning "make haste slowly." The motto of many people, including the Emperor Augustus. Its contemporary implication extols the wisdom of proceeding cautiously when creating complex designs.

festoon A string or chain of any kind of material suspended between two points to form a curved or inverted arc drop. A sculptured garland of leaves, flowers, or fruits suspended between two points. A favorite classical, Renaissance, and neoclassical motif.

fête galante A French 18th-century romantic version of a picnic with ladies and their escorts, in rich court apparel, flirting and playing musical instruments and games in a garden or idealized version of nature; the theme appears in murals, tapestries, textiles, and painting.

fiber A natural or synthetic thread or filament that can be sewn, woven, or spun into yarn. See *Table 2* and *Table 3*.

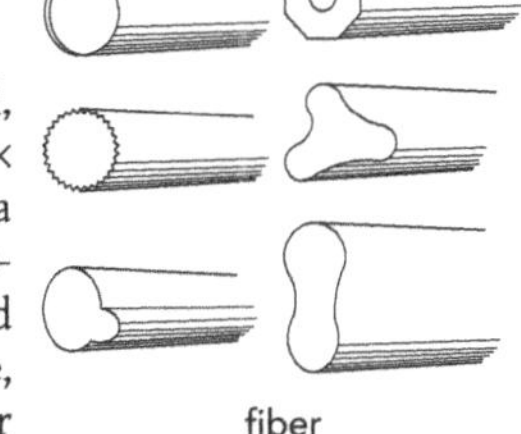
fiber

fiberboard A pulped wood panel, usually 4 feet by 8 feet (120 cm × 240 cm), compressed to form a rigid, strong, no-grain construction material. Many trademarked types are available: Masonite, Beaverboard, and Homosote, for example. Used for partitions, ceilings, and the interior construction of inexpensive furniture.

fiberfill Soft, synthetic material used as cushioning in upholstered furniture, bedding, and comforters. Usually consisting of polyester filaments. Often wrapped around foam to form upholstered furniture cushions.

fiberglass or fibreglass Fine filaments of pure glass, and the textiles woven from them. The filament is strong, soft, lightweight, and pliable and resists heat, chemicals, and soil. Initially manufactured by Owens-Corning Fiberglas Corp., Pittsburgh Plate Glass, and Johns Manville Corp. for a variety of construction and surfacing uses.

fiberglass objects Planters, shaped seats, and other dimensional forms made of fine filaments of glass saturated with polyester plastics that are poured into and formed in molds of the desired shape and size. Excellent for outdoor use and in contract design.

fiber rug A reversible floor covering woven of kraft or sisal filaments, sometimes combined with wool or other threads. Available in assorted sizes, colors, patterns, and shapes for use as independent floor coverings or a continuous carpet.

fiddleback A wood grain effect having a fine, even ripple running at right angles to the direction of the grain of the wood. Used for veneers. Often appears in maple and mahogany.

fiddleback chair A Queen Anne–style, American colonial seat. The back splat is shaped like the musical instrument or a vase, and the seat is usually made of rush. The chair has cabriole or bandy legs. A similar chair appears in Louis XV furniture.

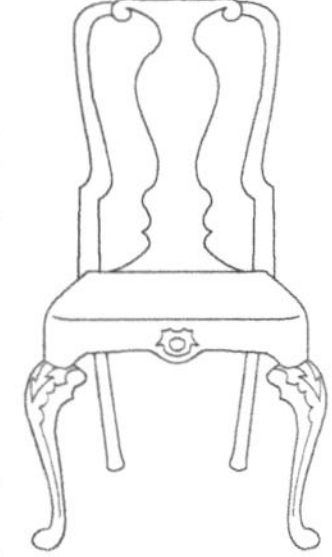
fiddleback chair

∞fiddle-braced back See BRACED BACK.

fiddle-string back or stick-back (adj.) A name sometimes applied to a Windsor chair or any other chair in which the back consists of many rods or thin turnings that resemble the strings of the bowed musical instrument.

field The surface of a panel that lies on the same level as the surrounding woodwork and is defined or outlined by a sunken bevel or applied molding. A panel with such a field is called a fielded panel.

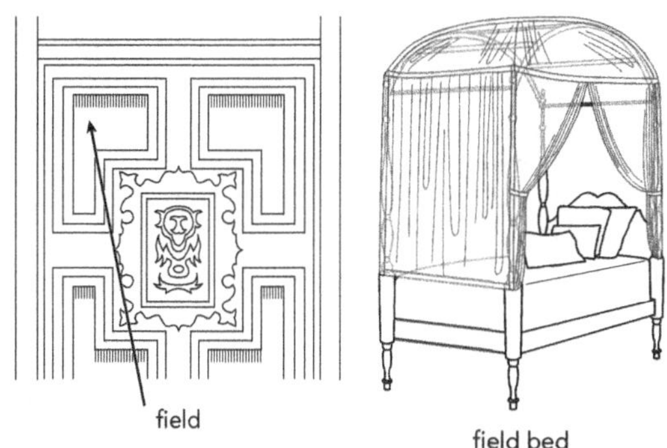
field

field bed

field bed (1) A small-scaled, arched canopy sleeping platform originally intended to be moved from place to place. Used by army officers on campaigns. (2) In 18th-century design, a sleeping device with a small tester and less imposing bedposts. (3) In tropical environments, a sleeping arrangement with high posts and with hinged arches in the longitudinal direction, for hanging mosquito netting.

figure (1) The highlights or cross-graining in a piece of wood or veneer. (2) Also, shapes created by the abnormal growth of a tree. See BURL. The vertical graining of a piece of wood is described as the PATTERN.

filament A yarn made up of a number of fine continuous strands lightly twisted together. Usually made of acetate, rayon, or other synthetic fiber. It is sold by the denier size.

fil de bois (French) Veneer used in a full, uninterrupted length on a piece of furniture.

fil d'or (French) Gold thread. A gilded silver thread originally made in Genoa and used in tapestries from the Middle Ages up to the 18th century.

filet A square-meshed, net fabric.

filet lace A type of open fabric in which the design is created by embroidering on net with a thread similar to that used in making the net. See LACE.

filigree Decorative openwork. Usually fine, lacelike work done in gold or silver wire.

filler (1) Threads that run across the width of the fabric from selvage to selvage. Another term for the weft. In weaving, the filler is the thread carried by the shuttle. (2) In woodwork, a liquid or paste, often pigmented, that is used to repair the pores or irregularities in coarse or open-grained woods. After using the filler, the wood is finished and polished.

fillet A molding with a small, flat, vertical surface as seen in section, usually used above and below a curved molding. The fillet is also the upright band between the flutings of a column. The term also refers to the uppermost member of a cornice.

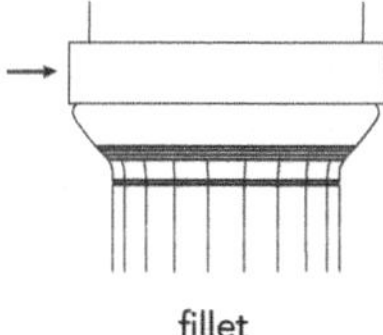
fillet

filling The weft or woof yarns. Used in the shuttle that moves back and forth across the lengthwise threads of a loom. Also, the pick threads. In carpetmaking, the threads that cross the warp and fill up the spaces between knots or tufts. See PICK WEAVE and WEFT.

films Synthetic fabrics made from liquids that adhere to backing materials. The liquid is applied directly to a formed or molded piece of plastic furniture. The applied layer supplies a fabric-like surface texture to the piece and thus substitutes for a fabric covering on the unit.

fin de siècle (French, end of the century) This phrase denotes the end of the 19th century and the ART NOUVEAU period.

finger joint A movable, interlocking connection mainly used between the movable and fixed parts of a bracket or fly rail, such as one used to support the leaves of a drop-leaf table in a horizontal position. See KNUCKLE JOINT.

finial The terminating ornament on a post, pediment, or intersection of furniture and architecture. A pineapple, urn, knob, or a cluster of foliage are among commonly used shapes.

finish (1) In fabrics, the treatment given to produce a desired surface: napping, embossing, glazing, waterproofing, or wrinkle resistance, for example. The treatment contributes to the fabric's feel or hand. (2) In cabinetry, a treatment applied to wood to protect the surface; to make it durable and resistant to stains and burns; to accentuate the grain; to lighten or deepen the color; to make the surface appear dull or glossy; or to change the color, by painting, lacquering, or distressing.

fir A soft, textured wood used for commercial plywood and interior trims. Not usually used for solid work in furniture. See *Table 5.*

firebacks Metal liners or screens, often decorative, placed behind the area of the fireplace where logs are burned. They reflected the heat into the room and protected the masonry. Popular in the 17th and 18th centuries, these were usually made of cast iron.

fireclay A heat-resistant material used to make firebricks for lining fireplaces.

fire division wall A partition that subdivides a building and resists the spread of fire but does not extend continuously through the building as does a fire wall.

∞fire dogs See ANDIRONS.

fire irons Hearth accessories: the poker, tongs, and shovel used to tend burning logs.

fire-retardant wired glass Sheet vitreous material with a wire mesh, chromium-dipped to ensure clean wire and a firm adhesion, which is embedded, as closely as possible, in its center. Produced by a continuous rolling process and made in many patterns, types, and finishes. Also used as a decorative material.

fire screen An ornamental panel set in front of an open hearth to keep sparks from flying into the room and to provide protection from intense heat.

fireside chair An upholstered seat, usually skirted, with a high rollover back that flares out as it rises up. The arms sweep away from the chair back and scroll around. The pillow seat of this 20th-century design is often T-shaped (wider at the front).

fire screen

fireside figures Fire screens made of wood or canvas, representing contemporary human profiles just under life size. Often females dressed in exotic costumes. These representations were also called "picture board dummies" and were popular in the late 17th century. See DUMMY BOARD FIGURES.

fire wall A partition constructed of fire-retarding material. It extends from the foundation up to and above the roof of a building, completely dividing it, and is designed to hinder the spread of fire for a defined period of time.

firing In pottery making, the heating of clay in a kiln to harden it.

∞First Plantagenet period See EARLY ENGLISH PERIOD.

∞First Pointed period See EARLY ENGLISH PERIOD.

fish tail A carved detail in the shape of a the posterior appendage of an aquatic animal that sometimes appeared on the top rail of spindle-back or banister-back chairs of 18th- and 19th-century American design.

fitments (British usage) Units such as bookcases and cabinets that are designed and built to accommodate the particular dimensions of a room.

fittings Metal hardware, mounts, escutcheons, etc.

flag A long grass that is twisted and woven into provincial-type seats. See RUSH.

flagstone Large, flat pieces of solid mineral matter, square or irregular in shape, used as flooring or pavement material. Slate is often used for flagstone floors. See *Table 3.*

flaked (adj.) Describes a wood figure or grain of oak that has been quarter-cut. Horizontal highlights streak across the grain of the wood. A breaking or loosening is called broken flake.

flambeau A flame or flaming torch used as a decorative motif. Popular in the 18th and early 19th centuries in England and France.

flamboyant (adj.) (French, flaming) Gothic style that included window tracery designed in conventionalized flamelike forms with reversed curved lines. See TRACERY. This appeared during the late Gothic period in English and French architecture (the 14th and 15th centuries).

flame carving A finial carved in a swirling, spiral effect to simulate a component of fire. Used to decorate urns in the late 17th and early 18th centuries.

flâneuse (From French *flâner,* to lounge) A garden-type lounge chair with a footrest, similar to the current deck chair. The flâneuse usually had a caned seat, back, and footrest.

flap table An early-17th-century surface-creating piece with a fixed center slab and two side wings that can be lowered by folding back the legs that support them. A form of GATELEG TABLE or EIGHT-LEGGED TABLE. Also called a DROP-LEAF TABLE.

flap table

flare An outward spread, as in a chair seat that is wider at the front than at the back.

flat (1) A dull, nonglossy paint finish. (2) A basic unit of stage scenery; a vertical frame with a covering of either wood or muslin. Broadway flats are thin because of limited space. Hollywood flats have larger supports that are perpendicular to the covering.

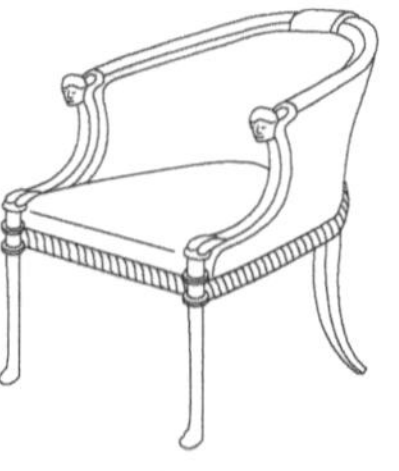
flare

flat-cut veneer A combination straight-grain and heart-figure flitch produced by slicing half of a log directly through the center, or heart.

flatted (adj.) Painted. Describes painted furniture that was popular in the Louis XV and Louis XVI periods.

flatting agent A substance added to varnishes, paints, and other coating materials to reduce the gloss.

flax The fiber from the inner bark of the herbaceous plant, used in the manufacture of linen. More expensive than cotton but more absorbent and with a crisper, firmer hand. Resists mildew. See *Table 2.*

Flemish Referring to Flanders, the historical name for the region that is now Belgium, Holland, and parts of northern France whose inhabitants speak a Dutch dialect.

Flemish bond In masonry, an arrangement of brick in which headers and stretchers are used alternately in the same course. In the next course, the arrangement is alternated so that the headers are centered over the stretchers below. A single Flemish bond is used for facing only. See BOND, DOUBLE STRETCHER FLEMISH BOND, and FLEMISH CROSS-BOND.

Flemish chair A late-17th-century English high-backed seat, with or without arms. The splat was a panel of cane, upholstery, laths, or balusters surmounted with carved cresting. Scroll feet supported the legs, which had straight backs with bold curves in front. The stretcher consisted of two concave curves joined by a convex curve in the center. See FLEMISH SCROLL.

Flemish cross-bond In masonry, alternating Flemish and stretcher courses, with the headers in vertical lines and the stretcher courses crossed. See BOND, DOUBLE STRETCHER FLEMISH BOND, and FLEMISH BOND.

∞Flemish ear A late French Renaissance and Baroque furniture foot, similar to the Flemish scroll foot, except that the S or C design is inverted. Appears on some furniture of the Louis XIV period. See FLEMISH FOOT and FLEMISH SCROLL.

∞Flemish foot A scroll-like ending to an S- or C-curved leg, popular in the 17th century in Flanders, England, and France.

Flemish chair and Flemish foot

Flemish scroll An S- or C-curved ornamental form in which an angle breaks a scroll, used in Flemish Renaissance furniture and in the English Carolean and William and Mary periods.

Flemish spiral bond In masonry, Flemish courses laid out so that the headers break joint over each other and form diagonal bands on the face of the wall. See BOND and FLEMISH BOND.

fleur-de-lis or fleur-de-lys (French) A decorative, conventionalized iris flower that has symbolized royalty and the French Bourbon kings in particular.

fleur-de-lis or fleur-de-lys

fleurette (French, small flower) A motif carved on Louis XVI furniture and accessories.

∞fleuretted treillage (Anglicized French) Beflowered trellis. A popular decorative motif in French Rococo, German Rococo, and Louis XV furniture and accessories.

fleuron A small, flower-like decoration set on the abacus of the Corinthian capital. It appears to spring from a small bud above the middle leaf in the capital.

fliers In a plan, the rectangular steps in staircase construction.

flight A series of steps uninterrupted by a landing.

flip-top table A contemporary expansion surface-piece with two leaves, one set on top of the other. When the top leaf is raised and set down even with the plane of the lower leaf, the surface area doubles.

flitch A part of the log that is sliced into veneer.

floating construction Solid wood furniture that is built so it can expand and contract without damage, by placing the screws that hold the sides and top together in slotted screw holes.

floating furniture Modern storage units hung or suspended from the walls. The case pieces do not have legs and are bracketed off stiles or upright wall standards bolted to the wall.

flock Finely powdered wool or other short-clipped fibers that are glued onto paper, fabric, wood, etc. to provide a suede or velvet finish or applied in a design to create a velvet effect. See FLOCKING.

flokati (flokates) Greek rugs loomed from long fibers of sheep wool into a thick shag, usually left in its natural creamy, off-white color. See SHAG RUG.

flocking A technique for applying non-integral short fibers. Originally, powdered wool was scattered over a surface; the particles adhered to the part of the surface that was treated with glue. The rest of the material was blown off. Developed during the Middle Ages, it was applied to paper in the 17th century and called velvet paper. Powdered color sprinkled on in place of flock resulted in a paper called counterfeit flock. In 1634, Jerome Lanyer received a patent for flocking.

floorcloth An early-18th-century rug made of heavy linen or canvas, heavily sized and coated and then painted or ornamented. Similar to WACHSTUCH-TAPETE.

floor covering See *Table 3.*

floreated (adj.) Describes Gothic tracery and ornaments that used floral and leaf motifs in flowing, rhythmic lines.

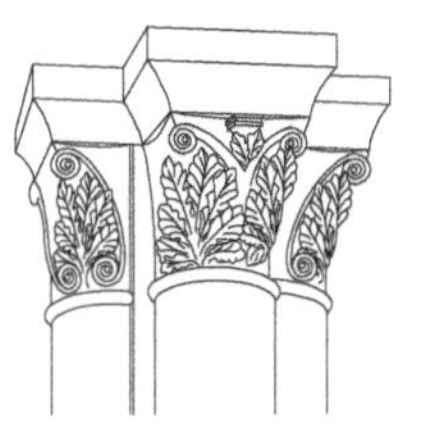

floreated

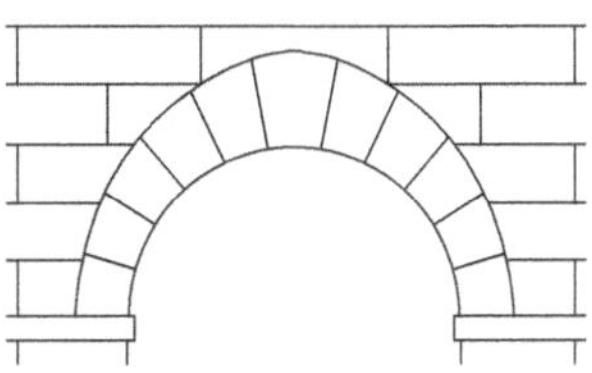

Florentine arch

Florentine arch A Renaissance architectural feature. A semicircular structural element springing directly from a column, pier, or capital and trimmed with an architrave. The outer curved element, or extrados, is pointed, whereas the inner arch, or intrados, is semicircular. Frequently used in a series. See ARCADE.

floor plan A horizontal building section. See PLAN.

flow The energy, commodities, people, and waste as they circulate into, through, and out of a structure. Traffic flow in a room, home, or office is important for safety reasons.

flue The enclosed portion of a chimney stack that carries the smoke upward and out of the building.

fluorescent lighting An illumination device consisting of a glass tube coated on its inner surface with a substance that glows when a gas-conducted current is induced in the presence of mercury.

flush (adj.) Describes a surface that is even, or at the same level, with adjoining surfaces.

flush bead A molding in which the sunk circular form is even with the surface adjacent to it.

fluting Continuous parallel hollows or channels, usually cut perpendicularly, as in a column, pilaster shaft, or furniture leg. Narrow concave moldings used in parallel lines. The spiral version is sometimes used on columns and furniture supports. Short flutings are often used on friezes as ornamentation. Also called cannellation. The opposite of REEDING.

fluting

fly ash A by-product of coal-fired power plants, used in the making of PORTLAND CEMENT, asphalt concrete, BRICK, and other products.

fly bracket An extended support, used to support a drop-leaf on a Pembroke or library table. The bracket sometimes had shaped or diagonally cut ends. See LOPER.

flying buttress A structural element, separated from the walls, that counteracts the thrust of an internal vault, especially in Gothic cathedrals.

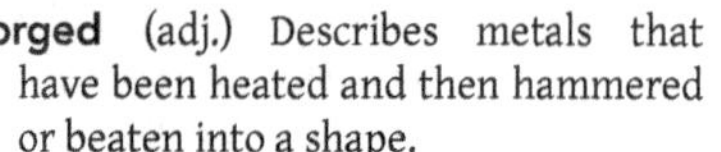

flying buttress

fly rail The folding bracket support for the flap or drop-leaf of a table.

FM Acronym for FACILITY MANAGER.

foam rubber Product made from the sap of the latex-producing tree, which is whipped with air to create a light, porous material. The firmness of the material depends on its air content. Used for mattresses, pillows, upholstery filling, and carpet backing. Also called LATEX.

foil The small arc used in Gothic tracery. Cusps separate foils. See CUSP and MULTIFOIL.

folding furniture Collapsible seating that can double over by way of hinges into a compact unit: a folding stool, folding chair, folding table, or folding bed. This principle was employed by the ancient Egyptians, Greeks, Nubians, and Romans and has continued in popularity up to present-day bridge sets.

folding furniture

folding table An early English Renaissance multilegged surface on supports. Often had from twelve to twenty legs, and the entire surface could be folded to one-third of its full size. The forerunner of the gateleg table, it functioned on the same principle of expansion.

fold over A desk or table with a leaf that bends over the upper surface. Used in late-18th-century France and England.

foliation See FEATHERING.

folly A garden or park structure resembling a classical or Gothic ruin, specially built to create a view or a charming effect. Popular in 18th-century France. Designer Bernard Tschumi brought the tradition into the late 20th century.

fondeur (French, metal caster) One who makes metal mounts, hardware, furniture embellishments, and accessories.

foot The bottom element of a furniture leg, or one of the cubes or spheres on which legless furniture rests.

footboard A supporting wooden piece at the lower end of a bed that connects with the two side rails. It can be an important decorative feature when carved and ornamented, or it may be a simple horizontal rail, depending upon the style or period. On Egyptian beds, it is more prominent than the headboard. A HOLLYWOOD BED omits the footboard.

footcandle A unit of photometry, based on the amount of luminous intensity produced by a standard candle at a distance of one foot from the source.

footrail The lower supporting stretcher between two legs of a chair or table, of the chair's front elevation.

footstool (1) Originally an accompanying step for high throne seats, and later used as an independent rest for the lower appendages. (2) A small, low HASSOCK.

footstool

forged (adj.) Describes metals that have been heated and then hammered or beaten into a shape.

form A long, backless bench or seat of the Jacobean period, often furnished with loose pillows.

formal Regular, symmetrical, and traditional in effect. Usually describes an arrangement or placement of furniture or decoration that is stately and carefully balanced. The opposite of a haphazard or whimsical effect.

Fortisan Trademark name for a strong yarn made from regenerated cellulose. It was initially produced by the Celanese Corporation. The yarn combines with silk, cotton, or linen to make sheer fabrics used for curtains. The resulting fabrics are strong, drapable, and resistant to changes in humidity.

Fortrel A polyester fiber produced by Fiber Industries, Inc., with properties similar to DuPont's Dacron: it is wrinkle resistant, is quick-drying, and has good wash-and-wear performance.

forum The large, open, public space at the center of an ancient Roman city.

four-poster bedstead A sleeping platform with two verticals in front and two in back; or uprights rising from a carved or paneled footboard and headboard. It was sometimes made to support a tester and drapery or a fabric canopy. See CANOPY BED and TESTER.

four-way center and butt match A pattern of veneer, such as the DIAMOND MATCH-VENEER, that usually uses butt, crotch, or stump slices. The design brings out the full interest of the graining.

foyer An area between the entrance and a main room of a home, apartment, or public building. Similar to the Roman vestibulum.

∞fractur (or fraktur) painting Decorative birth and marriage certificates created by the 18th- and 19th-century Pennsylvania Dutch.

frailero A Spanish Renaissance monk's chair, usually made of walnut, with plain legs and a broad front stretcher. Decorative nailheads secured the leather seat to the two side rails and affixed the back panel between the two uprights. The arms were wide and simple. The most typical chair of the Spanish Renaissance. See MISSION STYLE.

frame (1) The skeleton or basic structure of a piece of furniture that is later filled in with webbing, stuffing, muslin, upholstery, etc. See CARCASE. (2) A surrounding case or structure for the protection and enhancement of drawings, paintings, photos, and mirrors. Can be made of wood or metal, trimmed with moldings, or embellished with GESSO composition.

Francophile One who is enamored of all things French. In design, an aesthete who considers 18th-century French furniture to be one of civilization's highest achievements.

Franklin stove A combination cooking device and fireplace invented by Benjamin Franklin in the mid 18th century. It burned wood set on andirons and had a decorative front. Originally called a Pennsylvania stove.

free address Related to new concepts of work and workplace design which aren't based on working for a legacy corporation in a bricks-and-mortar office. A choice-based work environment requires flexible office space. Other related vocabulary terms include heads-down spaces, benching, and collaborative spaces. The free address worker chooses to work in a space that fits their functional and personal needs, including mood, need for interaction, and energy level.

free form An irregular, flowing abstract shape used in modern cocktail tabletops, accent area rugs, wall decorations, etc. These amorphous shapes may also be used in paintings and gardens.

free spirited typography A celebration within the world of typeface of bold, eye-catching fonts. The mostly sans serif letters, and the graphics of which they are a part, are seen as punchy, fun, full of swagger, and eye-catching; they often feature bold underlining or swash and appear hand-written. The graphic trend is rounded, chunky, and looks as though the 1960s and 1970s have been nudged in a high-tech direction. In interiors, the trend is impacting chiefly reception rooms, wayfinding systems, and retail signage.

freestanding column A vertical structural device with clear or open space surrounding it.

freestanding poles Metal or wood vertical elements with sleeve connections to make them longer or shorter. An adjustable insert sits at the bottom of the pole and rests on the floor, while another sleeve sits on top with its disk against the ceiling. The vertical remains erect because pressure is exerted upward and downward. Modern designer George Nelson's Omni system is based on the use of these poles. These elements are also used for pole lights and traveling display units.

∞French bed An early-19th-century Empire sleeping platform with S-scrolled headboard and footboard. Elegant versions were made of rosewood, had legs carved in the shape of dolphins or cornucopias, and were embellished with ormolu designs or medallions. See SLEIGH BED.

French bracket foot A support with a concave curve down the mitred edge, which gives a splayed effect. Almost always combined with a valanced skirt or apron. Both the inner and outer edges of the leg are curved, giving the appearance of a stunted CABRIOLE LEG. Also called a French foot. Popular in 18th-century English and American furniture.

French burl A Persian walnut wood with an interesting curly grain favored for inserts in cabinetwork.

∞French chair A general name for upholstered chairs in mid-18th-century England. The term does not apply to any particular style or decoration but to a general type of Rococo chair such as the BERGÈRE. See also CABRIOLET.

French Directoire The era in France from 1789 to 1804. It followed the Louis XVI period and served as the transition from the Greek style of Louis XVI to the austere Egyptian and Roman styles of the EMPIRE period. A continuation of the classical tradition of Louis XVI with the addition of Revolutionary motifs: symbols of liberty, triumphal arches, spirit levels, pikes, oak boughs, and clasped hands. Related to the democratic French government the Directory. See also DIRECTORY PERIOD.

French Early Renaissance period The period from approximately 1484 to 1547, covering the reigns of Charles VIII, Louis XII, and Francis I. A transitional period that blended outgoing Gothic structural forms with Italian Renaissance architectural details and ornaments.

French heading The gathering of a drapery or valance into regularly spaced folds. The folds are usually stitched in place to give a set appearance.

French Late Renaissance period The period from approximately 1589 to 1643, covering the reigns of Henry IV and Louis XIII and contemporary to the reign of Elizabeth I. The Italian Renaissance continued to dominate the architecture and decorations of the period, along with Dutch and Flemish influences. In interiors, wall paneling became more prevalent, and designs became more formal.

French Middle Renaissance period The reigns of Henry II, François II, Charles IX, and Henry III, covering the years 1547 to 1589. Catherine de Medici dominated the period, and local variations were added to the dominant use of Italian ornament and Renaissance architectural details. Gothic forms gradually disappeared.

French Provincial The term usually refers to simplified furniture of the Louis XV or Rococo style. However, plain furniture was made in the provinces in all times and styles, usually of walnut, oak, or fruitwood. PROVINCIAL furniture is simpler in line than the prevailing high fashion, and it is rarely veneered or decorated with marquetry or ornate carving. See COUNTRY FRENCH.

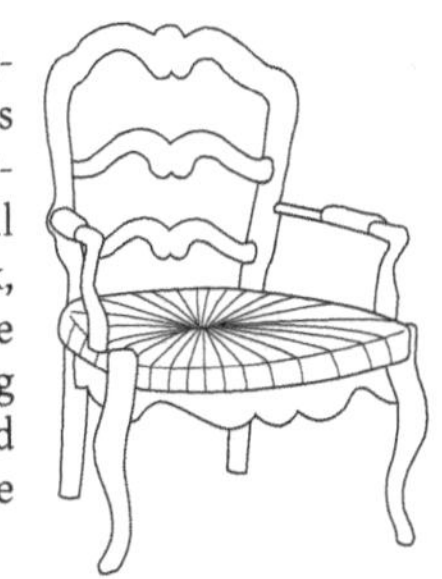
French Provincial

French Régence or Regency The transitional era (1700 to 1730) between the Louis XIV Baroque period and Louis XV Rococo. Louis Philippe, Duc d'Orléans, was Regent of France. Flat, curved paneling was used for ornament. Ribbon ornaments served as embellishments, and curved or CABRIOLE legs replaced straight ones. The BOMBÉ commode made its appearance, and polished walnut, mahogany, and rosewood replaced ebony as the favored wood. The period has no relationship to the English Regency period.

French Restoration period (1830–1870) The era after the French monarchy was restored, including the reigns of Louis XVIII, Charles X, Louis-Philippe, and Napoleon III. Characteristic of the time were eclectic designs, cheaper machine production, and a perception that the level of craftsmanship had declined. See also SECOND EMPIRE PERIOD. Also called Late Empire period.

French seam An especially fine finish in tailoring and upholstering, in which two rows of stitching cover the raw edges of the fabric being sewn.

French whorl foot A furniture termination that swirled or curled forward and rested on a shoe. It most often appeared as the termination of a cabriole leg in the Régence and Louis XV periods.

French windows A pair of multipaned, door-like glazed openings that extend down to the floor and, like hinged doors, are used for access to, or egress from, a room.

fresco (Italian, fresh) A wall painting in a watercolor-like medium (such as tempera) on wet plaster. The CARTOON (full-sized sketch) is drawn on the plaster surface. Using pigments mixed with water or lime water, the artist paints directly on the damp plaster. The color dries lighter and becomes integrated into the wall or ceiling. Made in Italy in the 14th century and perfected in the 16th century. Raphael's frescoes in the *Stanze* of the Vatican are fine examples of the art form.

fresquera A hanging food cupboard with Spanish latticework or spindle decoration. The openwork of the cupboard door allowed for ventilation.

fret A border motif or geometric band of Greek origin. It is made up of interfacing and interlocking lines and forms. Also called CHINESE KEY DESIGN or MEANDER.

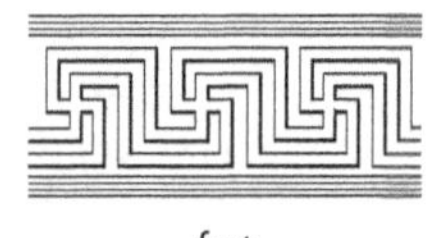

fret

fretwork Ornamental woodwork cut to represent small interlacing fillets or trellis work. Usually made in a complicated, repeating, geometric pattern. A favored technique of Chippendale in his Chinese pieces.

friar's chair See FRAILERO.

friesian A simple technique for carving with a chisel, usually used to create basic geometric forms. A popular technique in Colonial American woodwork. Also called Frisian.

Friesland A province in the Netherlands noted for its 17th-century carved Baroque furniture.

frieze (1) The central portion of the classic architectural entablature, located above the architrave and below the cornice. It usually has a flat surface embellished with decorative sculpture or carving. (2) Also, a painted or sculptured horizontal motif. (3) In furniture, the underframing of a table between the top surface and the legs. See APRON, FRONT, or SKIRT.

frieze

friezé or frisé (French *frisé*, curled) (1) A pile fabric with uncut loops, originally made in Friesland, Holland. The fabric is sometimes patterned by shearing the loops at different levels. Usually made of wool, mohair, or heavy cotton. (2) In carpet manufacture, rugs made of hard-twist, heavy, brushed wool yarns. See *Table 1*.

frieze drawer The top opening of a chest which extends forward over the main body. Usually supported by columns or pilasters. An Empire and Biedermeier early-19th-century design.

frieze rail In a door made up of three horizontal rows of panels, the horizontal raised element between the middle and top panels. See also PICTURE MOLDING or RAIL.

fringe An ornamental edging used to finish or trim drapery, upholstery, etc. A continuous band or ribbon with hanging twisted threads, loops, and tassels. Made in various styles, such as cut, looped, BULLION, or TASSEL.

frisé See FRIEZÉ.

frit (1) The mixture of silica and flux that is fused at high temperature to make a glass or ceramic material. It can also be in the form of paint. (2) The coating that serves as the base for a glaze or enamel. (3) A colored material that is applied to glass for a decorative effect.

front The principal, forward-facing surface of a piece of furniture. The principal elevation of a furniture piece may be a flat rectangle or consist of several planes, BOMBÉ (convex), BLOCK FRONT, BREAKFRONT, or SERPENTINE.

frosted glass See ETCHED GLASS.

frosting A slightly pitted surface in glassware.

fruit festoon Garland of angiosperms, leaves, and flowers, tied with ribbons and draped between two rosettes to form a downward curve. A popular Roman motif that Renaissance artists revived.

fruitwood Natural material from angiosperm-bearing trees such as cherry, apple, and pear, largely used in provincial furniture. An 18th-century favorite. See *Table 5*.

fruitwood finish A light, honey-brown surface treatment applied to soft woods to simulate fruitwood. The natural grain of the wood shows through, and the wood is often distressed.

Fujian A type of cypress tree native to Vietnam and southeastern China; the area is mountainous, forested, and known for the production of flower-scented teas. Used for partitions, roof materials, art works, and furniture.

fulcrum A Roman headrest on which a seated person could lean.

full-lead crystal The homogeneous solid substance that is at least 24 percent lead.

fully tempered glass Vitreous material that is three to five times more resistant to breakage than annealed glass. The material is heated almost to the softening point and then quickly cooled with air or in a liquid bath. The fully tempered version qualifies as safety glass.

fumed oak A furniture finish of the late 19th and early 20th centuries. Ammonia vapor stained the oak wood, rendering the graining more pronounced and deeper in color. A large quantity of mission furniture as well as late English Victorian pieces were produced in the material.

fumeuse A smoking chair. An 18th-century variation on the voyelle. The broad crest rail on the narrow, shaped back often had compartments that held smoking items such as tobacco, pipes, and flints. A person straddled the chair, facing the chair back and the equipped rail. See COCKFIGHT CHAIR and VOYELLE.

functional furniture Utilitarian furniture in which use and purpose are the driving forces of the design and the aesthetics derive from their operational values.

functionalism An early-20th-century design approach that sought to create designs appropriate for modern industrial society. Its proponents believed that good design should be readily available to all classes and would improve the standard of living. The resulting designs did not expressly represent narrative subjects or carry semiotic meanings.

furoshiki (Japanese, bath spread) A traditional Japanese cloth used to carry items. It is used to bundle up clothes at *sentos*, or bath houses.

furring A method of finishing the inside of a masonry wall by either applying plaster directly to clay tiles or attaching metal or wood strips to a lathed wall. The purpose is to provide an air space for insulation, to level wall irregularities, or to create a perfectly shaped room in which perimeter walls reconcile the geometry with the structure. The construction method also prevents the transfer of moisture.

fustian A sturdy cotton fabric with a pile similar to suede or velvet. A twill-weave fabric.

fustic A light yellow wood from the West Indies. In the 17th and 18th centuries it was used for marquetry and inlay.

futon (Japanese) A folded mattress in a frame that can be folded up for seating or folded down to form a sleeping surface. An inexpensive alternative to a sofa bed.

Futurism An Italian movement inspired by technology and Utopian urbanism that took a dynamic view of daily life. It helped spawn the Italian modern furniture and design industries. Related to CUBISM and RUSSIAN CONSTRUCTIVISM.

gabardine (Spanish, protection against the elements) A hard-finished twill fabric with a steep diagonal effect. Produced from wool, cotton, rayon, or mixed fibers.

gable The triangular space of wall enclosed at the side of a building by a sharply pitched roof.

gaboon A soft, straight-grained wood, golden to pinkish-brown in color, used in Europe for plywood, furniture, and interior work. Lightweight and fairly strong. Native to the African west coast. See SAMARA.

gadroon (French, *godron*) A series of elongated egg or ovoid forms in a band. Similar to bead molding in that it projects above the surface it ornaments. When used around a circular object, the oval form of ornament is called splayed gadroon. See NULLING.

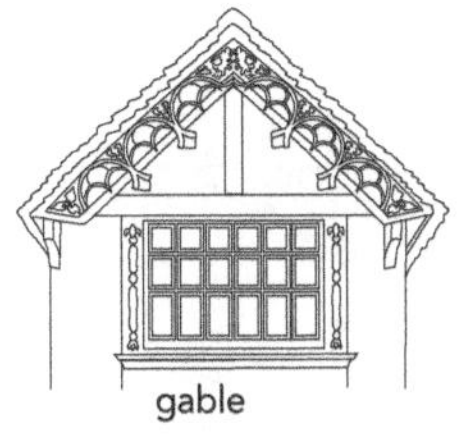

gable

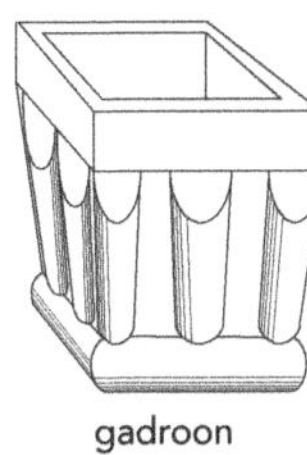

gadroon

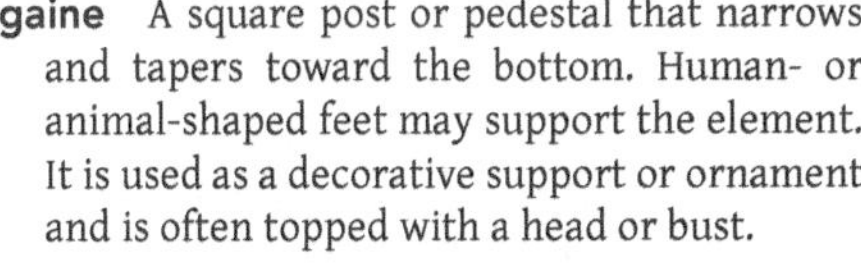

gaine

gaine A square post or pedestal that narrows and tapers toward the bottom. Human- or animal-shaped feet may support the element. It is used as a decorative support or ornament and is often topped with a head or bust.

gallery (1) A wide corridor walled in on one side only and usually located on the upper story. (2) The metal rod and support at the back of a sideboard of the late 18th century in England. (3) In furniture, the raised metal or carved rim along the edge of a shelf or around a tabletop or server, as in gallery-top tables.

galloon or galon (1) A narrow, closely woven braid used for trimming draperies and upholstery. Frequently used in the early 18th century to finish off rough upholstery work. (2) A lace or embroidered band with a scalloped edge on two sides. See GIMP.

galvanized iron A zinc-coated version of the most common element on earth. The coating process renders the chemical element rust-resistant.

gamification Applying the look and process of video entertainment to other areas; a conceptual and aesthetic move from video games to other activities, bringing game-mechanics to non-gaming situations. Qualities that are important in digital entertainment include scoring, competition, points, badges, and play rules. The design impact is playing out in fast-food restaurants, exhibition design, Web design, interior design apps, reception areas, and building entrances.

garde-manger (French) A food cupboard; a larder or cupboard.

garden apartment (1) A multiple-dwelling unit, usually two stories high and set in a landscaped area in a suburban residential area. (2) Sometimes a euphemism for a suite of rooms in a basement.

garden seat An Asian outdoor object for sitting made in the shape of a small keg, barrel, or drum. Originally the pieces were carved of stone; later, produced in porcelain and sometimes heated. Made with a lattice-like wooden center part and with a solid top and bottom.

garderobe An ARMOIRE or a WARDROBE.

garderobe

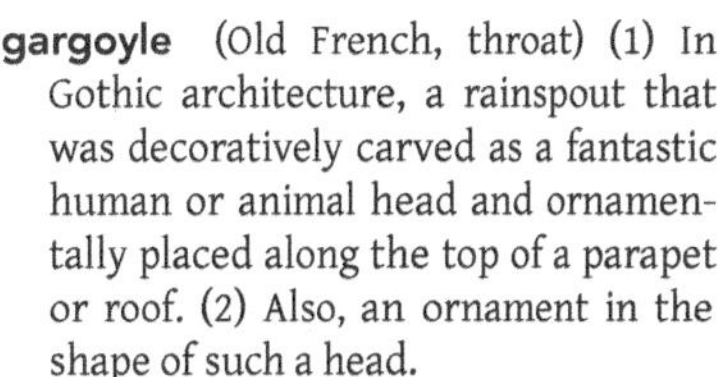

gargoyle (Old French, throat) (1) In Gothic architecture, a rainspout that was decoratively carved as a fantastic human or animal head and ornamentally placed along the top of a parapet or roof. (2) Also, an ornament in the shape of such a head.

gargoyle

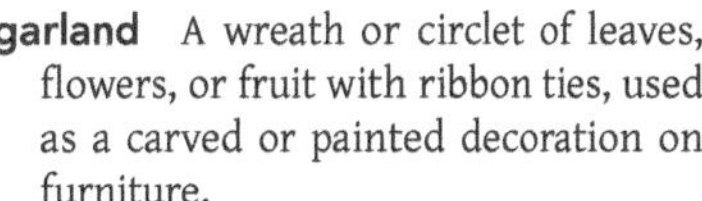

garland A wreath or circlet of leaves, flowers, or fruit with ribbon ties, used as a carved or painted decoration on furniture.

garniture Any motif used for enriching a surface or area. The embellishing or decorating may be painted, carved, inlaid, applied, etc.

garreting A surface finish of small stones or pebbles pressed into a mortar joint while it is still soft.

garrett (Old French, place of refuge or lookout) A room constructed in the roof of a building. An attic.

gatch An Asian and Middle Eastern term for decorative elements made in molded plaster. See ANAGLYPTA and CARTON-PIERRE.

gateleg table A drop-leaf dining surface with oval or rounded ends. Single or double wing legs or gates support the leaves. Introduced in mid-17th-century Jacobean furniture and was popular in English colonies. See EIGHT-LEGGED TABLE, FOLDING TABLE, and THOUSAND-LEG TABLE.

gateleg table

gauge The thickness of a material.

gauze A thin, transparent fabric made of a netlike weave, a plain weave, or a combination of the two. Originated in Gaza, Palestine. The material can be made of silk, cotton, linen, wool, synthetic fibers, or combinations of these fibers. Often used for GLASS CURTAINS.

gauze, theatrical A semitransparent loosely woven cotton or linen fabric with a shimmering appearance.

gazebo

gazebo (1) The turret on the roof of a lattice-constructed garden house. (2) Also, the entire garden house structure. An ornamental, open summerhouse.

gebs White, lacy, hand-chiseled plaster designs. The result of a decorative technique in which plaster is chiseled at various depths (instead of poured into a mold) and sometimes highlighted with colors. The technique can be used with any kind of motif, either geometric or representational, as well as calligraphy. Unlike conventional plaster work, which is done off site, gebs are done in situ, by applying a thick layer of slow-setting plaster over the surface to be decorated.

general lighting The overall illumination plan that creates a virtually shadowless interior, covering an area with an even distribution of foot-candles or lux for a designated amount of space. See SECONDARY LIGHTING.

generative design A creative approach with multiple foci, although focused on successful outcomes of the architecture, design, and construction process. This includes a studied use of materials, particularly in façade assemblies. The approach is related to wellness and healthcare design but also employee performance and satisfaction, as well as organizational performance, so workplace design is expanded to address communal quality of life.

generative space Designs that improve over time and that incorporate the knowledge, experience, and best practices of the healthcare industry. Such an area builds on improvements in healthcare and healthcare settings to date. Its goal is an environmental design that enables individuals to flourish in their communities. This transdisciplinary collaboration integrates the physical and social sciences; academic research and professional practice; and environmental design to produce systemic and sustainable environments.

Genoa velvet A multicolored, patterned plush textile on a satin ground.

genuine leather Only full-grain animal hide and top-grain animal hide may be labeled and sold as *genuine leather.*

Georgian sidechair

Georgian period The golden era of English furniture design and architecture, during the reigns of George I through George IV and the Regency (approximately 1714 through 1811). Some dominant designers and architects of this time were the Adam brothers, Chippendale, Shearer, Hepplewhite, and Sheraton. Usually divided into three separate periods: Early Georgian, 1714–1750; Middle Georgian, 1750–1770; and Late Georgian, 1770–1820. (The period coincides with the life of George Washington, 1730–1799, in the United States.)

German silver An alloy of copper, nickel, and zinc.

gesamtkunstwerk (German, unity of the arts) A nonhierarchical philosophy of interiors in which all arenas of design are valid and collaboration across professional boundaries is promoted.

gesso (1) A dense and brilliant white coating of gypsum or plaster with a high degree of absorbency that is used as a ground for tempera painting. The panels to be painted are treated with several coats of the material and size. (2) Also, a plaster-like composition molded to form a raised or bas-relief applied ornament on walls, furniture, frames, and moldings. Often painted and gilded. See ANAGLYPTA, CARTON-PIERRE, and COMPOSITION ORNAMENT.

Gewirkter Teppich or Tapete (German) Tapestry or arras.

ghiordes knot One of the two traditional cord fastenings used for hand-tying pile yarn in Oriental rugs over two warp threads and up between them. Also called the Turkish knot. See SEHNA KNOT.

gig economy The circulation of goods, services, and financial resources in the digital age. The new office is flexible, workers are freelance, and client and customers talk via online platforms. This involves independent contractors instead of legacy corporations, and flexible lifestyles for workers. Famous examples are Uber and Airbnb. Fast internet is a must and the sector is more urban than rural. This has resulted in millions of square feet of new office space that follow new design paradigms.

giglio (Italian) A decorative element similar to a FLEUR-DE-LIS, usually associated with Florence, Italy.

gilded or gilt furniture Seating, casework, or work surface pieces finished by covering with gold, gold leaf, or gold paint, an early-17th-century finish adopted in England during the early Queen Anne period, and also in France. William Kent was a leading designer. See GILDING.

gilded leather A popular treatment for animal skin hangings from the 16th through the 18th centuries. The hide was sized, then covered with gold or silver leaf. Sometimes the surface was tooled or embossed with chisels or patterned punches called irons. Tiny roses, rosettes, squares, circles, arabesques, and heraldic motifs were popular designs. During the 17th century, the Dutch often used colored grounds and bronzed or gilded fruits and cherubs. See also CORDOVAN LEATHER, GUADAMICIL, and MOROCCAN (MAROQUIN) TAPESTRY.

gilding

gilding The art of ornamenting furniture, accessories, and architectural details with gold leaf or gold dust.

gimp (or guimpe) Originally a woven silk braid of assorted designs. A binding material used on the outer edges of upholstered furniture to cover fabric joints or upholstery tacks or as an enrichment. Gimp is also used as a trim on draperies, bedspreads, etc. See also GALLOON.

ginkgo A species of plant that is described as a living fossil because its biological structure has remained unchanged from the prehistoric Permian period. Especially prevalent in China and Japan, used for food, medicine, and high-end paneling.

gingham A lightweight, yarn-dyed, cotton material woven in checks or stripes.

girandole A multibranched wall sconce that holds candles and is often mirrored. A late-17th- and 18th-century accessory and lighting device that sparkled and shimmered. Often paired with a console and mirror. In the 19th century, the term described a circular convex mirror, with or without sconces. In the American designs, the mirror was capped with an eagle. Also any branched candlestick. See APPLIQUÉ and BULL'S EYE MIRROR.

girder A heavy beam used over wide spans as part of a ceiling or floor structural system. It supports small beams or concentrated weights.

glamping A combination of *glamour* and *camping;* camping with style. An outdoor recreational activity in which the participants (glampers) leave their urban home regions to enjoy nature. They spend several nights outdoors surrounded by upscale amenities. Articles on the glamorous five-star camping style are a popular subect in interior design journals.

glamping

glass brick A hollow block, composed of two halves of molded soda-lime vitreous material. The pieces are sealed together with a vacuum between and can then be mortared together into wall units.

glass curtains Window coverings made of sheer, semitransparent fabrics that hang against a windowpane or vitreous surface. They may be used with blinds or shades or be over-hung with draperies.

∞Glastonbury chair A 16th-century ecclesiastic seat with X-shaped legs and sloping arms and back.

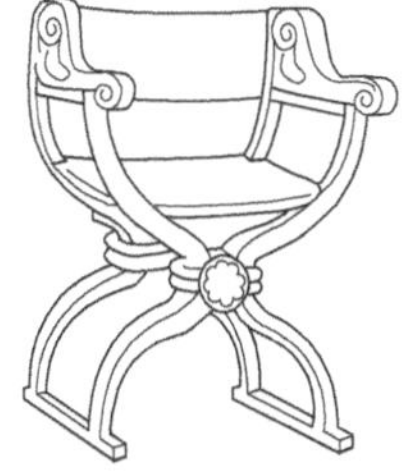
Glastonbury chair

glaze (1) In pottery, a thin coating of glass fired onto the pottery to give it color or a glossy appearance. (2) A sheen applied to a textile.

glazed chintz A printed, plain or colored cotton fabric given a crisp feel and a sheen by means of calendering or by treatment with paraffin. See CALENDERING.

glazed door A closure made of panes of glass and framed in wood molding strips, similar to a French door. In furniture, movable panels made of glass panes and held together in a decorative framework. Used in cabinets, secretaries, and bookcases.

glazed door

glazing A method of giving a smooth, high-polished finish to fabrics such as chintz or tarletan. The fabrics can be treated with starch, glue, shellac, or paraffin and then run between hot friction rollers. The finish will not withstand washings, unless synthetic resin or something similar is baked in at high temperatures.

glazing bars The wood or metal strips that form the framework around individual panes of glass in a window or door. Also called MUNTIN or MUNTING.

globe stand A favored 18th-century accessory. Usually a carved tripod to hold a rotating sphere miniature of the world. Smaller platforms stood on tables or desks; larger units stood directly on the floor.

gloss Degree of shine, sheen, or luster in a finish.

glyph A shallow, vertical groove cut into a flat or carved surface. A form of fluting. A feature of classical Doric architecture. See TRIGLYPH.

Gobelins A tapestry factory in Paris in the 16th century owned by a family of dyers. In 1662 Louis XIV purchased the factory, and Charles Le Brun was made director, whose plant produced textiles, metalwork, silverwork, wood carvings, and frescoes. The Savonnerie rug factory merged with the Gobelins. Among the famous artists and artisans who worked at the Manufacture Nationale des Gobelins were Nicholas Poussin, Louis and Charles Le Brun, and Antoine and Charles Coypel. See *Designers and Architects.*

Gobelins chair upholstery

going The horizontal distance between one riser face and the next, in stairway construction.

gold leaf Originally, an amalgam of tin and copper. The bright, shiny, thin sheet is laid over a surface that has been made tacky by a shellac, adhesive, or sizing. The sheet then adheres to the surface. Also called mosaic gold or Dutch gold. See GILDING.

gold plating A process whereby particles of the precious material are made to coat a baser metal unit, usually accomplished electrolytically.

gonçalo alves A Brazilian wood with a decidedly black-brown streak on a red-brown ground. It is hard and horny and sometimes develops surface cracks. Also called BOSSONA.

gondola An upholstered armchair with a concave, semicircular arched back. Also called a TUB CHAIR.

∞gondola bed A 19th-century Empire couch with foot and head boards that appear to scroll or roll over, like the ends of the venetian flat-bottomed boat. See BOAT BED and SLEIGH BED.

gondola chair A low seat for a writing desk, or a sofa whose back curves downward to form the arms. The sweeping, curving line resembles the boat.

gondole (French) The footrest accompanying a CHAISE LONGUE or DUCHESSE BRISÉE. With its curved upholstered sides, it can also serve as a small seat.

gooseneck lamp A light fixture with a metal pipe shaft constructed to be flexible and bendable. It is possible to alter the direction of the beam of light by twisting the corrugated pipe right or left, up or down.

gooseneck pediment A double-curved triangular-shaped vertical termination popular in 18th-century English and American furniture. It is also referred to as broken arch or swan neck. See BROKEN ARCH and SWAN NECK PEDIMENT.

Gothic arch A semicircular pointed structural shape that emphasizes the vertical dimension. It is produced by butting two arcs together, a process which reduces the lateral thrust.

Gothic period The era from approximately 1150 to 1500 in Europe. A time of outstanding ecclesiastic architecture and art, and the only European architectural style that is not based on classical forms. Named by the Italians, who preferred Greek and Roman architecture and assumed that only German "barbarians," the Goths, could admire such a style. The period is also referred to as the Middle Ages. Its

Gothic arch

central feature is a pointed arch. The phrase "height and light" accurately describes the effects of Gothic architecture.

Gothic Revival The renewed interest in the architecture and art of the 12th to 16th centuries during the 19th century in England, Continental Europe, and English colonies. John Britton's 1807 *The Architectural Antiquities of Great Britain* along with Walter Scott's novels fostered an interest in the medieval period. Augustus Welby Pugin was the advocate of the Gothic revival in England and decorated the interiors of the Houses of Parliament, London. See ROMANTIC EPOCH and ARTS AND CRAFTS MOVEMENT.

gouache (1) An opaque watercolor paint similar to poster paint. It dries lighter than it appears when wet. Also called TEMPERA (Italian). (2) Also a technique for making studies for oil paintings that was popular in the 18th century.

∞gout chair An 18th-century seat devised for sufferers of the painful ailment. The footstool could be pulled out from below the seat, so that the affected leg could rest on it in an extended position. When not in use, the trundle-like footrest retreated into the seat rail. See also GOUTY STOOL.

goût grec The fashion for ancient Greek artifacts and for Greek motifs. This preceded NEOCLASSICISM.

∞gouty stool A leg rest with an adjustable top on which a user suffering from inflammation could rest an afflicted leg. An 18th-century English design. See also GOUT CHAIR.

gouty stool

∞Governor Winthrop desk A typical fall-front writing surface of Colonial America (c. 1750), concurrent with Chippendale's English designs. The piece has two to four graduated drawers running the depth of the unit with bat-wing or willow brasses. Usually supported by bracket feet. The interior includes pigeonholes and a single or double tier of small drawers. The name is confusing because several governors named Winthrop lived in the 17th century.

Governor Winthrop desk

graffito ware Heavy pottery decorated with a primitively scratched or scribed design. See SGRAFFITO (GRAFFITO).

grain The fiber lines in wood. The figure, or pattern, inherent in the wood, which is the product of annual growth rings. The cells and pores of the tree.

grained furniture Inexpensive surface or volume-creating pieces of the late 19th century that were painted in a dark color and artificially finished to simulate oak wood. See GRAINING.

graining A painted imitation of the natural markings of wood. Often the appearance of an expensive or rare wood is simulated on a less expensive or painted surface.

grandfather chair A large, roomy, upholstered seat developed from the 17th-century WING CHAIR. Popular in the Queen Anne period.

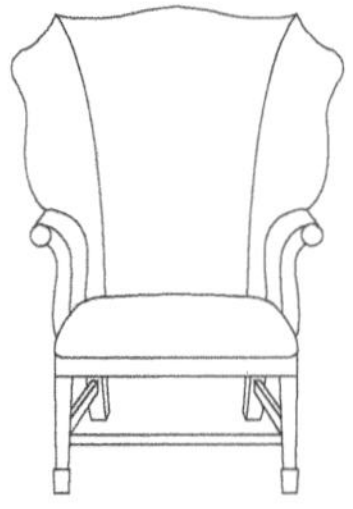

grandfather chair

grandfather (long case) clock A floor-standing timepiece with a wood enclosure that consists of a hood, a waist, and a base. The pendulum and the weights are protected inside the device, which usually stands over 6 feet high (1.8 m). Introduced into England after the Restoration, the stately pieces were popular in the 18th century.

grandmother clock A smaller-scaled, refined version of the grandfather clock. See GRANDFATHER (LONG CASE) CLOCK.

granite The hardest and most durable of building stones. A granular, crystalline rock of quartz, feldspar, and mica. See *Table 3.*

graphic arts The aesthetic activities, both analog and digital, that include drawing, engraving, etching, block-printing, and painting and that can involve text and image in creating an overall two-dimensional composition.

grandfather clock

grass cloth A wall-covering material glued onto a paper or fabric backing. The woven, coarse vegetable fibers create a horizontal effect and a nubby, irregular texture. The cloth may be simulated as a printed, embossed paper cloth or as a vinyl material.

grass mats Rugs of assorted shapes and sizes made of long blades of vegetal material braided or woven into either lacy openwork patterns or close weaves. Produced in geometric patterns or florals and in assorted natural colors or trimmed with dyed sheathing leaves.

grating See GRILLE.

gray goods Cloth as it comes from the loom without wet or dry finishing, before it is dyed. In the silk and rayon industries, this material is called greige goods.

great hall A large, two-storied central room used for dining and entertainment in the medieval castle and later in English country houses. The former was often open to the outside air, while the latter is entirely enclosed.

great monad or ovum mundi A circle with a horizontal S shape dividing it into two equal areas. This symbol represents the union of two basic and seemingly opposite principles: the material and the spiritual, or the feminine and the masculine. Similar to the Asian symbol for yin and yang.

great room A large enclosed space that serves as both a living room and a family room, common in American homes since the MCMANSION became popular in the 1990s. Often located in the center of a home and featuring a tall ceiling with exposed beams.

∞Grecian sofa The head portion is higher than the rest of the couch, and it curves over, as does the lower portion, or foot end. Also called an Empire couch. See RÉCAMIER.

Greco-Roman period The classical style from about 200 B.C.E. to C.E. 200. Its Romanized Greek forms, as unearthed in Pompeii and Herculaneum, are the basis of many 18th-century neoclassical designs.

Greek cross A geometric shape consisting of two lines of equal length bisecting each other at their centers.

Grecian sofa Greek cross

Greek key A fret design. A continuous band decoration of interlacing, hooked squares.

Greek Revival A renewed interest in the classical art and architecture of the area known as Hellas, in the 18th and 19th centuries. It overlaps with the Directoire, English Regency, and Empire periods.

green roof A top surface of a building constructed of multiple layers and covered with vegetation. The benefits of the ecological feature are water absorption, insulation, reduced indoor air temperature, and a nature-inspired aesthetic.

greenware Clay that has not been fired.

greige A neutral grayish-beige color.

grenadine A leno-weave fabric similar to marquisette but finer in texture. It is either plain or woven with dots or figures and is made of silk and cotton, silk and wool, or all cotton. See LENO WEAVE, and MARQUISETTE.

Grenfell cloth A closely woven, waterproof, windproof fabric. A sturdy twill weave.

greywood Artificially dyed English harewood, or, in America, dyed maple wood.

griffin A decorative device in the shape of a monster with the head and wings of an eagle and the body of a lion. In antiquity, the figure was associated with fire and thus often appears on friezes with candelabras. In heraldry, it represents wisdom and watchfulness. Popular in Gothic and Empire designs.

griffin

grille A metal lattice or trellis, usually brass, used in place of glass on cabinet doors. Often rosettes and other ornaments were added to the intersections of the crisscrossing wires or rods.

grisaille A monochromatic painting in grays or beiges, which gives the effect of a sculptured relief panel. Popular as a TROMPE L'OEIL painting technique for overdoors or overmantels in the Louis XVI period. Piat Joseph Sauvage was an outstanding painter of the technique. A grisaille may also serve as a first stage for an oil painting or as a model for an engraver.

groin The curved, sharp edge that is formed by the meeting of two vaulted surfaces.

groin rib An exposed intersection that is expressed (like a welt or bead) and that follows the perimeter line of the circular segment of a vaulted surface. See RIB and VAULT.

groin

groin rib

groove-and-rabbet joint See BAREFACED TONGUE JOINT.

grosgrain A heavy, ribbed fabric made of silk or rayon. The cords are close together and rounder than those of FAILLE. Used for draperies and ribbon decorations.

gros point A coarse tapestry effect produced by cross-stitching through net, canvas, or coarse linen. The embroidery threads are usually woolen, and there are approximately twelve stitches to the linear inch.

grotesques (grottesques) Decorations in antiquity, such as sphinxes or masks, that freely combined human forms with plant and animal forms. Winged females, mermaids, and fantastic monsters are some examples. The classical ornaments were rediscovered in grottos, hence the name *grotesques.* Raphael was one of the first Renaissance artists to make use of them. In Italian, grotteschi.

grotesques

grotto A cave or recess, either natural or artificial.

ground The rough wood framing on or in a wall, upon which paneling is applied.

ground color The background dye of a fabric, wallpaper, carpet, etc., on which other hues (the top colors) are applied. In screened or printed materials, the background is the ground color.

grout A liquid-like mortar or concrete that dries hard and solid. It is used as a filler or fixing agent for tiles and mosaics and between blocks of stones.

groutite A finer mortar than standard grout, used for small mosaic work such as contemporary tabletops, plaques, and decorative accessories. See GROUT.

guadamicil A leather tapestry or decorated hanging. Moroccan Arabs introduced the technique into Europe in the 11th century. Leather decorated in this way was first produced in Guadamicileria, Spain, in the 16th century. In the 17th and 18th centuries, leather tapestries were produced in France, the Netherlands, England, Germany, and Italy under such names as CORDOVAN LEATHER or MOROCCAN (MAROQUIN) TAPESTRY. See GILDED LEATHER.

guanacaste A tropical hardwood. See KELOBRA.

guéridon A small ornamental stand or pedestal. A round table popular in the Queen Anne period, adopted from France, where it appeared during the reign of Louis XIII. See TORCHÈRE.

∞**guéridon à crémaillère** A small round table or candleholder of the Louis XVI period. Adjustable to various heights by means of a toothed (crémaillère) support, which set into three supporting feet. Usually made of mahogany with a marble top.

guerilla design A purposely marginalized artistic movement that takes advantage of vacant lots or public spaces, where artists and designers create their works without official authorization.

∞**guerite** (French, sentry box) A high-backed, hooded armchair that enveloped the seated person and kept out drafts. Wicker versions in the 18th century were popular as pieces of garden furniture. Today this type of wicker furniture is a feature on the beaches of high-end resorts.

guéridon

guilloche A classical geometric band or border pattern of overlapping or interlacing circular forms. The circles themselves are sometimes filled with ornamental designs. Common in Renaissance and Victorian Renaissance Revival furniture.

guilloche

guinea holes or pockets Dished or scooped-out recesses in a gaming table that hold money or chips. An 18th-century English device. See DISHED.

gumwood A pink to reddish-brown wood with a heavy, strong texture. Its wild figures provide pleasing contrast to its ground color. If the wood is quarter-cut, it can produce a ribbon stripe veneer. The heartwood, or red gum, is used for cabinetmaking and for both indoor and outdoor architecture. The sapwood, however, called "sap gum," is not durable and is used only for plywood, furniture carcass lumber, and woodwork that receives a painted finish. See *Table 5.*

gusset A triangular insert between two pieces of fabric, to enlarge or strengthen the whole structure.

Gustavian A period in the 18th century named after Gustav III of Sweden, with interiors marked by white and light pastel colors. A Swedish variant of neoclassicism.

guttae Small conical ornaments under the TRIGLYPHS and MUTULES of classical Doric entablatures.

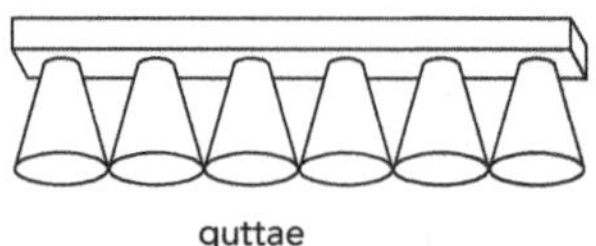
guttae

gypsum Hydrous calcium sulfate, which is used in making plaster of paris.

gypsum board or gyp board A wall material with a core of processed hydrated calcium sulfate (gypsum), encased in a tough, heavyweight paper. The smooth surface can be treated with paint, wallpaper, etc., after it has been primed. Comes in various thicknesses, ¼ inch to ½ inch (12.7 mm × 15.9 mm) and with squared, tapered, or beveled edges. The panels are typically 4 feet to 8 feet tall (122 cm × 244 cm). Also called plasterboard or drywall.

H hinge A swinging connector shaped like the aspirated consonant with one upright attached to the jamb and the other attached to the door. The horizontal piece works as a pivot; similar to an HL HINGE.

H stretcher A reinforcing element for chair, table, and case furniture legs. A wooden piece, or turning, connects each front leg with the leg immediately behind it; a crosspiece between the two connecting pieces forms an H.

hacha (Spanish) Squat element used in Mesoamerican ball games attached to a yoke around the waist; now popular with collectors and often featured in Southwestern-style interiors.

H stretcher

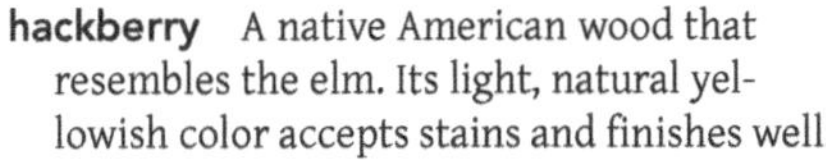

hackberry A native American wood that resembles the elm. Its light, natural yellowish color accepts stains and finishes well.

Hadley chest An early American (c. 1700), New England storage unit on four legs. The space-containing piece of furniture had one, two, or three drawers and would vary in height from 32 inches to 46 inches (80 cm–115 cm). The units were decorated with simple incised carvings and stained red, mulberry, or black. The owner's initials were often carved on the central panel. The top, body of drawers, and back were usually made of pine. See BLANKET CHEST and CONNECTICUT CHEST.

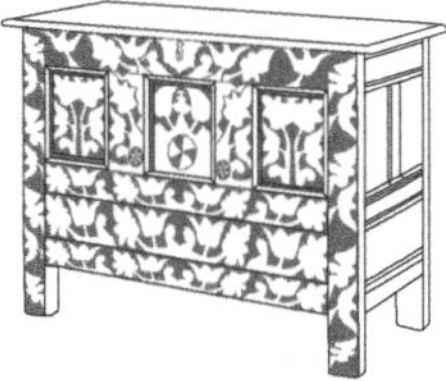

Hadley chest

haircloth A stiff, wiry fabric made of cotton with a horsehair, mohair, or human hair filling, woven plain, striped, or with small patterns. Durable, and is usually woven in narrow widths. Popular for upholstery in mid-19th-century England and America and used today for interlining and stiffening.

half column A rounded pilaster or a vertical structural element partially engaged in a wall. See ENGAGED COLUMN.

half turning See SPLIT SPINDLE.

∞half-headed bed A sleeping platform with short posts at the four ends and no canopy.

half-round slicing veneer A method similar to the rotary method for cutting flitches from the log. The shaving goes slightly across the annual growth rings, producing a wavy look.

half-timber A form of medieval house construction in which heavy beams and posts form the visible skeleton on the interior as well as the exterior. The areas between the wood construction were filled with wattle and daub, plaster, stone, or brick.

half-timber

half column

halftone An intermediate color between white and black in value.

hall chair Formal English seats from the 18th century, usually with decorative backs, originated by Manwaring. See LIGHT CHAIR and SIDE CHAIR.

hallmark The mark or stamp of official approval of a standard of purity, originally from the Goldsmith's Company of London. Now a mark of quality or genuineness that appears on metalwork and other items.

halogen A subcategory of incandescent lighting that emits a crisp, white light and that has a tungsten filament in the bulb filled with gas, creating a longer life than an incandescent bulb.

hall chair

halved joint A connection formed by two pieces of wood, the end of each sunk to half its depth. They are placed at right angles to each other; thus the projection of one fits into the sinking or groove of the other. This method is called "halving in."

hamman Turkish bath, a wet version of a sauna, associated with the Middle East but dating back to the Romans and now a feature of Islamic countries. A user progresses through a processional series of spaces, starting with an entry and transitional area, eventually relaxing in rooms devoted to cleansing, scrubbing, soaking, rinsing and massage.

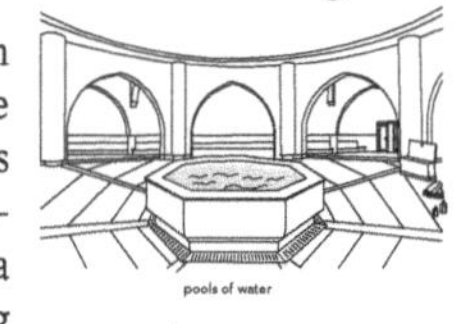

hamman

hammer brace The vertical member that supports the noncontinuous hammer beam.

hammer-beam roof A Gothic form of ceiling construction in which the rafters are supported by a horizontal beam which projects from the wall but does not join up with the corresponding projections from the opposite wall. The hammer beam is marked *A*.

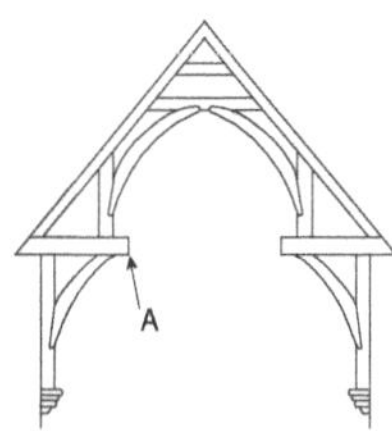

hammer-beam roof

hammer-beam truss An early English Renaissance form of roof support. A Tudor arch form in wood, each end of which rested on a large wooden bracket, which was usually carved.

hand The "feel" of the fabric, including subsidiary qualities including resilience, flexibility, and drapability. See FINISH.

hand blocking A method of printing a design on a surface. A design is carved or incised on a wood, linoleum, or other type of rectangular unit. The flat surface is the design; the gouged-out areas will not print. Paint or dye is rolled on the surface of the block with a brayer, and then pressure is exerted as it makes its imprint.

hand-blown glass Handmade vitreous ware using a blowpipe. Also known as "free-blown glass."

hand prints Wallpapers, murals, fabrics, accessories, etc., individually worked rather than a machine process.

hand screening A printing process for applying designs to paper, fabrics, vinyls, or wood. The design is prepared on silk meshes in wood frames. The silk is covered with a nonporous film which is cut away in the areas to be printed. A squeegee is rolled in paint and then over the screen, which is set down on the material to be printed. Each succeeding screen must be lined up to previous screens in order to create the intended design.

handkerchief table A triangular surface, designed to fit into the corner of a room. A second triangular top is hinged on so that, when the second triangle is flipped back, a rectangular table surface results.

handles Knobs or pulls used on furniture. In the Jacobean period in England, wood turnings and wrought iron were favored. Brass mounts were introduced during the William and Mary period. In France, mounts and other hardware were chased and engraved and made of ormolu. See HARDWARE.

handrail The top horizontal or inclined element (tubular or rectangular) into which the tops of banisters are set. It follows the incline of the stairs and serves as a support for persons taking the stairs.

hanging shelves Wall-attached units used for the display of books, plates, and china collections. Popular in the late 17th and through the 18th century in France and England, and in Japan. In the Victorian period, hanging whatnots or knickknack shelves were the vogue.

hanging shelves

hangings Draperies on tester beds or window curtains and draperies. Also wall tapestries or arras. The fabric embellishment may be made of damask, brocade, cotton, linen, wool, leather, etc. See ARRAS, GUADAMICIL, and WACHSTUCH-TAPETE.

hank A coiled yarn or fabric, or a unit of measurement.

hanok A traditional Korean house that dates back to the 14th century and the Joseon Dynasty. Shapes vary regionally, with the three common configurations being 1, L, or square shaped. Common features include thin screens, gravel and stone pathways, ladders, lofts, and a makgeolli shelf. Materials include wood, stone and earth, roof thatch or tile. Also called traditional Korean house or Joseon house. Falling out of favor after WWII as a residential choice, some now serve as boutique hotels.

hanok

hard core A rubble filling placed under a concrete ground floor and directly over the ground. It prevents the damp or moisture from rising.

hard flooring Material for horizontal surfaces made from subsidiary materials such as wood, bamboo, stone, ceramic, and glass. In contrast to any textiles such as rugs and carpets.

hard paste True porcelain made of kaolin or china clay. See CHINA and KAOLIN.

hardanger A drawn thread technique used to embellish fabric; a traditional handicraft.

hardboard Wood fibers are bonded with lignin, the natural bonding substance found in wood.

Hardoy chair A 20th-century version of the folding wood and canvas Italian officer's seat. Made of metal (not collapsible) and canvas or leather and originally manufactured by Knoll in 1947, and designed by Antonio Bonnet, Jorge Ferrari Hardoy, and Juan Urchin; also called the BKF chair.

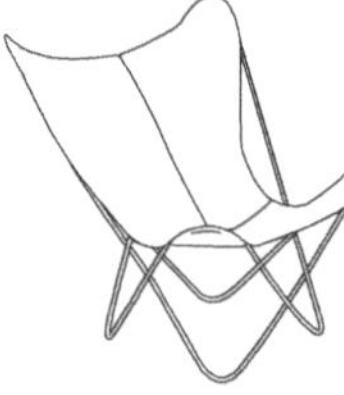
Hardoy chair

hardware In cabinetry, metal handles, pulls, escutcheons, hinges, decorative push plates, etc. Also called mounts. See ORMOLU and ESCUTCHEON.

hardwood A general term for the lumber of broad-leafed trees, in contrast to the conifers, which are termed softwoods. The name has no connection with the hardness of the wood. The furniture hardwoods are porous, and include oak, walnut, mahogany, beech, maple, and gum. See *Table 5.*

harewood A creamy white natural material (English sycamore) that dyes a silvery gray. It has a close, curly figure and a dense grain with a tendency to lose the dye on exposure to strong light. Plain, curly, fiddleback, finger roll, or heavy cross-fire figures are all possible in veneers depending upon the slicing method. Used in cabinetwork and turns a grayish green when stained with oxide of iron.

haricot (French, bean) A small crescent- or bean-shaped Louis XV table with cabriole legs and shallow drawers set into the curved apron.

harlequin table A complicated dressing-writing surface, of the end of the 18th century. It was designed with hidden compartments, pigeonholes, small drawers, etc.

harlequin table

harp A triangular instrument played by plucking its strings; stands on a heavy base with pedals that influence the tone. In furniture, it is the shaped metal piece that extends up from the lamp base and to which the lampshade is affixed. The harp is usually bowed in the center to allow the bulb to be screwed inside the socket to which the harp is attached.

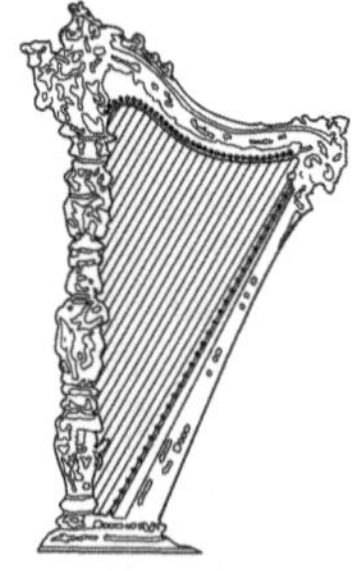
harp

harpsichord A piano-like instrument that preceded the pianoforte of the 18th century. The strings are plucked by means of quills attached to levers. It works on the same principle as the spinet and virginal.

∞Harvard chair An early American (17th century) version of a Gothic-type three-cornered seat made of wood turnings. A material celebration of the lathe.

Harvard frame A trademark name for a steel bed support. See BED FRAME and HOLLYWOOD FRAME.

harvest table A long, narrow, drop-leaf work surface. The legs may be straight or turned, and the flaps either have squared ends or are gently rounded. The design is usually associated with 18th-century American furniture.

hasp In a hinge lock, the hinged part that swings over the pin. In Spanish Gothic chests, the hasp was typically an ornate piece of metalwork.

hassock A heavy cushion or thick mat used as a footstool or ottoman.

hatching In drawing, a method of shading by means of close parallel lines. "Cross-hatching" is a field of crisscrossed sets of parallel lines.

∞haut relief In sculpture and ornament, high relief as opposed to bas-relief. See HIGH RELIEF.

hautelisse (French, high warp) A tapestry woven with an upright warp.

headboard The panel that rises above the mattress at the head of the bed. It can be made of wood or metal, upholstered, or inset with cane or leather panels, etc., simple or ornate, modern or traditional in style. A back support when a person is sitting up in bed. See FOOTBOARD.

header The end of a brick usually laid perpendicular to the face of the wall. It is used to tie two thicknesses of masonry together.

header bond In masonry, a brick pattern made up of the short end of bricks only. See HEADER.

headwall The architectural partition behind a patient's bed in healthcare facilities that contains heating, power, and data communications.

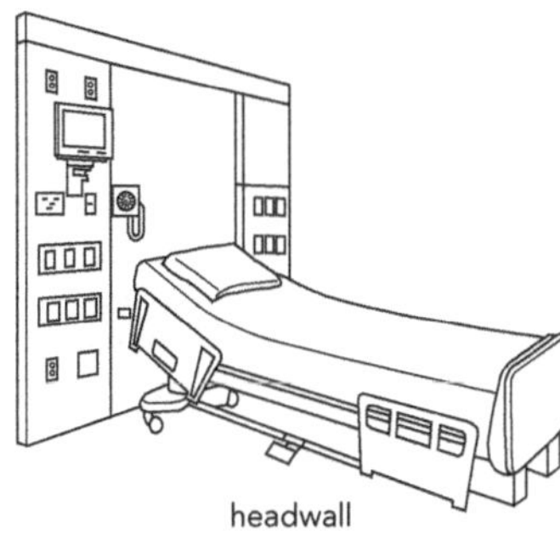

headwall

heart and crown A pierced motif carved on the cresting of a baluster chair of the late 17th century in England.

hearth The brick, stone, or tile pavement beneath the opening in a chimney and inside the fireplace; where the fire is made.

hearth

heart-shaped chair back A typical 18th-century Hepplewhite shield chair vertical that resembles the symbol of love.

heat-resistant glass Vitreous material that resists breakage when exposed to temperature extremes.

heat-strengthened glass Twice as resistant to breakage as the annealed material. It is only partially tempered.

heaving In wood finishing, a defect caused by partial softening of the undercoat that raises the surface of the top film.

helix A small spiral element beneath the abacus of a Corinthian capital.

helix

hellenistic (adj.) A period in ancient Greek art. Describes artwork under Alexander in the 3rd century B.C.E. In contrast to its predecessor, it is more elaborate, elegant, and delicate. This sometimes emotional form of art survived into the Roman period.

hemlock A wood that resembles white pine. It is strong, lightweight, and easy to work.

hemp A plant fiber that is a fast-growing biomass requiring little pesticide and is thus environmentally friendly and used for a variety of purposes including textiles, construction insulation, and fuel.

hemp sapele A fiber made from a large tropical African hardwood tree that produces a reddish-brown timber that can resemble mahogany.

henge Neolithic monument in a circular form, created with banks, ditches, and stone or timber. See TRABEATED CONSTRUCTION.

Herculon An olefin fiber produced by Hercules, Inc., used for indoor-outdoor carpeting, contract carpeting, and upholstery fabrics. Has a waxy feel and fair soil and stain repellancy. Highly heat-sensitive, it melts at temperatures above 200°F.

Hereke rug An extremely fine Oriental floor covering made of silk yarns and metallic threads hand-knotted into an intricate overall design.

∞herma A stone pillar, usually square, that tapers downward and is topped by a bust of Hermes. The Romans used it as a boundary marker and also as an outdoor decoration. Sometimes with no lower body parts other than prominent genitalia. Similar to a TERM.

∞hermes or herms See TERM.

herringbone Woodwork, brickwork, or stonework in which the material is laid at angles, so that the alternate courses point in opposite directions. Inlay, marquetry, and parquetry are sometimes done in this pattern.

herringbone

herringbone match Two V-match veneer or wood panels butted together to form a series of horizontal valleys and peaks.

hetre French for beechwood. A popular wood for fine 18th-century chairs.

hex sign A Pennsylvania Dutch motif for good luck, or to ward off evil spirits, usually a variation on a circle with a six-pointed star or another geometric motif enclosed in the circle. Painted on barns and houses and on chests, etc.; usually in bright, pure colors.

hickory A hard, tough, and heavy wood of the walnut family. It is not usually used decoratively, but it is elastic and bonds easily. Effective where thinness and strength are required; often used for bent and molded plywood. See *Table 5.*

HID lighting Acronym for HIGH-INTENSITY DISCHARGE, in which the electric current passes through a gas, usually mercury, metal halide, or high-pressure sodium. Provides illumination at reduced energy costs. See MERCURY HALIDE LAMP and SODIUM VAPOR LAMP.

hideaway bed Broad category of sleep furniture that includes several sub-types. See MURPHY BED and TRUNDLE BED.

∞hieracosphinx A recumbent sculpted Egyptian lion's form with the head of a hawk.

hieratic An abridged form of hieroglyphics used for religious writings.

hieroglyphs A system of picture writing and phonetic indications the ancient Egyptians used.

∞high daddy An 18th-century American tall chest unit of six or more drawers, graduated in size.

high relief Sculpture, the figures of which are carved out from the background to the extent of at least half their total mass, so that they appear almost detached or full round. See HAUT RELIEF.

highboy A tall chest of four or five drawers, on legs, with a cornice or pediment crown. It was originally mounted on a dressing table. Introduced from Holland into England during the William and Mary period and popular in America through the 18th century. The name might have been derived from the French *hautbois* (high wood).

high-gloss finish Wood furniture process that results in an external surface with a high sheen or shine. Normally requires a number of successive coats.

High Gothic Medieval architectural period (late 12th century to late 14th century). The pointed arch is the cornerstone of the religious architectural style that in the later period increasingly focused on refinements in addition to "height and light." Significant examples include Strasbourg Cathedral and Chartres Cathedral.

high-riser An armless and backless couch, usually 75 inches long (190 cm) by 30 to 36 inches deep (76 cm–91 cm), with a shorter and narrower mattress on a collapsed frame beneath it. The under-unit can be retracted and raised level with the upper mattress to sleep two people. When the under-unit is not in use, the high-riser has the footprint of an ordinary couch.

high-tech A term describing furniture and furnishings that are, or appear to be, constructed of factory or industrial parts and pieces: grids, pipes, metal stampings, expanded metals, vacuum-formed elements, etc. The design and its elements suggest commercial or heavy-duty use, although adapted to the home, office, or retail store.

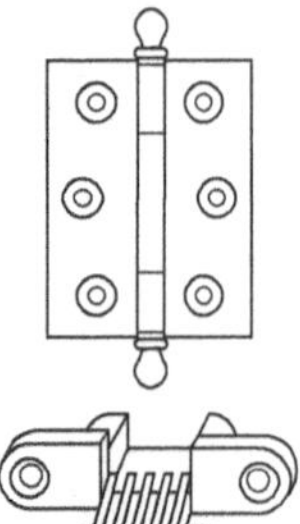

hinges

hinge A metal device consisting of two plates joined by a pin that pivots. Types include the BUTT HINGE, where the two plates are fixed inside the door or chest unit and only the pin is visible; the invisible hinge, which is concealed when in use; and the DOUBLE-ACTING HINGE, which makes it possible to swing a door almost a full 360 degrees. Some hinges are decorative and both plates are exposed for their beauty as well as their use.

hip In architecture, the angle formed by the meeting of two sloping roof surfaces, one of the most common type of roof structure. In furniture, the knee of the cabriole leg. The extensions above the chair rail in early-18th-century English cabriole-legged chairs were called hips.

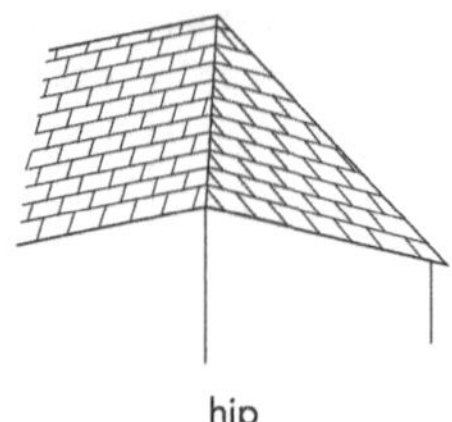

hip

hipster (adjective and noun) A trend in fashion, personal identity, and interior design. Countercultural but not oppositional, its followers deny being part of a trend and follow the creed "I don't care, but I look fabulous." Related to hippie, punk, and grunge, its attributes include quirky, trendy, and urban. This conflation of interests has resulted in new looks for coffee shops, hotels, and grocery stores. Design strategies include mismatching, artisanal appreciation, industrial touches, and nostalgia. Related to upcycling, it's the new bohemian look.

Hispano-Mauresque Spanish art influenced by Moorish (North African Islamic) designs. It was a part of the Gothic or Medieval period in Spain and lasted for several hundred years. Typical of the Moorish craftsman's influence on Spanish architecture: horseshoe arches, pierced stonework, tracery, and rich surface decoration.

historiated Ornamented with figures, animals, etc., which are representational or symbolic. Historiated initials were a popular ornament in medieval manuscripts.

Hitchcock chairs A popular style of seat LAMBERT HITCHCOCK developed in the early-to-mid 18th century but not realizing mass popularity until the mid 20th century. See *Designers and Architects.*

HL hinge A provincial movable connection usually made of forged or wrought iron. The design resembles an uppercase I attached by a short crosspiece to an uppercase L. The pivot joint between the I and the L creates the H in the name. See H HINGE.

hoarding A psychological condition marked by a deleterious tendency to collect and accumulate an overabundance of items. A pathological extreme of collecting that is the subject of multiple voyeuristic reality television shows.

hock leg Also called broken cabriole. The curve is broken below the knee on the inner side. The sides of the knees are sometimes ornamented with carved spiral scrolls called ears. See CABRIOLE LEG.

hock leg

hogarth chair A decorated Queen Anne seat with heavy knees and modified cabriole legs. The hoop back is usually hollow-crested and has a pierced splat.

holistic In design, an approach that views systems as a whole, with each depending on the other to exist rather than as a collection of autonomous parts and individually made decisions.

Holland shade cloth A plain cotton or linen textile finished with sizing or starch and oil to make it opaque; used to make window shades.

hollow wall A partition containing an air space, the facing and backing bonded together with masonry units. See CAVITY WALL.

holly, white A native American wood. The whitest and least grained wood available, used for marquetry, inlays, and stringing and banding. It turns brown with age and exposure.

Hollywood bed Sleep furniture without a footboard, the spring and mattress set on a metal bed-frame unit, often equipped with casters. A headboard can be attached to the frame, or the headboard can be attached to the wall and the frame then hooked on to it. The size varies from twin to king. See HARVARD FRAME and BED FRAME.

hom The Assyrian "tree of life" pattern.

homasote Brand of CELLULOSE-based fiber wall board, a material sheet made from recycled paper and compressed under high heat and pressure.

home theater A configuration including a large flat-screen television, DVD player, DVR, internet connection, MP3 dock, stereo receiver, and speakers to simulate the effect of a motion picture theater in a domestic setting.

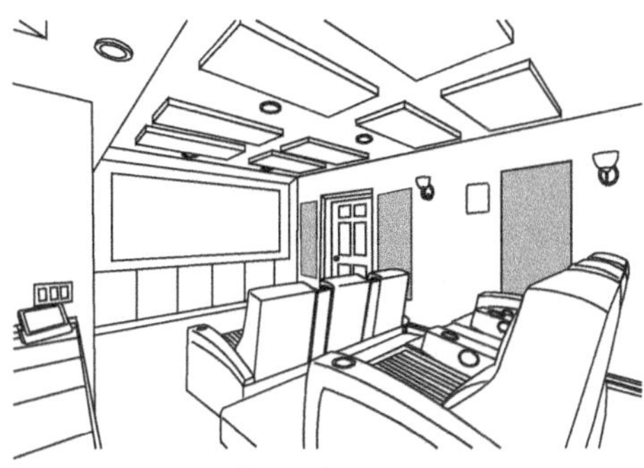

home theater

homespun Originally a fabric loomed by hand domestically, but now the name of a loose, rough fabric with a tweedy look that is obtained by using unevenly spun fibers of cotton, rayon, or wool. Used for curtains and upholstery.

honeysuckle A Greek decoration resembling a conventionalized fanlike arrangement of petals. Often called the anthemion. It appears on Renaissance furniture as a carved enrichment. A swag of the vegetal motifs can decorate panels, girandoles, furniture, etc.

honeysuckle

hood In furniture, the case enclosing the dial and works of a grandfather or long case clock. Also see HOODED TOP. In architecture, a sheltering overhang.

hooded top The rounded pinnacle of cabinets, especially those of the early Queen Anne period (early-18th-century England). Also called domed, curved, rounded, or semicircular. See BONNET TOP.

hoof foot See CLOVEN FOOT, DOE'S FOOT LEG, and PIED DE BICHE.

hooked rug A pile-surfaced floor covering made of loops of yarn or strips of cloth pushed through a canvas backing. Color and patterns are unlimited. Made by machine as well as by hand. See BRAIDED RUG.

hoop-back chair A seat in which the uprights and top rail of the back form a continuous curve. First appears in the Queen Anne period.

hoop-back chair

hope chest See CASSONE and CEDAR CHEST.

hopper light The upper section of a casement window that is hinged at the bottom and opens inward.

hopper window A casement opening that is hinged along its bottom edge so that it opens out and backward, usually part of a larger unit of fenestration.

horror vacui (Latin) Fear or dislike of undecorated space.

horse A simple vertical support for a trestle table. It may be an inverted V or a shaped piece.

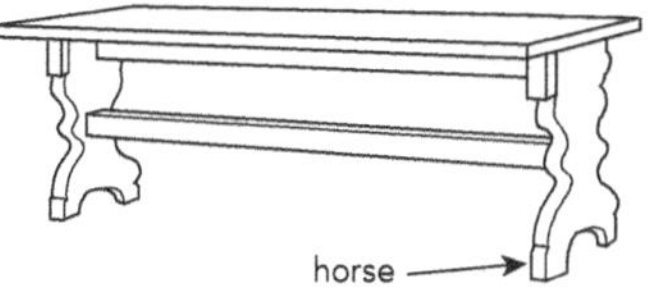

∞**horse screen** (English) A cheval screen. A fire protection device with two bracketed feet. See CHEVAL SCREEN.

horsehair A furniture covering woven from the threadlike outgrowth of the epidermis of the ungulate mammal's tail and mane. Hepplewhite used it as an upholstery material; it was prominent in the Victorian period and on Biedermeier seats. Stiff, sturdy, and generally dark if not black in color.

horseshoe arch A structural element with a curve greater than a semicircle or 180 degrees, prominent in Moorish, Spanish, and Islamic architecture and designs. See ISLAMIC and ISLAMIC ARCH.

horseshoe table A curved U-shaped dining surface, about 30 inches wide (76 cm) that was popular in the late 18th century. See HUNT TABLE and WINE TABLE.

hot desking Facilities management strategy in which more than one worker is assigned to a workstation or in which workplaces are assigned on an as-needed basis. See HOTELLING and NOMADS.

hot tubs Originally, large vats made of redwood or other closely grained woods that were filled with steaming water and used out-of-doors by one or several persons. The soaking device now may have seats inside. Some are equipped with Jacuzzi-like attachments that circulate streams of hot water around the inside of the tub, like a whirlpool. Also available in molded plastics, metal, and porcelain. Can be used indoors as well as out. See JACUZZI.

hôtel A French townhouse; an *hôtel particulier* is a private residence; an *hôtel de tourisme* is for paying guests; an *hôtel de ville* is a town hall.

hotelling A space-planning strategy in which workers, such as salespeople, do not have assigned places but use private spaces designated for multiple people in succession. Can refer to workstations or private offices; a method of supporting unassigned seating; related to HOT DESKING. Also see NOMADS.

hothouse A greenhouse. See CONSERVATORY and ORANGERY.

houndstooth A fabric and wallpaper design. A medium-sized broken-check motif often used in tweeds.

hourglass base A typically Regency base for stools, benches, and sometimes chairs. Made up of two curved elements, one set on top of the other to create a rounded X shape.

hourglass base

housed joint A socketed connection as opposed to a butt joint. One piece is grooved out to fit into the grooved part of the other.

∞housse The French term for slipcover.

howdah or houdah (Hindi) An ornate carriage used to ride an elephant; often designed like a piece of furniture.

∞huchiers-menuisiers (French, hutch carpenters) Makers of simple furniture of the early Renaissance period.

howdah

Hudson River School A 19th-century (1825–1870) American group of romantic landscape painters who glorified nature, many of whom were active in the riverine areas of New York State. Thomas Cole, Frederick Edwin Church, and Albert Bierstadt were major artists of the group.

hue A color. A tint is a color with white added. A shade is a color with black added.

humanism A mode of thought that rejects religion and focuses on innate personal and collective value; a focus on design for the domestic and civic realms instead of the ecclesiastical world.

humpback sofa GEORGIAN multiple-seating element with a prominent rounded back whose profile resembles a camel.

hung ceiling A horizontal plane installed below another by setting a new series of cross strips of wood or metal lower than the existing ceiling, then sheathing this framework with acoustic tiles, plasterboard, plastic panels, special light units, etc. Also called a suspended ceiling. See DROPPED CEILING.

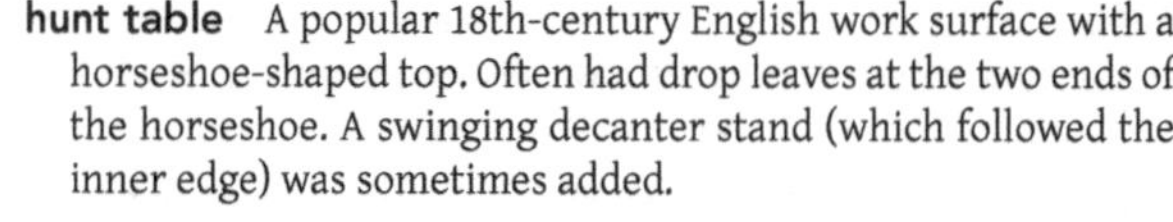

hunt table A popular 18th-century English work surface with a horseshoe-shaped top. Often had drop leaves at the two ends of the horseshoe. A swinging decanter stand (which followed the inner edge) was sometimes added.

∞hunting chair An 18th-century Sheraton seat design with a special wood strip or footrest in front.

hurricane lamp A tall, glass cylinder shade set over a candlestick to protect the flame, introduced in the late 17th century and used through the 18th century. In current décor, hurricane lamps are often used in pairs trimmed with prisms, and flame-shaped bulbs have replaced the candles. Similar to the 19th-century GIRANDOLE or LUSTRE.

Hushalon A wool felt material used for wall covering, with acoustical and thermal insulating properties. Moth- and flameproof, soil-resistant, and colorfast.

husk ornament A decorative element representation of the dry outer covering of oats when ripe. The spreading of the external protection into two halves makes it possible to create a chain-like pattern by having husk drooping from husk. This motif was popular in England in the neoclassical revivals. It was used as an inlay design, as a composition ornament of walls and ceilings in painted decoration, and by Wedgwood on his Jasper ware. See BELLFLOWER ORNAMENT.

∞hutch or huche *Huche* is Old French for bin or chest. Originally a Gothic chest. In current usage, a cabinet or cupboard placed over a buffet unit. The cupboard part may be left completely open or have doors on two sides with an open shelving area in the middle. See MÉNAGÈRE.

hutch or huche

hutong (Chinese) Refers to narrow alleys in historic neighborhoods; also indicates city areas formed of traditional courtyard houses.

hydria A Greek three-handled water jar.

hypocaust A plenum under the floor of a Roman building that distributes heat.

hypostyle hall A space with many rows of columns supporting a flat roof. A feature of Egyptian temples, Islamic mosques, and modern convention centers. See MOSQUE.

I beam A rolled steel structural element shaped like the capital letter I with pronounced top and bottom strokes.

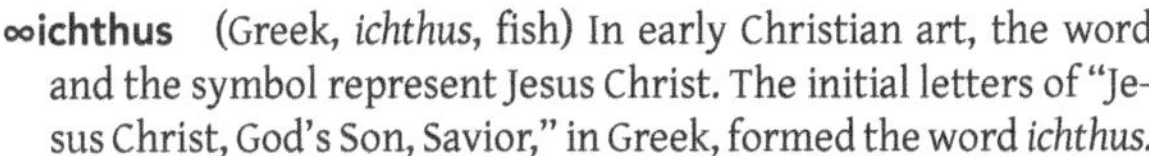
I beam

IAQ Acronym for INDOOR AIR QUALITY.

IBC Acronym for INTERNATIONAL BUILDING CODE.

Iberian Refers to the peninsula where Spain and Portugal are located.

∞ichthus (Greek, *ichthus*, fish) In early Christian art, the word and the symbol represent Jesus Christ. The initial letters of "Jesus Christ, God's Son, Savior," in Greek, formed the word *ichthus.*

icon or ikon (Greek, *eiko—n*, image) A religious painting of Christ, Mary, or a saint, typically on a rigid panel. The sacred image prompts a relationship between the devotee and the represented religious figure.

iconoclasm Purposeful destruction of art or architecture, often in the name of religion.

Iconoclastic period Era of the early 8th century, when Byzantine Emperor Leo III prohibited sculptural representations of humans or animals because he feared that statues foster paganism and idolatry. The resultant Byzantine and Near Eastern decoration emphasized floral and geometric patterns in rich color and texture.

iconograph A ground plan; a horizontal section.

ICU Acronym for INTENSIVE CARE UNIT.

ideograph The illustration of an idea, word, or object.

ikat Textile-dyeing technique of resist-dyeing on warp or weft fibers, resulting in a colored pattern. Threads are bound and resist-dyed before being woven into the fabric.

illumination The medieval art of hand-decorating manuscripts with scrolls, arabesques, foliage, etc. in rich color and gold and silver. Religious manuscripts were often enriched with colored illumination. See HISTORIATED.

illusionism A method of representation that renders its technologies undetectable. See TROMPE L'OEIL.

I.M. Acronym for the INNER MEASUREMENT OF A UNIT as opposed to the outer measurement (O.M.). The I.M. of a hollow pipe is the diameter measured between opposite points on the inside surface; the O.M. is the diameter measured between opposite points on the outside surface. See O.M.

image d'Épinal A simple reproduced representation used as decoration, in a variety of media. Originally religious in nature, many were patriotic and related to WWI. A genre of naive, traditional, sentimental imagery. Also imagerie d'Épinal and Épinal prints.

imari A type of Japanese pottery with blue and iron-red enamel and gold.

imbricate To place in overlapping tiers or to give a fish-scale-like appearance. A technique used for tile roofs and on columns, walls, etc.

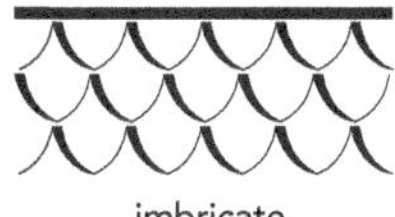
imbricate

imbuya Brazilian walnut. The wood varies in color from olive to a deep, rich, red-brown color and is used for veneering fine-grade furniture. It is fine-grained, hard, and heavy.

impasto An oil-painting technique Titian developed. Thin layers of opaque pigment and oil glazes are used to create a depth of color. When many layers are applied that make the paint thick or lumpy, and the brushstrokes are evident, the painting is described as "heavily impasted."

impluvium The cistern or pool in the atrium of a Roman house, used to collect rainwater.

impost The member just below the springing line of an arch, on which the arch rests.

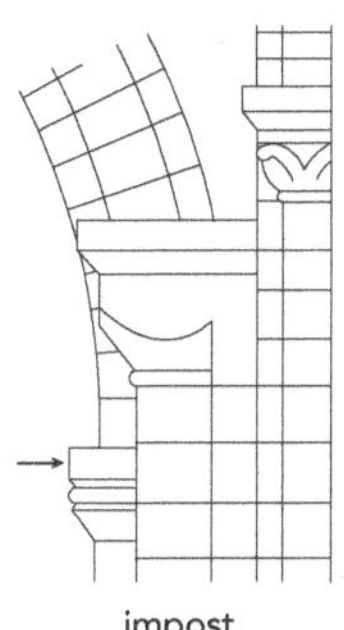
impost

Impressionism A 19th-century modern art movement. The aim of its promoters was to achieve greater naturalism by analysis of tone and color and the rendering of light on surfaces. Paint was often dabbed on in bright colors, even in the shadows. Major Impressionists were Claude Monet, Camille Pissarro, and Alfred Sisley. Although different in outlook, it was contemporary with the design movement of Arts and Crafts.

∞in antis Columns between the projecting side walls of a building.

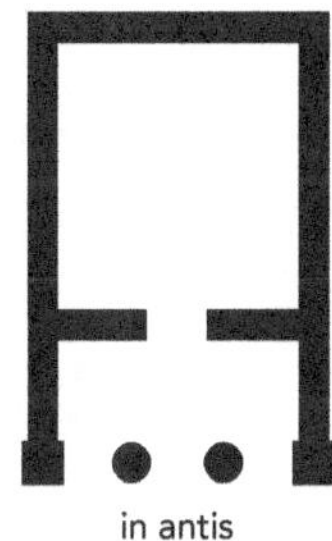
in antis

in situ (Latin, *in situ*, in place) Work done directly on the locale of the job and not made in a workshop for later installation.

incandescent light A sealed glass container with a filament that produces light (and heat) when an electric current passes through it.

∞incarnadine A 17th-century English term to describe a light crimson to a pale fleshy pink color.

incised The opposite of relief carving. The pattern is produced by cutting or etching into the material. The design is engraved below the surface. See INTAGLIO. See CHARLES L. EASTLAKE, JR. in *Designers and Architects.*

incised lacquer Several coats of a hard finish are applied to create a certain thickness. A design is then cut or carved into the built-up thickness. This form of decoration was used on Chinese-style furniture and screens.

India papers Chinese sheafs imported into Europe in the mid-17th century by means of the Dutch, French, and English East India companies; hence the name "India papers." Also called Japan papers. See CHINESE WALLPAPER.

India print A cotton fabric with a Persian or Moghul pattern hand-blocked in bright colors on a white or natural ground. It is used for draperies, bed throws, wall hangings, etc.

Indian red A soft reddish-brown or terra-cotta color, often used on American provincial pine furniture in the 18th century.

Indian rugs Oriental floor coverings handmade in the region of the subcontinent, usually of Persian design. They frequently have flora, vein-like patterns, or tree of life designs.

Indienne fabrics The French interpretation of India print cottons made during the late 17th and the 18th centuries. See TOILES D'INDY.

indirect lighting Illumination arrangement in which light is directed up to the ceiling or another reflective surface, from which it bounces back to softly illuminate the general area.

indoor air quality (IAQ) The relative health of the gaseous substances of an interior environment. The measurement is negatively impacted by off-gassing of VOCs, including formaldehyde from carpet, paints, ceiling tiles, adhesives, and furnishings.

indoor-outdoor carpets See HERCULON and POLYPROPYLENE-OLEFIN.

influencer A lifestyle expert on social media who assists customers in making purchasing decisions. Includes cuisine, fashion, interior design, mixology, and entertainment, often in combination. Some design gurus cover niche subjects and act as official or unofficial brand ambassadors as a means of marketing, paid or unpaid. Their sway represents a decline in the efficacy of traditional advertising and design. Their authority is by way of personal image, knowledge, reputation, and style. There are subcategories of mega, macro, micro, and nano-influencers.

infographic Visual representations of information, data, or knowledge, at a midpoint between pure text and pure image or symbol. The imagery may include symbols, charts, and small amounts of text. The goal is to create striking, engaging, and effective graphics, which leverage the legibility of signage and wayfinding and present complex information quickly and clearly. For interiors, the effects are evident in reception areas, airports, hospitals and retail. The shift from text to visual is transforming how designers communicate to clients.

inglenook A wide, recessed chimney opening usually furnished with benches at either side. A Scottish term for chimney corner.

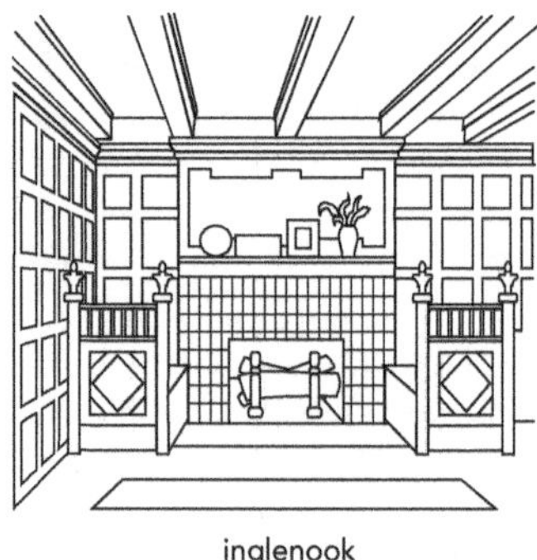

inglenook

ingrain A reversible, flat-woven wool or wool and cotton carpet made on a jacquard loom. The ground color on one side becomes the top or design color on the reverse side. Ingrain is also a woven, multicolored fabric with a flat weave. The threads are dyed before they are woven. See JACQUARD.

injection mold Manufacturing process using a form made of aluminum or steel. Thermoplastic or thermosetting plastic is forced into the cavity with an injector; the material assumes the form of the cavity when it dries or hardens. A technically complicated process, used for prototypes and mass manufacturing.

inlay A technique in which a design is cut out of the surface to be decorated and then filled in with contrasting materials cut to fit exactly into these openings. The contrast of color or materials creates the decoration. Inserts may be of wood veneer, metal, mother-of-pearl, ivory, etc. See BOULLE WORK, CERTOSINA, INTARSIA, and MARQUETRY.

innerspring mattress A 1924 innovation in which the thick sleeping pad has a center core of springs for buoyancy and resilience, with protective upholstered coverings on either side of it. These pads keep the felted cotton, short-fiber cotton, curled hair, or other soft material from becoming entwined in the coils. A tough fabric, like ticking, encases the whole unit. The construction, methods of tying or casing the coils, quilting material, etc. vary.

inset pilaster A flat half column set against a flush surface, usually at the front corners of a chest, cabinet, or other case piece.

Institutional Recycling Network (IRN) A micro-level effort at reusing furnishings and materials within one organization or commercial venture.

∞insula An ancient Roman apartment block housing multiple families and tenants, occupied by the lower and middle classes.

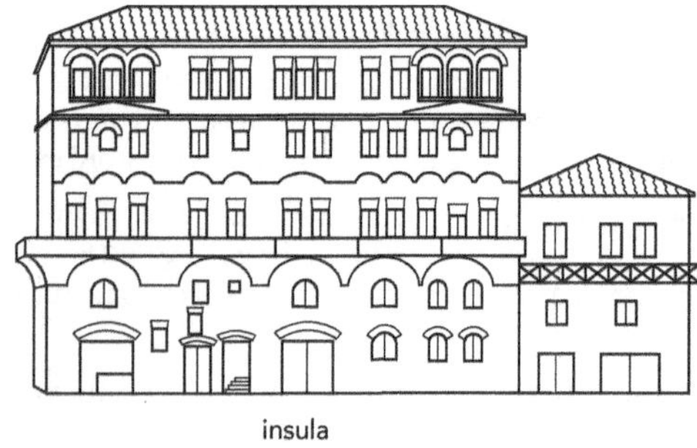

insula

insulating glass Window material that has been double or triple glazed, sometimes with an additional non-vitreous interstitial material.

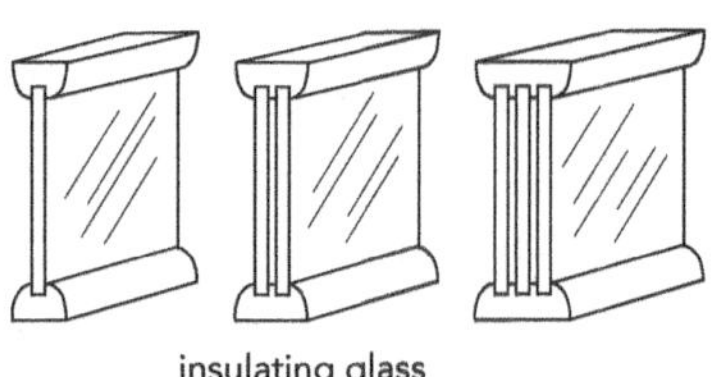

insulating glass

insulation The application of materials that keep in warmth, keep down sound vibration, and generally protect a structure from the outside elements. May be built into the building or added as facing materials to the inside surfaces. See EMISSIVITY.

intaglio Designs cut out of a surface, leaving a relief in reverse. The finished design is below the plane that has been worked upon.

intaglio engraving Distinguished from other metal plate engraving techniques by the printing process used. The ink lies in the engraved furrows, rather than on the smooth surface. A piece of paper is dampened and laid on the plate, and both are rolled through a mangle-like heavy press. The damp paper is forced into the furrows and picks up the ink. When the paper is dry, the engraved inked lines stand up in relief. See AQUATINT, DRYPOINT ENGRAVING, ETCHING, LINE ENGRAVING, and MEZZOTINT.

intarsia Incised work inlaid with contrasting materials to form a type of mosaic. Italian designers in the early Renaissance period used shell, bone, and ivory inserts. Also called tarsia. See CERTOSINA, INLAY, INTARSIO, and NONSUCH FURNITURE.

intarsio Pictures executed in wood veneers and inlays. A highly sophisticated form of inlay.

intarsio

intelligent house Domestic structure that relies on sustainable practices to be cool in summer and warm in winter.

intensive care unit (ICU) A specialized area in hospitals that provides 24-hour care for seriously injured or ill patients; the collaboration of designers and healthcare professionals results in ways to improve patient outcomes in these areas.

interior design A multifaceted profession in which creative and technical solutions are applied within a structure to achieve a built interior environment. These solutions are functional, enhance the quality of life and culture of the occupants, and are aesthetically attractive (as defined by the National Council of Interior Design Qualification).

interlaced chair back An elaborate design of strap or ribbon-back similar in character to fretwork. It was used in late-18th-century French furniture and in Chippendale and Hepplewhite pieces.

interlaced chair back

International Building Code (IBC) The work of the International Code Council (ICC) is to preserve public health, safety, and welfare of the built environment and its construction processes. It is intended not to replace but to work in tandem with local, state, and national codes. Unlike traditional codes which are the result of decades of iterations, the IBC aims for ease of use and embraces new technology as part of its global strategy.

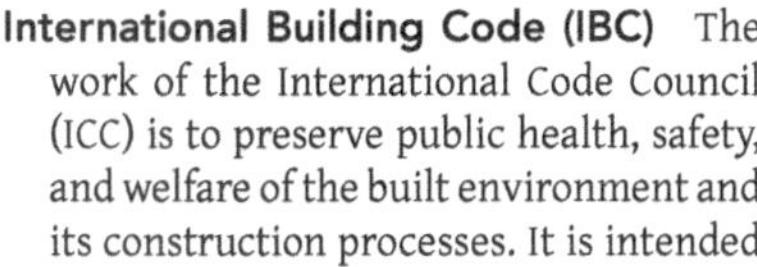

International Energy Conservation Code Building regulation established by the International Code Council to promote power efficiency through smart building practices, conservation, and reduced energy use.

International WELL Building Institute (IWBI) A global approach to health, with an organization leading it, that fosters a situation in which buildings and the people who use them are poised to thrive. The associated WELL Building Standards were released in 2014. The organization and its products support and advocate for comfort, health and wellness, problem solving, brainstorming, support and advice, and human comfort.

International Style An aspirational moniker for a strand of MODERNISM that emphasizes global similarities; the opposite of regionalism.

interpenetrations In Gothic vaulting, moldings intersecting each other and appearing to run through one another.

in-glaze decoration A technique used in ceramics where the embellishment is applied to the surface of the glaze before firing.

intonaco The final layer of wet plaster upon which the fresco artist works. The final coat is applied only to the area that the painter will be able to cover before the plaster dries. See FRESCO.

intrados The inner curve or surface of an arch. The soffit of an arch. See EXTRADOS.

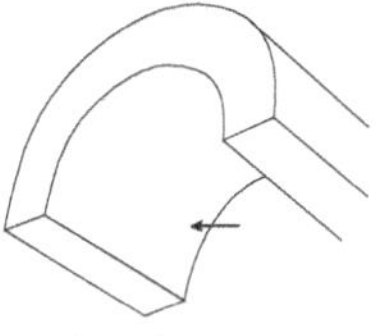
intrados

inverted cup A detail in the wood-turned shaped legs of the WILLIAM AND MARY PERIOD in England resembling an inverted drinking vessel.

invisible architecture Entities that contribute to a spatial ambience, such as light, sound levels, and scents, that are neither material or tactile but are detectible by hearing, seeing, and smelling.

Ionic order A classical category of architecture and decoration. The spiral-shaped volute or scroll is characteristic of the capital. The Romans proportioned the columns at nine diameters high.

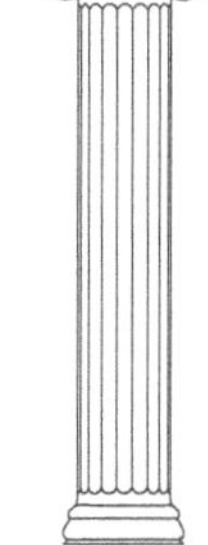
Ionic order

ireme Also called African teak or black afara. Native to Ghana, ireme is a pale yellow to light brown, faintly ribbon-striped wood. It has noticeable rays and an intermediate grain.

iridescent fabrics Textiles with contrasting colored warps and filling yarns, producing a changeable colored effect, as in TAFETTA.

Irish Chippendale Mahogany furniture made in Ireland in the mid 18th century, based on the published drawings of the cabinetmaker. The furniture lacked the level of execution and lightness of the original pieces. Lion masks and paw feet are often found on Irish Chippendale furniture.

Irish point A net curtain material with an appliqué design similar to DUCHESS.

IRN Acronym for INSTITUTIONAL RECYCLING NETWORK.

iroko A durable tropical African wood sometimes mislabeled African oak or teak. It bleaches on exposure, though the natural color ranges from light yellow-brown to deep reddish-brown. Iroko is used as a veneer wood and is also called KAMBALA.

ironwood A collective term for many varieties of exceptionally hard wood, such as the South American olive wood. The American variety is a brown-gray wood that is hard, heavy, and strong.

ironstone A type of semi-vitreous ware.

∞Isabellina The Spanish term for the Gothic phase of minute, detailed, patterned design. The Renaissance phase was termed PLATERESCO. MANUELINO is the Portuguese counterpart of Isabellina.

isinglass Thin, translucent sheets of mica that were sometimes used for fenestration in 18th- and 19th-century homes.

Islamic A variety of religious and secular designs related to Muslim populations around the world, especially North Africa, the Middle East, Spain, and Southeast Asia. There are many regional variations.

Islamic arch A semicircular pointed arch, often extending further than 180 degrees; also known as a horseshoe arch; in Spain, also known as a MOORISH ARCH.

island A designed unit that stands free and independent, away from walls, and can be approached from any direction. It can be furniture, a freestanding piece of equipment, or a design made of multiple parts.

Islamic arch

island bed A sleeping unit placed in the middle of a room and not in contact with any of the perimeter walls. A designer may back the head of the bed with a screen or wall of cabinets or shelves, making it less of an island bed.

Islon A trademark name for an all-nylon fabric with the soft look of velvet. It has body and is drapable, soil-resistant, durable, and color stable.

isometric projection A scalable three-dimensional view of an object that gives the impression of the object being in perspective. Line lengths are true to the original, although angles are changed. The plan is first set at an angle, and vertical lines are projected from it in scale. Not to be confused with AXONOMETRIC.

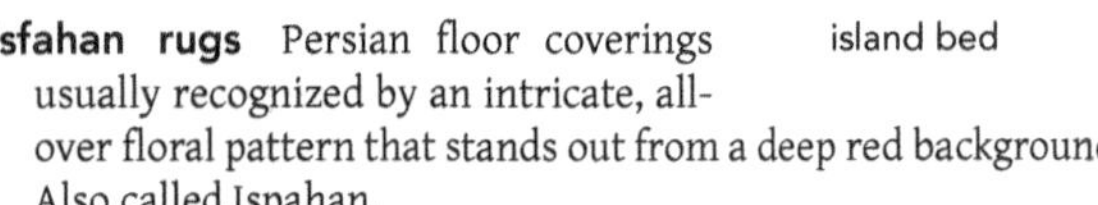
island bed

Isfahan rugs Persian floor coverings usually recognized by an intricate, all-over floral pattern that stands out from a deep red background. Also called Ispahan.

Italian neoclassical style A late-18th-century furniture style inspired by Greek and Roman antique designs. The rediscovery of Pompeii and the contemporary popularity of Louis XVI in France, and the Adam brothers, Hepplewhite, and Sheraton in England, prompted an Italian variant with its own unique flair.

Italian Provincial style A misnomer for modern Italian versions of late-18th- and early-19th-century popular Directoire and Empire works, as updated and adapted to contemporary tastes and mass production techniques. Popular in the United States in the 1950s and 1960s. Also called the PALLADIAN style.

ivory The tusks of elephants used for decorative inlay work and carving. It is a rare material that has been imitated in plastics. Trade in tusks from African and Asian elephants is illegal.

ivy A decorative leaf design, the symbol of friendship. It was sacred to Bacchus and therefore appears on many ancient vases. Usually broad and five-lobed, this design often appears at the end of long shoots in lance-like forms.

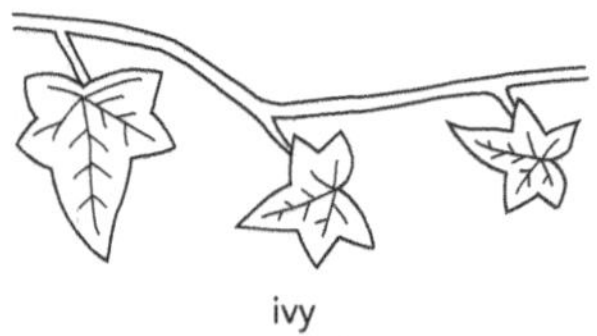
ivy

IWBI Acronym for INTERNATIONAL WELL BUILDING INSTITUTE

jabot A ruffle or frill. The cascading side pieces of a swag.

jabot

jacaranda See ROSEWOOD, BRAZILIAN.

∞jackknife sofa bed See SOFA BED.

Jacobean ornament Bands of molding applied to furniture in geometric patterns to create a paneled effect; elaborate turnings on stretchers, legs, and backs; chronologically related to the 17th century.

Jacobean period The era (1603–1649) in English art, architecture, and decorative arts that extends over the reigns of James I and Charles I. Stylistically the era merges TUDOR PERIOD designs and motifs with the RENAISSANCE and hints at BAROQUE developments to come.

jacquard In carpeting, the pattern-control device on the continuous Wilton loom. Joseph-Marie Jacquard in Brussels, Belgium, invented the mechanism that was adapted for the Wilton loom in 1825.

jacquard weave A textile construction with intricate, multicolored patterns produced on the type of loom created by Joseph-Marie Jacquard in the early 19th century. Damasks, tapestries, and brocades are all in the jacquard family. See JOSEPH-MARIE JACQUARD in *Designers and Architects*.

∞Jacquemart and Bénard French wallpaper manufacturers from 1791 to 1840. They were successors to Réveillon.

Jacuzzi A trademarked plumbing system designed to produce strong jets of water that circulate through a tub or vat. The powerful circulating movement in a hot-water bath relaxes aching muscles and encourages blood circulation. See HOT TUBS.

jalee In India, the decorated pierced marble or stonework such as was used in the Taj Mahal and other monuments of the Mughal elite. See MUGHAL. Also see EDWARD DURRELL STONE in *Designers and Architects*.

jalee

jalousie A French word for louvers, similar to Venetian blinds. A room equipped with the devices is fenestrated with louvered windows or panels. See LIGHTING LOUVERS.

jalousie window An opening with numerous horizontal slats of glass that tilt to a desired angle, in the manner of a Venetian blind. The multitude of panels decreases the window's visibility and renders it stronger to resist wind loads. See AWNING WINDOWS.

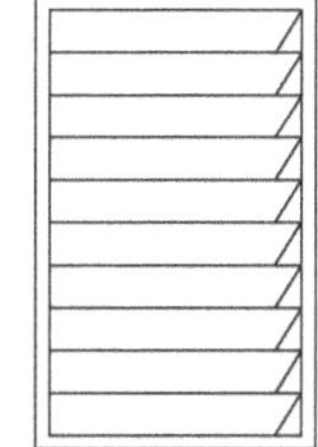

jalousie window

jamb The interior side of a door or window frame.

janissary Describes Turkish or Turkish inspired music (and other cultural forms); Byzantine, Ottoman, and Turkish interiors often include janissary objects, such as an OTTOMAN.

japanning An 18th-century finishing process. Furniture and metalwork were enameled with shellac, the decoration shaped in relief and painted in color and gilt. The technique imitated the brilliant lacquered work of the East Asian archipelago imported by the Dutch into Europe in the 17th century. Also refers to any European lacquer inspired by Asian techniques. See LACQUER. Also see MARTIN BROTHERS in *Designers and Architects*.

japonisme The European cult of Japanese-inspired artworks, especially of the Arts and Crafts period. See ARTS AND CRAFTS MOVEMENT.

japonisme

jardinière (French) A plant container or stand made of wood, metal, or porcelain. The piece reached the height of its popularity during the latter part of the 18th century in France and England.

jardinière velvet A silk short-piled textile having several depths of uncut loops set against a damask or silk background. It is usually a multicolored pattern resembling a flower arrangement against a satin background. Originally produced in Genoa, Italy.

jaspé In carpeting, irregular warp stripes of two hues of a color in a surface yarn, in either a patterned or plain fabric. In fabric, a streaked or mottled effect produced by an uneven dyeing of warp threads. It resembles the jasper stone.

jasper An opaque quartz; it can be red, yellow, or brown. The opaque silica is used on vases, seals, and snuff boxes.

jasper ware An 18th-century type of hard biscuit goods (pottery), introduced by Wedgwood in England, whose colors are inspired by the mineral.

Jeffersonian Neoclassical and Federal period design in the United States that resembles the work of President Thomas Jefferson. See NEOCLASSICISM and FEDERAL PERIOD.

∞Jenny Lind bed A spool-turned sleeping platform named for the soprano Jenny Lind, the "Swedish Nightingale," who was visiting America at the time it was designed (1850–1852). It features a low headboard and modest bedposts.

jersey knit Weft construction with no distinct rib. Sometimes called "single knits."

jesting beam A decorative or ornamental horizontal element, not necessarily a structural member.

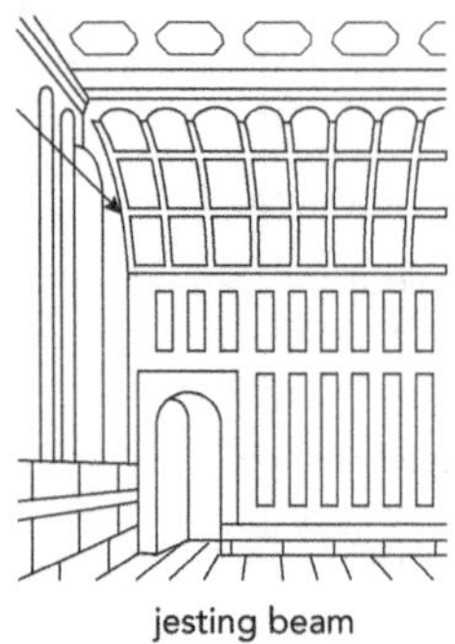
jesting beam

jeweling Any small, ornamental feature carved on furniture or a building, either above or below the surface, to resemble a polished or cut precious or semiprecious stone.

jian (Chinese) A bay in the Chinese architectural proportional system. Can also indicate the central room of the main hall of a traditional courtyard house. See HUTONG.

jib door A flush opening that is painted or papered over to make it as inconspicuous as possible; sometimes spelled gib door. There are famous examples at Versailles and the White House.

jigsaw detail A cutout or fretwork design made with an early power-operated tool. The embellishment was used for the enhancement of buildings of the mid and late 19th century. Bargework was often made with the precise cutting device. Gingerbread and steamboat Gothic of the late VICTORIAN PERIOD are examples of the work in extreme forms.

jigsaw mirror A framed reflective device popular in the 18th and 19th centuries in America and England. The earlier examples were hand cut and had detailed scrolls, while 19th-century pieces were cut on an early power-operated tool.

jigsaw mirror

joiner An artisan or draftsman skilled in connecting woods together by means of joints, glue, nails, etc. Does not do fine veneer work and usually works in a shop, not on-site. See JOINERY.

joinery The craft of assembling woodwork by means of mortise and tenons, dovetails, tongue and grooves, dowels, etc. See DOVETAIL, MORTISE AND TENON JOINT, and TONGUE AND GROOVE.

joint The junction at which two pieces of lumber unite to form a continuous element, support or to make a closure.

∞joint stool A 17th- and 18th-century simple seat made of turnings and connected.

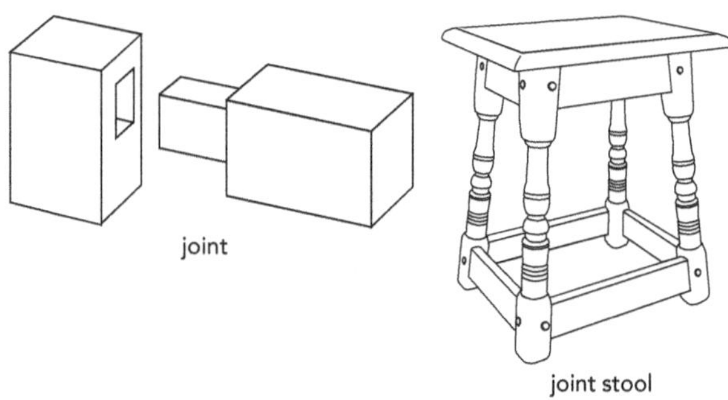
joint

joint stool

joist A horizontal construction member used to support a floor or ceiling; subsidiary to BEAMS.

Jouy A textile; see TOILE DE JOUY.

judge's chair An 18th-century high-back seat. The upholstered back is raised up from the seat and curved to cradle the head and shoulders. The upholstered arms curve around at the same level as the bottom of the chair back. The arm stumps and back chair rails are exposed. The squarish legs bracket out at the seat. BOX STRETCHERs connect the four legs.

Jugendstil German for young or youth-related style. The period in Austrian and German design was contemporary with ART NOUVEAU of France (1895–1912).

jute The fibrous skin between the bark and the stalk of a tiliaceous plant grown in India. The long, tough fibers are carded and spun into strong, durable yarns used as stuffer warps, backing, and binding and filling wefts. The yarns add strength, weight, and stiffness to carpets. See *Table 2.*

kakemono An unframed Japanese painting mounted on brocade, usually equipped with bamboo rods, top and bottom. Used as a wall hanging.

kambala Type of African wood used for flooring and objects. See IROKO.

kang Historically a heated platform in China; a low table placed on top of the platform that resembles a modern coffee table.

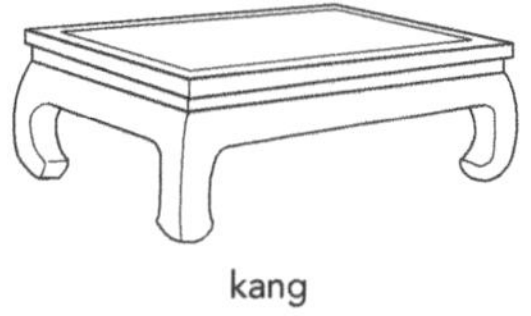

kang

kaolin A white clay used in making true porcelain. Also called china clay. Hard paste is made of this clay. See also CHINA and HARD PASTE.

kapok Silky fibers, obtained from the seed pods of the kapok tree. Used as a stuffing material for mattresses, cushions, etc. Also called SILK FLOSS. See *Table 2.*

Kappa shell A trademark name for fine sheets of ocean pearl nacré, iridescent in color. Available in assorted sizes and thicknesses and can be used for walls, furniture tops, lamps, light fixtures, screen inserts, etc. The material is similar to mother-of-pearl.

Karabagh rugs Geometric patterned floor coverings from the Caucasus. Typically woven in bold color combinations and with a coarse primitive texture. Also produced in long, narrow shapes for use as runners.

Karl Johans style The Empire or late neoclassical style in Sweden (early 19th century). See EMPIRE PERIOD.

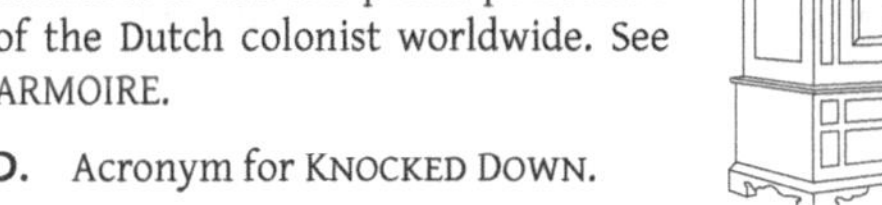

kas (Dutch) Chest or cupboard. A tall, upright cabinet, clothespress, or wardrobe. It usually had ball feet, a plain heavy cornice, and doors that opened outward. It was the proud possession of the Dutch colonist worldwide. See ARMOIRE.

kas

K.D. Acronym for KNOCKED DOWN.

keel arch A curved structural element that rises to a point. An OGEE arch.

keel molding See OGEE.

kelobra A wood native to Central America and Mexico and primarily used as a veneer. It is a neutral brown color and is also called guanacaste and genisero.

kemp Short, wavy, coarse wool or hair fiber, not usable for dyeing or spinning. Often used as carpet wool.

Kente cloth West African strip textile, associated with Ghana. Initially used in fashion, it is increasingly used for bed linens and accessories. Originally associated with the Asante ethnic group, it has come to represent Africa writ large and is used by many African Americans.

Keralite A trademarked type of exceedingly thin glass-ceramic that is heat-resistant and fire rated.

kerf A saw cut. Several adjacent saw cuts, when made against the grain of a wood plank, sometimes make it possible to bend the wood into a curve or arc.

Kerman rugs Gentle, pastel-toned, fine wool floor coverings from Iran. Usually have a central medallion on a soft ground color, surrounded by a border design. The border may be straight-lined or convoluted. The favored background colors are cream, rose, and light blue.

∞kettle base A bombé lower half of a piece of furniture that has an outward-swelling front and sides. This shape appears in English and American furniture in the mid-to-late 18th century. See BOMBÉ.

kettle base commode

key A wall or ceiling surface that has been scratched or gouged so that plaster will adhere. Also, any roughened surface that aids in adhesion.

key cornered A rectangular panel whose corners are broken by right angles. Paterae or rosettes are sometimes used to decorate these opened corners. This type of paneling was used in the LOUIS XVI, DIRECTOIRE, and EMPIRE periods and in the English REGENCY.

key pattern A Greek geometric band or border design. See FRET.

keying A method of closing securely by means of interlocking. Dovetailing is one example of this type of reinforcement.

keystone The central wedge-shaped block at the top of the curve of an arch. See VOUSSOIR.

kilims or khilims Handwoven Middle Eastern tapestries, without pile; lightweight enough to be hung on the wall or used as bedspreads and durable enough to be used as rugs.

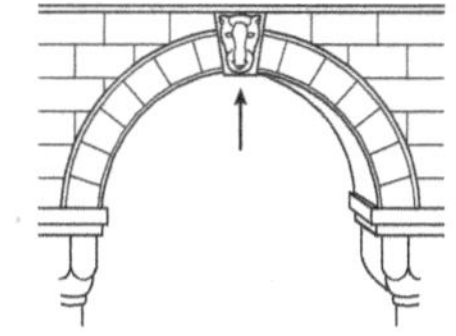

keystone

Khmer An ethnic designation that refers to the ancient Cambodian empire that reached its peak in the 9th to 12th centuries and to statues and other objects from that period.

kick pleat An inverted fold of fabric used at the corners of skirts of upholstered pieces.

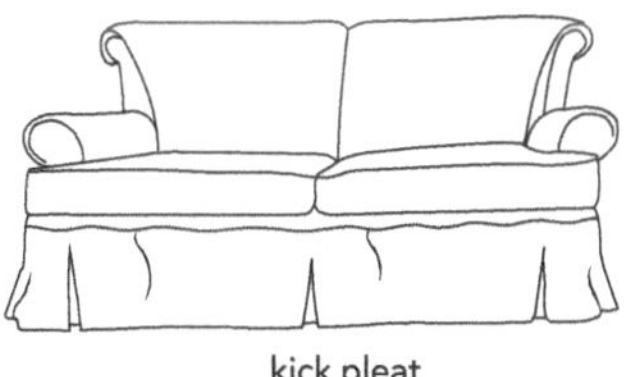

kick pleat

kickplate An applied surface, usually of metal or plastic, placed on the lower rail of a door to prevent scuffing.

kidney desk or table An ornamental kidney-shaped work surface with the concave side toward the sitter, who is semi-surrounded by the curved front. The shape was used as a kneehole-type desk or dressing table by Sheraton and as a POUDREUSE in the Louis XV period.

kidney desk or table

kiln-dried Lumber that has been artificially desiccated in heated chambers, rather than air-dried in the open. When artificially accomplished in an oven, the lumber is less subject to warping or checking because the moisture content is easily controlled. See CHECK.

king-size bed A double sleeping platform that can be made up of two twin-sized box springs and mattresses pushed together or one oversized spring and mattress. Usually 72 inches to 78 inches wide by 76 inches to 84 inches long (183 cm × 203 cm) and with one headboard.

kingwood A dark, purplish-brown natural material with black and golden-yellow streaks. It is a fine cabinet wood native to Sumatra and Brazil, also called BOIS DE VIOLETTE. Popular in the Louis XV and Louis XVI periods. It was decorated with SÈVRES plaques and ORMOLU mounts.

kiosk (French, *kiosque*) A small shelter or pavilion. The word is usually associated with a newsstand or other retail function.

Kirman rugs See KERMAN RUGS.

kitchenette A small cooking or service area, usually equipped with a stove, sink, and small refrigerator.

kiosk

∞kline A multipurpose ancient Greek piece of furniture that served as a sofa, dining couch, and bed. It resembles an oversized bed with a sweeping curved back at one end. The front legs curved forward, and the rear legs curved out behind. The back of the unit resembles the KLISMOS chair.

klismos A classic Greek chair with a concave curved back rail and curved legs that splay out front and back. This design appears again in the Directoire, Empire, and Regency periods. See also CATHEDRA.

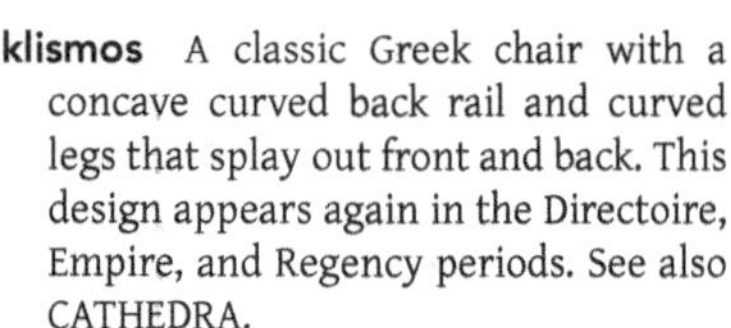

klismos chair

knee The upper convex curve of the cabriole leg, sometimes embellished with carved decorations like a shell, lion's head, etc. See CABRIOLE LEG and HIP.

kneehole desk

kneehole desk A work surface with a central open space below the writing area for legroom. Either side of the opening is solid or filled in with drawers or storage, which may continue down to the floor.

kneehole panel Part of a desk assembly. See MODESTY PANEL.

knife box A decorative wooden chest, with vertical slots for kitchen utensils. Usually used in pairs on top of sideboards, they were popular in 18th-century England. See PRONG BOX.

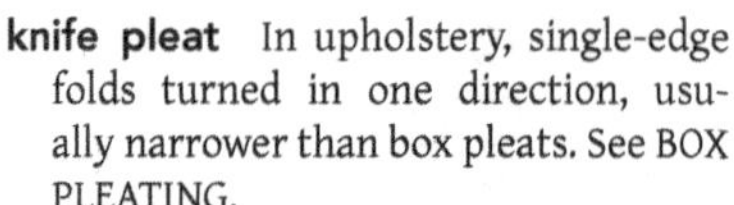

knife pleat In upholstery, single-edge folds turned in one direction, usually narrower than box pleats. See BOX PLEATING.

knife urns Ornamental vase-like forms resting on top of pedestals set at either end of an Adam side table. The urns held serving and eating utensils or hot or iced water. The urns were later replaced by knife boxes.

knife urn

knitted carpet Pile and backing yarns are integrated in one operation. Needles interlace yarns in a series of connecting loops.

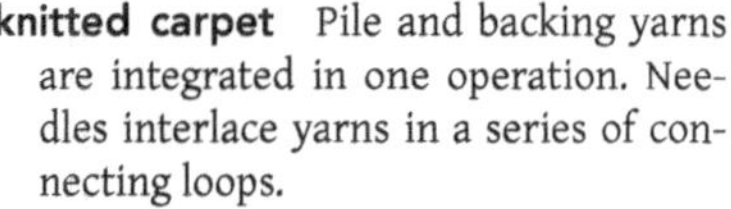

knob turning Lathe-work resembling a series of balls, used for furniture legs and stretchers during the 17th century. A feature of Jacobean and Baroque furniture.

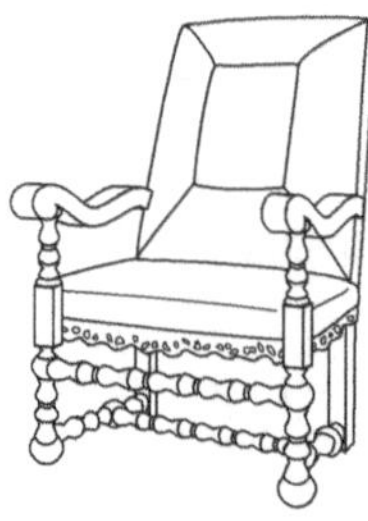
knob turning

knocked down (K.D.) The practice of shipping furniture unassembled, or in several parts, that must be put together at the point of use. An economy of space, labor, and shipping costs is effected when a unit is thusly shipped.

knop An archaic spelling for knob. A handle or holding device to open doors, drawers, etc. The term also describes a small bouquet of leaves or flowers. Also the bowl of a drinking or serving vessel, especially in ecclesiastical settings, or carved elements that copy the form of a chalice.

knot or knob A cluster or nosegay of flowers and/or leaves used as a boss or pendant at the intersection of vaulting ribs. See BOSS. A knot is also a dark round or oval interruption in the grain of wood that marks where a branch grew.

knotted rug An Oriental floor covering with a pile surface formed by the ends of threads tied around the warps. The weft threads serve as spacers.

knotty pine Pinewood showing grain markings or dark oval shapes, often accentuated by pickling the pinewood (whiting the wood). Used for Early American reproductions and for paneling informal rooms. The wood grows in Idaho, Washington, and Montana.

knubstol A Norwegian provincial tree-trunk chair.

knuckle carving The shaping often found on the outer edges of the arms of Chippendale chairs. It resembles the finger joints of the human hand.

knuckle joint The hinged connection of a drop-leaf table. Functions in the same way that the connections between the phalanges of the finger do. See FINGER JOINT and PEMBROKE TABLE.

koa A showy Hawaiian wood used for decorative effects. It takes a fine, lustrous finish. Koa has a reddish stripe on a yellow-brown ground with a decided cross ripple or curl, which gives it a plaid effect. It is used on fine furniture, for art objects, and for musical instruments.

Kodel The trademark name for a polyester fiber initially manufactured by Eastman. Not as strong as Dacron, it has less abrasion resistance, but it dyes well, dries quickly, resists wrinkling, and is considered more stable and heat-resistant than other polyesters.

∞**korai** Statues of women in early Greek art, usually heroic in scale.

Korean decoration See SAKAIDA KAKIEMON in *Designers and Architects.*

Korina A trademark name for limba, a light, golden blond wood that resembles primavera. It is available in long, wide panels uniform in color and satin-like in appearance. A stripe or crossfire figured veneer is also available. Also called AFARA.

Koroseal A trademark name for flexible synthetic fabrics or wall coverings derived from coal, limestone, and salt. Like leatherette or Naugahyde. They were initially produced by the B.F. Goodrich Company.

kotatsu A short-legged table with a removable top and a heater underneath found in Japanese homes.

∞**kouroi** (pl.; sing. is kouros) Early Greek life-sized or larger statues of nude youths that were made between c. 650 B.C.E. and 480 B.C.E.

Koylon The trademark name for latex-rubber foam initially produced by the United States Rubber Company.

∞**krater** An ancient Greek two-handled bowl used for mixing wine and water.

kunstwollen (German, will to form) Art historian Alois Riegl's concept of artistic volition. For design, a conceptualization of stylistic change that envisions that an object's shape was predetermined by the object itself and not the person who made it.

K-value (or K-factor) Numerical value indicating a structure's ability to transfer heat—that is, its ability to let heat to flow through. K-value equals the thickness of the structure divided by its R-value (resistance to heat flow). See R-VALUE.

kyanize To make wood decay-resistant; a process in which the lumber is impregnated with mercuric chloride.

kylin A fantastic dragon-like beast used in Chinese decorations. Also spelled qilin.

∞**kylix** An ancient Greek drinking cup. It is usually flat and two-handled and rises off of a slender foot or stem.

labrum (archaic) A stone bath of ancient Rome.

laburnum A hard yellow to reddish-brown wood, native to southern Europe. Takes a fine polish; used in the Queen Anne period for inlay and veneer.

labyrinth A complicated, intricate maze. In ancient Greece, an edifice composed of passageways that twisted, turned, and intersected one another. The original labyrinth is said to be the Labyrinth of Crete, built by architect Daedalus for King Minos to imprison the Minotaur. It was part of the Palace of Knossos; also a feature of garden designs from the Renaissance through the 20th century.

labyrinth

lace An openwork fabric consisting of a network of threads formed into a design made by hand bobbins, needles, or hooks. The ornamental openwork is also made by machine. See FILET LACE, NOTTINGHAM LACE, RETICELLA, and VALENCIENNES LACE.

lacewood An Australian decorative veneer wood with a pocked flaked surface that resembles filigree. Pink to light brown in color, and with a silky sheen, the material is used in small decorative areas for borders, inlays, etc.

lacquer A colored or translucent varnish made of shellac dissolved in alcohol, sometimes with pigment added. The Chinese and Japanese variants are hard varnishes made from tree sap. It has a shiny, lustrous quality. See JAPANNING, VERNIS MARTIN, and *Table 4*.

lacquer work Articles covered with a hard finish on which flat or relief designs are drawn. A fashionable furniture finish and form of decoration in Europe from the mid 17th century to the present day; also found on wall panels and screens.

lacquer work on a Chinoiserie bed

lacunaria See CAISSONS and COFFERED PANEL.

ladder-back A chair vertical support that resembles the multirung vertical movement device. Two vertical chairback stiles contain a series of horizontal rails, replacing the usual vertical splat. Often found in provincial furniture. See SLAT-BACK.

ladder-back

lag A resinous material deposited on trees by an insect *(Coccus lacca)*. This material is treated and converted into shellac and also used in fine varnishes.

lambelle A lightweight, damask, textured fabric with coarser contrasting weft threads. The warp is usually made of fine, mercerized threads.

lambrequin A valance board for draperies. Usually a horizontal stiff covering for curtain or drapery headings, as well as rods, hooks, and other hardware. Also called a PELMET or PALMETTE; originally the lambrequin was a fabric unit, but it was reproduced in carved wood panels with applied moldings or metal work decorations. See CANTONNIÈRE and PENTES.

lambris d'appui (French) Paneling that reaches to waist or elbow height.

lambris de hauteur (French) Paneling that reaches up to the cornice or picture rail.

laminated glass Heat-resistant vitreous product made of thin sheets fused together: a dense core covered with a thin coating of clear glass or transparent plastic is itself then laminated between two or more layers of untreated glass.

lamination A bonding or gluing together of various layers of wood, often with a veneer on top to form a permanent unit. Fabric may be glued to other materials in certain assemblies. See PLYWOOD.

lampadaire A classic pedestal designed to hold a small light fixture or candlestick.

lampas A patterned textile with two warps and two or more fillers. The pattern is always a twill or plain weave, and the background is a plain or satin weave. The textile is similar to a two-colored damask and was popular during the 18th and 19th centuries. The patterns today are usually historicist in style. Originally lampas was an East Indian printed silk.

lampshade A covering or shield for a light bulb set in a base. Usually silk, rayon, parchment, or opaque board covers a metal frame that produces a cylindrical, oval, or bell-shaped shade. Used to diffuse the light, cut down the direct glare of the bulb, and/or direct the stream of light. Metal lampshades also exist. See BOUILLOTTE SHADE, HARP, and TÔLE SHADE.

lanai A Hawaiian term for an outdoor patio, terrace, or veranda; used in other regions as well.

∞Lancashire spindle-back chair A country-style turned-back seat of early-18th-century England. The uprights are turnings connected with a top rail embellished with a shell-like ornament in the middle. The back

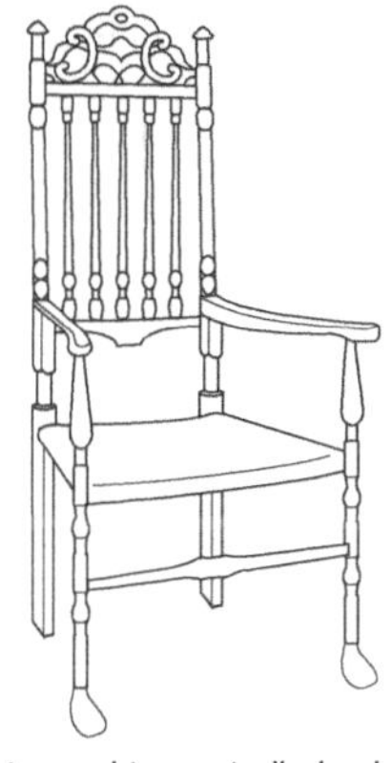

Lancashire spindle-back chair

consists of one or two rows of four or five lathed verticals contained by horizontal rails. The seat is typically rush, and the front stretcher is turned with a knob-like centerpiece.

∞**Lancastrian period** The Church of Fotheringhay, Northamptonshire, England, was built in this period. Design during the reigns of Henry IV, Henry V, and Henry VI. Late 14th through 15th centuries. See PERPENDICULAR STYLE.

lancet arch A narrow circular structural element that terminates at the top in a point. A feature of early Gothic architecture and furniture.

lancet window A narrow pointed opening. A feature of Gothic architecture.

landing A flat platform between two flights of stairs.

landmark An easy-to-spot object, building, or structure that serves as part of a wayfinding system, particularly important in airports and hospitals.

landscape (1) An outdoor scene depicted in art. (2) A planting arrangement. (3) A painting, mirror, panel, or digital image that is wider than it is tall.

lancet window

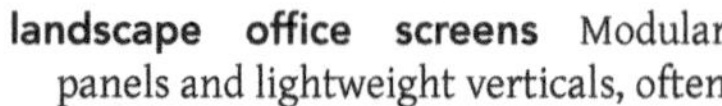

landscape office screens Modular panels and lightweight verticals, often made of soundproofing materials, that can be combined to differentiate work spaces in an open or free floorplan. Available from many manufacturers and in a variety of sizes, coverings, and colors. May include raceways for power and communication. Some panels are designed to incorporate shelves, files, task lights, etc. See OPEN PLAN.

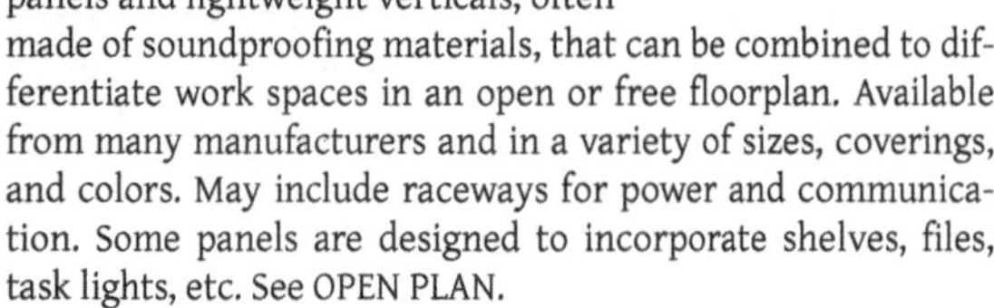

lantern In furniture, a case with a metal or wood framework furnished with panes of glass or other translucent materials. A lighted candle was originally inserted inside the framework. Today the devices are electrified. See LANTHORN.

∞**lantern clock** A rectangular or octagonal timepiece of the late 17th century. Resembling a light fixture, it is usually made of brass and glass; also called a birdcage clock.

lantern

lantern light A raised, vertical architectural protrusion that is set above the roof of a building. The panes of glass are vertical rather than arranged in a horizontal framework. Allows for natural illumination during the day.

∞**lanthorn** An archaic term for lantern. Horn was used instead of glass panes in the wood or metal framework.

lapis lazuli A semiprecious, azure stone of a rich blue color. An aluminous mineral resembling the blue carbonate of copper, it is used in inlay work and on decorative hardware. Popular in ancient Egypt and Renaissance Italy.

lap joint A form of joinery where two pieces of wood with identical grooved-out areas are laid one up and one down, so that they make a flush X arrangement when they are notched into each other at right angles.

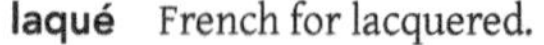

laqué French for lacquered.

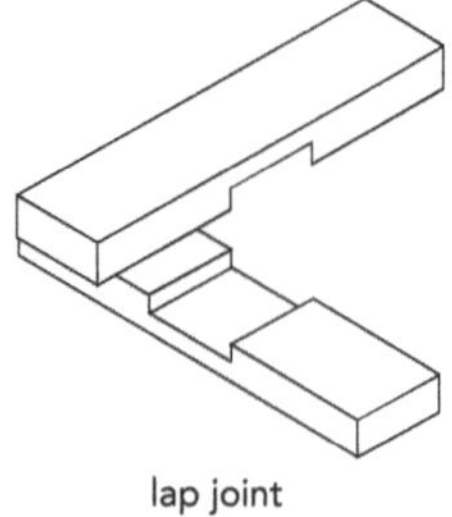

lap joint

L'art moderne A weekly periodical founded in Belgium in 1884. Its major premise was "Art is the eternally spontaneous and free action of man on his environment, for the purpose of transforming it and making it conform to a new idea." The periodical appeared until 1893 and brought together a group of avant-garde young Belgian artists known as "Les XX." The group included James Ensor, Ferdinand Knopff, Alfred William ("Willy") Finch, and Maus. See ART NOUVEAU.

Late Empire period See SECOND EMPIRE PERIOD.

lateral file An office storage piece in which documents are stored from side to side, rather than from front to back as in an upright file. Available in widths of 30 inches, 36 inches, 42 inches, and 48 inches (80, 90, 100, and 110 cm) and several tiers high. The traditional vertical file is usually 15 inches or 18 inches wide (42 cm and 47 cm), deeper than the lateral file. See VERTICAL FILES.

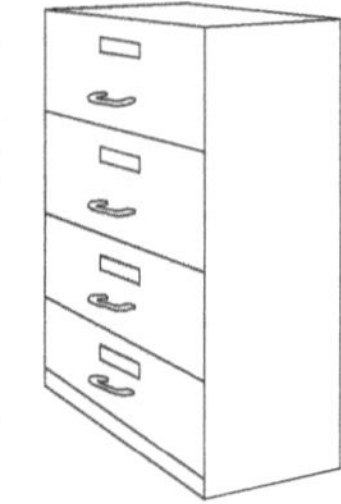

lateral file

latex A product made from rubber tree sap. It is a rubber coating used on carpet backings or to hold the yarn ends of tufted fabric onto the backing. See FOAM RUBBER.

latex paint A popular interior wall finish that uses a synthetic resin as the vehicle that carries the pigment. The fine particles disperse in water, and as the water evaporates they create a strong and durable film. The product dries quickly, is odorless, and covers well. When dry, it is water-resistant and scrubbable. An alternative to the oil-based variety.

lath A thin strip of flat wood used for understructures or as a support of a framework for finishing materials, like stucco.

lathe In cabinetry, an instrument for holding a rotating piece of wood or dowel against a tool that shapes it to make a wood turning.

Latin cross An overlain form with the vertical line longer than the horizontal one.

latten (German, laths or thin plates) A mixed metal of copper and zinc that resembles brass, used during the Gothic period for engraved panels and cast statues.

lattice An openwork criss-cross or fretwork made of wood laths or thin metal strips.

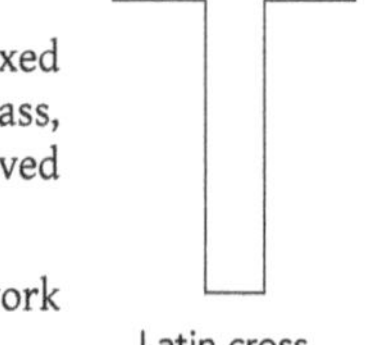

Latin cross

lattice window An element of fenestration with leaded glazing bars forming a gridded pattern with multiple openings. The panes are usually diamond- or lozenge-shaped.

latticework A chairback design by Thomas Sheraton and Robert Manwaring that consisted of wooden or metal strips crossing over each other diagonally. This name also applies to tracery on cabinet doors. Fretwork is usually smaller in scale than latticework. See TRELLISWORK. Also see THOMAS SHERATON in *Designers and Architects.*

latticework

lauan A reddish-brown Philippine hardwood that resembles mahogany. Sometimes called Philippine mahogany, it produces a handsome ribbon figure when quarter-sawed. See ALMON.

laurel An ornamental motif used as a symbol for glory. Singers and heroes in ancient times were crowned with the dark green glossy leaves. It was a common classical motif and also appears in 18th- and 19th-century European styles as an architectural or furniture decoration on friezes and in bands.

laurel wreath A crown made of leaves from the plant laurus nobilis, from the classical period, and a popular neoclassical motif that became an emblem of Napoleon's regime.

laurel wood An East Indian walnut, gray or brown, coarse-grained, hard and brittle, used as a veneer on fine cabinetry. The pattern may be striped, fiddlebacked, or figured, or it may have indistinct rays.

lavabo (French, washstand) A table and washstand, or a washbowl with a fountain, cistern, or water supply for handwashing. The lavabo is now often used as a planter in a decorative wall arrangement.

lavabo

lawn Originally a lightweight, fine linen fabric. Now also made of highly polished cotton yarn.

∞Lawson couch A simple, usually skirted, sofa or loveseat, with rollover arms that are mid-height between the seat and the top of the sofa back. A Lawson chair is similar in general line but seats only one person.

laylight A glass or translucent panel set flush into a ceiling to admit natural or artificial light.

lazy susan A revolving tabletop or tray for serving relishes and condiments. An American adaptation of the dumbwaiter of late-18th-century England.

leaded glazing Strips of the naturally occurring metal soldered together into a pattern, which hold small pieces of glass. Clear, colored, patterned, or textured glass can be used. Religious and educational institutions often have leaded-glass windows with pictorial representations composed of colored glass. See CAME and STAINED GLASS.

leaded glazing

lead glass Vitreous material that contains high levels of oxide of the naturally occurring metal and chemical element. Also called "flint glass" or "lead crystal."

leaf scroll foot A variation of the scroll foot. There is foliage carved on the face of the leg, and it sometimes hips out in front of the ankle.

leaf work Small collections of carved elements that resemble a plant's lateral appendages; used as decorative details on legs, splats, and cabinets during the last quarter of the 18th century in England.

leaf work

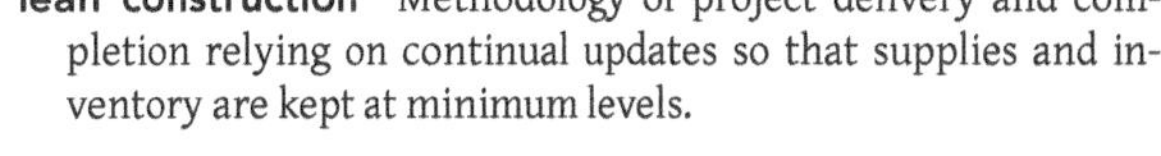

lean construction Methodology of project delivery and completion relying on continual updates so that supplies and inventory are kept at minimum levels.

learned irrelevance The situation in which a user forgets or fails to notice something, e.g., an exit sign, because on a daily basis it is not significant or relevant.

leather Animal hide used as an upholstery material, a wall hanging, a tabletop finish, a material to cover accessories or books, etc. Usually the hide of a steer is used, sliced or split five times. The three middle slices are used for upholstery.

leatherette An artificial leather made of nitrocellulose material with a heavy cotton backing. The top surface may be embossed or carved to simulate leather grainings. The material comes in a wide range of colors, textures, and weights and is used for upholstery and wall covering. See NAUGAHYDE.

leaves Additional flat panels that can be added to extend or increase the surface of a tabletop. Some are hinged to the table surface and must be raised to a horizontal position, as in the Pembroke or gateleg table. Others are drawn out from beneath the surface, as in the draw table. In other tables the framework is extended and the leaves put into the resulting space. See DRAW TABLE, EXTENSION TABLE, FOLDING TABLE, GATELEG TABLE, and PEMBROKE TABLE.

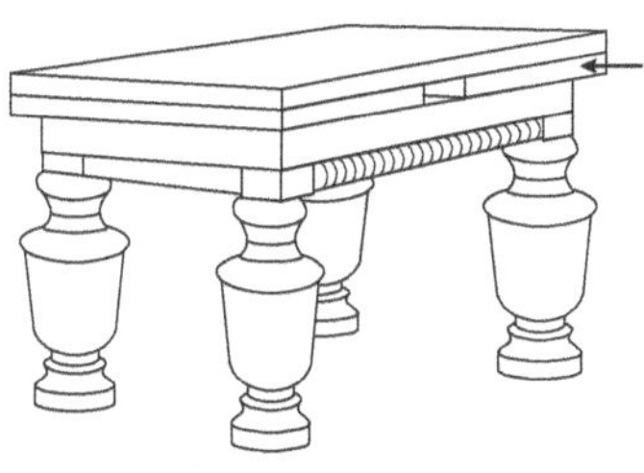

table with leaves

lectern A reading desk for a standing user. A carved or turned pedestal support for a Bible or a large book, such as a dictionary.

∞lectus A Roman bed or couch. The bed was sometimes equipped with a reading desk and cubicles to contain necessities.

LED Acronym for light-emitting diode. Light source used for a variety of purposes that, although more expensive, consumes less energy, has a longer lifetime, can be contained in smaller housing, and has a faster starting time than INCANDESCENT LIGHT.

ledge A simple horizontal structure, usually fixed across two vertical supports. A MANTEL is one type.

LEED Acronym for Leadership in Energy and Environmental Design, a rating system developed by the United States Green Building Council (USGBC) to measure green building designs and practices for built environments. Also, acts as an accreditation organization to authorize professionals who successfully take an exam about the rating system.

leg A furniture support. The vertical element of a chair usually starts at the seat rail and ends in a foot. It distributes the compressive forces of the seat to the ground.

∞lekythos (Greek, oil flask) A type of Greek pottery used to store oil named after the shape of seed vessels. Also spelled lecythis.

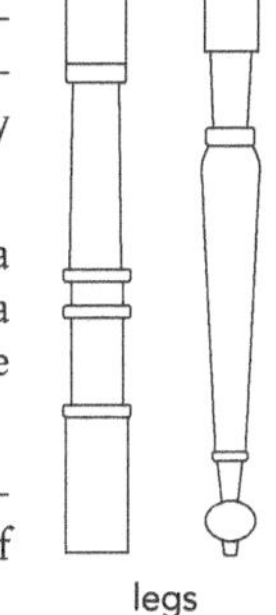

legs

le médaillon An oval-back chair of the Louis XVI period. The neoclassical chair had straight legs, and the arms were brought forward and fastened directly above the front legs. See CAMEO BACK and OVAL BACK.

lemoenhout South African furniture made from citrus wood.

leno weave A textile construction in which pairs of warp yarns wind around each other between picks or filler yarns, resulting in a netlike effect.

lenticular (adj.) Printed using a lens to create images with depth and movement effect. Materials include PVC, acrylic, and other base resin materials. Lenticular printing is used in a variety of forms, most commonly advertisements, novelty products, and façade elements.

leonine base A table, chair, or other furniture support carved to resemble the legs and paws of a lion.

letter wood A natural material native to Guiana, also called snakewood. The reddish-brown wood is distinguished by an irregular darker pattern.

letto Italian for bed.

letto con baldacchino Italian for a bed with a TESTER, or an upper, usually rectangular panel, supported by four posts.

lewan In Asian and Middle Eastern houses, a room with an open side that lets out into an inner court. See DIWAN.

library armchair A late-18th-century convertible seat with steps under the sitting platform. The seat flips over and becomes a small step unit.

∞library case A late-18th-century Hepplewhite term for a storage unit to house books.

∞library press bedstead A convertible sleeping element that folded up into a cupboard, bureau, or pseudo-bookcase. Popular in the 18th-century Sheraton, Shearer, and Hepplewhite periods for a sitting room that doubled as a bedroom.

library steps Many stepladder devices were used in the 18th century for getting at the uppermost shelves of the high built-in bookcases that often covered all the walls of a room that housed book collections.

library steps

library table Originally, the English term for a large pedestal or kneehole desk. Presently, a large work surface with drawers or a pedestal table. The kneehole desk has drawers on both sides of the opening. See PARTNERS' DESK.

library table

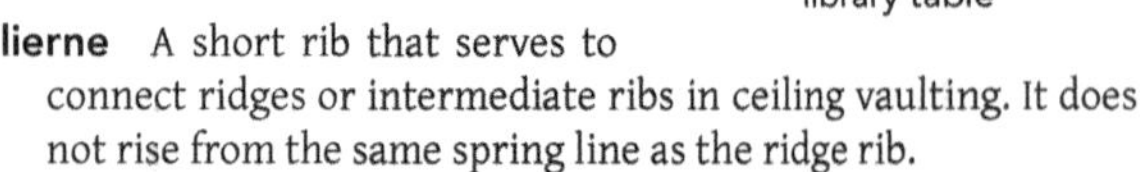

lierne A short rib that serves to connect ridges or intermediate ribs in ceiling vaulting. It does not rise from the same spring line as the ridge rib.

life cycle assessment A means of budgeting construction items that takes into account overall costs based on an extended period of use and not merely the cost at the time of construction or move-in. Often employed to explain the use of expensive items or materials.

∞light chair A lightweight, easily movable side chair. See HALL CHAIRS and SIDE CHAIR.

lighting louvers Plastic, metal, or glass filters set over electric bulbs to diffuse the light and soften the glare. They look like miniature Venetian blinds.

lignum vitae (New Latin, wood of life) A hard, heavy, greenish-brown wood used by the Dutch and Flemish in the 17th century for linen chests and cupboards. Durable, oily, waxy, with a fine interwoven grain, and difficult to work, this wood was introduced into Europe at the beginning of the 16th century for its medicinal value.

limba The French name for korina wood. See AFARA and KORINA.

lime Calcium oxide derived from burning limestone.

limed oak A special finish applied to the common natural material to give it a frosted or silvery-gray appearance. A whitish filler or paint is rubbed into the grain of the wood and then wiped off. This process accentuates the grain. Woods other than oak can also be limed.

lime mortar A masonry binding agent consisting of sand, water, and slaked lime.

lime-soda glass The most common type of vitreous material; made from sand and alkali.

limestone A building stone, usually gray or beige, that is mainly carbonate of lime or carbonate of calcium.

limewood An excellent carving material favored by GRINLING GIBBONS in the late 17th century (see *Designers and Architects*). It is close-grained and light in color.

linden (German, limewood) A fine, white-grained wood from the lime tree, excellent for carving. Many of Grinling Gibbons' mantels and trophies were carved in linden. The American basswood is sometimes referred to as linden. Not a fruit tree. See LIMEWOOD. Also see GRINLING GIBBONS in *Designers and Architects.*

line engraving A form of intaglio used for reproducing works of art. Dürer was one of the greatest artists to use this technique, which demands discipline and precision. A sharp graver creates V-shaped furrows on a copper plate.

linen A strong yarn made of smooth-surfaced flax fibers. It can be woven in a plain or damask weave fabric. There are many types: Belgian, English, Irish, handwoven, hand-blocked, hand-printed, homespun, satin, etc. Also used as a drawing material.

linenfold A carved Gothic panel embellishment that resembles a folded textile or a scroll. Popular in England in the mid-Tudor period, it was originally a Flemish motif. Another name for these panels is parchment panels.

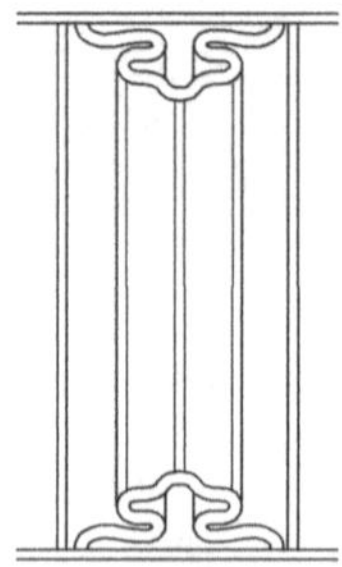

linenfold

linen press Cupboard or chest of drawers designed to hold household textiles. Name derives from a board-and-screw device originally used to smooth dampened fabrics, often made part of the chest.

lining (1) In furniture, a fine line of inlaid veneer, the same as "stringing." See BANDING. (2) In drapery and upholstery, a fabric used to back up the fine face fabric. It gives additional weight and body to the drapery and may serve as an insulating agent or protect the face fabric from sunlight. (3) Another name for carpet padding.

lining paper An inexpensive surfacing applied to a wall before the patterned or textured wallpaper is applied. It supplies a clean background for the wallpaper and helps prevent cracking.

linocut or linoleum cut A modern adaptation of the woodcut printing technique, using a piece of solidified resin fastened to a wood block as a surface into which the design is cut.

linoleum A manufactured floor-covering material cured by heating and therefore resistant to indentation and temperature changes. The wearing surface goes through to the backing, it is resistant to grease and oil, and it has some resiliency underfoot. The material will absorb moisture and is not recommended for humid areas. Usually manufactured in 6-foot widths (183 cm).

linseed oil The liquid substance processed or extracted from flaxseed, used in house paints and furniture finishes.

lintel A horizontal piece of wood or stone over a door, window, or other opening to support the weight above.

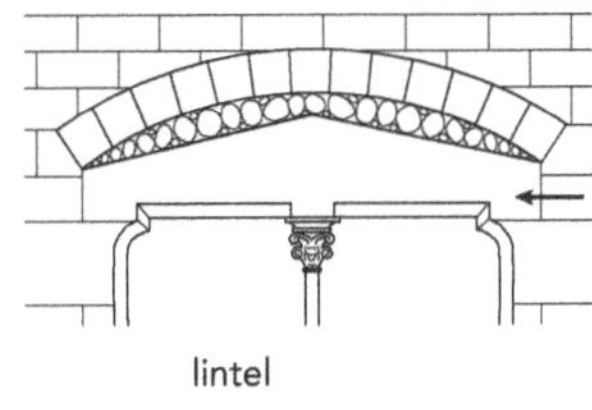
lintel

linters The short cotton fibers that stick to the cotton seed after the first ginning. They are used as stuffing for upholstery and mattresses and for producing cellulose sheets used in making rayon.

lion The "king of the beasts" and a favorite symbol in furniture, interiors, art, and architecture. In ancient Egypt, the tawny ferocious cat was associated with water and was usually shown at rest and with a stylized mane. In Greece and Rome, the feline carnivore symbolized the fallen hero and stood guard at gates. In Christian art, it represented the Redeemer, and in medieval heraldry seals, flags, shields, etc., the lion is a symbol of strength, courage, and royalty.

lion head A carved representation of the feline's visage used on furniture and in architecture. The motif served as a gargoyle on ancient classic temples and was often a knocker or handle on Gothic and Renaissance doors and cabinets. It also functioned as the holder of the end of a swag. See LION PERIOD.

Lion period The time from 1720 to 1735 in England when carved feline masks on the knees of cabriole legs and the arms of chairs and settees, and paws on furniture feet, were popular motifs.

lion's paw foot The carved representation of a furry feline appendage at the end of a furniture leg. Appeared in early Greek and Roman furniture and found in French, English, and Italian Renaissance designs. A prime decorating motif in 18th-century English furniture. See LION PERIOD.

lip molding A small convex molding found in Queen Anne and Chippendale chests and cabinets. Usually the decorative element was set around doors and drawers to act as a dust stop.

liquidy (adj.) Describes solid shapes with the qualities of liquids or gels; man-made designs that appear watery. These complicated forms lack clear-cut edges and straight lines. The result of complicated algorithms, they connote agility and nimbleness. They stem from interdisciplinary collaboration, with virtual representation at the center. Their creators are interested in bringing motion to statics, blurring the lines between organic and technical, and architecture as performance or journey. New digital capabilities have resulted in new furniture shapes and surface materials.

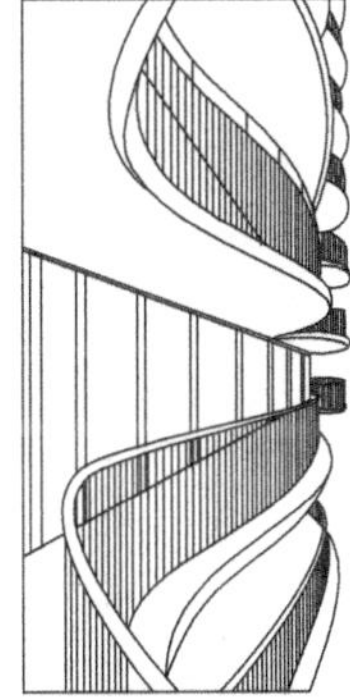
liquidy

∞**liseuse** (French) A Louis XVI reading table. A collapsible bookrest was set into the center top panel of the rectangular desk-like table. Often several small drawers were set into the apron of the table.

lisière (French, selvage) The outer woven edge of a textile or tapestry. See SELVAGE.

listel or list A border fillet molding.

lit The French word for bed.

lit à la française (French, French bed) A bed designed in the late 18th century that has a canopy and is placed sideways against a wall.

lit à la polonaise (French, Polish bed) A late-18th-century bed with a pointed crown canopy.

lit à travers (French) A sofa bed.

lit canapé (French) A sofa bed.

lit clos (French, enclosed bed) A bed with wood panels to enclose the sleeping area, often built against the wall; could be completely screened in. Found in French country estates from the 17th through the 19th century. See BOX BED and BUILT-IN FURNITURE.

lit d'ange (French, angel bed) An 18th-century French bed with a small canopy supported only by the headboard's posts. There are no front pillars, and the canopy extends partially over the bed. See ANGEL BED.

lit de repos (French) A daybed.

lit de repos à crosse (French) A daybed with outward, rollover scrolled ends. See CHAISE LONGUE.

lit duchesse (French) A bed of Louis XIV design with a large canopy supported by the four bedposts.

lit en bateau (French) A 19th-century French boat-shaped bed, similar to the SLEIGH BED.

lithic Refers to using stone.

lithograph A drawing or design done with a grease pencil or crayon on a special type of stone. A limited number of printed impressions are possible with this technique.

lits jumeaux (French) Twin beds. See SUMMER BED.

∞**livery cupboard** A 17th-century hall storage unit consisting of several open shelves for the display of plates. The lower chest was the receptacle for unused food. "Livery" is an old form of delivery and referred to the taking of food during the night, and therefore the livery cupboard was often found in the bedchamber. In churches, it was called a dole cupboard, and it held food for the poor. (The pediment top was added in the 18th century.)

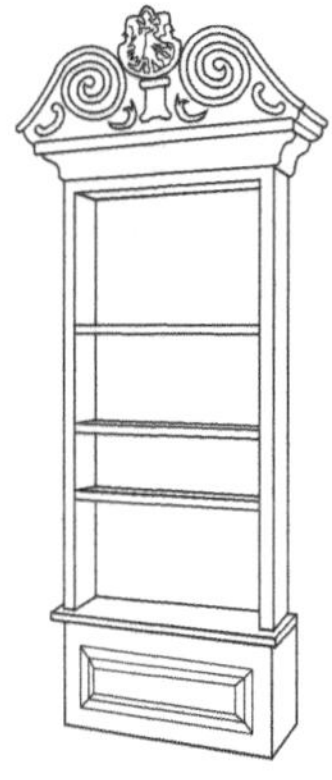
livery cupboard

∞**lobby chest** (archaic) Described by Sheraton in 1803 as a half-sized storage unit containing drawers about 3 feet tall (91.4 cm) and with four rows of drawers. A pullout writing board sometimes was provided beneath the top surface. This small unit was appropriate for studies, lobbies, or bedchambers.

lobe A circular element that is part of a foil in Gothic tracery. Example: clover leaves typically have three or four lobes. See FOILS.

lobing See GADROON.

locavore A person who chooses to consume (and eat) locally as a way of helping the environment and the local economy; includes using construction materials and finishes that do not travel long distances in order to reach a job site.

locker In 18th- and 19th-century furniture, a small central cupboard in the interior of a writing desk or secretary. A compartment or storage unit.

lock rail The middle horizontal element of a door, usually where the parts of the security device, strike, keyway, etc. are located.

loggia An Italian word for a room or area with an arcade or colonnade at one side. An arcaded gallery with a longitudinal side open to the outdoors.

loggia

Loma-Loom A trademark of Burlington Industries for a carpet of wool and nylon pile with a built-in sponge rubber cushion. The cushion is an integral part of the carpet that absorbs shocks and friction and gives the carpet extra resiliency.

Lombard style Northern Italian version of the Romanesque.

∞**long clock** An 18th-century hall or grandfather time device.

long house A traditional residential architecture characterized by a narrow dimension that fronts a commercial street and an attenuated length, found in Laos, Vietnam, and Native American communities, including the Iroquois. These narrow structures typically contained one family and one commercial function. A single opening is typically located at the end, within one of the short façades.

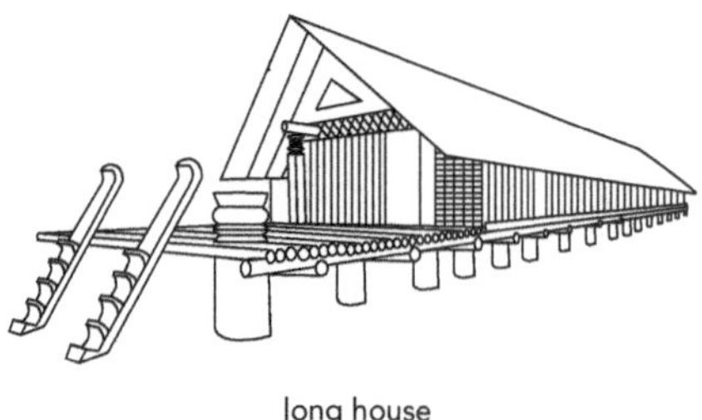
long house

loop back An oval chair vertical support or a Windsor bow back without arms.

loop pile A tufted carpet or rug surface in which the tied or knotted yarn circles are left uncut. See *Table 1*.

loose seat See SLIP SEAT.

loper The side support or runner under the drop-front or lid of a desk.

lossy (adj.) A pejorative term that indicates the dissipation of electromagnetic data. In information technology and data encoding, it is a term specific to imagery including design renders. It refers to a consequence of the compression process, or the attempt to reduce data size that incurs a loss of data quality for the purpose of storage, handling, or transmitting. For example, JPEGS that are jagged or pixelated. Lossless means compression with no discernible reduction of quality during the algorithmic process of compression.

lotus A Middle Eastern and Asian plant that is used as a decorative motif. The Egyptians used the flower form, both open and closed, for a column capital, on household utensils, and as a wall decoration motif. A feature of Thai gardens and floral arrangements, the bloom symbolizes purity and spiritual awakening.

Louis XIII style See FRENCH LATE RENAISSANCE PERIOD.

Louis XIV (1643–1715) Baroque The Golden Age of French arts and the reign of the Sun King. An artistic era based on classicism, although featuring complex curves, heavy draperies, and saturated colors. Rooms and furniture were enormous in scale. The ornamentation was rich and heavy, often gilded and with sharp accents. Compass-formed curves relieved the rectangular wooden wall panels, colors were saturated, and static objects suggested movement and emotion.

Louis XV (1715–1774) Rococo The reign of the great-grandson of Louis XIV in France. A period of gaiety, frivolity, and sentimentality. Rooms and furniture were human-scaled, and the result was comfortable and intimate. Curved free forms, S-shapes, asymmetrical compositions, and illusionism were dominant. The classical orders were sometimes replaced by the exotic including Chinoiserie; critics decried the era as effeminate. Lacquered, painted, and upholstered furniture added to the "age of the boudoir"; Madame de Pompadour was a guiding influence.

Louis XVI (1774–1793) Neoclassicism The reign of Louis XVI in France and a return to naturalism, simplicity, and reason in decoration. The classic architectural forms and orders were revived and strictly adhered to, with Pompeii, Herculaneum, Greece, and the Adam brothers of England as dominant influences. Straight lines and pure geometries returned, with symmetry and a severe classical quality. In art, the background was parallel to the picture plane; artists demonstrated a preference for simple shapes and primary colors.

Louis-Philippe period The reign in France of the former Duke of Chartres, 1830–1848, when the Rococo fashions and styles of Louis XV experienced a revival. The work was eclectic and occasionally lacked some of the grace and hand workmanship of the original period.

lounge A late-19th-century sofa or couch, often designed with one arm higher than the other, to serve as a headrest.

lounge chair A deep, fully upholstered seat designed to envelop and relax the seated individual; a comfortable seat into which one settles. May be of any style or period.

louver An opening in a wall or ceiling, covered with slats placed at an angle. Also, one of the slats.

louvered doors Enclosing devices with panels of overlapping horizontal slats, fixed or adjustable. The adjustable rails can be left open, closed, or in an intermediate position.

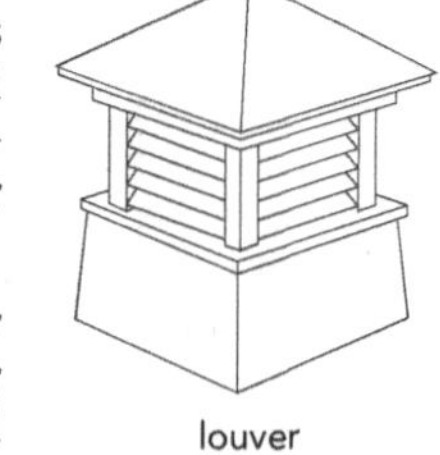
louver

love seat An upholstered settee for two persons. It first became popular in the Louis XIV period in France and in the Queen Anne period in England. The sofa for two is also called a "courting chair."

lovoa A tropical African wood that is yellow-brown to dark brown. Though it resembles Circassian walnut, it belongs to the mahogany family. In the veneer resulting from slicing a quartered log, there is a straight stripe with sharp color contrasts.

low-back chair A mid-17th-century term for the small side seats with short backs, which replaced stools and benches in middle-class homes. Cromwellian and Farthingale chairs are examples.

low-back chair

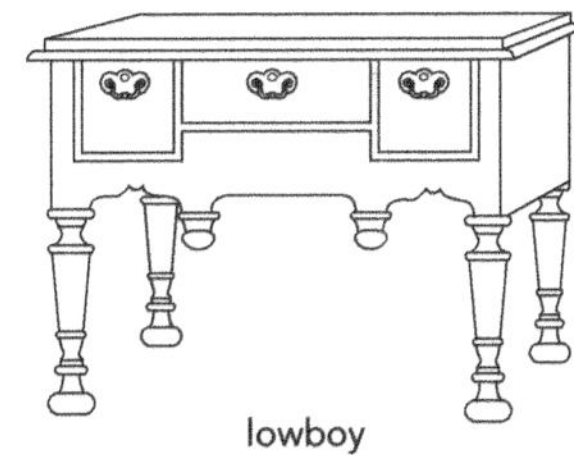
lowboy

lowboy A serving table or short chest of drawers without an upper tier of storage. With one to three ranges of drawers.

low-e Abbreviation for a reduced amount of emissivity. Relating to lesser levels of thermal heat-energy radiated by a surface. Glass has high emissivity, so coatings are utilized to improve thermal efficiency.

lozenge A conventional diamond-shaped motif. The Normans used the diamond shape in lozenge and billet molding. A product of the first part of the 17th century, the shape also appears in the French Directoire period. See DIAMOND ORNAMENT.

lozenge

lucarne French for a dormer window.

lug A small projecting element on a building material, which makes fixing the material into place easier and the resultant setting secure. On ceramic tiles, this projection is called a nib. It supplies an extra surface to glue or cement in place and therefore an extra surface for adhesion.

lumens The amount of light a lamp or light source produces.

luminaire Flush ceiling-mounted lighting device with fluorescent lamps (bulbs). It includes the lampholder, power connections, and any internal devices such as reflectors. It is sometimes called a "fixture."

luminosity The quality of reflecting or giving light.

luminous panels Strips of lights with glass or plastic translucent panes placed over them.

lunette In architecture, a semicircular window area. Also, a subsidiary vault intersecting with a main vault or dome and having its crown at a lower level, resulting in a crescent-shaped groin. In furniture, a crescent or half-moon shape. It may be used in a repeated decorative band design or, in the Jacobean period, as a carved or inlaid motif. In the 18th century, some tables featured painted or inlaid versions of the rounded forms.

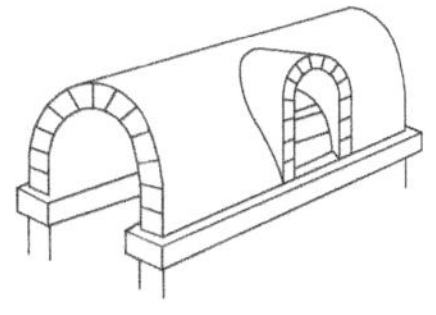
lunette

Lurex A trademark name for a non-tarnishing, aluminum-base metallic yarn often incorporated into upholstery, drapery, or curtain fabrics. Produced in various metallic colors by the Dobeckmun Company.

luster A thin metallic glaze applied to pottery to produce an iridescent color. Used on Persian ceramics, on Majolica ware, and on antique English and American ware.

lustre A table light or wall sconce in crystal or enriched with crystal drops or pendants.

lustre fabric In carpets, any pile-cut textile woven with surface yarns spun from soft types of staple and chemically washed to produce a bright sheen. The term also indicates a glossy finish achieved by heat or pressure.

lustre rugs See SHEEN RUGS.

luthern In classical buildings, a window (bull's-eye, square, arched, or semicircular) above the cornice, vertically in line with the front exterior of the structure.

lux (Latin, light) In the International System of Units (SI), a unit of illuminance that equals one lumen per square meter. It refers to the direct illumination on a surface from a single light source, whose intensity is calculated as one candle. It is a measurement of light intensity, or luminous flux per unit area. Not to be confused with the slang word for luxury, luxe. It is one of the terms interior designers use when creating ceiling plans with specific lighting requirements.

luxe depth A generous dimension for sofas and beds, a feature of oversized furniture.

lyre (1) A stringed instrument that appears in Greek decoration and was adapted in the Renaissance and in various forms in the 17th through the 19th centuries. (2) A popular furniture motif in the Empire period, and a particular favorite of the 19th-century American designer DUNCAN PHYFE. See *Designers and Architects*.

lyre-back chair A Duncan Phyfe early-19th-century American seat. The splat was an open-carved design of the ancient hand-held harp.

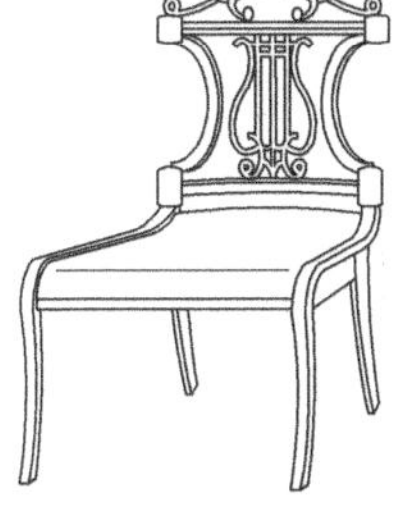
lyre-back chair

Macassar (1) A type of ebony, natural or dyed. (2) A type of oil. (3) The Indonesian seaport that heavily traded in the wood. Also called CALAMANDER and COROMANDEL.

macaroon or macaron A decorative rosette carving used to ornament Louis XVI furniture, named after the cake called in French macaron and in English macaroon. Usually an eight-petaled flower with a central bud, the motif was carved on the upper block of the chair leg or in the corners of the front seat-rail. See PATERA.

macaroon or macaron

macramé A technique used to produce wall hangings, decorative trimmings, and other designed objects made of knotted cotton yarns and twine. Usually conceived in a geometric pattern and executed by knotting or tying strands together to form an intricate openwork design.

∞**Madame Jumel chair** An early-19th-century Empire seat, without back stiles. The top rail of the back curves and sweeps forward to meet the front legs. The splat (central upright of the back) is often lyre- or vase-shaped. Similar to the Regency spoon-back chair. See SPOON-BACK and SPOON-BACK CHAIR.

Madame Jumel chair

madou See MAIDOU and PADOUK.

mad world The cultural and aesthetic world related to the English characters in *Brideshead Revisited,* written by Evelyn Waugh in 1945. From Madresfield Court, the home of the aristocratic Lygons, who are believed to have inspired Waugh's magnum opus. Architect/designer Geoffrey Bawa was a part of this scene. Interior design, specifically the philosophical differences between Victorians and moderns, was an onging theme in Waugh's fiction.

Magasin au Bon Marché The first complete modern glass-and-iron department store with natural light, built in Paris in 1876. It was designed by Louis Auguste Boileau and the engineer Alexandre Gustave Eiffel. The ground floor consists of a continuous line of show windows, and the corner of the store is a prominent pavilion. The interior is a combination of glass skylights, aerial bridges, and ornamental thin iron columns.

magnolia A straight-grained and generally uniformly textured wood, similar to yellow poplar but harder and heavier. Native to the southern United States, especially the Appalachians.

mahogany A longtime favorite furniture and interior wood with a reddish color and a handsome grain. It works easily, is wormproof, and takes a high polish. When figured, it may be plain or broken stripe, mottled, fiddlebacked, or swirled. Available in wide widths and long lengths. Among the varieties, those of tropical climes are considered the true mahoganies: African, Cuban, Peruvian, Brazilian, and tropical American. See ACAJOU MOÉ, AGE OF MAHOGANY, and PRIMAVERA. See also *Table 5.*

mahogany, Honduras A yellowish-white to salmon-pink to rich golden-brown wood, figured in a rich mottle or with a straight-grained moderate cross-fire. See BAYWOOD.

mahogany, Spanish One of the finest sub-species of the natural material. It is imported from Santo Domingo.

mahogany, white See PRIMAVERA.

maidou or madou A decorative veneer wood from Southeast Asia, found in a long grain, or an amboyna-like, fine burled figure. The color varies from pale straw yellow to red. Padouk burl wood is sold under the name maidou.

maître ébéniste A master cabinetmaker who specialized in surface-producing and space-containing furniture, including tables, desks, and wardrobes; in exclusion of seating. A maître ébéniste produced exquisitely crafted veneer work and was at the top of the furniture-making hierarchy. French kings bestowed the title on favored royal furniture designers. See ÉBÉNISTE.

majolica Italian and Spanish pottery coated with a tin enamel and decorated with bright colors. The name derives from the island of Majorca. See LUSTER.

makimono A Japanese painting in the form of a long scroll. See KAKEMONO.

makore or makori African cherrywood, pale pinkish-brown to dark red or purplish-brown in color, with a fine, smooth-surfaced texture, sometimes a mottled figure. Resembles American CHERRYWOOD. Used for furniture, cabinetry, and interior finishes.

maksura In an ISLAMIC mosque, a private sanctuary area within the structure with a perforated enclosure.

malachite A sea-green to dark green stone with intricately patterned scalloping whorls. Takes a high polish and was used in ancient Egypt for amulets. In Italy, known as the "peacock stone."

Maltese cross An object composed of four equal arms; each is wedge-shaped, and the points meet in the center.

manchette French term for a padded arm cushion. See ARM PADS.

mandala A Buddhist geometric pattern, diagrammatic of the cosmos.

man-made fibers SYNTHETIC hairlike strands used to create yarns. Manufactured and not of natural plant or animal origin.

Mannerism A 20th-century term that describes the painting style, especially in Italy, from 1520 to 1600. Art thusly named broke the rules of classical art. The human figure was distorted and elongated and struck tortured positions revealing strained and bulging muscles. Compositions were intentionally lopsided; perspective and scale were violently manipulated. Artists of the movement used bright, harsh colors that heightened the emotional effect. Tintoretto and El Greco are famous Mannerist artists.

Mansard roof A hipped attic or upper story enclosure with two slopes on each side. The first or lower slope is steep, and the upper angle is less extreme. Such an enclosure that is not hipped is a gambrel roof. Named for FRANÇOIS MANSART, the late French Renaissance architect. See *Designers and Architects.*

Mansard roof

mansonia An African wood that resembles walnut, often used as a walnut substitute in England. Sometimes called African black walnut. Usually straight-grained and fine-textured, it works and glues well and takes an excellent finish.

mantelpiece The stonework, brickwork, or woodwork surrounding a fireplace opening; may include a projecting shelf.

mantelpiece

Manuelino The Portuguese counterpart to ISABELLINA, the Gothic phase of minute, detailed, patterned designs.

maple A hard, strong, light-colored wood similar to birch. Straight-grained maple is excellent for interior finishes. The bird's-eye sub-species is curly grained, swirled, blistered, and/or quilted and works well as a veneering material. The natural material was used for marquetry and veneer in 17th- and 18th-century English furniture.

maquette French for a small-scale model.

marble A calcereous stone of compact texture that exists in most countries. The color, pattern, and textural effects are unlimited, and the material is used architecturally and decoratively. See *Table 3.*

marbling A painted imitation of the veining and texture of the hard crystalline form of limestone.

Marimekko Finnish company based in Helsinki and founded in 1951 that sells textiles, home décor, and apparel; it is best known for its signature brightly colored and bold textiles.

Marimekko

∞Marlborough leg A straight, grooved furniture support with a block as a foot that was used in mid-18th-century English and American furniture. It was especially favored by Chippendale. See BLOCK FOOT.

marquetry A representational design made by setting contrasting veneers into a surface. The resultant decoration is flush and level. Usually, the materials used are finely grained, colored woods. Popular in the Renaissance period and also in 18th-century England, France, and Germany. Lithographed transfers can imitate marquetry. See BOULLE WORK, INLAY, INTARSIA, and PARQUET.

marquise A projection or canopy over an entrance that is decorative and made of metal and glass. Sometimes referred to as a marquee.

marquise chair A completely upholstered small seat or sofa, prototype of the love seat, comparable to an overly wide BERGÈRE. Introduced in the Louis XV period in France, it was designed to accommodate wide skirts and panniers.

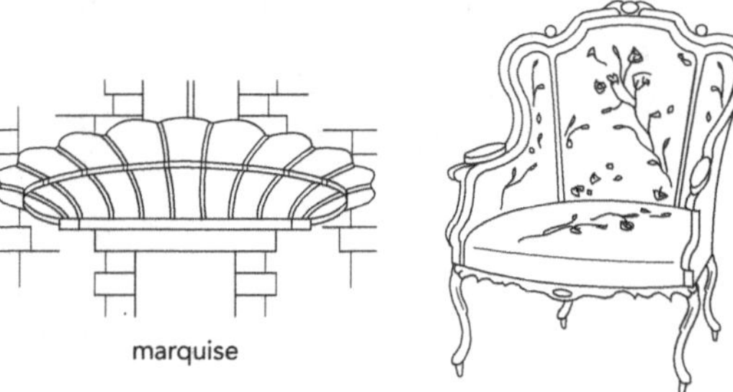
marquise

marquise chair

marquisette A lightweight open-mesh fabric in a leno weave. Similar to gauze in appearance and made of cotton, silk, rayon, or synthetics, it is often used for glass curtains.

marriage chest A CASSONE. An elaborately carved or painted Italian Renaissance long space-containing unit, used for storing household linens etc. and often placed at the foot of a bed.

marriage chest

∞Martha Washington chair A Sheraton or Hepplewhite type of Federal seat, with open arms and a high, fully upholstered back and seat. The legs were slender, tapered, and often inlaid; some seats were made with turned or reeded legs. See REEDING.

∞Martha Washington sewing table An oval-shaped surface-producing unit with deep semicircular end pockets that flank the legs. The top was hinged to allow access to the two rounded ends and the fitted central tray. The front, back, and sides of the pockets were either finely reeded to look like tambour work or covered with pleated fabric. Legs were turned or reeded. A late-18th-century, early-19th-century American design. See REEDING.

∞mascaron A grotesque mask or head used as a painted or carved ornament. It is usually distinguished from a MASQUE by being a grinning deformed caricature, distorted and sometimes terminating in foliage. A masque was often an idealized portrayal of nature. In the Gothic period, mascarons were caricatures. In the Renaissance and Baroque periods, the facial element accentuated a keystone in an arch or was used on chairbacks and other types of carved furniture. See GROTESQUES.

mascaron

Masland Duran A trademark of Masland Duraleather Company for a VINYL FABRIC with elastic backing, used for upholstery and produced in a wide range of colors, textures, and patterns.

masonite A compressed, rigid composite or building board made of wood fibers that resists puncture. The engineered product may be tempered for extra strength.

masonry Construction with stones, tiles, or bricks, natural or man-made, fitted together with MORTAR. In contrast to wood construction.

masques Exaggerated representations of the human face to suggest emotions or ideas such as those of comedy and tragedy. Used in antique classical architecture and decoration and popular during the Renaissance. They were often used as ornaments on the keystone of door or window arches. See MASCARON. Also in magnificently produced entertainments with splendid costumes, scenery, and floats.

mastaba An ancient, usually Egyptian, mud-brick tomb with a flat roof and sloping sides.

mastic An adhesive for fixing tiles, glass, and vinyl. Also, a gum or resin used in manufacturing varnish.

match boards Also called matched boards. Panels tongued and grooved together. The joint is either beaded or chamfered.

matchey (slang) A decorating scheme that relies too heavily on coordinated pieces and finishes. Sometimes matchey-matchey. See COORDINATED.

matelassé (French, padded or cushioned) A fabric with an embossed pattern that resembles quilting. Stitching or embossing can imitate the textile.

material ecology A process, an approach, and a philosophy that considers computation, fabrication, and material properties as integrated design components. It is interdisciplinary and fosters new ways of bridging the divide between the material and the virtual. It focuses on real objects, and related construction methods, with concerns for the digital and the organic. Inspired by natural processes and nature's successes, it asks designers to grow instead of to build. They focus on computation, additive manufacturing, biology, and biomimicry.

mate's chair CAPTAIN'S CHAIR without arms.

matte A dull, non-shiny finish. It hides imperfections and is less hard.

matted A term used to describe the rough, flat, sunk background of carving on oak furniture. Small dents or gouge marks often pitted the background.

mattress A filled pillow or pad placed over the springs or slats of a bed frame for comfort. Filled with any or a combination of the following: down, feathers, hair, cotton batting, foam rubber, etc.

Mauresque See MORESQUE. Moorish. Islamic art and design of the Iberian Peninsula.

MBD Acronym for MODEL-BASED DEFINITION.

McMansion Pejorative term for large upscale development houses that typically have multiple features, or bumps, including three-car garages, wine cellars, and home theaters. Contemporary versions of historicist styles.

McMansion

MDF Acronym for medium-density fiberboard. Engineered wood product made from wood residuals formed through high heat and pressure into wood fibers. It is a denser and stronger alternative to PLYWOOD and PARTICLEBOARD panels.

meander A decorative, geometric, repeating band. A Greek band. See FRET.

meander

mechanical card table An early-19th-century tripod game surface American furniture designer DUNCAN PHYFE created. The turned, foliage-carved, hollow, urn-shaped support conceals a steel rod. The rear legs and leaf brackets move into a supporting position when the top leaf, which lies atop the fixed leaf, is unfolded. The lower leaf attaches directly to the column. Usually made in pairs, of mahogany, they were also used as consoles. See *Designers and Architects.*

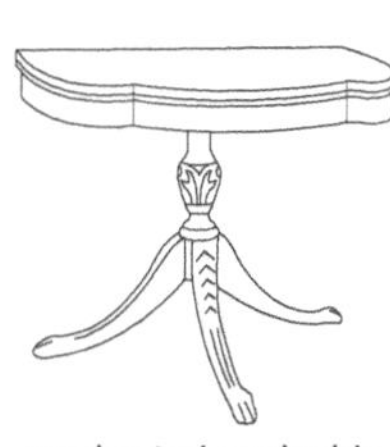

mechanical card table

médaillier A French 18th-century small cabinet or display case for medals and decorations.

medallion A central figural element, circular or oval, that acts as the organizing element in a pattern of stucco ceilings, rugs, tapestries, and quilts. Usually enclosed in an ornamented frame.

medallion

Medieval period Broad term that refers to the era after the fall of the Roman Empire and before the Renaissance, 5th to 14th centuries. See GOTHIC PERIOD.

Mediterranean style Commercial term for 20th-century furniture designs and motifs based upon countries of Europe and North Africa that touch the body of water. Ideas are drawn from French Provincial, Italian Renaissance, and especially Spanish influences, offering vigorous lines, deep moldings, metal ornamentation, molded as well as grilled panels, intricate carving, curved legs and spindles, and caning.

medium The liquid or vehicle in which pigments are mixed: water, oil, wax, egg, etc. The word is also used for a technique of creating or rendering a work of art: oils, tempera, marble, wood, bronze, etc.

megalith A prehistoric monument consisting of large, undressed stone blocks.

∞megaron Greek structure consisting of a single room with a central hearth and four columns; larger versions served as the central halls of Minoan and Mycenaean palaces. May be accompanied by a pronaos or porch.

Meissen A factory established at Dresden, Germany, then in 1710 removed to Meissen, by Augustus, King of Saxony. It used a process of copying Chinese porcelain credited to Johann Friedrich Böttger. The French Rococo period began to affect the designs by the middle of the 18th century, and copies of scenes by Jean-Antoine Watteau and Nicolas Lancret appeared. The factory produces expensive toleware, vases, statuettes, and other decorative pieces, with the trademark of crossed swords.

meisterfrauen (German) The wives of men (meister) who taught at the Bauhaus. The term recognizes that many women who married Bauhaus teachers were themselves talented designers whose abilities were often overlooked or whose contributions were mistakenly attributed to their husbands.

∞melon bulb A thick, swollen turning that resembles the fruit; retained from the Gothic period and used to support and embellish Elizabethan and Jacobean furniture.

∞melon bulb table A work and dining surface of the Tudor period (early 16th-century England) with conspicuous globular turned legs. The motif appeared on other pieces of furniture as well. See MELON BULB.

melon bulb table

∞melon turning See CUP-AND-COVER TURNING and MELON BULB.

memento mori (Latin, remember your mortality) A genre of art and objects used throughout history that depicts or reminds one of death; famous examples in residential libraries, such as those of JOHN SOANE (see *Designers and Architects*) and Horace Walpole, include human skulls, funerary urns, CANOPIC jars, and objects made of human hair.

memo A large sample, such as a piece of fabric, that is loaned to the designer and is to be returned to a showroom within a specified time frame.

ménagère A low dresser with open shelves for crockery. The open shelves were usually equipped with racks and guardrails. Also called a vaisselier. See HUTCH.

∞Mendlesham chair An early-19th-century variation of the Windsor chair that Daniel Day made in Mendlesham, England. The back had a narrow splat and a series of turned wood balls between the straight top rail and the lower cross-rail. The seat and legs were like those of the typical Windsor version. See DAN DAY CHAIR.

menhir A large, single, upright and undressed stone.

menhir

menuisier The French term for a craftsman who made weight-bearing pieces, including chairs, beds, sofas, stools, and other pieces out of solid woods rather than with veneer. Menuisiers also made furniture frames or CARCASES upon which ÉBÉNISTES worked. In prerevolutionary France, it was a classification lower in hierarchy then those who worked in veneers. Some specialized in architectural work, some in furniture.

mercerizing A process for treating cotton fibers or fabrics with a solution of caustic soda at a low temperature. The process makes the cotton stronger, more lustrous, susceptible to dye, and absorbent.

mercury halide lamp A high-intensity discharge light source. Light is produced by the radiation from mercury combined with the halides of metals such as sodium, thallium, and indium. More efficient than the mercury lamp and has generally acceptable color properties. The lamp has a life range from 7,500 to 15,000 hours.

méridienne A short sofa with one arm higher than the other. It was possible to recline in a half-sitting position on this particular sofa, which was popular at the end of the 18th and the early 19th centuries, especially in the EMPIRE period. It allowed a semi-recumbent human figure to elegantly relax in a semi-public setting.

merino The fine, cashmere-like wool obtained from the sheep, originally from Southwestern Spanish region Extremadura, later in Australia and the United States.

merisier French for wild cherrywood, or for a light fruitwood finish.

Merovingian A period of French architecture that predates ROMANESQUE, 5th–8th centuries. Part of the medieval period.

mesh fabrics Open loose-weave textiles of any fiber content.

mesolithic "Middle Stone Age" period, from the 7th to 8th millennia B.C.E. The transitional period from transitory hunter-gathers to established agriculturalists resulted in an increased number of designed objects, including axes, scrapers, pottery, and rudimentary pieces of furniture.

Mesopotamia The "Cradle of Civilization." The fertile plain area around the Lower Tigris and the Lower Euphrates in western Asia. Now known as Iraq, multiple early civilizations and cultures flourished in this area. The Babylonians or Chaldeans controlled the region from 4000 to 1275 B.C.E. From 1275 to 538 B.C.E., the Assyrians ruled, and the conquering Persians held sway from 538 to 333 B.C.E.

messaline A lightweight silk satin fabric.

metal mounts Furniture hardware. See MOUNTS.

metallic paints Finishes containing tiny flakes of any number of hard, shiny, malleable materials. The result is that the object so finished looks like it is composed of the mineral.

metates Pre-Columbian stone grinding platforms for spices and other foodstuffs, possibly used as seats or altars.

∞metoche The space between the dentils in the classical IONIC order.

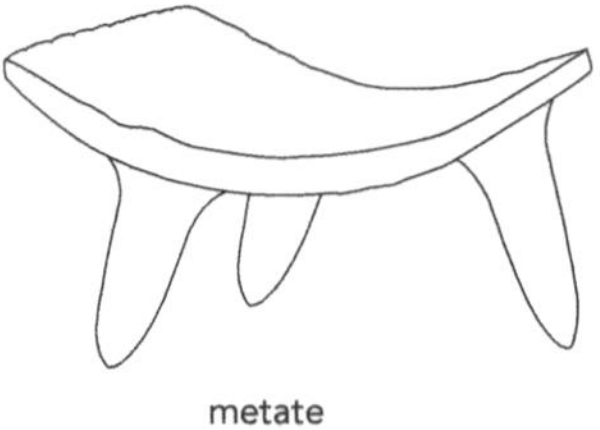
metate

∞metope The space between the TRIGLYPHS in the classical DORIC entablature. It is usually square and is decorated with designs or groups of figures. See DORIC ORDER.

meubles French for movable furniture as opposed to architectural furniture or built-in.

meubles à hauteur d'appui French low space-containing (storage) units, including secretaries, cupboards, or bookcases against which one could comfortably lean or rest.

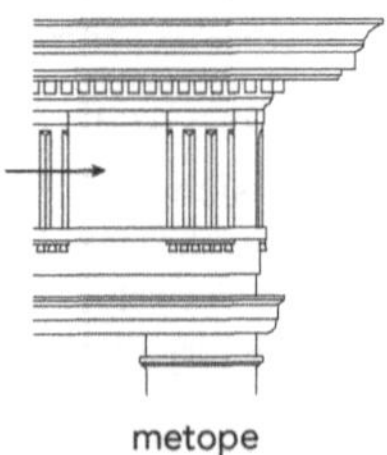
metope

meubles à transformations Mechanically designed convertible furniture of the late Louis XV period and also prevalent in late-18th-century English designs.

Mexican tiles Initially handmade ceramic pieces, dried in open fields, and fired in ovens. They are about 1 inch thick (25 mm), porous, and uneven. They must be sealed after installation. Commercially made versions also exist.

mezzanine A low-ceilinged story, usually above the ground floor. An ENTRESOL.

mezzanine

mezzotint The art reproduction process of the 18th century. It was especially popular in England where portraits by Sir Joshua Reynolds and Thomas Gainsborough were reproduced in the technique, which can produce halftones and highlights. A form of INTAGLIO ENGRAVING.

Micarta The trademark of the United States Plywood Corporation for vinyl sheet material used for lamination onto wood or walls, for tops and fronts of contemporary furniture, counters, service tables, etc.

mid-century modern The cutting-edge architecture, interiors, furniture, graphics, and product design in the years 1945–1965. Cara Greenberg coined the term in 1983 in her book *Midcentury Modern.* The designs depart from classical Modernism with their idiosyncrasies and wide appeal. It was an international phenomenon in which the USA loomed large. Major figures include Robin Day, George Nelson, and Florence Knoll. The trend was given a boost with the television series *Mad Men* (2007–2015) with its faithful recreations of modern offices.

mid-century modern

Middle Ages Broad term that refers to the era after the fall of the Roman Empire and before the Renaissance, 5th to 14th centuries. Preferred term instead of pejorative "The Dark Ages." See GOTHIC PERIOD and MEDIEVAL PERIOD.

∞**Middle Pointed period** See DECORATED PERIOD.

∞**mignatures** (1) Small-scaled sprig patterns for fabric Christophe-Philippe Oberkampf created at his factory in Jouy during the latter part of the 18th century. (2) Machine-made prints with small repeats printed on cotton.

mignonnettes Small, sometimes egg-shaped patterns found on the background of fabrics (toiles) produced in the early 19th century. These small shapes filled the spaces between the framed or paneled elements.

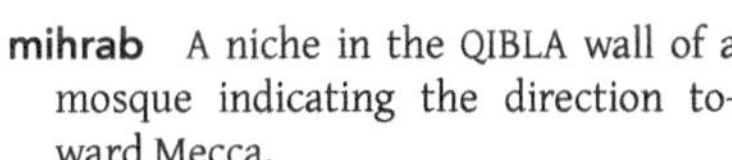

mihrab A niche in the QIBLA wall of a mosque indicating the direction toward Mecca.

mihrab

mild steel The iron alloy that contains some carbon and is not easily tempered.

milium A once-trademarked name for a metallized textile used for drapery linings. A metal in a resinous binder is sprayed on the fabric to give it a silvery look and a high reflectivity of radiant heat.

∞**milk or pie safes** These 19th-century American cupboards, found in Pennsylvania and the Midwest, were the forerunners to refrigerators. Doors with pierced tin panels allowed air to circulate. In Europe, early 16th-century, Tudor-Gothic oak cupboards were a forerunner of the volume-producing pieces of storage furniture.

milk or pie safe

mill ends Remnants or short pieces remaining from a run of fabric.

mille-fleurs (French, thousand flowers) A 15th-century Gothic tapestry pattern that contained a multitude of plants, leaves, and flowers. Also, later, multiple flower designs.

millwork The term used to describe architectural woodwork, including wall and ceiling panels, molding, door finishes, window trim, cabinetry, mantels, and built-in furniture. A professional term for the colloquial "carpentry."

minaret A tower adjacent to a mosque, used for the call to prayer.

minbar A pulpit in a mosque from where the sermon is delivered. Usually movable and made of wood.

minaret minbar

miniature Any very small painting, sculpture, or objet d'art. Includes small-scaled items intended for models and dollhouses.

mirador A Spanish term for a balcony with a view, a loggia, or a window overlooking a vista. See BELVEDERE.

mirror Looking glass. A highly polished smooth surface that reflects back an image. The earliest were polished silver reflecting devices of ancient Egypt. Metal versions were used during the Gothic period. The first silvered-glass ones were made in Venice in the early 14th century. Initially prohibitively expensive.

mise-en-scène The entirety of a production as the collaboration of the director and stage designers. The physical setting of a play, with FLATS, furniture, and props, and arranged with the actors as part of the spatial arrangement.

misericord A bracket on the underside of a hinged stall seat that is arranged to support a person when standing, after the seat has been raised. It is also called a miserere.

mission chair An early-20th-century inexpensive adaptation of the Spanish Renaissance frailero seat. A descendant of the Renaissance sedia. See FRAILERO and MISSION STYLE.

Mission style A popular design approach of the late 19th to early 20th century, based on the simple, massive furniture first made by priests and Native Americans for Christian residential organizations, such as ranches, convents, and abbeys, in the southwest United States and Mexico. Generally made of oak, with leather upholstery, trimmed with oversized nailheads, and stained dark. Named by GUSTAV STICKLEY, who designed bungalows and furniture. See *Designers and Artists.*

miter or mitre The corner junction of two pieces of wood cut at a similar angle, as in the corner of a picture frame. Usually the two pieces form a right angle.

mobile A form of moving sculpture originated by American artist Alexander Calder. It is usually a collection of shapes connected by wires in such a manner that the entire unit revolves and creates new arrangements of planes and solids in a three-dimensional movement.

modacrylic fibers Synthetic hairlike strands that are bulky and soft to touch and used to make fake fur fabrics and carpets. Chemical resistant and nonflammable, their heat resistance is poor. Yarns from the strands can be blended with cotton to produce a cashmere-like fabric. See ACRYLICS and *Table 2.*

model-based definition (MBD) A shift in digital product definition, in which building documentation and representation transition away from analog two-dimensional drawings but have at their core 3D visualizations that are rife with data. Part of 3D CAD software that moves beyond to a fully realized object-based paradigm. This impacts drawing production and construction. Significant features of MBD-produced files include geometry in one place; human and machine legibility; serving as single sources of truth with universally accessible definitions.

modern Baroque Efflorescent modernist designs, as described by a whimsical term, from the 1950s and 1960s. Also called California or Hollywood Regency.

moderne Term used for a style of interiors, furniture, and industrial products that appeared after the First World War (late 1920s). A transitional style between ART DECO and MODERNISM, with an aesthetic relationship to transportation, with streamlined forms, and often incorporating chrome and other new materials.

Modernism The architecture, furniture, and furnishings whose influence came to the fore in the 1920s in France, Germany, and around the world, especially Brazil, Japan, and Mexico. Artists of the movement reacted against ART NOUVEAU and VICTORIAN design and embraced industrial production. They broke down the barrier between art and manufacturing. Politically they supported socialistic goals of helping the poor. They opposed ornament and historicism, promoted functionalism, and embraced new materials, such as steel, glass, and concrete. See SCANDINAVIAN MODERN.

modernisme Spanish variant of ART NOUVEAU.

modesty panel A non-structural vertical element set into the exposed end of a pedestal or kneehole-type contemporary desk. The seated person's legs are shielded from view, and the desk has an enclosed appearance. A table desk purposely lacks the element.

modiglione Italian for a bracket or corbel; also called a MODILLION.

modillion The projecting decorated bracket used in a series to support the Corinthian cornice. It is one of the modillion band. Also called a CONSOLE.

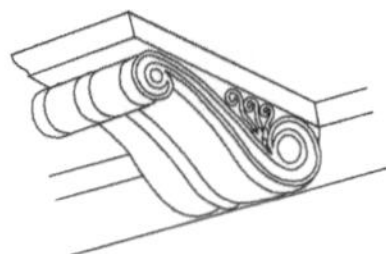
modillion

modular furniture A 20th-century concept in case goods and seating design. Correlated pieces are designed to a given set of dimensions (module) and also to fractions of that unit. The fractions and additional pieces can be stacked or butted together, and units can be added or taken away as needed. Connecting hardware combines individual pieces into larger units: there are modular case goods, modular seating, modular lighting panels, etc. See MODULE.

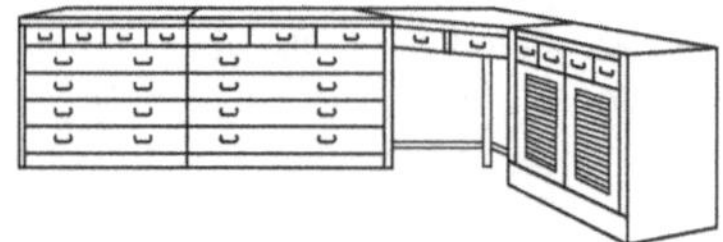
modular furniture

modular housing Dwellings erected of compact, self-contained units prefabricated in a factory, transported to a building site, and combined with other prefabricated units to form a complex of individual homes or a high-rise structure of apartments. See PREFABRICATED HOUSES and MODULE.

modular seating A sectional furniture element that supports the compressive forces of multiple sedentary humans. Intended for conversational areas or larger groups, made up of pieces designed to fit together to satisfy spatial and physical requirements especially in public spaces. The designed object may consist of seats without arms, seats with a right or left arm, corner seats, or backless seats. Each unit is of a shape and size that combines with other elements in the collection.

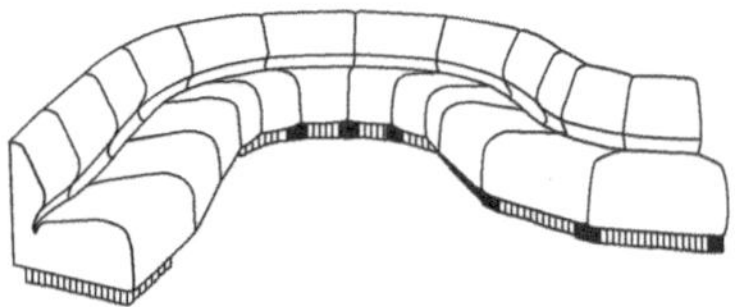
modular seating

module A measuring unit for an architectural or designed order. Basic units of the same size that can be used interchangeably, added to, or subtracted from. In office planning, makes for greater flexibility and mobility. Modules of lighting can be the same size as the ceiling panels and thus interchangeable. When based on similar dimensions, glass partitions, freestanding panels, files, walls, doors, etc. can more easily be rearranged.

modulor An image by the architect Le Corbusier of a human figure that he developed as an anthropometric scale and system of proportions. A man with raised arm, it promoted a harmony between designed spaces and the human body and forged a mathematical relationship based on human dimensions, nature and architecture. The figure, who was 6 feet tall (1.83 m) and Caucasian, played a role functionally and symbolically in Modernism as Leonardo da Vinci's *Vitruvian Man* did in the Renaissance.

modulor

mohair A cloth made from the fleece of the angora goat, woven in combination with cotton and linen. A resilient fiber, it adds body to other fabrics. Also a pile fabric of cut or uncut loops similar to frieze. It is strong and durable and was a popular upholstery fabric in 18th-century France. See *Table 2.*

moiré A waved or watered effect on fabric, especially rep or corded silks and synthetics. The fabric is pressed between engraved cylinders, which emboss the grained design onto the material. The pattern holds better on synthetic fabrics. See TABBY.

molded base The supporting platform of a piece of case furniture, made up of strips with a distinct profile or carved into a decorative molding.

molding or moulding A shaped strip (concave, convex, half-round, quarter-round, ogee, cyma, etc.), used on projecting or receding features of buildings, interiors, or furniture.

molding (moulding)

moleskin A heavy cotton fabric with a soft napped surface, used as a lining for synthetic leathers, oilcloths, vinyls, etc.

momie cloth A rough, pebbly surfaced fabric of cotton, rayon, or silk warp, usually with a woolen filling, used for draperies and upholstery.

Monel A trademark name for a metal alloy made of nickel and copper. Its main attribute is its resistance to corrosion.

money motif A series of overlapping disks (like coins) that forms an imbricated pattern or continuous border design.

money motif

∞monk's chair (archaic) See FRAILERO.

∞monk's cloth (archaic) Also called friar's cloth. A heavy, coarsely woven cotton fabric. Groups of warp and weft threads are interlaced in a plain or basket weave.

monk's seat (archaic) See TABLE CHAIR.

monochrome or monotone Tints or shades of one color. A complete range of one color from very light to very dark. Describes a designed ensemble that relies on one color, in contrast to POLYCHROME. See GRISAILLE.

monoxylous Made of one piece of a single material, such as Verner Panton's single-form injection molded plastic chairs. See INJECTION MOLD. Also see VERNER PANTON in *Designers and Architects.*

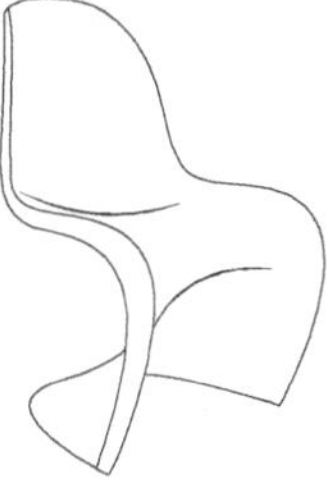
monoxylous

montage The placing of one layer over another or their juxtaposition. A design created by the overlapping or superimposing of initially independent decorative elements. See COLLAGE.

∞Montgolfier chair A Louis XVI seat with a balloon back designed to honor the Montgolfier brothers and their successful 1783 balloon ascension. The slat simulates the lines of an ascension balloon. Georges Jacob, noted French designer of the late 18th century, designed the original. See GEORGES JACOB in *Designers and Architects.*

Moorish arch A horseshoe-shaped structural element. The curve of the element is approximately three-quarters of a circle and springs from the column's capitals.

moquette An uncut pile fabric similar to frieze, with set patterns of assorted colors. It is made of mohair and wool, or heavy cotton, and is used for upholstery. During the 16th and 17th centuries, in France, it was made of wool. The Dutch version was called *velours d'Utrecht.* In France today, the term describes a Wilton carpet, woven on a loom similar to the English Wilton. The modern Axminster rug is a result of the moquette loom.

moreen See MORINE.

Moresque Decoration in the Moorish or Iberian Islamic style. The Moors possessed a large part of Spain and Portugal during the early Gothic period, and their influence is seen in art, architecture, and decoration. In carpet construction, it refers to the tweed or pepper-and-salt effect produced by twisting two different colored yarns together in the weaving process.

morine A thick wool upholstery material of the 17th and 18th centuries. Usually the warp was woolen, and the fillers were of linen, cotton, or wool. The material was either plain or figured. In the 19th century it was called moreen.

morning room A sitting or writing enclosed space in English architecture with a sunny exposure, used for a lady's morning activities: correspondence, etc.

Moroccan (maroquin) tapestries Decorated leather hangings. See GUADAMICIL.

Morris chair A large wooden slatted seat designed by William Morris, with loose cushions and an adjustable back. The seated person could lean back, after lifting the front edges of the chair's arms, and the back would decline to a semireclining position. See WILLIAM MORRIS in *Designers and Architects.*

Morris chair

mortar A bonding material used in bricklaying and masonry for bedding and pointing the various members. It is usually made of cement or lime mixed with sand and water. It dries hard and firm.

mortise A hole cut in a piece of wood that receives a tenon projecting from another piece of wood. Used in cabinet joinery. See JOINERY, MORTISE AND TENON JOINT, and TENON.

mortise and tenon joint A method of connecting two pieces of wood. The projecting extrusion (tenon) of one piece fits into the open shape (mortise) of the other. Often used to join stretchers to leg posts or seats to the back posts of chairs, as a glued joint.

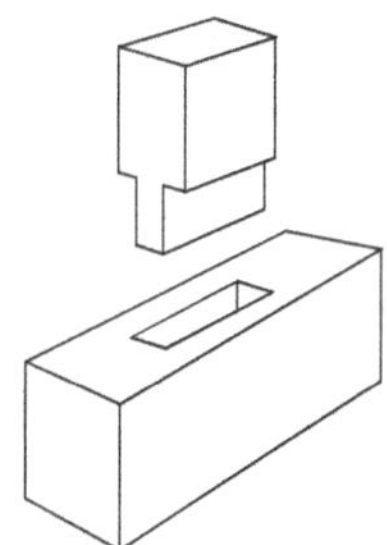
mortise and tenon joint

Mortlake tapestries Early-17th-century English silk textiles woven at the Mortlake Tapestry Factory. They did not compare in technique or color with products of the Gobelins Factory. See GOBELINS.

mosaic Small cubes (tesserae) of colored stones, marble, glass, etc. stuck into cement to form a pattern or design. The irregular surface quality catches light and reflects it at various angles. Much favored as a form of decoration in ancient Rome, and Early Christian and Byzantine churches. See PIETRA DURA.

mosaic

∞**moshee** An 18th-century term for decorative borders.

moso A type of bamboo with edible shoots. The plant grows very tall and is used for lightweight partitions, screens, and furniture.

mosque A Muslim temple or place of worship, derived from the Arabic "masjid." The home of the Prophet Muhammad was the first mosque. Important features of the religious structure include PRAYER HALL, MIHRAB, QIBLA, MINARET, and ABLUTIONS FOUNTAIN.

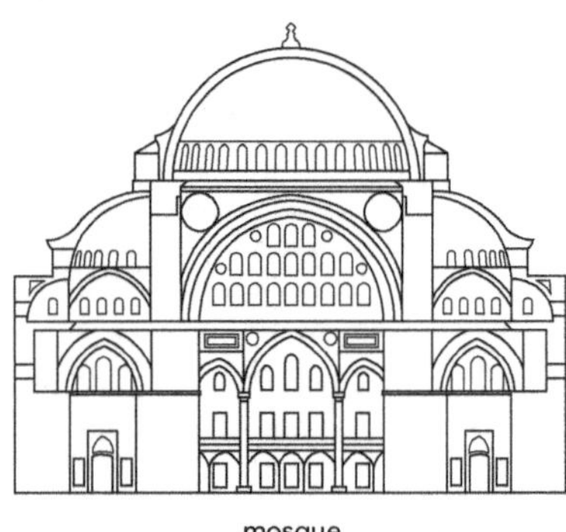
mosque

moss A chenille-like edging to a braid, used to finish and decorate pieces of upholstery and drapery.

mother-of-pearl The iridescent lining of the oyster and other shells, used for inlay work as well as small decorative items. See BOULLE WORK, INTARSIA, and NACRÉ.

motif or motive The theme or distinctive feature of a design, period, or style.

motion furniture Mechanized designed objects for seating allowing for the continual adjustment of user position such as a recliner, rocker, or cradle.

motion furniture

mottle A wood grain effect produced by short irregular wavy fibers across the face of the wood as cut.

mountings The base and harp (shade holder) that constitute an electrified lamp.

mounts Ornamental or functional hardware on cabinets or drawer units: handles, ESCUTCHEONS, drawer pulls, etc.

Moyen Age French for Middle Ages.

Mozarabic The art and design of Islamic Spain in which Christian, Gothic, and North African elements were vibrantly combined.

mud brick Building material consisting of wet earth compacted and sun-dried.

Mudejar A transitional art style of the 13th to 17th centuries in Spain, in which Moorish and Christian details were used together. It was the style of the Christianized Moor and was superimposed over Gothic and later Renaissance forms.

∞**muffin stand** A small tiered table to hold plates, used for teas and for other genteel entertaining. Popular in 18th- and 19th-century England and America.

Mughal Islamic dynastic rule of northern India and Pakistan, 16th to 19th centuries, known for the splendor of its decorations, and whose finest monuments include the Taj Mahal and the Red Fort.

muji (Japanese) Derived from *mujirushi ryohin* and translated as "no brand" quality goods; also a Japanese retail brand.

mule chest A massive space-containing object that resembles two storage units set side by side and sharing a single centered bracket foot; a forerunner of today's double dressers. The item often had handles on the sides for moving it around. It evolved from the coffer of the 17th century, which had a drawer or two under the lid.

mullion A slender vertical or horizontal bar between windows or glass panels. See also MUNTIN.

mullion

multifoil A pattern having multiple lobed or leaflike forms. An arch having more than five foils or arcuate divisions. A scalloped arch.

mummy cloth A silk or cotton fabric with an irregular warp figure. It has a light, fine texture.

Munsell System Albert F. Munsell's color categorization that designates and classifies colors and is widely used as a standard for color and color matching. Published as the *Munsell Book of Color.*

muntin or munting The central vertical part of a door that divides the panels above and below the middle rail. A vertical strip between two panels. The horizontal strip is called the lock rail. Also used to identify the wood strips that hold panes of glass in a glazed door or window.

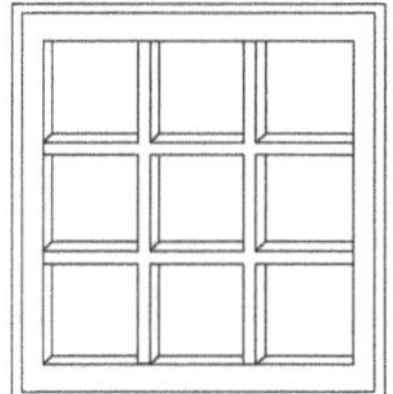
muntin or munting

mural Any kind of wall painting, either painted directly on the wall or printed on paper or canvas and then applied to the wall. It is not the same as a fresco, which becomes an integral part of the material of the wall. See FRESCO.

Murano glass Fine colored vitreous products produced in the Murano Glass Factory in Venice. Much of what is called Venetian glass is produced on the nearby island of Murano. Includes housewares such as vases and decanters, and chandeliers.

Murphy bed Originally, a falldown sleeping platform hidden away in a closet or in a covered recess in a wall. Later, the term for many space-saving beds consisting of a rigid frame with a mattress that fits into a closet, bookcase, or architectural setback when not in use. Also called a cabinet bed, wall bed, or HIDEAWAY BED.

Murphy bed

∞**murrhine** Ancient Roman glassware, fragile and opalescent.

muslin A plain-weave fabric that may be bleached or unbleached. It is used as undercovering on upholstered pieces to tie in the stuffing and padding materials prior to putting on the final upholstery fabric. The textile may be dyed or printed and used for curtains, bedspreads, etc.

muted Refers to colors that are soft, restrained, or dulled down.

∞mutule Any projection from the surface of a wall. It describes especially the square block, like the end of a beam, that appears at regular intervals above the frieze of a Doric building.

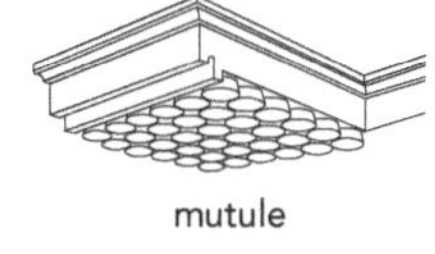
mutule

Mylar A trademark name for a polyester film made into metallic yarns. The polyester film is metallized by aluminum deposited on its surface, and the entire fiber is sandwiched in clear film. It is usually used with Nylomar Fortisan, as Mylar is a weak yarn that stretches easily. Non-tarnishing and soft in hand, it is used to decorate upholstery and drapery fabrics. Also a man-made drawing material similar to VELLUM.

mycelium The vegetal part of various fungus types, including mushrooms and yeast. A focus of recent developments as part of a rethink of fiber construction, in creating textiles and materials for industrial production; this represents a shift from technical industrial construction to biological fabrication. It carries with it the potential to impact design from fibers to large structures, but it is particularly important regarding microscopic filaments, new fiber development, and new tools of microassembly.

myrtle burl A highly figured, blond to golden-brown wood of widely varying designs, native to the western U.S. Hard and strong and used for cabinetwork, inlay, and veneer.

nacré The lustrous, iridescent material that lines some seashells. Called mother-of-pearl, it has long been popular as an inlay material on tabletops, chair frames, cabinets, barometers, and small accessories. The Victorians found the resilient natural material irresistible as an inlay decoration on papier-mâché objects.

nailheads Fasteners or brads with plain or decorated oversized flat ends made of brass, copper, or other metals, used to secure leather or fabric upholstery. They may be used to embellish leather panels. Functionally the part of the fastener that receives and distributes the compressive loads (the hammering), they became a form of ornamentation, especially in the Spanish and Italian Gothic eras. See STUD.

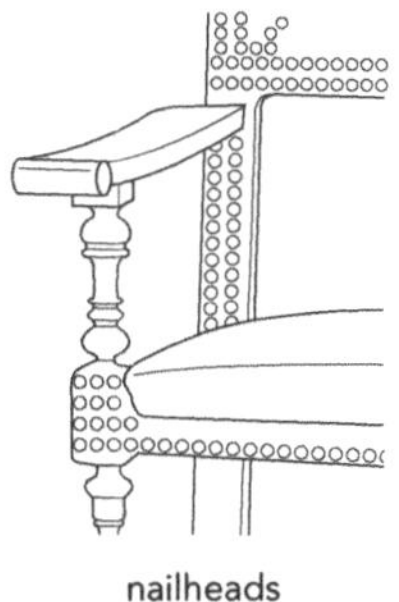

nailheads

nakora A trademark name for a Japanese blond hardwood. Extremely light in color, it has a definite grain pattern when rotary-cut.

nanmu A Chinese aromatic wood that turns rich brown in color as it ages. Also called Persian cedar.

nano material An extremely small substance having particles or constituents of or at molecular dimensions, or one that is produced by nanotechnology.

nap Fibers raised on the surface of a fabric to create a downy or fuzzy appearance. Differs from pile on a fabric. See PILE. MOLESKIN and flannel are napped textiles.

narrawood A Philippine hardwood that varies from light-golden tones to brown and also from light to dark red. The natural material may resemble mahogany or satinwood because it has ripples and also a fine mottled effect. Excellent for furniture production and interior veneer.

∞**narthex** The entry chamber or vestibule of a church, directionally transverse to the NAVE. Dates to the early Christian and Byzantine periods.

National Electrical Code (NEC) Also NFPA 70, a U.S. standard enacted into the legal framework for the purpose of ensuring safe practices for the use of wiring and equipment.

Native American rugs Tapestry wall coverings woven by the Navajo, Cheyenne, Hopi, and other ethnic groups. The ends of the filling yarns are woven in so the rugs are reversible. Sometimes referred to as American Indian rugs.

nattes A surface texture or decoration that resembles a plaited, basketweave design.

nattes

natural fiber Hairlike strands that come from plant, animal, and mineral resources. See *Table 2*.

Naugahyde Vinyl upholstery and wall-covering fabrics that imitate leather, initially produced by the United States Rubber Company.

Naugaweave United States Rubber's trademark name for breathable vinyl upholstery fabrics.

Navajo rugs Floor coverings handwoven by people of the ethnic group from the Southwestern United States, traditionally characterized by bold geometric patterns in black, gray, and white with strong accents of bright red.

nave The principal central bay of a cruciform church. It is usually flanked by aisles and terminates in an apse. See APSE and TRANSEPT.

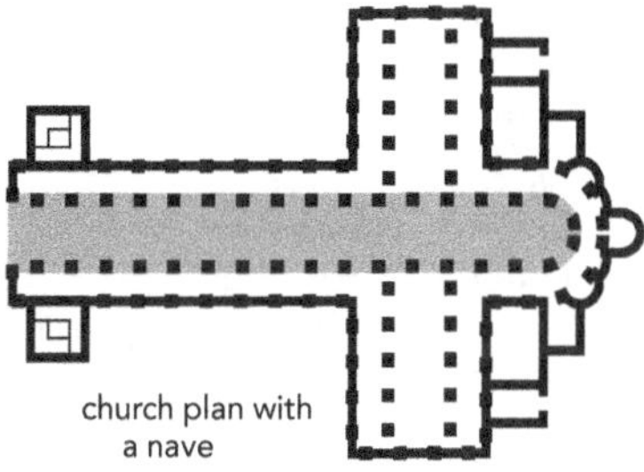

church plan with a nave

∞**nebule ornament** A Norman form of decoration that consisted of a continuous wavy line, used to enrich moldings.

NEC Acronym for NATIONAL ELECTRICAL CODE.

∞**nécessaire** A French term for a small writing or toilet accessory case.

necessary stool See CLOSE CHAIR.

necking See COLLAR.

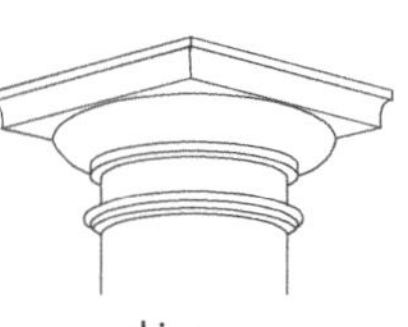

necking

∞**necropolis** Greek term for a large ancient burial ground.

needlepoint A dense cross-stitch embroidery done on net, heavy canvas, or coarse linen. It resembles a coarse tapestry. From the 15th century on, used as an upholstery covering for chairs, sofas, etc. See GROS POINT and PETIT POINT.

needlepoint

needlepunched carpet Floor covering that is made with barbed needles that are repeatedly inserted into a fiber web to tangle the fibers; a scrim may be added for strength and stability. Commonly used as indoor-outdoor carpeting.

neoclassicism A movement that originated in Rome in the mid 18th century as a reaction against the excesses of the

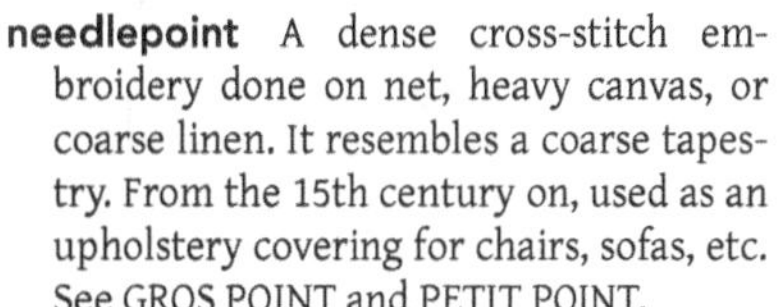

baroque and rococo styles and that quickly spread across Europe. The discoveries at Herculaneum and Pompeii gave impetus to a return to the art and architecture of classical Greece and Rome. The Louis XVI style in France and the Regency style in England were part of this trend. Also important in Denmark, Germany, Russia, Sweden, and elsewhere.

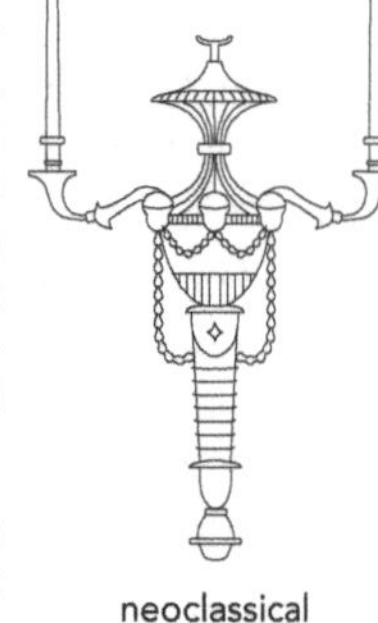
neoclassical sconce

néo-Grec style The French form of the new Greek style during the Louis XVI period, influenced by the discoveries at Herculaneum and Pompeii. Greek motifs, including caryatids and other classic detailing, became popular for furniture and interior decorations. A subset of neoclassicism that favored ancient Greek forms over Roman ones.

néo-Greek period A rarely used term for the American period of art and architecture (from 1815 to 1845), which was heavily flavored with classical Greek motifs.

Neolithic Referring to the "New Stone Age" period, from the 3rd to the 1st millennia B.C.E., characterized by the use of refined stone implements, extensive use of pottery, and early pieces of furniture.

nest To place one object within another, for example a set of tables or containers of different sizes that provide multiple surfaces or volumes that store compactly.

nested tables A series of small surface-creating pieces, graduated in size, so that one can be set inside the other. They may serve as adjuncts to sofas and are made in a variety of styles. See QUARTETTE TABLES.

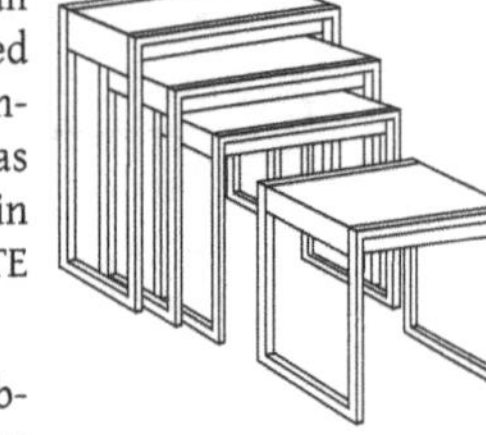
nested tables

net An open-weave, meshlike fabric used for GLASS CURTAINS. May be made of cotton, linen, or synthetic fibers.

net zero Requiring no additional energy input from outside sources.

neutral In colors, characterized by no definite character or personality. A thusly named finish usually blends well with most true colors. White, black, gray, and beige are neutrals.

New Colonial or Modern Colonial period An early-20th-century style of reproduction furniture. The features from both the colonial era and the later Federal and American Empire styles were retained, but the ostentatious ORMOLU and brass mounts were omitted. The S-shaped scroll, scroll foot, lion's paw foot, and classical columns were often in evidence. Mass-produced in Grand Rapids, Michigan, and elsewhere. Better pieces were made in mahogany.

New Colonial period

new urbanism The community design strain of postmodernism that rejected urban Modernism and sought to reshape town planning by relying on traditional civic principles; related to historicist and traditional interior designs.

newel or newel post A heavy upright or turning at the end of a handrail of a stairway.

nib See LUG.

niche A recessed or hollowed-out space in a wall, usually intended to hold a statue, vase, or ornament.

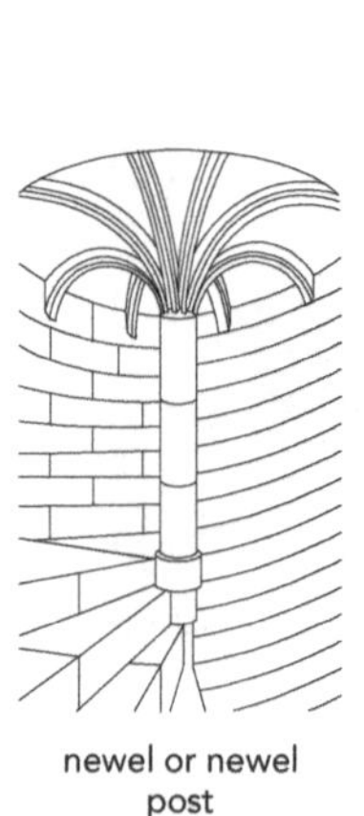
newel or newel post

niche

nicking A notched or gouged ornamenting technique used on 17th-century English oak furniture.

niello A method of decorating metal surfaces by engraving lines and infilling them with a black material which makes the design stand out.

night stool See CLOSE CHAIR.

night table A bedside surface piece, usually small, with or without a drawer or shelf, used to hold a lamp, ashtray, clock, etc. In period rooms, small commodes can serve in place of the items. See CHEVET.

nimbus A circular halo, a ring of gold, around a painted or carved representation of the head of Christ, the Madonna, or a saint.

NIMBY Acronym for "not in my back yard." Expression used by residents who oppose the development in their neighborhood of what they consider unfavorable projects, such as public housing, landfills, etc.

ninon A smooth, sheer, closely woven voile, usually of rayon, used for GLASS CURTAINS. Sometimes called triple voile.

no-fines A concrete composed of cement and coarse aggregate.

nogging In the construction of a partition, the placing of a horizontal piece between two vertical studs.

nogging

noil Discarded short fibers combed from wool, cotton, or silk in making high-quality yarns. Used for yarns of lower quality or for padding and stuffing.

nomads Office workers without stationary or permanent spatial assignments. See HOT DESKING and HOTELLING.

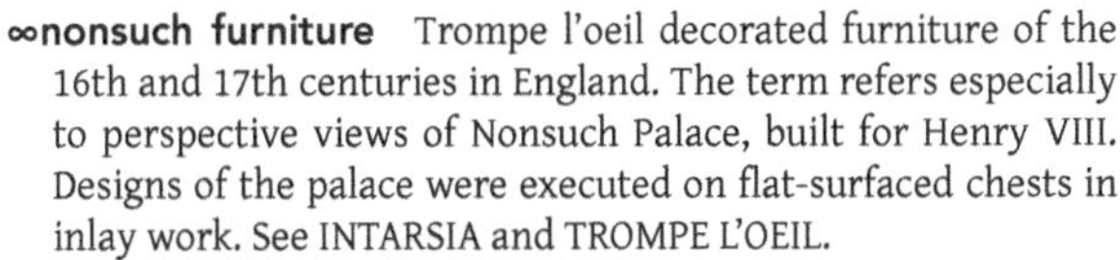
nomad

nonbearing Describing a wall or partition that does not support a load or resist a force or thrust from above. A filler section.

∞**nonsuch furniture** Trompe l'oeil decorated furniture of the 16th and 17th centuries in England. The term refers especially to perspective views of Nonsuch Palace, built for Henry VIII. Designs of the palace were executed on flat-surfaced chests in inlay work. See INTARSIA and TROMPE L'OEIL.

nonwoven Fabric made directly from fibers. Felt is an example as it is compressed.

Norman period The era in England under the Norman kings, dating approximately from 1066 to 1189. The architecture is characterized by massive constructions; rough, thick-jointed masonry; rounded arches; projecting parapets carried on a corbel table; wide buttresses of slight projection; and assorted carved capitals. The prominent motifs in decoration were the chevron, star, billet, zigzag, and bird-beak moldings. ROMANESQUE is the Continental name for Norman.

Normandy A province of France that produced charming, simple, country-style furniture in the 18th century. It was similar to colonial New England designs of the same time.

nosing The curved or shaped front edge of a stair tread.

notching See NICKING.

Nottingham lace A general name given to a machine-made flat knit textile, particularly tablecloths or curtains that are constructed in one piece. Originally a handmade product.

nub yarn See SLUB YARN.

∞**nulling** A Jacobean wood-carving technique that produced an effect similar to repoussé or chased metalwork. The patterns were created by a series of small projections or recessions from the surface (like a boss or bead) of the wood.

numdah Felted rug made in India, usually from cow's hair. Decorating their surface are allover designs of vines and blossoms that are embroidered in brightly colored wool yarns. Also known as a drugget.

∞**nursing chair** An English term for an anthropomorphic designed object with a low seat. See CHAFFEUSE. Originally an 18th-century term, its relevance was restored with the popularity of lactation rooms in the 21st-century workplace.

nylon A protein-like chemical that can be manufactured as fibers, in sheets, or as bristles. Tough, elastic, and strong, it is often used to create synthetic fabrics which originally derived from silk or rayon yarns. Also used as a carpet fiber. It provides a high degree of abrasion resistance, dries quickly, and is easy to care for. See *Table 2* and *Table 3*.

oak A hard, durable wood of a red or whitish color that lends itself to carving or paneling. Because it is porous, it must be treated with a filler before it is stained. European oaks are finer-grained than the American varieties.

oak, pollard English brown wood, nut-brown to deep brown in color, and spotted in black. The figure is often tortoiseshell in effect. The wood has a medium-hard texture.

oak, quartered Planks of wood sawed toward or through the center of the tree trunk, resulting in a decorative plank or veneer. The wood has a flake pattern, which is caused by the wide rays that reflect the light. Generally, oak is heavy, hard, and strong, and it has prominent pores in the spring-cut variety.

obelisk A tall, tapering column or structure, square or rectangular in section, with a pyramid-shaped top. It is often used as a commemorative monument or in a small version as a decorative object. First prominent in Egyptian and Roman monuments, neoclassical designers turned to the form with gusto.

objet d'art A small designed item whose aesthetics were more important than its function: miniature painting, sculpture, vase, snuffbox, etc. See BIBELOTS.

objet de vertu (English phrase made of French words) A curiosity, or collectible item of interest, prized for reasons of its history or craftsmanship; a bibelot or knickknack.

oblique arch See SKEW ARCH.

∞**obscure glass** A translucent rather than transparent vitreous material. It allows in light but does not permit a clear, uninterrupted view.

obelisk

obverse The main face of a medal, ornament, coin, etc. The opposite side is the "reverse" side.

O.C. An abbreviation for "on center." When dimensions or measurements are given in relating one structural element to another, the distance is sometimes given from the center point of one to the center point of the other.

occasional chair A small, pull-up seat of any style or period, usually used in a living or sitting room. Usually armless. See PULL-UP CHAIR.

occasional table A general term for a small surface creating piece of furniture that can have one or several purposes, such as accompanying a sofa at its lateral extremes, standing in front of it to support a coffee surface, or holding a lamp or cocktail accoutrements.

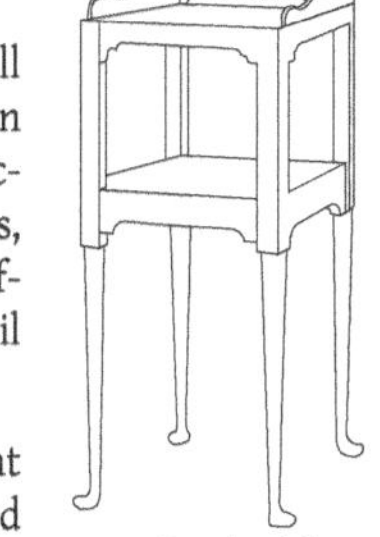
occasional table

oculus A circular opening such as might appear in the crown of a dome. A round window.

odalisque A female slave or concubine in a SERAGLIO. Because of its exotic and erotic connotations, the odalisque was a popular decorative motif during the reign of Louis XV and was often represented reclining on a couch.

∞**odeum** A small ancient Greek and Roman semicircular theater where public music and poetry competitions took place.

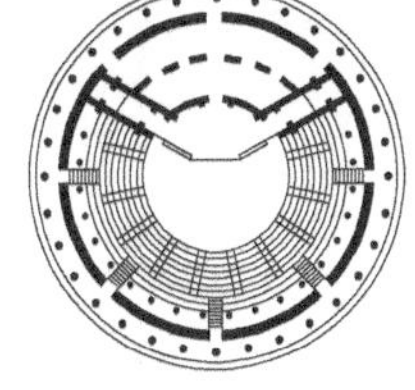
odeum

oeil de boeuf (French: bull's eye) A small round or oval window with a prominent frame, of masonry, metal or wood, in domestic and public architecture, typically found in an upper story if not the attic. Often found as dormer windows in a mansard roof. Prominent in European architectural eras from the Renaissance through Beaux-Arts. Famous examples sporting the bovine ocular fenestration include St. Peter's Basilica, Versailles, and Mt. Vernon.

oeil de boeuf

off-gassing Emission of harmful vapors or volatile organic compounds from a building or material that can degrade indoor air quality.

offset A small projection, ledge, or lip.

off-white Finish that is lightly tinted with a color: bluish-white, yellowish-white, etc.

∞**ogee** A molding made up of a concave and a convex curve. Also called an ogive or keel molding. In architecture, an ogee arch consists of two opposed ogee curves meeting in a point at the top. It was popularly used in the English Decorated Gothic period. Also called a KEEL ARCH.

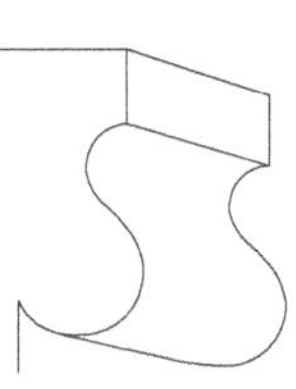
ogee

oiled silk A sheer fabric made of natural protein fibers excreted by larvae; it is rendered waterproof by being soaked in oil and then dried.

oil finish A wood surface treatment accomplished by repeated polishing with the fatty solvent procured from boiling linseed, a flax product. A low, satin-like luster results, and the wood resists stains. A popular finish on walnut and teak. Can yellow over time. See *Table 4*.

oil painting An art technique for which pigment is ground in a fatty medium and applied to a slightly absorbent surface or to a primed canvas. It is traditionally the technique for large and important pictures. The use of oil mixtures for house and/or decorative painting dates back to antiquity.

∞oinochoe A Greek wine jug. The word is from the Greek for "to pour out wine." The spout was shaped in a triangular form, which made pouring easy and accurate. See LAGYNOS and ARYBALLOS.

olefin A light synthetic fiber, soil-resistant and an excellent insulator, used to produce outdoor carpets, wallpaper, and sturdy upholstery fabrics that resist abrasion, pilling, fading, and aging. Sensitive to heat and susceptible to shrinkage. There are multiple trademark names: Fiberglas, Polycrest, Durel PP, and Murress III. See *Table 2* and *Table 3*.

olive wood Natural material from a small Italian tree that, as a veneer, can be used only in small, closely matched patterns. Also used as a decorative inlay. Light yellow with greenish-yellow figures, somewhat like English ash. See *Table 5*.

O.M. An abbreviation for "outer measurement." A measurement of distance between outer surfaces of a hollow object, rather than of distance between inner surfaces (inner measurement or I.M.). Outside measurement includes the thickness of the shell. See I.M.

ombré (French, shadowed) A shaded or graduated one-color pattern, usually in a striped effect. It is a range of tints to shades of a single color.

one-point perspective The mathematical drawing process developed in the Italian Renaissance for representing three-dimensional space on a two-dimensional surface, with all lines converging to a single vanishing point.

onion dome A bulb-like roof structure ending in a point that covers a cupola or tower, often in Eastern European Orthodox churches.

∞onion foot A furniture foot that resembles the bulbs of plants of the genus Allium, of the Early Renaissance; not common after the William and Mary period.

onion dome

chest with onion feet

onlay A decorative overlay or facing like a sheathing or a veneer.

on-the-glaze A colored design applied over fired and treated biscuit pottery, as in MAJOLICA pottery.

onyx A semiprecious gem, a variant of chalcedony, with two or more layers of strongly contrasting colors or marked with white and stratified with opaque and translucent lines. It is an agate stone used for cameos and inlay work.

opacity (1) The hiding power of paint, or its coverage ability. (2) In translucent materials, the ability to block light.

Op Art A style of abstract painting in the 1950s and 1960s that relied on visual sensations and optical illusions, often related to mental processes. Can be seen as an attempt to visually represent psychological processes, including the effects of hallucinogens.

opalescent Showing an iridescent reflection of light, opal-like in its play of color; having a rainbow-like or pearly appearance. Having the qualities of the mineraloid form of silica.

open back A chair's rear vertical surface that has an un-upholstered void between the top and side rails, or a decorative frame back with one or more voids or piercings.

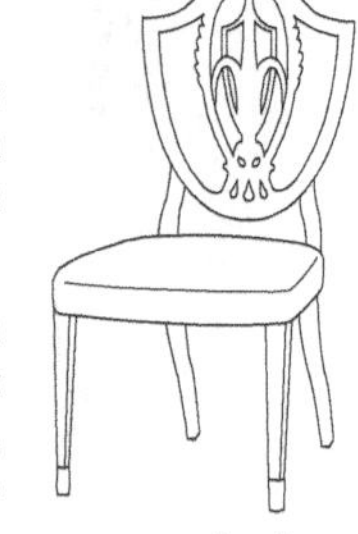

open back

open plan; open planning A concept in store and office layout without permanent constructed walls or partitions. Large, flexible areas are created, which can be divided, as needed, with movable panels, screens, or fixtures and case furniture. Made possible by the modern separation of structure from space-defining elements. See also CLOSED PLAN.

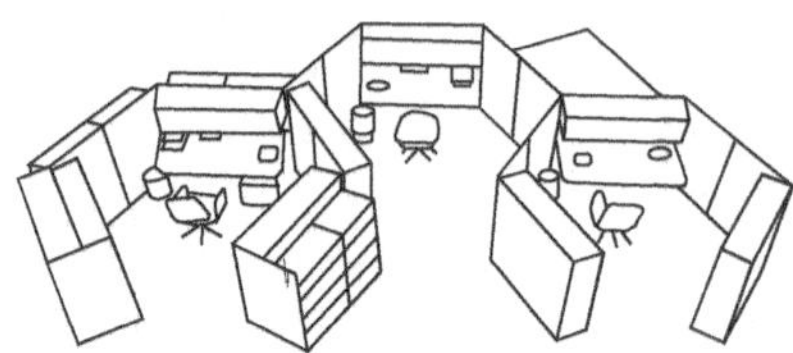

open planning

open-source Concept originating with computer software for which the source code is freely available; generally refers to a collaborative and transparent approach to business that is not centralized and relies on publicly available info, materials, and staffing.

open stock Furniture that is regularly warehoused and is available for immediate delivery. Not custom-made or specially finished. It is possible to buy parts of suites rather than complete groups from open stock.

open-well stair A vertical circulation element which consists of two or more flights surrounding an open space.

operationalize To clarify a concept, problem, or situation and make it measurable, especially in work space-planning and construction.

operatory In a dentist's office or surgery, a room or area with special equipment and facilities, for patient treatment or surgery.

∞opus alexandrinum (Latin) The mosaic work used on floors (and walls) in BYZANTINE and ROMANESQUE churches.

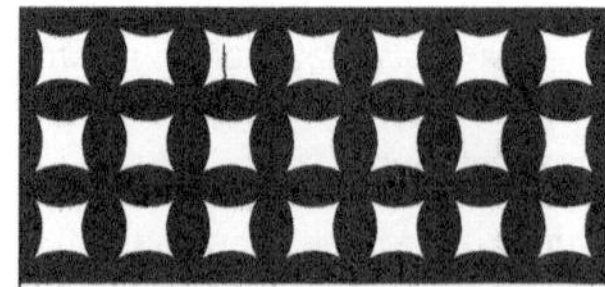

opus alexandrinum

∞opus sectile (Latin) Roman mosaics made up of large pieces of stone or tile that form geometric patterns.

∞opus spicatum (Latin) A Roman method of facing a wall with stones diagonally set to form a herringbone design.

∞**opus tesselatum** Latin term for a mosaic pavement that has TESSERAE laid into patterns or pictures. Tessellated pavements or floors.

∞**opus vermiculatum** (Latin) A type of Roman mosaic work that employed diamond-shaped or long, irregularly shaped stones. It was especially adapted for pictorial designs: hair, drapery folds, features, etc.

orangery or orangerie A hothouse for growing citrus trees. A glassed-in house for plants.

orchestra In the ancient Greek theater, the space in front of the stage where the chorus sang and danced. In present-day auditoriums, the main floor, which is usually pitched so that the level of the front row is below the surface of the stage and the rows behind rise progressively higher.

orders of architecture The classical architectural categories were differentiated notably in the expected characteristics of the pedestal, the column, and the entablature. The Greek systems were Doric, Ionic, and Corinthian. The Roman orders included the three plus the Tuscan and the Composite. See CLASSIC.

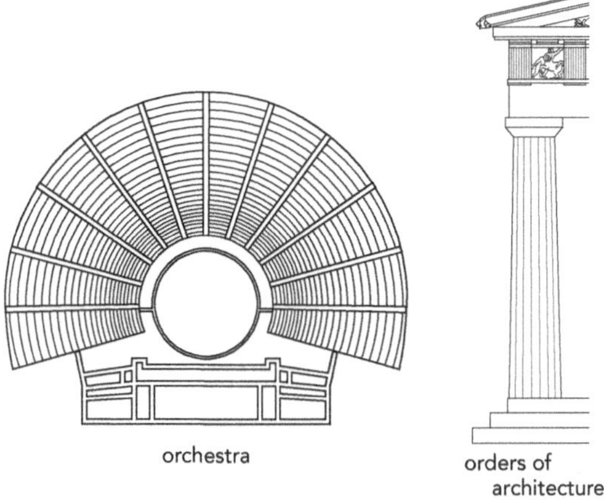

orchestra

orders of architecture

organdy (organdie) A thin, translucent, stiff, and wiry cotton muslin. It can be piece-dyed or printed. The Swiss variant is chemically treated to maintain its crisp, sheer finish.

organic architecture Frank Lloyd Wright's term, which he conceived as a conceptual whole, with the various parts relating to one another and in harmony with the environment.

organzine A two-ply silk yarn twisted in the opposite direction from the single yarn from which it is produced.

oriel window A large projecting wall opening supported by a corbeled brick or stone construction.

∞**Oriental** An outdated term describing the Middle and Far East, its culture and peoples. People from the Far East and Asia are now referred to as Asians. It is still acceptable to refer to objects such as rugs as Oriental.

orientalism A fabrication or idealization of Asian culture by those in the West; can involve art, literature, politics. As an approach to Asian artifacts and history, it is a glossing over, a superficial knowledge, and a failure to know. CHINOISERIE is one example. Often the attributes of one Asian culture are transferred to objects of another.

oriel window

∞**Oriental Modern** A furniture and interior trend in the mid-1950s. The basic Japanese and Chinese lines and geometric designs combine well with the low, sleek, un-cluttered modern lines. Teak and bamboo are used with walnut and rosewood. Heroic bronze, brass, and pewter hardware serve as decorative accents.

Oriental rug Hand-loomed floor coverings made from natural materials (wool, camel's hair, silk, cotton) produced in countries of the East, including Iran, Afghanistan, India, China, Pakistan, Romania, Russia, Turkey, and Tibet. Handcrafted with pile made of yarns tied into knots of two distinct types. Designs may be geometric; mystical or mythical; shapes of plants, foliage, and flowers; and animals. With or without borders. See ARDABIL RUG, CAUCASIAN RUGS, CHINESE RUGS, DHURRIES, FERAGHAN RUGS, ISFAHAN RUGS, KARABAGH RUGS, KERMAN RUGS, KHILIMS, OUSHAK, PERSIAN RUGS, PRAYER RUGS, SARABEND RUGS, SAROUK RUGS, TABRIZ RUGS, TURKISH RUGS, and TURKOMAN RUGS.

Oriental wood A hard-textured Australian natural material of brown to pink-gray color, sometimes with a pinkish cast or streaks. A strong, distinctive striped figure. A member of the laurel family, also called Australian laurel, Australian walnut, and Oriental walnut.

orientation The establishment of a relationship between the position of a wall or a piece of furniture to a point of the compass, a natural landmark, or another major interior design element.

origami Japanese traditional art of paper folding to make a figure or sculpture without cutting or gluing. Influential for designers creating lightweight concrete and other tensile structures.

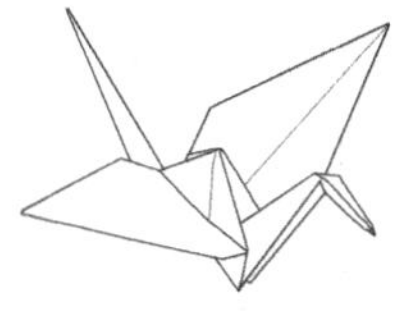

origami

Orlon A DuPont trademark for an acrylic fiber with at least 85 percent acrylonitrile. The fiber adds warmth without weight, and it resists sun fading and some chemical reactions. Orlon has a wool-like hand and takes a brilliant dye.

ormolu or ormoulu Gilded bronze. A bright gold-like metallic alloy with a high percentage of copper plus zinc and tin. Also bronze ornaments, hand-chased and surfaced with gilt, particularly popular in France in the 17th and 18th centuries. Mounts, moldings, and medallions were used as applied decoration on furniture. The manufacture of this material produced toxic gases. See BRONZE DORÉ.

ormolu or ormoulu

ornament A decoration, trimming, enhancement, or embellishment.

∞**os de mouton** (French, mutton bone) A carved motif popular in the period of Louis XIII in France, used for the legs and arms of chairs and sofas. The line is similar to that of a cabriole leg but heavier and stumpier.

osnaburg The plain, coarse cotton fabric from which cretonne is produced. See CRETONNE.

Ostwald system The principles of color classification that Wilhelm Ostwald of Germany devised. See MUNSELL SYSTEM.

ottoman (1) Originally a backless, long, cushioned seat, couch, or divan. In current usage, an oversized upholstered footrest, often designed to relate to a club or easy chair. The contemporary use and proportion developed during the Victorian period. See HASSOCK. (2) A heavy corded fabric like faille but with heavier and rounder ribs.

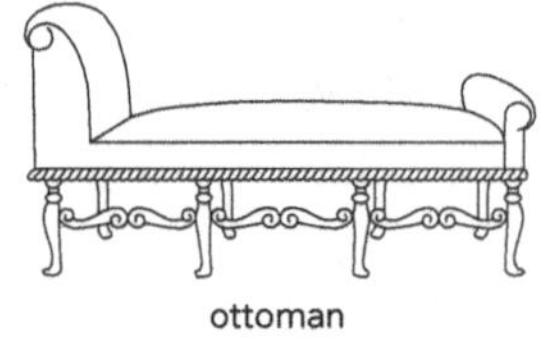
ottoman

ottomane A French upholstered CANAPÉ or SETTEE introduced in the Louis XV period. The curved enclosing side pieces are a continuation of the rounded back. A CANAPÉ À CORBEILLE.

oushak An Oriental rug of near-East origin, now available largely in reproduction. Originals are rare collector's items. Characteristically made in beige, gold, and soft orange and earth tones, with geometric designs contained by a wide border.

outrounded corners The perimeter elements of a square or rectangular tabletop, or panel, shaped into semicircular curves or quarter arcs. See SEGMENTAL CORNERS.

oval back A Hepplewhite chair vertical surface similar to French chairbacks of the Louis XVI period. Also referred to as LE MÉDAILLON. See also CAMEO BACK.

overdoor An architectural design or artwork set over an opening or passageway; the glazed variety is made of wood or lead mullions. In the 18th century in England and the American South, windowed transoms were greatly admired. Paintings can serve as overdoors, such as those François Boucher created for Madame de Pompadour. See FANLIGHT.

overdoor

overdrape An opaque window treatment that is combined with a sheer curtain.

overhead track See TRACK LIGHTING.

oversailing A continuous row of corbels that supports a load. See CORBEL TABLE.

overstuffed Heavily upholstered pieces of furniture, usually with concealed frames; a word associated with furniture with all visible parts upholstered.

ovolo A quarter-round convex molding, often decorated with an EGG AND DART motif.

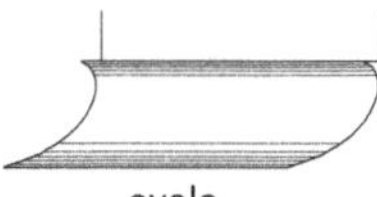
ovolo

∞oxbow chest See YOKE-FRONT CHEST.

∞ox-eye A round or oval window.

oyster grain A peculiarly figured walnut veneer that resembles the inside of a shell. A busy, splotchy, swirly pattern that was popular in the Queen Anne period in England (early 18th century). See OYSTERING.

oystering The process of veneering furniture with burr veneers during the early 18th century. See OYSTERPIECES.

oysterpieces Transverse slices through the gnarled boughs or roots of walnut and other trees.

oysterwood See OYSTERING.

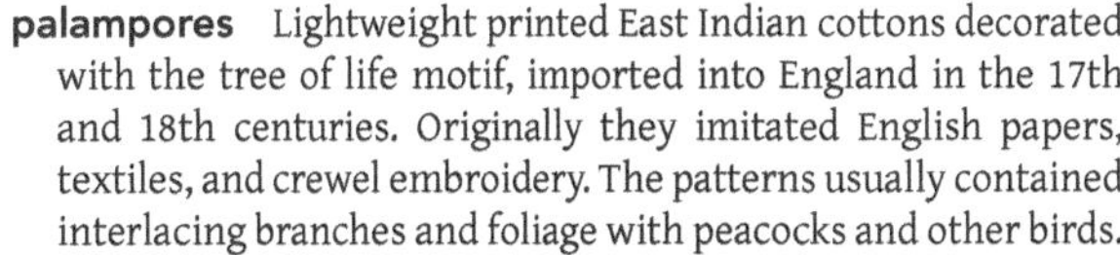

palampores Lightweight printed East Indian cottons decorated with the tree of life motif, imported into England in the 17th and 18th centuries. Originally they imitated English papers, textiles, and crewel embroidery. The patterns usually contained interlacing branches and foliage with peacocks and other birds.

palanquin A covered carriage for one person that was carried on the shoulders of four or more persons by means of poles that projected fore and aft on both sides with the carriage suspended between the poles. It was a form of conveyance that originated in Asia and was also used in 17th- and 18th-century Europe. See SEDAN CHAIR.

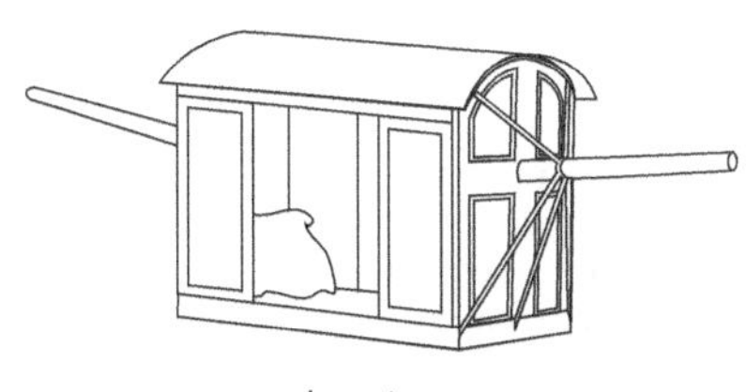

palanquin

pad foot A flattened disk-like support often found under a cabriole leg. Similar to a CLUB FOOT.

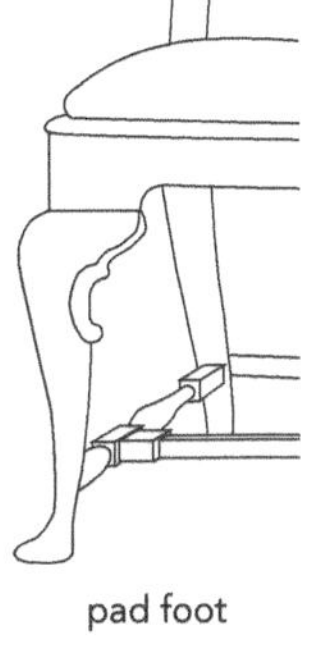

pad foot

padouk A hard, firm-textured durable Burmese wood similar to rosewood. Varies from pinkish tones to a deep reddish-brown, often with darker streaks, highly decorative. Also grows in Africa, Brazil, and the Andaman Islands. Sometimes sold under the name madou. See VERMILION.

pagoda A Chinese tower having several stories, each with its own upswept roof. Each succeeding roof seems to umbrella out and graduate up from the one below and the roofs get smaller as they go up. Initially a hybrid between defensive tower architecture and commemorative stupa design. The pagoda was adapted into an 18th-century decorative element of CHINOISERIE.

pagoda

paillasse Bottom mattress of a series made of coarse husks or other rough materials.

paillon The base coat for transparent lacquer, which is often a reflecting metallic surface or a gilded base, then treated with transparent coloring.

pailou In Chinese architecture, a gateway constructed of wood (or stone in imitation of wood) with a swooping curved tile roof.

paisley A printed or woven fabric design that imitates a Scottish shawl pattern created in the town of that name in the west central lowlands of Scotland. The amoeba- and paramecium-shaped elements were originally Persian in concept.

paktong A silvery alloy of copper, nickel, and zinc that was imported from China in the 18th century. Hard and resonant, it was used for fire grates, fenders, fire irons, etc. Called "white copper."

palazzo An Italian large public building or residence.

payload A Philippine wood of a variable tan ground with black to brown streaks. It has a hard texture and a striped or mottled figure.

Paleolithic "Old Stone Age" period, before the 8th millennium B.C.E, characterized by the first development of stone implements.

∞polestar In ancient Greece and Rome, a public exercise facility for training athletes.

palette (1) A board or tray for mixing paint colors. (2) A range of colors available in fabrics, papers, carpets, etc. (3) A color scheme for a specific project.

palimpsest An original page from a book, a scroll, or artwork in which a text or image has been removed and the base material used again; the process leaves traces of the original image, and the resulting collapsing of layers of initially unrelated images or text can have a pleasing effect.

palisade construction A wall assembly of interlocking vertical planks or logs of wood. It was the type of enclosure made at the Virginian colony of Jamestown.

palisade The French name for East Indian rosewood, dark brown with a violet cast and a definite combed grain stripe. The wood takes a high polish. See ROSEWOOD, HONDURAS.

palisade construction

Palladian Referring to the works or designs of Andrea Palladio and the classical Roman antiques he uncovered and recorded. It is also a generic term for the 18th-century architecture influenced by his research. See the entries that follow. Also see ANDREA PALLADIO in *Designers and Architects*.

Palladian motif An architectural device designed by Palladio and illustrated in the Basilica at Vicenza, Italy, where twin columns support the arches in a rhythmic arcade. The Palladian window is based on the same motif.

Palladian motif

Palladian window A three-part window design usually consisting of four pilasters or columns marking off three tall window areas. The two outer windows have a straight cornice, and the taller central window features an arched semicircular cornice. Popular in 18th- and 19th-century architecture in England and the United States, the Palladian window was characteristic of New England houses, where it lit up the central hallway.

palliative care An area of health maintenance and improvement that focuses on preventing and relieving patient suffering. In contrast to hospice care, it is intended for patients in all disease stages, including those with curable and chronic illnesses, as well as those near the end of life. New treatment developments require rethinking patient rooms and surgeries.

palm Leaves, branches, and the tree itself, used by early civilizations for decorative motifs. The tropical and subtropical flowering plant also served as a symbol of victory, triumph, and peace. The palm motif appeared in Egyptian, Greek, and Early Christian art and in the 20th century was favored by designers including Emilio Terry and Dorothy Draper.

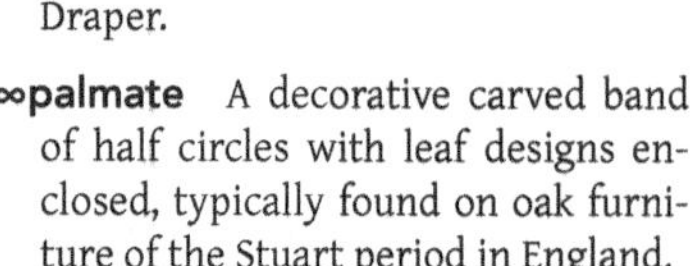
palm

∞palmate A decorative carved band of half circles with leaf designs enclosed, typically found on oak furniture of the Stuart period in England.

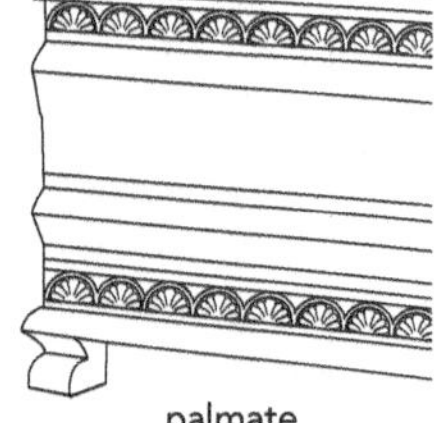
palmate

palmetto (1) A conventionalized fanlike branch of the palm used as a decorative motif. Similar to anthemion and fan motifs. (2) Also indicates a PELMET or LAMBREQUIN when they are thusly decorated.

palm vaulting See FAN VAULTING.

∞pamper A French term for a decorative composition of grapes and vine leaves that was a spiral element in the hollow areas of a twisting column.

∞pancetta An Italian Renaissance wooden stool with three splayed legs and a chip carved fanback. Similar to the sgabello but less elaborate and finished in its decoration. See SGABELLE.

pan daub (Hmong, flower cloth) Textile produced by the Hmong, involving sewing, quilting, and stitching. The resulting handiwork is used to form several different end products including pillows and wall hangings.

pane (1) A piece of glass set in a window or glazed door. (2) The space between timbers in a half-timbered building.

panel (1) In drapery, a width of fabric with hemmed edges and a finished top and bottom. The actual width varies (36 inches to 52 inches, or 91 cm to 132 cm), but in deciding how many are needed to cover an opening, one measures the finished pleated top. Two or three unpleated panels usually make one finished panel. (2) A flat surface, enclosed by a frame. Additional moldings, carvings, painting, applied fabric, wallpapers, etc. can further decorate a panel.

panel, bolection A raised central element, with the surface above and/or in front of the frame.

panel, sunk A recessed element, with the surface below or behind the frame or molding.

panel-back chair A massive, high oak seat with heavy legs, stretchers, and a frame and framed element vertical support usually decorated with carving. An early English Renaissance design. Also called a WAINSCOT CHAIR.

panel-back chair

panelglas A product originally made by the Johns Manville Corporation for acoustic panels made of vitreous fibers. The panels (2 feet × 2 feet or 2 feet × 4 feet or 60 cm × 122 cm) are mounted in simple overhead grids and help to diffuse light and absorb sound.

panel wall In building construction, a non-weight-bearing partition built between columns and piers that serves only to separate or otherwise define spaces.

∞panetière (French) A small hanging cupboard, originally used to store bread.

panne (French, shag, plush) A pile fabric with a shiny or lustrous surface. The finish is produced by pressing back the pile, which is longer than the velvet. Usually a silk or synthetic satin.

panneau (French, panel) Can describe a panel of paper, fabric, wood, etc., simple or elaborate.

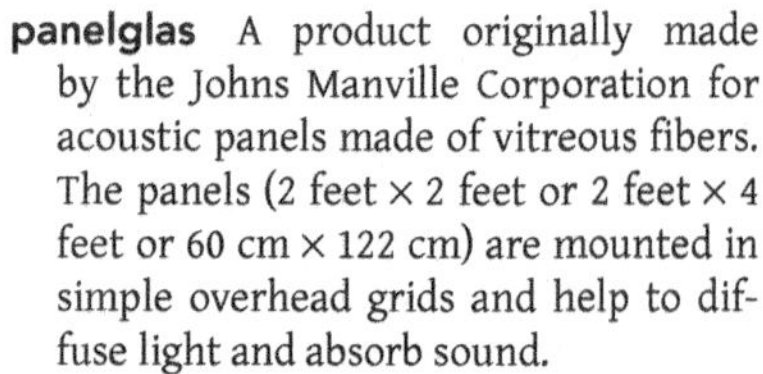
panneau

panne velvet A pile textile with a lustrous finish produced by flattening the yarns and making them lie in the same direction.

pantile A flattened S-shaped tile made of baked clay.

pantile

∞panurge French for a part of a harness. A bed design of the Louis XVI period in France.

∞papelera A small Spanish cabinet of the late 16th and early 17th centuries, with many compartments for papers and

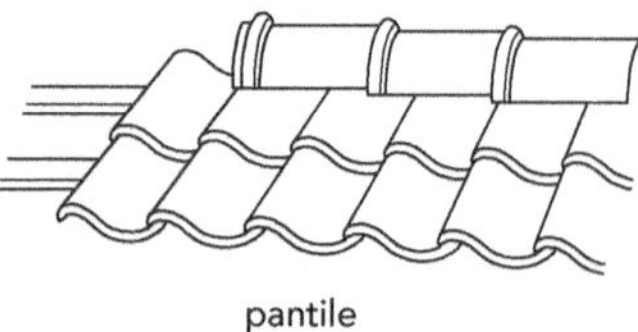

writing materials. Similar to the VARGUEÑO but without the drop-lid.

paper scroll A curved motif sometimes carved on the ends of the top rails of chairs, representing a rolled-up sheet of writing material, slightly uncurled. Popular in the mid-18th century. It is also called spiral whorl, spiral scroll, spiral volute, conical volute, and helicoidal volute.

papier-mâché A technique for making objects that originated in the Middle East and was revived in the mid-18th century in France. Pulped paper is mixed with whiting and glue. This semi-firm material can be shaped and molded, and it dries hard. Artisans of the technique were paperhangers, and they made frames, girandoles, and fancy boxes. Later, moldings and ceiling designs were made in the material and substituted for plaster. In the Victorian period, furniture and accessories were made of papier-mâché.

papier-mâché

papier peint The French term for early painted or printed WALLPAPER.

papyrus A plant symbolically and functionally important in the ancient Chinese and Egyptian civilizations. Paper was made from the plant, and the flower was used as a decorative motif in wall paintings, architecture, and domestic arts of the ancients and in later revivals.

paraline A category of analog architectural drawing that includes isometric, axonometric, and oblique drawings. These single-view drawings are characterized by being measurable and scalable. In contrast to three-dimensional perspectives or renderings, their defining feature is that sets of lines are parallel and do not converge. As a representational category, paraline lies conceptually at a midpoint between plans and elevations and three-dimensional renderings. Paraline images suggest the plastic qualities of architectural objects without attempting to replicate biological sight.

parametric The use of specific metrics to control computational data as generative algorithms. The resulting geometries can form textiles, interior finishes, architectural structures, and furniture pieces.

parametricism The design condition made possible by incorporating highly complex computer-generated geometries; finished designed products that evolve based on continual digital inputs; includes the use of the computer at all design stages, from conception to fabrication.

parametricism

∞parcel gilding A form of decorating in which selected parts of a frame, carving, or surface are embellished with gold. Practiced in the late 17th and early 18th centuries, it was popular during the Decorated Queen Anne period for mirror frames. Often accomplished with stencils.

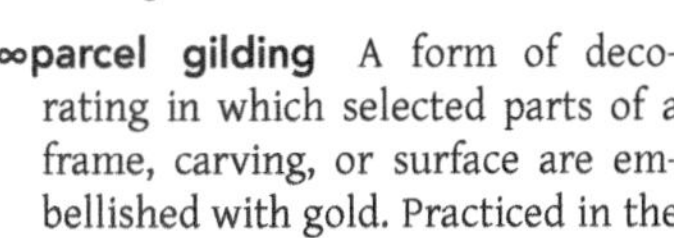

parchment (1) A writing material of antiquity, made by separating the inner side of a sheepskin from the outer woolly side. The peeled skin was treated to make the surface suitable for writing. (2) The warm beige-white color of the material.

∞parchment panel Another name for LINENFOLD paneling.

∞pargetry See PARGE WORK.

∞parge work Ornamental plaster or stucco design applied to a flat surface to create a bas-relief design, a late-16th-century development that attempted to emulate the ribs in a complicated fan- or star-vaulted ceiling. The element employed on the ceiling is decorative rather than structural.

parge work

parian ware Unglazed china, resembles marble.

∞Parliament chair An 18th-century Queen Anne side seat made of mahogany in the British colony of Bermuda. It had a high back with a shaped splat. The front legs were cabrioled with club feet.

parlor or parlour From the French *parloir,* a room where company is received. It is the present-day living room or drawing room. In Johnson's *Dictionary* (1755), it is defined as "a room on the first floor, elegantly furnished for reception or entertainment."

∞parlor lamp A late-19th-century Victorian light fixture on an ornate brass base, consisting of two bulbous globes set one on top of the other with a chimney projecting through the upper sphere. Both globes were usually painted or decorated with decals of lush, multicolored flowers.

parquet An inlaid wood floor, or a mosaic wood floor, with a nonrepresentational design created by strips of wood set out in a definite pattern. Sometimes different colored woods are used. MARQUETRY is similarly constructed, only the resulting figures represent scenes or objects.

parquet

parquetrie or parquetry Furniture inlay work in geometric patterns such as a checkerboard pattern, etc. See MARQUETRY.

Parson's table A simple, square piece of surface furniture design made famous by the Parson's School of Design's Paris studio. Attributed to Jean-Michel Frank, although other designers created similar tables, including Lilly Reich, Mart Stam, and Marcel Breuer. The square legs are continuous with the apron of the tabletop in a clean flow.

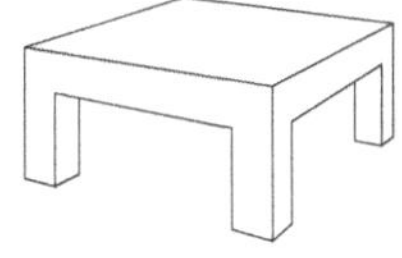

Parson's table

particleboard A construction material in which adhesives bond wood chips or fibers of any size and from any type of wood together in sheets. See MDF.

parting rail A wood divider between drawers on the front of case pieces. An important structural element. May be an important design feature when exposed.

partition An interior wall of one story or less in height.

∞partners' desk (archaic) An 18th-century extra-wide keyhole or pedestal work surface with drawers on both faces of the pedestal. It was therefore possible for two people to

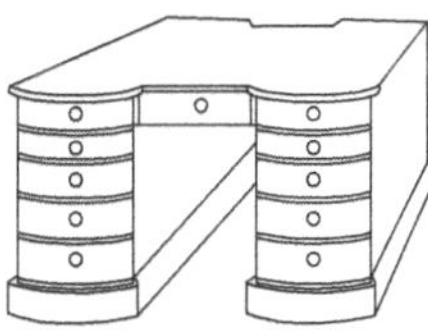

partners' desk

sit facing each other, one on either side of the desk. There is no front or back. The unit probably evolved from the large library tables of the early 18th century. The endpieces were paneled, and the desktop was often made of tooled leather.

partridge wood A Brazilian natural material with graining that resembles partridge feathers in its red and brown coloration. Used in the 17th century as inlay.

party wall A common partition between two structures, spatially separating each from the other but belonging to both units. In lieu of two walls that abut each other.

passementerie From the French *passement*, a strip of lace. A trimming or edging of braid, gimp, beads, or cording.

paste The body of pottery. Soft paste is produced by a glass mixture, while hard paste is a mixture of kaolin and feldspar.

pastels Sticks of dry powdered color mixed with enough gum to bind the powder into a chalk. When the sticks are rubbed on paper, they disintegrate, and the colored powder remains on the paper's surface. Properly used, the devices give the effect of a painting. Hard pastels are more closely related in effect to drawing. Quentin de La Tour, Jean-Baptiste-Siméon Chardin, and Edgar Degas were all skilled in their use.

pastiglia A bas-relief design achieved by adding successive layers of thin plaster over a surface covered with a fine fabric. The finishing details were achieved with a knife, and often the design was gilded and burnished. The three-dimensional technique was introduced in the Italian Renaissance. Also refers to molded plaster ornaments (gilded gesso work). See ANAGLYPTA, CARTON-PIERRE, and COMPOSITION ORNAMENT.

patera A round or oval disk usually decorated with a rosette or other ornament.

patera

patina or patine A greenish coating on the surface of old bronze. Also the mellowing of age on any object or material due to exposure or repeated waxings or polishings. Also the gloss on woodwork. See BRONZE.

patio An inner court, open to the sky. See ATRIUM.

pattern The vertical graining of wood and veneer, as opposed to the highlights or cross grains, which are called figures.

patterned rolled glass See DIFFUSING GLASS.

pavement Inside a building, a flooring of stone, marble, or tile.

pavers Unglazed porcelain or natural clay tiles. They are 6 square inches or more in size (15.25 cm).

pavilion (Latin, butterfly) A separate but related building, an integral part of the design of a larger or main building. The pavilion was originally a tent-like affair spread out like a butterfly's wings.

∞paw-and-ball foot A mid-18th-century replacement for the claw-and-ball leg support. See BALL-AND-CLAW FOOT.

paw foot Usually a carved representation of a lion's or bear's paw, decorated with foliage, and used as a furniture leg support in the late-17th- to early-18th-century French and English furniture. See BEAR'S PAW FOOT.

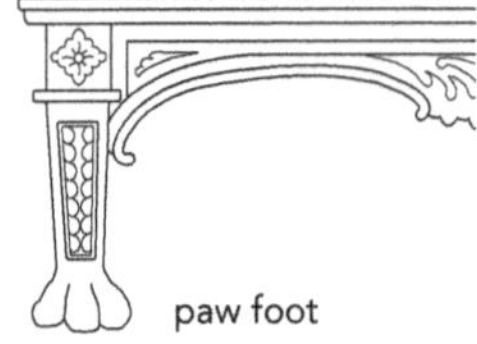
paw foot

paysages or paysages-décors An early-19th-century French term for wall murals featuring country landscapes, hunts, etc. These printed wallpaper designs were usually applied from the chair rail up to the cornice and formed a continuous scene around the room. They were not repeats of a scene but a continuous panorama. The English had developed a similar art in tempera-painted scenes on paper, which they called perspectives.

pé Plastic and wood composite material that works well for decking.

peacock chair A large, sweeping fanback seat woven of rattan or wicker and originally associated with Hong Kong. This mid-to-late-19th-century Victorian design is, with slight variations, still made today. Usually has an hourglass pedestal base with supporting uprights. See CROQUET CHAIR.

∞pear-drop ornament An embellishment usually decorating the upper section of a plain frieze. In Hepplewhite and Sheraton designs, it appears as a crystal-like lobe at the lower points of a series of Gothic arches in relief.

pearling A series of rounded forms of the same size, or graduated like a string of beads, used as a furniture embellishment, either in straight lines, arced, or in a SWAG.

pearls A string of beads, either of the same size or graduated, used as an ornament on furniture or wall décor. It may be a painted or carved representation, and it is often used in a swag-like arrangement. Popular in mid-and-late-18th-century French and English designs.

pearwood A pinkish-brown, finely grained natural material similar to boxwood, often used for inlay and fine cabinetwork. In the 16th and 17th centuries, it was used for country-made furniture and was sometimes stained to simulate ebony. See *Table 5.*

peasant weave See HOMESPUN.

pebble dashing Stucco or mortar that is surfaced with partially embedded small stones.

pecan A south-central U.S. wood of the HICKORY family. It resembles walnut with its strong grain pattern and is often used in conjunction with walnut on exposed areas of furniture.

∞péché mortel (French, deadly sin) A mid-18th-century term for a chaise longue that was sometimes made in two parts, an oversized easy chair with an upholstered stool, and joined in the middle. See CHAISE LONGUE and DUCHESSE.

pecky cypress A scarred, pitted, crumbly textured cypress wood used for interior wood paneling. It is worm-eaten in appearance, and it is structurally weak, but its uneven surface quality has a striking effect.

pedestal (1) A supporting base or block for a statue, vase, etc. (2) In architecture, the lowest portion of a classical order, consisting of a base, dado, and cornice. (3) In commercial furniture, denotes a 24 inch high by 15 inch wide narrow file with drawers (60 cm × 39 cm).

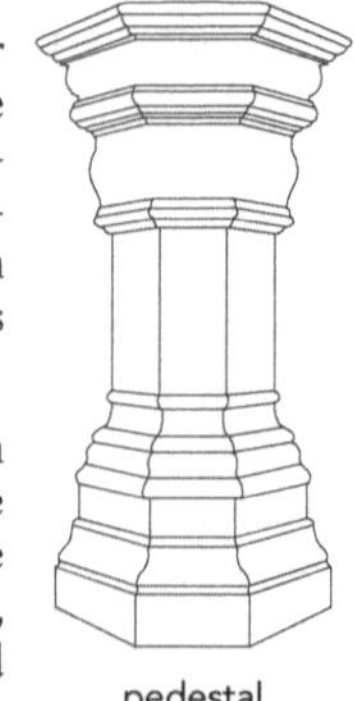
pedestal

pedestal chair A 20th-century seat design with the horizontal load-bearing surface on a single support with a flaring base. The support is usually made of metal, wood, or plastic. Sometimes the seat is molded in one with the pedestal in a continuous sculpted design. See EERO SAARINEN in *Designers and Architects.*

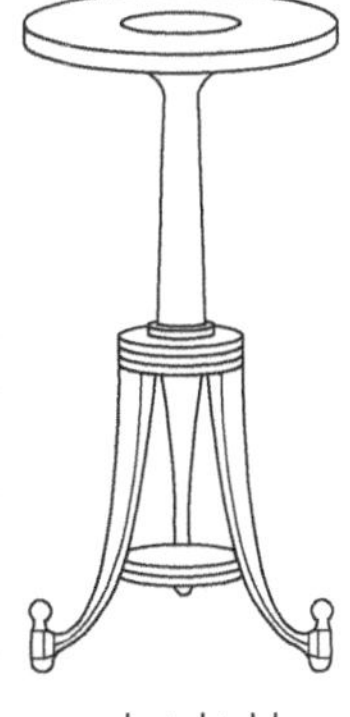
pedestal table

pedestal desk See KNEEHOLE DESK.

pedestal table Usually a round or an oval work surface supported by a single member base. This support is often a column or turning that ends in a heavy base with spreading feet. Although found in 18th-century English furniture, as well as in 19th-century Regency and Duncan Phyfe designs, it is also a popular modern design, with the work surface resting on a thin support that flares outward at the floor.

pediment (1) In Greek architecture, a triangular form at the roof line of temples or other structures that was accentuated by the moldings of the entablature. (2) In 18th-century furniture designs, the cap or finishing design on case pieces, bookcases, chests, cabinets, secretaries, etc. The pediment may vary in design: swan, segmented, broken scroll, etc.

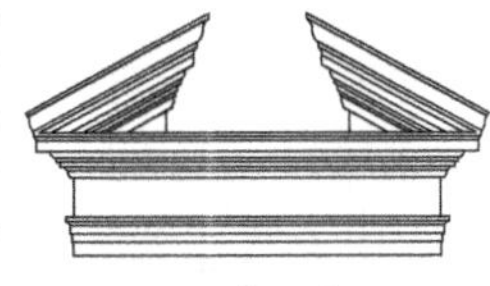
pediment

peg A wooden pin, dowel, or spike used for fastening or joining furniture, wood panels, floors, etc. in place of a nail. A joint that is accomplished with pegs is referred to as a doweled joint.

pellet ornament A Norman and Gothic ornament that resembles flattened balls or disks. See GOTHIC PERIOD and NORMAN PERIOD.

∞**pelmet** An element similar to a valance, such as a rail, rod, or side panel, that hides curtain fixtures. See LAMBREQUIN.

∞**Pembroke table** An 18th-century occasional piece of surface furniture with two wide drop leaves, and a drawer set in the apron. Brackets set into the top frame support the drop leaves. The central, fixed surface is twice as wide as the drop leaves. Named for the tenth Earl of Pembroke.

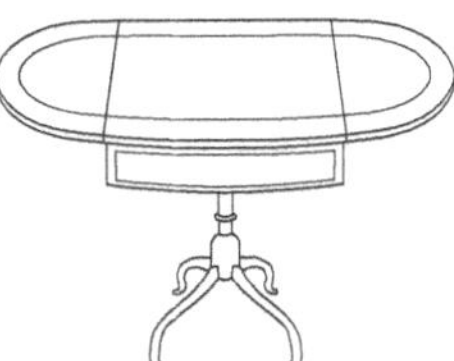
Pembroke table

pencil and pearl Another name for bead and reel molding, made up of alternating round and elongated forms.

pencil stripe A wood-grain effect similar to a ribbon striation. The elongated elements are fine and close together. Sometimes found in walnut.

pendant (1) A drop, or a hanging ornament, on furniture, light fixtures, etc. It may be a pendant sphere, pendant finial, or pendant husk. (2) A boss or projection hanging down from a vault or ceiling. See BOSS and CUL-DE-LAMPE.

pendentive A triangular element that transitions from a wall, pier, or column to the base of a dome. A famous example is found in Hagia Sophia, Istanbul, Turkey.

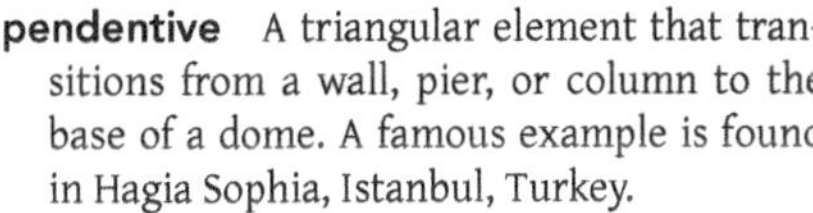

pendant

∞**pendule à gaine** (French) A tall clock or grandfather clock. See GAINE.

penne d'oiseau (archaic) (French, bird's feather) A carved ornament on wooden furniture of the mid-French Renaissance period.

pennon A streamer, ribbon, or label, used as a decorative motif.

Pennsylvania Dutch Name given to German and Swiss Mennonites who settled in the Northeastern United States near York, Lancaster, and Germantown at the end of the 17th century. "Deutsch" (German) became "Dutch," hence the misnomer. Using simple, functional lines, they decorated their furniture, homes, and utensils in bright, gay colors. Among their favorite motifs were circular geometric hex signs, peacocks, hearts, tulips, rosettes, roosters, hens, reindeer, and leaves. Their furniture was similar in construction to other 18th-century Colonial American designs.

Pennsylvania stove See FRANKLIN STOVE.

∞**pentes** A 15th-century term for lambrequins, ornamental draperies, valances, or scalloped fabric treatments for use on the upper part of a window, across the top of a doorway, or on mantels. See LAMBREQUIN.

penthouse A medieval term meaning a hanging roof, or a lean-to bracketed out from a wall. In present-day usage, a dwelling on the uppermost story of a high building or an additional structure set on a roof. The habitable space usually sits back from the main building wall, which allows for a terrace or walk area.

percale A medium-weight cotton fabric made of carded yarns with a firm, plain weave and a dull, smooth finish, often printed.

perforated metal A sheet of material with dots, dashes, or other simple designs punched out, creating a cane-like or lattice effect.

peristyle A colonnade surrounding a building or enclosing a court, especially in classical architecture.

Performalism Design where shapes have been liberated from a reliance on right angles and that disengages the exterior from the interior. The building's skin can thus respond to climate conditions in a variety of ways and can even move, while the building behind remains economically and functionally pragmatic. A 21st-century variant of the BRISE-SOLEIL.

performance architecture Buildings that have moved beyond the requirement of permanence; in a business context, an organization's social and administrative infrastructure (not necessarily buildings) that uses theoretical models to improve economic performance with measurable value.

pergola (Italian. arbor) A balcony or lattice framework covered with vines or shrubs. A latticed structure used as a summerhouse or shade area. A bower. See GAZEBO.

period A roughly defined era when a particular influence or style prevailed. Styles usually started before and lasted past the time of a designated period. Often there are transitional swaths of time during which the incoming and outgoing styles mix.

period furniture Newly made household objects of a style other than that of the present day. Such designs do not have to be authentic reproductions of historical styles but have the scale, details, or motifs of an era. Examples of popular period furniture include Empire, Chippendale, and Queen Anne. Historicist, and not modern or contemporary.

∞**periwig chair** A tall-back seat of the late 17th century (William and Mary period in England) that had an elaborate pierced and/or carved cresting to accommodate and provide a setting for elaborate headdresses of the day. Designed with turned walnut supports, and with or without arms. The back was usually caned.

perlon A synthetic fiber, similar to nylon, manufactured in Germany.

peroba A pale ROSEWOOD of South America that is identified by its streaks. The streaks may fade under exposure to strong light.

∞Perpendicular style The last phase (1377–1485) of the Gothic period in England. It is noted for the large windowed spaces and the slender vertical lines that appear on the interiors in tracery, moldings, and other decorations. Also called rectilinear, late pointed, and Lancastrian.

perron A landing at the head of a flight of stairs and directly in front of an entrance door of a building.

persane A French 18th-century printed fabric inspired by Persian originals; a pseudo-Oriental design.

∞persiana Venetian-blind-like elements used in Spain. See PERSIENNE.

Persian cedar See NANMU.

Persian knot See SEHNA KNOT.

Persian rugs An admired category of Middle Eastern floor coverings, noted for their magnificent designs, beautiful colors, and expert craftsmanship. Today, they are produced in Iran (formerly Persia). Among the best known are SAROUK, KERMAN, SARABEND, ISFAHAN, and FERAGHAN floor coverings. (See individual entries.) Each province produces its own traditional and characteristic style, theme, and type. Antique examples are especially prized. Examples from neighboring countries are sometimes mistakenly called "Persians."

∞persienne A French word for an external Venetian blind. A shutter of thin laths in a wood frame. See PERSIANA.

perspective The representation of three-dimensional objects in spatial recession on a two-dimensional surface. The assumption is that parallel lines never meet, but they appear to do so at a vanishing point on the horizon.

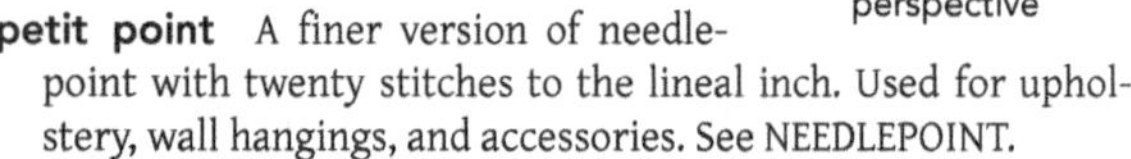

perspective

perspectives See PAYSAGES.

petite commode A small table and storage unit, usually with three drawers set one under the other.

petit point A finer version of needlepoint with twenty stitches to the lineal inch. Used for upholstery, wall hangings, and accessories. See NEEDLEPOINT.

petticoat mirror A console looking glass set over a low console or pier table. Often an Empire piece, ladies used them to see if their petticoats were showing. See CONSOLE MIRROR.

petticoat valance A fabric drape, full and shirred, used below the mattress on a canopy or tester bed. A dust ruffle.

pewter A metal alloy of tin and lead, dull gray in appearance, originally used as a silver substitute.

pharmacist's lamp A lightweight, floor-standing light fixture of brass or chrome with a semicircular shield. The shield can turn or twist to direct the light source, and the device was used in pharmacies in the early 20th century. The stem of the fixture is usually a narrow pipe. A modern adaptation was created.

Philadelphia chair A Windsor-style seat manufactured in the onetime American capital city in the 18th century. Gilbert and Robert Gaw were important manufacturers of this American seat. See WINDSOR CHAIR, AMERICAN.

Philadelphia chair construction A term for the construction used on Queen Anne and Chippendale seats made in the onetime colonial capital in the latter part of the 18th century. The side rails of the chair seat were mortised into the rear uprights.

Philadelphia Chippendale Chippendale-style furniture made of mahogany and produced in Pennsylvania's largest city in the latter half of the 18th century. William Savery and John Folwell were craftsmen who produced highboys, lowboys, and chairs rich in carved details.

Philadelphia peanut A bean-shaped cabochon ornament used as a decorative carved motif on 18th-century furniture made in the Northeastern American city.

philhellene One enamored of all things Greek. A lover, admirer, and supporter of Greece and Greek culture, especially the arts. Part of a general support of Greco-Roman design, some of these aficionados positioned themselves with their preference of Greece over Rome (Karl Friedrich Schinkel). Notable philhellenes throughout history include the emperor Hadrian, the dancer Isadora Duncan, and the designer T.H. Robsjohn-Gibbings. The latter saw connections between Art Deco, Greece, and modernism and created a contemporary version of the Klismos chair.

Philippine mahogany See LAUAN.

phosphorescent paints Opaque finishes that glow in the dark.

photoluminescent (adj.) Emitting light in the location where the substance first absorbs photons; used for egress marking, most notably in fire exit signage.

pianoforte A musical instrument invented by Cristofori in the early 18th century, a forerunner of the piano.

piano nobile The principal floor or main story of a building. In Renaissance structures a grand stairway led up to this main floor, which was not the ground floor. Also called BEL ÉTAGE.

piano stool A round, square, or rectangular seat with a screw pivot below so that it can be raised or lowered. The unit dates back to the late 18th century.

piano stool

piazza An Italian public urban space; also in English usage, particularly in the American South, a deck or balcony.

pick The single filling thread that goes completely across the loom and interlaces with the warp threads to weave a fabric. In carpet manufacturing, the weft threads (across the loom) tie in the yarn that forms the tufts and loops on the carpet's surface. The number of picks per inch indicates the closeness of the weave. In Axminster weaving, the word "row" means the same as "pick." See COUNT OF CLOTH and WEFT.

pickled (adj.) The result of rubbing white or off-white paint into previously stained and finished wood.

picot A purl on lace, or a small loop woven on the edge of ribbon.

∞picotage A printing technique used on toiles during the late 18th and early 19th centuries. Short metal wires were driven into the wood blocks used for printing, and these wires created a dotted background on the paper or fabric.

∞picoté A small-scale floral pattern Christophe-Philippe Oberkampf created at his factory in Jony, France, during the latter part of the 18th century. It featured a short-repeat pattern printed on cotton. Numerous dots surrounded the printed motif, which softened the silhouette. See CHRISTOPHE-PHILIPPE OBERKAMPF in *Designers and Architects.*

picture molding or rail A grooved extrusion on a wall placed close to the ceiling line, or the lowest border of a frieze, from which to suspend pictures. Also called a frieze rail.

picture rugs A modern Scandinavian development of woven abstract designs that may serve as dramatic floor coverings or may be mounted as wall decorations. They are modern floor tapestries or hand-knotted or hooked hangings. Some of the leading artists creating these floor coverings include the Danes Franka Rasmussen and Tusta Welfing and the Swedish weaver Brittan Valberg.

picture window A large single pane of glass similar to but somewhat smaller than the usual shop-front glass, used in an interior as a dramatic focal point of a room, usually a living room, where the outside surroundings provide an interesting scene to be viewed from within.

pie safes See MILK OR PIE SAFES.

piece-dyed Color transfer process in textiles after they have been woven. The opposite of yarn-dyed.

∞piecrust table A round pedestal work surface with the raised edge of the top surface carved in scallops, like the crimped edge of the crusted dessert. A common design in 18th-century England and America, especially in mahogany tripod tables.

pied-à-terre (French, foot on the ground) A second residence, usually in a different locale from the primary residence, used occasionally for the convenience of proximity to the sites of activities.

∞pied de biche (French, hind's foot) A decorative cloven-hoof-shaped foot for seating units, tables, etc., used in the late Renaissance in Italy, France, and England. Also called a CLOVEN FOOT.

pier An isolated, heavy, vertical masonry support, like a column or pilaster but lacking the proportions or details of either. The pier supports arches and beams, and it is attached to a wall at the point where a heavy load is imposed.

pier

pierced splat The center vertical panel of a chair back decorated with an openwork design, usually cut with a fretsaw. See FRETWORK.

pierced work Ornamental woodwork in which portions of the background are cut out, leaving an openwork design. Similar in appearance to fretwork. In Chippendale's Gothic-style chair, the process resulted in a popular form of decoration. It has also been used for windows etc. in Islamic architecture. It had a renaissance in the work of American architect Edward Durell Stone and the architects whose works are known as tropical Modernism. See EDWARD DURELL STONE in *Designers and Architects.*

pier glass Originally a mirror that stood on the floor against the wall, intended as a facing for vertical structural elements or to cover the space between windows. The term also describes mirrors set over console tables. See CHEVAL GLASS OR MIRROR.

pierced work

pier table A console usually used in conjunction with a glass or mirror. Originally intended to be used on the space (or pier) between two windows. Also called a CONSOLE TABLE.

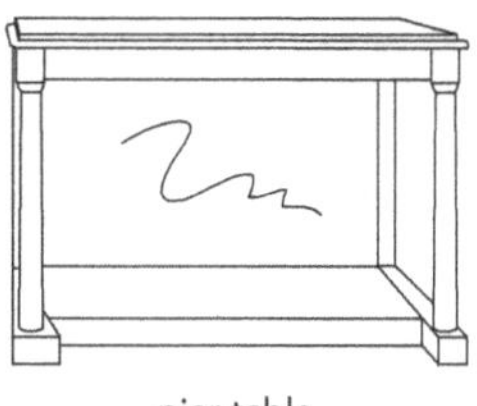

pier table

pietra dura or pietre dure (Italian or French) An Italian Renaissance mosaic inlay of marbles and assorted stones. Fine stones and marbles are inlaid or laminated into a stone base. The colors and markings are intricately used to create a pattern or picture. The pietra dura technique was used for tabletops, cabinet embellishments, etc. See INTARSIA and MOSAIC.

pigeonholes Small compartments in a bureau or secretary, often found in late-17th- and 18th-century pieces.

pigment Powdered coloring matter for paint, dye, or ink, made from natural or synthetic materials.

pigment volume concentration (PVC) The quantity of material color relative to resin in a paint. Higher amounts produce a textured, flatter appearance.

pilaster An engaged pier built as part of a wall and acting as a support for a cornice or pediment. A flat-faced vertical projection from a wall, sometimes with the proportions, details, base, and capital of a column. In furniture, the pilaster is a carved representation of the architectural feature, usually at the vertical ends of a cabinet, chest, or CONSOLE TABLE and it forms a support for an overhanging table surface or shelf drawer.

pilasters

pile In carpet construction, the uncut or cut loop tufts of surface yarn that form the wearing surface. In fabrics, the nap or top surface. See FRIEZE, PLUSH, VELVET, and *Table 1.*

pillar An upright member, usually a column. May not be cylindrical or have the proportions of a classical order. Also, a commemorative shaft.

pillar

∞pillar-and-claw table A pedestal work surface of the Chippendale style with a central column-like support terminating in splayed legs. The feet are usually carved lion or bear paws.

∞pillar-and-scroll A mantel clock case designed by the American clock designer Eli Terry, of Plymouth, Connecticut, in the early 19th century. It resembled the upper portion of a grandfather clock. The case had a scrolled top and skirt with columns or pillars at either side. The dial was opaque and enameled. Often a picture embellished the glass area below the dial.

∞pillowback chair One version of the 19th-century Hitchcock seat with the typical rush support, decorated or stenciled rails, and turned front legs. The distinguishing characteristic is the upholstered block in the middle of the top rail with turned decorations on either side. A favorite Sheraton motif.

pillow capital A Byzantine or Romanesque simplified version of the Corinthian capital. It is a square block, rounded at the corners, that resembles the head support in its form and is decorated in low bas-relief sculpture.

pillow capital

pilotis Cylindrical or oval freestanding columns associated with Le Corbusier, Alvar Aalto, and other modernists.

pinched trailing See QUILLWORK.

pincushion chair See COMPASS SEAT.

pine The abundant and popular American wood, with an interesting grain. It is economical, easy to work, and used for furniture as well as interior finishes. See *Table 5.*

pine, pickled A finish for interior walls or furniture that is a whitish patina or rub on knotty pine. Probably developed from the custom of scraping paint off old English furniture. The residue paint that accented the graining gave the old furniture a mellow quality now emulated in reproductions.

pine, white A soft wood. The grain is usually uninteresting, and the wood, which is generally used for structural and finishing purposes, is often painted. See *Table 5.*

pine, yellow Hard wood, stronger and heavier than white pine, and good for inexpensive flooring, trim, doors, and furniture. Usually painted. See *Table 5.*

pineapple A decorative carved stylized finial resembling the juicy tropical fruit, often used as a terminal piece on bedposts, newel posts, in pediments over doorways, etc. In early-19th-century America it was a symbol of wealth, prosperity, and hospitality.

pink noise A sound frequency that is not as strong as white noise but similarly intended to mask out undesirable sounds. Also known as flicker noise and produced by some electronics.

pinnacle A cone-shaped or pyramidal turret used in Gothic architecture to top roofs and buttresses. The pointed termination of a spire is often decorated with *crockets.* The device may be used decoratively as an ending or a finial at the crest or top of a piece of furniture.

pinnacle

pinwale An integral narrow rib or ridge in a fabric, as in a type of corduroy.

piping A tubular edging used to trim and decorate upholstery and draperies. The tube may have a cord filler, which lends the piping roundness and a firm appearance.

∞pipkin An 18th-century English term for a metal coal container used at the fireside. See COAL SCUTTLE.

piqua An African satin-textured wood with a uniform pinkish-brown color. See BOSSE.

piqué (French, quilted) (1) A heavy cotton fabric with raised cords running lengthwise. Also called Bedford cloth. (2) In inlaying, gold or silver, shell, mother-of-pearl, or ivory, set in points or strips. This inlay technique was popular in the 17th and 18th centuries in France for decorating small accessory pieces like snuffboxes, small cabinets, and jewel boxes.

pitch In the manufacturing of carpets, the number of warp threads per inch, measured across the width of the loom. The closer the warp threads, the finer the weave. The pitch is considered in connection with the "pick" or "rows" per inch. See PICK.

plaid Multicolored, checkered, or squared pattern created by bars of different colors and thicknesses crossing each other at right angles. The design may also be printed on fabric, paper, etc. Originally, the word meant the shawl worn by Scots, and the pattern was called tartan.

plain butt joint One piece of wood is held against another piece of wood using glue, nails, or screws. It is a poor-quality joint.

plain slicing veneer Consecutive slices cut from the half log or fitch parallel to a line through the center of the log. Usually results in a variegated figure.

plain weave A basic textile construction in which the warp and weft are the same size and alternate under and over each other in a regular manner. Used to make muslin, taffeta, etc.

plan The horizontal projection of any object. A drawing that shows the arrangement and horizontal measurements of a building or room. A plan is a horizontal section. What an architectural design with the roof removed would look like from a perfect bird's eye view.

plancer or planceer The finished underside or soffit of a cornice.

plane European sycamore wood, used for veneer and inlay.

plan

plank construction Assembly method of designed objects in which the original wooden materials remain visible and whose structure and manufacture are apparent by observation.

plank flooring Wood materials that lie atop the structure made of lumber pieces that are 3 to 8 inches wide (8 cm × 20 cm) and uncovered by other materials.

plank construction

plantation shutters A type of window covering with wide blades.

planted molding A cut and applied continuous decoration, as distinct from a stuck molding (which is formed on the surface and which is an integral part of the wall material). See APPLIED MOLDING and STUCK MOLDING.

plantscaping The art of decorating with an interior space with greenery as accents and space-defining elements.

plaque A plate or panel of wood, metal, glass, stone, pottery, etc. with a surface ornamentation or inscription. In furniture, an ornamental disc or plate of porcelain, lacquer, finely chased ormolu, inlay, Wedgwood, etc. used as an enhancement. See CARTOUCHE.

plaque

plaque striée (archaic) A striped panel, usually of bronze, which appeared as a decorative banding on aprons and legs of tables and commodes in the late Louis XVI period and through the Regency period in England.

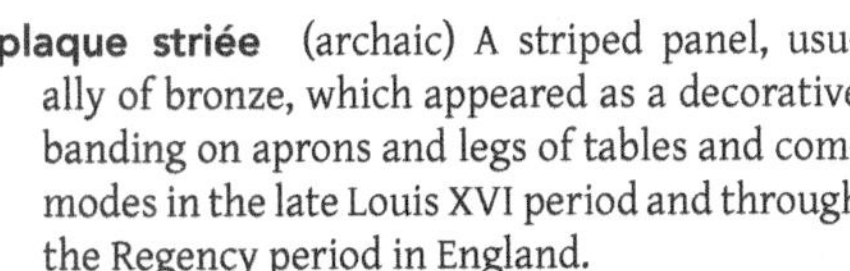

plaquette A strong shape of contrasting veneer inlay in a veneer surface. The shape usually has a decorative inlaid detail such as an eagle or an urn.

plaster A wall and ceiling surfacing material, made of lime, water, sand, and sometimes plaster of Paris. On occasions, hair is added as a reinforcing agent. May be smooth or textured.

plasterboard See BUILDING BOARD and GYPSUM BOARD.

plaster of paris A composition of calcined and ground gypsum or calcium sulfate hemihydrate. It is worked when moistened and hardens as it dries.

plastic (adj.) Modeled, as opposed to carved. (noun) A general term for a man-made resinous material that is chemically produced. It may be molded, formed, extruded, or shaped by heat or pressure. See THERMOPLASTIC, THERMOSETTING, and the generic names for trademarked materials.

plateau A decorative stand, set on low feet, used to raise a centerpiece above the table's surface, popular in the early 19th century. Often made of papier-mâché but also of wood, brass, or glass. Similar to a large trivet.

plate glass Vitreous material rolled in large sheets, made with soda, lime, and silica. The surfaces are ground and polished. A mid-19th-century development making possible large window panes and mirrors especially for storefronts.

plate warmer A metal-lined unit equipped with a heater that was placed in sideboards of late-18th-century English design. It later became a self-contained unit used on serving tables, similar to the current hot plate.

Plateresco The period in Spanish art dating from the first half of the 16th century. The style of ornament that prevailed was an imitation of the fine details of the silversmith's art. *Platero* is Spanish for silversmith.

Plateresque (Spanish, Plateresco) Highly ornamented design of the 16th century, related to Baroque. On the Iberian peninsula and in the Americas. See PLATERESCO.

platform bed A mattress set on top of a wood or plastic built-up surface. Sometimes the mattress is recessed into a frame on the top of the platform, and a shelf may go partially or completely around the perimeter. In other designs, the mattress appears to float over a base that is recessed below it. A platform bed may be used against a wall or stand as an "island" in a room. See ISLAND BED.

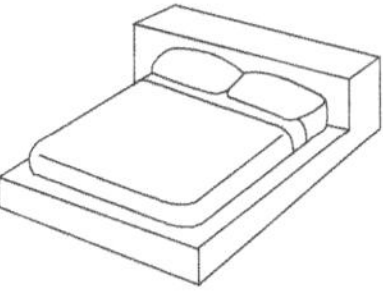
platform bed

pleating The folding or doubling over of fabric to create fullness. There are various methods: pinch pleating, box pleating, accordion pleating, etc. Each technique creates a different heading effect. Pleating is more formal than shirring. See LINENFOLD.

plexiform A surface design that resembles basket weaving or plaiting. It was often used to decorate Romanesque and Celtic architecture. See NATTES.

Plexiglas A trademarked name for a group of plastic sheet products produced in a variety of sizes, colors, thicknesses, and patterns, usually transparent. The generic term is plexiglass.

pliant (French, flexible) A cross-legged folding stool, campstool, or deck chair. See FAUDESTEUIL.

plinth The square part of the base of a column or a pedestal piece of case furniture that is set solidly flat on the floor. It is the molded projection base of a structure or a pedestal without elaborate moldings.

pliant

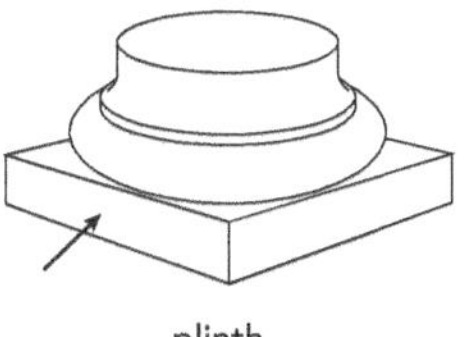
plinth

plinth block A small rectangle of wood used at the bottom of a door jamb trim. The baseboard butts against it.

∞pliqué à jour enameling A 14th-century finishing process that created a small-scale stained-glass effect. Vitreous, translucent glass pastes were set into a fine metal network or mesh, without backing.

plisse A crinkled surface in stripes or patterns that results from a method of printing on plain-weave cotton and rayon fabrics.

plum wood A dark red natural material, like mahogany, which was used up to the 18th century.

plush A long-pile velvet. Deeper and lusher than velvet or velour, it may be made of silk, mohair, or synthetic fibers. Used as an upholstery fabric. Velvet pile is less than ⅛ inch thick (3.175 mm), and plush pile is longer than ⅛ inch. See *Table 1*.

plush carpet Floor covering distinguished by a slightly higher pile than a velvet carpet; usually less dense. Because the surface is not as smooth as the velvet, the pile absorbs some light, resulting in a low reflection and a warm, textured appearance. See *Table 1*.

ply The number of twists, folds, strands, or layers in yarns, papers, and woods.

plywood Strong layered panel, consisting of a thick, semi-porous core, on both sides of which are laminated thin veneers, 1/16 inch thick or less (1.6 mm), with the grain running perpendicular to the grain of the core, an arrangement called crossbanding. A finish layer is applied on top: a veneer with the grain running parallel with that of the core. This makes a "plaid" with the tensions pulling in different directions, resulting in the panel's strength. See LAMINATION.

pocket door A standard-size closure that is opened by sliding the element sideways out of sight, into an opening in the supporting wall. A popular device in the 19th century when a pair of such doors closed off a parlor or dining room.

podium A pedestal or platform. A continuous base supporting a series of columns. See STYLOBATE.

POE Acronym for POSTOCCUPANCY EVALUATION.

point d'hongrie (1) Needlepoint with a design that resembles an irregular series of chevron forms. It is usually made of silk and used as an upholstery fabric. (2) A common layout of parquet floors.

pointing The process of gouging out part of the mortar that was used for the bedding of bricks or masonry (up to ¾ inch) and replacing it with a compound that resists moisture.

∞pole screen A fire protection device with two round verticals that frame and support a panel, of the same or different materials. See BANNER SCREEN.

∞pole table See POTE TABLE.

∞Polish bed See DOME BED.

pollard oak (walnut) Oak or walnut trees that are "polled," i.e. cut at the top to secure a bushier grain.

pollinator Animals, notably insects, who acquire, convey, and deposit pollen and perform a vital service in the fertilization of flora. Support for the beleaguered biological couriers is part of an effort to bolster healthy ecosystems. The delivery service of the biosphere includes birds, bees, butterflies, and small mammals. When visiting flowers, they move pollen grains from male to female parts of plants. They are of increasing interest to those who design sustainable ecologies, from green roofs to green houses.

polycarbonate A synthetic resin in which the polymer units are linked through carbonate groups; used in many molding materials and films.

polychrome Multicolored; of any period or location but particularly associated with the Mughal and Victorian eras.

polychromy The state of having multiple colors.

polyester A manufactured fiber produced from coal, air, water, and petroleum elements. Has the following characteristics: strength, wrinkle resistance, shrink resistance, shape retention, high stretch, abrasion resistance. It also is quick-drying, dyes well, and requires minimum care. Used in fabrics, containers, and finishes. See *Table 2* and *Table 3.*

polyether See POLYFOAM and POLYURETHANE FOAM.

polyethylene An olefin or polyolefin fiber that can be paraffin-based. Waxy in hand, resists dyeing, and has excellent chemical and solar resistance. Lighter than water and therefore floats.

polyfoam A synthetic resin that simulates latex foam rubber. Used for upholstery pieces, mattresses, pillow filling, etc. Also called polyurethane foam or polyether.

polymer A chainlike molecular structure composed of monomers, the basis of synthetic fibers like nylon, Dacron, Acrilan, Dynel, Creslan, etc.

polypropylene Similar to polyethylene, this is a paraffin-based textile that is called an olefin. This durable thermoplastic polymer is stronger, lighter, and less heat-sensitive than polyethylene, and is abrasion-resistant. It is used in packaging, textiles, plastic assembly parts, inexpensive furniture and other uses. Robin Day's stacking "polyprop" chair sold in the millions.

polypropylene-olefin carpets Floor coverings made of a synthetic fiber either by pile construction or felting. The material has a high resistance to moisture, mildew, rot, stains, and wear from abrasion. Their weather resistance makes them ideal for indoor-outdoor use.

polystyrene Rigid plastic material that is injection molded. Used for decorative panels, trays, drawer fronts and drawers, corner blocks, and structural parts.

polyurethane Synthetic material used to refinish floors instead of varnish. Also used as foam, adhesives, sealants, and a hard plastic.

polyurethane foam Also called polyfoam or polyether. A synthetic resin that simulates foam rubber and can be substituted for it. See FOAM RUBBER.

polyvinyl chloride (PVC) A durable, inexpensive, and commonly produced plastic used in construction, upholstery, apparel, electrical cables, pipes, and numerous other products. Resists color fading, moisture, and mildew.

∞Pombalino or Pompeline A Portuguese style of the mid-18th century, based on the French Rococo. It was named after the Marquis de Pombal, who was responsible for the rebuilding of Lisbon after a tidal wave struck the city in 1755.

pomegranate A decorative ornament based on the fruit, which is apple-shaped with a hard rind and a pronounced crown-like ending. Used in classical times as a fertility symbol.

pommes (French, apples) A finial-shaped arrangement of apples on a plate, used on bedstead posts. In the late 17th century, pommes were the ornaments Daniel Marot used to finish the corners of his testers. See DANIEL MAROT in *Designers and Architects.*

Pompeii A Greco-Roman city that was completely covered with ashes after Mt. Vesuvius erupted in 79 C.E. In the mid-18th century, extensive excavations at Pompeii and Herculaneum uncovered great decorative works and art treasures that influenced artists, architects, and designers. These finds inspired generations of neoclassical designers.

Pompeiian Based on motifs or designs uncovered by the excavation of the ancient city on the outskirts of Naples in the mid-18th century.

ponderosa pine A light-colored wood with a soft, even texture and a faint grain pattern. It is light in weight, easy to work, and takes paint and stains well. Often used as "knotty pine." From the western U.S.

pongee A fabric of plain weave made from wild silk in its natural, beige-tan color, with an interesting slubby texture. The name derives from the Chinese *pen chi,* which means woven at home on one's own loom (*pen,* own; *chi,* loom). Now also produced from synthetic fibers.

∞ponteuse (French) A gaming chair that one straddled. The back rail sometimes contained small compartments for chips, money, and cards. See FUMEUSE.

pontil An iron rod used to carry hot materials in manufacturing glass. In the hand-blown glass technique, the device supports the bottom of the piece being blown.

∞**pontypool** An English term for a method of japanning or lacquering on metal originated by Thomas Algood at Pontypool, England, in about 1660. See JAPANNING.

Pop Art Originally, the popular arts of mass culture. Later applied to works in the fine arts, using themes conspicuous in a consumer society: movie actors, sport heroes, film strips, commercial packaging, advertising, photography, and automobiles. Practioners of this movement included Andy Warhol, Roy Lichtenstein, and Claes Oldenburg. Pop Art peaked in the late 1950s and early 1960s in the United States.

poplar A pale-colored wood with an exceptionally fine grain, sometimes used for paneling in the Stuart period. In the 16th and 17th centuries, used for inlay work. See WHITEWOOD.

poplin A plain-weave fabric with fine cross-ribs. The warp threads are finer than the fillers. It is similar to broadcloth, but it carries a heavier rib.

poppy head The decorative end of a Gothic bench. It was often carved with fleurs de lis, animals, figures, etc.

porcelain A hard, vitreous, nonporous ceramic ware made of kaolin. See CHINA, HARD PASTE, and KAOLIN.

porcelaine noir Black china (or porceline) that results from metal oxides in the clay and firing in a special kiln.

porphyry A type of marble, consisting of a compact feldspathic base through which crystals of feldspar disseminate. The crystals are lighter than the base, often white. Red, green, and purple varieties exist. Popular for architectural and ornamental use, especially in ancient Egypt and Rome.

portal

portal An entrance to a large, important structure. See POSTERN.

porte-cochère (French) An extension porch from a building that provided shelter for passengers alighting from carriages. A gateway for carriages leading into the courtyard of a major building, characteristic of French Renaissance architecture. In contemporary architecture, a roofed but not enclosed parking area. Frank Lloyd Wright and others favored the device.

porte-cochère

∞**porter chair** An enclosed chair of the 18th century with a bowed top and sides, which was often set in entry halls to accommodate porters or footmen and to protect them from drafts in the waiting area. See also DRAFT CHAIR and SEDAN CHAIR.

portico An open space covered with a roof supported on columns. A porch-like structure in front of a building that is fronted with columns.

portière A curtain or drapery over an arch or doorway, or used in place of a door. A means of separating one area from another and providing privacy. It can separate an alcove from a room.

portico

portland cement A synthetic material made from lime and clay. It is a high-strength material that when added to an aggregate results in concrete.

Portland stone An English limestone that is white or creamy in color.

Portland vase A Roman ceramic container whose design features blue-black glass with superimposed opaque white figures. Josiah Wedgwood reproduced it in black porcelain in the late 18th century, as well as in the typical blue Wedgwood color scheme.

∞**Portuguese bulb** A ovular, knobby turning of Iberian origin, for furniture supports, used in the William and Mary style in England. The stretcher would usually connect into one of these distinctive knobs, rather than a cube shape. The stretcher itself was a bulging prominence.

post A short piece of wall that is about as long as it is thick. When a post acts as a support, it is called a pedestal.

post and lintel The elemental form of construction that depends upon a horizontal member (the lintel) resting upon two uprights (the posts).

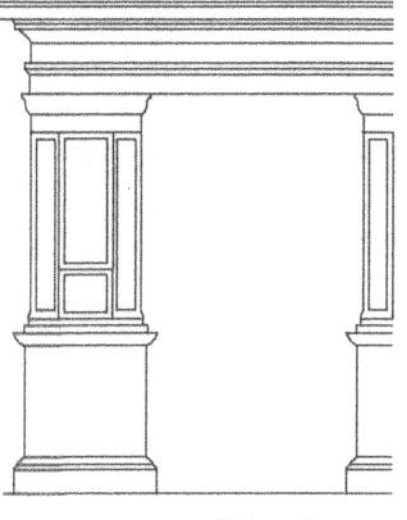
post and lintel

post-digital materiality An affirmation of physicality in the virtual realm. This focus is mediated by technologies; it flattens distinctions between physical and digital. The approach considers the virtual aspect of the real and the potential physicality of encoded data. This moves beyond a binary of the woodshop and the computer lab and involves representation and fabrication. Design ramifications include soft bricks as surface not structure; interior finishes used externally; expensive materials used extensively; and historical mash-ups, such as Baroque and California modern.

postern The back door or back entrance as opposed to the portal. See PORTAL.

postoccupancy evaluation (POE) A systematic method of obtaining feedback after construction in order to determine how successful the workplace is in supporting the organization and individual end-user requirements. A POE can also assess whether a project brief's parameters have been met.

postern

Postmodernism A stylistic rejection of Modernism and a return to historically inspired forms, of the late 1970s and 1980s; related to a philosophy in which truths are not inherent but socially constructed and dependent on context.

∞**posture furniture** An out-of-date term for chairs designed to give proper back support and encourage correct body positions. See ERGONOMIC DESIGN.

pot board The lowest shelf (closest to the floor) of a dresser.

pot cupboard See BEDSIDE CUPBOARD.

∞pote table A narrow, cylindrical surface-creating piece designed in the 18th century that resembled the lower portion of a fluted column. The cylinder was a single pedestal, either with exposed shelves on one face or with a tambour door. Also called a POLE TABLE or BOOK TABLE.

∞pouch table A small, elegant lady's work surface of the late 18th century. It contained various fittings and a silk pouch to hold needlework. The Sheraton period combined worktables with writing tables in elaborate variations. Sheraton described a pouch table as "a table with a bag, used by ladies to work at, in which bag they deposit their fancy needlework." Also called a BAG TABLE.

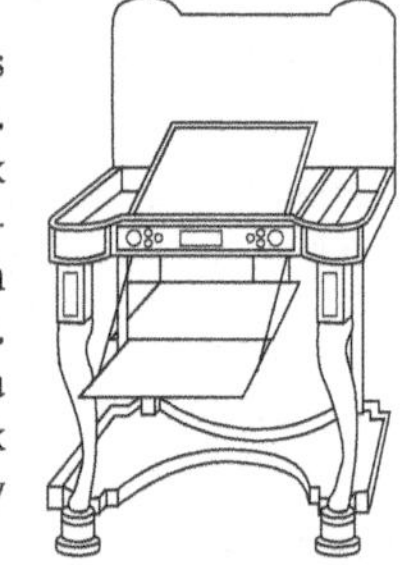
pouch table

∞poudreuse A lady's powder or toilet table, often equipped with a mirrored lid in the center that lifts up. A Louis XV period innovation. See also COIFFEUSE and TABLE À COIFFER.

pouf An ottoman made entirely of textiles, leather, or straw with no rigid materials.

poufed curtains Drapery panels where the fabric is gathered horizontally to create puffs that are held in place with cords, tiebacks, or stitching. Also called "bishop's sleeve" treatments.

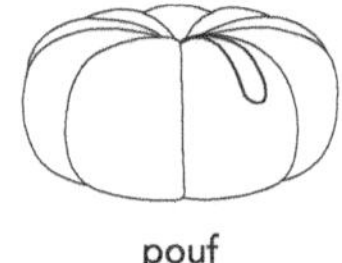
pouf

powder coat An applied outer layer usually used on metal that creates a protective, hard finish of fine dry particles that is more durable than paint.

powder room Originally, a corner or small closet in the bedroom of an 18th-century house where one could euphemistically attend to one's hair. In current usage, a ladies' lavatory.

power pole A wooden, metal, or plastic vertical member that goes from floor to ceiling and carries charged electrical wires and data cables. Electric outlets are spaced along the pole into which electrical equipment can be plugged. Particularly useful in open-office layouts or landscapes, as the electric power can be brought from the perimeter wall out to the middle of the space through the raceways in the bottom of panels.

power raceway A channel provided in open-office panels through which electrical power lines and communication cables can be drawn to provide power in the freestanding, out-in-the-open work stations. Also called an electrical raceway. See OPEN PLAN and ACOUSTICAL PANELS.

poyntell A floor pattern or pavement made up of square tiles or blocks laid diagonally or of diamond-shaped tiles.

Prague chair A simple, modern classic chair made of steambent birchwood combined with almost white handwoven cane. The squarish seat and chair back have gently rounded corners. The raked back chair legs continue up to form the frame for the subtly bowed back.

Prairie Style Midwestern American architecture movement whose most prominent figure was Frank Lloyd Wright; related to the ARTS AND CRAFTS MOVEMENT and MODERNISM.

prayer hall The central space of a mosque, often with many columns. See HYPOSTYLE HALL.

prayer rugs Small rugs originally designed for an individual to kneel on for Islamic prayers. See TURKISH RUGS.

preconsumer waste A part of the material stream cycle that involves materials discarded before consumer use. As a phase of manufacturing, some materials are discarded after assembly and before consumer use. Attention to the sector involves attempts to divert and reduce materials that do not contribute to product creation but negatively impact the environment. Manufacturers' scrap, construction site waste, textile clippings, sawdust, and demolition debris all produce quantities of materials that do not contribute to the consumer experience.

predella (1) A footstool. (2) In Italian art, the narrow panel at the back of the altar that served as a base for the altarpiece. Often the entire grouping consisted of several small, related paintings grouped together with the major painting set above.

prefab The vernacular term for PREFABRICATED.

prefabricated Units used in construction or decoration that are shaped, formed, and finished in a locale other than the site of construction or installation. Examples are purchased windows and doors made to fit doorways and frames being constructed on site.

prefabricated houses Dwellings made up of many manufactured elements brought to the building site and there assembled.

∞première partie A Boulle marquetry in which the tortoiseshell predominates and forms the groundwork for the metal inserts. See BOULLE WORK and CONTREPARTIE.

Pre-Raphaelite Brotherhood In the 19th century, a group of English artists, writers, and poets who revolted against the mechanization and eclecticism of the Victorian arts and the decline of craftsmanship. Their movement started a trend back to the styles of medieval Italian art that predated the famed Renaissance painter. Major figures included Dante Gabriel Rossetti, John Everett Millais, John Ruskin, and Edward Burne-Jones. The Arts and Crafts movement, whose leading figure was William Morris, was an outgrowth of the Brotherhood.

preshrunk A term applied to fabrics processed for shrinkage before being marketed. After such treatment (Sanforizing is one trademark process), changes in size in future washings is minimal.

press A cupboard or armoire in which clothes or linens were stored. In the mid and late 17th century, used to describe the case in which books were stored; also used as a term for bookshelves. The volume-containing unit was also known as a press cupboard, great cupboard, or wainscot cupboard.

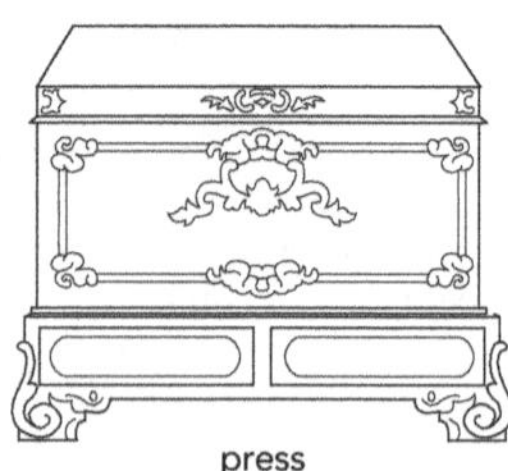
press

press bed A supported mattress that folds up and hides inside a cabinet. See MURPHY BED.

pressed glass Vitreous objects shaped by a fast and inexpensive method of pouring the molten silica into a mold. A plunger is pressed inside the mold and creates the inner contours of the object. An ideal technique for producing flat dishes, bowls, saucers, and plates. An inexpensive method to produce objects similar to cut glass, although the edges are less distinct.

∞pricket candlestick An early form of a light fixture with a spike projecting above the rim. The wax cylinder was impaled on the spike and thus held erect.

prie-dieu chair A seat designed to accommodate a person at prayer. A carved armchair with a high back; a low, hinged seat; and a receptacle for a prayer book. Also, a low chair without arms but with a broad upholstered shelf in place of the top rail. A person kneeling in prayer can rest his or her arms on the shelflike projection.

primary colors The basic colors from which all other hues can be mixed. The commonly accepted theory of pigment, as opposed to light, is that red, yellow, and blue are the three primary colors. Red and yellow make orange, blue and red produce violet, and yellow and blue form green. (Black and white are not considered colors; they are neutrals.) See SECONDARY COLORS and HUE. In light theory, red, blue, and green are the primary colors.

primary lighting The basic, elemental lighting in a store or commercial space. Usually devoid of special lighting effects such as spots, filters, floods, or washers and thus lacking in any attempt to affect atmosphere or mood. See GENERAL LIGHTING.

primavera A yellow-white mahogany with a striped or crossfire figure. Mexico and Guatemala produce a similar pale yellow-brown, birch-colored wood with a mahogany grain. It is a handsome and easily worked fine cabinet wood. See ACAJOU and MAHOGANY.

priming The application of a primary or first coat of paint or sealer on a wall, piece of woodwork, furniture, or floor. The use of a preparatory surfacing material.

primitive art Art of either deliberate or unconscious naiveté, characterized by more or less unsophisticated technique. A term also applied to the art of the 15th century in Italy, to the productions of some 17th- to 19th-century American itinerant artists, and to the work of modern artists including Henri Rousseau and Grandma Moses. Can also refer to prehistoric art and the art of regions remote from European, Western, or Chinese art developments. Considered by some as a derogatory term.

Prince of Wales feathers A chairback ornament of the Hepplewhite period. It was a carved representation of the three ostrich plumes that were the badge of the heir to the throne.

princewood A Spanish elm imported from the West Indies. Its reddish color made it popular in late-17th-century English furniture.

print A surface having a pattern imposed with ink or dye by means of stencils, rollers, blocks, or screens. Applies to fabric, paper, and wood.

print fidelity A measurement of the degree of congruence between a graphic strike and its originating plates; can refer to graphics and textiles.

print room An enclosed space decorated with lithographs and etchings, which were stylish wall decorations in mid-18th-century England. The graphic elements, in contrast to original paintings, were sometimes pasted directly onto the walls with ornamental paper borders around them serving as mountings or frames. Cutout borders, frets, ribbons, and festoons of wallpaper were used to accent and dramatize wall arrangements. Horace Walpole had a famous print room at Strawberry Hill.

priscilla curtain A drapery, usually sheer, with a ruffle of the same material on three sides of each panel. Two panels are set on two rods, one behind the other, with the long unruffled sides against the window frame. The panels are pulled back to the window, creating an overlap. The tie to the window frame can also be ruffled pieces of material. This curtain may be a simple pullback curtain with the two panels meeting in the middle.

prismatic glass A translucent rolled vitreous sheet with one smooth surface and one textured, with parallel prisms. The sheet refracts light, and the angle of refraction is determined by the way the light hits the prism.

prong box A receptacle for table silver placed in or on an 18th-century sideboard. See KNIFE BOX.

pronk An object of conspicuous luxury and cost. Its signifying attributes, such as wealth and craftsmanship, are more important than its function.

propaedeutic Related to the work of Italian-born Brazilian architect, furniture designer, and journalist Lina Bo Bardi. Serving as a preliminary instruction, her philosophy and design theory promoted works that were resolutely modern, although she celebrated the original state of natural materials, and her designs borrowed freely from history. See LINA BO BARDI in *Designers and Architects.*

proportion The relative size of one part to the whole or to other parts of a composition.

proprietary Of or relating to an owner or ownership, including legal protections and rights of use, e.g. proprietary textile and furniture designs.

propylene See POLYPROPYLENE.

propylon A large gateway between two towers that stood before the entrance to temples and important buildings in ancient Egypt.

proscenium The part of the stage in front of the drop curtain. Originally, in the Greek theater, the word meant the stage itself. In this arrangement, the audience is at one of the four sides of a performance space.

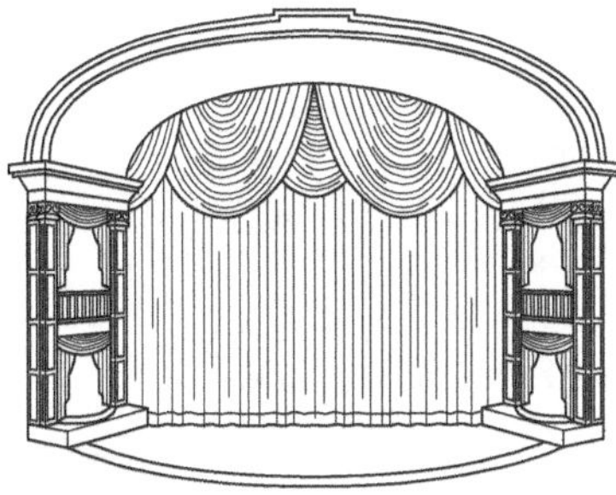

proscenium

proscenium arch The frame or arched opening that holds the drop curtain and through which the audience sees the performance. Conceptual theatrical terms of third and fourth walls relate to the proscenium as a boundary between performers and audience. See PROSCENIUM.

protein fibers Synthetic hairlike strands derived from peanuts, soybeans, caseins, cornmeal, or other molecular sources. See *Table 2.*

prototyping This approach makes central to product and industrial design a process of continual trial and error. Conceptually, it moves design and fabrication away from a linear process. It derives from DESIGN THINKING and focuses on user experience and on testing and retesting ideas. It favors building, collaborating, and trials over thinking, hierarchy, and representing. Assess, reposition, and make again, with a series of incremental improvements. Its origins lie in the English Arts and Crafts movement and the Bauhaus.

provincial Of the provinces. Colonial or country-made and/or country-styled. Simple and rustic. Often simplified versions of more elaborate urban pieces. See FRENCH PROVINCIAL.

proxemics The study of personal space and the effects of adjacencies and distances between people; refers to the function and symbolism of space and how a person individually perceives and uses space. Proxemics is concerned with culturally specific processes at the crossroads of the public and private realms. Edward T. Hall coined the term in 1963.

psyche (1) An Empire cheval mirror that stood on the floor and could be tilted forward or backward. See CHEVAL GLASS OR MIRROR. (2) An early-19th-century upholstered sofa with Greek curves.

puce (French word, flea) A dark brown or brownish-violet color.

puddling A formal drapery treatment in which the hemline falls below floor level so that the excess fabric is arranged to billow on the floor.

∞puente stand A carved trestle table that was designed to support the mainstay of Spanish Renaissance furniture, the VARGUEÑO.

puff New England term that refers to a down comforter with a removable cover. More commonly called a DUVET.

pull brackets Movable arms located on either side of and below a retractable writing surface of a desk or secretary. When extended, the brackets support the writing surface.

pulldown front A lid or covering on a secretary or bureau that, when lowered, covers, encloses, and secures the writing area and its fittings. Other types are cylinder, roll, and TAMBOUR.

pullman kitchen A shallow alcove or recess, often screened off from a living area, equipped with a compact arrangement of fixtures for food preparation (sink, stove, refrigerator, etc.). It is sometimes one wall of a room that is camouflaged to hide its utilitarian features.

pulls Handles for drawers, cabinets, etc. See HARDWARE.

pull-up chair A small, light-scaled seat used in living rooms and bedrooms. An occasional chair that can be designed in a period or contemporary style. In commercial interiors, a guest chair or side chair in a workstation, or one of two seats for guests or co-workers in front of a desk.

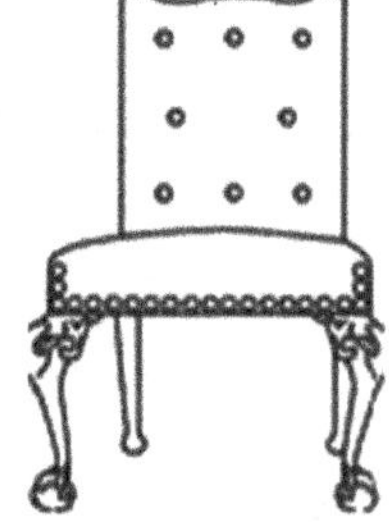

pull-up chair

∞pulvinaria The pillow-like elements on the side of an Ionic capital that end in the volutes. Pulvinar (the singular form) also refers to the pillow on which the statue of a god was set in classical temples.

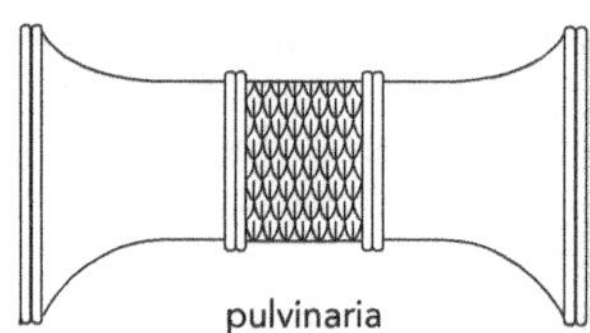

pulvinaria

pulvinated Describing a frieze with a convex profile.

punch list An inspection and resulting compilation of items that need to be completed at a project's end; a term in the construction industry for one of the final stages of a project.

punchwork A form of simple carved decoration. The background is made stipple-textured by the use of a fine steel workpiece that pierces or deforms the ground material.

purfled Having a surface ornament of drapery, lacework, or embroidery or one that simulates such an effect.

purple wood A purplish-colored Brazilian natural material used for inlay work, popular in the 18th century. Also called violet wood. See AMARANTH.

putto (plural, putti) A figure of a young boy, like a wingless cherub or cupid. Popular subject for decoration and sculpture in the Italian Renaissance and later.

putto

PVC Acronym for POLYVINYL CHLORIDE.

PVC Acronym for PIGMENT VOLUME CONCENTRATION.

pylon A truncated pyramidal tower flanking the entrance to an Egyptian temple or similar structure. Can describe bridges and their components as well.

pyramid A geometric solid shape composed of inclined triangles that meet at a point. One of the noted structures in ancient Egypt and Mesoamerica that has a square base and four triangular sides meeting at an apex.

pyroxylin A cellulose product that when applied to cotton or rayon fabrics renders them stain-resistant and waterproof.

qibla The wall of a Mosque that is oriented toward Mecca and contains the MIHRAB.

quadra A square architectural molded frame used to accent a relief sculpture. Also, the plinth block of a podium or platform.

quadrant brackets or quadrants Quarter-circle bands of metal attached to the pulldown front of a secretary or bureau. When the front is down, these bands support it.

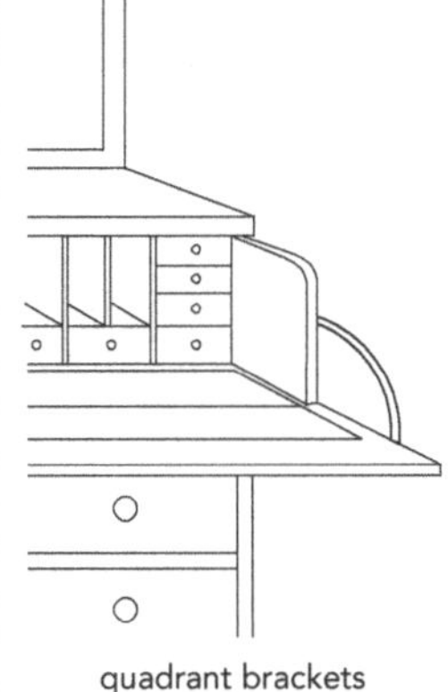

quadrant brackets

∞quadratura A 17th- and 18th-century type of TROMPE L'OEIL mural painting. Architectural elements like columns, cornices, entablatures, cupolas, and colonnades were painted on flat walls and ceilings to create foreshortened perspective views of exterior scenes. Painters who specialized in this art were known as quadraturisti or quadratisti.

quadrature See ILLUSIONISM and TROMPE L'OEIL.

quarrel or quarry A square or diamond-shaped pane of glass. The term also refers to a square paving stone or tile.

quarry ornament A surface treatment of crisscrossing or reticulated lines that form quadrangular or diamond-shaped spaces.

quarry tile A steadfast paving material made of unglazed ceramic, appropriate for demanding situations.

quarter landing A square platform that makes a 45-degree turn in a stairway.

quarter round A convex molding that, in profile, is one quarter of a circle. See ECHINUS.

quarrel or quarry

quarter-sliced veneer A fourth of a log sliced in parallel lines at right angles to the annual growth rings. This produces striped or straight grains on the slices.

∞quartette tables A set of four light surface-creating furniture pieces made to be stored by nesting one inside the other. See NESTED TABLES. Sheraton, one of the originators of this device, called them quartetto tables.

quatrefoil A four-lobed ornament, like a stylized four-leaf clover. A Gothic symbol for the cross and the four Evangelists, it was often used in window tracery and carved wood decoration on interiors and on Gothic furniture. See CUSPS.

quatrefoil

quattrocento (Italian) The 15th century or 1400s.

Queen Anne The furniture and interiors of England during the reign of Queen Anne (1702–1714). The early years were a continuation of William and Mary designs, while the late years herald the George I period. The cabriole leg, clubbed foot, shell carvings, and the swan's neck were popular motifs. Some consider it to be the finest period of English furniture. The monarch contributed little to the style that bears her name. See DECORATED QUEEN ANNE PERIOD.

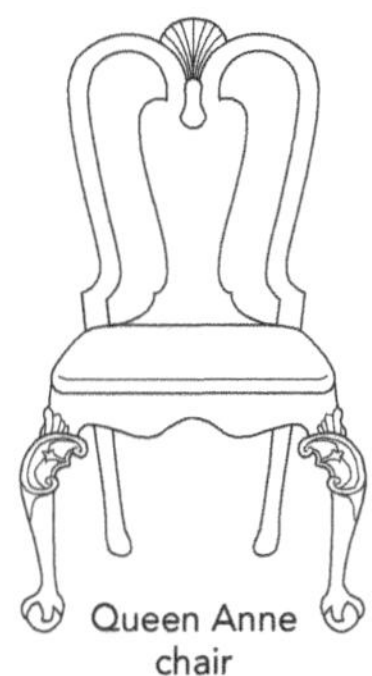

Queen Anne chair

queen-size bed A sleeping platform with a single mattress that sleeps two; approximately 60 inches wide by 76 inches to 84 inches in length (152 cm × 203 cm).

quillwork Decorative applied wavy bands of glass, especially on American and English glass. The vitreous material is pinched as it is being applied, and thus the wavy line forms.

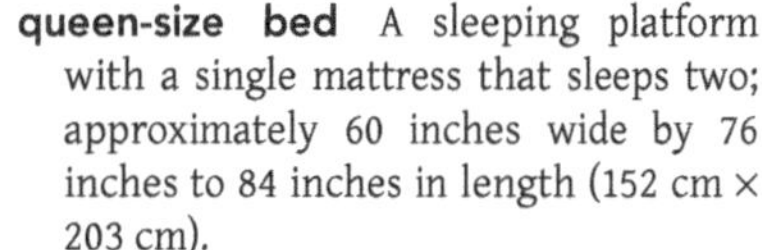

quilted figure See BLISTER.

quilting Two layers of fabric with padding between the layers, held in place by stitches that typically follow a definite pattern. The raised or tufted areas between the stitches give the textile its characteristic bumpy surface. Papers and fabrics can be embossed to create the effect.

∞quimperware Simple pottery ornamented in bright colors with scenes and figures produced by local craftspeople during the mid to late 18th century in France. A French Provincial decorative accessory.

quincunx An arrangement of five objects, with four at the corners of a square and one in the middle.

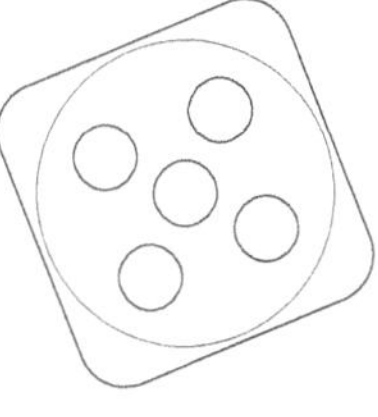

quincunx

quirk A sharp, incised groove in a molding. It is sometimes referred to as a "sunken fillet."

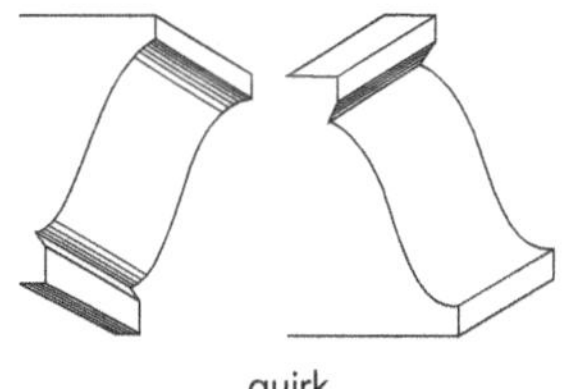

quirk

quoin (1) The corner angle of a building. (2) Also, the brick or stone laid at the corner angle. The cornerstone may be a decorative element. (3) A corner cabinet or table.

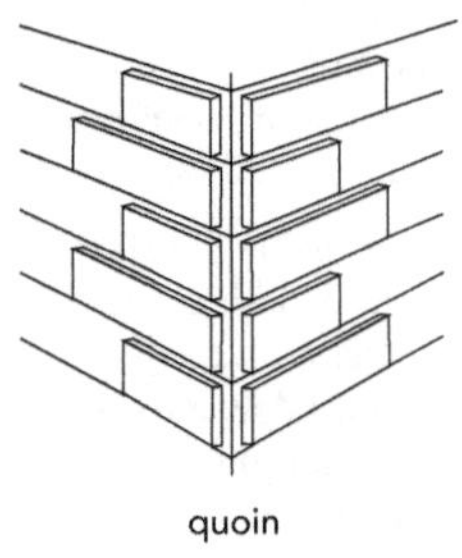
quoin

quysshen (archaic) A 16th-century term for cushion. Example from a probate inventory: "one longe quysshen of purple velvett."

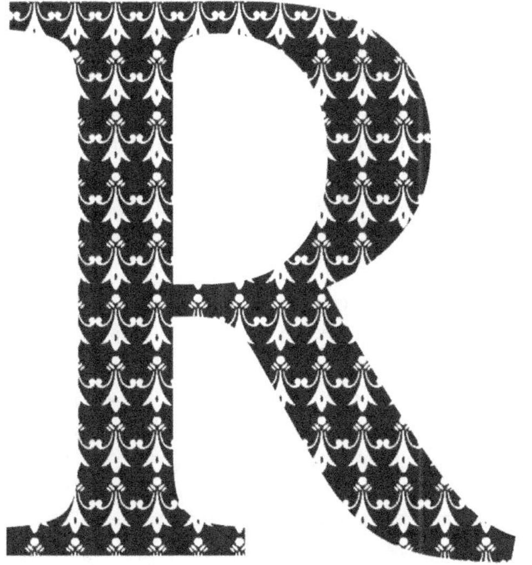

rabbet A continuous rectangular groove cut along the edge of a piece of wood or metal. It is usually cut to receive the edge of another piece of wood or metal, e.g., a rabbet is sometimes cut on the inner edges of a chair's seat frame to receive a slip seat.

rabbet joint In construction, a form of joinery in which a recess or groove is cut in one piece of wood to form a bed for another piece of wood; also called a DADO JOINT.

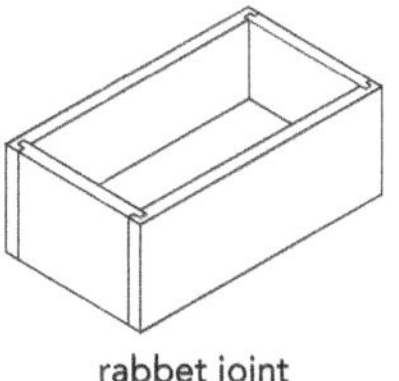

rabbet joint

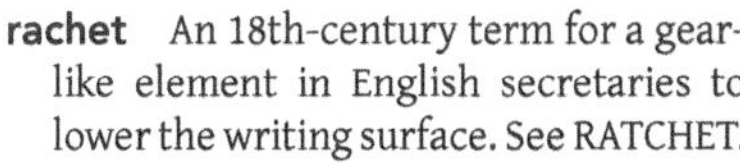

rachet An 18th-century term for a gear-like element in English secretaries to lower the writing surface. See RATCHET.

rack An angled frame or stand to hold music, books, magazines, etc. A grooved frame or a stand (with or without brackets) that holds guns, cups, etc.

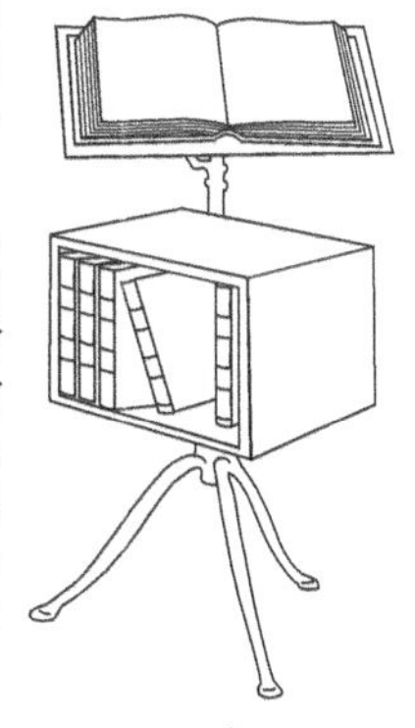

rack

radial rubber flooring Heavy-duty commercial tile covering patterned with raised circles or rectangles of the same color as the background of the tile. The raised pattern provides a greater life span for the material and also increases traction, reducing the possibility of slipping. Fashionable for high-tech interiors. See HIGH-TECH.

radiant heating A system of climate control by setting coils in the floor, walls, or both; when these areas are heated, the entire room warms up.

radio frequency identification (RFID) Denoting technologies that use wavelengths of electromagnetic radiation to identify people or objects carrying encoded microchips when they enter a building. Particularly useful for facilities management.

radius edge A rounded corner equivalent to a quarter of a circle that connects a straight vertical plane with a straight horizontal one. A 6-inch-radius edge is one-fourth of a 12-inch-diameter circle.

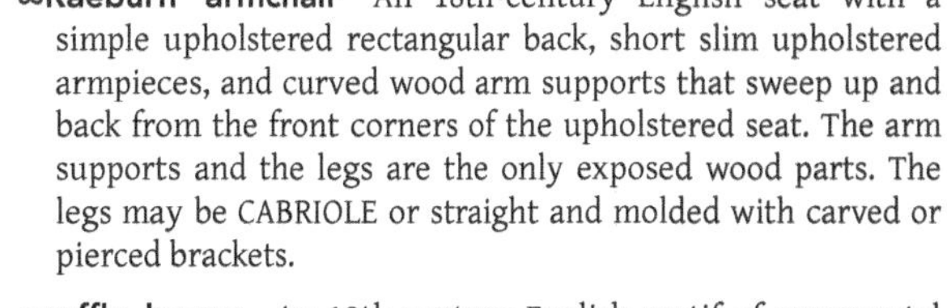

∞**Raeburn armchair** An 18th-century English seat with a simple upholstered rectangular back, short slim upholstered armpieces, and curved wood arm supports that sweep up and back from the front corners of the upholstered seat. The arm supports and the legs are the only exposed wood parts. The legs may be CABRIOLE or straight and molded with carved or pierced brackets.

∞**raffle leaves** An 18th-century English motif of ornamental foliage with serrated edges similar to the acanthus leaf. Originally found in Italian designs and adapted by English designers.

∞**rafraîchissoir or servante** A small Louis XV rectangular serving table set on casters, often marble-topped, with rounded corners and a drawer below and two shelves set between the legs. The top featured two silverplated receptacles that, when filled with cold water, kept wine bottles chilled. Canabas designed many such tables in solid mahogany. Variations appear in the Louis XVI period. See DUMBWAITER.

rafters The sloping beams that support the upper part of a roof, sometimes kept visible for design purposes in an interior.

rag rug A floor covering woven of strips of discarded textiles or other fabric scraps. The fabrics are sometimes plaited or braided and then sewn into a circle or oval area floor textile, and the results often purposely resemble Early American handmade floor coverings. See BRAIDED RUG.

rail (1) The horizontal strip of a frame or a panel. (2) The horizontal tie bar in the framing of a piece of furniture, such as the top of a chair back, or a stretcher. (3) A metal bar on a spinning or twisting machine.

rainscreen A thin exterior wall surface exposed to weathering and whose vertical elements stand at a remove from the structural supporting wall.

Rajput A Hindu military caste that emphasized the importance of heritage and that preceded and followed MUGHAL power.

rake An inward slant or slope from a 90° upright, like the slope of a chair back. An outward slope is a SPLAY.

raking cornice In architecture and furniture, the series of moldings on the angled sides of a pediment.

raku Low-fired, lead-glazed Japanese earthenware associated with the tea ceremony. It was frequently molded by hand.

ramie China grass. A fiber, similar to flax, that is derived from a stalk plant grown in the U.S. and in Asia. See BAST FIBERS and *Table 2*.

ramp (1) An inclined surface that joins two different levels, or the part of a staircase handrail that rises at a sharper angle than the normal handrail. (2) In furniture, a sharp curve ending in an angle at the end of an upright.

ram's head A classical decorative motif that represents the crown of the big horn sheep, reintroduced in the 18th century by Robert Adam on his furniture and in his decorative accessories. See ADAM BROTHERS in *Designers and Architects*.

ram's horn stump A double-curved arm support that resembles the twisted hard outgrowth of the formidable beast.

ranch house In contemporary usage, a residence built on one level. All the living, sleeping, and service rooms are on the ground. The structure may have a cellar or basement and a crawl-space attic.

ranch windows Wide but short openings placed higher up from the floor than the traditional double-hung or casement type. This permits the placement of furniture beneath them; ranch windows do not afford much of a view. Also called strip or ribbon windows.

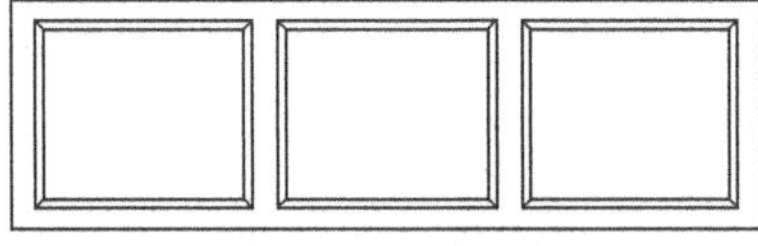
ranch windows

random match In veneering or decorative surfacing, a casual, unmatched effect with no attempt at a symmetrical or repetitive pattern.

random rubble In masonry, stones of assorted shapes and sizes, roughly surfaced, that are set in not clearly defined courses.

random width In woodworking, assorted dimensions of planks used vertically or horizontally to create an irregular pattern.

range tables A late-18th-century term for rectangular surface-creating pieces of the same size that could be combined to form a longer table. The outer corners of the end sections were sometimes rounded.

rapid re-housing (RRH) Related to homelessness and its solution, permanent residency. The moment an inventory is taken at a shelter focuses on three factors: the population to be served, the bed count, and available housing resources. RRH concerns people who are transitioning from homelessness to stable living. RRH is an intervention designed to help individuals and families who do not require intensive support to exit homelessness. Designers are turning to such projects to emphasize that their talents contribute to the societal good.

raster image A category of representation in interior design graphics, related to ray trace rendering and raster graphics. A bit map is a grid of individual pixels or squares that collectively compose an image. In contrast to a vector, the bit map includes countless tiny squares; each pixel is coded a shade and hue and from a distance represents the desired object. The term is related to the phenomenon of design clients increasingly expecting photorealistic renderings before signing off on a project.

ratchet A tooth or detent that is used in conjunction with a wheel for many purposes, including the raising and lowering of desk surfaces, lids, etc. The wheel has inclined teeth around the outer rim. When the ratchet is released, it catches onto one of the angled teeth and thus keeps the wheel from turning any farther. This maintains a writing surface at a set angle and height. For Sheraton's ratchet mechanism, see HARLEQUIN TABLE.

ratchet chair An 18th-century English reclining seat. A high-backed wing chair with MARLBOROUGH LEGs and curved arm stumps supporting covered armrests. The movable back was attached to the armrest by means of a ratchet device which made possible several changes in the degree of incline.

∞rat-claw foot A mid-and-late-18th-century English and American furniture termination that resembled the sharp spiny claws of a rodent clutching a ball.

ratiné A loose, plain-weave fabric with a nubby, uneven surface. The warp of the fabric is a special knotty yarn.

rattan The long, solid, round stems of a species of palm found in India and the East. The unbranched stems are pliable and tough, and are used in wickerwork furniture. Though it does not stain readily, rattan can be lacquered or painted.

rawhide An untanned animal skin.

rayon The name for any number of synthetic fibers having a cellulose base. It is lustrous, stiffer, absorbent, and less expensive than silk and may be used in combination with other synthetic or natural fibers. See *Table 2* and *Table 3.*

rayonnant (French, radiant or beaming) The name given to 13th-century French Gothic architecture, which was characterized by wheel tracery and circular windows, such as were used in Bourges, Amiens, and Rheims.

rayonnant

ray trace rendering A representation in digital graphics that involves a virtual camera that looks at an object through an image plane. Paths of light are traced from camera to object to light source, with important intersection points on the gridded plane where they are expressed as pixels. Algorithms provide increasingly sophisticated techniques of materiality and lighting based on how light interacts with objects and moves through space. This has impacted the fields of architecture, interior design, and animation.

RCL Acronym for ROLLING COMPLETION LIST.

reading stand or reading desk A popular piece of furniture of the late 18th century. Hepplewhite described one of his designs as a "tripod stand having a staff slide on the stem (fixed with a screw), supporting an adjustable book holder or table." The usage of the term increased in the late 20th century with a re-invigorated interest in ergonomics in office furniture.

ready-to-assemble (RTA) furniture Surface-creating and volume-producing pieces shipped from the manufacturer in parts to be put together by the retailer or consumer. Also called K.D. (KNOCKED DOWN) or flat pack, with flat pack referring to its ability to be shipped in low-profile, economical shipping cartons.

rebate See RABBET.

∞Récamier In furniture, a French 19th-century Directoire or Empire chaise longue named for Madame Juliette Récamier, whom the artist David painted. A classical reclining couch, with one end higher than the other and gracefully curved. Also called a GRECIAN SOFA.

recess A niche or alcove. An area set back from or into a wall.

recessed fixture A lighting element that is essentially hidden in the architecture, often the ceiling, and whose exposed parts are flush with the surrounding material.

recessed stretcher In furniture, the stabilizer that unites the two side stretchers rather than the front legs. This creates a setback that allows room for the sitter's heels. See H STRETCHER; STRETCHER; and X-SHAPED STRETCHERS.

∞réchampi A French term for relief decoration in gilt or color, or a combination of the two.

reclining chair A mechanically operated seat with a back that goes down and a footrest that rises up. By dropping the back and raising the footrest, the seated person assumes a semi-horizontal

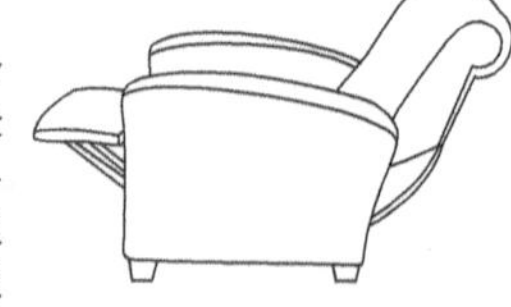
reclining chair

position. A 20th-century integrated version of the 18th-century duchesse brissée.

Rectilinear period The late Gothic period in England (approximately 1377–1485). See PERPENDICULAR STYLE.

red filler An Early American furniture finish used until about 1830. Applied on country-made pieces, it consisted of Spanish brown pigment mixed with raw linseed oil.

red gum A fine-grained wood of an ocher-brown color used for veneer for doors, and general interior finishes. Stained, the material imitates walnut, mahogany, or maple. See *Table 5.*

redwood A handsome, uniformly colored natural material that takes paint and stains well. Wide widths of planking are available. Found in tropical regions. See BRAZILWOOD. See *Table 5.*

reed The cores of the rattan vine. More commonly it refers to items made by weaving swamp grasses. Early American wicker chairs are made from the natural material.

reeding Rows of beading or semicylindrical convex moldings used in close parallel lines. When concave moldings are used, it is called FLUTING. The motif recalls a column's origin as bundled reeds.

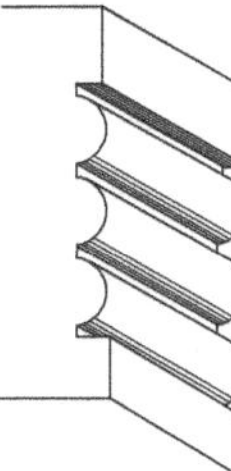
reeding

refectory The dining room in an institution or school, particularly in religious settings. Often furnished with long continuous tables and benches.

refectory

refectory table A long, narrow dining surface. In the early Gothic period, it was a slab of wood or several fitted planks on trestles. This developed into a firm, massive horizontal surface with bulbous legs, heavy stretchers, and ornate carving.

reflecting dressing table A complex, mechanically ingenious desk outfitted with mirrors and drawers, whose purpose is to assist the user in attending to their appearance, regarding make-up, coiffure, and clothing. From the mid 18th century. See RUDD'S DRESSING TABLE.

reflective glass A vitreous element where a thin film of transparent metal or metal oxides is bonded to the surface to reflect the rays of the sun.

Régence See FRENCH RÉGENCE or REGENCY PERIOD. The French regency occurred in the 18th century, and the English one in the 19th. The former is a transitional style between baroque and Rococo, the latter is a neoclassical variant.

Regency (English) period The era in England from 1811 to 1820 when the future George IV was prince regent. In furniture and interior designs, the era resembles the concurrent French Directoire and Empire. Noted for its extensive use of painted stucco and Greek, Roman, and Egyptian motifs. Thomas Hope, Sir John Soane, and John Nash were the leading designers. Nash's Brighton Pavilion demonstrates the period's stylistic range. See THOMAS HOPE and SIR JOHN SOANE in *Designers and Architects.*

Regency armchair A seat with cross-stretchers, curved back, and slightly curved legs.

reglet A narrow band or fillet that separates two moldings.

regula The short band between the tenia and the guttae in a Doric ENTABLATURE.

∞régulateur The French term for a REGULATOR clock.

regulator A grandfather clock or a long, wall-hanging case that houses a timepiece.

∞Reignier work Decorative inlays of colored woods similar in concept to buhl or BOULLE WORK. See REISNER WORK.

reinforced concrete Construction material strengthened by steel members or wire mesh, which are embedded when it is being poured. Also called ferroconcrete.

Reisner work A 17th-century German ornamenting technique of inlaying colored woods and metals, similar to BOULLE WORK and REIGNIER WORK.

regulator

relief A carved or applied ornament above the level of a surface. It may be high or low relief.

reliquary A small container, usually of precious metals and ornamented with jewels, that holds a sacred relic, e.g. a saint's or martyr's bodily remains.

relief

rematerial To use old products and substances and give them a new purpose in a project; the process reduces the amount of waste a project produces.

remote work Economic activity for service industries that shifts from the office to the domestic realm or elsewhere. This includes telecommuting, co-working, teleconferencing, and the flexible workplace. Employees in the new scenario do not commute to a central place but work from home. Described as anywhere, anytime, any device. What was already a cultural shift of import received renewed attention during the COVID-19 crisis of 2020. Upending both the home and office environments, the impact on interior design is far reaching.

Renaissance The period in Europe, from the 15th century to the end of the 17th century, when art, architecture, philosophy, and literature underwent a rebirth based on classic Greek and Roman models. The intellectual movement began in the 14th century with the writings of Dante,

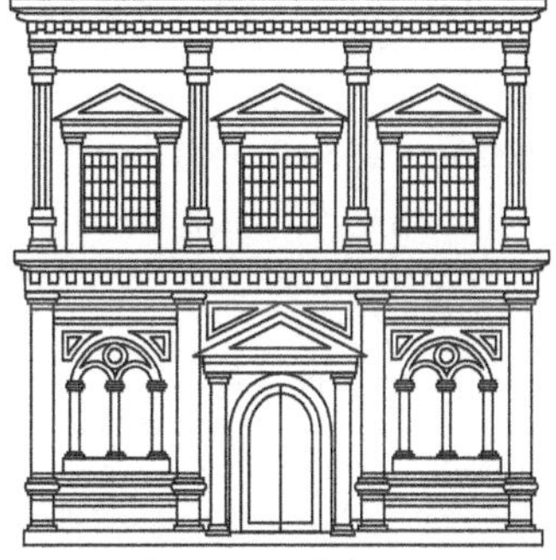
Renaissance Palazzo

Petrarch, and Boccaccio. Vitruvius' *Treatise on Architecture*, originally written in the time of Augustus, was issued in Rome in Latin in 1486 and translated into Italian in 1521.

Renaissance Revival One of several historically based styles in the eclectic 19th century. Works of architecture took their cues from famous structures, mostly Italian palazzi. Sir Charles Barry was a noteworthy exponent of the fashion.

∞rent table A round or octagonal pedestal work surface with drawers set into the apron under the top, usually seven in number, marked with the days of the week. In 18th-century England, landlords used this piece for collecting and filing lease payments.

rep A plain-weave fabric with a heavy filler thread that gives the fabric a corded effect, a definite crosswise rib. The textile can be made of most natural or synthetic fibers and can be used for upholstery and draperies.

repeat pattern An identical shape or image that occurs in a set sequence on a wall covering or textile.

replica An exact reproduction or copy that seeks to fool viewers into thinking that it is original. See TROMPE L'OEIL.

repoussé Relief work on metal materials. The design is produced by hammering or pressing on the material on the reverse side so that the desired form appears raised on the front. See CHASING and EMBOSSED.

repp See REP.

reproduction A faithful copy acknowledged as such, of the form, workmanship, and ornamentation of an original; not an attempt at a counterfeit or a fake.

repurpose A new approach for the cycle of materials and products as an offshoot of sustainability. It proffers a solution by extending the longevity of materials and considering the life of products beyond initial use. This long-term view considers a new or second life for existing products. Related topics include recycling, reusing materials, and upcycling. This has had a big impact on residential design and has the potential to change the dynamics of commercial design.

resiliency The capacity of a fabric or material to spring back after being crushed or bent; the capacity to resist creasing. Chemical treatment can render fabrics more crease-resistant.

resilient flooring A covering that provides shock absorption and more give than hard surfaces. It includes natural and synthetic surfaces such as vinyl, rubber, linoleum, cork, asphalt, combinations, and laminates.

resin The hydrocarbon secretion of trees and other plants that is used in the production of varnishes, adhesives, etc., which, when applied as a finish, gives the appearance of a hard lacquer.

resistance dimmer See DIMMER.

respond In architecture, the corbel or half column that supports one end of the last arch in an arcade.

restoration Repairing of broken parts or replacing of missing pieces or worn materials, to return an antique object or building as close as possible to its original appearance and condition.

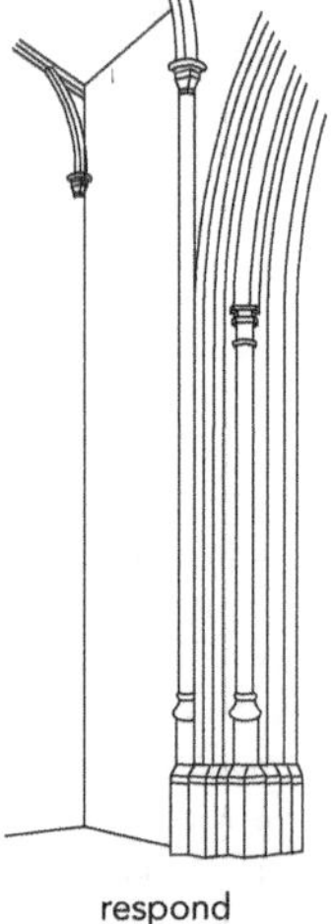
respond

∞Restoration chair A high-backed, cane-paneled seat of the Carolean period (late-17th-century England). The legs as well as the uprights were usually spiral turnings. The chair often had a carved cresting representing the crown, supported by cherubs and adorned with acanthus leaves and roses. The motif was sometimes repeated on the front stretcher. See RESTORATION PERIOD.

Restoration period The period from 1660 to 1688 in England. In 1660 the monarchy was restored, Charles II became king, and the Age of Walnut began in furniture. Though the furniture remained relatively simple and rectangular in outline, it became ornate and decorative in finish. This was the antithesis of the puritanical quality of the preceding CROMWELLIAN or COMMONWEALTH era. French and Flemish designs were popular.

Restoration period chair

restorative cities A movement initially focused on justice, it has made inroads to other fields, including interior design. It started as a desire to formulate fair justice based on a dialogue between victims, offenders, and law enforcement. A new means of conflict resolution, as its scope grew, it expanded to schools, workplaces, and housing. Its advocates call for a cultural and social change. Proponents encourage inclusion, participation, respect, and solidarity. Examples include interior healing gardens and spaces for acupuncture, yoga, and ecotherapy.

reticella A type of lace using a combination of drawn and cut work. See LACE.

reticulated A surface decorated with a lattice-like design similar to the meshes of a net.

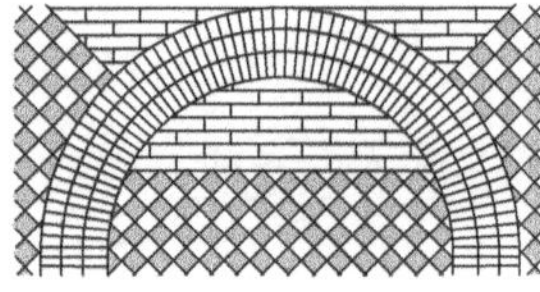
reticulated

Retro Futurism A 20th-century design trend until about 1960, depicting future styles spurred by science fiction novels, movies, and technology. Admiration of the visuals by later generations is thusly named.

return (1) A change in direction of any continuous surface. An example would be the turning of a cornice at the angle of a building and its continuance on the adjacent side of the building. (2) In commercial furniture, the work surface at the user's side. In a previous era, this might have supported a typewriter.

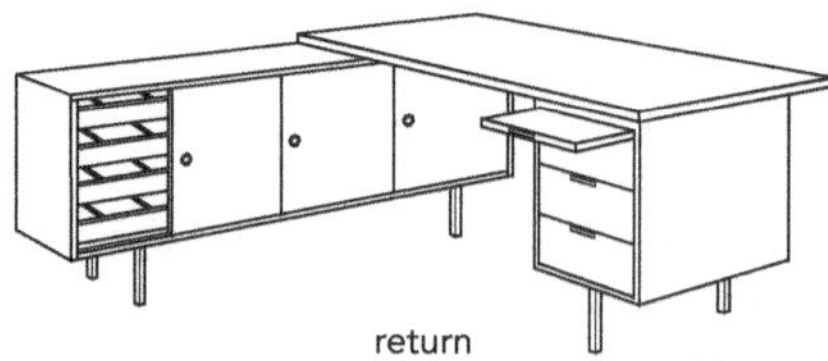
return

reveal The recessed area of a designed object that connects two features. Its recession casts the area in shadow and thereby hides flaws and allows slight changes in dimension. Waisted

Chinese furniture connects the horizontal surface to the apron with such a device.

reverse box match A decorative veneer technique similar to a reverse diamond match but angled to create a cross-patterned center with right-angled patterns going off in four directions.

reverse diamond match Four wedges of wood or veneer set together to form an X at the center with consecutively smaller V's radiating out from the center in all four directions.

reverse serpentine The opposite of a simple S-shaped curve. The ends and center are concave, while the area between is convex. See SERPENTINE.

revetment A veneering, facing, or sheathing of stone or metal on a structure or architectural element for protection or adornment. Also called a retaining wall.

revivalism The return of aspects of a previous historic period in an eclectic way; typically associated with the Victorian era, i.e. the 19th century.

rez-de-chaussée French for the ground floor or ground level. Americans refer to this as the "first floor."

riad or ryad A private house, villa, or pavilion in the Arab world.

rib A projecting band on a ceiling or vault. See GROIN RIB and VAULT.

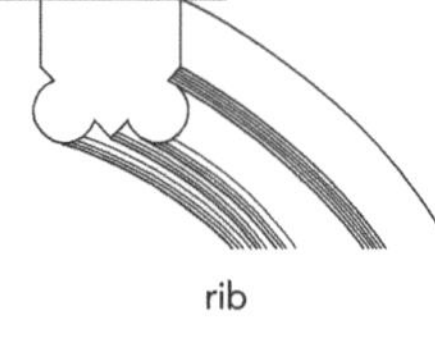
rib

ribband back A Chippendale chair style. The chair vertical that supports the upper torso is carved to resemble a pattern of interlacing ribbons. The motif also appears in the Louis XVI style and in German Rococo ornament. See also RIBBON BACK.

ribbed vault An extruded arch supported, or seemingly supported, by its projecting bands.

ribbon Narrow finished width of fabric used for trimming, manufactured in many widths, weaves, fibers, and colors. The decorative motif appears with foliage and flowers in garlands and festoons. The form is called a label when it bears an inscription. Antique labels are often simple and terminate in balls. Gothic labels are curled and quaint. Renaissance labels are free and elegant and are often divided at the ends like pennons. See FESTOON and PENNON.

ribbon back A carved chair vertical support representing puckered textile strips tied in bows, a decorative splat for a chair or settee. Popular in the Louis XV period and adapted by Chippendale and Manwaring. See also RIBBAND BACK. Also, a wood grain or figure of wide, unbroken, alternating light and dark stripes, mainly found in quarter-sliced mahogany.

rice pattern A ceramic decoration where small holes are cut in the clay and covered with glaze to form transparent spots.

Richardsonian Romanesque American revival style of medieval architecture that predated the Gothic period; architecture, interiors, and furniture, associated with Henry Hobson Richardson, that paradoxically contributed to the development of the skyscraper and Modernism itself. See HENRY HOBSON RICHARDSON in *Designers and Architects.*

rickrack A flat braid in a chevron motif. A zigzag pattern used as applied trimming.

Ricky Clifton side chair Seat sold by the Johnson Trading Gallery and inspired by ancient Egyptian campaign furniture and Roman copies of them.

rift cut A method for slicing OAK wood. A comb-grained effect is produced by slicing perpendicularly to the medullary rays, which radiate from the center of the log like wheel spokes.

rilievo stiacciato A shallow relief produced by scratches and incisions, described by Vasari as a "low or flattened relief."

rim In furniture, a border, edge, or gallery around a tabletop that is molded, carved, or fretted.

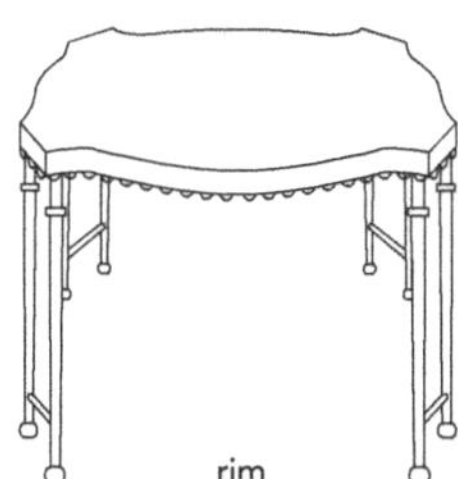
rim

rinceau (French, scroll ornament) Sometimes called an arabesque. It is usually a symmetrical, horizontal composition of scroll and leaf ornaments applied to a frieze, panel, or other architectural feature. Often combined with cartouches and grotesques.

rinceau

riser In a stairway, the vertical or elevating part of a step.

rising stretchers X-shaped connecting crosspieces between the legs of furniture that curve upward toward the intersection. A single stabilizer that curves upward is an arched or hooped stretcher. The devices are also called SALTIREs.

∞**rocaille** A French term for an outdoor artificial grotto decorated with oddly shaped stones and shells and that often had a water feature. The architectural composition gave rise to the term by which much mid-18th-century art is known, Rococo.

rocking chair A chair set on bowed runners, allowing the sitter to move to and fro. A popular chair in the United States since 1800.

Rococo The style of Louis XV. The word derives from ROCAILLE (rockeries) and coquille (cockleshell), motifs that first appeared in the 16th century. Juste-Aurèle Meissonnier was a major figure who produced a book of engraved designs. The period was distinguished by ornate, asymmetrical carvings, and painted decorations using foliage, shells, and scrolls. Chinese and other exotic motifs were often incorporated. Artists explored illusionism, and its cohort, deception, in this nonclassical movement. See JUSTE-AURÈLE MEISSONNIER in *Designers and Architects.*

Rococo mirror

roll In wallpaper, 36 square feet (3.34 square meters). Wallpaper widths may be 18 inches, 22 inches, 28 inches, 30 inches, or 36 inches (45.7, 56, 71, 76, and 91.4 cm). Lengths vary, but the roll will usually average 36 square feet. Several rolls are included in a bundle or stick.

rolled glass A vitreous material that is extruded between two tubular metal roll surfaces spinning in opposite directions to extract a continuous viscous sheet. The vitreous sheet has a small cross-section in contrast to its length, and it passes through a heating process and then solidifies. A pattern may be pressed on one of the surfaces.

rolling completion list (RCL) The managing of unfinished items of a construction project over time, related to the PUNCH LIST and an accelerated construction schedule.

roll molding A round three-dimensional shaped decorative strip. In Gothic architecture it is referred to as a BOWTELL.

rollover arms Upholstered chair armrests that start at the side seat rails and rise and turn over in a full, bold sweep. These padded scrolls turn outward laterally and attach to the chair back. Thus forming an enclosed seat area. Originated in France in the early 16th century and adapted by the English in the RESTORATION PERIOD (1660–1689).

rollover arms

rolltop desk See PULLDOWN FRONT.

Roman architecture The building tradition of the Roman republic and Empire, based on the classical orders: TUSCAN, DORIC, IONIC, CORINTHIAN, and COMPOSITE. The arch, vault, and dome were all prominent features. Favored materials were brick and concrete, with marble used as a surface material. A fusion of indigenous Etruscan and imported Greek traditions.

Roman eagle A decorative motif used by many countries and for many centuries. For citizens of the Roman Empire, the dignified bird of prey symbolized the deification of their emperors, and the apex predators were a feature on the standards of their armies. Napoleon I, emulating the Roman emperors, gave his armies the French eagle in 1804. The eagle appears in Louis XVI, Directoire, and Empire designs.

Romanesque A medieval European period (9th to 12th centuries), predominantly an era of ecclesiastic arts and building. According to Sir Banister Fletcher, the style included "the phases of European architecture which were based on Roman art from the departure of the Romans up to the end of the 12th century, when the pointed arch was introduced. It includes the Norman, Lombard and Byzantine periods, and was the basis for the ensuing Gothic styles."

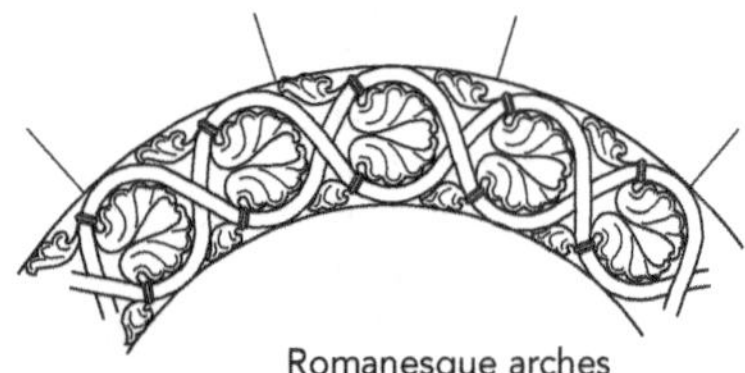
Romanesque arches

Romanesque arch A semicircular structural element, executed in masonry, similar to the ancient Roman arch.

Roman shade A window covering that, when raised, is accordian folded. It does not work on the usual spring roller associated with window coverings; cords at one end control the raising and lowering. Made of many different fabrics, this window covering is decorative and sometimes takes the place of curtains.

Romantic epoch The period of idealized medievalism that started in England, France, and Germany around 1830; an attempt to break away from neoclassicism and a perceived superficiality of revivals. In the arts, Eugène Viollet-le-Duc, and others, promoted Gothic revival. See EUGÈNE VIOLLET-LE-DUC in *Designers and Architects.*

Romanticism A 19th-century literary and arts movement that emphasized emotion rather than formal principles and intellect; its adherents expressed an interest in nature and nationalistic pride, while they eschewed classicism and prescribed rules in general.

∞**romayne work** Carved medallions, heads, or knobs used in the Jacobean and Restoration periods as furniture knobs and pulls. Also an early Renaissance motif (16th century) of classical Roman heads carved in medallions.

rondel A round outline or design in a flat or low-relief pattern made possible by the use of compasses; a feature of Romanesque furniture.

rope bed A sleeping platform and frame with cords laced back and forth to form a spring upon which a mattress is set.

rope molding A half-round or quarter-round decoration that is carved or embossed to resemble a robust cord. See CABLE FLUTING.

rosace A decorative rosette or circular centerpiece in a ceiling.

rose window A circular glazed opening with tracery mullions radiating like spokes of a wheel from a central point. Stained or colored glass fills the areas between the mullions. A feature in Gothic architecture. Also called a WHEEL WINDOW.

Rosetta stone A black basalt stele uncovered in 1798 near Rosetta, Egypt. The same inscription is written in hieroglyphs, Demotic, and Greek. The granodiorite monolith became the key to other hieroglyphic records of ancient Egypt. Found during Napoleon's Egyptian campaigns, it belongs to the group of artifacts that influenced artists of the Directoire and Empire periods.

rosetta wood An East Indian natural material Spanish and Indian craftsmen used during the 17th and 18th centuries in the Americas. It was also used for panels on early American chests because of its brilliant red color and black graining.

rosettes (French, little roses) A floral decorative device, usually a circle with petals developing out from a central point. The outer contour may be round, elliptical, or square. The element has been a popular motif since the Gothic period. See PATERA.

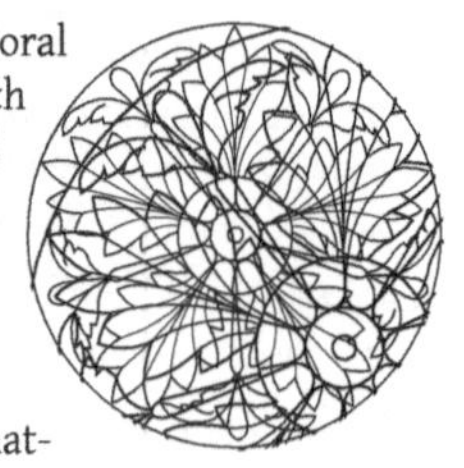
rosette

rosewood, Brazilian A hard, heavy natural material, mainly of a purplish-brown hue with black streaks. When freshly cut, it exudes an aroma reminiscent of the fragrant flower. Also called jacaranda. Popular during the English Empire period for cabinets and musical instruments.

rosewood, Honduras A lighter and more uniformly grained natural material than Brazilian rosewood. See PALISANDER.

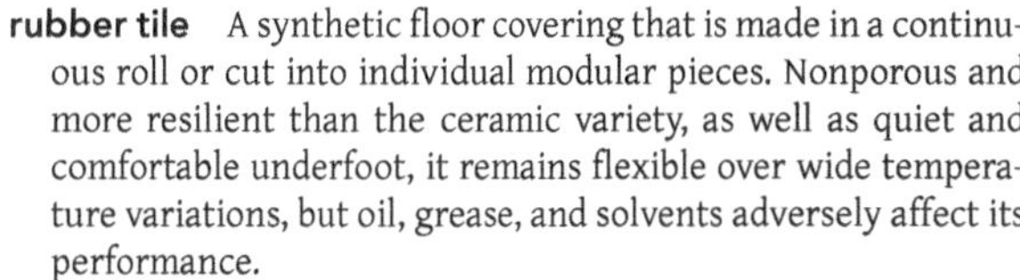

roshan

roshan In Islamic domestic architecture, a protruding window with open screens, allowing for air to circulate but preventing visual access.

rostrum (Latin, beak of a ship) A raised speaker's platform. The raised tribune in the Roman Forum from which the orators spoke was decorated with the prows of ships, which were trophies of war.

rotary-cut veneer A thin slice of wood made by slicing a log in a circular manner around the circumference. It is similar to the unwinding of a roll of paper. The procedure results in a bold, variegated grain as the cut follows the log's growth rings.

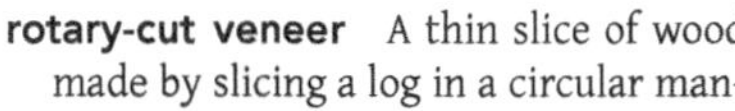

rottenstone A finely powdered siliceous limestone (originally called Tripoli after its place of origin). The soft porous rock can be used with oil to polish wood and also for grinding and polishing sculpture, etc.

rotunda A round building such as the Pantheon in Rome, or the central part of a round building. The room may be a round central hall, surmounted with a dome, as in the Capitol in Washington, D.C.

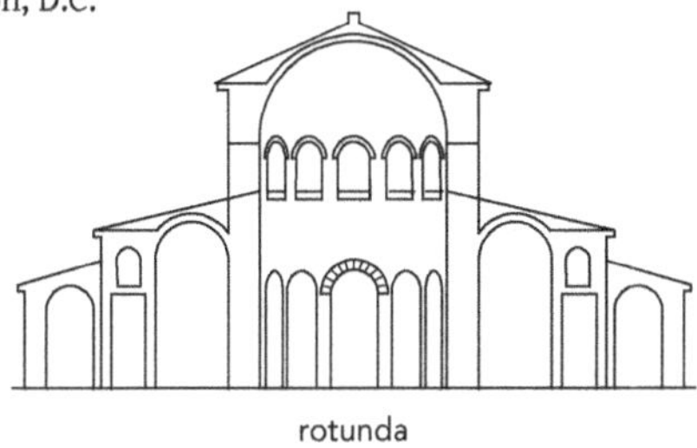

rotunda

∞**roundabout** A 19th-century three-seater furniture piece. In plan, the three seats form a circle, and the three individual chairbacks radiate and curve out from the central point. The seated persons must turn their heads to see and talk to the others who sit on the same piece of furniture. See TÊTE-À-TÊTE.

∞**roundabout chair** Usually designed to fit into a corner, the square seat was diagonally set and the back extended across two adjoining sides. Thus, the chair has a leg in front, one in back, and one at either side. Sometimes referred to as a corner or writing-arm chair. See FAUTEUIL DE BUREAU.

roundabout chair

roundel (1) A round, flat or low-relief form like a patera, medallion, or plaque. (2) A circular disk of stained glass in a leaded window.

rovana A group of synthetic products, previously trademarked by Dow Chemical Company, that includes Saran microtape. Can be extruded as a fiber and used in fabrics. It is flame-resistant, has excellent resistance to abrasion, and keeps its shape. Used mainly for warp threads in drapery fabrics.

RRH Acronym for RAPID RE-HOUSING.

RTA Acronym for READY-TO-ASSEMBLE.

rubbed brickwork An English Renaissance masonry installation that used soft fired clay units that could be cut into exact shapes and sizes. The finely fitted construction blocks were rubbed down to make a smooth, even surface. Sir Christopher Wren employed the technique at Hampton Court.

rubber tile A synthetic floor covering that is made in a continuous roll or cut into individual modular pieces. Nonporous and more resilient than the ceramic variety, as well as quiet and comfortable underfoot, it remains flexible over wide temperature variations, but oil, grease, and solvents adversely affect its performance.

rubble Irregularly shaped stones set into a wall, with or without mortar.

rudder A wooden support for the leaf of a drop-leaf table or shelf that resembles a ship's steering device; similar to a BUTTERFLY support.

∞**Rudd's dressing table** A mid-18th-century English horizontal surface which served the work of attending to one's appearance, regarding make-up, hair, and dress. Hepplewhite described as it "possessing every convenience which can be wanted; or mechanism and ingenuity supply." It was named for a noted personality, Margaret Caroline Rudd, an orphan who parlayed her good looks and charm into riches. The piece of furniture is associated with a profligate lifestyle that connects appearance to luxury.

∞**rule joint** A dustproof and draft-proof hinged connection on late Queen Anne furniture, screens, tabletops, etc. A hinged assembly. See KNUCKLE JOINT.

runcible (adj.) Having the features of another piece of cutlery, e.g., a spoon with prongs, a curved fork, or a spoon with a cutting edge. Sometimes considered a nonsense term. Can indicate an item that has the qualities of an item that it is not.

runic knot An ornamental motif of the Celtic, Scandinavian, and German Romanesque periods. It is an interlaced design using the magical symbols of ancient northern European civilizations.

runner foot A pair of straight legs that a horizontal rail or stretcher connects at their base. The legs appear to end on this crosspiece. A popular chair support in the Italian Renaissance period. Sometimes carved lion's paws decorate the ends of the crossbar. A user can rest their feet on the rail.

running bond See STRETCHER BOND.

∞**running dog** A continuous scroll or wavelike design. Also called the VITRUVIAN SCROLL.

rush A long grass that is twisted and woven to make seats for provincial chairs. The seats are also known as flag seats. Seats made from the natural and sustainable material have been used from the earliest times, and the material is often woven into mats.

Russian Constructivism A post-revolutionary avant-garde movement; a utilitarian and technological form of Modernism that was related to CUBISM. The movement started in 1915 and was a cultural force into the 1920s. Major figures included Vladimir Tatlin and Alexander Rodchenko. Regarding form, it was a precursor to Deconstruction.

rustication A form of masonry popular in the Renaissance, Baroque, and Mannerist periods using stonework or bricks that have recessed or chamfered edges. A decorative, wide-jointed appearance is created. Manipulated stucco can resemble this rough-cut masonry.

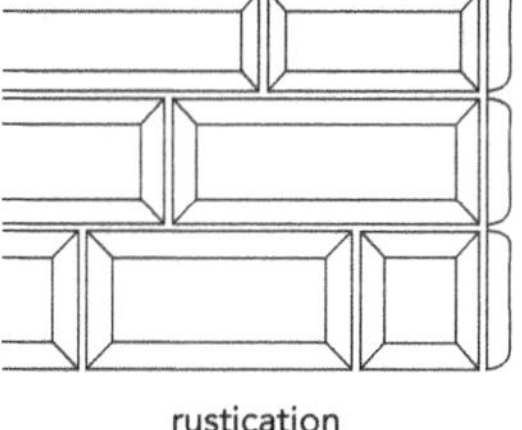

rustication

rustic furniture English garden furniture of the mid 18th century that simulated natural twigs and branches, gnarled with an effect of fantasy. Prepared lumber was carved to resemble tree branchlets and underbranches.

rustic stonework Masonry in which the face of the rock is roughened, but the block is carefully shaped, leveled, and set in straight courses. The edges are often smoothed out to emphasize the rough face of the hard mineral building material.

R-value (R-factor) Numerical value indicating how effectively a structure resists heat flow—that is, its efficacy in insulating and preventing heat exchange. R-value equals the thickness of the structure divided by its K-value (i.e., its ability to transfer heat).

rya rug (Scandinavian, rough or shaggy) A high-pile, shaggy floor covering based on a Scandinavian craft that predates 3000 B.C.E. It was originally a dowry item and was used as a blanket for warmth. Used today in contemporary and provincial rooms as a decorative floor textile.

RYB color model A conceptual framework of chromatic theory and pigment mixing, based on three primary colors: red, yellow, and blue. Its origins predate the 20th century and scientific color theory. Its initiators included Claude Boutet. Bauhaus instructors, including Josef Albers, furthered it with their research. It is frequently represented as a diagrammatic ring, with the primary colors equally spread apart and with secondary and tertiary colors between them. Of the color palettes available to designers, it is one of the most vibrant.

ryokan Traditional Japanese inn. Typical features of the small-scale projects include tatami mats, communal baths, shoki, and futons. They share features in common with Japanese historic houses. Many were on the highway between Edo (Tokyo) and Kyoto. Dating back to the 8th century C.E., the first known hotel was a ryokan. Today they are in the category of boutique hotels.

saber legs Fine splayed supports found on early-19th-century Sheraton chairs in the Grecian style. The front vertical supports flare forward, and the rear vertical supports curve out behind, as in the Greek KLISMOS chair.

sabicu A pink to red wood that resembles mahogany. Hard and heavy, with a low luster, the wood is native to Cuba and Central America.

sabot foot See SPADE FOOT.

∞sabots (French, wooden shoes) Decorative metal coverings for the feet of wood furniture. They were designed to enhance as well as protect the foot, and they serve the same purpose that chutes do on the angles and legs of wood furniture. They appeared in the 18th century and were made of BRONZE DORÉ, brass, or other metals. See also CHUTES.

∞sack back The double-bowed back of a WINDSOR CHAIR.

sacristy A room or rooms in a church where vessels and vestments are stored. Made famous as a hiding place for the characters in Puccini's opera *Tosca.*

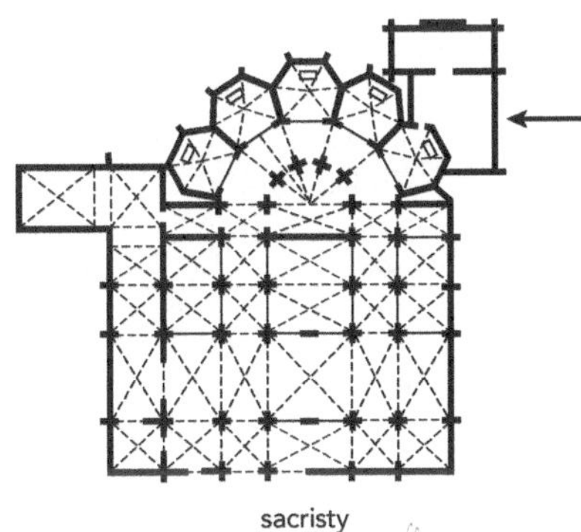

sacristy

saddle Board or stone slab at the bottom of a door. See SILL.

∞saddle-check chair A bedroom easy chair of the wing (forty-winks) type designed by Hepplewhite and others in mid- and late-18th-century England and the United States. See WING CHAIR.

saddle seat A scooped-out support that resembles the contour of the common equestrian equipment. The support is convex at the sides and back and concave in the center, and it rises to a central ridge toward the front. Often found in WINDSOR CHAIRS with thick pine horizontal planes.

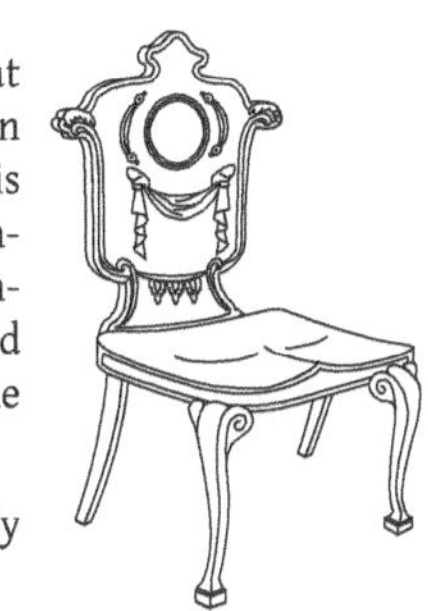

saddle seat

sailcloth A strong, durable, firmly woven cotton canvas.

Salem rocker An early-19th-century New England piece of MOTION FURNITURE with a heavy scrolled seat, top rail, and arms. The spindle-back is straight and not as high as that of a BOSTON ROCKER.

salon A large apartment or room in a house or palace, used for entertaining and conversing. It was the center of cultural and political society from the late 18th through the 19th centuries. Many salons were made famous by the hostesses who presided over them, including Juliette Récamier.

salt glaze A surface of thin glass on pottery or brick that is produced by throwing the white crystalline substance into the oven during the firing process. The glass finish results from the thermochemical reaction of silicates in the clay body with the sodium of the sodium/chlorine compound.

saltires X-shaped stretchers of Italian origin, used to reinforce the legs of tables and chairs. See RISING STRETCHERS and STRETCHERS.

samara A reddish-brown hardwood from French Equatorial Africa. It is rotary-cut and usually has a large swirled grain pattern. Also called GABOON.

same-handed rooms In healthcare design, patient areas that have identical configuration to reduce employee error and improve productivity. In plan, individual patient areas are not book matched.

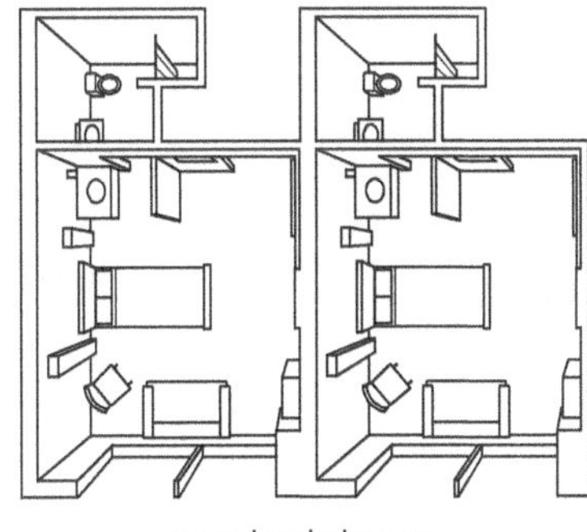

same-handed rooms

samite A heavy silk fabric of the Middle Ages, usually interwoven with gold and heavily embroidered. It was used mainly for upholstery and garments.

sampler A needlework exercise a child or novice performed in embroidery. Especially in vogue during the 18th and 19th centuries, the textile often featured an alphabet or quotation embroidered in a variety of stitches and colors.

sanctuary The most sacred area of a house of worship, typically surrounding the high altar.

sandalwood An East Indian and Pacific Islands wood that is hard, yellow, and close-grained. It is used for ornamental objects and inlays rather than for furniture.

sandblasting A method of cleaning or polishing a stone surface by bombarding it with fine mineral particles propelled by jets of steam or air. Also, a technique for cutting or engraving glass or crystal in a similar manner. The treated area is usually cloudy and gray and not as smooth to the touch as polished glass.

sand shaking A 17th-century Dutch technique for deepening or shading the color of pieces of wood inlay by dipping them into hot sand.

sanguine (French, bloody) (noun) A reddish-brown or terracotta color chalk used for drawing. Many Renaissance artists produced drawings or studies for paintings wielding this soft, pastel-like medium.

sapele or sapeli An African wood that resembles mahogany in color and texture but is more evenly striped and harder, heavier, and tougher than African mahogany. The natural material is usually dark red-brown in color. Also called tiama.

sappanwood A natural material that closely resembles brazilwood and is native to Indonesia, Sri Lanka, and India. Used for furniture produced in the Dutch colonies during the 17th and 18th centuries, based on models and designs from Europe.

sarabend rug A style of Persian floor covering that has a rose-colored or medium-blue background, with palm leaves as the major decorative motif.

saracenic (adj.) Showing an Islamic influence. The Mohammedan Saracens greatly influenced Spanish arts and architecture from the 8th century, when they swept from Morocco into Spain. Saracenic Spanish arts are also called Moorish. Motifs were chiefly abstract geometric and interlaced patterns. See ISLAMIC.

Saran The trademarked name for polyvinylidene chloride (PVDC), from which multifilaments are extruded for use in tough, heavy-duty fabrics. Stiff, sunlight- and weather-resistant, and excellent for outdoor use. See *Table 2.*

sarcophagus (1) A stone coffin originated by the ancients. (2) In the 18th century, a wine cooler made of mahogany with a lead liner and often part of a sideboard. It was also called a cellarette or garde du vin. See CELLARETTE.

sarcophagus

sarouk rug A style of Persian floor covering that is predominantly knotted in deep, dark blues and reds, with floral designs that stand out in lighter colors.

sash The movable or fixed framework of a window.

sash bar The strip of wood or metal that subdivides the panes of glass in the frame of a window. See MULLION, MUNTIN, and TRACERY.

sash curtains Sheer or semi-sheer draperies mounted on a rod attached to the frame of a window or door. Sometimes the drapery has two slots for rods, on both the top and the bottom, and the fabric is shirred and pulled taut.

sash window Usually a double-hung framed opening that is opened and shut by raising or lowering one of the windows.

sateen or satine A cotton fabric with a satin weave, a lustrous face, and a dull back. Commonly used as a lining material for draperies.

sash window

satin A fabric originally made of silk and imported from China. It was first known as Zaytun, after the Chinese seaport by that name. It is a basic weave, and the face of the fabric is smooth and glossy, while the back is dull. Blending the silk fibers with linen or cotton weft results in a stronger fabric. There are many types of satins. See SATIN, ANTIQUE; SATIN, CHARMEUSE; SATIN, HAMMERED; SATIN, RIBBED; and SATIN, SLIPPER.

satin, antique A rich, heavy fabric with a dull, uneven texture. Used for upholstery and drapery. It may be made of silk, cotton, rayon, or a blend of silk and cotton.

satin, charmeuse A shiny silk fabric with an organzine warp and a spun silk weft.

satin, hammered A glossy silk fabric that has been treated to have a textured surface effect similar to that of beaten metal.

satin, ribbed Bengaline or faille fabric woven with face protrusions, which gives the fabric a lustrous, unbroken surface. It can also be given a moiré finish. See MOIRÉ.

satin, slipper A heavyweight fabric of silk or synthetic fibers with a cotton back, originally used to make slippers in the 18th and 19th centuries. It is currently used as an upholstery and drapery fabric.

satine See SATEEN OR SATINE.

satine rubanne A straight-grained, strong, durable, South African wood with ribbon-like markings. Used for inlays and decorative banding. Also called capomo.

satin finish A smooth, low-luster surface treatment on fabric, paper, paint, etc.

satin weave One of the basic textile constructions, producing a face almost completely of warp, evenly spaced, and therefore lustrous.

satinwood A highly figured, close-grained, hard, durable natural material native to Sri Lanka and Southeast Asia. It is light yellow to golden brown in color, with a lustrous satin-like quality. A favorite wood in the Louis XV and Louis XVI periods, often use for inlay and veneering. See AGE OF SATINWOOD. Also see SEDDON, GEORGE, in *Designers and Architects.*

saturation A noun that describes a color's level of intensity. The degree of purity of color, especially of shades although not tints. The result of soaking (the time that a textile is in contact with the dye) or a chemical treatment by which colors are fully absorbed or have maximum percentages of pigment to the full extent. Used in the context of textile construction, biology, and chemistry. Often describes colors that appear dark, such as those of the Victorian era.

satyr A human figure with a goat's legs and appendages, such as ears, horns, and tail. A common feature of neoclassical decorative arts, including works by Wedgwood and Flaxman.

satyr mask A Germanic motif that reached the height of its popularity in England from 1730 to 1740. Carved on the knees of furniture legs and also used decoratively on other areas.

Originally a classical motif, it also appears in French and Italian Renaissance designs.

sauna Room, roomette, or closet, usually lined in wood and provided with benches for sitting or stretching out. Can be filled with dry heat that is thermostatically controlled or that is produced by hot bricks or stones contained within the sauna. Originally a Scandinavian innovation to relax and refresh its users.

sausage turning Wood lathe-work which resembled links of the European culinary staple, typical of machined-wood elements (vertical or horizontal) in German Renaissance, Jacobean, and 19th-century American furniture.

∞Savonarola chair An early Italian Renaissance X-shaped piece of furniture. The seat was often made of interlaced strips of wood, and the back was carved or decorated with simple inlay work. Named for the martyred Italian monk Girolamo Savonarola (1452–1498) who championed abstinence and austerity. His eponymous seat is appropriately restrained in form and decoration.

Savonarola chair

Savonnerie (1) A famous rug and tapestry factory in France, founded in 1604. (2) Also, the high-pile, hand-woven rugs produced in this factory, which were often decorated with pastel floral and scroll designs.

∞sawbuck table A simple dining surface of 17th-century Europe and America that rested on X-shaped trestles or two-legged standards. Also called a trestle table.

saxony A carpet texture longer than plush but shorter than shag. No twist is set into the pile. The pile is tall enough to stand up but may flatten out when subjected to heavy traffic. Usually produced with thick yarns for a nubby, casual look. See *Table 1.*

SBS Acronym for SICK BUILDING SYNDROME.

scaffolding A temporary skeletal framework built around a structure or object or on one side of it. The short-term architectural appendage provides a means of working on the outside of a building or inside a large unplatformed area. Also a framework around a piece of sculpture.

∞scagliola An imitation marble made of gypsum or plaster of paris, chips of marble, and coloring matter. Invented in Italy in the 17th century, scagliola was used to make chimneypieces in 18th-century England, and the Adam brothers used this technique widely.

scale (1) The dimensions of a unit in relation to the height and width of the area in which it is to be placed. The relationship between one piece of furniture and another in size and proportion. (2) A ratio that indicates the relationship of the length of lines in a drawing to the actual length of objects in reality. In a scale drawing, the drawing is proportionately reduced or enlarged in relation to a given ratio, for example, ¼ inch may be equivalent to 1 foot.

∞scale-back chair A Queen Anne seat with an imbricated pattern carved onto the chair's splat and uprights. See SCALING and IMBRICATE.

scaling A surface finish that resembles the exterior of a fish. A technique used by architects and designers to fill in the background of small panels. See IMBRICATE.

scalloped arch An arch having more than five foils, a design found in MOORISH architecture. See FOIL.

scalloped borders See CUTOUT BORDERS.

scalloped edge An edge or border that has been marked or cut into segments of a circle. An outer profile that resembles the wavy, fluted contour of a scallop shell.

scalloping

scalloping A decorative motif reminiscent of shells and featuring incised curves. See also CONCHA.

scallop shell Semicircular shell shape with ridges radiating from a point at the center bottom, used as a decoration. Popular in the late Renaissance, Louis XIV, Louis XV, Queen Anne, and Georgian periods. It was often found on Goddard 18th-century kneehole desks and cabriole-legged highboys (See GODDARD, JOHN) and on the knees of cabriole legs, on aprons, on crests of furniture, and also as a hood on architectural pieces of case goods. Also called a COCKLESHELL. See *Designers and Architects.*

sidechair with scallop shell

Scandi wellness A lifestyle trend with housewares and interior design at its core. It originated in the Scandinavian countries but quickly spread worldwide. The Danish and Norwegian word is hygge. It is contemporary, fun, relaxed, and cozy. The approach emphasizes the comfort and small moments of joy that derive from simple pleasures, such as having snuggly socks and candles. Although related to mindfulness, it isn't solitary but outward looking. IKEA products demonstrate its retail base.

Scandinavian modern A simple, chaste, refined version of the traditional Empire style, introduced in the 1930s as Swedish or Danish modern. With Alvar and Aino Aalto as its famous acolytes, there is an almost complete lack of applied decorative elements; hardware is simple. Even as pieces became increasingly modern, they avoided the criticism of coldness because of their use of regional woods, including walnut and teak. The pieces have gracefully tapered legs and gently curved arms and backs.

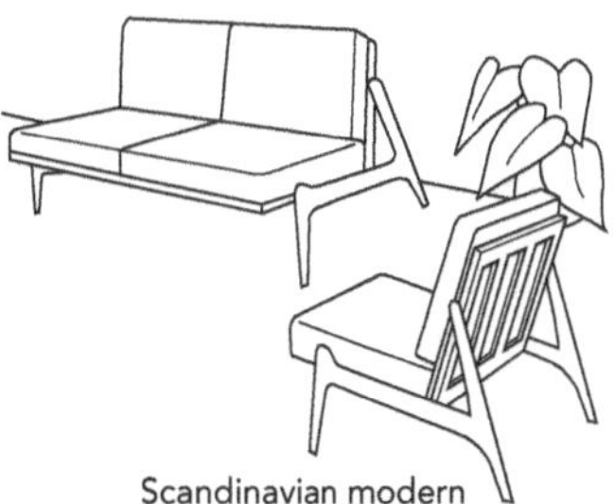
Scandinavian modern

∞scaramouche A decorative representation of a buffoon or clown of 17th- and 18th-century Italian comedy. The figure was usually represented in black with a black cape and hat and a grotesque mask. A decorative element in 18th-century English, French, and Italian designs.

scarf joint In cabinetry, two beveled edges laid one over the other to form a continuous level plane. An overlapping joint.

scarves Pieces of fabric used on the tops of dressers and cabinets. May be any shape, but frequently sized to fit.

scatter rug A small floor covering used as an accent, often at the bedside or in entries and hallways. Available in many sizes, shapes, colors, patterns, and fibers, such as wool, nylon, Acrilan, cotton and sisal.

school A group of artists or designers whose work shows similar characteristics owing to the influence of an individual master or body of theory. The art of a region or country, not always literally related to an academic institution. See, for example, HUDSON RIVER SCHOOL.

schreinerizing A process for producing a high luster on fabric by passing it between rollers, one smooth and one engraved with fine lines, to increase the surface area for light reflection.

scissors chair A folding X-shaped chair used in ancient Egypt, Greece, Nubia, and Rome. The prototype of the DANTE CHAIR and the SAVONAROLA CHAIR.

sconce (Latin, *abscondere*, to hide) An ornamental wall bracket used to hold candles or electric bulbs. Originally, a sconce was a shield or protection for a flame or a lantern to protect a light. See APPLIQUÉ and GIRANDOLE.

scissors chair

sconce

scoop seat A slightly concave seat, dipped to accommodate the contour of a seated person. It is found in classic chairs and reappears in the late 18th century in Sheraton's work and the Empire style. A variation appears in present-day contour and molded plywood chairs. Also called a DROPPED SEAT.

scoops and vents The topography and openings in surfaces produced by parametric design and digital fabrication. See PARAMETRIC.

scoops and vents

Scotchgard A trademark name for a fluorochemical process applied to fabrics to make them resistant to dirt, water, and oil. The process allows the fabric to breathe and does not impair the hand or color. Originally produced by the Perma Dry Company and now owned by 3M Company.

scotia A concave molding that resembles the S curve made by two connecting curves of different radii.

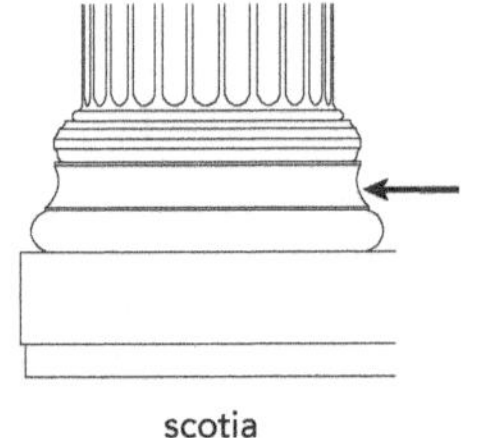

scotia

scratch carving A simple country-style incising done with a V-shaped chisel.

scratch coat A rough, first coat of plaster that is abraded and scored before it is dry. The finish, or smooth coat, adheres better to this coarse texture.

screed The guide band applied to a surface before the application of plaster, the final layer of a concrete floor, or the finishing material of a roof, such as tile or asphalt.

screen A separating device or divider. A partition or enclosure of wood, metal, or stone that can be decorative, functional, or both.

∞screen table A late-18th-century Sheraton design for a lady's desk with a vertical element set behind the desk surface. It permitted the lady to work near a fire and yet be protected from flying embers. The device let down into a slot opening, making a level surface when it was not in use. A drawer was placed below the slider.

screw stair A spiral staircase that twists around a slender pole.

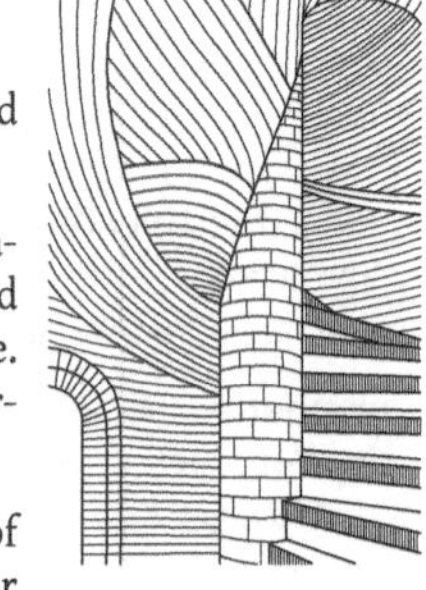

screw stair

∞scribanne An imposing desk-cupboard of the Louis XIV period.

scribe (verb) In carpentry, to fit one material to another, as the side of a shaped wooden strip to an uneven wall surface. The strip has to be shaped to fit the irregular surface contour of the wall.

scribe molding A small, pliable strip of wood used to cover an irregular joint or crack.

scribing A technique of fitting frames, moldings, etc. onto irregular surfaces. The unit to be applied must be cut and shaped to fit these irregularities.

scrim A lightweight, open-weave, coarse cotton fabric similar to marquisette, usually white, cream, or ecru and used for needlework. Sometimes the textile has larger openings (¼ inch by ¼ inch) and is heavily sized. A form of scrim is also used to cover and hold the joints between plasterboards before plastering.

∞scrinium A round box of the classical Roman period that held scrolls. Such boxes were generally made of beechwood and could be locked or sealed and carried about. The device could be a library case or a collection of scrolls.

∞scritoire (French) Writing table.

scroll An S- or C-curved design. An artistic invention in ornamentation, used with such motifs as ACANTHUS LEAF, laurel, oak, ivy, and wheat. A spiraling and convoluting line, like a rolled piece of paper, makes the scroll.

scroll bed See GONDOLA BED and SLEIGH BED.

scrolled-top mirror A Chippendale design found in America in the mid-18th century, similar to a silhouette or fretwork mirror but characterized by a broken pediment with a central carved ornament. Often made of mahogany with gilt decoration.

scroll foot A flattened rolled element at the end of a cabriole leg, which originated in the Louis XIV period. Appears in England in the William and Mary period.

scroll molding Applied trim that resembles a curled piece of paper. Popular in English Gothic architecture.

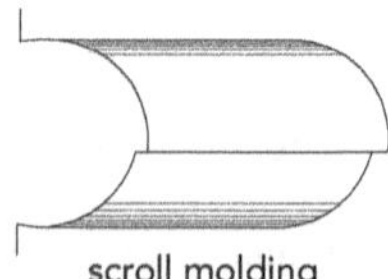

scroll molding

scroll pediment A broken triangular roof in which each half is a reverse curve that ends in a scroll at the outside end. The open center area usually is trimmed with a finial.

scrollwork Ornate, lacelike wood cutouts made with a jigsaw. It was a popular decoration in the Steamboat Gothic period in the 19th-century United States. See JIGSAW DETAIL.

∞scrowled chair An English chair of the mid 16th to the mid 17th centuries, with a heavy, high panel back. It usually had a heavy top rail, and cresting that was partly supported by brackets was attached to the upper sides of the stiles. Flat-shaped arms attached to the front supports, and it had baluster legs and low-placed stretchers. See WAINSCOT CHAIR.

scrubbed pine A provincial furniture finish for Early American and French "antiques," consisting of light oil on a natural pine wood, which approximates an unfinished look.

∞scrutoire A writing desk. Often a slope-front desk which has a lid that opens to form a horizontal writing surface.

sculpture The art of creating forms and decorations in three dimensions or in relief. Carving is the process of freeing the form from the material. Modeling is the building up of the form from some plastic material such as clay, wax, or plasteline and then cast in plaster or metal, usually bronze. Carving is usually done in wood, stone, or marble.

sculpture

sculptured rug See CARVED RUG.

∞scutcheon See ESCUTCHEON.

seam The joining of two surfaces. Some examples are the butt or overlap of two pieces of wallpaper, the sewn line of two pieces of fabric in a drapery, or the hairline between two joined pieces of wood or veneer.

seasoned lumber Wood that has been dried in the air or in a kiln to improve its durability for furniture construction and to control warping and checking. See CHECK and KILN-DRIED.

seaweed marquetry A popular form of ornament during the William and Mary and the Queen Anne periods in England. An inlay of various woods in an arabesque pattern of small leaves and oceanic botanical forms. Probably based on BOULLE WORK. Also called ENDIVE MARQUETRY.

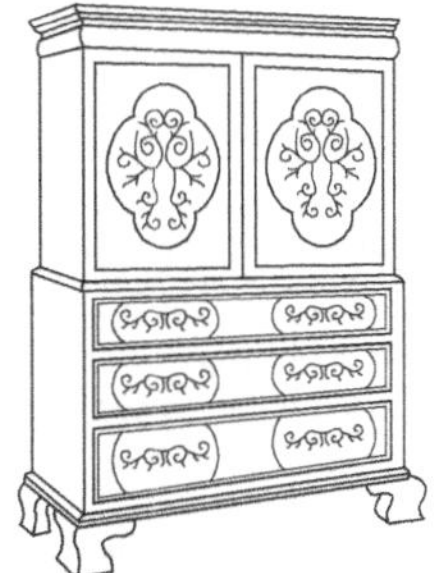
seaweed marquetry

Secession Movement See SEZESSION.

Secessionists The group of artists who sought to unite the arts, embrace manufacturing processes, and oppose Art Nouveau and 19th-century historicism. They were multidisciplinary, early modernists centered in Berlin, Munich, and Vienna.

secondary colors The three colors produced by mixing any two of the three primary colors. Red combined with yellow produces orange, blue and yellow make green, and blue mixed with red forms violet. Therefore, the three secondary colors are orange, green, and violet.

secondary lighting Additional illumination of an interior that goes beyond the basic, primary, or general lighting plan. The use of spotlights, floods, filters, wall-washers, and indirect lighting techniques to add depth, dimension, and atmosphere. See AMBIENCE LIGHTING and INDIRECT LIGHTING.

Second Empire period or Late Empire period The period in France approximately between 1852 and 1871, which produced massive scrolled and rollover-type furniture that blended the Empire with Louis XV motifs, rather than with classic elements. In the United States, Duncan Phyfe produced ungainly butcher furniture in this style. See BUTCHER FURNITURE.

secrétaire (French, desk) See SECRETARY.

secrétaire à abattant (French) A desk with a drop-lid.

secretary A desk surface with a space for writing appliances that is combined with a drawer base below and a bookcase cabinet above. In the 17th century, it was essentially a bureau: a writing table on a chest of drawers with a hinged desk arrangement equipped with brass quadrants. During the 18th century, the bookcase or shell units were added over the desk surface. See BUREAU, SCRITOIRE, and SCRUTOIRE.

section A vertically sliced view through a structure or a formed part, such as a molding. Gives a clear impression of the silhouette as well as the internal construction of the object. The section view can also give dimensions.

sectional furniture Upholstered or case furniture made in modules, or small units, that can be pulled together in a variety of ways to make larger units that turn corners, for example. Usually refers to a sectional sofa, which is composed of two, three, or more parts, one of which is a curved or angled corner piece. Each part of the sectional couch can be a finished piece that may be used individually.

sedan chair An 18th-century enclosed chair, usually carried by four men, as a form of transportation. Originated in Sedan, France, in the 17th century and popular in England in the 17th and 18th centuries. Also called a CHAISE À PORTEURS or a PALANQUIN.

sedia (Italian) A chair. Often specifically, a Renaissance armchair.

segmental arch An arch shaped as a wedge of a circle but less than a semicircle. An elliptical arch.

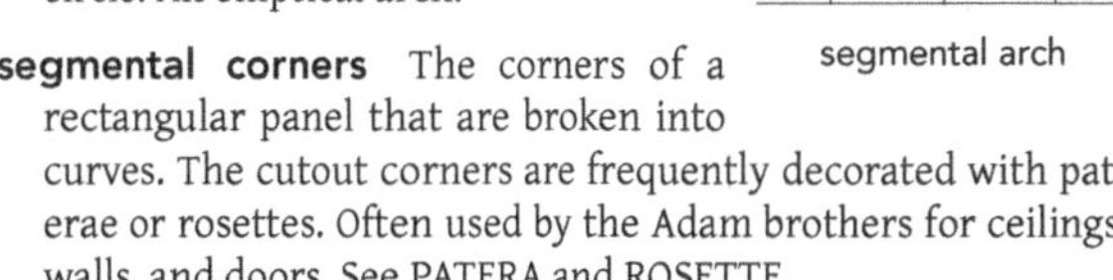
segmental arch

segmental corners The corners of a rectangular panel that are broken into curves. The cutout corners are frequently decorated with paterae or rosettes. Often used by the Adam brothers for ceilings, walls, and doors. See PATERA and ROSETTE.

segmental front See BOW FRONT and SWELL FRONT.

sehna knot A method of hand-tying pile yarns in Oriental rugs: over one warp thread and under a second. Also called the Persian knot. See GHIORDES KNOT, the other traditional knot.

∞seigneurial chair A chair of state. In the Gothic and Renaissance periods, it was usually high-backed and had solid arm supports and a solid base. The chair was often canopied and elaborately carved. Less imposing versions were used for the master of the manor or castle. See CANOPY CHAIR.

seigneurial chair

self-covered seat deck The area under the loose cushions on a piece of upholstered furniture that is covered in the same fabric as the rest of the piece. Also called a self-covered deck.

∞sella curulis An ancient Roman X-shaped folding chair favored by officials and dignitaries.

selvage or selvedge The reinforced, vertical, outer edges of a fabric. Also, the unpatterned or unprinted margin of wallpaper (on either side of the design), usually imprinted with the pattern name, product number, manufacturer's name, and instructions.

∞semainier A tall bedroom chest with seven drawers, introduced in the Louis XV period. The drawers were originally intended one for each day of the week. It was similar to a chiffonier, which is wider and does not have a specified number of drawers. See CHIFFONIER.

∞semé (French: sown, as seeds are sown) A minute floral motif scattered over the background of a brocaded fabric. In the Louis XVI period, tiny rosebuds were often found within or around satin and faille stripes woven on the fabric.

semi-lead crystal High-end vitreous material that contains 10 to 12 percent lead.

semi-vitreous (adj.) Describes ware that is somewhat like glass.

sepia print A pattern or image with a reddish-brown tint. The color is a brownish pigment originally made from the cuttlefish.

seraglio (1) An enclosed or protected area in a house. (2) A harem in a Turkish palace.

seriographs Fine, silk-screened prints that are created in a limited number. See SILK-SCREEN.

serpentine (1) (adj.) Snakelike. (2) (noun) A sinuous line created by juxtaposing a concave form and a convex form; two connected CYMA CURVES. Usually the center curve is convex and prominent. When the center curve is concave and receding, the line is called a reverse serpentine. The serpentine line was used in Louis XV commodes and also in 18th-century English cupboards, desks, and chests.

serrated edge A ZIGZAG, toothed, or DENTIL edge. A series of inverted V's in a continuous band.

∞serre-papiers See TABLE À GRADIN.

servante See RAFRAÎCHISSOIR.

server or serving table An auxiliary piece of furniture in a dining room, used to hold or contain dishes, glassware, silver, table linens, and bottles. It usually has drawers and may also contain cabinet space. The larger units are similar to buffets, and the smaller pieces are like rafraîchissoirs, servantes, or dumbwaiters. The top surface holds food, platters, and other service pieces.

∞serviteur fidèle (French, loyal servant) The French version of a dumbwaiter; a multitiered table. See DUMBWAITER and RAFRAÎCHISSOIR.

set Sufficient dishes to serve four or more people. Usually offered at a considerable price advantage when compared to individual pieces or place settings.

settee A seating device that developed from the SETTLE. Long, with a carved or upholstered back, arms, and a soft seat, it was intended to hold two or more persons. Usually it matched the individual chairs of the period in contour and chairback decoration. Often described as two-, three-, or four-chairback settees. A front leg was provided between each chairback; thus a three-chairback settee would have four legs in front to delineate the three seats. Popular in the late 17th and early 18th centuries.

settle A bench, usually of oak, for two or more people. A settle usually had a high back and arms, and sometimes there were ears or wings at either end. Originally a popular seating device in the Middle Ages, often carved, paneled, and richly decorated. A settle with a hinged seat over a chest is a BOX SETTLE. A canopied settle was called a CANAPÉ.

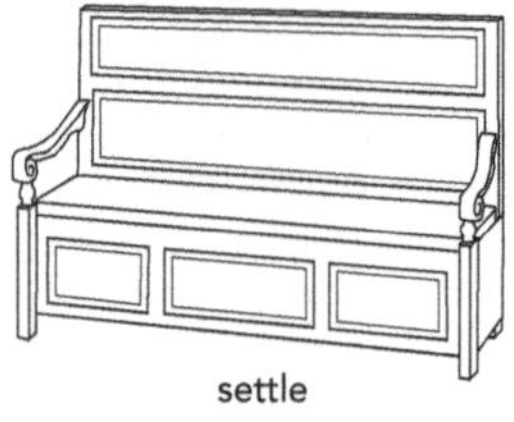
settle

settle chair A box-shaped Tudor seat similar to the Italian Renaissance SEDIA.

Sèvres (1) A porcelain factory at Sèvres, near Paris, founded in 1756. Mademoiselle de Pompadour obtained royal patronage for it during the reign of Louis XV. Here were produced magnificent vases and plaques for furniture and table inserts. (2) *Sèvres* also describes the products of the factory, including the vases and urns of a special rose color, as well as pieces in King's blue.

sewing table A popular, small working table of the mid and late 18th century. Usually equipped with drawers, trays, spool racks, and a cloth bag below for sewing materials. French Louis XVI and Empire designs were also created to satisfy this need. Also called a POUCH TABLE.

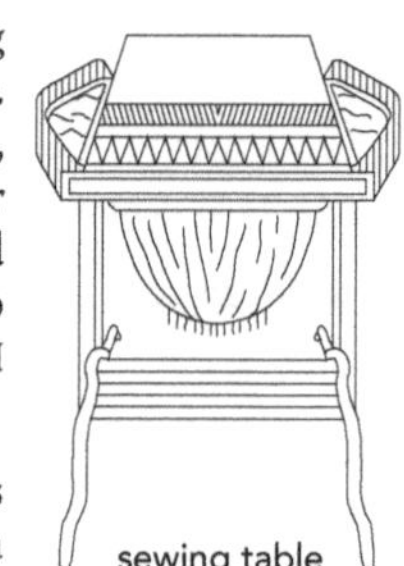
sewing table

Sezession A series of artistic revolutions that occurred in Germany and Austria during the last decade of the 19th century. Avant-garde artists left the old academic societies and organized forward-looking exhibitions of their own. Three major eruptions took place: Munich, 1892; Vienna, 1897; and Berlin, 1899. This dramatic cultural shift constituted the beginnings of Modernism. Also called the Secession Movement. See ART NOUVEAU and JUGENDSTIL.

∞sgabelle or sgabello A small 16th-century Italian Renaissance seat usually identified by its carved back splat, octagonal seat, and carved trestle supports instead of legs. A highly decorated version of a simple stool.

∞sgraffito (graffito) (Italian, scratcher) A decorative technique of 16th-century Italy, in which tinted plaster was covered by white plaster (or vice versa), and the top layer was scratched to reveal the bottom layer. Arabesques were popular designs in the technique. See GRAFFITO WARE.

shade (1) A color with black added, as opposed to a tint, which is a color with white added. See TINT. (2) Also, a protection or covering for light fixtures and windows. See LAMPSHADE and WINDOW SHADE.

sgabello

shade cloth See HOLLAND SHADE CLOTH.

shading Paint-texturizing technique in which color values from light to dark are blended across a wall or ceiling.

shaft The central portion of a column or pilaster, between the capital and the base.

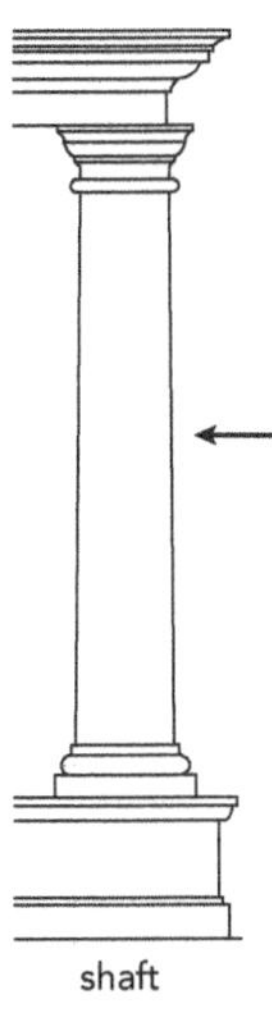

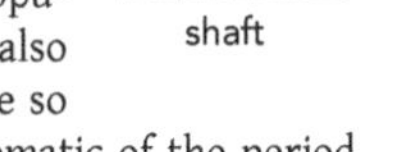

shaft

shagreen The untanned skins of horses, mules, or sharks that were finished with a granular surface and dyed green. It was sometimes used for covering small pieces of furniture in the 18th century and again in the 1920s.

shag rug Floor covering with a long pile, usually textured loop, cut, or a mixture of the two. The longer the pile, the more it lies down and mats. In luxurious versions, the pile is long and dense and does not flatten as readily. Nylon and various polyester shags are popular, though the hairy floor coverings are also available in wool and acrylics. These were so popular in the 1960s that they are emblematic of the period. See *Table 1*.

shake A rough, split-wood shingle favored in the western United States.

Shaker A religious group in the United States in the late 18th century and early 19th century who preferred simple, plain, functional furniture devoid of decoration. The clean, straight lines of their designs resemble 20th-century modern, and their concept of built-in is also prophetic. Design for the Shakers, however, was not a matter of style but a philosophical and spiritual approach to life that revealed itself in the straightforward designed objects they produced.

Shaker modern A simple, chaste, up-to-date version of early-19th-century Shaker furniture. Clean, straight-lined, with gentle tapers. The pegging and dovetailing details are the sole embellishments. Maple, cherry, and other fruitwoods were often used and given an oil finish.

shakkei Wood louvers in Japanese designs that filter light and permit air flow.

shams Pillow covers that match quilts or comforters.

shantung A heavy grade of pongee, an unbleached textile originally made in Shandong, China. It is usually manufactured from wild silk, cotton, or a combination of the two. See PONGEE.

sharing economy An economic model and commercial activity of capitalism that concerns goods and services and that creates new models for living and working. It is less hierarchical, with multiple peer-to-peer interactions. It offers an alternative means of acquiring, or providing access to, domestic and commercial space. All-important are developing online communities, social power, commerce at the scale of individual transactions, and that sharing is a virtue. It is an unusual model for design services that addresses a number of contemporary issues, such as the cost of living in expensive urban centers.

shaving mirror A popular device of the 18th century. A framed reflective surface that can be tilted within a stand, often fitted with drawers below to hold razors, jewelry, etc. The unit can stand on top of a chest. See STANDING MIRROR.

shaving table A clever, complex dressing device of the Chippendale period. Often equipped with hinged side-table surfaces, a basin area, a spring-up mirror, drawers, and compartments. Also called a REFLECTING DRESSING TABLE or RUDD'S DRESSING TABLE.

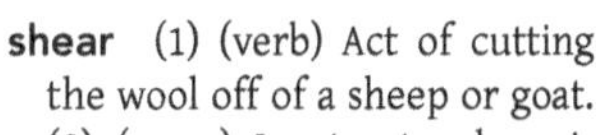

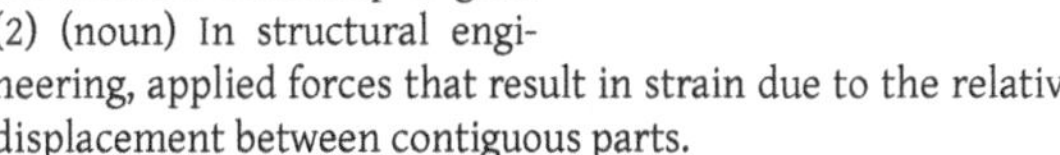

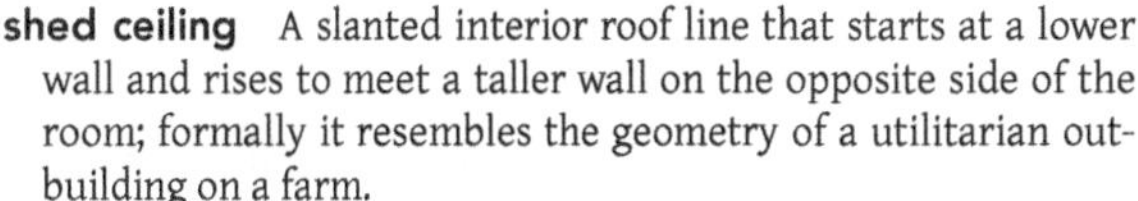

shaving table

∞sheaf back A delicate late-18th-century French chair whose vertical support features a bundle of stylized wheat spikes that fanned out to meet the top rail. These chairs usually had rush or cane seats.

shear (1) (verb) Act of cutting the wool off of a sheep or goat. (2) (noun) In structural engineering, applied forces that result in strain due to the relative displacement between contiguous parts.

shed ceiling A slanted interior roof line that starts at a lower wall and rises to meet a taller wall on the opposite side of the room; formally it resembles the geometry of a utilitarian outbuilding on a farm.

sheen rug An inexpensive floor covering in which a shine is chemically produced. Also called a lustre rug.

sheer Any lightweight, gauzy, transparent fabric such as CHINA SILK, MARQUISETTE, NET, or maline. May be woven of natural or synthetic fibers.

sheet glass Vitreous material that is cut into sheets. The base material is produced either by machine or by hand; the rectangular piece is lengthened and flattened by drawing, casting, blowing, floating, or rolling. Not plate glass.

sheetrock Plasterboard composed of gypsum placed between sheets of paper.

∞Sheldon's tapestries Woven wallcoverings produced in the time of Elizabeth I by Flemish weavers working in England under the supervision of William Sheldon.

shell (1) In furniture construction, the framework or basic structure. The unadorned, unsheathed unit. (2) A decorative motif. For specific motifs, see COCKLESHELL, ROCAILLE, and SCALLOP SHELL.

shellac A natural resin that is soluble in alcohol. When applied to wood, it produces a shiny surface. Often used as a prime coat on unfinished wood pieces, as a sealer. See *Table 4*.

shell chairs Molded fiberglass seats with sides, backs, and bottoms formed of plastic material, often continuous. May have metal pipe legs or a molded plastic pedestal base. See TULIP CHAIR.

∞sheveret An elegant drawing room writing table with a small shelf in back for books. The front portion of the top was hinged so it could be turned over, and the front legs were pulled out to support it, thus forming a writing surface. Originally a Louis XVI design and anglicized at the end of the 18th century.

shield back A chair vertical support shaped like the defensive apparatus that was popularized by Hepplewhite in mid-18th-century England. The piece resembles a heraldic frame with a tapered point at the center bottom. The element sometimes included a carved splat representing the feathers of the Prince of Wales or a sheaf of wheat.

shiki In fabric, a heavy silk or rayon rep made with irregular-shaped filling threads. In wallpaper, a paper-backed fabric with

silk threads on the face, to simulate the actual shiki silk, or an embossed paper that simulates the texture of the fabric.

shingles Thin wood tiles, usually of cedar, used as overlapping plaques for facing exterior walls and roofs. Produced today in synthetic materials.

shingle style A domestic architectural innovation of about 1870 based on the Queen Anne stick style of Norman Shaw of England and on Japanese forms. Buildings were sheathed in thin pieces of construction material over a wood frame in curved and straight sweeps. Ground-floor plans were open, and porches were noticeable external features. An accomplished example was McKim, Meade, and White's Low House.

Shinto (1) Indigenous religion of Japan that predates Buddhism and Confucianism. It involves polytheism and the worship of forces and forms of nature. (2) Shinto items were favorite collectibles of many 19th-century ARTS AND CRAFTS designers. See JAPONISM.

shirring A gathered effect of fabric drawn on a thread or a rod, resulting in many small folds. A fine example of a controlled shirred effect is the AUSTRIAN DRAPE.

shoe or shoe piece (1) The part of the back seat rail of a chair that projects out to support the bottom of the splat, often found on brace-back Windsor chairs. (2) Also, the disk often found under the foot of a furniture leg, called a FERRULE.

shoji A simple Japanese geometric frame, subdivided into smaller rectangular panels. The framework is usually made of narrow black lacquered wood strips, and the open rectangular spaces are filled with translucent materials such as paper, polyplastex, plastics, and fabrics. Shoji panels serve as screens, dividers, Japanese doors (which slide behind one another on a track), and window coverings.

shoring A temporary wooden framework used to support an unstable wall or a building that is being repaired.

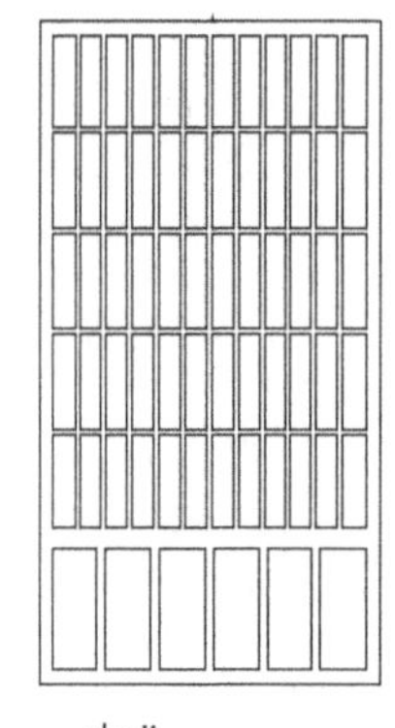
shoji

shot In carpet construction, the relationship of weft threads (across the loom) to the tufts or loops of surface yarn. A "two-shot" carpet means there are two weft threads between each row of surface tufts. The larger the number, the more material, and therefore the denser the carpet construction and the stronger the weave.

shouldered arch A structural device with a rectangular lintel supported by shaped corbels. The curved inner edges of the CORBELS create the archlike effect.

show wood The exposed, finished natural material on upholstered furniture, in contrast to unexposed parts such as the carcass.

shutter An interior or exterior covering for a window that may be flat, paneled, louvered, or a fabric-covered frame. May be made of wood, metal, plastic, or vinyl. Once largely protective, shutters now serve mainly as both interior and exterior decoration.

shuttering The use of temporary wood or metal walls to enclose poured concrete. These temporary pieces are removed after the concrete sets. The visual impression of the wood grain onto the concrete was considered desirable in Brutalist architecture.

siamoise An S-shaped two-seater of the mid 19th century, either an upholstered sofa or a double armchair. When seated, two people face in opposite directions, and they look over their shoulders in order to converse. This design was named after the Siamese twins Chang and Eng, two Thai nationals of Chinese heritage who created a sensation in Britain and the United States. Also called a TÊTE-À-TÊTE.

sick building syndrome (SBS) An acute human illness caused by time spent in a building with mold, fungus, toxic air particles, or other harmful substances.

sideboard An auxiliary case piece in the dining room that consists of drawers and cupboards that hold the items needed to furnish the dining table. Its present form was evolved by Shearer and perfected by Hepplewhite and Sheraton in the late 18th century. Also see BUFFET, CRÉDENCE, and CREDENZA.

side chair An armless seat. This category evolved in the 17th century, when these pieces of support furniture replaced the stools and benches intended for people other than nobility or the heads of families. The lack of arms accommodated voluminous ball gowns. In commercial interiors, they serve as chairs for guests in front of, or at the side of, a desk. See HALL CHAIRS and LIGHT CHAIR.

∞siden glass Lopsided glassware.

side table Originally an ornate serving surface that was combined with a pedestal to form a sideboard. William Kent, in the 18th century, designed many magnificently carved and decorated tables, often topped with marble.

side table

silencer A thick, flannel-like, heavily napped fabric used under a tablecloth to protect the table and to dampen noise from plates and cutlery.

silent valet Skeleton-like wood or metal framework designed to hold a man's complete change of clothing. It may contain a jewelry tray and is often combined with a chair.

silhouette (1) The outline of an object. (2) A profile or outline drawing in which the outline is completely filled in with a single color.

∞silhouette mirror A scrolled mahogany frame for a reflective device of the Chippendale period. The frame was carved and gilded, and a decorative ornament was applied to the cresting. Also called a FRETWORK MIRROR.

silk A natural fiber extruded from a silkworm as it spins its cocoon. The name is probably derived from that given to the people in the part of China where the material was first known. The resulting fabric of natural protein may be used alone or blended with other natural or synthetic fibers. It has a fine hand, drapes beautifully, and takes a brilliant dye. See *Table 2.*

silk floss The tangled waste strands of protein fiber that results from larvae. The term is often misused to describe KAPOK, an upholstery filling.

Silk Road A transportation route from Asia to Europe, from China to Venice, and including parts of Turkey, northern Africa, and the Middle East. It was a route for trade goods, including spices and textiles, and is usually invoked in reference to eras before the 18th century. While parts of the Silk Road are actual transportation routes, it is not literally a single road. The early version of globalization included the cities of Xi'an, Samarkand, and Constantinople. See ORIENTALISM.

silk-screen Originally, an old Chinese method of handprinting colors through stencil-like designs on meshes made of a fine textile tautly stretched on rigid wooden frames. As in lithography, wood blocks, and etchings, each color requires a separate printing frame with only the part of the design that is to appear in that particular color. See HAND SCREENING and SERIOGRAPHS.

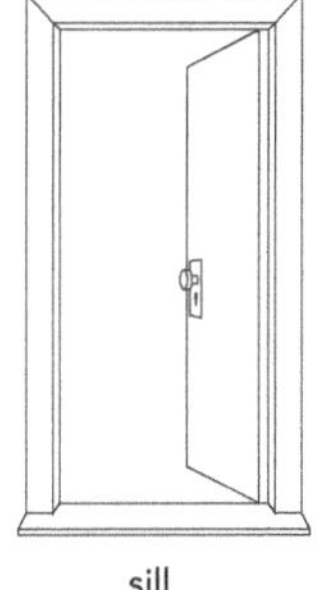
sill

sill In construction, a horizontal strip forming the bottom of a structure, usually the board at the bottom of a window frame. A door sill is also called a SADDLE.

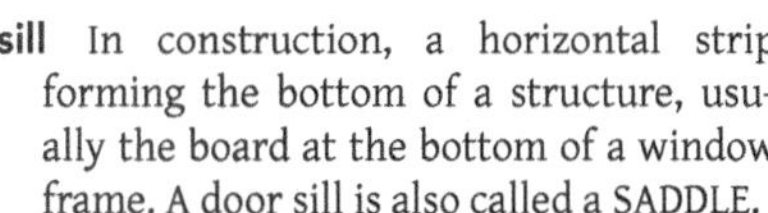

silo In corporate organizational culture, a department that communicates with departmental subdivisions above and below it in a hierarchy but does not communicate with other departments. In contrast to a horizontal or T-shaped corporate relationship. The layouts and specifications of offices and workstations can either promote or hinder development of the desired organizational relationships.

∞**sillón frailero** Spanish Renaissance chair with a hung leather seat, sometimes hinged. It is similar to the Italian Renaissance sedia, although with geometric decoration.

silvering glass A late-17th-century process for making mirrors. A sheet of tin was laid on a backing and covered with a layer of quicksilver and then with a piece of vitreous material. Pressure was applied to affix the quicksilver. The layer of mercury was easily injured which resulted in a loss of the reflective properties.

silver plate A thin layer of the chemical element Ag that is applied over a base metal or alloy. One such process is electroplating.

singerie A decorative motif with the monkey as an ornament or an element in a mural, fabric, or wallpaper design. The monkey was often combined with chinoiserie in gay, delicate designs. Such murals often decorated dadoes and cornices. Singerie was popular in France and England during the 18th century because of the popularity of exotic subjects. See HUET, CHRISTOPHE, in *Designers and Architects.*

single arch molding A small half-round applied strip used around drawers in case furniture of the William and Mary period in England. See COCK BEADING or MOLDING.

single bed A sleeping device that is usually 39 inches wide by 78 inches to 84 inches long (92 cm by 187–203 cm). Some sleeping platforms may be as narrow as 30–33 or 36 inches (76–91 cm). Two standard-size single beds pushed together make a king-size bed. Also called a TWIN-SIZE BED.

single gate table A drop-leaf work surface with only one leaf, which can be raised to a horizontal plane by extending the one gate, or supporting member. Also called a TUCKAWAY TABLE.

sinicize To make Chinese in character. The process whereby non-Chinese communities, and their cultural products, become Chinese. Relates to the designed objects of Chinoiserie; famous examples include Chippendale's line of Chinese-inspired furniture and accessories. Also describes China's adoption and adaptation of Western objects such as table-height chairs, in contrast to mat-sitting.

sisal A hard fiber, larger and stiffer than jute, flax, or hemp, used to make summer carpets, hard floor mats, etc. See *Table 2.*

six-legged highboy A tall chest of drawers peculiar to the William and Mary period in England.

size A gelatin-like solution that stiffens textiles and glazing papers. The gelatinous material is also used to prime coat a wall before painting and papering it. A new paper or paint holds better on a wall that has been sized. See BUCKRAM.

skein-dyed (adj.) Fibers that receive pigment before they are spun into a yarn.

skein-dyed yarn Lengths of interlocked fibers which were infused with pigment before being spun. The surface version is spun from white wool or worsted staple and then given color in skein form by immersion in kettles or vats. See VAT-DYED.

skeuomorph A form or entity that remains after the technology that generated the form becomes outmoded; for example, a cell phone that rings like a dial telephone.

sketch A rough draft for a composition or a design. A trial run by the artist or designer. This preliminary attempt may later serve as reference material; a pictorial note or memo.

skew arch A rounded structural device in which the axis is not at right angles to the face of the curve. The courses that make up the element are not parallel with the axis but at right angles to the face. The resultant form is inclined inward toward the horizon.

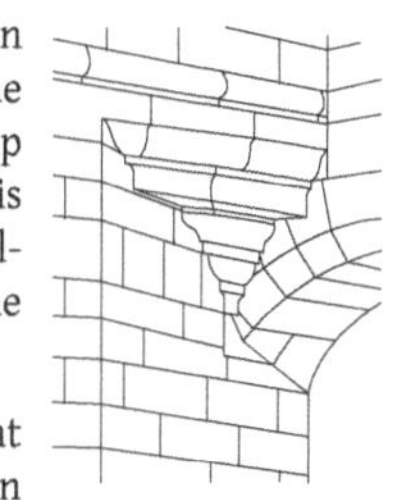
skew arch

skirting A molded strip that covers the joint where the wall and the floor meet, often made of wood but may also be made of vinyl, tile, or rubber. Also called a cove base or COVED SKIRTING.

skirt or skirting piece (1) The wood strip or panel, usually shaped, that lies below a sill, shelf, or tabletop. Also called an APRON or FRIEZE. (2) Also a fabric valance around the base of an upholstered chair or couch to hide the legs and wood construction of the seat. The element may be pleated, shirred, or tailored (fitted and plain).

skylight A window or glass structure set into the ceiling of a room (under a roof) to provide additional light without detracting from the privacy of the room.

slant-top desk A work surface, usually 18th-century English or American, with a drop-front writing section, set at an angle, which rests on a base made up of several drawers. Similar to a SECRETARY without the bookcase element.

slat (1) A horizontal bar connecting the upright members of a chair back. It is sometimes used as a single feature, or it may be used to hold the vertical splat. The top rail is considered a slat. A slat is also called a horizontal splat. (2) Also, a thin, narrow piece of wood such as a lath, one of the many metal or wood strips in a VENETIAN BLIND.

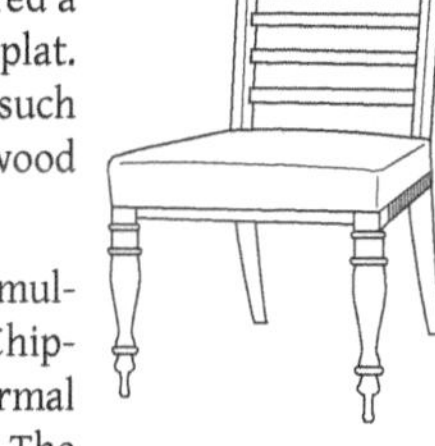
slat-back

slat-back A chair rear support with multiple horizontal rails or crossbars. Chippendale and Sheraton designed formal versions of this country-style chair. The typically armless chair was popular in Early American furniture. See LADDER-BACK.

slate (1) A fine-grained stone formed of compressed clays which readily splits into plates or tiles. The stone is used as a high-end roofing material, usually set in an overlapping manner, and it is also used for flooring and pavements. (2) Also a 16th-century English term for sheeting. See *Table 3.*

slatted wood A seating foundation that does not rely on springs. It is made entirely of strips of the hard fibrous natural material.

sleep chair or sleeping chair A seat with a concealed mattress that extends out to form a platform for a user who desires rest.

sleeper sofa A seating unit that looks like a traditional sofa. It has a concealed spring mechanism and a mattress that pulls out to form a bed, usually the size of a double bed.

∞Sleepy Hollow chair A mid-19th-century American seat that is upholstered and has a curved back and low, comfortable arms. The seat is usually scooped out. It is typical of the Louis XV influence on Victorian design.

sleigh bed A 19th-century American adaptation of the Empire scrolled sleeping device. The resemblance of the curved foot and headboard to the front and back ends of the winter vehicle gave the weight-supporting piece of furniture its name. See EMPIRE BED.

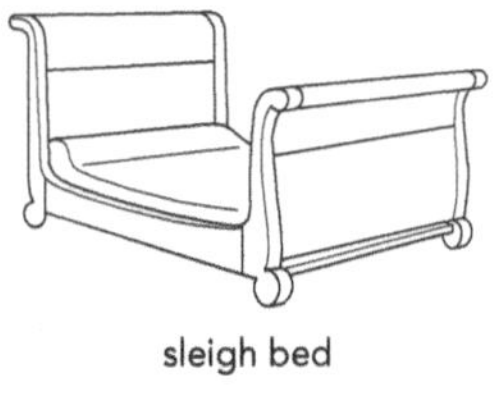

sleigh bed

sley The number of warp threads or ends per inch of woven fabric.

slide The pullout shelf of a desk, secretary, writing table, or serving table.

sliding casements Windows that open and close by moving laterally on horizontal tracks.

sling chair A 20th-century canvas or leather seat with metal rods. The wrought-iron base is shaped like two bent butterfly paper clips with two peaks in the front and two higher peaks in the back. The canvas cover has four pockets that fit over these peaks. The stretched textile makes a concave sweep from the rear peaks to the front peaks. Also called a butterfly chair. See HARDOY CHAIR.

slip Clay and water that have been mixed to a creamlike consistency. It is applied to pottery to produce a glaze or colored effect.

slipcover A removable fitted envelope made to protect upholstery fabric, to conceal worn upholstery, or to provide a change for a new season. Floral chintzes were considered appropriate for spring and summer. May be made also of cotton, linen, silk, or synthetics. The idea of temporarily draping upholstered furniture became popular in the Louis XV period.

slip match A veneering pattern created by joining the veneer sheets side by side so that the figure is repeated over and over in a continuous manner.

∞slipper chair Any short-legged resting platform with a low seat. The seat is usually only 12 inches to 15 inches off the ground (30–38 cm). A regular seat height is about 18 inches (46 cm).

slipper foot A club furniture leg support with a pointed and protruding toe. It was a popular furniture leg base in the Queen Anne period in England.

∞slip seat A resting platform for a user that lifts out from the frame of a chair and can be readily recovered. See FAUTEUIL À CHÂSSIS.

slope-front desk A drop-front or drop-lid work surface. The surface slants upward and backward when closed, thus creating a sloped or angled front. It appeared in 18th-century English and American designs. See DROP-LID.

slow living A lifestyle trend that is an antidote to a frenzied pace of constant acquisition. It developed first in food as a reaction against the time-consuming preparations of haute cuisine, with simple dishes that take a long time to cook. This resulted in a general approach to living in the modern world. It moved into fashion with ramifications for interior design and travel. It includes decluttering, consuming less, and rejecting existing business models.

slub yarn A strand of fibers with a thickness caused by wrapping or twisting one strand around another several times. The resultant irregularly thickened strand or thread adds a distinctive quality when woven into a fabric. The sewing and weaving material is also called nub yarn and thick-and-thin yarn.

smart materials Composite designs that sense and react to environmental conditions or other stimuli and are therefore "intelligent." This is a result of nanotechnology, materials not used in their natural state, although designs can contain biologic materials. The stimuli include stress, moisture, light, heat, and magnetic waves. The results include textile coatings, memory polymers, and spatially continuous materials. Important for aerospace industry and healthcare. Has resulted in bathing suits that change color and drapery that responds to light.

smart window Fenestration made of translucent materials that develop gradations of opacity based on an electric current and response to input data, such as amount of light. Also called smart glass, EGlass, switchable glass, or switchable windows. Used in windows, skylights, and translucent partitions. The electrically switchable glass or glazing changes light transmission properties when voltage is applied. Flip a switch and a conference room with smart windows becomes private or a suspect cannot see those who witness an interrogation.

smoke detector A device that sounds an alarm when it senses airborne toxins above specified levels.

smooshing Paint-texturizing technique that creates a marbled effect. A thin piece of plastic is applied to a wall of wet paint, rubbed with the hands, and peeled off.

snake foot (1) A furniture termination carved to resemble the head of a limbless reptile. It is actually a club foot with an elongated toe, as in a SLIPPER FOOT, and it appears in 18th-century English and American furniture. (2) Also, a yellow-brown or red-brown wood with dark spots and markings, popular for inlay work in the late 18th century.

snap table A small tripod work surface with a hinged top held in a horizontal position by a spring catch. Also called a tip-up table. Designed in the mid 18th century in England and America.

socketing An inexpensive method of joinery. The end of one piece of wood is shaped to wedge tightly into a cavity cut in a second piece, like a chair leg pegged into the round cavity on the bottom of a wood seat of a kitchen chair.

socle (1) A plain, unmolded square pedestal for a statue or superstructure. (2) Also the base of case furniture.

sodium vapor lamp A light source used in street lighting. An electric discharge into a mist of the element in an excited state produces a yellow light, approximating the maximum luminosity in the spectrum. This lighting is efficient and can have a life of up to 20,000 hours, but it is not desirable lighting for merchandise presentation; it is not complimentary to the human complexion, as it changes the color of the object it lights.

sofa (Arabic, *suffah*) An upholstered daybed, usually with two arms and a back. A couch to which a back has been added. It appeared in France in the Louis XIV period. See also SUFFAH.

sofa bed A seating unit in which the back drops down, becomes parallel with the seat, and makes a sleeping surface 43 inches to 49 inches wide (109–125 cm). Also called a jackknife bed. May be designed in a traditional or modern style, and varies in size from a love seat (48-inch sleeping area or 122 cm) to a standard 7 feet or longer sofa (213 cm) that opens to a 54-inch or 60-inch sleeping surface (137 or 152 cm).

sofa table An oblong or narrow rectangular work surface with flaps at the short ends that are supported by hinged brackets, similar to a Pembroke table. The drawers are in the longer side of the table frame. This type of table appeared at the end of the 18th century.

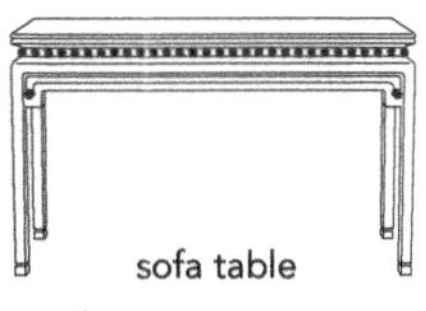
sofa table

soffit (1) The underside of an arch, cornice, beam, or lintel. (2) The furred-out space between the top of an upper range of wall-hung cabinets and the ceiling.

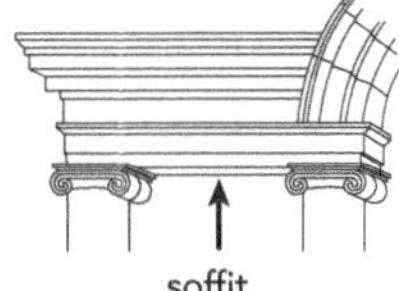
soffit

softwood In general, the natural material from conifers, including cypress, pine, and fir. The term has no relation to the relative density of the lumber in comparison to hardwoods. See HARDWOOD and *Table 5*.

solarium A room or porch enclosed with large areas of glass to allow in sunlight.

solar lamp A mid-19th-century fuel-burning light fixture based on the Argand model. The fuel supply was set under the burner. The lighting device usually consisted of a metal or marble column topped with a large globe. Prisms frequently decorated the base of the globe. See ARGAND LAMP and ASTRAL LAMP. Historically the devices used fuel, but similar-looking versions appeared in the 20th century that relied on free energy of the sun, particularly in the context of camping.

soldier A brick laid on its end so that it appears vertical (height exceeds width) in the bond.

soldier arch A flat structural device made of bricks that are laid on edge. Often used as a facing for a lintel-type construction, that is, over window and door openings. It is an element of post-and-lintel construction and not the curved element associated with Roman brickwork.

solid modelers The computer visualization of solid objects which are geometrically correct in multiple respects. It is a move beyond wireframe means of designing and representing 3D objects. Drawn objects can be seen (and sliced) inside and outside, with accurate information about intermediary surfaces between edges. This complicated technology is more geometrically accurate than existing methods. It impacts all representational arenas of interior design, from renderings in the design phases to construction documents. The scale ranges from objects to interiors and architecture.

solid vinyl tiles Modular flooring pieces made of often colored polyvinyl chloride with a small amount of additive. The color is continuous through the depth of the material. Typically 12 inches × 12 inches (30.5 cm × 30.5 cm).

∞**solium** A sarcophagus for an eminent person, made of marble with impressive sculpture. A significant designed object in its own right, also represented as a part of decorations from ancient Egypt through the 19th century. Some serving pieces took the form of the item.

solution-dyed (adj.) A synthetic fiber that receives pigment while in its liquid stage, through soaking or chemical reactions. In contrast to PIECE-DYED. See VAT-DYED.

sonora A heavy, Philippine hardwood, yellow-white to pale brown, with a medium-fine texture.

soutache A narrow, rounded braid with a herringbone effect, used as a trimming or edging material in multiple textiles, including draperies and beddings.

Southwestern A contemporary decorating trend that is an offshoot of Spanish colonial design, from the area that was New Spain in the 16th century. It includes Native American textiles and objects, brightly colored accents (yellow, orange, turquoise, adobe red) set against earth tones, and a prodigious use of terra-cotta as floor tiles, pottery, and roof tiles. Includes custom work such as countertops and sinks made from tiles. Projects have stucco walls, exposed beam ceilings, and wrought-iron accents.

space-as-a-service A real estate model that shifted from asset ownership to monetization of access to space and related services. It has significantly impacted a number of stalwarts of the interior design field, including retail (Amazon), hospitality (Airbnb), and office interiors (WeWork).

space heater A portable gas or electric unit that can be used when needed to provide energy transferral. Sometimes installed semi-permanently, to provide for extra warmth where the overall building climate system is not completely effective.

spackling A plaster or a putty-like substance used to fill up holes or correct surface imperfections in a piece of wood or on a wall or ceiling. When the added material has dried, excess material is sanded off, and the smooth surface is ready for the finishing coat. Typically made from gypsum plaster from hydrated calcium sulfate and glue; also of vinyl.

spade foot A rectangular, tapered termination found in Hepplewhite and Sheraton's designs. It is separated from the rest of the leg by a slight projection. Also called a sabot foot. See TAPER LEG, THERM LEG, and THIMBLE FOOT.

∞**spallière** A decorative painting on a chair back. The stenciled top rail of a Hitchcock chair.

span The open or clear space between two supporting elements in architecture or designed objects. The space between two columns, piers, etc. The space covered by an arch.

spandrel (1) In furniture, a triangular or rectangular piece spanning the space between a vertical support and

spandrel

a horizontal piece or rail or between two verticals. (2) In architecture, the horizontal elements that connect columns or piers.

spandrel wall In architecture, the non-structural part of the curtain wall above the top of the window of one story and below the bottom of the windowsill of the story above. This area may consist of several courses of masonry, or it may be glass, metal, plastic, or a combination spandrel panel, such as those used in modern curtain wall constructions. Common types include aluminum or glazed metal.

spandrel steps Stairs that have triangular treads.

∞Spanish chair A late-16th-century English piece of furniture with a high upholstered back and seat. The top rail or cresting was usually ornate and richly carved.

Spanish colonial furniture The provincial furniture of the colonies, including the American Southwest. Based on styles that originated in the Iberian peninsula, the furniture is heavy, massive, and rectilinear, with simple carving and decorations. Native woods are used and stained dark. Used in whitewashed and stuccoed, low-ceilinged rooms that are trimmed with exposed ceiling beams. Decorative accessories are a combination of Native American, Mexican, and Moorish motifs in bright colors and feature geometric forms, flowers, birds, and other animals.

Spanish furniture Pieces designed in the 16th, 17th, and 18th centuries. Moorish influences persisted, notably in the use of tooled and colored CORDOVAN LEATHER for covers, seats, and decorations; ornamentation featured colors, geometric motifs, inlay, and gilding. Iberian versions of Italian and French Renaissance forms tended to be heavy with brusque outlines. Chairs were rectangular and heavy, with wide arms and high backs. Walnut, chestnut, oak, and others were used. Iron served ornamental and structural purposes.

Spanish scroll foot A hoof-like, grooved, and flared furniture leg base that ends in an inward-curving roll. It was introduced from Portugal during the Restoration period and used in 18th-century English and American furniture. Also called a Braganza toe.

sparking lamps Small non-electrical light fixtures of the early 19th century that burned sperm oil or whale oil and gave off a small, flickering light. Particularly favored by courting couples; hence, the name is derived from a slang word for courting.

∞sparver A CANOPY or TESTER over a bed.

spathe The leafy part of a plant that encloses a flower. Often a feature in carved floral decoration of many periods and cultures, including Greek and Roman, Gothic, Islamic, Renaissance, Arts and Crafts, and Art Nouveau.

spattering Paint-texturizing technique in which uneven spots are achieved by loading a brush and flipping the paint onto the base color.

specifications The exact details, measurements, materials, equipment, etc. stipulated for a given project, job, or construction. The extensive legal documentation includes text and image and is often compiled in book form as an additional contract document to the working drawings.

spectral colors Colors produced by a beam of white light as refracted through a prism. They are usually called violet, indigo, blue, green, yellow, orange, and red; as wavelengths that humans perceive as colors, they perform differently than pigments.

speed stripe A horizontal band that is a typical motif in American Art Deco.

sphinx A mythical monster that combines a human head and woman's bust with the body of a lion. Originally an ancient Egyptian motif. In the Roman era, wings were added. During the Renaissance, Adamesque, Empire, and Regency periods, the being was used as a carved or painted decoration. It was particularly popular as a furniture support during the Empire and Regency periods, when Egyptian objects mixed with Greek and Roman motifs. See also ANDROSPHINX and CRIOSPHINX.

sphinx

∞spider-leg table An 18th-century English drop-leaf horizontal surface of Sheraton design with eight thin vertical supports. A variation on the GATELEG TABLE or the EIGHT-LEGGED TABLE.

spindle A long, slender rod, often ornamented with turned moldings or swellings; part of furniture of architectural millwork.

spindle and bead An ornamental molding resembling a string of sausage-like members separated by round or elliptical globes.

spindled panels Interior shutters made of delicate rods. Common in Spanish window treatments.

spiral A curve that winds around a fixed point and does not backtrack on itself. Each whorl is a complete turn of the curve around the axis and may be on one plane or in an ascending or conical shape like a shell. The curvilinear form is the basis for the volutes of classical capitals, scrolls, and twisted rope turnings.

spiral leg A furniture support resembling a twisted rope, or a support with a winding, descending flute or groove. Originally of Portuguese and Indian origin, it became popular in England during the Restoration. See BARLEY-SUGAR TURNING.

spiral staircase Vertical circulation unit that winds around a central shaft as it rises from one level to another. Also called a winding staircase.

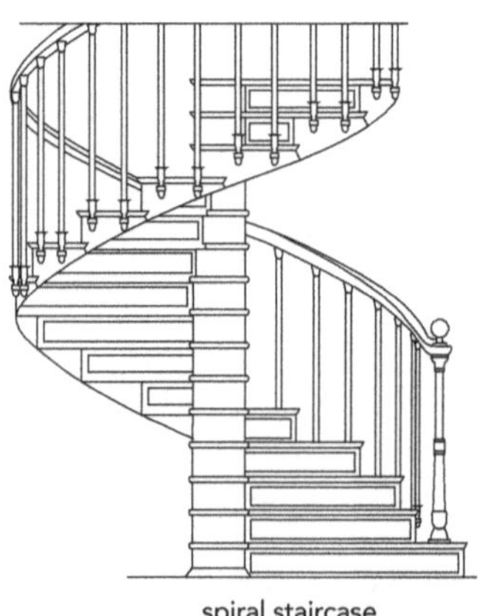

spiral staircase

spire The pointed termination of a structure, of a designed object including furniture, or architecture, interior or exterior, such as a finial, usually conical or pyramidal in form.

spire

∞splad An 18th-century English spelling of SPLAT.

splanch A split-level, ranch-style house, on two levels, and with half a story between the two, or a two-level exterior that contains a three-level interior. Popular in the New York metropolitan region from the 1950s to the 1970s. See RANCH HOUSE and SPLIT-LEVEL HOUSE.

splat The central, upright wood panel of a chair back, serving as a back rest. May be vase-shaped or fiddle-shaped, embellished with carving and marquetry, and decorated with fretwork, pierced designs, or tracery. Usually not the entirety of the chair back but a figural element paired with verticals.

splay (English, shortened form of *display*) (1) A bevel or chamfer. (2) A surface that is spread out or set at a slant. (3) A large chamfer or diagonal surface formed by cutting away an angle of a wall. See BEVEL, CHAMFER, and RAKE.

splay leg A vertical support that angles or flares out from a chair, table, chest, or other piece.

spline (1) In cabinetry, a method of strengthening a joint by means of a small strip of wood inserted between and projecting into the two pieces of wood that form the joint. (2) Also, a method of dropped ceiling in which ceiling tiles are held in place with a gridded support system.

splay

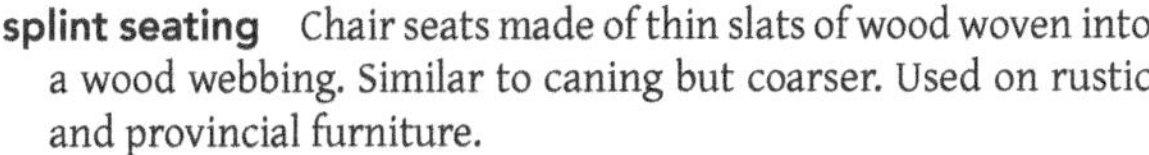

splint seating Chair seats made of thin slats of wood woven into a wood webbing. Similar to caning but coarser. Used on rustic and provincial furniture.

split spindle An applied ornament of 17th-century English and American furniture. A delicate, slender turning was cut in half lengthwise, thus creating two half-round moldings. It was applied to cabinets, cupboards, and other pieces. In Jacobean furniture, the shaped forms were used for chairbacks with the smooth, cut side toward the sitter's back.

split-level house A dwelling built on a series of levels rather than complete stories. The main level usually has the living and dining rooms, the kitchen, and sometimes a study. Several steps up from this level are the sleeping quarters, while several steps down are the utilities, recreation or family room, maid's quarters, and storage. Of many eras, but associated with the 1970s.

spolia Items seized in warfare and used to commemorate victory; booty or plunder. Representations of spolia are often a motif in classical and neoclassical furniture and decorative arts. See BOOTY.

sponge painting A surface finishing technique using cleaning devices in lieu of brushes or rollers in order to create a broken, splotchy effect.

∞spool furniture Turned designed objects (chiefly seating and surface-creating pieces) that were mass-produced in the United States in the mid 18th century, distinguished by turnings that resemble a string of cylindrical devices or buttons. Often made of pine and stained to resemble mahogany, although better pieces were made of maple, cherry, or walnut. See JENNY LIND BED.

∞spoon-back chair An early-19th-century Regency and Biedermeier (neoclassical) seat with a curved wood back. The low-set arms rise from the seat above the front legs and make a continuous and rising sweep up to form the top rail. The center splat is plain or may be urn- or vase-shaped. Similar to the American Empire chair called the MADAME JUMEL.

∞spoon foot A CLUB FOOT or DUTCH FOOT. The base of a cabriole leg that flares and spreads out; usually it is set on a pad. Popular in the Queen Anne period.

spot or spotlight (1) A fixture of illumination that focuses on a particular point or object. (2) Also, a small discolored area on a substrate.

spring line The imaginary horizontal plane at which an arch or vault begins to curve.

springs Flat, zigzag, or coiled devices of high-quality steel that add to the resiliency of upholstered furniture or of beds. In beds, the spiral forms may be used under or within the mattress.

spruce A type of pine closely related to fir. A soft, light, strong, straight-grained wood used for interior and exterior work. See *Table 5.*

spun silk Yarn made from waste fibers and damaged or pierced silkworm cocoons. Heavier and less lustrous than first-grade yarn.

spun yarn Strand made from short or staple fibers.

spur The triangular filler between the round shaft and the square base of a Gothic column. The item might be in the form of a spray of foliage, a tongue, or a GROTESQUE.

spur stone A mineral block specially shaped and set at the corner of a structure to prevent injury to the corner from passing traffic.

squab A loose, stuffed cushion used for seats of chairs, settees, and long stools. The comfort-giving items were replaced by upholstered seats toward the end of the 17th century, but they are still used on luxurious armchairs and sofas. Also called a CARREAU.

squinch In furniture, a corner cupboard. See ENCOIGNURE.

S-scroll A popular CYMA CURVE of the French Rococo (Louis XV) and English Chippendale periods. Sometimes used broken or stepped in the center.

squab

S-scroll legs A 17th-century furniture support of Dutch design. The leg was S-shaped and ended in an S-shaped scroll. Usually it was heavily embellished with carving.

stabile A freestanding abstract sculpture or structure, typically made of wire or sheet metal, that is built in the style of a mobile but is rigid and stationary. Alexander Calder is the most famous artist known for producing these artworks that contrasted with moving sculptures.

stacking chairs Modest seats designed to be stored on top of one another. Used in contract design for setting up temporary auditoriums, fashion shows, and dining accommodations, for example.

stained glass Designs or pictures made of colored vitreous material and held

stacking chairs

together by strips of lead that form the outlines of the design. It was a Byzantine invention that became a distinctly medieval art form. The colored planar material is made either by adding metallic oxides to molten glass (pot metal) or by fusing the colored variety onto plain glass (flashing).

staining (1) In wood finishing, the process of applying coloring matter to the outer surfaces of wood to enhance characteristic grain, provide uniform overall color, or to imitate or match other cabinet woods. (2) Also a textile treatment for the purpose of identifying the fibers present. See *Table 4*.

stainless steel An iron and carbon alloy that is a bright silvery color and is resistant to tarnish, rust, and corrosion. Used to make cutlery and in architecture where its lustrous surface is prized.

stair rods Metal poles, often brass, that hold a carpet runner on a flight of stairs. The narrow cylinders secure the carpet close to the bottom of each riser, across the face of the carpet, so there is no need of nails or tacks.

stalactite Small, vertical, polygonal or curved niches projecting in rows above one another to create an effect that resembles the naturally occurring formation in caves. This type of ornament was used to create Moorish capitals.

stamping The use of a die to create designs in pottery and other artforms. Dies press and pound metal or other material into its desired shape.

stanchion A vertical member against a wall, such as a pier or engaged column, made of any material, that supports a load carried onto it by a beam.

stand A framework, small table, or lowboy on which chests, cabinets, drawers, and basins were placed. DANIEL MAROT, GRINLING GIBBONS, and WILLIAM KENT carved magnificent gilded bases in the 17th and 18th centuries. See *Designers and Architects*.

standard-size bed A double sleeping platform, usually 53 inches to 54 inches wide, by 75 inches long (138 cm × 188 cm).

standing mirror An oval, shield-shaped, or rectangular framed reflective surface set on a chest or table, usually equipped with a drawer that serves as its base. An 18th-century design. Also called a shaving mirror.

stanze (Italian, rooms) A suite of rooms or an interior project. For example, Raphael's *Stanze* in the Vatican.

starburst A five-pointed star with raylike emanations. A decorative motif.

star molding A sculpted decoration with a concave decagon motif, popular in Romanesque architecture.

stationary curtains Sheer textile panels used under draperies. Also called under-curtains or GLASS CURTAINS.

stayed mast (1) A heavy, high post supported by means of stabilizing cables. These vertical elements are often erected at ports and naval yards with proper main and top yards for training purposes. (2) A designed object that is supported laterally for stability, in a manner similar to the maritime assembly.

Steamboat Gothic A revival style using lacy, ornate, elaborately embellished woodwork, with turnings, balls, finials, gables, bargeboards, and gingerbread on wood and shingle structures built in the United States at the end of the 19th century. The inspiration for this extravagant use of the jigsaw were the floating palaces on the Mississippi River in the mid-19th century, hence the name. See JIGSAW DETAIL.

steel engraving An art reproduction technique introduced in the second quarter of the 19th century. A microscopic film of iron/carbon alloy was deposited on the softer copper plate by means of electrolysis. The hard plate made it possible to print large editions without destroying details of the plate. This method was soon superseded by photoengraving.

steel furniture Pieces produced in limited quantities in the 17th and 18th centuries in Europe by gunsmiths and ironworkers. Most of the known designs are of the Directoire or Early Empire periods and were created for Napoleon's campaigns, in which the strong and easily transported folding chairs and collapsible tables, beds, and desks proved useful. The designs were often embellished with BRONZE DORÉ rosettes and medallions, as well as chiseled and chased details. See ORMOLU.

stela or stele A stone slab or pillar used as a commemorative or grave marker in ancient Greece.

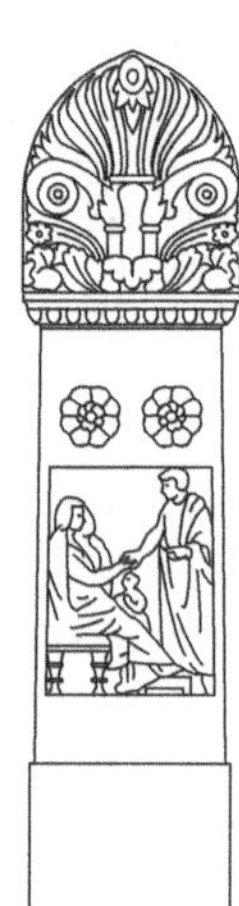

stela or stele

stemware Drinking glasses that consist of a bowl, vertical support or stanchion, and foot.

stencil A pattern made by brushing or wiping ink or paint over a shield of metal or paper in which the design has been cut. The paint will go only through the resultant voids. The design can be reproduced many times over on walls, ceilings, furniture, and floors. In the 19th century, it was used in place of wallpaper as a method of achieving an allover design. The top rails of Hitchcock chairs were usually embellished with gold using the method.

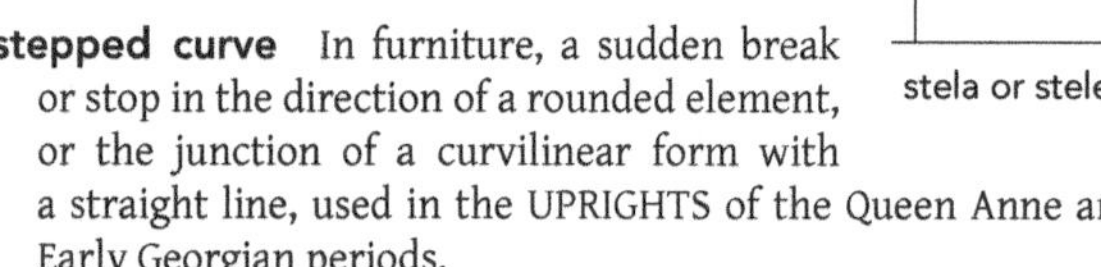

stepped curve In furniture, a sudden break or stop in the direction of a rounded element, or the junction of a curvilinear form with a straight line, used in the UPRIGHTS of the Queen Anne and Early Georgian periods.

step table A two-tiered, rectangular, surface-creating designed object with a smaller surface above, suggesting a pair of invisible risers and treds.

stereobate (1) The basement or foundation of a building. (2) Also a continuous pedestal under a plain wall.

stereochromy A technique of painting on stone or marble with pigments in water glass, a sodium-silicate compound.

sterling (1) A standard of pure silver content. (2) Also, silverware, jewelry, and other items made of silver that is at least 92.5 percent pure, meeting the standard.

stick (1) In wallpaper, a set of several rolls. (2) Also a bobbin, as on a sewing machine. (3) Also the rods or spindles that constitute the back of a Windsor chair. See STICK-BACK.

∞stick-back The back of a Windsor chair, made up of many rods or spindles. These elements are called sticks or fiddle strings. See FIDDLE-STRING BACK and STICK.

stick-back

Stick style A romantic 19th-century English style of architecture that features the structure and patterns of framing sticks. A revival of a medieval technique, it is a variation on the half-timber house, WATTLE AND DAUB,

TUDOR or FACHWERK, with the wood strips left exposed to form the major pattern and decoration.

stick table A combination pedestal work surface and lamp. The lamp base is usually a turning or column that appears to be a continuation of the surface support and extends through the horizontal surface. A lampshade is set atop this decorated cylinder. Appears in traditional styles as well as in modern designs.

stile (1) In furniture, the vertical strips of the frame of a panel or case piece of furniture. (2) Also the outer uprights of some panel-back chairs.

Stile Liberty (Italian) See ART NOUVEAU.

still life A painting or representation of an arrangement of flowers, fruit, books, musical instruments, vases, and so on. In certain periods, the composition included hunting trophies.

stinkwood A South African natural material with a distinctly unpleasant odor when freshly cut. Resembles walnut and has a reddish cast. Used in the 17th and 18th centuries by furniture makers to reproduce Dutch designs.

stipple engraving or crayon engraving A combination of ETCHING and intaglio printing popular in the 18th century for reproducing portrait drawings of famous personalities. The representation consisted of making dots on a grounded plate with an etching needle. Can also be a printing method on textiles. See ENGRAVING, INTAGLIO, and INTAGLIO ENGRAVING. Reintroduced in the 20th century by the *Wall Street Journal*.

stippling A painting technique for surfacing a wall, object, or textile with a multitude of tiny dots, spots, or blobs. It can be accomplished with various tools, such as the stiff bristles of a brush, a fine sponge, or crumpled tissue paper.

stitched up A 17th-century French upholstery technique. The upholstery of the seat is drawn over the seat rails and attached to the rails underneath the chair. See STUFFOVER SEAT.

∞**stoa** (1) A colonnade around an agora, an ancient Greek marketplace. (2) An I-, L-, or U-shaped detached colonnade or portico. See COLONNADE and PORTICO.

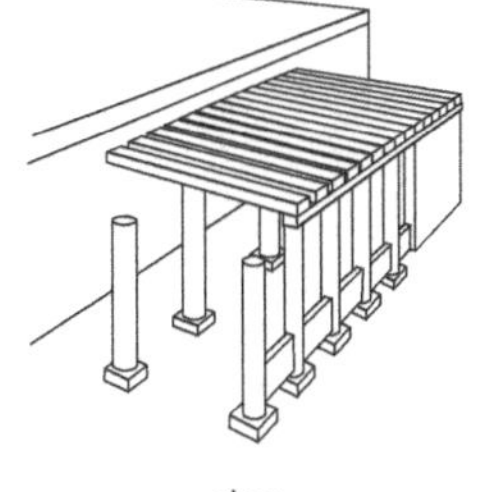
stoa

stock-dyed (adj.) A fiber that receives its pigment before it is spun or otherwise manufactured into thread or yarn. See SKEIN-DYED.

stoneware A heavy, opaque, nonporous, and nonabsorbent pottery made from siliceous paste.

stool A backless and armless seat that was replaced in the 17th century by small chairs or side chairs in formal situations. The modest piece of furniture is now used as a small decorative seat, or a very low design serves as a footrest. See PIANO STOOL.

stool

stopped channel fluting A series of equidistant concave vertical depressions with straight or rounded ends. Originally a decoration on classical architecture. In the 18th century it was used as a FRIEZE decoration on cabinets and furniture.

storage bed A sleeping platform with a space-containing element below. The mattress is placed on a base fitted with drawers or cabinets. A contemporary version of a captain's bed, a bunk bed with drawers below that was used on 19th-century whaling ships. See CAPTAIN'S BED.

storage wall A series of modular units that can be arranged in a variety of ways against a partition or can serve as the vertical space-defining element. A 20th-century invention introduced by George Nelson and Henry Wright in 1945 as a space-saving answer to storage problems. Later developed into a collection of storage units produced by Herman Miller. Many variations exist, from wall-hung to self-standing units and from modern styles to medieval and Spanish-inspired units.

story or storey The space between two floors of a building, or between the top floor and the roof.

story post A weight-carrying structural element or column that extends through the separate floors of a building.

straddle chair A seat that one sits spread-legged across, with the vertical back element between one's knees. The back rail can serve as an armrest. See COCKFIGHT CHAIR and VOYELLE.

straight match Wall covering pattern in which the left side of the strip meets and is identical to elements of the right side of the previous strip.

straight stair A flight of vertical circulation uninterrupted by turns or landings.

straining An early-17th-century technique of tightly stretching and gluing the upholstery fabric to the whole of the woodwork, as in the stately beds designed by DANIEL MAROT in the William and Mary period. See *Designers and Architects*.

∞**strapontin** A bracket or jump seat used in carriages, cars, or in public buildings. A flap or fold-down seat.

strapwork (1) A carved, wooden, arabesque that has a flat stem of a scroll in section, or an ornament that resembles a pattern cut from leather. An interlaced pattern that resembles a crisscross or braided design that resembles strips of leather. In the Elizabethan and Jacobean periods, the decorative motif consisted of carved decorated panels with ribbon-like bands in repeating and interlacing designs, especially on ceilings. Also appears in the splats of chairs. (2) Also, darned lace. See RIBBAND BACK.

straw chairs Originally, provincial seats with rush or woven seats. They were adapted for more formal and decorative uses in the 17th and 18th centuries.

straw marquetry An Asian technique which was used in France in the 17th century. Two layers of flattened and tinted vegetal material were placed one on top of the other and cut through together, as in MARQUETRY, and the cutout shapes were applied to wooden or papier-mâché objects. Some designs were executed like mosaics, others were engraved, and in some extraordinary units, minute pieces were built up into low-relief decorations.

stretcher (1) In masonry, the two long vertical surfaces of a brick when used in its typical fashion, rather than the short end, which is the header. A stretcher course is one which is composed only of stretchers laid in a continuous row and is the most common. (2) The crosspiece that connects, braces, and strengthens the legs of tables, chairs, chests, etc. See ARCHED STRETCHER, RISING STRETCHERS, SALTIRES, and X-SHAPED STRETCHERS.

stretcher bond In masonry, a method of bricklaying with only the stretchers showing. The stretchers in the succeeding courses appear to overlap one another, and the vertical joints fall in alternate courses instead of one directly under the other for the structural integrity of the wall. The overlap may be only ¼ of the length of the brick. See BOND.

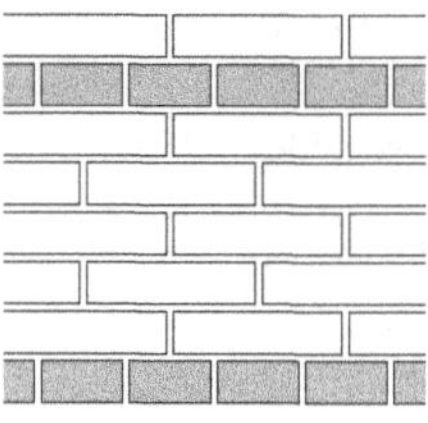

stretcher bond

stretcher course See STRETCHER and STRETCHER BOND.

strié A fabric with an uneven color or streaked effect produced by using warp threads of varying tones. It is possible in this manner to produce a two-toned effect in taffeta, satin, or corded upholstery fabrics. See JASPÉ.

striges (sing, strix) The vertical fluting on a classical column. See FLUTING and STRIX.

strike One pass of a printing process; the result of a print pass on a textile, wallpaper, or other material, after contact with a printing plate.

string In stair construction, the angled member or sides into which the treads and risers are fixed.

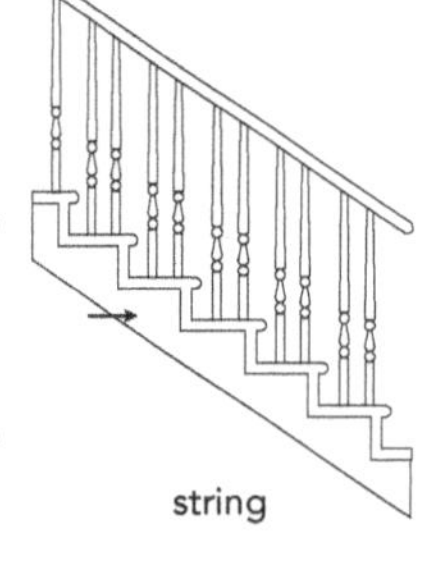

string

string course A horizontal band of ornamental masonry across the front of a structure that may enclose decorative elements and may be either flush with the wall or projecting from it. It may be differentiated from the rest of the façade by virtue of material, texture, or color.

stringing A narrow band or strip of contrasting veneer used as a decorative border. Also called BANDING or LINING.

stripe A veneer pattern with straight line effects in shades of dark and light, seen in walnut and mahogany. A design consisting of bands or straight lines against a plain background.

strip flooring Horizontal covering with bands or boards that are usually 2 inches wide and $^{25}/_{32}$ inches thick (5 cm × 2 cm). Strips may be as narrow as 1 inch (2.54 cm).

strip lighting A metal or plastic rail with a series of exposed sockets and a single plug or switch. Can be used to frame a mirror, outline a window, follow a ceiling line, or create a decorative pattern of lamps in lines. Usually used as an accent light.

stripping Removing old paint, lacquer, varnish, or any other finish from a piece of furniture, a treated surface, or textile. The first step in refinishing a piece of furniture.

strix A channel or groove in a fluted column. See FLUTING and STRIGES.

structural clay tile A hollow ceramic unit with parallel air cells. It may be made of burned clay, shale, fire clay, or mixtures of these materials.

structural luminaries Lighting that is permanently installed. It includes wall and ceiling fixtures that are installed to permanent wiring. Sometimes called ARCHITECTURAL LIGHTING.

strut A horizontal building construction member that is set between two verticals, or a vertical member that is set between two horizontal members, to hold them apart. A chair or table stretcher acts as a strut.

Stuart period English architecture and design from approximately 1625 to 1690, which coincided with the beginning of the reign of Charles I into that of William and Mary.

stucco A plaster or cement used for interior or exterior walls. It can be decoratively textured or coated, and the surfacing material can be tinted. See COMPO and GESSO.

stuck molding A trim piece that forms part of the surface it adorns, in contrast to a molding that is applied to or planted on a surface and not an integral part of the unit. See PLANTED MOLDING.

stud (1) A wooden post, nominally 2 inches by 4 inches (38 × 89 mm), used to form the skeleton of a wall or partition. The posts support the joists and receive the lath or sheet material, which finishes the wall. (2) Also a copper, brass, or gilt nailhead used for decorative purposes on chests, cabinets, and door panels or for securing leather or fabric to chairs, panels, chests, or cabinets. Originally nailheads were functional rather than decorative.

student lamp A late-19th-century brass illumination device with the fuel reservoir higher than the burner, as in an ASTRAL LAMP. The chimney, which was set around the projecting burner, was partially covered by a tôle shade to direct the light downward. The lampstand itself sometimes had a ring on top to make it portable. Electrified versions were also developed.

studio couch (1) A seating device that converts into a sleeping unit by means of removable cushions or bolsters and retractable springs. An informal bed unit. (2) A couch with an auxiliary set of spring and mattress that are stored, trundle-bed fashion, under the main spring and mattress; when the auxiliary set is pulled out, it converts into two twin beds.

study (1) In art, a drawing or painting of a detail made as a learning exercise and used as part of a larger composition. (2) In interior design, a library or den, usually a room with a desk, comfortable chairs, and bookshelves. Serves as a retreat.

stuffer In carpet construction, a strong coarse fiber such as jute that runs lengthwise on the loom and is woven in with the filling and warp threads. It adds a thick protective backing to the finished carpet.

stuffover seat The fixed upholstery of a chair formed by drawing the fabric or leather over the rails and securing it with nails along the underside. A galloon or a brass molding finishes off the joint. See STITCHED UP.

stump bedstead A bedstead without posts.

stump foot A furniture leg that proceeds directly down to the floor without any special foot, pad, or disk.

stump grain See BUTTWOOD VENEER.

∞stumpwork A relief effect in embroidery created by stitching with wool or silk threads over padding. A quilting or trapunto effect in vogue during the late Tudor and Jacobean periods. See TRAPUNTO.

stupa A dome-shaped earthen monument that houses Buddhist relics.

style (1) The characteristics of a design. (2) The motifs, techniques, and materials typical of a certain period of time or of a particularly successful designer.

∞stylobate (1) The stone blocks or steps of a Greek temple on which the columns rest. (2) A basement or platform on which columns are placed to raise them above the level of the ground or floor. (3) A continuous, unbroken pedestal for a range of columns or an ARCADE.

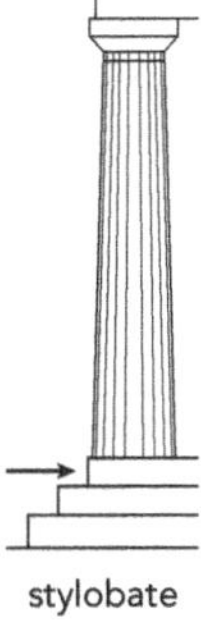

stylobate

subacute (adj.) Describes a sector of the healthcare industry. The area of a hospital that is designed to treat patients afflicted with illnesses of recent onset or with somewhat rapid change in a medical condition. In contrast, acute conditions are characterized by sudden onset and rapid change; chronic conditions are characterized by indefinite duration or virtually no change in medical condition. Successful collaboration between interior designers and healthcare professionals improves patient outcomes in subacute treatment areas.

suede cloth (1) A synthetic fabric with the look and feel of the napped side of leather. (2) Also, any fabric with the raised nap and matte finish that suggests the soft velvety leather.

suffah (Arabic) A place or couch for reclining before the door of a house. The word from which *sofa* is derived.

sugar pine or white pine A product of California and southern Oregon, it ranges in color from creamy white to pale brown faintly tinged with pink. Little flecks and intermittent lines of a darker shade run parallel with the grain. Knots have a purplish band around their edges. A close-grained wood that works well and holds a shape. See *Table 5.*

sugi finish A Japanese wood-finishing technique. The surface is charred and rubbed with a wire brush to create a driftwood effect.

summer beam (French, *sommier,* rafter) A large horizontal timber used as a bearing support. It usually spans the width of a room. In the Colonial American home, the structural element ran from the central stone chimney to a post on the opposite side of the room.

∞summer bed A Sheraton design that consisted of two single, four-poster beds separated by a space but connected at the cornice, which ran straight across the two beds.

sunburst An ornamental motif that may be carved, painted, or inlaid, with straight or jagged rays radiating from a central point. It was associated with Louis XIV, who was known as "the Sun King."

sunfast Describes a dyed fabric that resists fading under exposure to sunlight.

sunk top A table surface that is set below an edge or rim, as in gallery tables and tables on ocean liners. See GALLERY and PIECRUST TABLE.

Sunsum (1) The Golden Stool of Ashanti (or Asante) legend, which is believed to contain the spirit of the Ashanti people. (2) Also, the name for the spirit that signifies one's interaction with the world and connects the human body to the soul, a belief held by the Ashanti and by other Akran (Ghanaian) groups.

supergraphics Environmental designs of a huge scale, often executed with a bright palette. Generally uses simple, bold, repetitive lines and forms. Used on walls, ceilings, columns, and doors to break the perceived dullness of box-like interiors, accentuate areas, create movement or flow among rooms or spaces, camouflage dated architectural details, or decorate a wall without using wallpapers, graphics, or wall arrangements. A late-20th-century concept associated with the 1960s and 1970s.

superimposed order An architectural design in which each successive story of a colonnaded building has its columns, pilasters, or antae treated with a different classic order. Doric is usually on the lowest level, Ionic on the second, and Corinthian on the third story. The Romans used this device in the façade of the Colosseum in Rome, and it reappeared during the Renaissance.

super lamp A compact fluorescent lamp initially created by Philips to replace incandescent lighting. Promises a life span seven to ten times longer than the traditional incandescent bulb and an energy savings of up to 70 percent. The lamp's spiral shape is intended to fit into fixtures initially designed for incandescent lamps.

supermullions The upright bars or MULLIONS above the starting point of the foliation of a Gothic TRACERY window.

supporting column A vertical member at a front corner of a cabinet or chest that supports an overhanging FRIEZE drawer. This motif is usually associated with Empire, Regency, and Biedermeier styles.

surah A soft silk fabric, usually twill, woven in a plaid design. It can be made from synthetics or a combination of fibers.

surbase molding In cabinetry, the decorative trim on the base or pedestal of a piece of furniture. The molding may be carved, inlaid, or otherwise decorated, and the pedestal can contain drawers.

surrealism A 20th-century school of art that began in the weird and fantastic works of Hieronymus Bosch and Henry Fuseli. It was influenced by the nihilism of Dada and aspects of early-20th-century cubism. The word was first coined in France, and André Breton, the founder of surrealism, defined it as "pure psychic *automatism.*" Surrealists provided an alternative to the strict functionalism of Modernism. Major figures included Salvador Dali, Paul Klee, and Frida Kahlo.

sustainability A broad approach to design that maintains an ecological balance between the natural and built environments. A comprehensive attempt to minimize the negative effects of design and construction on the biosphere.

suwer (Wolof) West African tradition of painting on glass that originated as an Islamic art form and became secularized. See VERRE ÉGLOMISÉ.

swag (1) Cloth draped in a looped garland effect. (2) A carved or painted decoration in a pendant curve. The composition may be a festoon or a garland of fruits, flowers, leaves, or ribbons. See CATENARY and FRUIT FESTOON.

swag

swag light A lamp or fixture hooked onto the ceiling, in which the electric cord, usually decorated with a metal chain, is draped from the hanging point to the nearest wall and then down to the floor outlet where it is plugged in. Provides overhead light without installing electrical outlets or boxes in the ceiling.

∞**swan bed** A French Empire sleeping platform with carved birds of the genus Cygnus on either side of the headboard. The front or footboard consisted of a pair of cornucopia-type legs and a carved fruit arrangement. The entire bed was raised up from the floor on a heavily carved dais.

swan neck A general term for moldings or members with an ogee curve, as in the shape of a curved handrail ending that resembles the head support of the graceful waterfowl. See OGEE.

swan neck pediment A broken roof form in which the raking lines are composed of two opposed S curves. The upper ends are scrolled over with paterae on their faces. The pediment usually has a small central pedestal, sometimes topped with an ornamental feature such as a vase or pineapple. Popular in the earlier Queen Anne period. See also BROKEN ARCH and GOOSENECK PEDIMENT.

swastika A cross composed of four equal L-shaped arms at right angles to each other. It was an ancient symbol of good luck and was used in ancient Greece and Rome as part of a fret or Greek key design. In the 20th century, Germany's Nazi Party appropriated the motif.

swatch A small sample of cloth or material, also called a clipping or cutting. Used as a specimen of the color, pattern, and texture of a fabric, as an aid to making choices or specifications, or as the original against which new fabric runs are compared.

Swede cloth A napped fabric that resembles suede leather.

sweep front A piece of furniture with a flat, bowed, or slightly curved principal elevation.

swell front A cabinet, credenza, or chest of drawers, with a segmented or bow-shaped principal elevation. See BOW FRONT.

swing glass See CHEVAL GLASS OR MIRROR.

swing-leg table A work surface with a hinged rail attached to a single support. The vertical element sweeps out in a curve and assumes a position at a right angle where it supports a dropped leaf, which is raised parallel with the floor. See DROP-LEAF TABLE, FLAP TABLE, EIGHT-LEGGED TABLE, GATELEG TABLE, THOUSAND-LEG TABLE, and TUCKAWAY TABLE.

swing room A space used on a temporary basis to house occupants during a construction or reconstruction project.

swirl A wood-grain effect that appears around knots or crotches. An irregular, eddying grain.

Swiss fabric A fine, sheer cotton textile that originated in Switzerland. It may be plain, embroidered, or patterned with dots and is often used for GLASS CURTAINS. See DOTTED SWISS.

swivel A revolving mechanism below the seat of a chair or below the surface of a tabletop that swings the surface around in a wide arc, sometimes a full 360 degrees. Used in the LAZY SUSAN and the DUMBWAITER.

swivel

sycamore, English A heavy white to light brown wood that is tough and strong. Usually used for finishing work. When stained with iron oxide, it becomes a greenish-gray color. Popular as a veneering wood in the late 18th century. Also called HAREWOOD.

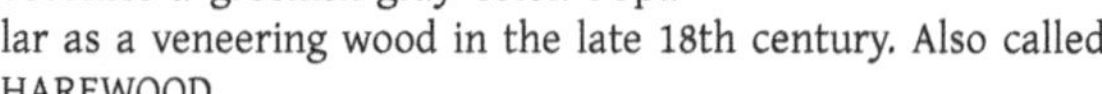

sylmerized (adj.) Describes fabric that has undergone a chemical treatment to make it stain-resistant. The process does not affect the color, feel, or hand.

symbol In furniture and interior decoration, a pictorial representation of an intangible, that is, an idea, quality, virtue, group, or trade. A decorative grouping of items that represent a concept or association beyond their literal reference. Symbols are used widely as carved, painted, and appliquéd decorations. See TROPHY.

symmetrical (1) A balance of mirror images. (2) An ensemble composed of two units of exactly equal shape, size, and mass and set equidistant on either side of a central point or axis line. There are three types: bilateral, radial, and translational.

symposium Originally, an all-male dining and drinking social event made famous in Plato's descriptions. The social event involved a layout of Roman beds and tripod tables set at right angles in a TRICLINIUM.

synthetic (adj.) Refers to man-made fibers, wood finishes, etc. Materials that are produced chemically in a laboratory rather than from natural growth or development in nature. New materials can be made from natural elements as cotton, wood pulp, or coal that are combined with man-made chemicals, tars, or resins. See *Table 2.*

synthetic resins Chemical compounds used in finishing textiles to give them desired resiliency, hand, and fade resistance. Also used on coated plastic fabrics.

tabaret A stout, satin-striped silk fabric used for upholstery.

tabby (1) A watered silk or moiré effect on fabric. (2) Also the name of an 18th-century English wallpaper ground. See MOIRÉ.

taberna (Latin, plural, *tabernae*) A Roman shop, in a market or off the street; often covered by a barrel vault. The ancient predecessor of a fast-food restaurant.

tabernacle frame The entire trim or decoration of a door, window, niche, or chimney. It consists of columns or pilasters with an entablature and pediment.

tabernacle mirror See CONSTITUTION MIRROR.

table (1) Before the mid 16th century, an index, a pocket-book, or a tablet. (2) In the 14th century, a religious carving or painting in a church. (3) Today, a flat, horizontal surface, raised on legs, trestles, or a pedestal.

table à coiffer (French) A dressing table, introduced in the period of Louis XV. Usually the center sliding panel contained a mirror with a drawer below. Deep wells on either side contained cosmetic containers, washbasins, etc. Also called a COIFFEUSE or POUDREUSE.

∞table à gradin (French) A tiered desk of the 18th century. A second tier of boxes or compartments was set on the flat writing surface. It was similar to a BONHEUR DU JOUR.

table à jeu (French) A gaming or card table.

∞table à l'Anglaise (French) An extension dining table of the LOUIS XIV (1774–1793) NEOCLASSICISM period.

table à l'architecte (French) A hinged and adjustable work surface supported on trestles or legs. See ARCHITECT'S TABLE.

∞table à milieu A center table. A table occupying the center of a room, such as an entry hall, without chairs, whose purpose is to hold flowers or other decorative objects.

table à ouvrage (French) A worktable. Usually a small table with an undershelf or drawer, often equipped with spaces for writing materials. See POUCH TABLE.

table à rognon (French) A kidney-shaped table, especially popular in the Louis XV period. See KIDNEY DESK.

tableaux (French) Pictures, paintings, or scenes.

∞tableaux tentures (French) A set of wallpaper panels that, when put up together, makes one large panoramic scene or a series of coordinated scenes. A wallpaper mural of many panels, popular in the early 19th century.

table chair An armchair or settle of the 16th and 17th centuries with a hinged top for a back. The back, when tilted down and lowered over the arms, became a useable horizontal surface. Sometimes has one drawer.

table chair

∞table de chevet (French) A night table that probably originated in the period of Louis XV. See CHEVET.

table de dame (French) A lady's small dressing or powder table of the 18th century, especially popular in the Louis XV period. See POUDREUSE.

table desk A writing surface without a modesty panel or a pedestal for file storage. See BUREAU PLAT.

∞table jardinière (French) A table with a sunken well in the surface to hold a plant container. SÈVRES plaques sometimes decorated the earliest examples.

tablero (Spanish) A framed stone upper panel, typical in Mesoamerican design.

tablet chair A seat with a wide flat arm that serves as a shelf or writing surface. It appeared on 18th-century American Windsor chairs, and a popular 20th-century version appeared in many schoolrooms. Also called a writing armchair.

tableware A broad range of products used for decorating the table, serving food, and dining.

∞tablinum (Latin) The principal living and socializing area of an ancient Roman house, with one side open to the atrium, sometimes with access to the rear garden. Used to receive visitors and vendors; it functioned like an office, including storage of family records.

tabonuco A light-colored, beautifully grained West Indian hardwood.

taboo furniture A colorful furniture collection made of recycled garbage bags and plastic bottles. Designed by Ayse Birsel and Bibi Seck, and made in Dakar, Senegal. The low stools are contemporary yet grow out of West African traditions.

∞taboret (French, *tabouret*) A low upholstered sitting stool. In 17th-century France, it was a distinguished seat for a lady of the court to sit on before the King and Queen. Also in the court of Queen Anne in England. In the 18th century, the side chair replaced the taboret. May also be an un-upholstered stool that functions as a stand or table.

taboret

Tabriz rugs Floor coverings with classic Persian border designs, many dating back to the 16th century. Often with a central medallion, sometimes incorporating shapes of stylized hunters, animals, flowers, and birds. Colors are usually soft and muted.

tackless strip Pin-holding band used in stretch-in carpet installation projects.

taffeta (Persian, *taftah*, silk or linen) A plain, basic weave, as well as the crisp fabric produced with this weave. The warp and filling threads are of equal size, and the resulting fabric is smooth on both sides with a lustrous surface. May also be woven in a manner that produces an iridescent effect. Also called taffety. See PLAIN WEAVE.

taffeta, antique A stiff, plain-weave fabric made of duppion to simulate 18th-century taffeta. See DOUPPIONI.

taffeta, faille Taffeta woven with a pronounced crosswise rib.

taffeta, moiré Rayon or silk taffeta with a watered or wavy effect. See MOIRÉ.

taffeta, paper A lightweight taffeta treated to create a crisp, paper-like finish.

taffeta, tissue A lightweight, semitransparent fabric.

tagout A sign or other warning device attached to a machine signifying that the equipment should not be operated. Ensures the safety of employees. A facilities management term.

taille-douce (French, line engraving) See ENGRAVING.

tailpiece A projection, on the back of the seat of certain Windsor chairs which receives the spindle braces.

tallboy A piece of furniture in which one smaller chest of drawers sits on top of another larger chest. This design first appeared at the end of the 17th century. See CHEST ON CHEST, DOUBLE CHEST, and HIGHBOY.

talud (Spanish) A Mesoamerican wall base, frequently sloped, that supports an upper framed panel.

tambour (French, drum) A flexible roll-over-top, or rolltop, desk or table. Small molding strips or reeds are transversely glued onto a heavy canvas backing, the ends of which fit into grooves on the inner sides of the piece of furniture. It may be used as a vertical rolling or horizontal sliding door on a cabinet or chest.

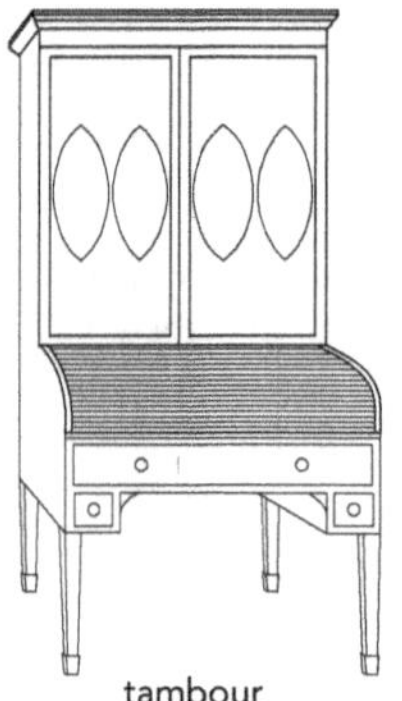
tambour

tambour curtain Panels of fine, sheer cotton fabric (such as BATISTE, MUSLIN, or LAWN) that usually have embroidered borders or an allover pattern.

tambour embroidery A chainstitch form of stitch work that is done on special tambour frames. Today, it is a machine technique that resembles the handmade product. It is used to decorate fine LAWN, BATISTE, and MUSLIN fabric panels used as curtains. See TAMBOUR CURTAIN.

tamo Japanese ash. A figured blond wood with varying patterns: fiddleback, mottle, swirls, and peanutshell figures. Tamo bends easily, glues well, and takes a beautiful finish.

tanguile A dark, red-brown hardwood from the Philippines, similar to other lauan woods of Southeast Asia. It is sometimes marketed as Philippine mahogany.

tansu Traditional Japanese chests and cabinetry. The cabinets serve as mobile storage units.

tantrika Abstract paintings related to ancient tantric principles; simple devices on paper that encourage meditation. These small paintings (approx. 12 square inches) have been a common decorative element in Indian homes, from the medieval period to the present. Usually wall-hung, and sometimes serving as a backdrop for a Buddha.

tapa cloth A fiber textile made in the South Seas, usually block-printed in bright allover native designs with vegetable and animal dyes. The fibers are usually derived from mulberry bark.

taper leg A straight, rectangular furniture support whose cross-section becomes increasingly smaller as it approaches the bottom or foot. See THERM FOOT.

tapestry (French, *tapisser*, to line) A handwoven fabric with a ribbed surface such as a rep and a design woven in during the manufacturing, making it an integral part of the fabric structure. Pictorial tapestries were originally made of wool accented with silk and metallic threads. They hung on the cold, drafty walls of medieval castles and fortresses. A handmade tapestry is reversible if the loose threads are snipped off. At the end of the 19th century, William Morris revived the fashion of wall decorating in England. The earliest English wallpapers were referred to as "paper tapestries." See ARRAS and MORTLAKE TAPESTRIES.

tapestry

tapet A late Gothic, early Renaissance term for a carpet, which at that time meant a table covering.

tarlatan A stiff, gauzelike fabric.

tarsia See INTARSIA.

task lighting Illumination for specific purposes; brighter, more direct, or more concentrated light directed at an area where an activity is being performed or an object is on display. Specific and concentrated light.

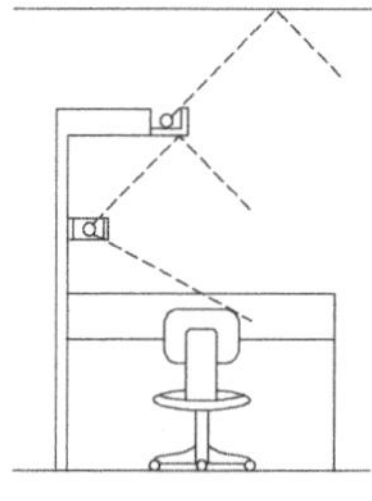
task lighting

task seating Commercial chairs designed for a specific purpose. For example: a typing chair, a tall stool for a drafting table, a chair with a writing arm, or a swivel chair or chair that tilts. Seats are designed to accommodate the work to be performed and to make the worker as comfortable and productive as possible.

Taslan The trademarked name for a textured, air-bulked yarn originally made by DuPont.

tassel A pendent ornament, usually twisted threads around a roundish core, with a thick fringe of the twisted threads falling below the core. Applied to the corners of pillows on upholstery pieces, along the edges of draperies, on cornices, and, famously, by EMILE-JACQUES RUHLMANN as drawer pulls. See *Designers and Architects.*

tatami A natural straw matting woven in uneven rows, often bound in black tape. Used by Japanese architects, arranged in certain patterns, for wall coverings as well as floor coverings. The texture of the tatami mat has been reproduced in vinyl.

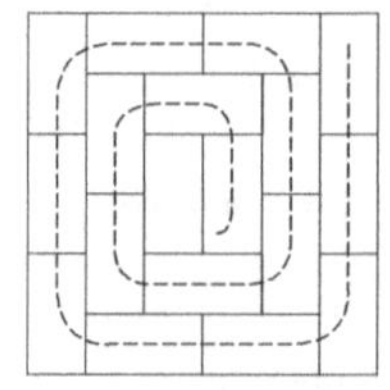
tatami

taupe (French, mole; moleskin) A dark, brownish, gray-purple color.

tavern table (1) A simple, leafless dining surface of the 17th and 18th centuries, such as a REFECTORY TABLE. (2) Also a table with stretchers, or a turned table.

tea caddy A container of elegant design made of wood, china, earthenware, pewter, or silver. In 18th-century England, the leading decorators and designers created these important household items.

tea table Small-surface furniture, either round or rectangular, with a GALLERY, or rim, around the top.

tea wagon A small, movable table on wheels with a shelf or two below the top table surface. Often equipped with handles and an extension.

teak A light tobacco-brown wood with fine black streaks. (The blackish cast often associated with teak is a stain.) Teak is important in tropical countries where exposure to moisture, heat, and insects are important factors in furniture construction. The wood has a rippled or mottled figure, and the color deepens with age. Native to India, Myanmar (Burma), Java, and the Malay Peninsula.

teakettle stand A small tripod table with a central column support and a gallery around the edge of the table surface.

teapoy (Hindustani, tripod) A small, low table, most usually a tripod but sometimes four-legged, popular in the 18th century. A large tea chest on legs, with a lift-up top under which nestled the tea caddies.

teardrop brasses Teardrop-shaped pendants or drops used as pulls or handles on drawers, doors, and cabinets.

teaser Short marketing materials created by prospective employees and design firms, in print or digital form, 2D and/or 3D. A teaser is a digital addition to the standard items of job hunting: a cover letter and a portfolio. Whereas a portfolio might have ten to twenty items in it, the shorter and economical teaser has three to five. Intended to quickly entice clients and prospective employers through a representative, not comprehensive, sampling. Important for visually and materially focused professions, including interior design.

tectonics An architectural concept in which the relationships among designed form, function, and material qualities are expressed in the building design. Historically related to the English architecture firm the Tecton Group and to one of its principals, Denys Lasdun. Also related to the concrete work of LE CORBUSIER. See BRUTALISM. See *Designers and Architects.*

∞telamones (Latin) Male caryatids. The Roman term for atlantes. See ATLANTES and CARYATIDS.

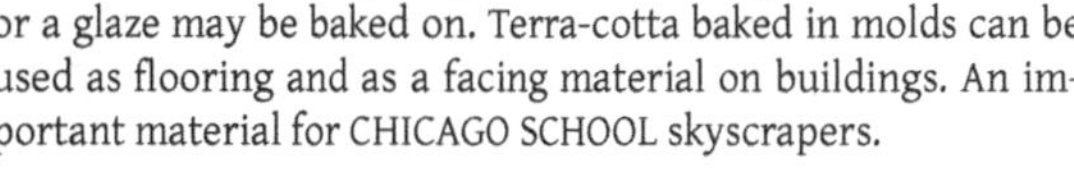

telamon

teleconferencing A business practice of holding meetings by phone, video, Skype, Zoom, or other methods, to include people who are in various locations. Related to other office innovations such as BENCHING, HOT DESKING, HOTELLING, and NOMADS.

tempera A common painting technique used up to the 16th century. Powdered color is mixed with egg yolk, thinned with water, and then applied to a panel prepared with gesso. It dries quickly and the color lightens, resulting in a tough and permanent finish. Tempera is much like the current gouache technique. See GESSO and GOUACHE.

tempered glass Vitreous material that has been strengthened with the addition of other ingredients to prevent breakage.

template or templet A pattern for a construction or decoration. A contour drawing of the exact shape and size of a form to be created. The template is often made of durable material and used as a guide for a repeating pattern or to ensure standard dimensions.

tenacity Fiber strength.

tenia The flat band at the top of a Doric ARCHITRAVE upon which the triglyphs rest. See TRIGLYPH.

tenon In carpentry, a projection at the end of a piece of wood that is shaped to fit into a specific opening (a mortise) of a corresponding shape in another piece of wood. Used in joinery. See MORTISE AND TENON JOINT.

tensegrity The structural design concept of objects that are simultaneously under compression and tension. The term was coined by Buckminster Fuller, who created the geodesic dome. Also called tensional integrity or floating compression.

tensegrity

tensile strength The ability of a material to resist breaking under stress.

tent bed An 18th-century variation of the camp bed or field bed. A four-poster with a tester that resembles a tent top. See FIELD BED.

tenture (French) A tapestry, wall hanging, colored wallpaper, or set or series of tapestries on one particular subject.

term (1) A pedestal that tapers toward the base. (2) Sometimes refers to both the pedestal and the bust that stands on it. Used as a decorative device in the Renaissance and Rococo periods.

terminal figures Human figures, natural or grotesque, often carved in high relief, and used to embellish prominent features on furniture, such as a term. See TERM.

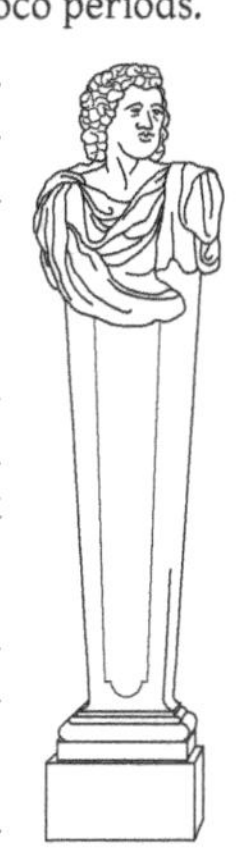

terminal figure

tern foot A triple-scrolled foot. See TRIFID.

terrace (1) A raised outdoor area or platform usually surrounded by a balustrade or low fence. (2) A continuous row of houses. (3) Also a graded bank of earth covered with sod.

terracescape An outdoor landscape created with various levels, or terraces, that are enhanced with plants, shrubs, and paving materials.

terra-cotta (Italian, baked earth) Clay fashioned into ornaments, vessels, tiles, etc. and then baked. Finished pieces vary in color from a gray-brown to a brick red. The clay may be colored with paint, or a glaze may be baked on. Terra-cotta baked in molds can be used as flooring and as a facing material on buildings. An important material for CHICAGO SCHOOL skyscrapers.

terrazzo A type of concrete made up of small pieces of crushed marble and cement. Used for pavements, floors, and walls, and sometimes accented with metal feature strips. See *Table 3.*

terre-cuite See FAÏENCE and TERRA-COTTA.

terry cloth A slack-tension warp pile fabric with uncut loops on one or both sides, traditionally made of cotton.

tertiary colors Colors produced by mixing a primary color with an adjacent secondary color; for example, red and orange mixed together produce a red-orange color. See PRIMARY COLORS and SECONDARY COLORS.

tessellated (adj.) Describes a surface, such as a wall, that is treated with a mosaic design composed of small cubes, or tesserae, of stone, glass, marble, or tile. See TESSERA.

tessellated

tessera (plural, *tesserae*) A small cube of glass, marble, stone, or ceramic used in mosaic designs. See TESSELLATED.

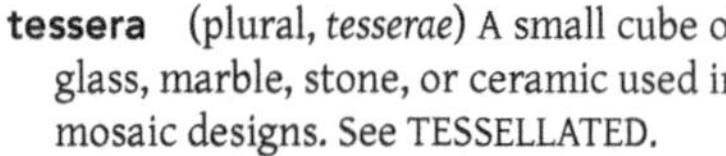

tester (French, *testière*, or headpiece) A canopy on a four-post or draped bed. Originally, a flat wooden canopy, paneled and carved, used as a roof for Tudor and Stuart bedsteads. This was replaced by a wooden framework heavily draped and swathed with valances. In the mid 18th century, it became a small wood cornice with a valance and curtains. See CANAPÉ and CANOPY.

tête-à-tête (French) An S-curved sofa for two, also called a siamoise. A 19th-century design in which the seated persons sit shoulder to shoulder and face in opposite directions. See SIAMOISE.

têtes d'anges (French) Angel heads with wings. Decorative sculptured forms, sometimes set in medallions or rondels, or on pilasters. Used in Renaissance architecture and furniture, and also in late-18th-century France and England. See also CHERUB HEAD.

tetradic Adj. based on the twelve-color wheel, it is a scheme of four colors equally spaced apart. This involves either two sets of complementary colors or is the result of the colors that correlate to a square being overlain on the wheel. Red, green, blue-purple, and yellow-orange is an example. The resulting schemes are fun, loud, and vibrant but not peaceful or restful. Such palettes have existed throughout history but are associated with the Bauhaus and other modern movements.

Texas depth furniture Oversized furniture intended to fill MCMANSIONS of the 1990s. Also relates to obesity.

textiles Fabrics. Woven or unwoven materials used in interiors for upholstery, drapery, wall coverings, etc. Fabrics may be made of natural fibers such as wool, silk, cotton, and linen; or synthetic fibers for example, rayon, nylon, and Dacron; or combinations of natural and synthetic fibers. See *Table 2*.

Textolite A trademarked name for a plastic material originally manufactured by General Electric in a wide range of colors, patterns, and textural effects. It is easy to clean, resists stains and scratches, and is used for laminating on tabletops, countertops, walls, and shelves.

texture The feel and the appearance, or the tactile effect, of the surface of a material. The quality may be described as smooth, rough, pebbly, and so on. Also applies to the grain in wood. See EMBOSSED.

texture paint A water-based paint with a silica sand additive that creates a stucco-like texture on the wall, and that hides surface imperfections.

thatch A roof covering of straw or reeds.

theatrical gauze A plain-weave, open, lightweight, semi-sheer cotton or linen fabric, usually stiffened with size to give it body. Also called opera gauze. Used mainly for GLASS CURTAINS.

therm foot A rectangular, tapering foot for a chair, table, or cabinet leg. Favored by mid- and late-18th-century designers. Also called a SPADE FOOT.

therm leg A four-sided tapering leg. A favorite furniture support of Hepplewhite and other mid-to-late-18th-century English designers. Could be highly decorated. Also called a TAPER LEG.

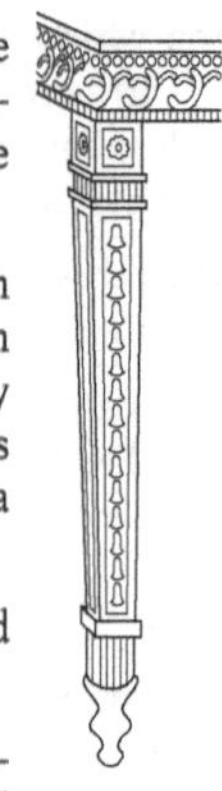
therm leg

thermoform A manufacturing process in which a plastic sheet is heated until it is pliable, then shaped to a specific profile in a mold, and finally trimmed to create a useful product. The process is used to create interior panels, light fixtures, and a variety of designed objects.

thermopane A double-glass insulating pane used on doors and windows.

thermoplastic polymer A plastic material or synthetic resin that softens at high temperatures and returns to a solid state upon cooling, in contrast to a THERMOSETTING POLYMER, OR THERMOSET.

thermosetting polymer, or thermoset A plastic or synthetic resin that hardens and sets permanently at high temperatures. The opposite of a THERMOPLASTIC POLYMER.

thermostatic Adj. that refers to a high-tech device in residential or commercial settings that automatically responds to temperature changes, which activates adjustments to the device. Concerns heating, cooling, and refrigeration.

thimble foot A spade foot or sabot foot, but one that is turned rather than rectangular. See SPADE FOOT.

∞**thirteen-state tracery** A late-18th-century fretwork or carving made up of thirteen elements. The openwork originated in China, and the concept of the thirteen original American colonies was superimposed on the design. Used to decorate glass panels of secretaries and bookcases of the late 18th century.

thousand-leg table A variation of the gateleg dining surface that dates back to the first half of the 17th century. It had a central drawer, two extra swinging legs that folded in under the braces of the tabletop, and two leaves that dropped down. When the table was opened, it reached 5 feet in diameter. See EIGHT-LEGGED TABLE and GATELEG TABLE.

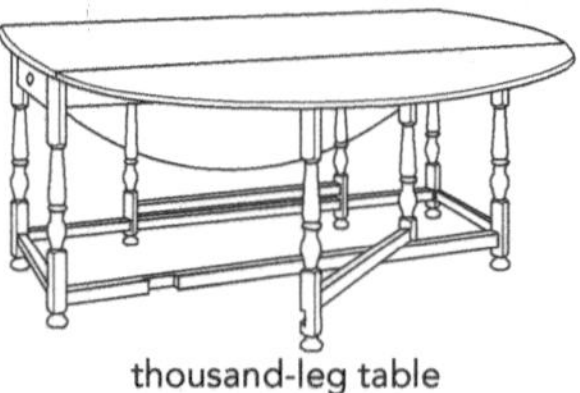
thousand-leg table

thread count The number of threads in 1 square inch of fabric.

∞**three-back Windsor chair** See COMB BACK.

3D depth Increasingly realistic interior design renderings which focus on the illusion of depth in 2D images. Algorithmic software provides greater depth perception and precise geometric information. A result of new generations of sophisticated visualization; phases in image creation include content generation, data compression, and transmission. Also important in gaming and animation, the new image category has had a profound impact on clients who increasingly expect photorealism. Replete with detail, successful images in the category earn the descriptor "awesome."

three-quarter width In carpet construction, one-quarter of a yard, or 9 inches, is a unit of loom width, and a standard carpet is "three-quarters wide," or 27 inches wide. In Europe, a three-quarter width is referred to as an ell.

threshold A plank-like element customarily placed under a door. It may be constructed from various materials, such as wood, metal, or stone.

∞thronos (Greek) An ornamental ancient Greek chair with a high seat and back and rectangular turned, or curved, legs that end in animal feet.

thrust The force exerted by an arch on each side.

thrust stage A theater configuration in which the audience sits on three sides of the performance area.

ThruVu blinds Trademarked name for vertical strip blinds used over windows, made of lightweight metal or fabric. Used to control light and air, as in a traditional horizontal VENETIAN BLIND. Originally designed by GEORGE NELSON and Henry Wright, these blinds have since been imitated, adapted, and improved under other names. Sometimes called Boston blinds. See also *Designers and Architects.*

thumb molding A convex applied strip with a flattened curved profile. Also referred to as LIP MOLDING.

thuya A hard, dark, red-brown wood native to North Africa, usually with a BIRD'S EYE figure. Takes a high polish, and is used for cabinetwork. Used by the ancient Greeks and Chinese, and a popular veneer in 18th-century England.

tiama See SAPELE or SAPELI.

ticking A closely woven cotton fabric with a twill or satin weave, usually woven in stripes, but may be printed. A sturdy fabric for mattress covers, and also used decoratively for drapery, upholstery, and wall covering.

tidy (plural, tidies) A small doily, often crocheted or elaborately embroidered, or a large runner, used on chairbacks and arms. A popular decorative conceit during the Victorian period. Also called ANTIMACASSAR.

tieback An object that restrains a drapery. May be a fabric sash or cord with tassels, or a decorative hook, rosette, or bar made of metal, glass, or wood. When the drapery is tied back to one or both sides of a window, doorway, or other opening, a decorative swelling of fabric appears above the tieback, and the fabric cascades downward.

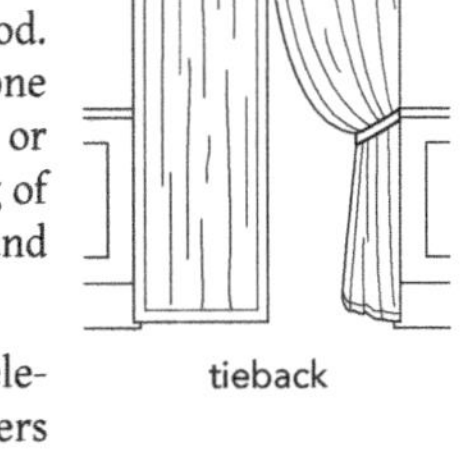
tieback

tie beam A horizontal structural element that connects the ceiling rafters and keeps them from spreading. The tie beam is used in truss construction to counteract the outward thrust of the slanting members. May be left visible in an interior.

tie-dyed Fabric imbued with pigment with this hand-craft resist technique: areas of fabric or yarn are knotted, or bound with string or rubber bands, before being dyed. Also called bound resist.

tier curtains Two or more rows of short draperies hung one over the other to cover a window. Sometimes the lower tier is longer and made of a decorative or more opaque fabric.

tier table A small round table consisting of two or more surfaces or shelves set one over the other, with the largest one at the bottom. A serving table. See SERVITEUR FIDÈLE, DUMBWAITER, and RAFRAÎCHISSOIR.

Tiffany lamp Illumination device designed by LOUIS COMFORT TIFFANY, with motifs derived from plant forms. The undulating curves of the glass shade were emphasized through the use of iridescent violets, mauves, ochers, and greens. See *Designers and Architects.*

tigerwood A West African wood of a grayish-brown to golden-brown color, accented with black streaks and a definite ribbon stripe, used for cabinetry and paneling. Also called African walnut and Nigerian golden walnut.

tile A thin slab of baked clay. May be glazed or ornamented. Used for a variety of surfaces, such as roofs, walls, floors, counters, backsplashes, patios, and exterior façades.

till A small drawer or compartment in a table, desk, or chest, for money, jewelry, or valuable papers. Often equipped with secret springs or locks.

tilt-top table A pedestal table with a hinged horizontal surface that can drop vertically when not in use. See SNAP TABLE.

tint A color with white added, which in effect lightens or pales the color to a pastel. The opposite of shade, which is a color with black added. See SHADE.

tiny house An extremely small dwelling, measuring only about 100 to 150 square feet, and favored as an environmental statement. Jay Shafer is a major figure in the movement that supports such housing.

tip-up table A double-leaved table that folds like a book (the hinged leaves hang down on either side of a central spine). Similar to a SNAP TABLE or TILT-TOP TABLE.

tissue Semi-sheer crisp fabric made of silk or synthetic yarns.

toddy table A small table of the Georgian period in England. See URN STAND.

toile (French) (1) A linen- or canvas-like fabric. (2) Also a fabric used for painting, or a painting or picture on such fabric. (3) A fabric with pictures printed all over it. See TOILE DE JOUY.

toile de Jouy Originally, a hand-blocked cotton or linen fabric with repeating printed pastoral scenes, in one color, on a white or natural background. A factory founded by CHRISTOPHE-PHILIPPE OBERKAMPF at Jouy, near Versailles, France, produced these fabrics in the mid 18th century. Oberkampf designed pictorial groups in one color (red, blue, green, or eggplant) and printed them on natural cream-colored cotton. They showed groups of peasants or aristocrats dressed in different costumes and engaged in everyday activities, as well as scenes from fables and historical scenes. The original Jouy prints were marked *Bon Teint* on the selvage, which means COLORFAST.

toile d'Indy Cotton or linen printed with a floral or pictorial design. Originally imported into France during the late 17th century from India and Persia and later manufactured in Europe as well. See INDIENNE FABRICS.

toilet mirror (archaic) A cheval mirror with dressing table compartments. Also called a DRESSING MIRROR.

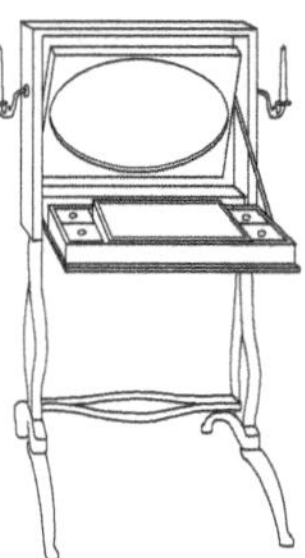
toilet mirror

tokonoma (Japanese) A recessed space or alcove in a Japanese interior reception room, for the purpose of displaying artwork, including bonsai (dwarfed trees), calligraphic scrolls, or ikebana (floral arrangements).

tokonoma

tôle (French, sheet iron) Objects made of tin or other metal and ornamented with painted or enameled patterns. Eighteenth-century lamps, boxes, and trays were often made of tôle.

tôle shade A lampshade made of sheet metal, often decorated with painted or decal artwork. Usually associated with Early American, early-19th-century, and provincial lamp designs. See BOUILLOTTE SHADE.

toleware Decorated metal goods made of tin, iron, or other metal that was painted or lacquered. Originated in France, then made worldwide.

tonal value The relative strength of a color based on its degree of light absorption.

tondo (Italian) A circular picture, popular in Italy in the mid 15th century.

tongue and groove A joint in which a long, narrow, straight projection (the tongue) fits into a corresponding groove in the adjacent piece. Used extensively in flooring. See JOINERY.

Tontine A washable fabric used for window shades and bed linens, originally trademarked by DuPont.

top color In printed or screened fabrics, papers, etc., the pigment applied over the ground color of the material to produce the design or decoration.

topiary art The clipping and shaping of plants, shrubs, and trees into formal or fanciful shapes: geometric shapes, birds, and other animal forms are commonly used. Topiary trees have been featured in formal gardens from the 16th century to the present.

topos A traditional theme or formula in literature or art.

top rail (1) The uppermost horizontal member of a door. (2) A horizontal bar or rail that connects the uprights of a chair back, and supports the cresting, if any. In some historical periods, the top rail appears to be a continuation of the uprights in that it is a curve, serpentine, or bow-shape. Also called the CRESTING RAIL.

torch A flambeau, or flaming brand. A Roman motif that reappeared in the Renaissance, Directoire, and Empire periods. See FLAMBEAU.

torchère (1) Originally, a small table designed to hold a candlestick, candelabrum or other light-giving object. The table surface was usually mounted on a pillar or light framework and embellished with carvings and gilt. A French design of the Louis XV period. (2) Today, a standing floor lamp, usually with a bowl shade to cast light upward. The slender light fixture was also called a GUÉRIDON.

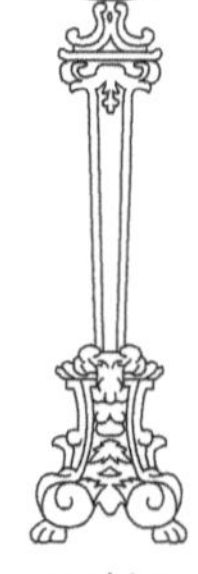

torchère

toron In West African Islamic architecture, the permanent wooden stakes that project from exterior walls and are used as scaffolding during and after construction. Unlike European scaffolding, they are a permanent part of the building.

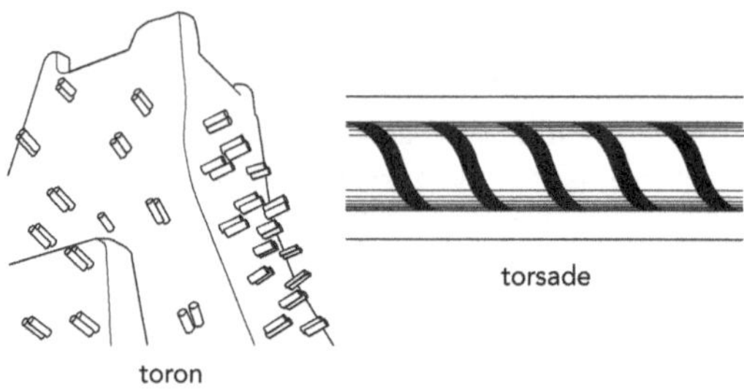

toron

torsade

torsade A molding with a twisted, ropelike or cable design. See CABLE.

torso (1) The trunk of the human body. (2) The main part of a designed object.

tortoiseshell The back plates of a sea turtle, flattened out and joined together under heat and pressure. Used in antiquity as a veneering material for furniture. It became popular again during the period of Louis XIV, thanks to ANDRÉ-CHARLES BOULLE and his inlay technique. Usually a mottled brown, gold, and black semitranslucent material. See BOULLE WORK. See *Designers and Architects*.

∞**torus** A convex, semicircular molding, often found at the base of a column.

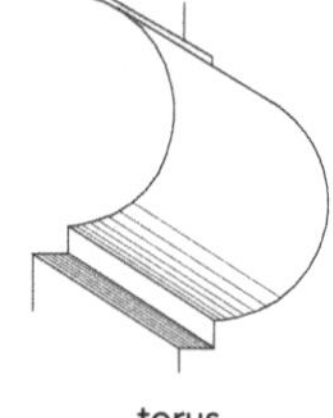

torus

touchstone A black marble from Namur, Belgium, used on chimneypieces and mantels in the late 16th and early 17th centuries. NICHOLAS STONE often used the material. See *Designers and Architects*.

towel horse or towel rail A slender wood frame with several crossbars used to hold towels, usually on two or more legs. In vogue in England in the mid 18th century.

towel horse or towel rail A slender wood frame with several crossbars used to hold towels, usually on two or more legs.

t-pillow A seat cushion for a chair or sofa that is wider in front than at the back, because the arms of the upholstered unit do not extend to the front of the seat. The two rectangular projections of the pillow (the crosspiece of the unvoiced consonant letter) fill up the space between the end of the armpiece and the front of the chair. A sofa with two pillows will have only one projection or ear on each pillow.

trabeated construction Basic building assembly using vertical posts and horizontal lintels. Stonehenge is a famous example.

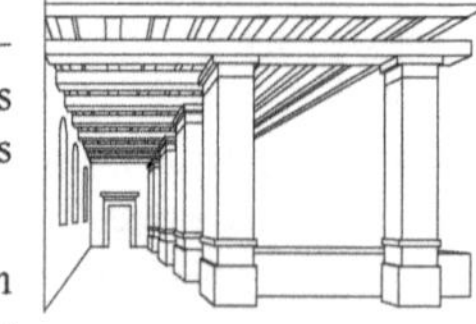

trabeated construction

tracery Originally, the MULLIONS in Gothic windows and between choir stalls. A decorative form composed of arcs and circles, and sometimes plant motifs, in intricate patterns. The design was important but not the material, so similar ornamentation exists in metal, wood, and stone. In Chippendale Gothic works, tracery appears in chairbacks. See BAR TRACERY.

∞trachelium The neck of a Greek Doric column, between the ANNULET and the hypotrachelium.

track lighting The arrangement of spotlights or flood-lights in decorative housings on a channel or track attached to a ceiling, wall, or other surface, with one end wired into an electrical source. The length of channel can be extended. Fixtures can be moved anywhere along the track, aimed at different positions, and may be turned on and off individually. Used for selective illuminating or TASK LIGHTING. See also CABLE SYSTEM.

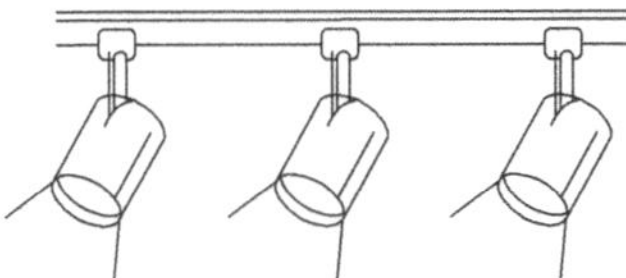

track lighting

traditional (adj.) In interior decoration, usually describes a style of a bygone age, historicist, in contrast to a CONTEMPORARY or modern style.

transept In church architecture, the part that crosses the nave at right angles near the apse of the building. See APSE and NAVE.

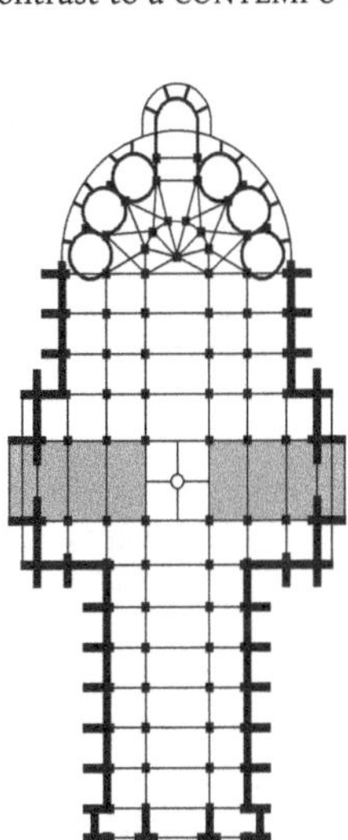

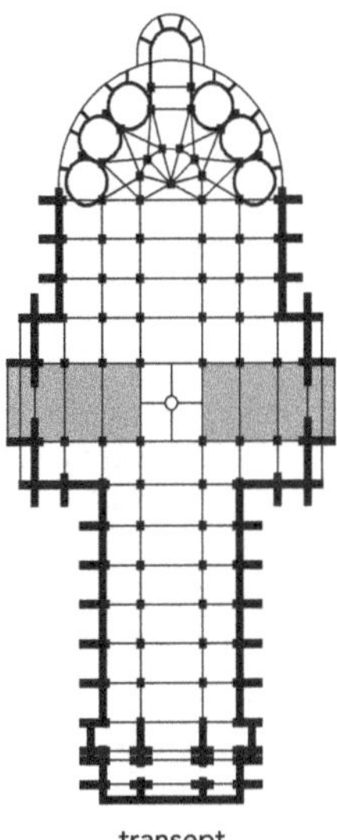

transept

transfer printing A method of applying one-color designs to pottery. The pattern is printed on paper by means of a copperplate engraving and then conveyed to the pottery, as in a decal. See DECALCOMANIA.

transitional (adj.) A style that combines new elements with elements that are already established. An example is the French Régence period, which was a transition from the Louis XIV style to the Louis XV style.

transitional housing A non-permanent living situation. Refers to a temporal state as it intersects with domestic environments. It meets basic living needs but requires support for education and counseling. Often a first home after jail; a place of addiction treatment; or a mental health facility. It is related to homelessness and is also discussed in the context of veterans. Can include a variety of homes, although usually small-scale in contrast to institutions. Related to halfway houses.

transitional Tulbagh chair A simplified wooden version of the South African TULBAGH CHAIR.

translucent (adj.) Describes a material such as fabric or glass that allows light to pass through but diffuses it so that objects cannot be seen clearly. See OBSCURE GLASS.

transom The upper part of a window, or the window over a doorway, usually constructed to allow in air.

transverse ribs In arch vaulting, the main protrusions which mark or delineate a vault's contour.

trapunto A type of quilting that gives a raised relief effect to a stitched design. The design is usually outlined with single stitches and then filled from behind. The method often embellishes the pillow backs of upholstered pieces. Also called STUMPWORK.

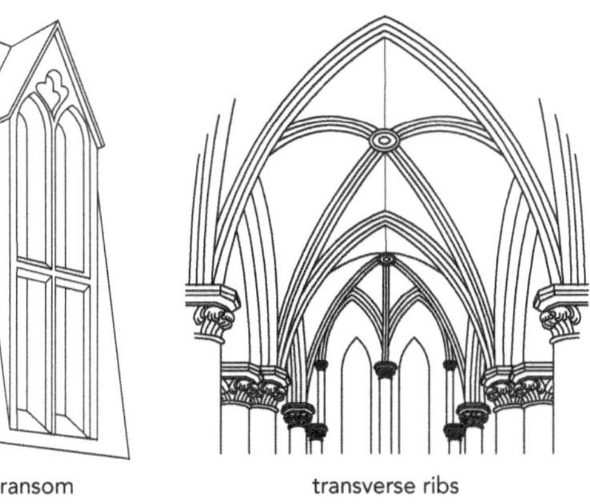

transom transverse ribs

travertine A cream-colored, onyx-like stone that is pockmarked or full of irregularly shaped depressions. See *Table 3.*

tray A type of inside drawer behind a door or doors, usually without hardware.

tray table A collapsible stand that, when opened, supports a a horizontal serving surface. The removable framed element serves as the tabletop. See BUTLER'S TABLE.

∞trayle or trail A running vine with grape clusters and leaves. It appeared as a decorative element in Tudor England. See also VINETTE.

tray-top table A small table with a low gallery or skirting around three or all four sides, popular in the mid to late 18th century.

tread In stair construction, the flat, horizontal part of the step between two risers.

trecento The 1300s, that is, the 14th century, specifically in Italian art and design.

tree of life A motif based on a plant or vine, with branches, leaves, flowers, and small animals. Originated by the ancient Assyrians and used as a decorative motif by Persians and Indians. Used in English Renaissance design. See HOM and PALAMPORES.

trefoil A three-lobed, clover-like ornament used with Gothic tracery and decoration. Cusps separate the three arcs. It was the Gothic symbol for the Holy Trinity in Christianity. See CUSP.

trefoil

trelliswork A crossbarred or lattice element in wood. A pierced or fretted woodwork design with a reticulated appearance. See also FRETWORK.

∞treenail or trenail Wooden pegs that have been rounded and tapered to a point. Used in the construction of finer 18th-century pieces.

∞trencher A large wooden serving platter. Originally, a slice of bread on which food was placed.

trelliswork

trestle (Old French, *trestel*, a beam) A supporting frame, in contrast to a leg. In the Tudor period, the elements supported large boards to form a TRESTLE TABLE. A saw horse is one example.

trestle table See SAWBUCK TABLE.

triacetate A derivative cellulosic fiber. See *Table 2*.

triadic Three related items or people. With color, it initially referred to the primary colors red, blue, and yellow and their position on the color wheel; they are equally spaced apart. Such color schemes exist in interiors, textiles, and designed objects. Examples are the Burger King logo and Superman's costume. Also refers to related harmonic schemes with similarly positioned colors, such as orange-violet-green. Famous examples include the Triadisches Ballet at the Bauhaus and Gerrit Rietveld's Schröder House.

triangle seat Sometimes called a corner stool or a BOFFET OR BOFFET CHAIR. The latter was a Scandinavian design that was made in England in the early 17th century. Three-sided chairs were also made in the Queen Anne period and afterward, with splats on the two sides under the semicircular arm and a backrest that encircled the two sides of the triangle. See BARBER'S CHAIR.

triclinium (Latin) The dining room of a Roman house; often elaborately decorated and furnished with couches.

tricot (1) An inexpensive tapestry fabric, the underside of which differs from the top side. Usually made of cotton or rayon. (2) A warp-knit fabric, also with different sides, and made of nylon.

∞tricoteuse (French) A small sewing table or worktable, usually with a gallery around the top. The table often had several shelves under the top surface. Appeared in the Louis XVI period and continued through the Directoire period and on into the 19th century. See POUCH TABLE.

∞trictrac table A backgammon table. A popular gaming table of the Régence, Louis XV, and Louis XVI periods. In the Louis XVI period, they were made of mahogany with removable tabletops. Sometimes one side of this removable top was covered with leather and the reverse side was covered in baize. The top was removed to reveal the interior, a gaming area with a backgammon board, sockets for candles, and compartments for dice and counters. See BAIZE.

∞tri-darn A Welsh court cupboard of the 16th century, with two tiers of cupboards and, above them, an open, spindle-sided dresser. See DEU-DARN.

∞trifid A three-toed furniture foot of the 18th century that was used in England and the United States. See TERN FOOT.

trifoil See TREFOIL.

trifold mirror A reflecting device that stood on a dresser top, with a large center section and two hinged side panels. Also called a triplex or a wing mirror.

triforium In a Gothic or Renaissance church, an arcaded gallery above the side aisles and below the clerestory. An elaborate version graces the upper level of St. Paul's Cathedral, London.

triglyph In a Doric entablature, the set of upright channels in the spaces between the METOPES. The two elements together form the frieze. To the extent that classical stone construction reflects the methods of earlier buildings in wood, these elements represent the ends of ceiling rafters. See also GLYPH.

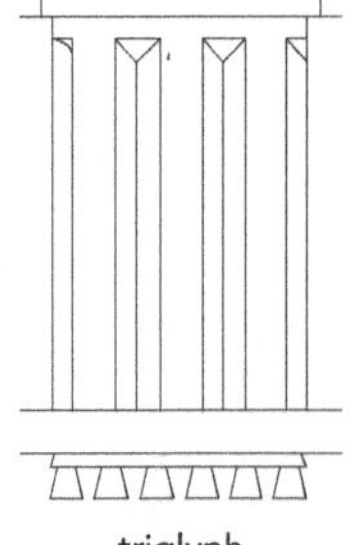
triglyph

Trilok A trademarked name for a corrugated, three-dimensional fabric made of monofilament yarns. A durable, serviceable fabric used for upholstery in homes, autos, and public areas. First patented by the United States Rubber Company.

trimetric A category of architectural drawing that suggests 3D volumes in space, yet not in a perspectival or photorealistic way. The three spatial axes, x, y and z, are unequally defined, with each at a different scale that creates a distorted although scalable image. This is in contrast to a dimetric drawing, which has two similar axes, x and y. One of three types of axonometric projection, a stalwart in the field of architectural drawing.

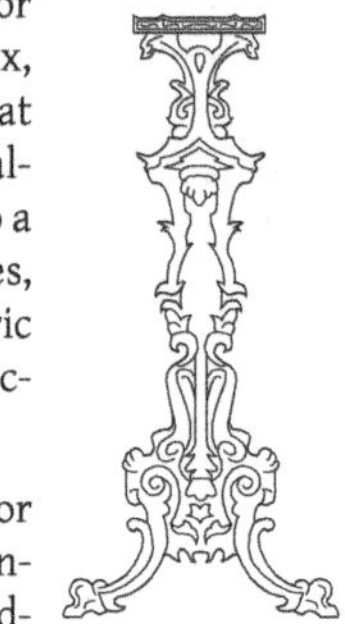
tripod stand

tripod stand A very small table with a flat or gallery-top surface that rests on a column-like shaft, which ends in a triple spread-legged support. A favorite of the 18th century in England and the United States.

tripod table A round Roman stand supported by three outward-curving legs.

tripod table

triptych Any three-panel or threefold picture, screen, or mirror, especially a three-panel religious painting used on an altar.

triquetra An ornamental interlaced pattern that consists of three pointed lobes.

trivet A small, openwork, three-legged frame in metal, originally hung on the bars of a grate to keep a kettle or dish hot. Today, a three-legged stand that raises a hot container off the surface of a table or server. A large trivet is called a footman. The items became fashionable in the mid 18th century.

troffer A trough-shaped reflector that holds fluorescent lamps. Part of a light fixture, or the light fixture itself.

trompe l'oeil (French, deceive the eye) A technique of using pictorial elements, perspective, foreshortening, and shadows to render objects in paint or inlay so realistically that they appear to be three-dimensional. See QUADRATURE and REPLICA.

trophy A token of victory. A decorative arrangement of symbols of battle set on a panel or a pilaster. May be painted, carved, or inlaid. The symbols included weapons, horns, banners, spears, shields, and laurel leaves. Renaissance artists' trophies were executed in INTARSIA or TARSIA, woven fabric, and TAPESTRY. Other types are used today: musical instruments, flowers, fruit, fish, animals, and professional symbols. See SYMBOL. Also see GIBBONS, GRINLING, in *Designers and Architects*.

∞trotter See PHILADELPHIA CHIPPENDALE.

trumeau (French, pier; or the wall between windows) Overmantel or overdoor paneling, usually filled with mirrors or paintings. The paintings were often made to look like grisaille, or relief sculpture in the 18th century. Trumeau was part of the exquisite boiserie of the Louis XV and Louis XVI periods. See GRISAILLE.

trumeau mirror A framed reflective device of the late 18th century, usually a tall rectangular mirror set into an overmantel or hung in the space between windows. A characteristic element was a painted scene in the upper section, or a carved panel. The decoration was often more prominent than the reflective surface. See CONSTITUTION MIRROR and PIER GLASS.

∞trumpet turning A carving with a flared end that resembles the bell of the musical wind instrument. A 17th-century motif.

trundle bed A small-scaled sleeping platform on casters for children or servants which rolled under a full-size bed when not in use. Originally a Gothic design, it was often used in Colonial and Early American homes. Today, a pullout on casters somewhat smaller than the piece of furniture under which it is set. Similar to a HIDEAWAY BED.

truss In furniture construction, a BRACKET, CONSOLE, or CORBEL.

tub chair A late-18th-century English seat for relaxation with a rounded back and wide wings, similar to a BARREL CHAIR but wider, taller, and more enveloping. In the Regency period (early 19th century) the design changed, and it more closely resembled the SPOON-BACK CHAIR, except that instead of having a splat, the entire back was enclosed with cane or upholstery.

∞tub sofa A fully upholstered French designed seating object. The ends sweep around in curves, and they feature arm pads, or MANCHETTES. The people seated at either end of the couch are slightly turned toward each other. Similar to a kidney-shaped couch.

tubular furniture Contemporary casework and seating with structural parts made of plastic or metal rods or tubes, including the chair and table legs, chair arms, and back rests. Outdoor furniture is often made of polyvinyl chloride (PVC) or aluminum, with plastic webbing or plastic-covered pillows. A result of the early modernists' interest in bicycle tubing as a furniture material.

tuckaway table An 18th-century American folding work surface with crossed or scissored legs. The top leaves dropped close together, making a compact, storable unit. A forerunner of the snack table.

Tudor arch A four-centered, flat-pointed structural device, characteristic of the English Medieval, Gothic, and early Renaissance periods.

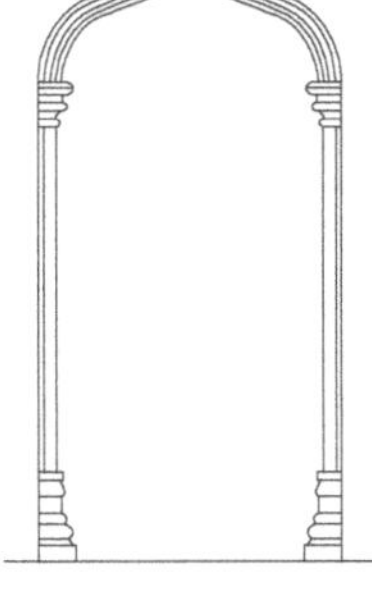
Tudor arch

Tudor–Elizabethan period The English era from 1485 to 1603, during which new Renaissance forms combined with established Gothic and medieval forms. Generally, furniture was massive, with straight lines, and was elaborately carved. Beds were huge, bedposts highly ornate, and chairs and tables had underbracing. Features included the MELON BULB turning, the TUDOR ROSE, the carved ACANTHUS LEAF, and the LINENFOLD motif.

Tudor flower See BRATTISHING.

Tudor period The reign of the royal family in England from Henry VII through the reign of Elizabeth I (1485–1603). It was a transitional era in architecture and decoration from the late Gothic to the Renaissance. A time of secular building that combined elements of the late GOTHIC perpendicular with NORMAN castellated motifs.

Tudor rose An English Renaissance decorative motif that consisted of a conventionalized five-petaled flower with a smaller bloom set in its center. The royal emblem of England, it symbolized the marriage of Henry VII of Lancaster (red) to Elizabeth of York (white).

Tudor rose

tufa A lightweight volcanic stone, or a rock with a rough, irregular, cellular structure. It may also be formed as a calcareous deposit from water. The ancient Romans used the naturally occurring material to make concrete.

tuft In carpet construction, a single yarn in a surface pile of a carpet. Twisting together the fiber strands produces the yarn.

tufting (1) An upholstery technique in which the covering fabric and the padding are sewn in a pattern of pillows and depressions. The process is fastened with buttons. The process makes the fabric conform to the curves of the unit. It is used on leather or imitation leather, where the material is not easily worked. (2) A new form of carpet construction. Multineedled machines sew pile yarns onto a wide fabric. A jute or canvas backing and latex are used.

Tulbagh chair A caned seat unique to South Africa and based on a QUEEN ANNE chair and a Dutch BOX CHAIR; often with a vase-shaped splat and box stretchers.

Tulbagh chair

tulip chair An influential seat by Eero Saarinen. A curved, molded plastic form continuous with a pedestal base and with an affixed upholstered seat pad. Similar to a COGNAC CHAIR.

tulip wood A yellowish natural material with red and purple stripes from a small Brazilian tree, a member of the rosewood family. Used mainly for inlays and banding. See BOIS (OR BOISE) DE ROSE.

Tunbridge ware A veneer made at Tunbridge Wells, England. It resembled minute mosaic work. Many small rods or dowels of wood were arranged in a design, and they were then glued in place, like pieces of spaghetti. This cluster of rods was then thinly sliced, horizontally, and the design appeared on each fine sectional slice of veneer.

tungsten halogen lamp An incandescent lightbulb that contains the gas form of the reactive nonmetallic elements in addition to a tungsten wire filament. The gas recycles the tungsten (which would ordinarily collect on the bulb wall) back onto the filament. Supplies an almost constant light output throughout the life of the bulb. Emits a slightly whiter light than an incandescent fixture.

tupelo A gumwood of a light gray color that tends to warp unless it is properly dried. Will take a mahogany or walnut stain. Often used for inexpensive furniture, interior trims, and plywood construction. Also called black gum. See *Table 5.*

turkey rocker An overstuffed, liberally tufted easy chair on a spring base, popular at the end of the 19th century. See TUFTING.

Turkey work A Middle Eastern type of fabric or rug, or more frequently, European imitations of it. Worsted yarns were pulled through a coarse, open-textured cloth, then knotted and cut. The patterns were executed in bright colors, and the fabric was used to cover the backs and seats of chairs after the mid 17th century.

Turkish corner An exuberant, overstuffed, overdecorated, overpillowed, and overcanopied area in a late Victorian home. It was a fanciful and idealized vision of the informal, luxurious, exotic East, an already ornate and heavily patterned period. The corner was equipped with a large daybed, sometimes with a canopy, myriad cushions, carved tables and stands, incense burners, vases with peacock feathers, water pipes, pictures, trophies, and an occasional animal skin.

Turkish knot See GHIORDES KNOT.

Turkish rug Hand-knotted floor coverings that are more geometric in character than traditional Persian rug designs, even when floral patterns are used. Muslims use small versions of these as prayer rugs. The rug has a niche or mihrab element included in the overall design that is pointed toward the Islamic holy city of Mecca when the rug is used for prayer.

Turkmen or Turkoman rugs Short, close-pile wool floor coverings made by nomadic tribes of Turkestan in Central Asia. Their dominant color is blood red, combined with cream, black, brown, and blue in overall geometric patterns that vary with the different ethnic groups. Bokhara is the most well-known example; the term is often used inaccurately in the West.

turned (adj.) Constructed with wood pieces that are carved while being rotated, for example on a lathe.

turned chair A JACOBEAN seat based on a medieval triangular stool and rendered elaborate with decoration on the vertical supports and stretchers.

turning An ornamental or structural element of furniture produced by rotating a wood dowel on a lathe and shaping the dowel with cutting tools into a series of nodules, swellings, disks, etc. See SPINDLE.

turnip dome A spherical roof or cupola most often appearing in Russian, Eastern European, Near Eastern, and Islamic architecture and ornaments. It resembles a bulbous inverted turnip, overlaps the turret or drum below, and tapers to a graceful point above. Also called an ONION DOME.

∞turnip foot A 17th-century variation on the ball foot. The general appearance is that of an inverted root vegetable with a flattened end. A collar usually separated the ball from the floor. See BALL FOOT.

turnkey (adj.) Describes the provision of a complete product or service that is ready for immediate use after a specified time. The term derives from a symbolic moment of handing over a key, indicating project readiness and ownership.

turpentine A resinous fluid used as a solvent and dryer in paint mixing.

turquoise (Old French, Turkish) A type of daybed or settee introduced in the Louis XV period based on a Middle Eastern or Persian divan. The piece had a mattress-like cushion, no back, and equally high ends. The daybed was usually placed with the long end against the wall, and bolsters supplied additional comfort. Smaller round bolsters were placed next to the rising end panels. A forerunner of the STUDIO COUCH.

Tuscan A Roman variation of the Doric order. See DORIC ORDER and ETRUSCAN ORDER.

Tuscan

tussah silk Material made from the cocoons of wild silkworms, usually light brown in color. Used for weaving PONGEE, SHIKI, and SHANTUNG. Coarse, strong, slubby, and uneven in texture.

tuxedo sofa A contemporary clean-lined, simple, upholstered seating unit with thin sides that flare out slightly. The upholstered sides are the same height as the back, creating a continuous line. Can be finished with a skirt.

tweed A rough-surfaced material with a homespun effect. The yarn is usually dyed before weaving, and it is often woven in two or more colors to obtain a pattern such as plaid, check, or herringbone.

tweed carpets Floor coverings loomed with shag, looped or twisted yarns in a variety of colors. The surface may be an even texture or a mixture of high and low pile. Such floor textiles are usually recommended where soiling may be a problem, as the mixed colors camouflage stains and dirt.

twig furniture Designed household objects, including seating, made of branches, or dowels carved to resemble branches, popularized with the Adirondack style in the early-20th-century United States.

twill A basic weave, and the fabric produced by this weave. It has a distinct diagonal line because the filling yarn passes over one or more warp yarns and then under two or more. The herringbone is one variation.

twining stem molding A linear decoration that simulates a stylized tendril wound around a plant stalk.

twin-size bed A standard sleeping unit for one person, which is 39 inches wide by 75 inches long (99 cm × 190 cm). Two such beds may be used together with a large headboard to make a unit about the size of a KING-SIZE BED. See also SINGLE BED.

twist carpet A floor covering made of uncut pile. Yarns of different colors are intertwined to form the pile loops.

twisted column A decorative vertical element, structural or decorative, that appears to rotate around its vertical axis. Popular in the French, German, and Italian Renaissance and Baroque periods, and in the 19th century. Also called a wreathed column.

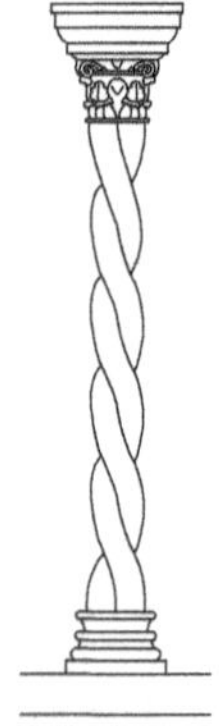
twisted column

twist turning A spiral form used in France and Holland in the late 16th and early 17th centuries. Introduced into England in the mid 17th century, it appeared during the Restoration period as legs, uprights, and so on. See SPIRAL LEG.

two-chairback settee See COURTING CHAIR.

tympanum (1) The (usually) triangular surface of a pediment bounded by the lower molding and the sloping sides, often featuring relief sculpture. (2) Also, a sculpted panel above a door, triangular, round, or rectangular.

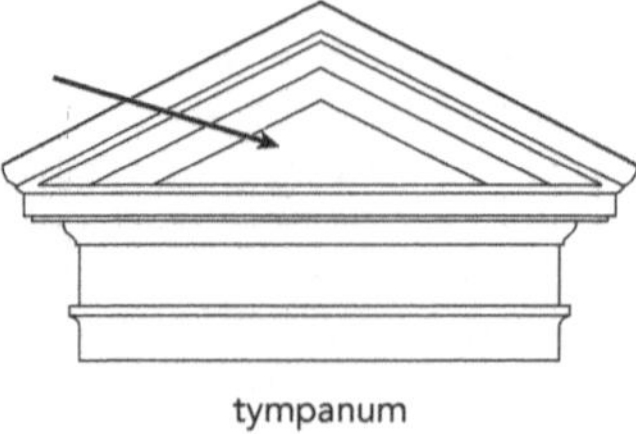
tympanum

UBC Acronym for UNIFORM BUILDING CODE.

UL Acronym for UNDERWRITERS LABORATORIES INC.

ultrasuede A synthetic microfiber fabric made of polyester and used in upholstery and wall panels. The fabric feels like the natural product but with the advantages of washability, durability, and stain resistance. Associated with the styles of the 1970s, particularly the fashion and interior design work of the designer Halston.

ultraviolet (UV) light Invisible electromagnetic radiation in the spectrum between visible violet light and X-rays. About 5 percent of the sun's radiation consists of it. Most spectral energy is absorbed by the Earth's ozone layer; by air impurities such as dust, water, and smoke; and by window glass and clothing. UV light has the ability to kill germs; it is used in healthcare to sterilize rooms, body tissue, blood plasma, and vaccines. Overexposure, however, harms human tissue and textiles.

umbrella setup An architectural firm consisting of architects, engineers, landscape designers, interior designers, and other specialists. The firm is thus able to provide complete design coverage for both the interior and the exterior of a structure.

underbracing The arrangement of stretchers, braces, or spandrels below the horizontal surface of chairs, tables, and chests, used to reinforce and strengthen the units. See STRETCHER.

underdrapery A curtain panel that hangs closer to the window than the outer curtain. Often made of a fabric such as a SHEER that is lighter in weight.

underframe The part of furniture supported by the legs or feet, which carries the superstructure. For example, the boxy skeleton under a tabletop, or the square support under a chair seat, called the seat frame or the seat rails. The structural ensemble may be painted or carved or decorated with an apron or pendants. See APRON, and SKIRT or SKIRTING PIECE.

underglaze color A mineral pigment used for pottery decoration. It is applied before the glazing, and resists the high temperature of the firing process.

underlayment The backing and padding used with a floor covering. See CARPET PADDING.

Underwriters Laboratories Inc. (UL) The UL label on electrical components indicates the approval of the organization, an independent group that tests the safety of electric components.

unhoused The state of having no accommodation or a lack of domestic shelter. The word is a less pejorative alternative to "homeless." It references an insecure housing situation and assumes a societal obligation that everyone has housing. It connotes respect, dignity, and care.

unicorn A single-horned, mythological animal of antiquity that looks like a horse with a long horn protruding from its forehead. Found in numerous applications, from tapestries and other textiles to the decoration on housewares and furniture. Also a popular decorative motif in the Renaissance and neoclassical periods.

Unidure A trademark name for a permanent, wrinkle-resistant finish applied to spun rayon and blended fabrics. The United Piece Dye Works patented it.

Uniform Building Code (UBC) A United States law requiring that certain standards be followed in architectural construction. The UBC includes specifics regarding the use of space, materials, and layout to ensure safety, security, and habitability. For example the, UBC provides guidelines for the use of fire exits and fire-prevention devices, as well as procedures for natural disasters and building egress. The text also requires structural, architectural, and materials documentation.

uninterruptible power supply (UPS) A system designed for continuous operation in the event of a disturbance or failure in the main electrical generating unit.

universal hospital unit A healthcare architectural setup in which an intensive-care patient would not have to move to a different area of the facility once his or her condition improves slightly.

universal design A list of principles written by a group of architects, product designers, engineers, and environmental researchers that is meant to guide and improve the conceptualization of products, environments, and communications. The main principles of the approach include equitable use, flexibility in use, simple and intuitive design, perceptible information, tolerance for error, low physical effort, and appropriate size and space for use by all people. This results in a built environment that accommodates all people.

universal joint A connection that allows one or both of the conjoined units to move in all directions.

universal table An all-purpose work surface that could be used for dining or storing tea, sugar, etc. Usually made of mahogany and equipped with two leaves that slipped under the main table surface. A drawer at one side was fitted with twelve storage bins plus a writing shelf. A Sheraton design of the late 18th century.

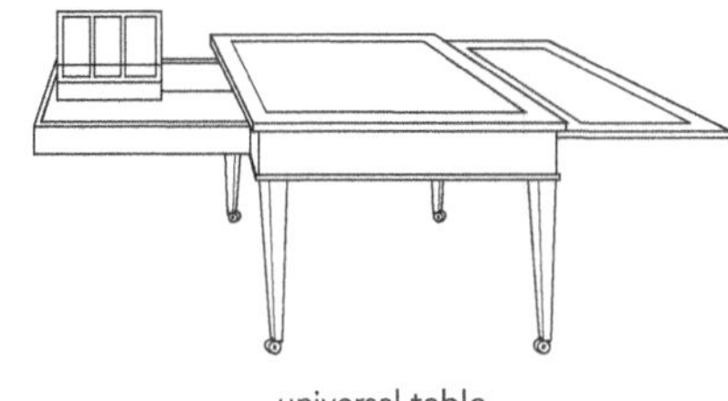

universal table

upcycling A 21st-century term for the utilization of waste in useful products. The initial idea dates from 1963, when the Heineken brewery developed a bottle that was intended to become a construction material after its initial use. See WOBO.

∞upholder An upholsterer. An 18th-century term.

upholstered walls Interior vertical surfaces that are covered first with a soft filler material, and then with a finishing fabric. Sometimes tufted with buttons or marked off into billowing panels or squares. These sound-absorbing vertical planes are also soft and yielding to the touch. Ceilings can be treated similarly.

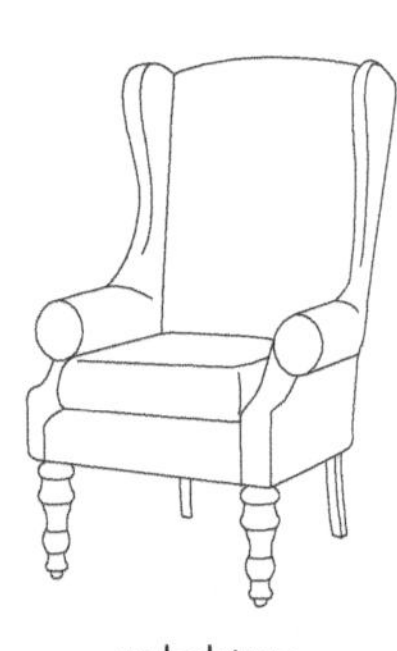

upholstery

upholstery (1) The materials used in stuffing, padding, and covering chairs, sofas, and other pieces. (2) The craft of creating furniture that includes elements of padded textiles.

uplight A light fixture that casts light onto the ceiling, where it is reflected back into the room.

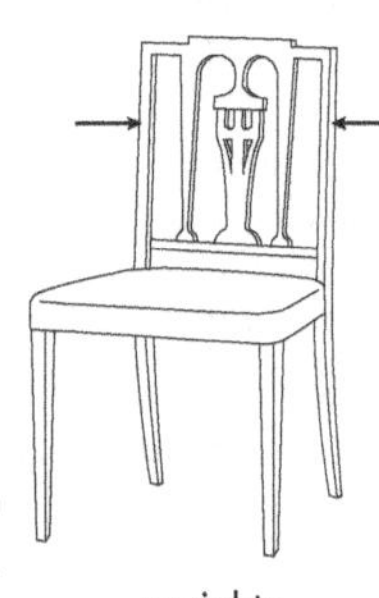

uprights

uprights In chair construction, the outer vertical rails or stiles that extend up from the back legs of the chair and support the chair back. The top rail braces and connects these vertical members. The posts can be turned, straight, or shaped, depending on the period and the style of the furniture.

UPS Acronym for UNINTERRUPTIBLE POWER SUPPLY.

∞Upson board See FIBERBOARD.

∞uraeus A serpent used as the symbol of royalty in ancient Egyptian art and decoration.

urn A large decorative container made of metal, pottery, stone, or other material. In furniture, a large, wooden, vase-like container that was usually set on a pedestal on either side of a side table. Such shapes were used as decorative turnings at the cross-points of stretchers in 16th- and 17th-century furniture designs. An urn was often set on the central pedestal in a swan neck pediment. See KNIFE URNS and VASE.

urn stand A small table designed to hold silver or Sheffield plate containers. It often featured a pullout shelf to hold a teapot or coffeepot. These surface-creating pieces of furniture made their appearance in the 18th century.

urn-shaped splat A wood chair back, cut out and shaped like a vase or other vessel. A popular decorative device in 18th-century English and American furniture, it was sometimes pierced for an openwork or lattice effect.

Utrecht velvet A mohair textile with a pattern created by pressing down some of the pile. The pile that has not been pressed down has the usual plush feel.

UV Acronym for ULTRAVIOLET

V-match Veneer that is cut and butted together to form a decorative pattern in which the wood grain radiates from a center line to form a pattern resembling a series of chevrons. Also called an angle match.

∞**vaisselier** (French) An 18th-century French dining room cabinet or dresser with shelves. See MÉNAGÈRE.

valance A decorative finishing device over the top portion of draperies. Made of fabric, wood, and other materials, it can be designed to lie over window frames, doorways, or bed draperies. See CANTONNIÈRE, LAMBREQUIN, PELMET, and PENTES.

valance

Valenciennes lace An elaborate bobbin-made material in which the ornaments and fabric are of identical thread, similar in technique to those used to make CLUNY LACE, DUCHESSE LACE, and CHANTILLY LACE.

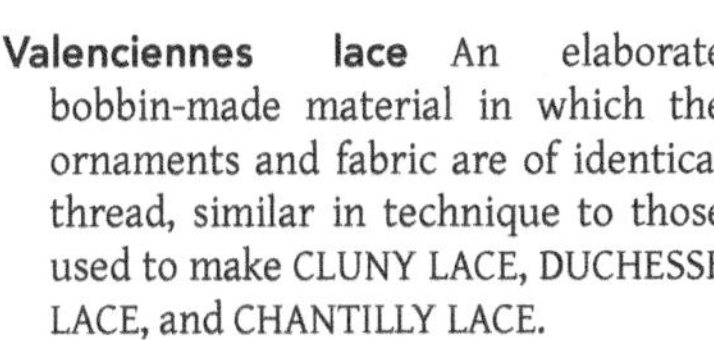

Valois period The Renaissance era in French architecture, which dates from about 1483 to 1589, during the reigns of Charles VIII, Louis XII, François I, Henri II, Henri III, and Charles IX.

values The gradations of tone from light to dark under the play of light on a solid object.

vane A metal device installed on the highest point of a structure that indicates the wind's direction. It moves freely on its axis, around which it is balanced. Both halves weigh the same, although have different surface areas. The smaller surface area, an arrow, points into the wind. Common motifs are a rooster, hence the alternate name weathercock. Also a goose, witch, fox or santa. Now a collectible.

vane

vanity A modern dressing surface that surrounds the washbasin in a bathroom. Usually made of marble, tile, formica, or other washable material. Drawers are sometimes set into the apron, and a cabinet hides the plumbing under the sink. Also called a vanitory.

vargueño A Spanish cabinet and desk with a drop-lid. It was introduced during the Plateresco period of the Spanish Renaissance, during the 16th and 17th centuries. Movable pieces reveal an interior that is divided into drawers and compartments. The storage and work surface unit was originally made of walnut and later mahogany. The front was elaborately inlaid with pierced metal mounts, velvet panels, NACRÉ, and other materials. The hardware was large, elaborate, and gilded. Many come from Spain's Islamic period.

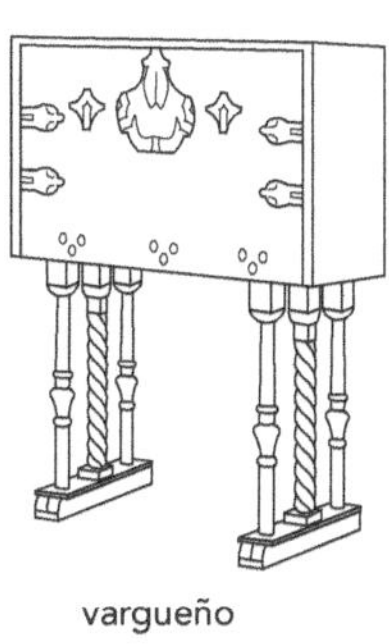
vargueño

varnish A finishing coat made of resinous matter in oil or alcohol, which is applied to woodwork to create a glossy, transparent, washable surface. In the 16th and 17th centuries, the oil-based finish sank into the wood. By the early 18th century, lac dissolved in wine spirits was used. *Vernis Martin* became a popular finish in the mid 18th century. See LACQUER and SHELLAC. Also see *Table 4.*

vase A decorative vessel or urn. A shaped container made of precious metals, bronze, brass, porcelain, china, or glass. A popular decorative motif in the 18th century.

vase-shaped splat An urn-shaped central element of a chair back, under the top rail, and between the uprights. Similar to the FIDDLEBACK CHAIR.

∞**vaisselier** See MÉNAGÈRE.

vat-dyed (adj.) Fibers that are infused with pigment using a process that produces a permanent, fast color. Each fiber of the fabric has the colors of the container chemically induced and fixed into it. The fastness varies from color to color. Used mainly for cotton, rayon, linen, and some blended fibers. (Not used for silks, vinyls, nylons, polyesters, or glass fibers.) Also called SOLUTION-DYED.

vault (1) A roof constructed according to the principle of the arch. (2) An underground room or burial place.

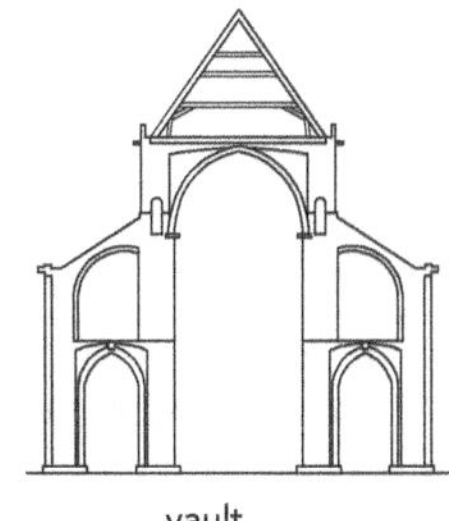
vault

Vauxhall glassworks A noted mirror and vitreous products factory that the Duke of Buckingham established near London, England, in 1670.

veduta (Italian, view) A painting or drawing of a place, town, or vista. Giambattista Piranesi was an outstanding member of the *vedutisti*, and his "Views of Rome" prints are a part of many commercial and residential interiors.

∞**veilleuse** (French, watcher; one who sits up to watch or look after) A chaise longue of the Louis XV period in which typically the side intended to support the user's head is higher than the other side.

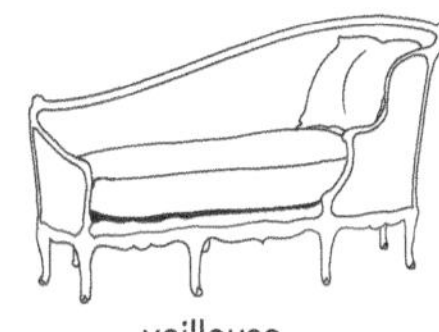
veilleuse

Velcro The trademarked name of the product invented by Velcro Industries: a fabric fastener that, like the zipper, connects two pieces. Two strips of specially devised fabric, one with tiny hooks and the other with loose loops, are sewn on the pieces to be connected. The two strips adhere to each other; to open the fabric piece, one pulls the strips apart. An example of BIOMIMICRY.

vellum (1) An ancient writing material made from a calf, lamb, or kid skin that has been treated with lime. (2) Today, a translucent parchment-like paper. See PARCHMENT.

Velon (1) A trademarked name for extruded plastic filaments used in making fabrics and webbing. The trademark was held by the Firestone Plastics Company. (2) Also, a plastic upholstery fabric.

velour (French, a velvet fabric) A soft, closely woven, smooth fabric with a short, thick pile. See *Table 1.*

velours d'Utrecht A 17th-century wool velvet produced in the city in Holland. See MOQUETTE and UTRECHT VELVET.

velours de Gênes A silk velvet made originally in Genoa, Italy, usually with an allover pattern. See GENOA VELVET.

velure An 18th-century American word for velour. See VELOUR.

velvet A fabric with a dense, short pile, less than ⅛ inch thick on the top surface, and a plain back. True velvet is made with two warps, one of which loops over a wire, which later cuts the loop into pile. Velvet can be plain, striped, or figured and can be made of wool, silk, cotton, nylon, or other fabric. Used for upholstery and drapery.

velvet, brocaded Velvet on which a pattern is created by removing part of the pile by means of heat and chemicals. Also called FAÇONNÉ.

velvet, chiffon A lightweight, soft velvet with a cut pile. It has a closer weave than transparent velvet.

velvet, giselé A version of the textile with a pattern created by the contrast between the cut and uncut loops.

velvet, Lyons A stiff, erect, thick-pile material usually made of silk, with a cotton or rayon back.

velvet, nacré A velvet that has one color for the backing and another for the pile, thus creating an iridescent, pearly appearance.

velvet, transparent Lightweight, soft, draping velvet made of silk or rayon, with rayon pile.

velvet carpet Plain velvet is a cut pile fabric woven on the velvet loom, the simplest form of carpet construction. Figured velvet is a cut pile fabric woven with wool or worsted surface yarns. All the pattern colors are drum-dyed before being placed on the loom. Bladed pile wires form the surface texture as in both plain and figure velvet. See *Table 1.*

velveteen Cotton velvet, woven like a sateen with filling threads floated loosely over the warp, which are then sheared to produce a fine, close pile. Used for upholstery and drapery.

veneer Thin slices of wood between $\frac{1}{16}$ inch and $\frac{1}{32}$ inch thick that are made by cutting through the cross-section or the vertical section of a FLITCH. These thin, continuous slices are almost identical in grain and figure and can be matched in various ways to create interesting surface patterns. Veneers are applied over a sturdy backing of a coarser, less decorative wood. The effect of veneered furniture or walls is that the area has been constructed completely of a fine-grained or attractively colored wood. During the 16th century in southern Europe, veneers were cut by hand to $\frac{1}{10}$ inch thickness. In the reign of William and Mary (late-17th-century England), burr walnut veneers were applied over oak. Chippendale, Sheraton, and Hepplewhite used mahogany and satinwoods as veneers, as well as in solid construction.

veneer matching See BOOK-MATCH VENEERING; BOX MATCH; CENTER MATCH; CHECKERBOARD MATCH; DIAMOND-MATCH VENEER; FOUR-WAY CENTER AND BUTT MATCH; HERRINGBONE MATCH; RANDOM MATCH; REVERSE BOX MATCH; REVERSE DIAMOND MATCH; SLIP MATCH; VERTICAL BUTT AND HORIZONTAL BOOK-LEAF MATCH; and V-MATCH.

veneering The method of gluing thin slices of wood over less expensive woods or other core products.

Venetian console (adj.) Describes the arts, architecture, and crafts of Venice, Italy, a seaport city, and once a major trading center. In the Byzantine and early Renaissance periods, art and artifacts demonstrated a blend of European and Eastern motifs. The Italian Rococo style is sometimes referred to as Venetian Rococo because of its flamboyant, fanciful, and ornamental quality; the furniture was elaborately painted, japanned, and gilded, and the exaggerated BOMBÉ was prevalent.

Venetian console

Venetian blind Window covering or shade consisting of horizontal wooden or metal slats strung together on tapes. May be raised or lowered as a unit, and the slats can be angled up or down to ensure privacy, at the same time allowing air and some light to seep in.

Venetian chinoiserie The Rococo furniture of the 18th century that was produced in Venice, Italy. Based on the Louis XV style, citizens of the port city added embossed textures and satin lacquers inspired by Asian finishes. Although chinoiserie was adopted throughout Europe, many of the finest Asian-inspired designs were created in Venice because it had direct trade with the Far East. See CHINOISERIE and SILK ROAD.

Venetian door An opening and enclosure with glass side panels incorporated into the frame.

Venetian furniture Late Italian Renaissance household objects, ornate and extravagantly curved and carved. It is a blend of styles: the grandiose Baroque, the whimsical Rococo, and the exotic Far East. See VENETIAN and VENETIAN CHINOISERIE.

Venetian glass A type of vitreous ware originating from Venice, Italy. The glass is fine and usually colored or ornamented.

Venetian gold or gilt A finish developed by early Italian Renaissance craftsmen of Venice and Florence. Gold leaf was applied over a red paint preparation and then burnished. Some of the undercoat came through and added brilliance and richness to the finish.

Venetian lace Needlepoint lace. The pattern is embroidered over base threads.

Venetian shu'iter A louvered shutter.

Venetian window A three-panel glazed opening with a large central panel and two narrow side panels.

Venetian window

veranda or verandah A long, covered porch, usually built against one side of a building.

verdigris (1) A grayish, blue-green coating or patina that, over time, forms on copper, brass, and bronze. (2) Also, the color of a finish used for wrought-iron furniture.

verditer paper (French, green of the earth) An 18th-century English wallpaper printed in cool bluish-green colors made from chalk and precipitated copper.

verdure tapestry A leafy tapestry design featuring forests, bushes, trees, and meadows, with only an occasional bird, animal, or human figure.

Verel A once-trademarked name for a modified acrylic fiber that has a soft hand, drapes well, and resists abrasion and the effects of sunlight. Used in carpeting, for fire-resistant drapery, and for synthetic fur fabrics. It is similar to DYNEL.

vermeil (French) (1) Silver gilt, or other gilded metal. (2) Also a vermilion-red color.

vermicular Stonework that is marked with squiggly, worm-like lines. An irregular textured design carved on the facing material of Renaissance buildings.

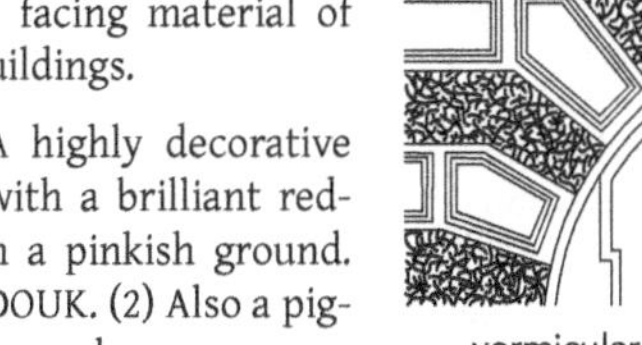
vermicular

vermilion (1) A highly decorative Indian wood with a brilliant red-orange hue on a pinkish ground. Also called PADOUK. (2) Also a pigment of the same color.

vernacular (A term from linguistics) In design, indigenous or humble buildings, and basic objects that are not consciously designed.

vernis de Gobelins A Japanese-inspired lacquer process introduced into France and the GOBELINS factory by GERHARD DAGLY in the late 17th century. See *Designers and Architects.*

vernis Martin A lacquer finish invented by the Martin brothers during the reign of Louis XV. It was an imitation of Chinese and Japanese relief work. See MARTIN BROTHERS in *Designers and Architects.*

verre églomisé (French, gilded glass) A process in which the back side of glass is gilded with gold or metal leaf. See SUWER.

verrier A glassware cabinet or a glass showcase with shelves. See VITRINE.

vertical blinds Non-textile window covering made of lightweight metal, vinyl, fabric, or wood slats. Used as window coverings or as dividers, or screens, or interior separators. Also called BOSTON BLINDS.

vertical butt and horizontal book-leaf match A veneer pattern in which small pieces of veneer (cut from a small log) are matched in two directions: vertically and horizontally. The pattern is a series of rectangles that create a butt design vertically and also form a book-leaf match horizontally.

vertical file The standard office storage device cabinet in which papers and records are arranged from front to back. Letter-size files are 15 inches wide, and legal-size files are 18 inches wide. A vertical file may be two, three, four, or five drawers high.

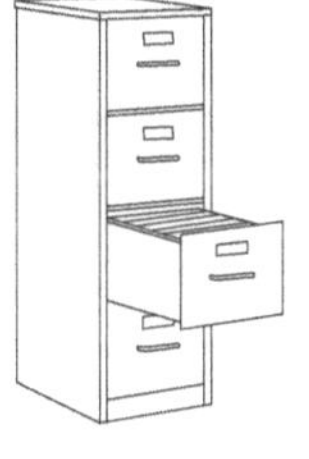
vertical file

vestal lamp A mid- to late-19th-century paraffin light fixture in the shape of an antique oil lamp set on a base and stand. The burner was raised above the fuel supply and covered with a chimney and a glass shade. It resembles a STUDENT LAMP.

vestibule An entrance hall or waiting room.

vibe (1) The character or mood of a designed space; how it makes one feel, related to one's personal associations with the design. (2) In advertising, a vernacular term that describes a branded environment; what a design communicates to its viewers.

Vicrtex Trademark for electronically fused vinyl sheeting for upholstery or wall covering, initially produced by L.E. Carpenter and Co.

Victorian Pertaining to the reign of Queen Victoria of England, from 1837 to 1901. Generally refers to florid decoration, historical revivals, eclecticism, and a culture of moral rectitude. See VICTORIAN CLASSICISM, VICTORIAN JACOBEAN, VICTORIAN RENAISSANCE, and VICTORIAN ROCOCO.

Victorian Classicism A revitalization of Louis XVI designs in the 1860s. The furniture had simple, delicate lines with restrained decorations.

Victorian Jacobean A minor furniture style of the 1870s characterized by strapwork, interlaced flat bands of carving, and the use of myriad small spindle turnings.

Victorian Renaissance The period from 1850 to about 1860, when the Italian Renaissance became the source of inspiration for eclectic Victorian furniture makers, designers, and architects. The pieces were massive and heavy in scale, with moldings, carvings, and marble lavishly applied. The classical motifs used were ponderous and richly embellished.

Victorian Rococo A popular furniture style from 1840 to 1860, also called the French style because it was adapted from the Louis XV Rococo era. The designs were full of curves, scrolls, and heavy carvings of birds, flowers, and fruits, often executed in rosewood, mahogany, and black walnut. JOHN HENRY BELTER of New York is the most famous American designer of this style. Not an authentic revival of Rococo forms. See *Designers and Architects.*

vieil (French, old or old-fashioned) The name of a silk brocade.

vignettes (French, small vines) (1) In Gothic ornament, a leaf and tendril decoration. (2) Also an ornamental motif, pattern, or design that is centered on a large field, and not confined by a border or edge. The design fades subtly into the background, and the composition has an unfinished quality.

vignettes

villa A country estate with a main house, outbuildings, and gardens.

vine A popular motif in classical and medieval ornament. In antiquity, it was associated with grapes, wine, and the god Bacchus. Ivy leaves were often combined with the vine. In the Middle Ages, the vine was used in ecclesiastical art, combined with wheat ears, to symbolize the blood and body of Christ.

vinette A continuous ornamental band of leaves and tendrils. See TRAYLE.

vinette

vinyl A synthetic compound used to make plastic material for a variety of interior finishes.

∞vinyl asbestos tile A sheet of flooring material similar to asphalt. Had excellent wearing qualities and resisted grease, oil, and acids. Vinyl asbestos was less expensive than homogeneous vinyl but not as resilient or as quiet. Since the identification of its principal material as a carcinogen, its only role in most projects is its expensive removal.

vinyl fabrics Textiles fused or coated with vinyl plastic. In the coated types, the vinyl is opaque, and the surface is printed or embossed.

vinyl tile A nonporous, homogeneous flooring material resembling rubber. It has excellent wear resistance and is comfortable to walk on. Resists grease, moisture, and mild acids, and is very resilient. Laminated, or backed, vinyl is not as expensive as homogeneous vinyl, and, though it has many of the advantages of homogeneous vinyl, it does not wear as well. Produced in a range of colors and in a wide selection of patterns, textures, gauges, and sizes.

violet wood See AMARANTH.

∞virginal A spinet. A musical instrument popular with young maidens in the 16th and 17th centuries, hence the name. See HARPSICHORD and SPINET.

virtual construction management (VCM) (1) The use of building information modeling (BIM) to manage a project digitally. (2) Also, a virtual construction team (VCT); a group of designers and architects who manage a building project primarily through the use of computers. See BUILDING INFORMATION MODELING.

∞vis-à-vis A 19th-century, S-shaped two-seater. The two seats faced in opposite directions, but were attached in the middle. Also called a DOS-À-DOS, SIAMOISE, and TÊTE-À-TÊTE.

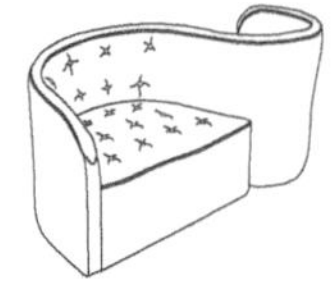
vis-à-vis

viscose The gluey, organic liquid that is used to make rayon and cellophane, resulting in a material with a soft, smooth touch. Also known as RAYON.

∞vis, or vise, or vice (archaic) A spiral staircase around a column called a NEWEL OR NEWEL POST. The staircase was usually constructed of stone.

vitreous (adj.) Like glass in appearance or physical properties; having the qualities of glass, e.g. transparent, hard, shiny.

vitreous enamel A shiny porcelain treatment of glass powder fused on metal.

vitrified Hardened clay products, such as tiles, that have been sufficiently fired so that all grains are fused and pores are closed. The end product is impervious to water.

vitrine A curio cabinet with a glass front, used for the display of china, glass, or objets d'art. See VERRIER.

∞Vitruvian scroll A series of undulating, wavelike rolled elements. A continuous band of horizontal scrolls. It was named after Vitruvius, the Roman architect and author.

∞voider An 18th-century English tray used for carrying dishes and utensils to and from the table.

voile A light, transparent fabric of plain weave, usually piece-dyed and then striped or figured. Can be made of cotton, wool, silk, or synthetic fibers. See SHEER.

volatile organic compounds (VOCs) An amalgamated substance in which naturally occurring elements have significant vapor pressures. VOCs can negatively affect human health and the environment.

volute (1) A scroll line or spiral form found on Ionic and Corinthian capitals. (2) A flat or rising spiral in furniture decoration, used at the ends of furniture legs and elsewhere. See EARPIECE and SCROLL.

Voronoi diagram In mathematics, a graphic model that is a special kind of decomposition of metric space determined by multiple distances to a specified discrete set of objects in space. This results in interior panels and textiles with innumerable variations of oval forms.

volute

voussoir A wedge-shaped block used in arch construction. The central block is the keystone, and it is marked *clef* in the design diagram. The lintel in the diagram is marked *linteau*.

voxel Element of computer-based modeling and graphic simulation. It is a value on a grid in 3D space. As an analogy, voxel is to 3D as pixels is to 2D. Where a pixel has x and y axes, a voxel has x, y and z axes. It is a unit of digital graphic information that designates a point in 3D space; each coordinate can indicate position, color, and density. Any discrete elements of the latest generation of interior design representation or rendering.

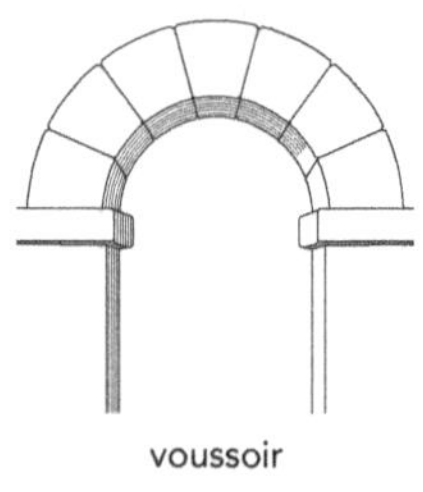
voussoir

∞voyelle A cockfight chair of the Louis XVI period. One straddles the chair, facing the chair back, and rests one's arms on the upholstered, shelflike top rail. See COCKFIGHT CHAIR.

∞voyeuse See COCKFIGHT CHAIR and VOYELLE.

Vycron Trademarked name for a dacronike fiber.

wabi sabi (Japanese) A lifestyle and aesthetic philosophy of accepting imperfection for a "perfectly imperfect life." One embraces life's unpredictability and thereby achieves peace and mindfulness. Aesthetically rustic and simple, with an understated elegance. Followers take a less-is-more position that aligns with minimalism and see beauty in everyday life as an alternative to the relentless pursuit of perfection. An example in interior design is a fired ceramic piece whose glaze cracks unevenly. It is not thrown out but admired for its authenticity.

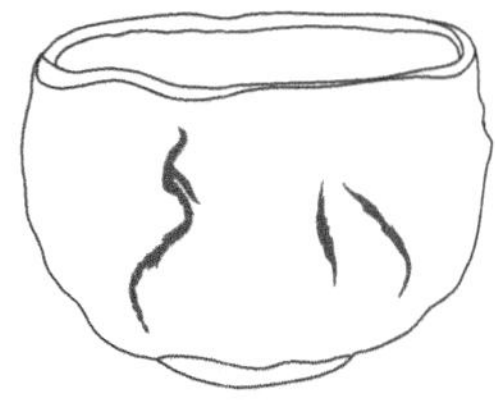
wabi sabi

Wachstuch-Tapete An 18th-century German variation on gilded leather tapestries. A heavy linen or canvas fabric served as the base, and the artwork was done on it in durable, brilliant color. CHINOISERIE was a popular motif of the elaborate worked textiles. At the end of the 18th century, English designers imitated the technique. It was a forerunner of modern plastic-ground or vinyl-ground wall coverings. See FLOORCLOTH.

wagon vault An architectural semi-cylindrical tubular extrusion of an arch. It resembles the covered transport that was a staple of preindustrial America. See BARREL VAULT.

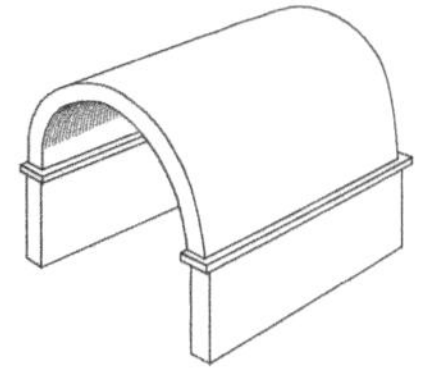
wagon vault

wagon In theater, a movable platform on wheels. Flats and other set pieces can be attached to this rolling device that are easily moved on and off stage during scene changes, rather than requiring several people to manually carry the scenery.

∞**wag-on-wall** A weight-driven clock with exposed weights and pendulum.

wainscot A wooden surfacing applied as paneling to interior walls. May or may not extend up to the ceiling. Made up of stiles and rails which form frames for large or small panels. The name, which predates the English Tudor period, refers to a superior grade of oak, close-grained and without knotholes.

wainscot chair An early-17th-century English and English colonial seat that resembled the similarly named wall. The panel splat was often carved or inlaid, and the seat stood high and required a footstool. It served as a chair of state in the Tudor and Jacobean periods. Also called a PANEL-BACK CHAIR.

wale A row or chain of loops running lengthwise in knitting. Also a ridge formed by a row of tight loops running lengthwise in woven fabric.

wallboard See BUILDING BOARD and GYPSUM BOARD.

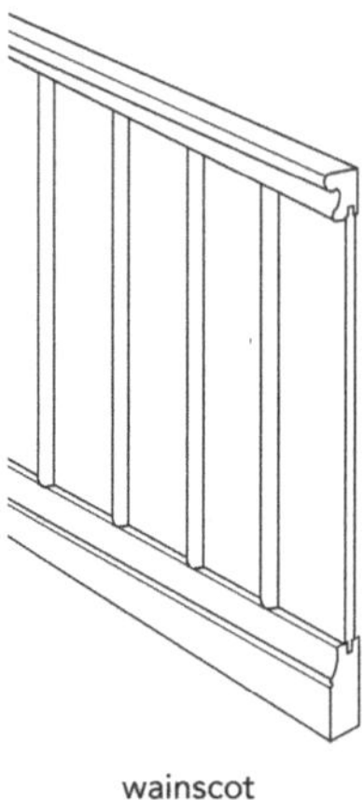
wainscot

wall furniture Architectural designed objects—such as cabinets, cupboards, beds, and seats—that are fashioned as an integral, built-in part of the room, in contrast to portable chairs and small tables. Before the Renaissance period, seats and beds were often stationary units.

wall-hung units Chests, cabinets, and shelves supported from a partition by means of brackets or attached directly to the structure. The brackets insert into continuously slotted upright bars, or standards, bolted into the vertical assembly, thus making the space-containing units adjustable. The pieces do not touch the floor. See FLOATING FURNITURE.

wall mirror See PIER GLASS.

wallpaper Thin sheets of cellulose fibers printed by hand or machine methods in a variety of patterns, textures, and colors and applied to vertical surfaces as a decorative and utilitarian covering. The earliest versions were Asian imports in the 17th century. The applied product today is also printed on vinyl and fabric grounds. See CHINESE WALLPAPER and DOMINO PAPERS. See FLOCKING.

wall system Any device or assembly that is bolted, screwed, or fastened into a vertical surface such as a partition, structural or not, and that does not depend upon legs or a base for support. A WALL-HUNG UNIT or set of units.

wall treatment The decoration applied to a vertical plane, rather than its actual surface. It may consist of a wide variety of objects—paintings, graphics, medallions, tiles, bracket clocks, mirrors, lavabos, and so on—grouped in various arrangements, either symmetrically or asymmetrically. The arrangement may be as simple as a large painting or mural that is papered or painted. In small foyers or entries, the treatment might include a mirror and console shelf with accessories.

wall upholstery Fabric overlain on foam or polyester padding that adhere to a vertical surface. Often tufted.

wall washer A light that bathes a vertical surface, rather than the floor or the general area. Includes angled TRACK LIGHTING and cove lighting. A form of INDIRECT LIGHTING. See COVE LIGHTING.

wall-to-wall carpet Textile that covers the floor completely and hides the horizontal surface. It is secured to the floor with stripping that hooks the material into place.

walnut A light brown wood grown throughout Asia, Africa, Europe, and America. The American variety has a coarser grain than its European cousins. It presents a tremendous range of figures, depending upon the method of slicing. See AGE OF WALNUT.

walnut, black A richly colored wood whose fine-grained quality makes it easy to carve. Takes a high polish. Fairly expensive because of its limited supply. Also called English walnut.

walnut, Circassian A beautiful curly grained brown wood from the Black Sea area. It is relatively expensive and used for furniture and interior paneling.

walnut, oiled The light brown wood when treated with a linseed finish, instead of varnish or lacquer. The rubbed finish gives the wood a smooth, dull satin feel, and it is more resistant to stains and heat than varnish or lacquer.

walnut, Oriental Eucalyptus wood. A pale reddish-yellow, figured wood.

walnut, white See BUTTERNUT.

wardrobe A clothes press and hanging cupboard in one unit. The volume-creating piece evolved from the medieval ward room (a place for hanging garments) to 17th-century hanging cupboards and closets to 18th-century tallboys. Serves as storage in architectural contexts that do not include built-in closets. See ARMOIRE, GARDEROBE, and KAS.

wardrobe

warisan (Indonesian and Malay) Heritage and inheritance. Refers to both individual property and shared cultural legacies.

warp (1) In textiles, the threads that run lengthwise on a loom. The vertical threads of a fabric. See WEAVE. (2) In furniture or woodworking, a distortion in shape. Changes in the moisture content can cause twisting or bulging of a piece of wood.

washi A Japanese paper used for various purposes, including wallpaper and calligraphy. Made from young kozo, mitsumata, and gampi trees. It is a common myth that Japanese calligraphy is done on rice paper.

washstand A furniture support for a basin. Prior to the 18th century, the basin stood on a small table or lowboy. See also BASIN STAND.

water bench See DRY SINK.

watercolor A painting technique that uses colored pigment ground up with water-soluble gums. When the pigment is moistened with the inorganic liquid (H_2O), it yields a transparent stain that is applied in washes to paper. Parts of the ground or paper are usually left unpainted to provide white highlights, and gradations of hue and tone are accomplished by adding washes. Joseph Turner and Alexander Cozens are among the masters of the medium.

washstand

watered silk See MOIRÉ.

Waterford glass Fine Irish vitreous ware and crystal that originates from the port city of the Republic of Ireland.

water leaf An ornamental motif that resembles an elongated appendage of the laurel plant and often enriches a CYMA REVERSA molding. In the 18th century, the motif was usually represented in low-relief carving.

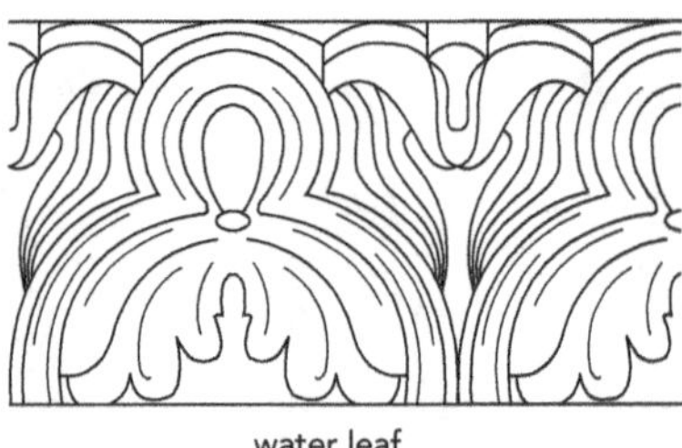
water leaf

wattage A unit of measurement of the electricity a lamp consumes.

wattle and daub Rudimentary construction made from twigs woven between poles and plastered with mud.

wave pattern A continuous horizontal band made up of conventionalized crests, also called a wave scroll. See VITRUVIAN SCROLL.

wayfinding (1) How individuals orient themselves and navigate within a space. (2) A system that relies on the placement of navigational tools, such as landmarks, signs, and descriptors. A feature of many projects but essential in hospitals and airports.

WBS Acronym for WELL BUILDING STANDARDS.

weather boarding Overlapping horizontal wood planks that are placed over the framework of a building. An exterior wall-facing technique. Also made from artificial materials including vinyl, aluminum, and fibrous cement.

weave (verb) To create fabric by interlacing warp (lengthwise) threads with weft, or filler (horizontal), threads at right angles to each other. Different patterns and textures result depending on the type of loom, the weaving pattern, and the yarns used.

webbing Strips of tightly woven burlap used in upholstery construction as a reinforcement and support for springs and cushions. The strips can also be made of linen, plastic, or nylon. In skeletal-type seats of inexpensive lawn or beach furniture, the webbing itself forms the finished seat or back rest.

web foot A heavy, clumsy base of a leg similar to the CLOVEN foot, club foot, and hoof foot. Sometimes used as a termination to a Queen Anne CABRIOLE LEG.

wedding chest See CASSONE and CEDAR CHEST.

weft The threads that run across the loom from selvage to selvage. These are woven in and out among the warp threads. Such threads are also called the fillers, or the woof. See FILLING.

Weldwood Flexwood A trademark of the United States Plywood Corporation for a wide selection of wood veneers on cloth backing, used as wall covering. Adaptable to curved and straight surfaces and applied like wallpaper. Installed, it resembles wood paneling.

well building standards (WBS) A set of performance-based quality assurance guidelines related to the health of a space's users, overseen by the International Well Building Institute (IWBI). Collectively they intend to measure, certify, and monitor aspects of the built environment. The concern is for the health and well-being of the people who use a building or interior space. Underlying the standards are seven focus areas: air, water, food, light, fitness, comfort, and mind. The guidelines are intended to foster healthier buildings, inside and out.

wellness A broad term related to healthcare that moves beyond a narrowly defined vision of medical health (with its focus on disease-free bodies) to a comprehensive attitude toward beneficial environments. Fundamental to this approach is that an individual's relationship to buildings and communities is fulfilling, promotes change and growth, and is in spiritual harmony with the environment. Attention to function and aesthetics is a given, but design attuned to wellness leverages a space to increase occupant comfort by being psychologically uplifting.

Welsh dresser A side table with cupboards and drawers, and with a POT BOARD below and shelves above. Popular in 17th-century England and based on the 16th-century French DRESSOIR DE SALLE À MANGER and the English TRI-DARN. See DUTCH DRESSER.

welting A strip sewn between two pieces of upholstery fabric to give a finished appearance to the seam. Usually made by covering a cord with a tube of fabric and sewing it into the seams so that the stuffed tube appears on the right side between the two joined pieces. Also called PIPING.

wenge A type of wood typically used for parquet flooring.

whatnot An ornamental shelf unit used to display bric-à-brac and objets d'art, particularly in the Victorian era. Sometimes designed to fit into the corner of a room. See CURIO CABINET and ENCOIGNURE.

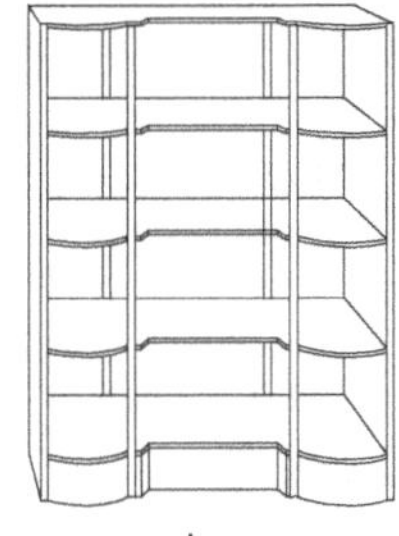
whatnot

wheat ear A decorative, carved, painted, or inlaid motif on Hepplewhite designs that resembles the spike of the grain of the edible cereal grass.

wheel-back chair A seat in which the back resembles the movable circular object with spokes radiating from a central BOSS, PATERA, or PLAQUE. Sometimes an oval replaced the central circle. Characteristic of the Adam brothers' 18th-century school.

wheel window A large circular wall opening with TRACERY radiating from the center. Similar to a rose window, with less pronounced spokes. A Gothic design. See ROSE WINDOW.

wheel window

whiplash line The typical curved line of the Art Nouveau period. A slow, lazy S that sinuously curves back on itself and resembles the snap curve of the device used for flogging and beating.

∞white lead A heavy, non-water-soluble substance formerly used as a base in house paint when mixed with linseed oil. No longer used because it is toxic. See BLANC DE PLOMB.

white noise A non-homogeneous mixture of sound waves covering a wide frequency range that softens or masks unwanted noise pollution (such as trains or snoring sleeping partners) during sleep and other times in which quiet is preferred.

whitewash An unpigmented fluid used to cover exterior structures such as walls, fences, and stables. It is usually impermanent and inexpensive and varies in composition, generally consisting of lime, flour, salt, glue, whiting, and water or sometimes soap. Occasionally used as calcimine for interiors by mixing with size and adding color.

Whitewood Refers to yellow poplar and cottonwood. It has a uniform, uninteresting grain and is used for the interior parts of furniture and as the core for veneer work. Soft, easy to work, and excellent for painted and lacquered finishes.

whorl A scroll or spiral effect on the feet or top rails of furniture.

wicker Small twigs or flexible strips of wood that are woven to become chairs, tables, screens, and baskets. See RATTAN.

Wiener Werkstätte (German, Vienna's Workshops) A community of artists, architects, and designers. Founded in 1903 by JOSEF HOFFMANN and KOLOMAN MOSER, it served as an outlet for graduates of Austria's Kunstgewerbeschule, or arts and crafts school. An offshoot of the Vienna SECESSIONISTS, its focus was the creation of art forms for daily life, such as jewelry, fabrics, furniture, ceramics, and other items. Products were marked by simple shapes, geometric patterns, and minimal decoration. See *Designers and Architects*.

wig stand A 17th- and 18th-century tripod table fitted with a small basin and drawers that held hair powder and a form to hold a headdress. Also called a demoiselle.

wild wall A vertical surface in a film set that can be removed in its entirety. When in place, it blocks undesired views and makes filming possible.

William and Mary period The period during which King William III and Queen Mary II ruled England, Scotland, and Ireland (1689–1702). Also called Early Queen Anne. Artisans introduced Dutch (William was a Dutch prince), Spanish, and Oriental motifs into English design. The furniture market welcomed French refugee artisans led by DANIEL MAROT, chief designer to the king. This conglomeration gave rise to a distinctly English school of furniture that influenced English colonies around the globe. See *Designers and Architects*.

William and Mary highboy

willow brasses Furniture hardware with plates that have scrolled outlines. An 18th-century decorative motif.

willow pattern A decorative transfer-print pattern for whiteware (the affordable version of china) that was widely used in the 1800s. The surface ornamentation typically depicted Chinese scenes in cobalt blue ink, and red and purple inks were also available.

willow pattern

Wilton carpet A pile floor covering woven on the Wilton loom, which is controlled by a jacquard pattern device. The loom draws up all yarns of a single color at a time, while the pile and the other colors remain hidden. The pile may be cut or uncut, or a combination of the two, and thus can accommodate a variety of textures. Wool Wiltons show excellent wear under severe conditions and have a sturdy foundation construction. See WIRES.

winder In staircase construction, a tapered step used at the angle where a stairway makes a turn but has no landing.

winding staircase A vertical circulation element that spirals around a

winding staircase

central shaft as it rises from one level to the next. Also called a SPIRAL STAIRCASE.

∞**window breast** In Gothic architecture, a thin, screen below a wall opening. The MULLIONS of the CLERESTORY window may be carried by this screen, and the screen itself may be decorated with a BLIND ARCADE. See SPANDREL WALL.

window frame The trim or jamb around an opening, often ornamental.

window mantel A cornice of wood and fabric trim set over a wall opening as a finishing piece for draperies or curtains. See CORNICE and LAMBREQUIN.

window seat (1) A small upholstered stool or bench made to fit into a recess or alcove that has a wall opening. (2) A built-in bench in a BAY WINDOW, BOW WINDOW, or window ALCOVE. The unit usually features pillows, and the top sometimes provides access to storage space underneath.

window shade A covering, usually made of heavy fabric, placed between the glass and the curtain. The fabric attaches to a roller with an internal spring mechanism. The roller is fixed to the window frame at the top. A pull on the cord unrolls the shade and covers all or part of the window. A quick tug at the cord causes the fabric to roll back up again onto the roller. See AUSTRIAN SHADE CLOTH and HOLLAND SHADE CLOTH.

window stool A Hepplewhite term for an upholstered settee or bench made to fit in an exterior wall recess. See WINDOW SEAT.

Windsor chair A domestic seat introduced in the 18th century in England. The back is made of vertical rods that create a fiddle-string or stick-back appearance. The legs, originally CABRIOLE, were later turned. The arms and rail connected in a continuous hoop. Developed during the reign of Queen Anne. The spindles and back were turned and cut originally near Windsor, England, hence the name. See COMB BACK, FIDDLE-STRING BACK, and WINDSOR CHAIR, AMERICAN.

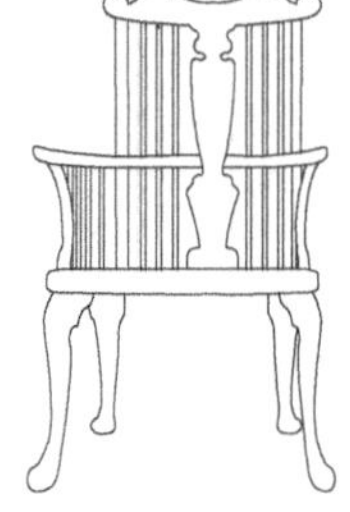
Windsor chair

Windsor chair, American Several versions of the seat were produced in the 18th and 19th centuries in America, with reproductions still made today. Early variations were light, graceful, and without the wide splat. Some Pennsylvania designs had ball feet. The variations are designated by the type of back: bow or loop back, fanback, low-back, and comb back. Some had a writing arm, and some had bamboo turnings. See BOW BACK, COMB BACK, HOOP-BACK CHAIR, and LOW-BACK CHAIR.

wine cooler A small, metal-lined stand designed to keep bottles chilled during a dinner. See CELLARETTE and SARCOPHAGUS.

wine cooler

wine table A horseshoe-shaped surface-creating piece of furniture designed to stand in front of a fireplace, with a curtain across the open end that faced the fire. People sat around the convex end of the table. A small decanter holder on a pivoting arm was attached to the curtain support so that the bottle could be reached from all parts of the horseshoe. See HORSESHOE TABLE.

∞**wing bookcase** See BLOCK FRONT and BROKEN FRONT.

wing chair A high-backed, upholstered comfortable seat with side wings, or ear pieces, on either side of the back. Originally a mid-17th-century design, it was a forerunner of the 18th-century grandfather chair. Also known as a forty-winks chair, saddle-back chair, GRANDFATHER CHAIR, or SADDLE-CHECK CHAIR.

∞**wing-and-claw foot** A massive carved furniture leg base used on Empire couches and other large pieces. Used in England and America in the early 19th century. Also called a winged paw foot.

wired glass See FIRE-RETARDANT WIRED GLASS.

wires In carpet construction, metal rods that are inserted across the loom at the same time the weft yarn is shuttled across the warp threads. When the filaments are withdrawn, the series of loops that remain form the pile of the carpet. In Wilton carpets, the metallic extrusions have a knife edge that cuts the loops into tufts as the wires withdraw. Wiltons usually have thirteen wires per inch.

WOBO Abbreviation for the Heineken World Bottle design. In an early attempt at sustainability, Alfred Heineken created the "brick that holds beer"—a beverage container that could also serve as a building material after its original use. Heineken's idea was ahead of its time, though unsuccessful in the 1960s.

woodcutting A printing method in which the surface of a block of natural material is gouged out everywhere except for the design that is to be reproduced. The untouched parts are covered with printing ink, and the block is pressed onto a sheet of paper or fabric. The ink prints only the ungouged surface of the block. Thousands of impressions, or STRIKES, are possible. This method was used to print early wallpapers, fabrics, and leather tapestries.

wood engraving A printing method in which a design is cut with a graver or burin (a sharp, pointed tool) on a block of wood, such as boxwood, that has been cut across the grain. The furrowed lines are filled with ink, the block is set against the paper, and pressure is applied. The ink transfers the design of the recessed lines onto the paper. Thomas Berwick popularized the technique in mid-18th-century England.

wood finishes See *Table 4.*

woods See *Table 5.*

woof See WEFT and WEAVE.

wool A natural, crumpled fiber from the hair of sheep and goats. The scaly surface of the fibers makes it possible to create felt. Warm and resilient, the resulting natural textile is used for upholstery, drapery, casement fabrics, and carpets. See *Table 2* and *Table 3.*

woolen yarn In carpets, a sheep filament that is spun from short fibers that are interlocked as much as possible and tightly twisted.

wool suede An all-natural, nonwoven fabric, similar to felt. Used as drapery, upholstery, and wall-covering material. Soil and flame-resistant, with excellent acoustical and insulating properties.

working drawing A carefully detailed scale drawing used in constructing interiors, including millwork, furniture, and other designed objects.

work station An enclosure or compartment made of freestanding furniture, screens, and panels. One unit in an open-office system, appropriate to the specific work that will be performed there, such as a desk with or without a return, a drafting table, a conference table, chairs, files, and storage. May be shared, individual, or collaborative. (A programmer may share a work station with one or more workers; an engineer or draftsperson may have an 8 foot by 8 foot work station furnished with the tables and storage units needed.)

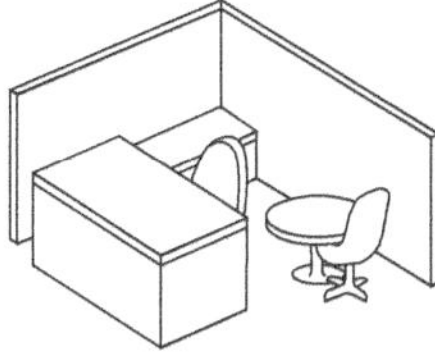

work station

wormholes Tiny, pinhead-sized, crooked pits often found in old pieces of furniture made of soft woods. Usually the depressions are the result of beetles or beetle larvae eating into the wood. In faux antiques, wormholes are artificially created, with buckshot or fine dental drills, and the holes extend straight through the wood rather than being crooked.

wormy chestnut Chestnut wood that is holey and pitted, as though affected by the chestnut blight. The rough, irregular texture and pleasing light brown color make it popular for paneling and provincial tabletops and cabinet panels. Too weak for structural woodwork.

worsted yarn In carpets, a filament spun from the longer types of staple, then carded to lay the fibers as nearly parallel as possible, and finally combed to extract the shortest fibers for use as NOIL. See WILTON CARPET.

Woven Wood A trademarked name for thin slats of natural material interlaced with various fibers into window shades, draperies, and roll-up shades. Some types of fibers used are wool, linen, cotton, nylon, and Lurex. The wood may be left in its natural color or lacquered in multiple colors. The vertical yarns of the composite piece can be manipulated to create exciting patterns.

wreath A closed or partially closed ring of foliage, fruit, or flowers. A classical motif, it was adopted in the Renaissance and neoclassical periods. In the Empire period, it became an important ornamental feature of architecture, interiors, and furniture, often enclosing the initial N, Napoleon's personal badge, or an eagle.

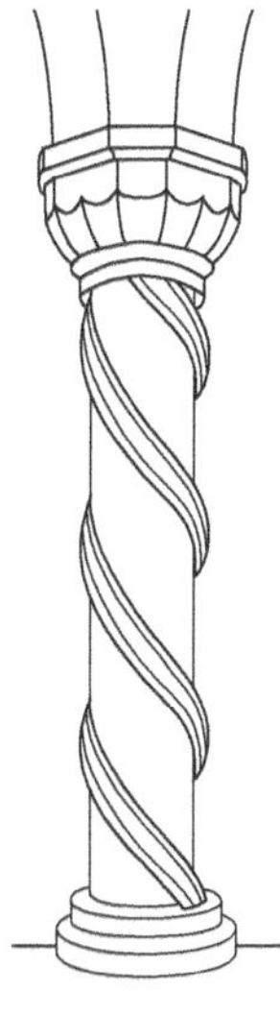

wreathed column

wreathed column See TWISTED COLUMN.

∞**writing armchair** See ROUNDABOUT CHAIR and TABLET CHAIR.

wrought iron Metallic element that has been worked, bent, twisted, and formed. The chemical element with the atomic number 26 contains a low percentage of carbon and is malleable—it can be drawn out and extended by beating. The worked metal can be used for decoration as well as for functional furniture parts. Used for centuries, it was particularly popular in the 19th century.

wunderschrank (German) Teutonic version of the French cabinet de curiosités. A tall, wide storage and display device, with shelves behind glass doors, sometimes with drawers; 16th to 19th centuries. It held notable objects, rare and curious items that prompted conversation and speculation. Containing private collections, it included artworks side by side with *natura*, including seashells, antlers, claws, and fossils, and taxidermized insects. This analog encyclopedia put disparate objects into proximity and encouraged viewers to make comparisons and form analogies.

Wyzenbeek test A method used to measure the abrasion resistance of textile fabrics. Also known as ASTM D 4157, or the oscillatory cylinder method. It is the principal method of determining a textile's durability.

X-frame chair A transportable folding seat, from ancient times to the present. See DANTE CHAIR, DIRECTOR'S CHAIR, SAVONAROLA CHAIR, and X-SHAPED CHAIR.

xenon arc lamp A light fixture that uses the colorless odorless atmospheric gas and requires high amounts of electricity. Created in Germany in the 1940s and favored for its precise focus. It was first used on a wide scale for movie projectors, and it is often used in microscopes and other instruments. The technology to create illumination from the noble gas still exists in some vehicle headlight assemblies.

X-shaped chair A folding sitting device similar to a camp stool or yacht chair, made with or without a back. The design is found in antiquity, also in Italian medieval furniture of the 14th century. High-backed, armed, and heavily sculptured X-shaped chairs were used in the 17th century and in Ming Dynasty China. See CURULE CHAIR, DANTE CHAIR, and SAVONAROLA CHAIR.

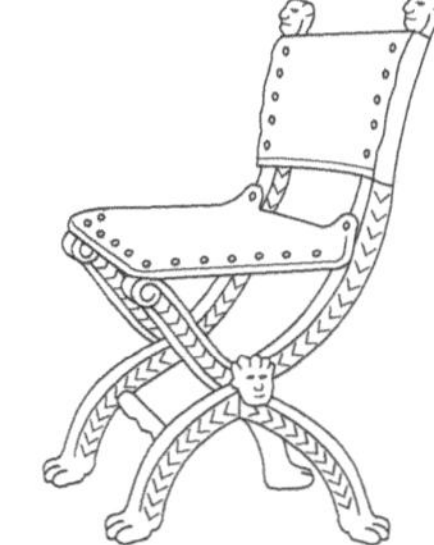

X-shaped chair

X-shaped stretchers Cross stabilizers made flat or curved upward in serpentine form, with knobs or other ornamentation at the intersection. As an assembly, they take the form of the eponymous letter. The structural intersections serve to connect and reinforce the four supports of a chair or piece of furniture. See SALTIRE.

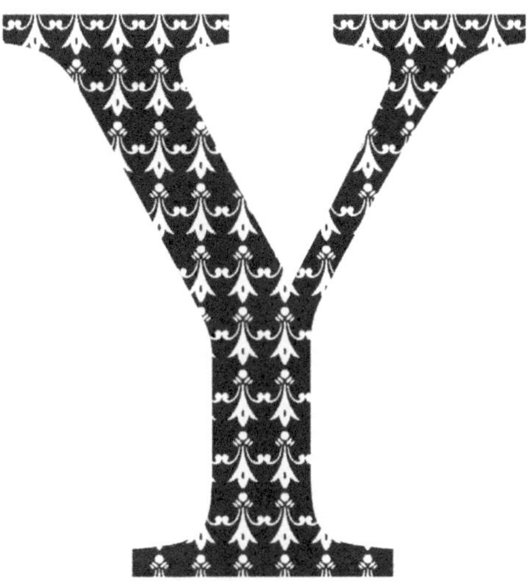

yarn Groupings of natural or manufactured fibers that are combined to form a continuous strand used to produce fabric.

yarn-dyed (adj.) Describes woven strands that are color treated in vats before they are woven into fabric; in contrast to piece-dyed.

yellow wood Light-colored natural material native to South Africa.

yeseria Small, colored, lacelike patterns of plaster relief used in Moorish interiors. See COMPOSITION ORNAMENT.

yew, English A hard, durable, pale reddish-brown wood with a fine, even, lustrous grain, used for furniture in England from the Tudor period to the present day. In the late 17th century, the wood was used for veneer as well as for long CASE CLOCKS.

yoke back

yoke back A crossbar with two reverse image S-shaped curves used as the top rail of Georgian chairs. The silhouette resembles an ox yoke.

∞yoke-front chest An 18th-century space-containing unit with a REVERSE SERPENTINE front. The sides swell out, and the center area is concave. Also referred to as an oxbow chest or U-shaped chest.

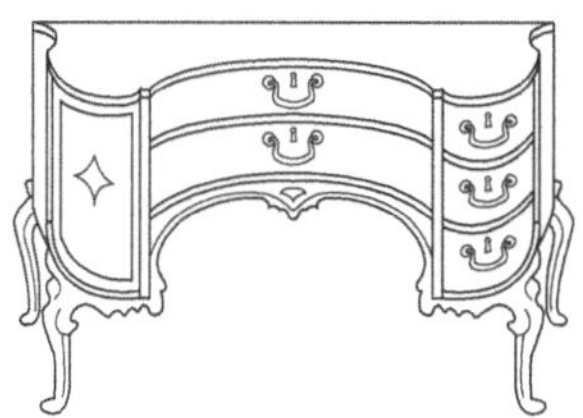
yoke-front chest

∞Yorkshire chair A small Jacobean seat with knob-turned legs and straight uprights ending in inward scrolls. The broad carved top rail and seat below were arched above and crescent cut below.

∞Yorkshire ladder-back chair An 18th-century domestic or provincial chair with a rush seat and a high back usually composed of five slats. The horizontal elements that constituted the back—the ladder—were plain or slightly shaped and curved.

zabuton Square Japanese cushions for sitting, traditionally used when resting on the floor.

zebrawood or zebrano An African natural material with a vigorous, pronounced brown stripe on a light brown ground. Used for ornamental cabinetwork and banding. Heavy and hard, with a coarse texture.

Zefran Trademarked name for an acrylic staple fiber produced by the Dow Chemical Company. A light, bulky fiber with a soft, woolly hand. Similar to ACRILAN and ORION. Stronger and more stable than many acrylics, although it has dyeing problems.

Zeftron Trademarked name for a nylon fiber produced by BASF SE, formerly Badische Anilin-und Soda-Fabrik, or Badische Corporation, in Germany. The nylon fiber is wool-like, soil-resistant, and colorfast. It has permanent shock control and wears well. Used for contract carpets. Originally called Zeflon.

Zelan Trademarked name of a finish applied to fabrics to make them resistant to water-based stains.

zellige or zellij An Islamic art consisting of mosaics made from small ceramic tiles produced in Morocco and elsewhere in North Africa and the Middle East. The mosaics are found on walls, ceilings, fountains, floors, pools, tables, and so on. Their abstract, geometric patterns underscore the belief that cosmic intelligence gives life order, even if people cannot always understand it. The abstract patterns reflect the impulse to understand God's creation through study rather than mimesis.

zellige

Zepel A trademarked name for a special finish applied to fabrics to make them soil-resistant and stain-resistant. See SCOTCHGARD.

zero net energy Applies to a process of manufacturer that consumes no outside power. For example, a building where energy is produced on site, that is, off the power grid, and that reduces the impact on the environment.

Zhuo table A Chinese rectangular surface-producing designed object from the Zhou Dynasty, with legs mitered at the corners rather than inset.

ziggurat A feature of Assyrian and Babylonian architecture. A solid structure made from one platform atop another, with each higher platform built successively smaller. The resulting squat tower has a series of setbacks with ramps connecting one level to the next. Each stage was set back and usually terraced. The exterior surface was often finished in colored glazed tiles.

zigzag A CHEVRON pattern. A Norman motif.

zigzag

Zip-a-Tone Sheets of graphic material used for applying shades of tonal value to line reproductions without the use of a screen, as in a halftone process, usually done by transfer. See BENDAY.

Zip-a-Tone

zoomorphic (adj.) Relating to the form and proportion of animals. Designed elements that use the images, proportions, or functions of animals or animal parts.

zoophorus A sculptured FRIEZE that combines animal and human figures. For example, see the WING-AND-CLAW FOOT and DRAKE FOOT.

appendix 1: designers and architects

It may seem counterintuitive that, in the age of the internet and social media, it can still be difficult to obtain information about the year a person was born, but so it is. When that information was not available, we indicate simply the decade of their birth, e.g. (b. 1950s), or the century in which the designer was first active, e.g. (20th century). We attempted to contact all the living designers in this appendix.

Aalto, Aino (1894–1949)
The first wife of Alvar Aalto, she worked with her husband on both architectural and interiors projects. Initially their furniture designs were simplified versions of neoclassical pieces. They became increasingly modern and experimented with tubular steel, although they are mostly known for their work in bent plywood furniture.

Aalto, Alvar (1898–1976)
Finnish architect and furniture designer. His designs initially grew out of Finnish design traditions, and his projects became more resolutely modern toward the end of the 1920s. He became famous as a furniture designer with his creations in laminated and bent wood. See AALTO STOOL.

Aalto, Elissa (1922–1994)
Alvar Aalto's second wife was also a furniture designer and architect. She worked with her husband to the end of his life, when he concentrated more on architecture and large-scale projects and less on furnishings.

Aarnio, Eero (b. 1932)
A Finnish architect and designer noted for his molded fiberglass furniture including the Cognac Chair and doughnut-shaped Eros Table. His Gyro Chair is a flattened sphere with a shaped depression contoured to hold the human body. His playful forms and use of plastic, velvet, and electronics made his pieces seem tailor-made for the rebellious years of the 1960s.

Abercrombie, Stanley (b. 1935)
An influential design editor, with degrees from MIT and Columbia. He served as editor of *Interiors* and *Interior Design.* A fellow of the American Academy in Rome, he taught at Harvard and wrote a book on the architecture of Gwathmey Siegel.

Adam brothers
John (1721–1792); Robert (1728–1792); James (1732–1794); William (1739–1822). Four Scottish architect-designers who influenced English interiors and furniture design during the middle and latter half of the 18th century. Robert and James were the most famous; they designed in a restrained, classical manner, much influenced by the discoveries at Pompeii and Herculaneum. The Adams used Wedgwood inserts, designed by John Flaxman, as well as other classical motifs in their designs for bas-relief ceilings and friezes. One of their many accomplished projects was Syon House, 1760–1769.

Adler, Jonathan (b. 1966)
Born in New Jersey, Adler was first interested in pottery. He studied art history at Brown University and started a pottery business that branched off into interior design and furniture design. Playful colors and patterns mark his modern luxury style that he describes as "maximalism" and "happy chic." His interior projects include luxury residences and boutiques, with product designs for various companies, including Lacoste and Starbucks. He served as a judge on *Top Design*, a reality television show (2007).

Affleck, Thomas (1740–1795)
One of the Philadelphia school of cabinetmakers of the mid 18th century in America, known for his highboys and lowboys and Georgian and early Chippendale-style chairs.

Aguessy, Kossi (b. 1977)
Aguessy was born in Lomé, Togo, of a Brazilian mother and African father. His multicultural roots greatly influence his design and the way he disregards boundaries in design. He received his design degree at Central St. Martins in London. Aguessy works with several different media and has lived in New York, London, Paris, and Rotterdam.

Alaton, Kalef (1940–1989)
Alaton was a Turkish-born interior designer who studied painting and sculpture at the École des Arts Modernes in Paris and the École des Beaux-Arts in Turkey, with the intention of becoming an artist. He turned to design and began studying with Russian designer Oscar Mourinsky. After relocating to the U.S., he focused on homes for the wealthy and designs for the hospitality sector that often featured custom furniture pieces. Frequently published in *Architectural Digest,* he was also a professional bodybuilder.

Albers, Anni (1899–1994)
Textile designer and printmaker, married to Bauhaus faculty member Josef Albers. As a student, she followed the Bauhaus when it moved from Weimar to Dessau. Her specialty was textiles made of unusual materials, such as cellophane and metallics. With her husband, she fled Germany and taught at Black Mountain College in North Carolina.

Alberti, Leon Battista (1404–1472)
A Florentine architect, sculptor, painter, musician, and poet of the Renaissance. Alberti wrote books on architecture, perspective, and painting that greatly influenced later craftsmen. His *De Re Aedificatoria* was the first book on architecture ever published.

Allen, Cindy (b. 20th cent.)
Allen has served over ten years as editor-in-chief of *Interior Design*. In her leadership position in design journalism, she organizes multiple design events and lectures. The New York School of Interior Design presented her with an honorary doctorate in fine arts in 2010.

Allen, Davis (1917–1999)
One of the first inductees into the Interior Design Hall of Fame in 1985, Allen was a significant figure for establishing the sub-discipline of modern commercial interiors. He worked for forty years for Skidmore, Owings & Merrill and established design standards and practices for the corporate environment. Notable projects include the Istanbul Hilton and the Inland Steel Co. headquarters in Chicago.

Andrei, Anda (b. 20th cent.)
Andrei is a longtime design partner and in-house architect of hospitality designer Ian Schrager. Their collaboration began in 1983 with Schrager's work for the Morgans Hotel Group. She served as design director until 2004, when she followed Schrager to his new company. She has collaborated with Philippe Starck and others. She favors the minimalistic, modern, fashionable style for which the Ian Schrager brand is renowned.

Andric, Nada (b. 1950s)
The Associate Director of interiors at Skidmore, Owings & Merrill, Andric has dedicated her design expertise to large-scale global design projects and earned her place in the Interior Design Hall of Fame. Her most well-known project is the world's tallest building, Burj Kalifa, Dubai.

Arad, Ron (b. 1951)
Arad is an architect, industrial designer, and artist and hails from Tel Aviv, Israel. After attending the Jerusalem Academy of Art and the Architectural Association in London, he founded Ron Arad and Associates along with Caroline Thorman in 1989. Kartell, Vitra, Moroso, Flos, and Alessi are some of the companies Arad has partnered with in the realization of his design work. Major projects include the Bookworm bookshelf in 1994 (Kartell) and the Maserati headquarters showroom in Italy. He has designed everything from perfume bottles to eyewear.

Ashbee, Charles Robert (1863–1942)
An English craftsman-designer and disciple of William Morris and the Arts and Crafts movement. He was a "medievalist" and in 1888 founded the Guild and School of Handicraft; he designed metal objects and furniture. Because of his disavowal of historic forms, he is also considered one of the early supporters of Art Nouveau.

Assadi, Felipe, and Francisca Pulido (b. 1971)
The architects founded their firm, Assadi + Pulido, in 1999. They both studied architecture at Finis Terrae University, graduating in 1996. Their work includes the 20x20 House, Arauco Express, and Teatro del Parque. The firm is based in Santiago, Chile, and the duo works on a variety of project types in Chile and internationally.

Audran, Claude III (1658–1734)
A French painter, decorator, and designer who created wall murals and tapestries, including the Régence decorations for the Luxembourg Palace. He was one of Watteau's instructors.

Aulenti, Gae (1927–2012)
Italian architect and interior and furniture designer. The project that brought her world renown was her refashioning of a Paris train station to become the Musée d'Orsay. She designed furniture for Zanotta and Fontana Arte, multiple showrooms for Fiat, and accessories for Louis Vuitton.

Baillie-Scott, Mackay Hugh (1865–1945)
One of the British designers with one foot in Arts and Crafts and one in Art Nouveau. Liberty's in London, an exclusive retailer, sold his geometrically shaped furniture.

Baldwin, Billy (1903–1983)
Baldwin was born in Baltimore in 1903 and started designing there until Ruby Ross Wood coaxed him to New York City. His designs managed to be timeless and bold, mixing in high-quality pieces with a client's other pieces. His notable works include Cole Porter's Waldorf Towers apartment, Diana Vreeland's "garden in hell," and the Slipper Chair. His design for Harvey Ladew's sitting room featured his favorite aubergine paint color. His clients included Paul Melon and Jacqueline Kennedy Onassis.

Balashova, Galina (b. 1931)
A Russian architect and designer who graduated from the Moscow Architectural Institute. Balashova is most well known for her contributions to the Soviet space program. She designed interior spaces and furniture for spacecraft as well as logos, murals, and memorabilia. She did interiors for the Soyuz and Mir Space Stations and the Buran Shuttle. She was one of a select group of designers who were expert at designing for zero- and low-gravity environments.

Ban, Shigeru (b. 1957)
Born in Tokyo, Ban attended the Southern California Institute of Architecture and Cooper Union before working for famed Japanese architect Arata Isozaki. In 1985 he began a private practice that includes architecture, exhibition design, and industrial design, including furniture, lighting, and product design. Ban is known for his paper tube structures and his experimental methods of using pre-existing materials in new ways. His ecological and low-cost methods led him to be a consultant for the United Nations High Commissioner for Refugees.

Bardi, Lina Bo (1914–1992)
The Italian-born Brazilian architect who in 1953 designed a plastic bowl-shaped chair set into a steel frame. Bardi's Bowl has gone through hundreds of iterations. In her revolutionary steel and glass house in Brazil, cage-like interiors enclosed a garden, and the floors were paved with glass mosaic tiles. She founded and edited the journal *Habitat*.

Barnes, Jhane (b.1954)
A rare figure in design who is active in both fashion and contract interiors. She was a graduate of the Fashion Institute of Technology. She has designed everything from furniture and carpets to clothing and eyeglasses. She did some of her early textile designs on an Atari computer and was one of the first designers to realize that computers had the possibility of larger patterns and complex repeats. She brought corporate textile design, most notably carpet tile and panel fabric, into the digital age.

Barragán, Luis (1902–1988)
A native of Guadalajara, Mexico, Barragán traveled to Europe, where he attended lectures by Le Corbusier and met the intellectual, painter, and architect Ferdinand Bac. He was enamored with the simplicity of Greek villages and found his ideal at the Alhambra, Spain. In his own work, he was renowned for his ability to capture quietude in his landscaping and architecture, through his use of stucco, cobblestones, and unfinished wood. His San Cristobal residence (1967–1968) in Mexico City features modular slabs surrounded by shallow pools of water. Many of his interiors feature the work of furniture designer Clara Porset. In 1979 he was awarded the International Pritzker Architectural Prize.

Barry, Barbara (b.1950s)
A Los Angeles-based interior and furniture designer who founded her own firm, Barbara Barry Incorporated, in 1985. Her style is characterized by simplicity, subdued colors, and restrained patterns contrasting with a 1940s Hollywood glamour and elegance.

Baughman, Milo (1925–2003)
A furniture designer who combined fine craftsmanship and mass production, often using steel and chrome with wood, and producing interesting textures and colors.

Bawa, Geoffrey (1919–2003)
A Sri Lankan architect and decorator, his life's work has two threads: large corporate or governmental commissions and more personal and locally oriented projects that focused on interiors, furnishings, and gardens. He developed a way to incorporate Asian antiques and indigenous pieces into modernist designs that created a subfield: the Asian Modern hotel interior.

Beardsley, Aubrey (1872–1898)
An English illustrator and high priest who grew out of the Arts and Crafts movement and whose graphics figure among the earliest Art Nouveau pieces. His body of work includes illustrations for Oscar Wilde's *Salome*, 1894. Beardsley's black-and-white designs were easily reproducible and influenced designers of furniture and interiors, including Edward Burne-Jones. See ART NOUVEAU.

Behar, Yves (b. 1967)
Swiss-born designer and entrepreneur Behar studied industrial design in Europe and the U.S. before founding fuseproject in San Francisco in 1999. A design agency, fuseproject covers all sectors of design including furniture, technology, fashion, environments, identity, product, Web, and print. Sustainable practices are a main component of his innovative work.

Bel Geddes, Norman (1893–1958)
An industrial designer with an impressive output who also did a series of acclaimed exhibit and set designs. He designed radio casings for Philco, an influential if unrealized teardrop-shaped automobile, and famously, the popular Futurama exhibit for General Motors at the 1939 New York World's Fair.

Bellini, Mario (b. 1935)
International architect Bellini was born in Milan in 1935 and attended Politecnico di Milano in 1959. In 1963 he began designing furniture; he then turned to architecture, urban design, and industrial design. He has designed products for B&B and Cassina, Vitra, Brionvega, and Yamaha.

Belter, John Henry (1804–1863)
A popular New York cabinet and furniture maker of the mid 19th century. He originated and worked with laminated plywood. Belter's Victorian Rococo Revival designs were constructed mainly in rosewood, oak, and walnut, employing a quasi-industrial process. His furniture, popular in the 1850s, had heavily carved and curved frames, roll moldings, and naturalistic flower details.

Beneman, Guillaume (1750–1811)
A French master cabinetmaker for Louis XVI. He worked for Marie Antoinette at St. Cloud and later executed Percier's designs in the Empire style. Beneman's style was severely classical and more in keeping with the later Empire period. Mahogany and elaborate gilt bronze mountings enriched his designs.

Bennett, Ward (1917–2003)
Born in New York, Bennett started working in the Garment District at the age of thirteen. After designing costumes at the Hattie Carnegie House of Fashion, he went to Paris in 1937. That led him to a career that included working as a window dresser, hat maker, and finally interior decorator. His career reached its height in the 1960s and 1970s and included creating furniture designs for Brickel Associates. He designed with industrial materials, combining elegance and minimalism. Bennett believed that he could design anything, including textiles, jewelry, sculpture, and furniture. Clients included Gianni Agnelli, David Rockefeller, and Tiffany's.

Bertoia, Harry (1915–1978)
An Italian by birth, Bertoia showed his affection for the U.S. with his adopted first name. A student at Cranbrook, he worked briefly for Charles and Ray Eames. His most famous furniture line was a series of molded wire mesh forms outfitted with pads that became a mainstay of Knoll's corporate business.

Bing, Siegfried (1838–1905)
German retailer active in Paris. His shop L'Art Nouveau lent its name to the style. Also a promoter of Japanese art. See JAPONISME.

Bishop, Dan (b. late 20th cent.)
Bishop was a production designer for the *Mad Men* television series, which ran from 2007–2015. It is widely credited with having reignited an interest in mid-century modern office interiors. His other work includes the movie *A Single Man* and TV show *Carnivàle*.

Blomstedt, Pauli (1900–1935)
A Finnish architecture turned furniture designer. He started out doing exceedingly simple versions of classical architecture, but he then turned in an uncompromising modernist direction. A number of tubular metal freestanding desks and armchairs are among his works. Along with his colleagues—including his wife, the architect Marta Blomstedt (1899–1982) he was a major figure in the group considered the Finnish equivalent of the Bauhaus.

Blondel, Jacques-François (1705–1774)
A French architect and theorist of the period of Louis XV. He designed in a refined Rococo manner, and his interior "boiserie," or wall panels, are recognized by their straight, elegant lines that terminate in Rococo corners and cornices.

Boffrand, Germain (1667–1754)
An architect and interior designer from Nancy, France, for decades he juggled a career with clients in his hometown and in Paris. He did mostly private houses. His remodeling of the Hôtel de Soubise in Paris, with two oval salons, is one of the major monuments of Rococo. He also consulted with Balthasar Neumann on the remodeling of the Residenz in Würzburg, Germany. As evidenced by his work at Soubise, he was particularly gifted at creating all-encompassing designs that included furnishings, mirrors, hardware, and exquisitely detailed walls and ceilings.

Botero, Samuel (b. 1945)
Born in Colombia and graduated from the Pratt Institute in New York City. He works in a variety of styles, with emphasis on color and nature. He has his own practice in New York and was named one of *Architectural Digest*'s Top 100 Designers. He designed a residence for the Princess Yasmin Aga Khan, as well as numerous restaurants, including Prima Donna, Café Japonais, and Orsini's.

Boulard, Jean-Baptiste (1725–1789)
A cabinetmaker (ébéniste) and sculptor of the Louis XVI period, noted for the magnificent bed he created for Fontainebleau.

Boulle, André-Charles (1642–1732)
Boulle and his four sons were French master cabinetmakers. Boulle designed rich, ornate, massive pieces that employed his veneer technique of inlays made of tortoiseshell, brass, pewter, copper, and ebony. In 1672, Boulle was appointed head cabinetmaker to Louis XIV. Besides his noted Boulle work technique, he designed parquet floors, mirrored walls, and inlaid panels at Versailles. His opulent designs were replete with scrolls, flowers, and arabesques. See BOULLE WORK.

Bouroullec, Erwan and Ronan (b. 1976 and 1971)
The Bouroullec brothers hail from Brittany, France. The first born, Ronan, began working as a designer, with Erwan joining later. Giulio Cappellini assisted them in their first industrial design projects in 1997, notably the Lit Clos and the Spring Chair. Their clients include Vitra, Kvadrat, Magis, Kartell, Established and Sons, Ligne Roset, Axor, and Issey Miyake. They were the subject of a career retrospective at the Museum of Contemporary Art, Chicago.

Boutros, Hany (b. late 20th cent.)
Boutros, along with Mario Elcid, owns the Mondo Collection, a design showroom in New York City. The furniture and design house includes furniture, lighting, and an interior design showroom. The collection houses worldwide designers, some from countries outside of the design mainstream.

Bradfield, Geoffrey (b. 1946)
Born in South Africa, Bradfield started his interior design company in Johannesburg before moving to New York in the 1970s. Bradfield designs luxury spaces, specializing in residences and smaller offices. He describes his style as "functional opulence" with projects including the Gertrude Vanderbilt Whitney estate on Long Island, King Hussein's estate in Maryland, and numerous jets, yachts, and celebrity residences. His work is inspired by world design, particularly the Asian decorative arts, African art, and Art Deco. He designed a line of textiles and wall coverings for Stark Carpet and also has his own line of furniture.

Breuer, Marcel Lajos (1902–1981)
An architect and designer who taught at the Bauhaus, he was born in Hungary. After he fled Germany, he designed many functionalist furniture pieces out of wood and metal for Isokon in Great Britain. In the U.S., Walter Gropius offered him a teaching position at Harvard, and he created the Butterfly house in 1949 for the Museum of Modern Art, New York. One of his earliest furniture designs, B32, commonly known as the Cesca chair, has sold in the millions. See BAUHAUS.

Briseux, Charles Étienne (1680–1754)
A French Rococo architect and interior designer. In his boiserie panels he preferred straight sides with a moderate amount of curvature on top.

Bromley, R. Scott (b. 1950s)
Born in a small town in rural Canada, the future architect later moved to Montreal. After graduating from McGill, he began his career at Philip Johnson's office. He started his practice in 1974, designing single-family homes and the infamous Studio 54 discotheque. Bromley teamed up with Robin Jacobsen and, later, Jerry Caldari to create several influential projects including the Abitare store in New York and the renovation of a Richard Neutra house. His roster of clients includes Robert Redford and Diana Ross.

Brown, Eleanor McMillen (1891–1991)
The interior designer founded McMillen Inc. in 1924 after attending Parsons School of Design in New York. She was well known for her sharp business sense and highly functional furniture arrangement as well as her work in the White House on Lyndon B. Johnson's family quarters.

Buatta, Mario (1936–2018)
Known as the "Prince of Chinz" due to the vibrant floral fabrics found in his signature designs. Buatta was popular for his English Regency-inspired rooms that gave an American twist to historicist designs with a bold use of color. His style is informed by his encyclopedic knowledge of antiques. In addition to his spatial design ability, he was an expert at staging projects for photo shoots.

Bunnag, Duangrit (b. 1966)
Thai hospitality designer known for a series of minimalist but luxurious boutique hotels. He also has done high-end residences and bars. He is an adroit user of social media to promote his firm and present his ideas about design. Stylistically, his projects range from industrial to hip, yet always with an eye to comfort.

Burdick, Bruce (b. 20th cent.)
Creates commercial office designs for Herman Miller, as well as residential furniture. His is known for freestanding non-panel systems furniture, some on aluminum bases.

Burn, Diane (b. late 20th cent.)
Burn renovated and decorated her own California mansion as her first taste of decorating. John Loring, the New York bureau chief for *Architectural Digest*, was at her home and was impressed with her work. That led to her home on the cover of *Architectural Digest* and the beginning of her decorating career. Burn describes her style as romantic design, transitional, and luxury. She works primarily with high-end residential interiors and is based in Panama, where she serves an international clientele.

Cabrera, Rafaell (b. 1952)
From Trinidad, Cabrera worked for the Hudson's Bay Company and has taught at Rhode Island School of Design (RISD). During his career, he has worked in set design and counts among his more visible projects multiple interiors for MAC Cosmetics.

Caffieri, Jean-Jacques (1725–1792)
A great French artisan of ormolu metal mounts for Rococo furniture. He worked under Jean-François Oeben, cabinetmaker to Louis XV.

Campana, Fernando and Humberto (b. 1953 and 1961)
Humberto was born in Rio Claro, Brazil, and graduated with a law degree. His older brother Fernando was born in Brotas and studied architecture at the São Paulo School of Fine Arts. Both served as instructors at the Brazilian Museum of Sculpture and Fundação Armando Alvares Penteado in São Paulo.

Cañas, Victor (b. 1947)
Born in San José Costa Rica, Cañas graduated from the Universidad Iberoamericana in Mexico City and DPU, London University for urban planning. His interior design work is resolutely contemporary in nature. He practices worldwide and is a popular lecturer and design professor.

Carlin, Martin (1730–1785)
A French master cabinetmaker to Louis XVI. He produced charming, delicate furniture in rosewood, with Sèvres porcelain inlays. Carlin was also a caster and chaser of metal furniture mounts and one of the earliest exponents of neoclassicism. He often used independent, or detached, balustrade columns to support the friezes of cabinets.

Carlson, Richard (b. 20th cent.)
Industrial design consultant, Richard Carlson has produced over 200 products, most notably the Décor Insulated BYO Wine Chiller, which is on permanent display at the Museum of Modern Art (MoMA). For that item, he was awarded the Prince Philip prize for Australian Design in 1980. The Design Institute of Australia awarded him the Inaugural Gold Medal for Industrial Design in 1984. He was named design director of Swanke Hayden Connell Architects.

Carr, Sue (b. 1940s)
Carr, interior designer and educator, is the principal of Carr Design Group, an architectural and interior design firm based in Australia. The firm's contemporary work focuses on details and includes projects such as the Adelaide Hilton, Australian Stock Exchange, and Melbourne's Westin Hotel.

Casas, Arthur (b. 1961)
After studying architecture and urbanism at Mackenzie University, São Paulo, Casas established Arthur Casas Studio, which manages offices in São Paulo and New York. He does residential, commercial, institutional, and furniture design. Casas is known for his interior work, which he describes as stemming from a contrast between essential rationality and through forms that have an individual if not idiosyncratic character. The designer is committed to being environmentally friendly, a goal he pursues throughout the design process. He is always looking to invent new ways of working with recycled and repurposed materials.

Casson, Hugh (1910–1999)
A British architect, interior designer, and artist. His early career was dedicated to teaching at Cambridge School of Architecture. Post-Second World War Casson was appointed director of architecture of the 1951 *Festival of Britain*. The Festival brought attention to Great Britain as a center of Modernism and fostered the careers of many including Robin and Lucienne Day.

Castaing, Madeleine (1895–1992)
Although she started her career as a respected actress in France's silent film industry, she turned to decorating. A Paris decorator and furniture dealer, Castaing was a proponent of a 19th-century approach to decorating even though she was active after the Second World War. She favored varieties of classicism, including Empire, English Regency, and Biedermeier. Her idiosyncratic style ranged from placing neoclassical antiques on leopard print carpets to her quirky fashion style: she wore a wig with a visible chin strap.

Chamaki, Johnny (b. 1969)
Chamaki was born in Tehran, Iran, and was raised in Sydney, Australia. He studied at the University of Technology in Sydney and is best known for his Outlaw Chair. He established the Johnny Chamaki design studio in 2002, which focuses on furniture design, interiors, and architecture. His past clients include Andreu World, Woodmark, and Clements International.

Chambers, Sir William (1723–1796)
An English architect of Scottish descent, Chambers was born in Sweden and led a peripatetic life of constant travel. He initially designed in the Palladian tradition. Like Chippendale, he adapted Chinese forms to furniture. In 1759, he published *Designs of Chinese Buildings, Furniture, Dresses, Machines and Utensils.* Also an author and furniture designer, Chambers was named chief architect to George III and was a leading authority on the Italian Renaissance. His Somerset House in London, 1776, is a classic of secular Renaissance design.

Chaowakul, Pitupong (b. 1975)
This Thai designer established a small but highly creative architecture and design firm, Supermachine Studio, in 2009. Many of his projects are related to performing arts, such as music festivals and stage design work. The firm has done art exhibitions, installations, and object design, including a whimsical bottle opener. Its interactive and often comical projects draw attention with modest budgets. One of the firm's prominent projects to date was a student lounge for Bangkok University.

Chermayeff, Serge (1900–1996)
He designed tubular steel furniture, including nesting chairs. He taught at Harvard, Yale, and the Illinois Institute of Technology (IIT).

Chi, Tony (b. 1960s)
Born in Taiwan, Chi moved to New York at a young age. He attended the High School of Art and Design and the Fashion Institute of Technology. He began working with Charles Morris Mount Design and started designing on his own in 1984. Tony Chi & Associates focuses on the hospitality sector. He has designed for chefs including Wolfgang Puck and Michael Mina. His notable hotel interior projects include Park Hyatt and Mandarin Orientals worldwide.

Chin, West (b. 1960s)
Chin is the principal architect of WCA, a New York City-based architecture, interior design, and decorating firm. WCA's style is modern, functional, and minimal, and his notable projects include Serge Normant at John Frieda Salon, Whym, Eatery, The Campbell, Lux Photography Studio, and numerous celebrity residences. In addition to residential and commercial design, WCA created a furniture and accessory line in 2006.

Chippendale, Thomas (1718–1779)
An English author, cabinetmaker, and interior designer. His earliest work was in the refined Georgian style, and in 1754 he published the *Gentleman* and *Cabinet-Maker's Director.* Chippendale worked in a variety of styles, including Queen Anne, Chinese, Rococo, and Gothic. He was noted for his chairs, girandoles, mirrors, frames, and assorted beds. Henry Copeland, William Ince, Thomas Johnson, Matthias Lock, Robert Manwaring, J. Mayhew, and others followed in the pluralistic tradition that he originated.

Chippendale, Thomas II (1749–1822)
The son of the noted Chippendale. He designed and executed furniture in the Regency or neoclassical style and worked in partnership with Thomas Haig. Harewood House and Stourhead are among his prominent commissions.

Cho, Minsuk (b. 1966)

With a master's degree in architecture from Columbia, Cho works out of offices in New York and Seoul. He previously worked for Polshek Partnership and Rem Koolhaas. His innovative and cutting-edge designs create a new vision of a nonhierarchical, postindustrial age. He exploits the possibilities and ambiguities of mass media in all phases of his small- to medium-scaled projects.

Churriguera, José de (1664–1725)

A Spanish architect who introduced Baroque stylings into Spanish architecture. Heroically scaled motifs were applied onto structures rather than planned as functioning parts of the construction. Columns and pilasters became spiral or baluster-form shafts; voluptuous volutes replaced pediments; and nudes, cherubim, plaster clouds, waterfalls, and draperies became lost in the mélange of swirls, curves, and fantasy. He worked with his brothers, Joaquín de Churriguera and Alberto de Churriguera. See CHURRIGUERESQUE.

Citterio, Antonio (b. 1950)

Citterio was born in Meda, Italy. He studied architecture at the Polytechnic University in Milan and in 1972 began work as a designer and consultant focusing on industrial design. He held a teaching position at Milan's Domus Academy. He opened his studio in 1972. Antonio Citterio and Partners has locations in Milan and Hamburg. He has collaborated with B&B Italia, Flos, Kartell, and Vitra. Notable works include the headquarters for Esprit, an industrial plant for Vitra, and Mobil storage for Kartell. His work is a part of the permanent collections of MoMA and the Centre Pompidou.

Clodagh (b. 1950s)

The Irish-born designer made waves in the design field since starting her Manhattan firm in the 1980s. Her projects celebrate "life-enhancing minimalism" and the belief that good design can influence physical and psychological well-being. Clodagh designs using methods including feng shui, chromatherapy, and biophilia.

Cochois, Jean-Baptiste (d. 1789)

A French master cabinetmaker *(ébéniste) to* Louis XVI. He was an inventor of dual-purpose mechanical furniture: e.g., a chiffonière that converted into a night table.

Colombo, Joe Cesare (1930–1971)

An Italian industrial designer. Colombo's career in design started with a proclivity for painting and sculpting. He is well known for embracing modern technologies and materials to create modular furniture befitting the space age. His use of curved forms and bold colors are characteristic of modern design of the 1960s and 1970s.

Cottam, Hilary (b. 1965)

Cottam, a UK-based social entrepreneur, founded Participle, an organization focusing on social change. She also initiated the enterprises School Works and the Do Tank and worked on such broad topics as aging, health, families, youth, and redesigning the prison system. Organizations she has collaborated with include the World Bank, UNICEF, and the UK central government and local authorities. She was named UK Designer of the Year in 2005.

Crane, Walter (1845–1915)

An English craftsman-designer and disciple of William Morris and the Arts and Crafts movement. He said, "The true root of all art lies in the handicrafts."

Cressent, Charles (1685–1768)

A leading French cabinetmaker of the Régence and Louis XV periods, noted for his ormolu trim and chased metalwork as well as his meticulously detailed marquetry. A student of Boulle, he designed clocks, wall decorations, and two- and three-drawer commodes that are considered by many to approach perfection. He incorporated floral forms, palm leaves, vines, garlands, cupids, lovers, monkeys, and grotesques into his sumptuous metal enrichments.

Cuvilliés, François de, the Elder (1695–1768)

A French furniture maker of Flemish ethnicity who made his career in Bavaria during the Louis XV period. He was an architect and engraver in an elaborate but refined Rococo style, which he brought with him when he relocated to Munich. Extremely short in stature, he found a success in Germany that eluded him in France; his influential projects include the Residenz in Würzburg and the Amalienburg Pavilion in Munich.

Cuvilliés, Jean François, the Younger (1731–1777)

A designer of ornaments and decorations, he published an influential anthology of drawings of his father's works.

Czarnecki, John (b. 1970s)

Czarnecki was born in Milwaukee and studied at the University of Wisconsin. He practiced architecture in Wisconsin and urban design in Toronto before entering the publishing field. He has worked for the American Institute of Architecture Students national journal, as senior acquisitions editor at John Wiley & Sons, and as associate editor at *Architectural Record*. In 2011 he became editor-in-chief of *Contract Magazine*.

Dagly, Gerhard (1653–c. 1714)

A French craftsman who introduced Japanese lacquer techniques into France. At the famous tapestry and furnishings factory, the method was used and known as *vernis de Gobelins*.

D'Aquino, Carl (b. 1960s)

D'Aquino believes that the most important part of a project is finding something personal about it and using materials in a new and interesting way such as making curtains out of paper or parachute cloth. D'Aquino and Francine Monaco met when D'Aquino needed to rent out space in his studio. The two worked independently until they collaborated on a project for a two-bedroom apartment above the Museum of Modern Art. The two complement each other well, with Monaco focusing on space-planning and D'Aquino considering the project as a whole and a visitor's experiential movement through the space.

D'Arcy White, Barbara (1928–2012)

A visual merchandiser known for her showrooms for Bloomingdales and other retailers. She popularized using steel and glass furniture in residential interiors. One of her window displays included inflatable furniture, and she designed the influential first floor of Bloomingdale's cosmetics department. One of her signature moves was using plaid curtains in children's rooms.

Davis, Arthur (1878–1951)

English student at the École des Beaux-Arts, where he met his future business partner, Charles Mewès. Their firm, Mewès and Davis, was responsible for the Ritz Hotels and for outfitting ocean liners for the Hamburg-Amerika Line and Cunard. Davis designed the English ships, including the *Aquitania*, which he considered his finest work, and the *Queen Mary*, an experience that caused him to leave the field.

Day, Lewis F. (1845–1910)

An English industrial designer. A pioneer of the modern movement, he recognized the inevitable influence of machinery on decorative art: "Whether we like it or not, machinery and steam power, and electricity for all we know, will have something to say concerning the ornament of the future."

Day, Robin (1915–2010) and Lucienne (1917–2010)
A pair of British designers who, like the Eames, were partners in life and in the design studio. Robin concentrated on furniture designs and Lucienne on textiles. A highlight of their career was the 1951 *Festival of Britain*. They created multiple pieces and layouts for Royal Festival Hall. Robin Day has the distinction of designing the Polyprop Chair, a modest metal and polypropylene chair that is one of the most successful chairs of all time. Lucienne Day initially considered herself a painter and amateur textile designer. But her playful textile designs drew their inspiration from modern abstract art and found a willing audience among customers who craved her avant-garde designs on everything from napkins to wallpaper.

Day, Thomas (1801–1861)
A free-black carpenter and furniture maker in Antebellum North Carolina. Day worked on both architectural millwork and furniture pieces, whose styles ranged from Empire to Victorian. At one point he employed twelve people, including white apprentices. His pieces are highly sought after today, and he was the subject of a major exhibition at the North Carolina History Museum.

Delanois, Louis (1731–1792)
A French master cabinetmaker under Louis XV and a protégé of Madame du Barry, Delanois designed much of the furniture at Versailles.

Deskey, Donald (1894–1989)
Deskey's most famous project was the interiors of New York's Radio City Music Hall. His projects, for interiors and furnishings, often included expensive materials, which was at odds with the works of his modernist contemporaries who sought to achieve high-quality design inexpensively. Also a noted product designer.

Desmalter, Jacob (1770–1841)
An important cabinetmaker of the early 19th-century French Empire period. He executed designs created by interior designer Charles Percier.

Despont, Thierry (b. 1948)
French interior designer Despont studied architecture at the École Nationale Supérieure des Beaux-Arts of Paris and urban design and city planning at Harvard. He founded Thierry W Despont, Ltd. based in New York, with luxury residential, museum, hotel, and historical restoration projects. Important works include the restoration of the Statue of Liberty, a flagship store for Ralph Lauren, and renovation of the Boca Raton Resort and Hotel.

Diallo, Cheick (b. 1960s)
Diallo was born in Mali and studied at the School of Architecture of Normandy as well as furniture design at the École Nationale Supérieure de Création Industrielle (ENSCI). He founded ADA, the Association of African Designers. Based in France, he opened his own furniture and accessories company, Diallo Design Atelier.

Diaz-Azcuy, Orlando (b. 1950s)
Diaz-Azcuy received multiple degrees including architecture from Catholic University in Washington, D.C., and master's degrees in landscape architecture and city and regional planning from the University of California. He worked at Gensler as design principal and then headed his own firm. His well-known projects at Gensler include the Levi Strauss & Co. headquarters in San Francisco and the United Bank of Denver.

Dione, Aicha (b. 1970s)
A Senegalese textile designer who crafts modern interpretations of traditional motif and weaving methods. Based in Dakar.

Dixon, Tom (b. 1959)
Dixon created his British design and manufacturing company in 2002, focusing on lighting and furniture.

Donghia, Angelo (1935–1985)
Donghia started his design career at Parsons School of Design. His design philosophy is centered upon a concern for the comfort of the user, although in a luxurious, occasionally over-the-top way. Trademark design moves include the use of silver gray, overscaled diamond patterns, sensuous textures, and "fat" furniture.

Downing, Andrew Jackson (1815–1852)
An American landscape architect and tastemaker of the period. He came from Newburgh, New York, and published *The Architecture of Country Houses* in 1850. The book had a great impact and contributed to the trend toward Italian-style villas and smaller houses. Downing also advocated Gothic cottages because they were not only "picturesque, but their floor plans are well suited to our informal world."

Draper, Dorothy (1889–1969)
A 20th-century American interior designer and businesswoman noted for her oversized architectural details and upholstered furniture in bold colors. Her work bridged the gap between historicism and Modernism and fell under the rubric of Hollywood Regency. She was known for the elaborate stucco work of her projects especially around door frames. One way that she gave historical projects a fresh feel was by using traditional textile patterns at a larger scale.

Du Cerceau, Jacques Androuet (c. 1515–1584)
A French Renaissance architect, draftsman, and furniture designer who studied in Italy under Bramante. In 1550 he published *Recueil Gravé de Meubles*, which set forth rules of proportion and ornamentation to be used on furniture. Du Cerceau originated the use of long columns on buffets and cupboards, the furniture equivalent of the colossal order.

Dufrene, Maurice (1876–1955)
A designer of jewelry and interiors, Dufrene is one of the designers whose stylistic range started with Art Nouveau and extended to Art Deco. He was a contributor to the exhibition in 1925 that gave Art Deco designers a visible platform.

Duquette, Tony (1914–1999)
An American designer who was active as an interior designer, a set designer, and a costume designer. He graduated from Chouinard Art Institute and was discovered and mentored by designer Elsie de Wolfe. Much of his notable work in Los Angeles was for major film companies such as Metro Goldwyn Mayer. He did set designs for the film *Kismet* (1955) and costume designs for the Broadway musical *Camelot* (1960).

Duret, Younes (b. 1980)
Duret is a Moroccan designer who received his degree from the French design school ENSCI in Paris. He created his own design agency called EXTRU-D. Duret was chosen to work as part of the Tasmeem Lab. Much of his work lies at the intersection of Eastern and Western culture. The firm produces furniture, lamps, and other objects, many of which are intended for retail environments.

D'Urso, Joseph (b. 1943)
A prominent designer who belonged to the 1980s "high-tech" movement. After studying at the Pratt Institute, the Royal College of Art in London, and the Manchester College of Art and Design he started designing private residences. His style tended towards bare and austere spaces with a single piece of modern furniture. Later he developed his own line of modern tables.

Eames, Charles (1907–1978)
An American architect and designer. He invented a process for molding laminated plywood into compound curves and joining the plywood to other plywood or steel members with rubber discs. Eames produced exquisite forms with carefully studied proportions, including wire frame chairs with snap-on upholstery for Herman Miller. Many of his designs were done in conjunction with his wife and business partner, Ray. The couple's firm in its final years focused on exhibition design, films, and corporate consulting. See EAMES CHAIR.

Eames, Ray (1912–1988)
Ray Kaiser, born in Sacramento, California, was an early abstract artist of America's first wave of modern art. She spent her formative years in New York. In 1940 she met Charles Eames at the Cranbrook Academy of Art. After marrying in 1941, the couple moved to Los Angeles. Inspired by wartime use of new materials and technologies, the Eameses designed low-cost modular furniture. They went on to design houses, exemplifying new ways for working with industry, and created partnerships with universities and government agencies as they moved to bigger and bigger projects.

Eastlake, Charles L., the Elder (1793–1865)
An advocate of the Gothic Revival in England during the 19th century. A painter, scholar, collector, and curator who served as president of the Royal Academy.

Eastlake, Charles L., the Younger (1836–1906)
Nephew of Eastlake the Elder, he similarly supported Gothic Revival design. He influenced design chiefly through his publications, including *Hints on Household Taste*, 1868. Eastlake pieces were produced with machine methods, resulting in assorted pieces of furniture that were embellished with heavy hardware, metal, and tile panel inserts. Heavy oak furniture influenced by him enjoyed enormous popularity in the U.S.

Easton, David (b. 1937)
Easton is a New York-based designer and is a master of many styles including neoclassicism. He mostly focuses on residences but has commercial and hospitality spaces to his credit as well. His designs are applied to a variety of products including fabric, trim, lighting, carpet, wall coverings, and outdoor furniture. Easton's inspiration comes from his travels, enthusiasm for history, and practicality.

Eichler, Joseph (1900–1974)
Eichler founded Eichler Homes and built over 10,000 middle-class subdivision homes in San Francisco and around 900 in Southern California from 1949 to 1966, doing his part as a developer to contribute to the phenomenon known as California Modern.

Elkins, Francis (1888–1953)
Elkins saw Modernism in a more sympathetic light than did her brother, the successful architect David Adler. She collaborated with Adler on many projects and also worked independently after she relocated to Monterey, California. She traveled to Europe with her brother and there met Jean-Michel Frank, who became a friend and whose pieces she incorporated into her designs. Her aesthetic opinions were many and included a preference for floral arrangements of pink and red carnations.

End, Henry (1915–2002)
End was born in England and attended the St. Martin's School of Design and the Royal College of Art in London. In 1946 he began working in the U.S., where he specialized in hotel and restaurant design. His publication *The Interiors Book of Hotels* is influential in the field. His projects include the Plaza in New York and the Carlton in London.

Ercolani, Lucian (1888–1976)
Ercolani was born in Italy, and his family later moved to London. In the 1890s, he studied drawing, design, and furniture construction at the Shoreditch Technical Institute. He founded the furniture company Ercol in 1920, known for steambending wood to form 20th-century versions of the classic Windsor chair. He preferring working with elm, and his most popular works are the Windsor and Evergreen furniture collections and the 1958 Ercol Butterfly Chair.

Ertegün, Mica (b. 1927)
New York socialite Ertegün formed MAC II in 1967 along with Chessy Rayner. The designers began designing luxury residences but later acquired projects including banks, shops, apartments, and offices. Clients include the Trade Development Bank in Geneva, Banco Safra in Brazil and Luxembourg, Warner Communications, and New York's Carlyle Hotel. Ertegün, a Romanian native, is known for her simple, but not minimalist, elegant designs.

Esrawe, Héctor (b. 1968)
A committed modernist, Esrawe studied industrial design at the Universidad Iberoamericana in 1992. He is known for using bright colors and crafting strong silhouettes in his furniture designs.

Featherston, Grant (1922–1995)
Featherston was born in Geelong, Victoria, Australia and is well known for creating a plywood shell contour chair in 1951. He is a founding member of what became the Design Institute of Australia. A notable project was furnishing the National Gallery of Victoria.

Follot, Paul (1877–1941)
A French designer of interiors, furniture, textiles, and various industrial projects. He was first associated with Art Deco, from which he transitioned to a severe version of classicism. His extensive body of work includes a stint designing for Wedgwood.

Fontaine, Pierre François Léonard (1762–1853)
A French architect-designer who, with Charles Percier, worked within the stylistic realm known as Empire for Napoleon at the start of the 19th century. They designed interiors and furniture for Malmaison, Saint-Cloud, the Tuileries, and the Louvre. Their creed was "simple lines, pure contours, correct shapes replacing... the curving and the irregular." The duo might be the first professional interior designers, as the profession became later known. See EMPIRE PERIOD.

Fornasetti, Piero (1913–1988)
An interior designer and industrial designer, he worked with Gio Ponti. A highpoint of his career was the commission to do the *Andrea Doria* interiors. His unorthodox approach to design includes an upholstery textile that resembles book bindings and a formica pattern that looks like newspaper clippings.

Fort-Brescia, Bernardo (b. 1951)
Fort-Brescia received his degree in architecture and urban planning from Princeton University and later his master's in architecture from Harvard University. He taught at Harvard University as well as the Urban Design School. Fort-Brescia has lectured around the globe, and his work has been on display in several museums in both the U.S. and Europe.

Fox, K. C. (b. 1960s)
Fox grew up in Los Angeles, and her early professional experience included a stained-glass apprenticeship and a stint as a poker dealer. Once introduced to the film industry, she found work as a set decorator for commercials, music videos, and films. With its deft use of classic modern furniture pieces, her *Legally Blonde 2* work landed her on the cover of *Architectural Digest*. She has designed for a wide range of films such as *The Girl with the Dragon Tattoo* and *The 40-Year-Old-Virgin*, focusing on layering to build background for characters.

Frank, Jean-Michel (1895–1941)
An interior designer and decorator. His fame started when he designed an all-white apartment for Elsa Schiaparelli in 1927. His designs were known for the use of exotic veneers, including snakeskin and sharkskin. He worked with Giacometti, Salvador Dali, and Emilio Terry. His was the kind of Art Deco that is thinly veiled classicism, stripped of its details, and flirting with Surrealism.

Frankl, Paul (1887–1958)
Born in Austria, Frankl will forever be associated with Art Deco, because of the numerous furniture pieces he made in the U.S. that were inspired by New York's skyscrapers.

Fukasawa, Naoto (b. 1956)
Born in Japan, Fukasawa studied art and product design at Tama Art University. He then worked at Seiki-Epson Corp. as a designer, before moving to San Francisco and joining ID two, later called IDEO. Moving back to Japan to implement an IDEO office there, he founded Naoto Fukasawa Design in Tokyo in 2003. That year he also founded the product brand ±0 and served on the advisory board for Japanese retailer MUJI. Fukasawa's designs include a wall-mounted CD player, an LED watch, Infobar A02 for KDDI, and numerous furniture and accessories.

Galle, Emile (1846–1904)
An Art Nouveau glass and furniture maker, Galle was from Nancy, which became a French center of Art Nouveau. In the 1870s and 1880s, Galle focused on techniques for making pigmented glass, which he fashioned into vases and other objects. The studio he opened expanded into furniture and at its height had 300 employees. The highlight of his career was a retrospective of his work at the 1900 Exposition Universelle.

Garcia, Jacques (b. 1947)
Born in France, Garcia studied at the Atelier Met de Penninghen School of Interior Design in Paris. His design career includes the Hotel Victor in South Beach, renovation of Champ de Bataille, the Marie Antoinette exhibition at the Musée Carnavalet, and the Rare restaurant in New York. His style ranges from contemporary to ornate and historical. He is an avid collector of furniture and royal objects, which is seen in his designs.

Gaudí i Cornet, Antoni (1852–1926)
The Catalan architect created unique architectural forms in keeping with Art Nouveau or Modernism. In his highly plastic architecture he introduced color and unusual materials, which achieved effects similar to those of Abstract Expressionism and Surrealism. Gaudí was a spirited innovator and favored the hyperbolic paraboloid form. The Church of the Holy Family has been under continual construction since work started in 1882 and is considered his masterpiece. Other works include Park Güell, Casa Battlé, and Casa Milá. See ART NOUVEAU.

Gehry, Frank (b. 1929)
The architectural superstar has designed multiple pieces of furniture throughout his career, first experimenting with plywood and cardboard. His *Easy Edges* furniture debuted in the 1970s. He was awarded the Pritzker Architecture Prize in 1989.

Gensler, Art (1935–2021)
The firm he started in 1965 is now the largest firm in the world. Gensler studied architecture at Cornell and founded the firm that bears his name in San Francisco in 1965. It has forty offices, 1,700 clients, and over 3,000 employees. It is now a global practice, with mostly corporate clients. The firm offers services in the sectors of architecture, branding, consulting, interior design, product design, planning, and urban design.

Gibbons, Grinling (1648–1721)
An English master wood-carver sculptor who was born in Rotterdam. He worked in close association with Sir Christopher Wren, and he created numerous carved trophy panels and mantels. Gibbons did much of the sculptured embellishment for the choir in St. Paul's Cathedral, as well as interior work on Kensington Palace, Hampton Court, and Windsor Castle. Gibbons sculptured realistically in high relief, with deep undercuts, and his motifs included fruit, vegetables, game, fish, leaves, and flowers crafted into swags, festoons, draperies, and frames.

Gibbs, James (1683–1754)
An English architect and furniture designer in the tradition of Sir Christopher Wren. Gibbs is most known for St. Martin-in-the-Fields in London (1721–1726).

Gillow, Robert (1704–1772) and Richard (1734–1811)
Furniture makers in the first half of the 18th century in England. Much of the furniture and cabinetwork they produced was exported to the West Indies.

Gostelowe, Jonathan (1744–1806)
An American cabinetmaker who worked in Philadelphia, Pennsylvania, in the Chippendale style. He produced many fine mahogany pieces.

Grange, Jacques (b. 1944)
Grange trained at the École Boulle and École Camondo and became a professional decorator in France and abroad. His clients included Pierre Berge, Yves Saint Laurent, Isabelle Adjani, Princess Caroline of Monaco, François Pinault, and Alain Ducasse. Grange bridges the gap between traditional and contemporary styles by following in the footsteps of Madeleine Castaing. One of his biggest projects was Colette's apartment at the Palais-Royal in Paris, France, where he updated the space without forgetting the palatial context.

Graves, Michael (1934–2015)
Initially a modernist, part of a group known as the New York Five. His winning competition entry for the Portland Public Services Building, 1982, caused an uproar with its unabashed reliance on historicist architecture, known as postmodernism. Known for his architecture, he designed a number of furniture and industrial pieces, including pieces for Target. Among his most important interior projects were his Sunar showrooms in the 1980s that highlighted the firm's contract textiles.

Gray, Eileen (1878–1976)
An Irish architect and designer whose modernist designs were admired by no less than Le Corbusier. Because she used expensive materials, she was long considered an Art Deco designer, but her pieces were always more modern than deco. She collaborated with Seizo Sugawara in creating lacquer finishes. Her reputation as an architect comes from the two houses she designed for

herself on the French Mediterranean, the more famous being E-1027. She also was known for incorporating African pieces into her designs.

Ginsberg, Alexandra Daisy (b. 1980s)
Ginsberg studied architecture at Cambridge University and design at Harvard and the Royal College of Art. Her work focuses on integrating science technology and design in a biotech future and her projects include The Synthetic Kingdom and E. chrome. She has taught at the Arts Science Bangalore and Cambridge. Her work is displayed in museums around the globe.

Girard, Alexander (1907–1995)
An architect, textile designer, and colorist, Girard was born in the U.S. but raised in Italy. Charles Eames recruited him to oversee Herman Miller's textiles department. His all-encompassing design work for Braniff Airlines constituted what now would be called branding. For the airline he designed or commissioned interiors, exteriors, logos, stationery, and dishes and flatware. He collaborated with Eero Saarinen. (See EERO SAARINEN in this appendix.)

Goddard, John (1723–1785)
Trained in England, this American designer and cabinetmaker worked in Newport, Rhode Island. In association with his son-in-law John Townsend, he produced a particular type of block front desk, secretary, and cabinet, usually with ogee bracket feet and shell ornaments. See BLOCK FRONT.

Godoy, Emiliano (b. 1974)
Industrial designer Godoy studied industrial design at Pratt, graduating in 2004. He also studied industrial design at the Universidad Iberoamericana and furniture design at the Danish School of Design. He founded his own practice, Godoy lab, and is the design director of Pirie, which manufacturer's furniture. He has worked for companies such as 3-form, Lacoste, and Novel.

Godwin, Edward William (1833–1886)
English architect and furniture and wallpaper designer. Godwin's work related to both English Arts and Crafts and Japonisme. He designed houses, often doing some of the interiors, paintings, and furnishings. His prominent commissions included work for his friends, the artists Frank Miles and James Whistler. He later focused on geometric furniture pieces known as Anglo-Japanese that were loosely inspired by his admiration for Japanese carpentry. He also did costume and stage designs, a result of commissions he received because of his relationship with the actress Ellen Terry.

Gomez, Didier (b. 1953)
Gomez created his first interior design agency in 1985 and has since started over with two new firms in 2003: Didier Gomez Design and Didier Gomez Interior Design. His firms, with headquarters in Paris, design apartments and residences, commercial spaces, hotels, and restaurants.

Greene, Charles Sumner (1868) and Henry Manther (1870–1954)
A pair of brothers working together in architecture, the firm of Greene and Greene designed bungalows and furniture and were leaders of the American Arts and Crafts movement. They were influenced by the writings of John Ruskin and William Morris and by the Japanese pavilion at the World's Columbian Exposition, 1893. They also shared an interest in California's Spanish and Mission architecture. Their masterpiece is the Gamble House, 1908.

Griffin, Marion Mahoney (1871–1961)
After studying architecture at MIT, Griffin worked in Frank Lloyd Wright's office and was an accomplished renderer; many of his perspectives that resembled Japanese etchings came from her hand. Later, she and her husband, Walter Burley Griffin, designed Australia's capital, Canberra. Griffin worked in Australia and India.

Grossman, Greta Magnusson (1906–1999)
Born in Sweden, Grossman began her design career with a woodworking apprenticeship, after which she began creating furniture, textiles, and ceramics. With classmate Eric Ulrich, she opened Studio, a store and workshop in Stockholm, where she took on furniture and interiors commissions, famously designing Sweden's Princess Brigitte's crib. After moving to the U.S., she opened a shop in Beverly Hills. She designed homes in Los Angeles and San Francisco in the 1950s and taught industrial design courses at the University of California, Los Angeles and the Art Center School in Los Angeles.

Gropius, Walter (1883–1969)
An architect and founder of the Bauhaus in Weimar. In 1909, Gropius worked out a memorandum on standardization and mass production of small houses. He became the head of the Bauhaus in 1919, the design school that was a community of architects, painters, and craftsmen working in a new spirit. After emigrating to the U.S., Gropius, along with Marcel Breuer, was responsible for a New England mid-century modern style of domestic architecture. See BAUHAUS.

Guimard, Hector-Germain (1867–1942)
A French architect and furniture designer. Greatly influenced by Victor Hortae, whom he knew personally, he became the French interpreter of Art Nouveau. One of his most noted commissions was the entrances to the Metro stations in Paris. The mass-produced cast-iron pieces were shaped into elegant, twisted, curving, flowerlike forms. In 1938, Guimard moved to New York. See ART NOUVEAU. See also HORTA, VICTOR in this appendix.

Haines, William (1900–1973)
An American actor who began a career in interior design after his acting career was cut short due to bias against his sexuality. Working with his spouse Jimmie Shields, he spent fifty years designing interiors for Hollywood's elite in a style that effortlessly combined both formal and casual living. Alternately referred to as California Modern or Hollywood Regency, Haines' work took the edge off Modernism and made it approachable and luxurious.

Hajj, Mona (b. 1958)
Hajj is a Baltimore-based interior designer with roots in Europe and Lebanon. She designs with attention to detail and creates residential interiors and custom cabinetry that span a range of design styles. She wrote the book *Interior Visions*, and her work has been recognized in many magazines.

Halfpenny, William (1735–1755)
An English carpenter and architect who helped popularize the Chinese trend in architecture and decoration. In collaboration with his son, he published many books during the early part of

the 18th century, including *The Modern Builder's Assistant* and *New Design for Chinese Temples, Triumphal Arches, Garden Seats, Railings, Etc.* A frequent feature of his designs was a pig-tailed Chinese mandarin holding onto an umbrella.

Hampton, Mark (1940–1998)
Although he started his career as an interior designer working for the innovative David Hicks, Hampton eschewed contemporary design and made his fame as a traditionalist. His tasteful designs came to epitomize the wealthy era of the 1980s, and his clients included Presidents Reagan and George H.W. Bush. In addition to the White House, Blair House, and Camp David, Hampton's projects included a suite of reception rooms at the State Department, Gracie Mansion, and the American Academy in Rome. His decorating books were successful, and the firm he founded is now in the capable hands of his daughter, Alexa Hampton.

Hansen, Fritz (firm founded in 1872)
Hansen founded his company in Copenhagen as a manufacturer of furniture parts. Now the company is internationally known, bringing Danish furniture design into the spotlight. Many important designers of the 20th century created designs for the firm, including Arne Jacobsen, Piero Lissoni, Bruno Mathsson, and Hans Wegner.

Haraszty, Eszter (1920–1994)
Haraszty was the head of Knoll Textiles from 1950 to 1955 and created its influential and popular Fibra design. She was one of the textile designers who took the principles of the Bauhaus and applied them to contract interiors.

Hardouin-Mansart, Jules (1646–1708)
Court architect to Louis XIV; one of those responsible for architecture, interiors, and furnishings of Versailles.

Hariri, Gisue and Mojgan (b. 1960s)
Hariri and Hariri were born in Iran and moved to the U.S. in the 1970s. Mojgan received bachelor's and master's degrees from Cornell. They founded their eponymous firm in 1986. Gisue studied architecture and urban design at Cornell, graduating in 1980. The works emanating from the sisters' New York-based firm have been described as sensual Modernism. Their work includes a residential mixed-use development in Austria and a chandelier for Swarovski. They have taught at Columbia University.

Harrison, Peter (1716–1775)
Harrison was one of the first professional American architects in that he prepared sketches for others to build from. His best-known works are in Newport, Rhode Island, which he made an architectural center of colonial New England. His masterpiece, the Synagogue of the Congregation Jeshuat Israel (known as Touro Synagogue), 1763, is the oldest temple in the U.S.

Hayek, Sami (b. 1974)
Mexican-born Hayek studied environmental design at the Art Center College of Design and founded his own studio in Los Angeles, Espacio Sami Hayek. His multidisciplinary design firm based in New York focuses on residential, commercial, furniture, and product design. His designs include furniture for Poltrona Frau, an accessory collection for Target, and a middle-income housing unit in Mexico.

Hays, Tyler (b. 1968)
Hays studied sculpture and painting at the University of Oregon, where he worked as a carpenter before moving to New York and starting his own furniture company, BDDW. The company creates quality solid-wood furniture with a twist.

Hecker, Paul (b. 1964)
With his business partner Hamish Guthrie (b. 1970), he founded Hecker Guthrie, a small architecture and interiors firm in Melbourne, Australia. The firm does projects in the hospitality, residential, and retail sectors and has won awards in and out of Australia.

Henkels, George J. (1819–1883)
An American cabinetmaker who operated out of Philadelphia, Henkels was known for Rococo and Renaissance Revival furniture.

Hepplewhite, George (1727?–1786)
An English neoclassical furniture designer. In 1788, his widow published the *Cabinet-Maker and Upholsterer's Guide.* Like Chippendale's publications, it was a comprehensive collection of standardized furniture pieces. His work was characterized by lightness of construction, elegant curvilinear forms, and perfection of workmanship. Hepplewhite used heart-shaped and shield chairbacks carved with wheat ears, fern leaves, honeysuckle, swags, and Prince of Wales feathers. Hepplewhite favored the spade foot for his delicately grooved and fluted chair legs.

Herrera, Juan de (1530–1597)
A Spanish architect who was responsible for the Desornamentado style. He worked under Phillip II, and his work was simple, severe, and almost harsh in relation to the Plateresque period that preceded him and the Baroque (or Churrigueresco) that followed. A pupil of Michelangelo, his greatest achievement is the Escorial, 30 miles from Madrid (50 km). He also added the southern portion to the Alcazar in Toledo, Spain.

Herter, Christian (1839–1883) and Gustave (1830–1898)
Cabinetmakers and decorators from Germany who were active in New York. They had an elite clientele for whom they designed in historicist traditions. Together they started the successful retail endeavor Herter Brothers.

Heurtaut, Nicolas (1720–1771)
A French furniture maker who specialized in the Rococo style popular during the reign of Louis XV.

Heywood, Levi (1800–1882)
Founder of the influential Heywood Brothers furniture company. Their innovations include a standardized loan of offerings and selling by catalog.

Hicks, Ashley (b. 1963)
Born in 1963, Hicks trained at the Architectural Association in London. He then worked for his father, well-known designer David Hicks, before beginning his own firm based in London. He created his first furniture collection called Jan-tar Mantar in 1997, which reinterpreted the Greek klismos chair. He designed shops for Allegra Hicks, his former wife, and works on high-end residential interiors worldwide.

Hicks, David (1929–1998)
Hicks was an English interior decorator whose signature design look came to define the 1970s. He used bold colors and combined antiques, contemporary art, and modern furnishings. After attending Charterhouse School and the Central College of Art, he began his career drawing cereal boxes for the advertising agency J. Walter Thompson. Hicks started to design patterned carpets and fabrics when he found all those on the market to be outdated. In

the 1970s and 1980s Hicks opened branches of his successful retail store in fifteen countries. Much imitated features of his work include displaying artwork on dark brown walls and the use of reflective wallpaper.

Hitchcock, Lambert (1795–1852)

An American furniture designer and cabinetmaker working in Connecticut, Hitchcock was the designer of the Hitchcock chair, derived from the Sheraton pillowback or oval-turned top-rail chair. The factory-produced chair usually was painted black and had a rush or cane seat; turned, splayed front legs; and gold stenciled fruit and flower decoration on the wide top rail. It was a chair based in neoclassicism, rendered affordable for the masses.

Ho, Jiun (b. 1972)

International interior and product designer Ho studied at the Chicago International Academy of Design. He established a design firm based in San Francisco that creates elegant and minimalistic residential and hotel interiors, furniture, and lighting design. Projects include the Renew boutique hotel in Honolulu with complete branding and interior work and the Revel Spa.

Hoffmann, Josef (1870–1956)

Austrian designer and architect born in Moravia, Czech lands, Hoffmann was the taste- and pace-setter for Austrian décor in the first three decades of the 20th century. The Palais Stoclet in Brussels (1905–1911) is his masterpiece, and in it one can see his subtle compositions based on simple rectangles and squares and with mosaics by Gustav Klimt. Hoffmann was a student of Otto Wagner.

Hope, Thomas (1769–1831)

The leading furniture designer, patron, and collector of the Empire style in England, which is correctly termed English Regency. His book of furniture designs, *Household Furniture and Interior Decorations*, 1807, moderated the extravagant pseudoclassical style. See REGENCY (ENGLISH).

Hoppen, Kelly (b. 1959)

Interior designer Hoppen was born in Cape Town, South Africa, and later opened her own design firm, Kelly Hoppen Interiors, in London. The firm specializes in high-end residential, commercial, aircraft, yacht, furniture, and product design. Projects include British Airways First Class, the Kelly Hoppen Home Collection of furniture, and Hotel Murmuri in Barcelona. She has written a number of books and appears regularly on television.

Horta, Victor (1861–1947)

A Belgian architect who created in the Art Nouveau style. Two of his most noted works are the home of Baron van Eetvelde (1895) and the Maison du Peuple (1895). The interior architecture of both structures is significant for the irregularly shaped rooms, which open freely onto one another at different levels. The iron balustrades are typically Art Nouveau in their twisted, plantlike elements. His other major projects include the Hôtel Tassel, 1892–1893, and the Hôtel Solvay, 1894–1900. See ART NOUVEAU.

Huet, Christophe (1700–1759)

A French artist during the reign of Louis XV. He created many chinoiserie-Rococo designs that included mandarins, pagodas, parasols, monkeys, ladders, and fantastic foliage.

Hunt, Holly (b. 1945)

Texan Hunt is president and CEO of Holly Hunt, a top luxury merchandiser. She began in 1983 with a small showroom in Chicago's Merchandise Mart with luxury designer collections. She also serves on the board of the School of the Art Institute.

Hustwit, Gary (b. 1960s)

Hustwit directed the films *Helvetica* and *Objectified. Helvetica* was his first movie as director, and he has also produced documentaries including *I Am Trying to Break Your Heart* and *Drive Well, Sleep Carefully*. Previously he worked with SST Records in the 1980s, ran Incommunicado Press in the 1990s, served as vice president of media website Salon.com in 2000, and started the DVD label Plexifilm in 2001.

Hwang, Doojin (b. 1963)

Korean architect, interior designer, and furniture and product designer. His firm takes advantage of social media and the Web for its publicity. His projects are resolutely contemporary, although with a feel for the grand history of Korean architecture. Projects such as Stone Residence and West Village Building, show his adept approach to materiality. He is also an advocate for the preservation of Korean modern architecture and is a frequent commentator on the richness of vernacular architecture and design.

Ince, William (1737–1804)

An English cabinetmaker and follower of Chippendale. With Thomas Mayhew, he published *The Universal System of Household Furniture*, from 1762 to 1763. It contained designs for lanthorns (lanterns), sideboard tables, bookcases, beds, and so on. Ince used fretwork, combined with Chinese and Gothic motifs, and chairbacks carved with ribbons and scrolls and patterned with brass nails. See MAYHEW, THOMAS.

Ïto, Ora (b. 1997)

A French designer who burst on the scene when, lacking work, he decided to design projects for top brands, including Louis Vuitton, Adidas, and Gucci—without being hired by them—and released his projects on the Web to create a stir. He is a furniture and product designer and has done a number of restaurants of note, including Marxito and Wallpaper. He has designed furniture for Cassina and Roche Bobois.

Iu, Carolyn (b. 1950s)

Iu was born and raised in Hong Kong, and received her design degree from Cornell University. In 1977 she joined Skidmore, Owings & Merrill and worked as an associate partner until 1994. She established Iu & Lewis Design in 1995, predominantly working on corporate interiors. Iu's style is simple, classic contemporary with a little bit of tension.

Jackson, Dakota (b. 1949)

Jackson performed as a dancer before becoming a furniture designer in the 1970s. He founded his own firm based in New York and creates interiors along with furniture design. Notable interiors work includes David Yurman's Madison Avenue Boutique in 1999, Kip's Bay Boy's and Girl's Club Decorator Showhouse, and Temple Jeremiah in Illinois. His quality high-end furniture can be seen in numerous showrooms worldwide.

Jacob, François Honoré Georges (1770–1841)

A French cabinetmaker of the Louis XVI and Directoire periods. He made and designed furniture for Napoleon.

Jacob, Georges (1739–1814)

The father of the equally famous François Honoré Georges Jacob. A noted cabinetmaker of the Louis XVI period.

Jacobsen, Arne (1902–1971)

A modern Danish designer and architect, Jacobsen designed multiple versions of a laminated plywood-and-steel chair. For the interiors of the SAS (Scandinavian Airlines System) Hotel, Copenhagen,

1958, which he designed, he created the Ant Chair, the Egg Chair, and the Swan Chair. For the airline itself, he designed a streamlined set of flatware.

Jacquard, Joseph-Marie (1752–1834)
The Frenchman who, in 1801, created the jacquard loom, which revolutionized the production of figural woven textiles. The loom made it possible to produce in expensive multicolored designs. In 1825, the loom was adapted for the carpet industry. Its automated processes make it a forerunner of the computer.

Jain, Bijoy (b. 1965)
An Indian architect and furniture designer, Bijoy is the founder of Studio Mumbai and studied architecture in the U.S. as a retail and color consultant. Her unusual wallpaper is, like all her work, modern but not minimalist.

Jeanneret, Charles Édouard (b. 1887–1965)
See LE CORBUSIER in this appendix.

Jeanneret, Pierre (1896–1967)
The Swiss cousin of Le Corbusier, he worked in the office when it produced the iconic tubular steel furniture pieces. He later collaborated with Jean Prouvé. He stayed in Chandigarh, India, from 1951–1965. Like Charlotte Perriand, he experimented with making modern furniture designs from cord and bamboo. See LE CORBUSIER and PERRIAND, CHARLOTTE and PROUVÉ, JEAN in this appendix.

Jiřičná, Eva (b. 1939)
Architect and designer, based in London and Prague, Jiřičná studied engineering and architecture until 1962, when she earned a master of arts at the Prague Academy of Fine Arts. Jiřičná integrated her engineering and architecture background with interior design. Known for her attention to detail and her steel and glass staircase, she is recognized for her innovative use of industrial materials in retail and commercial spaces. She previously worked for Norman Foster and Richard Rogers.

Johnson, Philip (1906–2005)
The eclectic American architect and designer was born in Cleveland, Ohio. One of his most famous buildings is his Glass House, 1949, in New Canaan, Connecticut. Johnson was associated with Mies van der Rohe in designing the Seagram Building in New York City and its Four Seasons restaurant. His biography is notable: he was a minor figure in the Harlem Renaissance, then one of the most ardent supporters of Modernism, neither of which prepares one for his stylistic about-face in the 1980s when he created the first major postmodern monument, the AT&T Building in New York, 1979.

Jongerius, Hella (b. 1963)
A Dutch industrial designer and owner of Jongeriuslab in Rotterdam. She has worked to design many products including textiles, housewares, furniture, and plane seating. These are typically characterized by combining opposites (new and old, industrial and craftsmen) as well as being highly textural. Gary Hustwit's 2009 film *Objectified* included interviews with all the top industrial designers, and hers is widely considered to stand out.

Joop, Jette (b. 1968)
German fashion and accessories designer, and colorist. After studying industrial design, Joop turned to kitchen and residential accessories. She designed her own stores, collaborates with several high-end housing developers, and has designed a restrained line of wallpapers. A sense of calm pervades her work that is at odds with her glamorous and provocative public persona.

Juhl, Finn (1911–1989)
A Danish architect and furniture designer. The legs, arms, backs, etc. of his furniture designs are beautiful and subtly sculpted wood elements, which is why his pieces are often described as primitive or organic. He contributed to the interiors of the United Nations Building, New York, and did a line for Baker Furniture.

Kagan, Vladimir (1927–2016)
Ethnically Russian, Kagan was born in Germany. His furniture design showroom attracted prominent corporate clients, including General Electric, General Motors, and American Express. His residential clientele included Marilyn Monroe and Lily Pons. His New York design firm was unusual at the time because it offered furniture and its own line of textiles. He taught at Parsons and was a prominent figure in the American Society of Interior Designers (ASID).

Kahane, Melanie (1910–1988)
An interior designer and member of the American Society of Interior Designers (ASID). A graduate of Parsons' Paris school, Kahane's clients included Lord and Taylor, NBC, NASA, and Shubert Theaters. She established herself as a bold colorist by creating a red kitchen stove. She brought the bright colors of the 1960s into historicist interiors. Her showroom in 1949 was black, white, and pumpkin and was one of the most photographed rooms of the year.

Kakiemon, Sakaida (1596–1666)
A Japanese pottery artist who developed the use of colored enamel designs on porcelain. Decorations done in this manner bear the name of this artist and are sometimes erroneously referred to as Korean Decoration.

Keller, Dale (1929–2016) and Patricia (b. 1926)
An interior design pair who reigned as the world's leading experts on high-end hotel interiors for decades. After graduating from the University of Washington they started their first firm in Tokyo and later had offices in Hong Kong, London, and New York. Their influential projects include the Tokyo Hilton, the Okura Hotel, and the Marunouchi Hotel.

Kelly, Ben (b. 1950s)
A British interior designer who has also been active in graphic design with several prominent record covers to his credit. He is most well known for his work on the Hacienda Nightclub in London, which started a trend of hospitality design as experience. His designs reflect his desire to retain the best features of existing conditions and reinvigorate old spaces with color, material, textures, and finishes.

Kent, William (1685–1748)
An English architect, furniture designer, painter, and landscape designer in the tradition of Inigo Jones. His furniture designs were in the ponderous Venetian style with classical detailing, and they served as a link between Queen Anne and Chippendale designs. Kent's furniture was produced in mahogany and gilt and trimmed with ornately carved scrolls, swags of fruit and flowers, and often an eagle's head terminating in a scroll. With the Earl of Burlington, he designed the Palladian Chiswick House. See ARCHITECTS' PERIOD.

Kenmochi, Isamu (1912–1971)
Japanese furniture designer. He collaborated with the American-Japanese sculptor and designer Noguchi to create the bamboo basket chair. See NOGUCHI, ISAMU.

Kilvert, Lilly (b. 1950)
An influential set designer. The two-time Oscar nominee worked on *The Last Samurai*, *Valkyrie*, and *City of Angels*.

Khanh, Quasar (1934–2016)
A Vietnamese engineer, inventor, and designer. Khanh is most well known for his inflatable line of furniture, *Aerospace*. His fame in the 1960s is explained by his bold products that were shocking in both color and form. He worked regularly in plastic and Plexiglas.

Kim, D. B. (b. 1960s)
South Korean-born Kim is a designer of hospitality, architecture, interiors, and product design and is a well-known design blogger. He joined the global interior design firm Pierre-Yves Rochon, Inc. of Chicago as an interior designer.

Kit, Ajax Law Ling (b. late 20th century)
One Plus Partnership is a Hong Kong design firm founded in 2004 by Kit and Virginia Lung. They designed the YOHO Midtown residential clubhouse and have designed many other project types including retail, hospitality, and residential.

Kita, Toshiyuki (b. 1942)
The Osaka-born furniture and product designer maintains offices in Japan and Italy. He has designed for Cassina, including the award-winning KICK table. He taught in Seattle and Vienna and has been exhibited worldwide.

Kjærholm, Poul (1929–1980)
A modern Danish furniture designer famous for his table and chair designs, particularly PK24, a sleek lounge chair. Rather than specializing in one material, he seemed to effortlessly change from working in wood to leather, steel, and wicker. He started his career in Copenhagen, and he later created designs for Herman Miller.

Knoll, Florence Schust (1917–2019)
Florence Knoll worked for Walter Gropius and also for Marcel Breuer, who was one of her instructors at Cranbrook. She also studied with Mies van der Rohe. In the years following her marriage to Hans Knoll in 1946, she became increasingly important to managing the company and formulating its design direction. In print and in person, she could be disarmingly modest about her design ability. After her husband's death, her leadership turned Knoll into a design force that rivaled Herman Miller.

Knoll, Hans (1914–1955)
The modernist credentials of the Knoll family start with the family factory in Weimar, Germany, where they produced pieces for Walter Gropius, Marcel Breuer, and Mies van der Rohe. In 1937 Hans Knoll opened a showroom in the U.S., and with his second wife, Florence Schust Knoll, the family business became one of the leaders of American interior design and furnishings. He died in an automobile accident in Cuba, and the firm was then led by Florence.

Korban, Ryan (b. 1985)
A self-described "untrained stylist" and blogger, based in New York, Korban is a well-connected interior designer. He counts James Franco and Alexander Wang among his clients.

Kruger, Nic (b. 1980s)
Kruger is a furniture designer based in Knysna, South Africa. His company, Shipwreck Furniture, follows sustainable practices with material sourced from found shipwrecks to create tables, benches, and other unique furniture.

Kuma, Kengo (b. 1954)
Kuma was born in Yokohama, Japan. He attended the University of Tokyo School of Architecture in 1979, and in 1987 he founded Kengo Kuma and Associates, which later opened a satellite office in Paris. Important works include the M2 building, Lotus House, and the Kitakami Canal Museum. One of the leading Japanese architects and interior designers of his generation, he is known for his hospitality projects.

Kuramata, Shiro (1934–1991)
After studying woodworking, Kuramata worked doing retail display design. He achieved international acclaim once he turned to interior and furniture design. Associated with the postmodern Memphis designers, he designed for Vitra and Cappellini. His expanded metal chair, How High the Moon, blurs the line between sculpture and furniture.

Kwami, Mark (b. 1966)
The German-Ghanaian Kwami was raised in Africa and today works out of Berlin. He studied product and industrial design at the University of Fine Arts, Berlin, and founded Numodus, a business management and market research company. He also cofounded the Made in Africa Collection, which imports African furniture and home accessories products for retail in the European Union.

Lahlou, Hicham (b. 1973)
Lahlou is an Arab-African designer from Morocco. He designs for a number of different business sectors, including hotels, residences, branding, retail, palaces, and strategic planning. He also works at a smaller scale designing watches, lighting, and tableware for international brands. Lahlou founded and served as president of the Moroccan Federation of Design and Industrial Design. He received his degree in 1995 in architecture and design from the Académie Charpentier in Paris.

Lamb, Max (b. 1980)
An installation and furniture designer who focuses on using natural materials in highly unusual ways. He uses traditional or even prehistoric methods of fabrication combined with digital design to create pieces that stretch natural materials like rock, sand, and wood to their limits. His all-terrazzo room at the Milan Furniture Fair, 2014, including walls, floor, and furniture, was a stand-out.

Lancaster, Nancy (1897–1994)
Born in Virginia, Lancaster moved to England in 1926. She popularized an English country look that relied heavily on chintz and was at once elegant yet comfortable. She is known for a yellow library in her London flat that she described as "buttah yellah." With John Fowler, she ran the firm of Colefax and Fowler that influenced residential design on both sides of the Atlantic.

Langley, Batty (1696–1751)
An English architect and designer who operated a drawing school for carpenters and whose own works frequently used ogee or cyma curves for moldings around doors and drawers. Langley's *Gothic Architecture Improved by Rules and Proportion* helped usher in the Gothic Revival. He also compiled *Ancient Masonry*, which provided inspiration for colonial American builders.

Langlois, Peter (18th cent.)
A late-18th-century French craftsman who brought the elaborate Boulle work techniques to England. See BOULLE WORK.

Lannuier, Charles-Honoré (1779–1819)
A French cabinetmaker and designer. Trained in France, he worked in New York in the Louis XVI neoclassical style and influenced the work of Duncan Phyfe.

Larsen, Jack Lenor (b. 1927)
An architect and interior designer who specialized in the design and manufacture of textiles that combine style, texture, and the finest hand craftsmanship with industrial production techniques. A onetime student at Cranbrook, he founded the Jack Lenor Larsen Textile House in 1952.

Lasalle, Philippe de (1720–1803)
A French designer and manufacturer of textiles, as well as the inventor of special weaving devices. During the Louis XVI period he was especially noted for his floral patterns and *lampas*. His artistry earned him the title "the Painter of Textiles."

Laszlo, Paul (1900–1993)
A successful hospitality and retail designer, when Laszlo turned to modernist residential interiors, his client list expanded to include Cary Grant, Barbara Stanwyck, and Elizabeth Taylor. As a designer for Herman Miller, he produced a successful matching circular sofa and coffee table. He also designed textiles and lamps.

Latrobe, Benjamin Henry (1764–1820)
An English-born American architect who worked in the Greek Revival style, greatly influenced by classical Greek and Roman architecture. Although his designs include work on the U.S. Capitol, the White House, and the Cathedral of Baltimore, he also designed Gothic Revival buildings, a popular stove for heating interiors, and some furniture pieces.

Lavoine, Sarah (b. 1973)
Lavoine is a Polish princess who became a French decorator. She opened her office in 2002 and soon thereafter a design boutique in Paris. Her projects tend to small residential, retail, and hospitality, in which she often uses a bright accent color.

Le Brun, Charles (1619–1690)
King Louis XIV's favorite painter and decorator. He created tall, elaborate, heroically scaled furniture. Among his achievements was the semicircular vaulted arch in the Hall of Mirrors (Galerie des Glaces) in Versailles, designed by Jules Hardouin-Mansart. As the director and chief designer of the Gobelins Factory, he oversaw the creation of multiple objects that were the embodiment of Louis XIV decoration.

Le Corbusier (pseudonym of Charles-Édouard Jeanneret) (1887–1965)
Born in Switzerland, he was an architect, painter, writer, and architectural critic, as well as one of the most influential architects and city planners of the 20th century. His conceptual structure, the Maison Dom-Ino, separated structure from space-defining elements. He started working on his iconic furniture designs in 1928 when CHARLOTTE PERRIAND started working in his atelier.

Lee, Gary (b. 1953)
After graduating with a Bachelor of Fine Arts with a focus on interior and graphic design at the University of Michigan, he became a partner at ISD, Incorporated, a firm that specialized in high-end commercial interiors. Lee opened his own firm in 1993 in Chicago. His practice includes corporate, residential, hospitality, retail, and product design, with clients including Armani Exchange and the Boston Consulting Group.

Lehrer, Mariana (b. 1970s), and Giselle Gutman (b. 1970s)
The architects established their firm Gutman+Lehrer Arquitectas in 1996 after graduating from the Universidad de Buenos Aires, Facultad de Arquitectura. They work on residential and commercial spaces with clients including MVZ Publicidad and The Leading Hotels of the World.

Leiserowitz, Nila (b. 1950s)
After graduating from the University of Minnesota, Leiserowitz worked as vice president focusing on interiors at Perkins+Will in Chicago. She ran a design firm in Minneapolis before she joined Gensler in 1995. She was central to the firm's move into the Chicago design market.

Lepautre, Jean (1617–1682)
An interior designer and clockmaker for Louis XIII and Louis XIV. He published several works on decorative furniture that had a great influence on Flemish and English styles. Louis XIV named Lepautre the Royal Architect.

Lewis, Sally Sirkin (b. 1930s)
The founder of the luxury home furniture manufacturer J. Robert Scott. She was the first woman to open a showroom on Melrose Avenue in the design district of Los Angeles. Over the course of her career she has received over 150 design patents for her furniture.

Liebes, Dorothy (1899–1972)
An accomplished American interior and textile designer. Her textiles were known for their bold, polychrome designs and were heavily textured. She used unusual materials in her work, including plastic and metal. Frank Lloyd Wright and Edward Durrell Stone used her textiles, several of which are part of the collections of design museums.

Lim, Kevin (b. 1976)
The son of William Lim, from Singapore, trained at the Architectural Association under Argentinian architect Ciro Najle and engineer Hanif Kara. One of Singapore's most accomplished architects of the 20th century, William Lim, acted as his mentor. As the founding principal of Studio SKLIM, Kevin Lim brought his clean aesthetic to a variety of small projects, including offices and residences. He has worked extensively in London, Singapore, Tokyo, and Beijing and has worked for Rem Koolhaas. *Interior Design* included one of his projects among its list of the best of 2012, and *Perspective* named him as one of its "40 under 40."

Lim, William (b. 1957)
Lim is a Chinese architect known for his interior architecture work. He studied at Cornell and became managing director at CL3 Architects Ltd. in 1993. The interior architecture firm specializes in hospitality, corporate, retail, and art installation projects. Clients include the Shangri-La Hotels Group, Marina Bay Sands Corp., Marco Polo Hotel Group, and Crown Hotel and Casino. Lim is also an avid art enthusiast and implements artwork into his projects.

Lin, Kris (b. late 20th cent.)
Kris Lin Interior Design (KLID) has done multiple projects, including a Japanese restaurant, a night club, and a real estate office. He describes his work as belonging to a "new Orientalism of Southeast Asian style." His real estate office is unexpectedly serene, while his night club has the appropriate balance of bling and bliss.

Ling, David (b. 1960s)
Ling trained as an associate with Richard Meier, I. M. Pei, and Emilio Ambasz and subsequently founded David Ling Architects, an international design practice, in 1992. His project types range from small offices to high-end residential and retail. Fluent in Chinese, English, and German, Ling has taught at Parsons School of Design and the University of Nuremburg.

Lissoni, Piero (b. 1956)
Lissoni studied architecture at the Politecnico di Milano. After graduating in 1985, he worked as a designer for furniture manufacturers. Along with Nicoletta Canesi, he established Lissoni Associati in 1996, which focuses on architecture, graphics, and industrial design projects. Their interior work includes hotels, showrooms, private houses, shops, and yachts, and products include furniture, lighting fixtures, and packaging. Clients include Alessi, Cassina, Fritz Hansen, Glas Italia, Kartell, and Knoll. Lissoni is also active as an art director, focusing on corporate identity, signage, and packaging.

Loewy, Raymond (1893–1986)
Born in France, this American industrial and interior designer first worked as a window dresser and fashion illustrator. A polymath, among his singular and evocative designs are the Coldspot refrigerator, a Greyhound bus, Studebaker automobiles, Skylab, a Lucky Strike cigarette package, and a Coca-Cola bottle. He also designed the distinctive light blue livery of Air Force One.

Loos, Adolf (1870–1933)
An Austrian architect born in the Czech lands who became one of the leaders in the modern movement of the early 20th century. He recognized the impact of machinery on ornament and design. His strong, austere quality influenced the development of the functional style in Austria and around the world. The sumptuousness of the materials he used in his American Bar, 1908, does little to prepare one for the provocative argument of his lecture "Ornament and Crime" in 1910.

Lotersztain, Alexander (b. 1977)
Lotersztain was born in Argentina and studied design at Griffith University and Queensland College of Art. He founded the international design studio Derlot in 2003, which focuses on sustainable furniture, interiors, object design, branding, and art direction. Clients include Nestlé, Covo, and Mizuno.

Lung, Virginia (b. 1970s)
One Plus Partnership is a Hong Kong design firm founded in 2004 by Ajax Law Ling Kit and Virginia Lung. They designed the YOHO Midtown residential clubhouse and also work on other project types including retail and hospitality.

Mackintosh, Charles Rennie (1868–1928)
A Scottish artist, architect, and furniture designer who designed and created in the Art Nouveau style. One of the earliest figures who can rightly be termed a modernist, his works included a series of nearly all-white tea rooms, and his masterpiece, the Glasgow School of Art, 1895. See ART NOUVEAU.

Mackintosh, Margaret Macdonald (1864–1933)
A Scottish designer who trained at the Glasgow School of Art. She collaborated with her sister, Frances Macdonald, and later with her husband, Charles Rennie Mackintosh. She worked in metal and textiles, forming a variety of panels, and designed objects, including lamp shades and light fixtures. Stylistically her works were related to Arts and Crafts, Art Nouveau, and the Vienna Secession. As with many of the 20th-century women who worked with their husbands, it is difficult to untangle the extent of her contributions to designs typically credited to the men, such as the Willow Tea Rooms.

Mackmurdo, Arthur Heygate (1851–1942)
Although trained as an architect, he found his professional success in graphics and furniture design. He worked with William Morris yet is considered an early advocate of Art Nouveau. To him is credited the first Art Nouveau piece of furniture, a chair with floral carvings that dates to 1882.

Maddox, Eva (b. 1943)
Maddox studied at the University of Cincinnati and has received numerous AIA and ASID awards. Her clients include AT&T, Owens Corning, Spiegel, Hayworth, and Helikon. She has been published in *Interiors*, *Interior Design*, and *Contract*. She partnered with Stanley Tigerman in founding an alternative graduate school of design, Archeworks. She retired from Perkins + Will as Design Principal in 2016.

Magistretti, Vico (1920–2006)
This architect and designer worked for the major Italian design firms and was one of the first furniture designers to work extensively with plastic.

Magnusson, Carl (b. 1940)
Born in Sweden, Magnusson grew up in Canada and studied architecture and design at the University of Idaho and the Chalmers Institute of Technology in Sweden. He moved to Los Angeles in 1966 and worked for Charles and Ray Eames. He joined Knoll in 1976 and remained there until becoming Senior Vice President in 1993. At Knoll, his most significant designs include the Magnusson Desk and RPM chair. He also has worked with BMW and Teknion.

Maharam, Michael (b. 1959)
Maharam took over the family's New York textile company in the late 1990s, as the fourth generation to lead the firm that transitioned from producing fabrics for theatrical productions to contract work. He has collaborated with a variety of 20th-century designers in producing textile designs, including Bruce Mau and Konstantin Grcic. His is one of the few firms to bridge the gap between contract work and fashion, collaborating with the menswear designer Paul Smith.

Majorelle, Louis (1859–1926)
Important French Art Nouveau furniture maker, he was born into a family of cabinetmakers in Nancy, France. Along with others, he established the northeastern French city as a major center of Art Nouveau furniture. Under his design leadership, the family factories progressed from reproducing 18th-century pieces to being on the forefront of design. He exhibited in multiple world fairs. After 1910, the firm's creative energies were spent, but it continued to be financially viable for a decade after his death.

Mallet-Stevens, Robert (1886–1945)
Trained as an architect, he created a few significant buildings in his career that flourished between the wars, most notably a striking cubist villa and garden for the Count and Countess de Noailles. He was also active as an interior and furniture designer; he was one of the designers in the 1925 Exposition Internationale des Arts Décoratifs. He was an early set designer for film.

Mansart, François (1598–1666)
French classical architect. Mansart's Hôtel de la Vrillière (1635) was long used as a model for elegant Paris houses. Mansart became Louis XIV's chief architect. At Versailles he built and oversaw the furnishing of the Galerie des Glaces and the Grand Trianon. Though not an invention of his, the Mansard roof honored its namesake through his frequent employment of it.

Mare, André (1885–1932)
An important figure in the early Art Deco movement, Mare was partners with Louis Süe, with whom he founded Süe et Mare, a company involved in the creation of many types of decorative arts, such as clocks, wallpaper, and larger furniture pieces. They exhibited at the 1925 Paris Exposition des Art Décoratifs et Industriels, from which the term "Art Deco" is derived. See ARTS AND CRAFTS MOVEMENT.

Marino, Peter (b. 1949)
This successful designer studied architecture at Cornell, after which he worked for SOM. His roster of diverse project types includes jet and helicopter interiors. His prominent projects include the residence for Ron Perelman, CEO of Revlon; offices in the Seagram building; and Pickfair, the home of Mary Pickford and Douglas Fairbanks. Marino is widely published, including articles in *House & Garden* and *Architectural Digest.*

Marot, Daniel (1661–1752)
A French designer of the Louis XIV period. Because of religious persecution, he fled from France to Holland, and then to England, where he became the chief designer to William III. His designs blend Louis XIV and Dutch styles. His position at court enabled him to direct a large group of refugee artisans into England. He designed mantels, sidewalls, cabinets, clocks, beds, and draperies.

Martin brothers (18th cent.)
French artisans (Guillaume, Étienne-Simon, Julien, and Robert) distinguished for their lacquer finishing in the Chinese manner. Their technique, called vernis Martin, employed a clear lacquer speckled with gold. Snuffboxes, furniture, and even complete rooms were finished in the technique. See VERNIS MARTIN.

Martin, Catherine (b. 1965)
Born in New South Wales, Martin is active as an interior designer and art director. She has won Academy and Tony Awards for her production costume designs. She worked on the films *Romeo+Juliet*, *Moulin Rouge*, and *Australia* and the Broadway production *La Bohéme.* Married to director Baz Luhrmann, she has a line of designer rugs, wallpaper, and paint and does branding and product design.

Martin, Robert (1706–1767)
A lacquerer who, along with his brothers Guillaume, Étienne-Simon, and Julien, studied Chinese lacquer and developed a comparable technique that came to be known as vernis Martin.

Mathsson, Bruno (1907–1988)
Mathsson was a Swedish furniture designer and architect. His most well-known works are the Grasshopper, Mimat, and Eva Chairs and the Super Elliptical Table. He used carving, bending, and laminating wood and also traditional handicraft methods in his modern furniture.

Matos, Sergio (b. 1979)
Matos was born in Paranatinga, Brazil, and is an industrial designer who incorporates Brazilian historic forms into his works. His most famous piece is the Hamper chair.

Matta, Roberto Sebastian (1911–2002)
A sculptor as much as a furniture designer, Matta started his career in Le Corbusier's office. He included among his friends René Magritte, Joan Miró, and Pablo Picasso. A politically active figure in his native Chile, he is known in the U.S. for the Malitte seating system, which is a demountable sculpture that turns into multiple-seating pieces, each made of a single piece of upholstered polyurethane foam.

Maugham, Syrie (1879–1955)
Maugham was born in London and opened a shop in 1922, when she began decorating projects. She was known for her glamorous rooms, luxurious materials, and furniture selections and for her own all-white drawing room, which she copied for clients multiple times. It was said that friends remembered her for kindness and her staff knew her for her temper. She influenced subsequent designers, particularly Elsie de Wolfe, Jean-Michel Frank, and Francis Elkins.

Mayhew, Thomas (d. 1804)
An English cabinetmaker who worked with WILLIAM INCE. Together they published a book of designs, *The Universal System of Household Furniture.* He was a contemporary of Chippendale.

M'Baye, Ousmane (b. 1975)
M'Baye is a designer in Dakar, Senegal, who creates furniture and also works as an event designer and decorator. He uses recycled materials such as metal tubing from water pipes and oil cans. He does not claim to be an artist but rather an artisan designer. He is self-taught and draws inspiration from working in his studio.

McClelland, Nancy (1877–1959)
One of the most influential American interior designers, because of her success as an author and her tireless efforts to promote design education, standards, and licensing. She started out as a journalist for the *Philadelphia Press* and moved on to oversee window displays for Wanamaker's. A polyglot, she was known for her expertise in antiques and wallpapers. She wrote numerous books and articles and served as the first president of the American Institute of Interior Designers, the forerunner to ASID.

McCobb, Paul (1917–1969)
An American furniture designer who had a lasting influence on American furniture during the 1950s and 1960s. He was especially active in creating modular furniture and coordinated groups that combined good design and craftsmanship with mass-production techniques.

McIntyre, Samuel (1757–1811)
An American wood-carver of Salem, Massachusetts, who created many mantelpieces and overdoors as well as carvings on furniture; for his designs he relied on Batty Langley's publications. Greatly influenced by Sheraton's later designs, he, like Duncan Phyfe, was a leading designer of the American Federal period.

Meeks, Joseph (1771–1868)
Founder of a successful New York furniture company, Joseph Meeks and Sons. The firm specialized in Rococo Revival furniture. After Joseph retired, his sons and later a grandson ran the firm.

Meissonnier, Juste-Aurèle (1695–1750)
The father of the Rococo style. French, he was born in Turin, Italy, and in his adulthood produced a book of engravings using the shell motif that captured the fancy of French craftsmen. They adapted and incorporated his designs into the period woodwork (boiserie) and furniture. Meissonnier became designer to

Louis XV in 1725. As a painter, goldsmith, architect, and interior designer, the talented artist carried the Rococo style to its extravagant limit.

Mies van der Rohe, Ludwig (1886–1969)
German-American architect. A pioneer of modern architecture, van der Rohe started out as an assistant to Peter Behrens. He was appointed director of the Bauhaus in 1930 and stayed until 1937, when he left to teach at the Armour Institute (now the Illinois Institute of Technology). Most of his work that meets the definition of interiors and furnishings comes from his years in Germany, including multiple examples of exhibition designs, which included custom furniture pieces. For the German Pavilion at the Barcelona World's Fair, 1928, he collaborated with Lilly Reich in producing an elegant set of polished chrome and white furniture, a set that included the Barcelona chair and stool.

Mizner, Addison (1872–1933)
American decorator, architect, furniture designer, and developer. Along with his brother Wilson, Mizner became a successful Florida developer. In addition to planning new neighborhoods, Mizner frequently did the architecture, the interiors, and the furnishings. He was a key figure for developing a Spanish colonial revival that came to represent an idealized vision of Florida's past.

Mogensen, Børg (1914–1972)
Born in Denmark, Mogensen began his career as a cabinetmaker in 1934. He studied furniture design at the Copenhagen School of Arts and Crafts and architecture at the Royal Academy of Fine Arts, where he graduated as an architect in 1942. In 1950, he started his design office, creating simple, functional furniture that played a large role in establishing Denmark as a center of modern furniture design.

Molyneux, Juan Pablo (b. 1946)
A Chilean-born interior designer who has designed interiors for private residences as well as public buildings and private clubs in four continents. His most famous designs are maximalist and classical in style including rooms for the Russian Federation and the United Nations Headquarters in Geneva.

Montoya, Juan (b. 1944)
Montoya was born and raised in Colombia. He studied architecture in Bogotá before graduating from Parsons School of Design, New York. After further studies in Milan and Paris, he returned to New York and founded his firm. Montoya's work is formally simple and tactile; he likes to juxtapose and layer textures, fabrics, and colors. He says most of his inspiration comes from different cultures, including Japan, Morocco, Scandinavia, and the Americas. Montoya focuses on the residential sector and has done furniture for Henredon.

Moore, Ian (b. 1958)
Born in New Zealand, Moore studied and worked as a structural engineer before turning to architecture and interiors. He has collaborated with Ove Arup and Norman Foster. His small firm is known for single-family and multi-family residential projects that have won numerous awards in Australia.

Morgan, Julia (1872–1957)
California's first licensed woman architect. San Francisco-born, a University of California graduate of engineering, Morgan was encouraged by Bernard Maybeck to pursue architecture. In 1898, after two years of failed applications, she entered the École des Beaux-Arts, Paris. She returned to America, and her career took off during the architectural boom that followed the San Francisco earthquake of 1906. She designed hundreds of residences, which do not reflect one definitive style. Her creations were client-centered and depended largely on materials available locally. She integrated the architectural traditions of the West with her sophisticated Beaux-Arts training. Her most prominent client was William Randolph Hearst (1863– 1951). She worked for decades on his immense private home, Hearst Castle, San Simeon, California (1919–1940).

Morris, May (1862–1938)
The daughter of William Morris was herself a designer. She specialized in embroidery, contributed to the designs of furniture produced by her father's firm, and was responsible for Arts and Crafts' popularity with women who pursued embroidery as a hobby.

Morris, William (1834–1896)
English producer and designer of wallpapers, furniture, tapestries, carpets, stained-glass windows, and home accessories. Morris was the leader of the Arts and Crafts movement, which looked to England's medieval past to find contemporary solutions. Greatly influenced by Dante Gabriel Rossetti and Edward Burne-Jones, Morris revolted against the eclecticism of the late 19th century. He created and designed the furnishings for his home, Red House. Morris said, "I don't want art for a few, any more than education for a few, or freedom for a few. What business have we with art at all unless all can share it?" He attempted to bring art back to the common man, in his home and its furnishings, but unfortunately his beautiful handmade products were extremely costly. See ART NOUVEAU and PRE-RAPHAELITE BROTHERHOOD. See also WEBB, PHILIP SPEAKMAN in this appendix.

Moser, Koloman (1868–1918)
Moser was a polymath, although he was most known for his graphic work. First a member of the Vienna Secession group, he and the like-minded artist Gustav Klimt seceded from the Secessionists. His body of work includes fashion, stained glass, ceramics, and furniture. He admired the Arts and Crafts artists.

Mourgue, Olivier (b. 1939)
Born in Paris, Mourgue studied design at École Boulle and then furniture design at l'École National Supérieure des Arts Décoratifs, graduating in 1960. His most well-known work is the Djinn chair, designed for Airborne International in France and featured in the movie *2001: A Space Odyssey*.

Mozer, Jordan (b. 1960s)
Mozer founded Jordan Mozer and Associates, a Chicago-based architecture and design firm specializing in high-end hospitality design. He is most known for designing restaurants in the 1980s in an over-the-top postmodern style, including the way over-the-top *Vivere Room*.

Muni, Shonibare (b. 1960s)
Muni is the past president of the Interior Designer Association of Nigeria. After graduating from the Istituto per l'Arte e il Restauro in Florence, Italy, and working at an architectural firm, she cofounded Avant Garde and Interior Options Ltd, an interior design firm and furniture manufacturing company. She has worked on major projects locally and internationally, with clients including the Hilton Hotels and AGIP. Along with her interior design endeavors, she manages Ethniki, an African-inspired furniture and accessories company.

Muthesius, Eckart (1904–1989)
The son of the famous author Hermann Muthesius, Muthesius the younger is a globally relatively unknown German modernist who did most of his work in India and for one client, the Maharaja of Indore. His designs are usually similar to those of his Bauhaus contemporaries, although some of them veer in the direction of being more Art Deco. His innovative armchair designs incorporated ashtrays and reading lights. He did interiors for trains, ships, and recreational vehicles.

Nakashima, George (1905–1990)
Nakashima was born in Spokane, Washington, and was a woodworker, architect, and furniture designer of the American Arts and Crafts movement. After studying architecture in the U.S. and France, he worked abroad including for Antonin Raymond in Japan. He is known for his butterfly joints, large-scale tables, natural edges, and use of traditional Japanese tools and techniques. As a Japanese American he was interned at a camp in Idaho during the Second World War.

Nelson, George (1908–1986)
One of the most important and prolific American designers of the 20th century. His leadership at Herman Miller guaranteed that the contract furniture company would live on after the tenure of Gilbert Rohde. Nelson introduced the slat bench, the adjustable headboard bed, and case furniture built on steel frames that were finished in a wide range of woods or lacquered colors. Nelson was one of the innovators of modular office and bedroom furniture. His OMNI office furniture was composed of interchangeable parts. His famous designs include the Marshmallow Sofa, the Coconut Chair, and a collection of clocks. See MODULAR FURNITURE.

Neutra, Richard (1892–1970)
An American architect born in Vienna in 1892. In the late 1920s he produced the Lovell House and the Lovell Beach House, which were combinations of Californian skeletal pavilions and European cubist designs. He knew Rudolph Schindler and met Frank Lloyd Wright while attending Louis Sullivan's funeral. He believed that the "constructed human environment should be an entity, and not split up by specialists." He designed furniture for his architectural work in the U.S. and for the German projects he turned to late in life.

Newson, Marc (b. 1963)
Interior and furniture designer Newson was born in Sydney and is best known for his aluminum Lockheed Lounge Chair. His work focuses on curves, color, and anthropomorphic forms. With his firm, Marc Newson Ltd., he creates interiors, furniture, transportation design, and products ranging from cameras to apparel. Notable interiors include the Qantas First Class Lounge and Hotel Puerta America in Spain.

Niamien, Vincent (b. 1956)
Niamien is a furniture designer who mixes modern and traditional styles and uses wood, his favorite material, and metal in a tasteful manner. He purposely combines wood and metal because one is a natural element while the other is man-made, therefore creating a balance. In 1996, a chair of his called Sie won the grand prize at the Biennale Internationale Design of Dakar. He was born in Côte d'Ivoire in a small village where his father was a wood-carver and his mother made pottery. His furniture work includes sofas and stools.

Ninivaggi, Krista (b.1979)
An interior designer known for her work in hospitality design. She is a graduate of Rhode Island School of Design and has worked for major companies such as the Rockwell Group, AvroKO, and ShoP Architects. Ninivaggi's designs are distinctive in their use of color and materiality.

Noguchi, Isamu (1904–1988)
An American landscape architect, sculptor, and furniture designer who created a figural free-form glass-topped table that rests on an intricately shaped abstract base, as well as a curving, armless sofa with a small backrest. Noguchi designed stage sets for Martha Graham and Merce Cunningham and furniture and lamps for Herman Miller and Knoll.

Oberkampf, Christophe-Philippe (1738–1815)
The founder of the fabric factory at Jouy near Versailles, and the creator of "toile de Jouy," a particular type of printed cotton fabric. See MIGNONNETTES, PICOTÉ, and TOILE DE JOUY.

Oeben, Jean-François (1721–1763)
A master cabinetmaker to King Louis XV. He created many beautiful pieces decorated with fine marquetry in colored woods. Oeben designed furniture for the Marquise de Pompadour, who preferred simpler pieces to the then-current Rococo style.

Olbrich, Joseph Maria (1867–1908)
Olbrich was one of the founding members of the Vienna Secession group and was the architect for the group's signature building, the Secession Exhibition Building. He first worked for Otto Wagner. He later relocated to Darmstadt, Germany, where he was a major figure in Jugendstil design. A firm believer in the ability of a designer to work in multiple realms, his life's work includes interiors, furniture, textile designs, and glass and silverware design.

Oppenord (or Oppenort), Gilles Marie (1672–1742)
A French designer of interiors, furniture, and metalwork. He was the director of styles during the Régence period and was partially responsible for introducing the craze for Rococo art. His painted panels resembled the works of French painters Jean-Antoine Watteau and Claude Gillot.

Oxman, Neri (b. 1976)
Oxman is an architect and designer and assistant professor of media arts and sciences at the MIT Media Lab, focusing on cutting-edge digital design and fabrication.

Pabst, Daniel (1826–1910)
An American cabinetmaker who produced excellent furniture and cabinets in his Philadelphia shop during the 1860s. His Victorian designs showed a distinct French Rococo influence; his work was mainly executed in black walnut.

Palladio, Andrea (1518–1580)
An Italian architect and excavator who, with Giacomo Barozzi da Vignola, rediscovered and standardized the proportions of the Roman architectural orders. His *I Quattro Libri dell'Architettura*, 1570, had great influence on architecture and design. Palladio also designed many buildings in the pure Italian Renaissance style.

Paniagua, Mauricio (b. 1969)
Paniagua is the co-founder of DFC, a Mexico City-based product design company. Paniagua is originally from Guatemala and studied industrial design. He met Tony Moxham in New York City and moved to Mexico in 2005 to start DFC. Their company combines traditional Mexican techniques and styles with modern design, employing Mexican artisans who use traditional local techniques. Their modern designs are bold, colorful, and eccentric.

Panton, Verner (1926–1998)
A furniture designer who pioneered in the use of molded plastics for lightweight colored portable chairs in interesting shapes and forms. His cantilevered, curved, and saddle-seated chair was designed to conform to the human body. His biggest success was a single-piece molded plastic stacking chair, which is now known as the Panton Chair.

Parente, Rodolphe (b. 1980)
A French designer who is best known for his residential work in Paris. He designs with a self-proclaimed "graphic quality" to his work and has said that he often tries to incorporate a show-stopping element that will provoke conversation amidst an elegant backdrop. One example is a studio whose floors he had lacquered cherry red.

Parish, Sister (1910–1994)
Born Dorothy May Kinnicutt, "Sister" was a nickname. A socialite and interior designer, she married Henry Parish II, an investment banker, Sister Parish rose to fame when Jacqueline Kennedy hired her in 1960 her to decorate the White House. Her work was nostalgic and charmingly innovative. One of her signature moves was painting floors. Parish used English and French antiques, and her rooms had elaborate but always matching coordinated color schemes and were replete with objets d'art.

Paulin, Pierre (1927–2009)
A French designer noted for his biomorphic furniture, usually made of chrome, foam, and stretch fabric. The units are sculptural in their appearance, lightweight, and comfortable. A testament to the futuristic quality of his designs was their use in the film *2001: A Space Odyssey*. His Tongue Chair is made from a single continuous element and is part of the permanent collection of the Museum of Modern Art and the Musée des Arts Décoratifs.

Pawson, John (b. 1949)
Born in Halifax, Yorkshire, Pawson went to Japan to teach English, where he visited the studio of architect and designer Shiro Kuramata and decided to pursue architecture. After returning to England, he began studying at the Architecture Association. He began his own practice in 1981. Prominent works include Calvin Klein's flagship store, airport lounges for Cathay Pacific in Hong Kong, and the Cistercian Monastery of Our Lady of Nový Dvůr in Bohemia. He also worked with Gae Aulenti and Ettore Sottsass.

Payne, Chris (b. 1960s), and Emma Campbell (b. 1970s)
British-born designers later based in Nairobi, Kenya, they are the head creative team at Interior IDEA, an interior and graphic design company. Their firm focuses on residences, camps, and hotels in East Africa. Projects include the Malewa River Lodge and Serengeti Safari Camp, which has been featured in *Architectural Digest*.

Percier, Charles (1764–1834)
French architect, decorator, and furniture designer to Napoleon I. With Pierre Fontaine, he helped create the Empire style of the early 19th century. Percier worked on Malmaison, Saint-Cloud, the Tuileries, and the Louvre. He designed furniture, textiles, ornaments, wallpapers, and accessories for these palaces. See EMPIRE PERIOD.

Pergolesi, Michelangelo (active 1777–1801)
A decorative painter, architect, and furniture designer. He worked with Robert Adam and painted ceilings, panels, and furniture for him. Pergolesi painted his designs on a flat tint, usually pale green or yellow, rather than on the natural wood itself.

Perriand, Charlotte (1903–1999)
After Le Corbusier admired her projects at the Salon des Artistes Décorateurs, she joined his firm in 1927. Her collaboration with Le Corbusier and his cousin, Pierre Jeanneret, in the 1920s and 1930s is considered the period when the famous modernist produced his iconic furniture pieces and refined his approach to residential interiors. The first furniture pieces were crafted out of tubular chrome and pony skin. She fled France before the Second World War for Japan and Vietnam, where she collaborated with designers and craftsmen in creating modern designs out of bamboo.

Pesce, Gaetano (b. 1939)
Pesce has been expanding the ideas and structures of Italian New Design throughout his career. He studied architecture and industrial design in Venice from 1958 to 1965. He went on to produce vibrant work in painting, sculpture, film, theater, design, and architecture. In the 1980s, he taught at Cooper Union in New York. He developed furniture designs for B&B Italia and Cassina.

Phyfe, Duncan (1768–1854)
A Scottish cabinetmaker who worked in America. His earliest works were in the classic Adam tradition. He is often presented in the context of the work of Sheraton and Hepplewhite. Phyfe personified the American Regency (neoclassicism) period. The lyre and the plume are two motifs often found in his designs. His sons Michael and James worked with him, and they counted the Astor family among their wealthy clients. See FEDERAL PERIOD.

Platner, Warren (1919–2006)
A Cornell graduate, Platner successively worked for Raymond Loewy, I. M. Pei, Roche and Dinkeloo, and Eero Saarinen. His eponymous furniture line is a set of chairs and tables that stand on cage-like wire bases.

Ponti, Gio (1897–1979)
A prolific designer and author whose education started at the Milan Polytechnic. He was one of the founders of the design magazine *Domus*, and one of his prominent projects was the interiors for the ill-fated ocean liner *Andrea Doria*. The furniture company Cassina produced his Superleggera Chair for decades.

Porset, Clara (1932–1981)
The Cuban-born designer worked for Luis Barragán and was responsible for the custom furniture pieces that he used in his projects. Porset's designs relied upon Mexican traditional manufacturing techniques yet managed to look contemporary, even when made out of rush, wood, and leather.

Propst, Robert (1921–2000)
Probst designed the first line of systems furniture, Action Office, for Herman Miller.

Prouvé, Jean (1901–1984)
Prouvé was a French architect, designer, manufacturer, and engineer. His father, Victor Prouvé, was a founding member of the Art Nouveau School of Nancy. Prouvé the younger began his career as an artist and blacksmith apprentice, later establishing Ateliers Jean Prouvé in 1931, making metal furniture. One large project was making furniture for the CPDE, the Paris power company. A new business, Construction Jean Prouvé, switched to larger-scaled projects. Prouvé helped the company became a leading manufacturer of lightweight curtain wall façades. A noteworthy project was La Maison Tropicale, a modular prefabricated housing system intended for France's colonies.

Pugin, Augustus Welby (1812–1852)
English architect and writer, the prime architectural force in the Gothic Revival period. He specialized in interiors and furniture. His publications includes the influential *Contrasts* which appeared in 1836.

Pushelberg, Glenn (20th cent.)
Pushelberg has no distinct style and tries to make each project have an unexpected yet defined twist. Pushelberg teamed up with George Yabu in Toronto, Canada, and together they have worked on a variety of projects. Experimenting with materials and the design process is a big part of their design technique. Some of their recent projects include the Four Seasons hotel in Tokyo, a redesign of Neiman Marcus in Las Vegas, and the renovation of Tiffany & Co.'s New York flagship.

Putman, Andrée (1925–2013)
A French interior designer who started out as a journalist in the 1960s. She worked as a marketing consultant for fashion companies, including the French chain store Prisunic. Soon she was designing home accessories and in 1978 embarked on a career in interior design. Putman gained renown for her ability to recognize the worth of furniture designed by modern luminaries such as Antoni Gaudí and Eileen Gray at a time when the pieces were not valued. Her interior designs are noted for being richly detailed while remaining modern. She has been commissioned to work on the interiors of museums, hotels, designer clothing shops, and the Concorde for Air France, among other projects.

Race, Ernest (1913–1964)
Race's first designs that received international attention blended abstract modernist patterns with traditional Indian textiles. He later focused on inexpensive and mass-produced contemporary furniture. His Antelope Chair and Table had its debut at the 1951 Festival of Britain. One of the most important British modernists, he is less well known outside of his home country.

Rams, Dieter (b. 1932)
Rams was born in 1932 in Germany and studied architecture in Wiesbaden. After graduation he began a long partnership with Braun in 1955, working as an architect, interior designer, and product designer. He was awarded the Order of Merit of the Federal Republic of Germany in 2002. His designs are known for their timeless aesthetic, function, and accessibility to the public. He is known for designing the Phonosuper SK4, a combination radio and record player, an early component audio system, a portable world-band radio, and furniture for Vitsœ.

Rashid, Karim (b. 1960)
Born in Cairo, the designer lived in London and studied industrial design at Carleton University, Canada, and the Associazione per il Disegno Industriale in Milan. In 1993, he opened a design studio in New York City, and the firm's services include interior design, product and furniture design, branding, fashion, and art. He is known for his bold use of color and organic shapes. The studio has 3,000 objects in production including seating, lighting, ceramic tiles, trash cans, water bottles, and vacuums. Clients include Alessi, Cappellini, Samsung, and Swarovski. Notable interiors projects are the Morimoto restaurant in Philadelphia, Samurais Hotel in Athens, and the Silk Road Restaurant in Las Vegas.

Ravenhall, Brendan (b. 1979)
The furniture and product designer was born in Côte d'Ivoire, grew up in Washington D.C., and later moved to Los Angeles. He graduated from the Rhode Island School of Design. His projects include the cord lamp.

Raymond, Antonin (1888–1976)
Antonin was born in the Czech lands and moved to New York, where he worked for Cass Gilbert. He then worked for Frank Lloyd Wright in Chicago, before the Prairie Style master sent him to Tokyo to oversee construction of the Imperial Hotel. Raymond's design aesthetic became increasingly modern. He opened his own firm in Tokyo and was influential in the world of Japanese architecture. From there he also did work in India.

Raymond, Noemi (1889–1955)
A French-speaking Swiss national, Noemi met her future husband Antonin in New York when she was an art student. She was a modernist who later designed rugs, furniture, silverware, and glassware. One of her textiles was specified for a Louis Kahn project.

Reich, Lilly (1885–1947)
Born in Berlin, the German designer is widely credited as the design force behind the furniture and interiors she produced in collaboration with Ludwig Mies van der Rohe. They designed a cantilevered chair with a tubular steel frame, and a similar chromed flat steel-frame chair, both known as Brno Chairs. For the German Pavilion at the 1929 Barcelona exhibit, they designed an X-frame armchair, stool, and table. For a residential project in Brno, the Tugendhat house, they designed an elegant and extravagant MR armchair. After Mies relocated to the U.S., Reich stayed in Berlin and continued to represent her former partner's business interests until her death.

Richardson, Henry Hobson (1838–1886)
Probably the most influential American architect of his generation. He studied at both Harvard and the École des Beaux-Arts. Trinity Church, Boston (1872–1877), the Marshall Field wholesale store, Chicago, and New Brattle Square church in Boston are principal works of his. Paradoxically, Richardson managed to develop a simple modern aesthetic while operating within the parameters of Romanesque revival. He also designed furniture.

Riesener, Jean-Henri (1734–1806)
A French master cabinetmaker. He trained under Jean-François Oeben during the Louis XV period, but most of his works have the classical look of the Louis XVI period: exquisite proportions, graceful lines, architectural motifs, and roses. Riesener's designs included fine marquetry details in deep tones on mahogany. He also used pictorial center panels, with allover patterns embellishing the sides of his units.

Rietveld, Gerrit Thomas (1888–1965)
Dutch architect and designer. Rietveld started out as a cabinetmaker and designed a chair that became a classic of modern furniture. His chair employed a dematerialized effect by emphasizing surface and the two dimensionality of applied color. From 1919 to 1931 he was a member of the de Stijl movement and moved on to architecture. The Schröder House, Utrecht (1924), is his most famous building for its impression of weightlessness and equilibrium reminiscent of Mondrian's paintings.

Risom, Jens (1916–2019)
A Danish designer/manufacturer who emigrated to the U.S. and produced fine modern furniture with high standards of craftsmanship. Many designs are scaled to the smaller home or apartment. Also a designer of contract furniture, his most famous pieces from his period as a Knoll designer were a variety of chairs made of woven webbing.

Robsjohn-Gibbings, Terence Harold (1905–1976)
A 20th-century furniture and interior designer. During his long career, he alternately worked out of New York, London, and Athens. He created pristine and elegant case goods and fine-lined seating units for Baker and Herman Miller. Ideologically, he managed to decry historicism and argue for Modernism, while he created a line of pieces that were inspired by antique Greek and Roman models. His clients included Doris Duke and Elizabeth Arden.

Rockwell, David (b. 1956)
Born in Chicago, he studied architecture at Syracuse University and the Architectural Association, London. In 1984 he established the architecture and design firm the Rockwell Group. Based in New York City, it focuses on international high-end experimental hospitality, retail, and entertainment. Designs include the Academy Awards set, JetBlue Terminal, the *Hairspray* Broadway set design, numerous hotels, and interactive installations.

Rodrigues, Sergio (1927–2014)
Rodrigues was an icon of modern Brazilian furniture design. He graduated from the National School of Architecture in Rio in 1952 and founded Oca in 1955. One of his best-known works is Poltrona Mole (soft armchair), which he created in 1957. Most of his projects are in Brazil.

Röntgen, Abraham (1711–1793) and David (1743–1807)
Marquetry and furniture designers of the Louis XV and the Louis XVI periods. The father and son team used light, bright-toned woods as inlays in mahogany, and their marquetry work has been compared to marble mosaic work. Their workshop produced highly intricate pieces of furniture with numerous compartments that opened and shut by means of clever mechanical devices. Their furniture was produced mainly in a factory at Neuwied, Germany. Chrétien Krause and Michael Rummer are credited with doing much of the marquetry, and Johann Roetig the mechanical devices. The Röntgens counted Marie Antoinette among their clients.

Rohde, Gilbert (1894–1944)
A native New Yorker and son of a cabinetmaker, Rohde began designing furniture after an inspiring trip to the Paris Exhibition in 1925. His early work was sold at Lord & Taylor. Exuberantly modern, his designs rescued the nearly bankrupt Herman Miller, a producer of historical furniture reproductions, by updating its image. He designed a successful line of modular office furniture for the company and went on to become its design director.

Rorimer, Louis (1872–1939)
Rorimer founded the Cleveland-based furniture manufacturer Rorimer-Brooks. The firm was highly successful, employing more than 100 people who made a variety of revival pieces, most notably copies of English Jacobean works. Attending the 1925 Art Deco exposition in Paris was a life-changing event for the designer, who afterward shifted the firm's design direction to be more eclectic and modern.

Rottet, Lauren (b. 1960s)
After receiving an architecture degree from the University of Texas, she worked at numerous firms, notably beginning Skidmore, Owings & Merrill's interiors practice in Los Angeles. In 2008 she established Rottet Studio, an international architecture and interior design firm focusing on corporate and hospitality design, and with offices in New York, Los Angeles, Houston, San Francisco, and Shanghai. Projects include the Surrey Hotel in New York, St. Regis Resort renovation in Aspen, and the Presidential Bungalows at the Beverly Hills Hotel. The American Institute of Architects and the International Interior Design Association gave Rottet Fellow status.

Rousseau de la Rottière, Jean-Siméon (1747–c. 1822)
A French designer of interiors and accessories of the Louis XVI period. He decorated the boudoir of Marie Antoinette in elegant, refined forms using golden tones. The panels ("Love Assisting at the Toilet of Grace"), which he used in this room, were done in subtle gradations of gold and silver. He also decorated the Queen's room at Versailles.

Rueda, Angelica (b. late 20th cent.)
Rueda created Casacor, an interior design show throughout South America, along with Javier Campos Malbrán, Ernesto Del Castilho, and Brazilian Yolanda Figueiredo. Casacor started in Brazil in 1987.

Ruhlmann, Emile-Jacques (1879–1933)
French furniture designer Ruhlmann came from a family that owned a painting and contracting firm. His forays into furniture began in 1910 when he designed pieces for his own apartment. In 1919 he began an interior design firm with Pierre Laurent making wallpaper, light fixtures, rugs, furniture, and other items. He was influenced early on by the Art Nouveau movement in France, but later moved on to design pieces more influenced by 18th-century sensibilities of craftsmanship and classical inspiration. Ruhlmann founded his cabinetmaking shop in 1923 and began the prolific stage of his career constructing precious pieces out of rare woods like Macassar ebony and Brazilian rosewood. These pieces were further distinguished with sumptuous materials, such as ivory and shagreen. His Elephant Chair garnered acclaim. A standard motif was his use of tassels for drawer pulls.

Ruskin, John (1819–1900)
An English writer and art critic, Ruskin wrote that "ornamentation is the principal part of architecture." Two of his several publications are *The Seven Lamps of Architecture*, 1849, and *The Stones of Venice*, 1851. He influenced the works of William Morris, Gustav Stickley, and Richard Norman Shaw.

Saarinen, Eero (1910–1961)
An influential modern architect and designer who was born in Finland and arrived in America in 1923. He regarded each problem as a new and individual challenge, and he sought to answer it with free, original forms, including the TWA terminal at Kennedy Airport and Dulles International Airport. He collaborated with Charles and Ray Eames, and among his many furniture designs the most famous ones were his pedestal chairs and tables. His designs for Knoll include the Womb Chair and the Grasshopper Chair.

Saarinen, Eliel (1873–1950)
A Finnish architect and city planner. He constructed the Helsinki railway station and many U.S. buildings. The father of the Finnish-American architect Eero Saarinen, the elder Saarinen served as the president of Cranbrook Academy outside of Detroit.

Salm, Isaac (b. 1978) and Jaime (b. 1978)
Isaac and Jaime Salm were born in Medellin, Colombia. Isaac serves as the business managing director, while Jaime acts as the creative director of their design firm. Jaime studied industrial design, graduating in 2001. They founded MIO in 2001, focusing on sustainability, product and furniture design, environments, and branding. They serve as consultants for companies as well as sell their own products, which include modular tiles, lighting, furniture, and accessories. They run offices in Philadelphia and Germany.

Sané, Édouard (b. late 20th cent.)
The Senegalese designer and restaurateur's most famous project is a bar, restaurant, and event space called Kadjinol Station.

Sato, Oki (b. 1977)
Born in Toronto, Sato received a master's degree in architecture from Waseda University in Tokyo in 2002. That same year in Tokyo, he established Nendo, which added an office in Milan a few years later. The firm focuses on architecture, interior, furniture and product design, and graphics with mostly luxury retail and restaurant design types. Clients include Fritz Hansen, Hermès, Cartier, Swarovski, and Moroso.

Saunier, Claude-Charles (1734–1807)
A French master ébéniste (cabinetmaker) who worked for Louis XV and Louis XVI. His marquetry was in the style of Jean-François Oeben.

Scarpa, Carlo (1906–1989)
An Italian architect who was also known for his furniture, interiors, and product designs. His showroom for Olivetti, the typewriter company, was the first of his interiors projects to garner worldwide acclaim. He created a line of seating for Knoll.

Schinkel, Karl Friedrich (1781–1841)
The architect, stage designer, and painter was also an accomplished furniture designer in the Biedermeier style.

Schrager, Ian (b. 1946)
A New York entrepreneur, real estate developer, and hotelier, Schrager changed the hotel industry with his high-end modern hotels. He began with Studio 54, the popular New York celebrity nightclub in the 1970s. Publicity for the Morgans Hotel introduced the term "boutique hotel." Hotel concepts introduced by Schrager include "lobby socializing," "cheap chic," "urban resorts," and "hotel as a lifestyle." After leaving the Morgans Hotel Group, he created the Ian Schrager Company in 2005. His memorable hotels include the Gramercy Park Hotel, the Mondrian, and the Hudson in Manhattan, as well as the Delano in South Beach, Miami.

Schütte-Lihotzky, Grete (1897–2000)
The Austrian-born designer found her greatest success when modernist architect Ernst May invited her to design kitchens for his housing projects. The resulting Frankfurt Kitchen, 1926, was reproduced at least 10,000 times. She used inexpensive and practical materials, such as linoleum and plywood painted a glossy finish. A laboratory for preparing foods, some of its simple innovations were drawer holes instead of pulls and drawers individually dedicated to staples and spices. After being imprisoned in the Second World War in Germany, she worked in Cuba and China.

Scott Brown, Denise (b. 1931)
In addition to working as an architect, Scott Brown is a planner, educator, writer, and principal of Venturi, Scott Brown and Associates in Philadelphia. She began her education in South Africa and later attended the Architectural Association in London. After her first husband's death in an automobile accident, Scott Brown finished her master's degree in planning and met Robert Venturi. Scott Brown and Venturi have taught at several schools including the University of Pennsylvania; University of California, Berkeley; UCLA; Yale University; and Harvard University. Their furniture designs were more postmodern collector's items than commercial successes. Their greatest success came with the commission to do an addition to London's National Gallery.

Seck, Bibi (b. 1970s)
Seck was born in Paris and also grew up in London and Dakar. He has designed car interiors for Renault, as well as a Tag Heuer watch. With Ayse Birsel, he founded Birsel+Seck with offices in New York, Dakar, and Istanbul. The product design company has collaborated with Target, Herman Miller, and Hewlett Packard. One prominent project designed and produced by Seck is the colorful Taboo furniture line made in Senegal from recycled garbage bags and plastic bottles.

Seddon, George (1727–1801)
An English cabinetmaker, furniture designer, and upholsterer who worked with his sons George and Thomas and his son-in-law, Thomas Shackleton. Seddon made rich, elegant pieces and favored satinwood.

Selldorf, Annabelle (b. 1960)
Selldorf was born in Cologne, Germany, and is the founder of Selldorf Architects, New York. She received her architecture degree from Pratt Institute and her master's degree from Syracuse University in Florence, Italy. Her noteworthy projects include the Neue Galerie, New York, and the Sterling and Francine Clark Art Institute renovation in Massachusetts. In *Architectural Digest*, Selldorf described her method as starting with austerity and to that adding humor and intuition.

Shah, Shamir (b. 1960s)
After graduating with a degree in architecture from Yale University in 1987, Shah opened his architecture and interiors firm, Shamir Shah Design, in 1999. Based in New York, the firm specializes in high-end residential work with custom detailing and furniture design. Notable projects include New York boutique hotels and a flagship store for the ceramicist Jonathan Adler.

Sheraton, Thomas (1751–1806)
The last of the great 18th-century furniture designers. He published *The Cabinet-Maker and Upholsterer's Drawing Book* from 1791 to 1794. Sheraton was influenced by Hepplewhite and Chippendale and even more by French neoclassical designers. He used satinwood veneers, straight lines, and inlays rather than painted decorations, and there was an overall elegance, grace, and refinement in the designs of his early and middle years. His later works took a more extravagant turn and featured urns, rosettes, festoons, scrolls, and pendant flowers.

Snelling, Douglas (1916–1985)
Snelling was born in England in 1916 but practiced in Australia as a furniture designer, architect, and graphic designer. He designed primarily residential interiors and is most known for his boomerang-shaped chair and the Snelling Line of furniture.

Soane, Sir John (1753–1837)
An English architect and one of the group chiefly responsible for introducing classical Greek architecture into England. He studied in Rome and found inspiration in the temples of the Caesars, which were built in the Greek style. See REGENCY (ENGLISH). Architecture students from across the globe honor his legacy by visiting his townhouse in London.

Sondresen, Ole (b. 1968)
Born in Norway, Sondresen went to the University of Oregon for architecture. He established a practice based in New York that designs custom furniture and lighting and a variety of project types from residential to airport design. His practice implements sustainability, which is the frequent topic of his popular lectures.

Sottsass, Ettore (1917–2007)
After working for George Nelson, the Italian designer developed a signature style. The founder of the influential Memphis Group rejected minimalist Modernism. Often described as a postmodernist, his works incorporated color and made reference to popular culture. His design work included Olivetti typewriters and furniture for Poltronova.

Stam, Mart (1899–1986)
The Dutch designer has the distinction in design history of having created the first cantilevered armchair made of tubular steel in 1926, beating out his rival, Marcel Breuer, by a matter of months. Breuer's competing Cesca chair became more well known, but it is similar to Stam's earlier chair. Stam's chair was used to furnish apartments in the influential Weissenhof housing exhibition in Stuttgart.

Starck, Philippe (b. 1949)
Starck is a French product and interior designer born in 1949 in Paris and educated at the École Camondo. He has his own company called Starck, where he creates ultra-modern and sometimes startling designs. He has worked with Target, Microsoft, Alessi, Kartell, Floss, and numerous other companies for product design. Famous pieces include the Louis Ghost Chair and the Bubble Club Sofa and Armchair. Notable interiors include Café Costes in Paris and the Royalton and Paramount hotels in New York.

Stefanidis, John (b. 1937)
Born in Alexandria, Egypt, Stefanidis studied at Oxford University. After a stint in advertising, he switched careers to interior design. In 1967 he began a London architecture and interior design practice. He primarily designs in the residential and hotel sector and uses bold colors and eclectic elements. He also designs fabrics, wallpapers, accessories, and furniture.

Stern, Robert A. M. (b. 1939)
American architect Stern was born in New York City and studied architecture at Yale. In 1970 he became a professor of architecture at Columbia University. His architectural career began in the mid-1960s. He is known for his postmodern architectural style, adapting historicist styles to contemporary buildings, as well as his ability to blend buildings into their surroundings. In 1998, he was named Dean of the Yale School of Architecture.

Stickley, Gustave (1858–1942)
Stickley was a furniture designer and manufacturer who was highly influenced by English Arts and Crafts and specifically the writings of William Morris and John Ruskin. In his journal *Craftsman*, he published designs for simple houses with clearly conceived interiors that resonated with the American public. See MISSION STYLE.

Stone, Edward Durell (1902–1978)
An American architect who designed many important buildings in and out of the U.S. His pierced screens and patterned concrete and clay tiles influenced interior designers. His playful modernist hotel interiors were popular with the public and scorned by architectural critics.

Süe, Marie Louis (1875–1968)
An important figure in the early Art Deco movement, Louis Süe was partners with André Mare, with whom he founded Süe et Mare, a company involved in the creation of decorative arts such as clocks, wallpaper, and larger furniture pieces. They exhibited their wares at the 1925 Paris *Exposition des Art Décoratifs et Industriels*, from which the term Art Deco is derived.

Sugimoto, Takashi (b. 1945)
Sugimoto was raised in Kochi on the island of Shikoku, an area of natural beauty and centuries-old traditions. He graduated in 1968 from the Tokyo National University of Fine Arts and Music, the country's top art school. Among his major projects is the influential bar Set/Off in Tokyo.

Sullivan, Louis Henry (1856–1924)
The father of modern American architecture. He attacked historicism and eclecticism and evolved skyscraper design by combining new technical means with aesthetic ideals. In 1873 he worked for William Le Baron Jenney, who later built the first all-steel-frame building. In 1881, Sullivan partnered with Dankmar Adler, and they completed the Auditorium Building in Chicago in 1889; the structure was an opera house, hotel, and office building within a steel-frame office block. The Carson, Pirie & Scott Department Store in Chicago (1899–1904) had an evocative contrast between the lush organic ironwork of the first two floors and the cellular upper floors. In his book *Ornament in Architecture* (1892), he stated, "Ornament is mentally a luxury, not a necessary" [*sic*].

Summers, Gerald (1899–1967)
British furniture maker and one of the earliest designers of functional furniture. In 1929 he formed Makers of Simple Furniture, Ltd., a company dedicated to producing modern, practical pieces. He is most famous for his swept-back, curving chair produced from a single sheet of bent plywood (1943). In 1939 he left furniture making to start a ball bearing company.

Szenasy, Susan (b.1939)
Editor-in-chief of *Metropolis* from 1986 to 2017. The brunt of her work as a writer and educator has been arguing for ethical, sustainable, and human-centered design. She shifted the direction of design journalism from aesthetics to advocacy.

Tabansi, Anselm (b. late 20th cent.)
The Nigerian designer first studied law but went into interior design and is now the managing director of Svengali Design Ltd., a furniture design and production company. He was named president of the Interior Designer Association of Nigeria.

Tayar, Ali (1959–2016)
Tayar was born in Istanbul and studied architecture at the University of Stuttgart and MIT. In 1993 she formed Parallel Design Partnership, based out of New York. The firm designs furniture, objects, and interiors. Notable interiors include the PoP Burger and Pizza Bar in New York City and Omnia Hotel in Zermatt, Switzerland.

Té, Maybelline (b. 1970s)
Té is a contemporary furniture designer and the creative director of Snug Furniture. She was born in the Philippines and was managing director of the furniture company Tequesta International, Inc. After acquiring a degree in business management from the University of the Philippines, she studied interior design at the Art Institute of Charlotte, North Carolina.

Terry, Emilio (1890–1969)
Cuban designer of furniture and accessories who also designed a few houses. Active in Paris. His designs departed from canonical Modernism in their use of evocative forms that often bore no relation to their function, e.g. a house shaped like a shell. He brought the art movement of Surrealism into the world of interior design. A signature piece of his is a console table whose legs are plaster palm fronds.

Thompson, Benjamin (1918–2002)
Born in St. Paul, Minnesota, Thompson was an architect, restaurateur, and proponent of good, affordable, modern design. He received a bachelor's degree in fine arts in 1941 from Yale and then joined the Navy in the Second World War. He approached Walter Gropius with the intent of forming an architectural practice with former classmates. The resulting firm was known as The Architect's Collaborative, or TAC. He later founded D/R, a chain modern European furniture retail store.

Thompson, Jim (1906–1977)
An American diplomat who managed to reinvent himself, late in life, as a silk manufacturer in Bangkok, Thailand. He is credited with creating a fashion among wealthy Thais for reconfigured traditional wooden homes and for collecting Asian antiques and artwork. He mysteriously disappeared while walking in the Malaysian highlands. Posthumously, his firm has successfully moved from selling silk to being a comprehensive source for luxury goods.

Thonet, Michael (1796–1871)
Prussian-born Austrian furniture manufacturer and designer. Among his many designs are two iconic pieces: a bentwood café chair and rocker. Many modernists, including Mies van der Rohe, Le Corbusier, and Aalto, used his furniture in their interior designs. His innovative manufacturing techniques including boiling, steaming, laminating, and bending wood.

Tiffany, Louis Comfort (1848–1933)
American artist and designer, born in New York City, the son of the founder of Tiffany & Company. Tiffany studied painting and founded an interior-decorating firm in New York. Its specialty was favrile glasswork, such as lamps, vases, and stained-glass windows, made in the Art Nouveau style with iridescent coloring and forms inspired by nature. See TIFFANY LAMP.

Tihany, Adam (b. 1948)
A commercial and residential interior designer, Tihany attended the Politecnico di Milano, School of Architecture and Urban Planning. He began Tihany Design in New York in 1976, and the firm's projects included commercial design, residential interiors, furniture, products, exhibitions, and graphics. In 1981, Tihany began specializing in hospitality design, creating restaurants for celebrity chefs. Notable work includes La Coupole, the Mandarin Oriental Las Vegas, Westin Chosun in Seoul, and One & Only Cape Town Resort, South Africa.

Townsend, John (1732–1809)
An American cabinetmaker, Townsend worked in the Chippendale style and also did Federal-style work.

Trubridge, David (b. 1950s)
Trubridge studied naval architecture at Newcastle University in northern England and graduated in 1972. A self-taught furniture maker, his commissions include projects for the Victoria and Albert Museum and St. Mary's Cathedral in Edinburgh. He traveled to New Zealand in 1985, where he established a manufacturing workshop. The Designer's Institute of New Zealand presented him with that nation's highest design award, the John Britten Award.

Tsao, Calvin (b. 1960s)
Tsao got his master's degree in architecture at Harvard's Graduate School of Design. His work ranges from luxury hotels and urban development projects to high-end residences and product design.

Tunthavorn, Bancha (b. 1980s)
Thai designer Tunthavorn studied visual communication at the Art Institute of Chicago. Tunthavorn worked as a production designer for OWN: The Oprah Winfrey Network and later as a graphic designer in the Bangkok office of AvroKO.

Urban, Joseph (1872–1933)
Trained as an architect, the Austrian-born designer was active in multiple disciplines related to theater during his years in New York. Considered a major figure of American Art Deco, Urban created multiple stage sets, bringing knowledge of Viennese stylistic innovations to the U.S. He designed a sumptuous residence in Palm Beach, FL, Mar-a-Lago.

Urquiola, Patricia (b. 1961)
Urquiola was born in Oviedo, Spain, studied architecture in Madrid, and graduated from Milan Polytechnic in 1989. She began her career in 1991 working with Italian furniture stalwart De Padova in Milan designing furniture. Two years later she created a studio with a few friends with a focus on interior architecture. In 2001 she established her own studio in Milan that focuses on product design, displays, and architecture. She has worked with B&B, Alessi, Kartell, and Flos.

Van de Velde, Henri (1863–1957)
A Belgian artist turned architect who campaigned for Art Moderne in Belgium, France, and Germany. Van de Velde was impressed with the importance of machinery and its ultimate effect on the design and ornamenting of architecture. A co-founder of the Bauhaus and vocal supporter of it, his own designs were more influenced by John Ruskin and William Morris. See ART NOUVEAU.

Vanderbyl, Michael (b. 1947)
The San Francisco-based multidisciplinary designer studied at the California College of the Arts. He has designed furniture for Teknion, Baker, HBF, and Bernhardt.

Venturi, Robert (1925–2018)
American architect, born in Philadelphia. A graduate of Princeton and an outspoken advocate for postmodernism, Venturi is most famous for the books *Complexity and Contradiction in Architecture* (1966) and *Learning from Las Vegas* (1972, co-authored with Denise Scott Brown and Steven Izenour). His architectural philosophy opposes the orthodoxy of modern architecture, supporting instead the validity and importance of American roadside strip buildings, with a hint of irony and humor. The most prominent commission of his firm Venturi, Rauch, and Scott Brown was the addition to London's National Gallery.

Vervoordt, Axel (b. 1947)
The designer's career started when he rehabbed a row of 16th-century houses in Antwerp, Belgium. Then he became a respected antiques dealer which allowed him to write a number of well-received books. After his turn to interior design, he became known for a minimalist look that was more rustic than high-tech. His projects often employ earth tones and neutral color palettes, and he favors traditional materials such as stone, concrete, and stucco. His roster of clients includes Kanye West and Kim Kardashian, Bill Gates, and Calvin Klein.

Vignelli, Massimo (1931–2014) and Lella (1934–2016)
Massimo was a designer and architect who was a major figure in the Memphis group and who, throughout his career, was awarded many honorary doctorates. Lella was a registered architect who started out in the interiors studio of Skidmore, Owings, and Merrill in Chicago. The married couple is known for their furniture

and graphic designs, and their distinguished client list includes Ford Motors, American Airlines, IBM, Knoll, and Xerox. Their masterwork remains the design of the New York City subway map.

Viñas, Ghislaine (b. 1968)
Born in the Netherlands although she bears a French given name and a Spanish surname, the interior designer was raised in South Africa and studied interior design at Philadelphia University. After graduation, she moved to New York, where she established Ghislaine Viñas Interior Design in 1999. She primarily works with residences, creating colorful townhouses and lofts across the country. She is skilled at creating color palettes that are, depending on the project, attention getting, appropriate, and fresh.

Viollet-le-Duc, Eugène Emmanuel (1814–1879)
A 19th-century French architect, archaeologist, and prolific writer noted for his dictionary of architecture. He was much enamored with the Gothic, and he engaged in restoring important medieval buildings including Notre Dame in Paris. He was a seminal figure in the 19th-century preservation movement. He played a role in France analogous to that played by Pugin and Ruskin in England.

von Nessen, Greta (1900–1978) and Walter (1889–1943)
Walter designed a variety of industrial products, including lamps, ash trays, and serving trays. His chrome swing-arm desk lamp from 1927 became a classic. He also did multiple designs for Herman Miller. After Walter's death, Greta ran their firm, promoting her husband's designs and creating new designs based on the direction set by the original pieces. She also collaborated with George Nelson.

Voysey, Charles Francis Annesley (1857–1941)
One of the most important links between the ornamentation of William Morris at the end of the 19th century and the 20th-century modern movement. Voysey believed in "discarding the mass of useless ornament." His austere, mostly white interiors draw on rural vernacular architecture and stand in sharp contrast to his multicolored wallpapers.

Vredeman de Vries, Hans (1527–c. 1604)
Flemish/Dutch architect who published pattern books of architectural ornament and details. His son Paulus reissued the pattern books in 1630. It is likely that his designs contributed to the Great Bed of Ware, 1590, a monument in the history of furniture.

Wagner, Otto (1841–1918)
Austrian architect and one of the first in the late 19th century to admire the machine and to understand its essential character and relation to design and ornament. Josef Hoffmann was one of his pupils. Wagner was impressed with the comfort and clean lines of English industrial art: "All modern forms must be in harmony with the new requirements of our time.... Nothing that is not practical can be beautiful."

Wai, Hunn (b. 1980)
Wai hails from Singapore, where he started his design education. After graduating from the National University, he studied at the Design Academy Eindhoven, Netherlands, where he met his partner, Francesca Lanzavecchia. Their firm L + W maintains offices in Italy and Singapore. *Newsweek* named Wai as one of five designers of the future. The highly conceptual design firm is unusually interested in designing for the aging, and among their designs are canes, crutches, and walkers. Wai designed a whimsical Ping-Pong dining room table out of Corian, and the firm's clients include Samsonite and Mercedes-Benz.

Wakefield, Cyrus (1811–1873)
Wakefield began a company that specialized in rattan furniture. When his nephew Cyrus Wakefield sold the company to the Heywood Brothers, the newly formulated company was named Heywood Brothers and Wakefield.

Walsh, Sally (1926–1992)
Walsh was inspired by her mother, whose interests ranged from art, architecture, poetry, and literature to international affairs. Her career at Knoll Associates began with her working as a typist. She moved into sales and progressed to providing all-around assistance to founder Hans Knoll. She moved to Houston and started her own firm designing offices, banks, academic facilities, showrooms, and plane interiors. With her commitment to classic modern pieces and to providing comfort, she was a natural to join the cadre of designers who worked for Braniff Airlines.

Walsh Grant, Margot (b. 1936)
Of Chippewa Indian and Scottish descent, she started her career at Skidmore, Owings and Merrill where she rose through the ranks. She then started working with Art Gensler, when his eponymous design firm had but a handful of employees. She ended her career as one of Gensler's vice presidents. She was known for managing large projects and for insisting that clients were aware of design decisions throughout the design and construction process. She oversaw a number of projects for Marine Midland Banks.

Wearstler, Kelly (b. 1967)
California-based interior designer and founder of Kelly Wearstler Interior Design. She is well known for her elegant and over-the-top designs for boutique hotels as well as celebrity private residences. She has since expanded from interior design to luxury brand furniture.

Webb, Philip Speakman (1831–1915)
An English architect who, with RICHARD NORMAN SHAW and William Eden Nesfield, brought about a revival of residential architecture based on Queen Anne and Georgian styles combined with vernacular traditions. The aim of these anti-Victorian architects was to create functional objects and spaces based on the intrinsic values of the materials used. Webb was a friend of William Morris, and he designed Red House at Upton in Kent for him. The planning and furnishing of this historic structure led to the establishment of the firm of Morris, Marshall, Faulkner and Company in 1861, a group important in the Arts and Crafts Movement. Webb designed architecture, furniture, tiles, and stained glass.

Weber, Kem (1889–1963)
American furniture and industrial designer, architect, art director, and teacher. Stylistically, his designs seemed more industrial than other Art Deco works yet more flamboyant than modern pieces. Working in metal, leather, wood, and textiles, his projects seemed to embody the spirit of the airline business, exemplified by his creation in 1934, the Airline Chair. He was one of the first modernist designers of distinction on the West Coast of the U.S.

Wegner, Hans (1914–2007)
A Danish furniture designer of exquisitely simple modern furniture who started his career in the office of Arne Jacobsen. His designs combine comfort with function and are executed with the exemplary craftsmanship of the best Scandinavian modern pieces. His famous pieces include the Chinese Chair, the Classic Chair, the Folding Chair, and the Peacock Chair.

Weinfeld, Isay (b. 1952)
Born in São Paulo, Weinfeld graduated from the School of Architecture at Mackenzie University. His modernist architecture, interiors, and furniture design company is based in Brazil and handles a variety of project types. Projects include the Mocoto Brazilian restaurant in London, a sideboard for Zezinho, and the Hotel Fasano.

Whistler, James Abbott McNeill (1834–1903)
American painter. Whistler traveled widely and spent significant periods of time in Europe. He contrived an image for himself as a dandy and socialite and was associated with artists' circles in Paris and London. Whistler's portrait of his mother (1872) is his most well-known work. He was involved in interior design on both sides of the Atlantic. In London, he hired E. W. Godwin to design his house. He designed and executed the Peacock Room for F. R. Leyland, a project as famous for the contentious relationship between client and designer as for its extravagance and exquisite craftmanship.

White, Stanford (1853–1906)
American architect, born in New York City. In 1879 he became a founding partner of the architecture firm McKim, Mead, and White. White specialized in interior design and furnishing and the decorative elements of building. Two of his works survive in New York City: the Washington Arch and the Century Club; and both reveal his interest in Renaissance ornament. White was shot and killed by Harry K. Thaw for his love affair with Thaw's wife, Evelyn Nesbit Thaw.

Wilkinson, Clive (b. 1954)
The South African interior designer and architect received his architecture degree from the University of Cape Town. He finished his studies at the Architectural Association in London, where he studied under Rem Koolhaas and Zaha Hadid. After working in Australia, he relocated to Los Angeles, where he served as a project manager for Frank Gehry on the Disney Concert Hall. His design work includes architecture, interiors, furniture, and graphics.

Williams, Bunny (b. 1944)
A renowned designer as well as an accomplished entrepreneur and author. Williams graduated from Garland Junior College in Boston and then moved to New York, eventually starting her own design firm while mentoring up and coming designers. Her style is characterized by refined beauty while maintaining livability and comfort.

Wolf, Vicente (b. 1946)
Wolf was born in Cuba. In New York, he founded Vicente Wolf Associates and VW Home, a showroom and retail store. He designs homes, stores, restaurants, hotels, and furniture and accessories. Prominent projects include the Ayya Hotel in New York, the Luxe Hotel Rodeo Drive and Café Rodeo in Beverly Hills, and an apartment for the Prince and Princess von Furstenberg. He has collaborated with Niedermaier, Henredon, and Tufenkian. He is the author of multiple books and has taught at Parsons School of Design.

Wolfe, Elsie de (1865–1950)
A leading interior designer of the early 20th century. She had a great influence both in America and in Europe fostering an updated version of 18th-century elegance. She later became Lady Mendl and collaborated with the architect Stanford White. She is one of those on both sides of the Atlantic who nudged historicist design in a contemporary direction.

Wood, Ruby Ross (1880–1950)
Wood was born in Monticello, Georgia, and moved to New York to be a reporter in the early 1900s. She began by ghostwriting articles for decorator Elsie de Wolfe in *The Delineator*. Her experience writing design articles led her to open a decorating shop, the Modernist Studios. After scant initial success with retail, she turned to decorating residences. Adventurous in her tastes, she was known for unusual yet stylish accessories.

Wormley, Edward (1907–1995)
Wormley, a well-known mid-century furniture designer, attended the Art Institute of Chicago in 1926. Due to insufficient finances, he left before graduating and started his career at the department store Marshall Field's design studio in 1928. His long partnership with Dunbar Company began in 1931. He continued to act as a consultant for the furniture company after opening his office in New York in 1945. Notable works includes the Precedent collection for Drexel and multiple designs for Dunbar.

Wright, Frank Lloyd (1869–1959)
The midwestern American designer and architect. He believed that a building should be an integral part of its site, and he expressed a respect for nature and natural materials. He began his career working for Louis Sullivan. In domestic architecture, he developed a concept of transparency that endeavored to break down the concept of distinct rooms in which people confined themselves. Wright employed continuous casement windows, lowered ceilings, and projecting, streamlined, horizontal overhangs. He designed many pieces of furniture throughout his career.

Wright, Russel (1904–1976)
The onetime stage designer was an instrumental figure in industrial design who sought to bring high-quality design to America's middle-classes. While he also designed furniture, he is most famous for the ceramics and glassware that he designed from the 1930s to the 1950s.

Yabu, George (b. 1953)
Yabu and partner Glenn Pushelberg founded their eponymous design firm in 1980. Both were design students at Ryerson Polytechnic in Toronto and created Yabu Pushelberg after pursuing individual private practices. Their firm has studios in New York and Toronto and focuses on luxury design, primarily hospitality. Notable work includes the Blue Fin Restaurant, Four Seasons, Tiffany & Co., and the W Hotel. The duo moved into large-scale residential development.

Yanagi, Sori (1915–2011)
One of Japan's preeminent designers of the 20th century. The young Yanagi's life received a professional boost during Charlotte Perriand's stay in Japan during the Second World War. He assisted her on her explorations of converting her metal designs to bamboo. His entry into the cannon of modernist furniture pieces is the Butterfly Stool, an elegant ensemble of plywood and metal rods that represents a synthesis of East and West that he developed during his stay in the U.S. in the 1950s.

Yoshioka, Tokujin (b. 1967)
A graduate of Japan's Kuwasawa Design Institute, Yoshioka is a well-known product designer, artist, and architect. After working with Shiro Kuramata, he began a long partnership as in-house designer for Issey Miyake in 1988. In 2000 he launched Tokujin Yoshioka Design. His clients include Hermès, Toyota, BMW, and Swarovski. His work covers everything from ceramic tiles to watches and furniture. His 2001 Honey-Pop paper chair is one of his well-known works.

Zak, Jakub (b. 1970s)
Zak was born in Canada and studied design there before completing his education in Berlin. He then moved to Milan, where he designed furniture for Patricia Urquiola. In 2001 he founded Oeuffice with Nicolas Bellavance-Lecompte, whom he knew from his student days. Oeuffice creates limited edition objects and furniture. Projects include the Ziggurat container and "totems for living" and are shown at Carwan, a Beirut gallery.

Zec, Amir Vuk (b. 1957)
Zec is an architect, set designer, interior designer, and product designer and is founder of New Way architect studio. He hails from Sarajevo, Bosnia, where many of his projects are located. His modernist projects typically include large amounts of glass, yet his façades have depth with elements that alternately protrude and recess. His projects include a modest but stylish Turkish cultural center and the Hotel Han.

Zeisel, Eva (1906–2011)
A Hungarian-born ceramicist, accessories designer, and sometime furniture designer. Her design productivity spanned nine decades and included periods working in Vienna, Berlin, and Leningrad. She and her husband emigrated to the U.S., and she taught at Pratt. Her tableware was not fancy, but her designs departed from strict Modernism with their recognition of historical forms and abstracted references to nature and human relationships. A version of her dinnerware was sold at Crate and Barrel.

appendix 2: organizations and associations

AAHID (American Academy of Healthcare Interior Designers): Founded in 2004, the group certifies interior designers in healthcare to protect the health, safety, and welfare of users of healthcare spaces. They focus on continuing education, research, and collaboration with the goal of improving outcomes and maximizing efficiency.

AAI (Asociación de arquitectos e interioristas de Mexico): It is a national association that promotes and professionalizes the strategic value of architecture and interior design, by establishing business alliances (networking) with design and architecture companies, suppliers, companies, plastic artists, and related journals and universities. It pursues multiple objectives: to establish a select group that brings together the best in interior design and architecture nationwide; to create and improve business associations; to certify and accredit interior design work; to encourage new talent; and to reward the best in architecture and interior design in Mexico.

ABD (Brazilian Association of Interior Designers): Founded in 1980, it regulates the professional title "Designer de Interiores." It is the major design organization in Latin America, and its recent initiative is to foster design subfields and specialities. An off-branch of the organization, ABD Acadêmico, works with design educational institutions to coordinate activities of volunteers, alumni, design professionals, educators, students, and manufacturers.

ACT (Association for Contract Textiles): The professional trade association was founded in 1985. The not-for-profit serves companies that design, develop, produce, promote, and sell contract textiles. Their activities include promoting value, developing voluntary performance guidelines, serving as an informational resource, monitoring legislation, and providing a forum for design professionals.

AIA (American Institute of Architects): The AIA was formed in 1857 as a national organization for licensed architects and emerging professionals. The group provides continuing education, contract documents, Web resources, and market research, promotes public advocacy, and hosts a convention. The organization serves as a voice of the profession and creates a high standard for design.

APDIQ (The Association of Professional Interior Designers of Quebec): A not-for-profit organization that promotes classification and certification in order to insure recognition and professional competency. It oversees an accreditation arm and controls the title "Designer d'intérieur certifié." Its 900 members comprise employees, volunteers, and consultants, all contributing to recognizing the profession and protecting the public.

ARIDO (Association of Registered Interior Designers of Ontario): Founded in 1934, ARIDO is a professional organization for designers in Ontario and is the largest professional association of its type in Canada. It started as the Society of Interior Decorators of Ontario and changed its name in 1984. The subsequent act gave interior designers the right to the title of Interior Designer in Ontario, thereby elevating the profession and helping consumers make informed decisions.

ASHE (American Society for Healthcare Engineering): With membership across the professions of architecture, engineering, construction, facility management, and healthcare, the organization focuses on the safety of the physical healthcare environment from the engineering perspective. ASHE offers opportunities in professional growth and provides member resources.

ASHRAE (American Society of Heating, Refrigeration, and Air-Conditioning Engineers): ASHRAE advances the building systems industry by providing technical and educational information and opportunity for professional growth. Founded in 1894, the society has more than 50,000 members who focus on heating, ventilating, air-conditioning, and refrigeration. A key mission is to improve sustainability and indoor air quality.

ASID (American Society of Interior Designers): The predecessor organizations to the largest community of professional interior designs were AID (American Institute of Interior Designers) and NSID (National Society of Interior Designers). The current organization was founded in 1975 and has 30,000 members in forty-eight chapters in the United States and Canada. The membership comprises designers, industry representatives, educators, and students. The group celebrates the power of design.

ASTM International: The group was previously known as the American Society for Testing & Materials, and the name change reflects its global outlook, as it now serves 150 countries. The organization is committed to developing and delivering voluntary consensus standards of materials. The goals of the recognized standards are to improve product quality, enhance safety, facilitate commerce, and build consumer confidence.

BIFMA (Business and Institutional Furniture Manufacturers Association): BIFMA is an organization that supports the North American office and institutional furniture industry. It promotes industry standards by developing voluntary product and industry standards, publishing information and industry statistics, and advocating for the profession.

BIID (British Institute of Interior Design): The United Kingdom's sole professional institute for interior designers. Its membership hails from both the commercial and residential sectors, running the gamut from heritage to cutting edge. In addition to rigorous entry requirements which assess training, experience, and professionalism, members continue their development throughout their career to ensure continued expertise in design process, practice, and regulatory matters.

BOMA (Building Owners and Managers Association International): BOMA serves the commercial real estate industry. Founded in 1907 as the National Association of Building Owners and Managers, the group later changed its name to reflect its global reach. Programs include advocacy, education, research, standards, industry trends, building codes, *The BOMA Magazine*, and conferences.

CFAI (French Council of Interior Designers): Some 1,000 Interior Designers follow the criteria defined by the council. The council regulates institutions of higher education that offer design education. It also organizes review of design projects, rallying the efforts of independent practicing professionals, architects, and those in design related disciplines. A landmark decision in 1981 established the authenticity of the interior design profession and its ability to provide services on an equal level with architects, in terms of creativity, technique, and professional deontology.

CHD (Center for Health Design): Founded in 1993, the CHD focuses on creating healthier and safer healthcare environments. The organization promotes evidence-based design (EBD), education, and advocacy. It holds symposia, publishes a journal, and maintains a popular website. The group also created an Evidence-based Design Accreditation and Certification (EDAC). The organization's belief is that healthcare facilities can contribute to quality of life and celebrate human spirit.

CIDA (Council for Interior Design Accreditation): The independent, not-for-profit quality assurance organization serves education programs at colleges and universities in the United States, Canada, and, increasingly, across the globe. For more than thirty-five years, this knowledge-driven organization has been committed to the enrichment of the interior design profession through identifying, developing, and promoting quality standards for design education.

CIIDA (China International Interior Design Association): The international professional association was initially registered in Hong Kong. It is a non-profit association which provides service to interior design institutions, designers, and colleges across the globe. It unites design agencies and designers in order to promote the research and development of the design industry, to enhance the level of Chinese interior design industry generally, and to promote professional and intellectual exchanges. It spares no effort in its charge to promote Chinese interior design.

CMG (Color Marketing Group): The CMG's purpose is to exchange information on color trends across industries. The group was founded in 1962 for color designers that profitably market goods and services. In addition to predicting trends, CMG works on merchandising and sales, education, and networking across industries including fashion, consumer goods, technology, transportation, home, and building environments.

CSI (Construction Specifications Institute): The CSI's purpose is to improve the quality of construction specifications. The national organization began in 1948 and promotes best practices, standards, certification, and education. Members include specifiers, architects, engineers, contractors, facility managers, product representatives, manufacturers, and owners who support the advancement of the profession.

DIA (Design Institute of Australia): It is the principal organization through which designers work for the future of Australia's design professions. It is the nation's peak industry body for professional design, and it represents Australian design and designers domestically and internationally. DIA members work to help professional designers succeed in business and to flourish in their working lives, while collectively growing the island nation's reputation as a global center of design.

DIFFA (Design Industries Foundation Fighting AIDS): The foundation started in 1984 and has three strands to its initiatives: preventative education programs, treatment and direct care, and public policy advocacy. Its members come from all fields involved in design and the visual arts. Its headquarters are in New York, and it has eight chapters across the United States.

FGI (Facilities Guidelines Institute): The FGI was founded in 1998 to set guidelines and provide organization within the revision process. These consensus-based guidelines are examined in publications and advised by sound research with the goal to advance quality health care. The FGI is a not-for-profit corporation.

FSC (Forest Stewardship Council): The FSC is an international not-for-profit established in 1993 that promotes responsible management of the world's forests.

German Design Council: Germany's leading authority on design and brands, the Council promotes societal awareness of design and supports companies on all matters relating to brand and design development. It serves as a forum for interdisciplinary knowledge transfer and gives its members a competitive edge, independently, internationally, and competently. It sponsors and participates in a number of design award programs with a goal of better positioning new products in the marketplace.

HKIDA (Hong Kong Interior Design Association): At its inception, The HKIDA set out to be a comprehensive platform dedicated to fostering exchange between industry professionals and the public at large. The organization is active regionally and internationally, with a focus on learning programs and exchange sessions with like-minded associations. It nurtures young design talent by providing support and a platform to showcase their works. It promotes professional standards and ethics for the design practice by the issuance of a certificate of Certified Interior Designer.

IALD (International Association of Lighting Designers): The IALD was founded in 1969 and works internationally to advance professional lighting designers and set a high standard for the profession. The group promotes the appreciation of lighting and the contributions of lighting designers as professionals who are responsive to natural and built environments.

IDC (Interior Designers of Canada): The organization was founded in 1972 and advocates for the interior design profession. Its ranks include students, educators, professionals, and other industry members.

IDEC (Interior Design Educators Council): IDEC is a professional association that advances interior design education, scholarship, and service. It serves interior design educators in a way analogous to the service provided by the Association of Collegiate Schools of Architecture (ASCA) to architecture educators. It started in 1962, and its role has consolidated around a scholarly journal and an annual conference.

IDSA (Industrial Designers Society of America): In 1965, the IDSA was formed out of the merger of three previously existing entities: the Industrial Designers Institute (IDI), the American Society of Industrial Designers (ASID), and the Industrial Designers Education Association (IDEA). All three trace their existence to an American response to the successful trade show held in Paris in 1925. The retailer Macy's subsequently held an Exposition of Art and Trade. The current organization promotes the practice and education of industrial design and advances the positive impact of design.

IES (Illuminating Engineering Society): Founded in 1906 to promote quality lighting and professionals active in the field, the group is an organization of lighting professionals who serve the public by improving lighted environments. It promotes the art and science of quality lighting to its members, allied professional organizations, and the public.

IFDA (International Furnishings and Design Association): The group was founded in 1947 and is an organization for members to provide services and products to the furnishings and design industry. The group is a way to give presence to the furnishings and design industry and provides tools and resources that enhance business.

IFI (International Federation of Interior Architects/Designers): The IFI facilitates the exchange of knowledge across the global design community. The federation was founded in 1963 in Copenhagen, Denmark, and is today present in 110 countries. The group offers education and promotes the profession. The IFI is a member of the International Design Alliance (IDA), the International Council of Societies of Industrial Design (ICSID), and the International Council of Graphic Design Associations (ICOGRADA).

IFMA (International Facility Management Association): Formed in 1980, the association certifies managers and advances the facility management profession. The group sponsors the world's largest facility management conference and exposition, conducts research, and provides continuing education.

IIDA (International Interior Design Association): The organization was founded in 1994 when two organizations, the Institute of Business Designers (IBD) and the Council of Federal Interior Designers (CFID), merged. The association elevates the profession and has 13,000 members in thirty-one chapters. It is a forum that promotes the health, safety, and well-being of the public.

IIID (Institute of Indian Interior Designers): The Institute was founded in 1972 to establish good professional and trade practices and ethics among its membership. It enhances the image of the interior design profession and organizes knowledge exchange events with similar organizations within the country and abroad. The IIID is a member of the Asia Pacific Space Designers Alliance and has over 8,000 members in thirty-one chapters across India.

LeadingAge: Formerly the American Association of Homes and Services for the Aging (AAHSA), the group advances the vision of healthy, affordable, ethical, long-term care. It represents 6,000 mission-driven, not-for-profit nursing homes, continuing-care retirement communities, assisted-living and senior housing facilities, and community service organizations; it serves approximately 2 million persons across the country.

NCIDQ (National Council for Interior Design Qualification): The NCIDQ oversees the registration of interior designers and its qualifying exam.

NEWH (Network of Executive Women in Hospitality): The networking resource for the hospitality industry dates back to 1984. The organization provides networking opportunities, education, and scholarships. The group spans all aspects of the hospitality industry, including professionals, students, management/operations, architecture, communications, design, distribution, education, manufacturing, production, purchasing, and sales of hospitality, food service, senior living, and related industries.

NOMA (National Organization of Minority Architects) and NOMAS (National Organization of Minority Architects Students): The allied organizations believe that they thrive when members eagerly contribute their time and resources. Their mission centers on a strong national organization, strong chapters, and engaged members with the joint goal of minimizing the effects of racism in the profession. Their efforts bolster the voices that speak out against apathy, bigotry, intolerance, and ignorance and abuse of the natural environment.

NTMA: National Terrazzo & Mosaic Association The NTMA establishes the standards for floor and wall systems and provides specifications, color plates, and general information for architects, interior designers, and other specifiers.

OBD (Organization of Black Designers): Formed in 1990 to give a presence to African Americans and other designers of color, the OBD promotes diversity in the design industry. The organization encourages multicultural and multidisciplinary designers and encourages awareness, visibility, and support.

OFDA (Office Furniture Dealers Alliance): The OFDA provides growth in the commercial furniture and interior products industry for American and Canadian dealers, manufacturers, and vendors. The association gives professionals tools for profitability including management education, business performance benchmarking services, and networking.

SIDA (Society of Interior Designers of Australia): Founded in 1951, the society advances the art of interior design services to the public, as well as assisting designers entering the field. SIDA, the earliest Australian design association, worked to advance the standards of interior designing and decoration and to uphold in practice a code of ethics and professional practices. By 1964, the society had members across Australia and became incorporated as a not-for-profit company. The society created a Diploma Course in Interior Design that commenced at Randwick College of TAFE in Sydney.

USGBC (U.S. Green Building Council): Formed in Washington, D.C., the USGBC includes builders, educators, students, environmentalists, and organizations. Through sustainable practices, the organization positively affects the built environment to improve the quality of life of its inhabitants. It operates programs that promote sustainable design, most notably the LEED green building certification system.

appendix 3: graphic and space standards

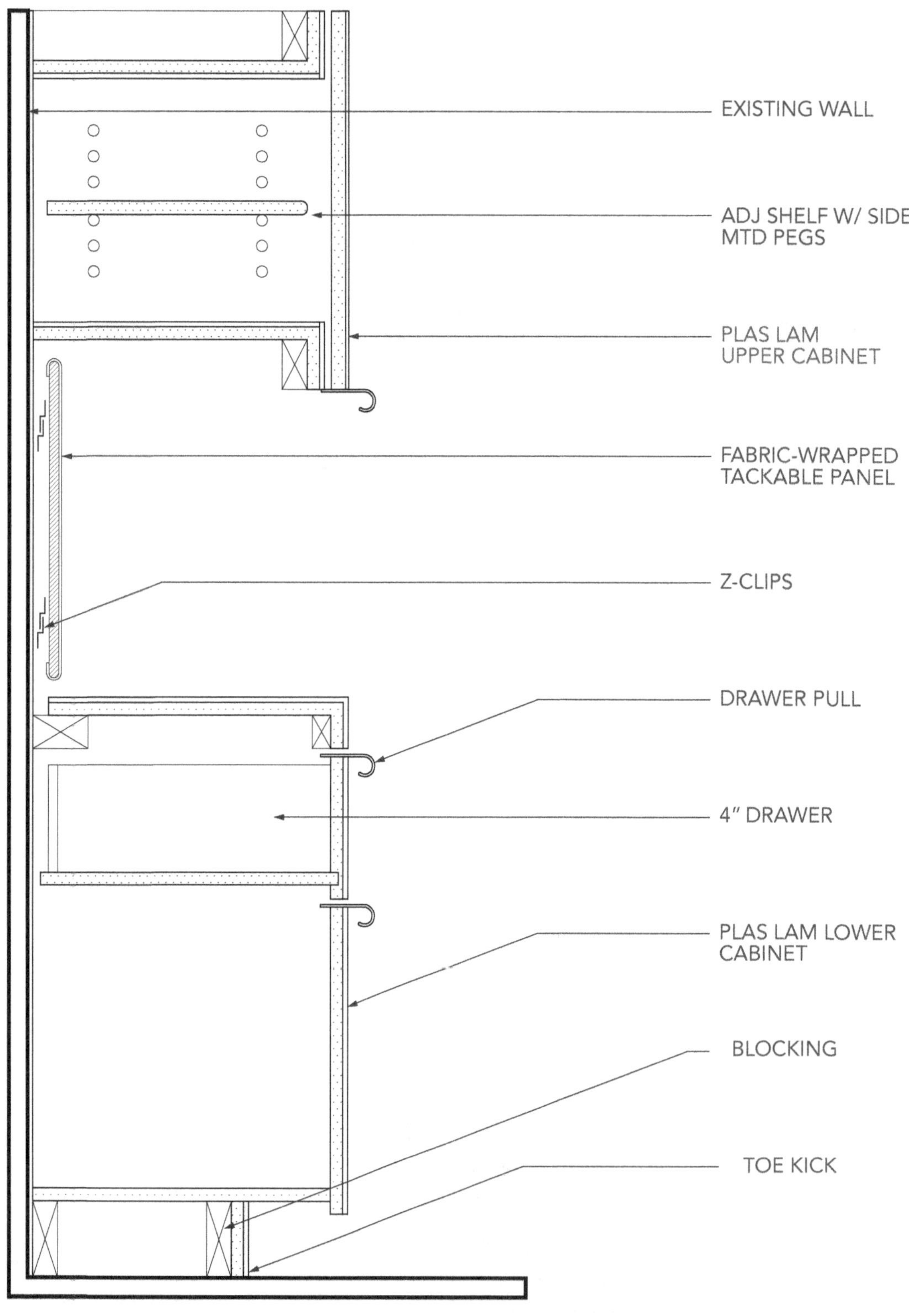

STANDARD UPPER AND LOWER CABINETS **M1**

Imperial	**Metric**
4"	10 cm

Imperial	Metric
2′-0″	61 cm
1′-4″	40.5 cm
3/4″	19 mm
1′-1/4″	31 cm
10-1/4″	26 cm
1-1/8″	28.5 mm
2″ × 4″	38 × 89 mm

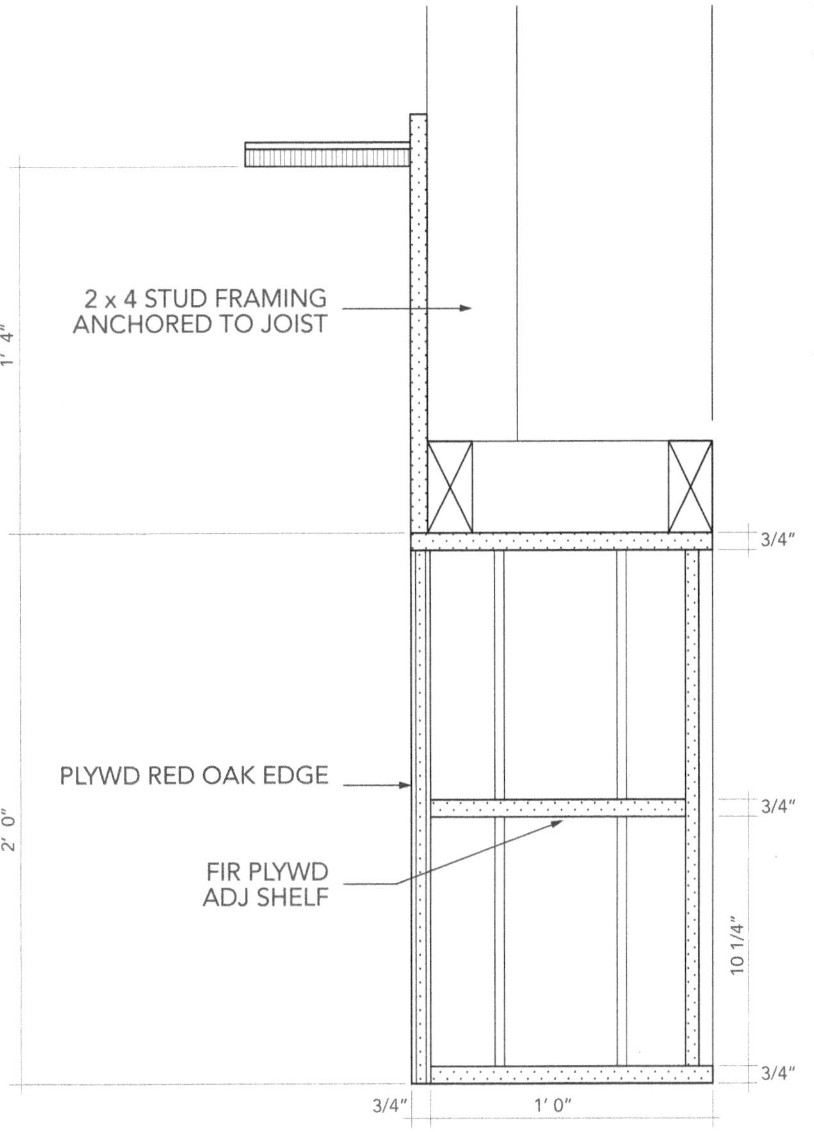

WALL CABINET

M2a

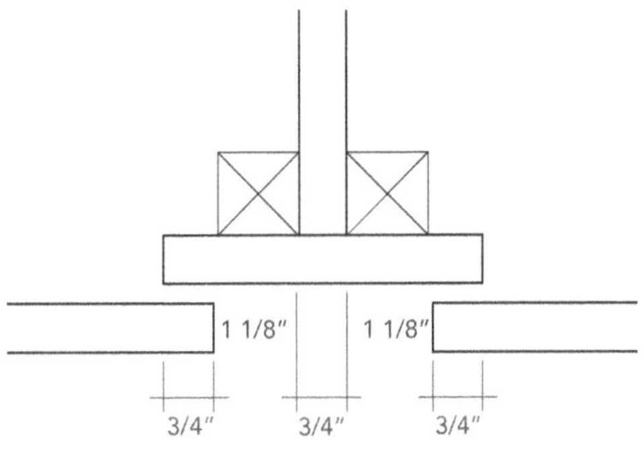

PLAN OF BASE CABINET DOOR

M2b

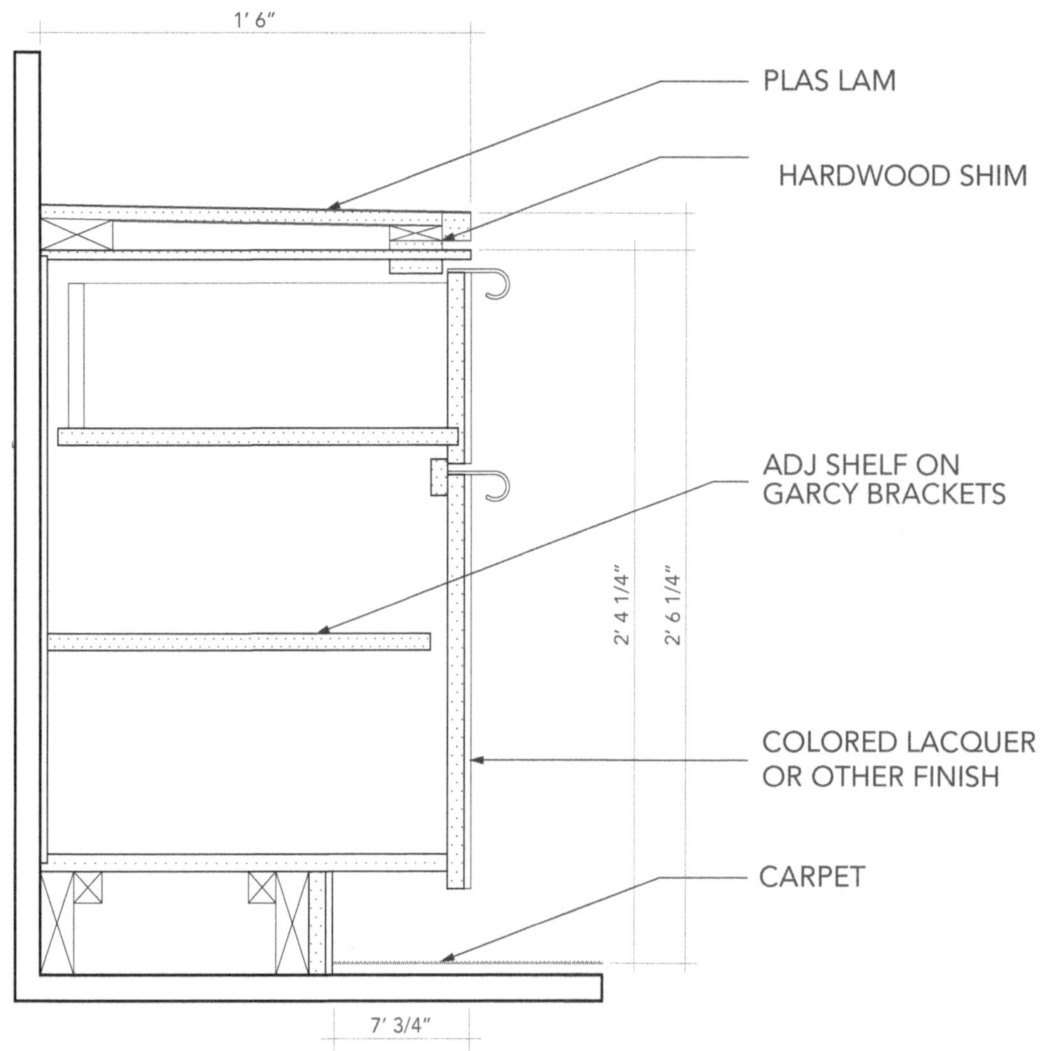

LOWER CABINET W/ ADJ SHELF

Imperial	Metric
1'-6"	46 cm
2'-4-1/4"	72 cm
2'-6-1/4"	77 cm
7-3/4"	18 cm

M3

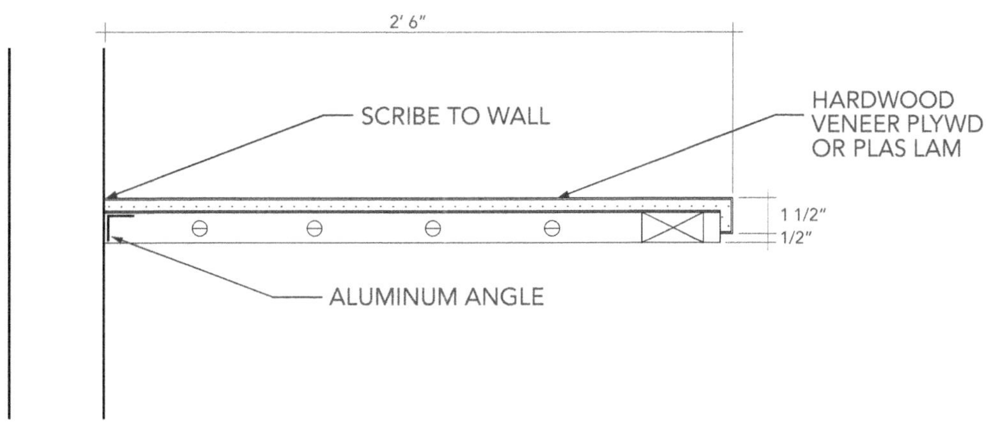

COUNTERTOP W/ ALUMINUM SUPPORT

M4a

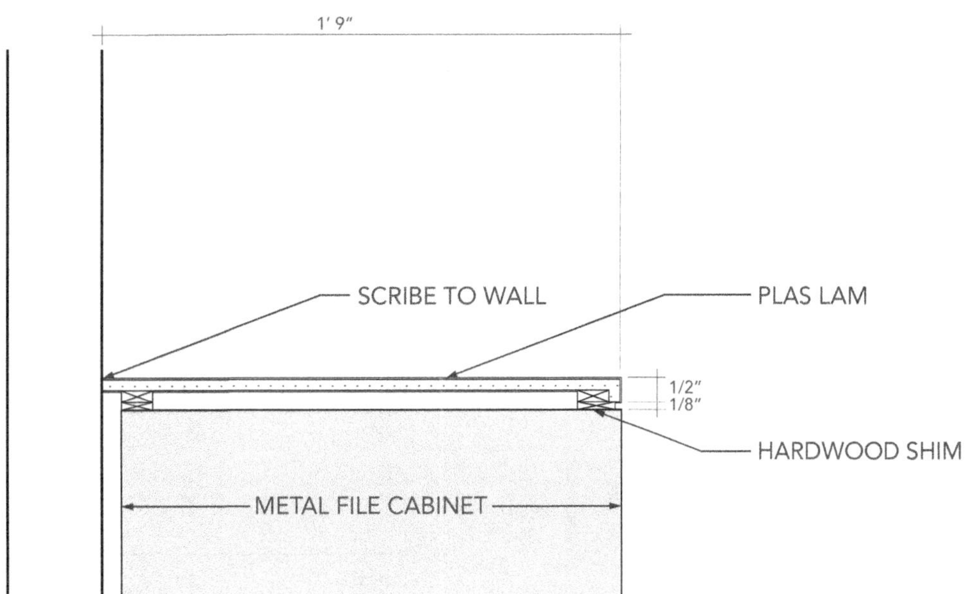

COUNTERTOP ON TOP OF FILES

M4b

Imperial	Metric
2′-6″	76 cm
1-1/2″	38 mm
1/2″	13 mm
1′-9″	53 mm
1/2″	13 mm
1/8″	3.175 mm

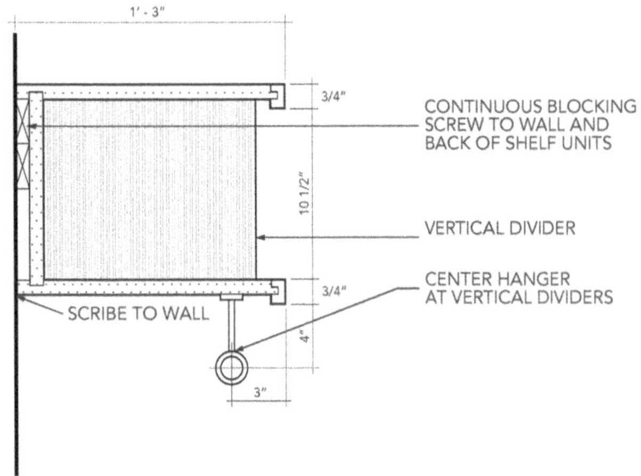

CLOSET SHELF W/ HANGER ROD **M5a**

Imperial	Metric
1′-3″	38 cm
¾″	19 mm
10-1/2″	27 cm
4″	102 mm
3″	76 mm

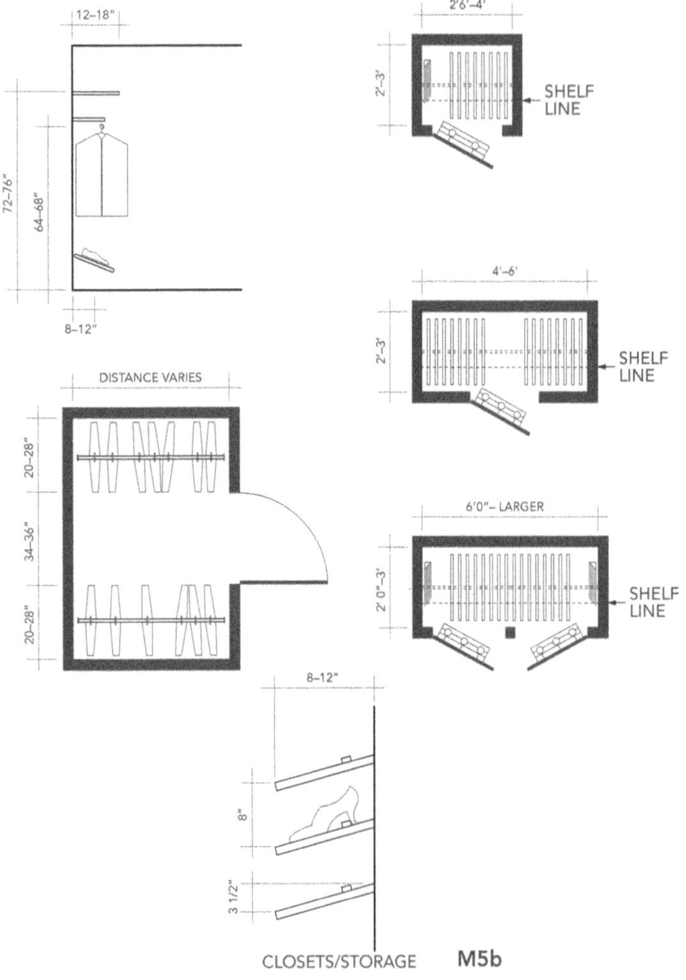

CLOSETS/STORAGE **M5b**

Imperial	Metric
72″–76″	183–193 cm
12″–18″	30.5–46 cm
64″–68″	162.6–173 cm
8″–12″	20–30.5 cm

Imperial	Metric
2′-6″–4′	76–122 cm
2′-3′	61–91 cm

Imperial	Metric
20″–28″	51–71 cm
34″–36″	86–91.5 cm
20″–28″	51–71 cm

Imperial	Metric
2′-3′	61–91 cm
4′-6′	122–183 cm

Imperial	Metric
2′-3′	61–91 cm
6′	183 cm

Imperial	Metric
3-1/2″	89 mm
8″	20 cm
8″–12″	20–30.5 cm

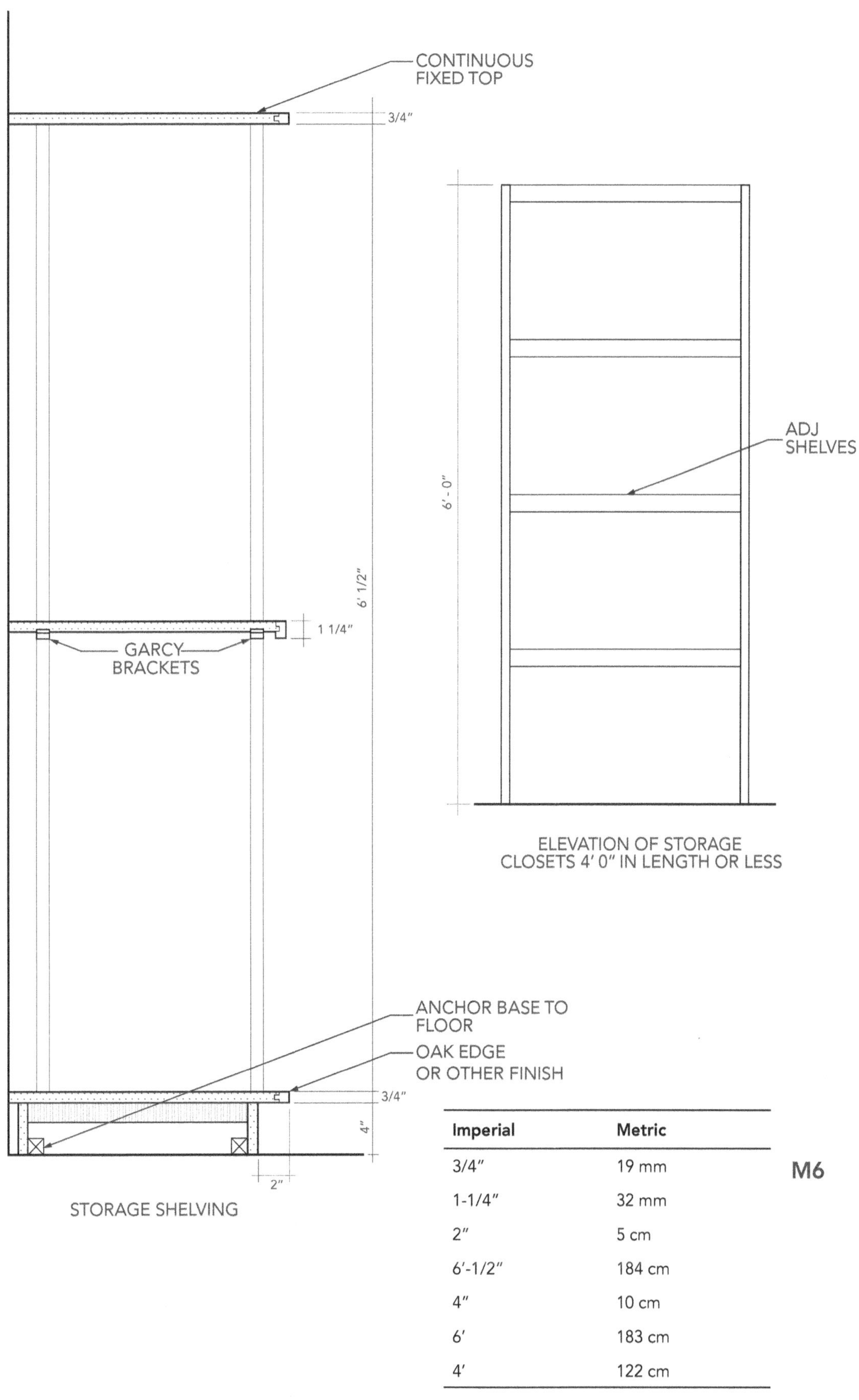

Imperial	Metric
3/4"	19 mm
1-1/4"	32 mm
2"	5 cm
6'-1/2"	184 cm
4"	10 cm
6'	183 cm
4'	122 cm

M6

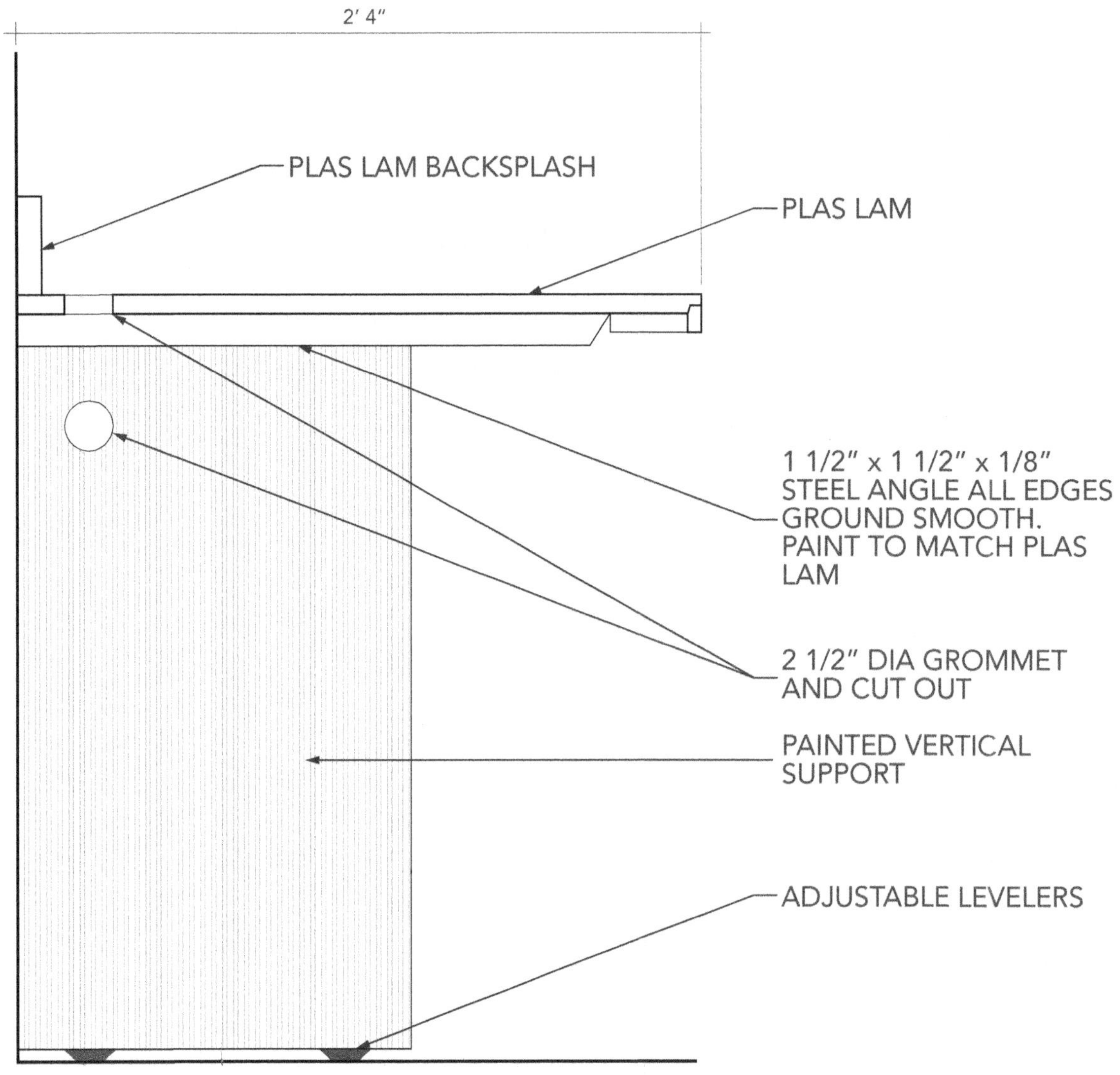

BASE AND WORK COUNTER

Imperial	Metric
2'-4"	71 cm
1-1/2"	38 mm
1/8"	3.2 mm
2-1/2"	63.5 mm

M7

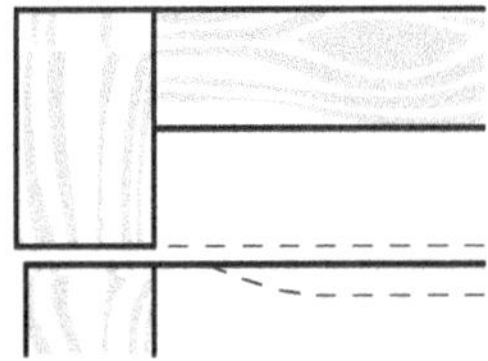

DRAWER FACE-PLAN
CUSTOM GRADE

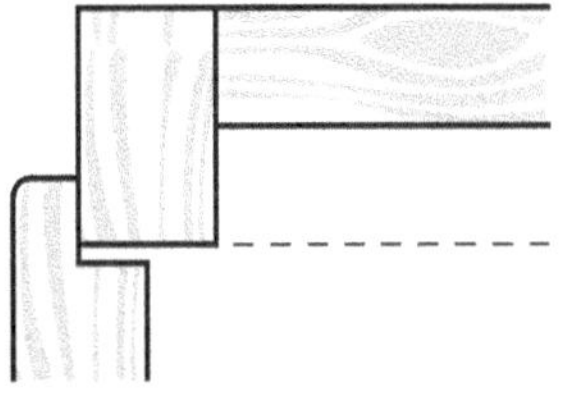

DRAWER FACE-PLAN
ECONOMY GRADE

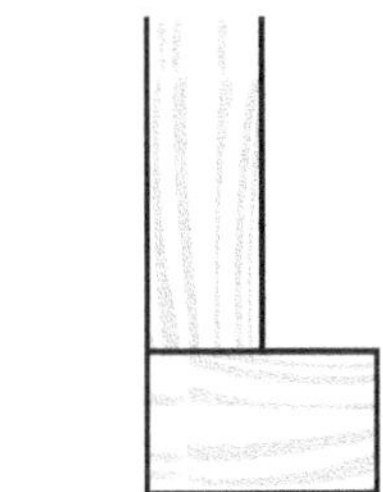

CABINET BASE CORNER DETAIL
CUSTOM

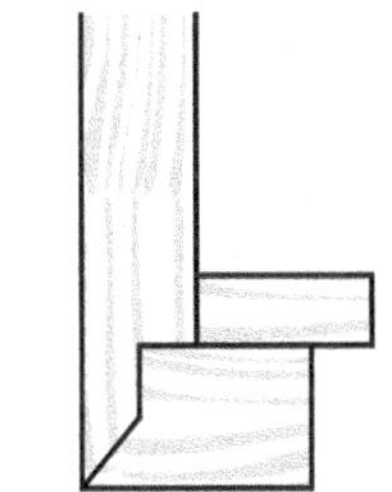

CABINET BASE CORNER DETAIL
PREMIUM

STANDARD JOINERY - BASE CABINET **M8**

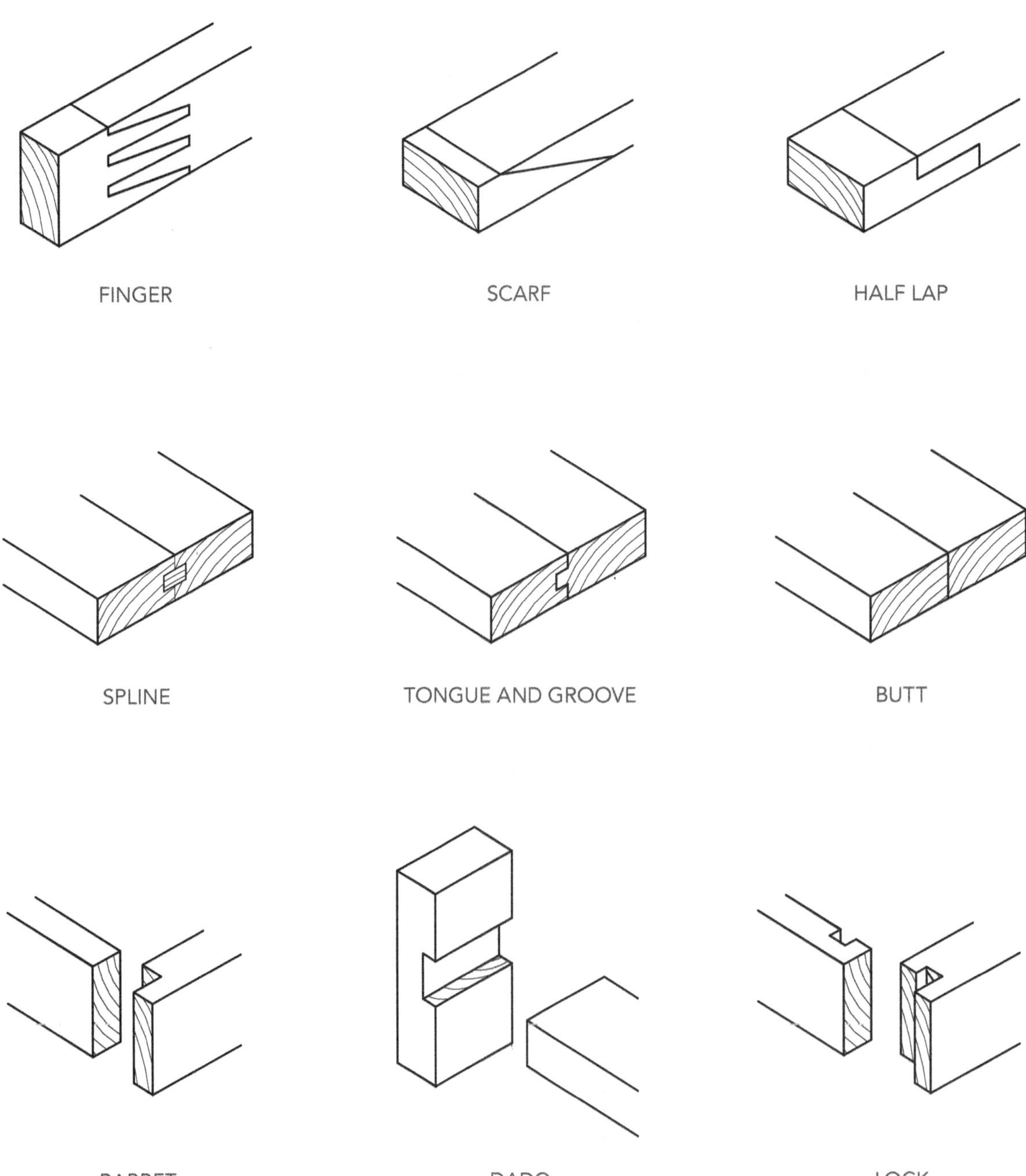

TYPICAL JOINT DETAILS

M9

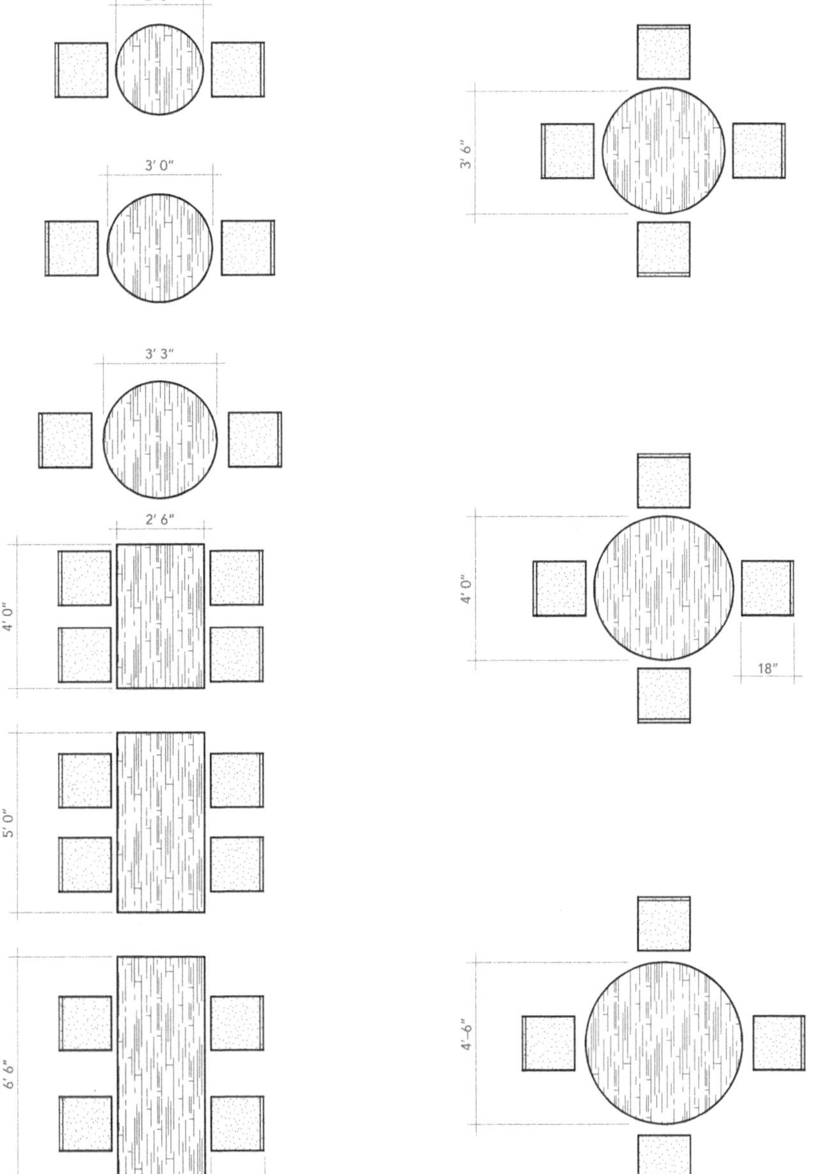

TABLE SIZE AND CONFIGURATION

F1

Imperial	Metric
2'-6"	76 cm
3'	91 cm
3'-3"	99 cm
4'	122 cm
5'	152 cm
6'-6"	198 cm
18"–24"	46–61 cm
3'-6"	107 cm
18"	46 cm
4'-6"	137 cm

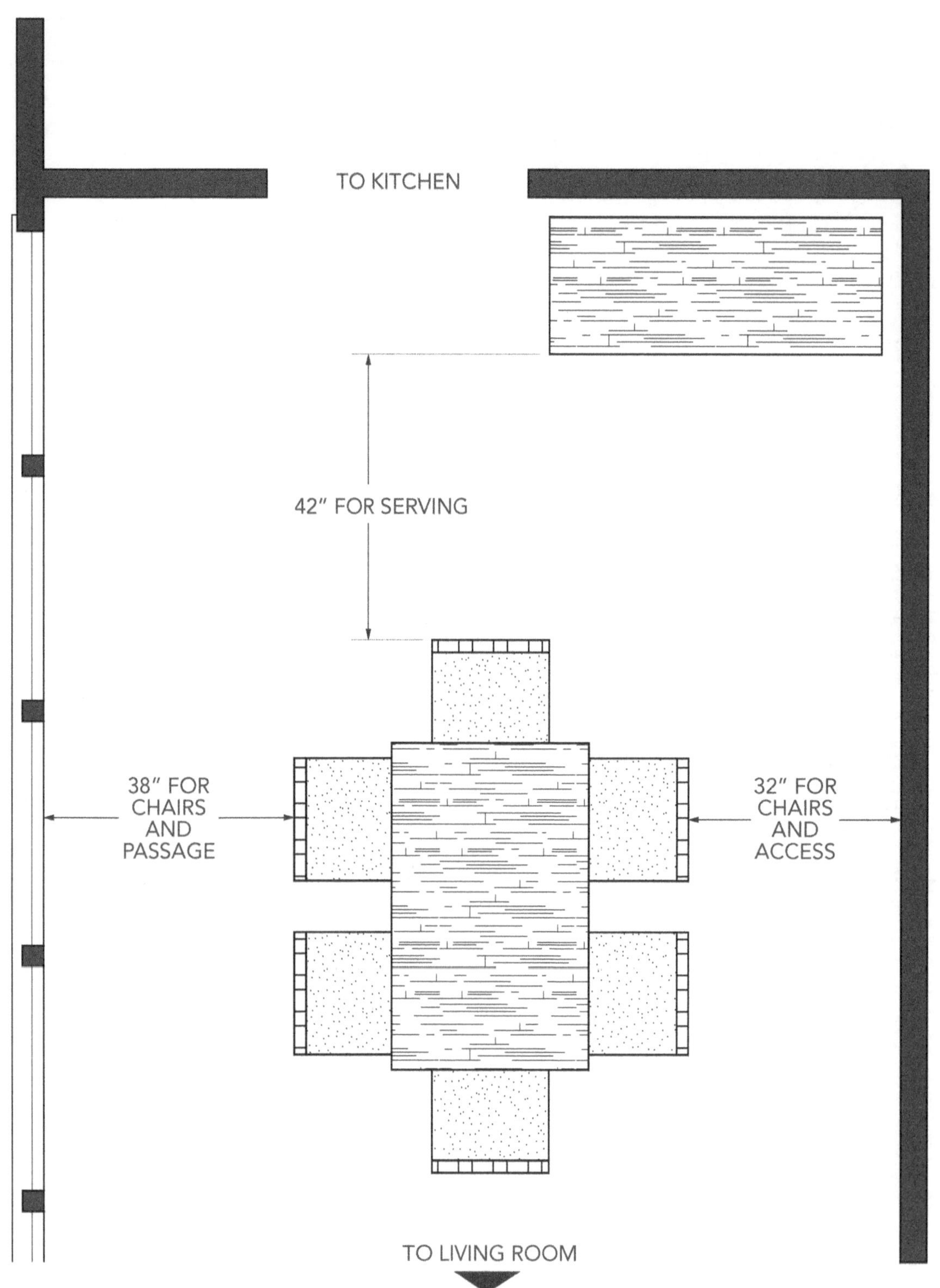

Imperial	Metric
38″	96.5 cm
42″	107 cm
32″	81 cm

FURNITURE CLEARANCES
DINING ROOM

F2

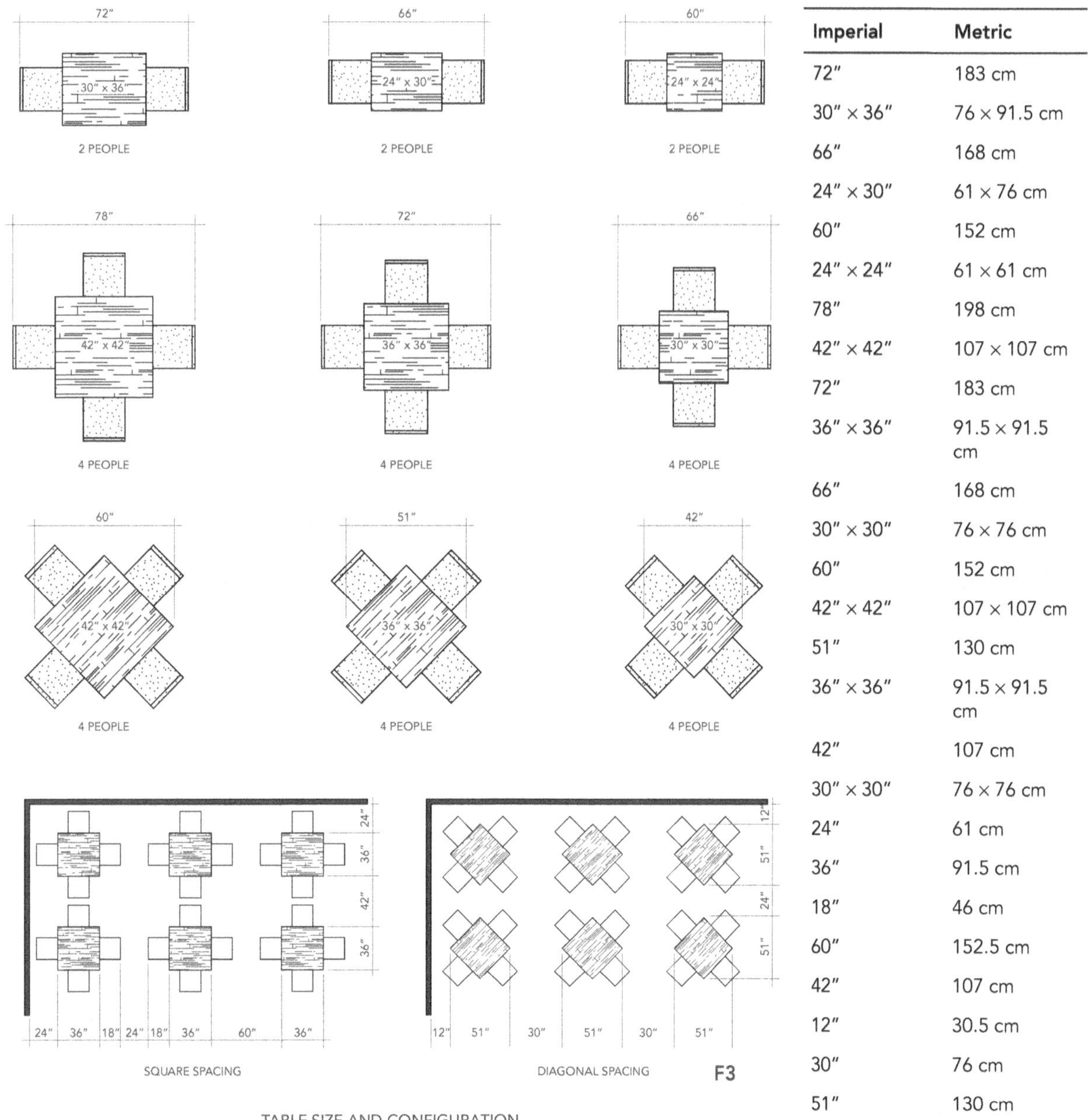

TABLE SIZE AND CONFIGURATION

Imperial	Metric
72″	183 cm
30″ × 36″	76 × 91.5 cm
66″	168 cm
24″ × 30″	61 × 76 cm
60″	152 cm
24″ × 24″	61 × 61 cm
78″	198 cm
42″ × 42″	107 × 107 cm
72″	183 cm
36″ × 36″	91.5 × 91.5 cm
66″	168 cm
30″ × 30″	76 × 76 cm
60″	152 cm
42″ × 42″	107 × 107 cm
51″	130 cm
36″ × 36″	91.5 × 91.5 cm
42″	107 cm
30″ × 30″	76 × 76 cm
24″	61 cm
36″	91.5 cm
18″	46 cm
60″	152.5 cm
42″	107 cm
12″	30.5 cm
30″	76 cm
51″	130 cm

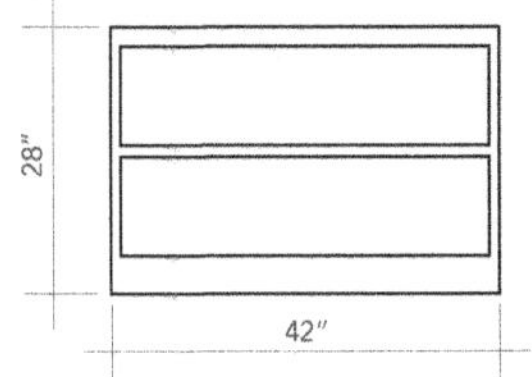

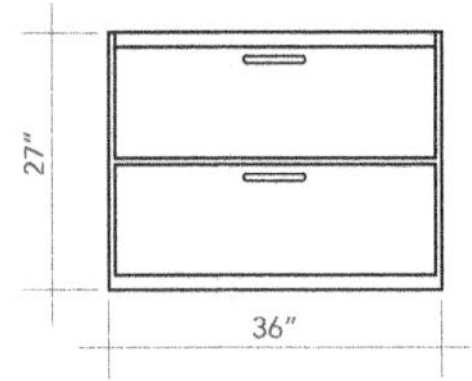

Imperial	Metric
28″	725 mm
42″	1,000 mm
27″	725 mm
30″ or 36″	690 or 800 mm

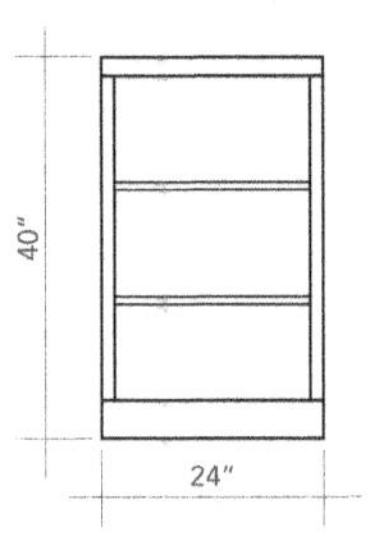

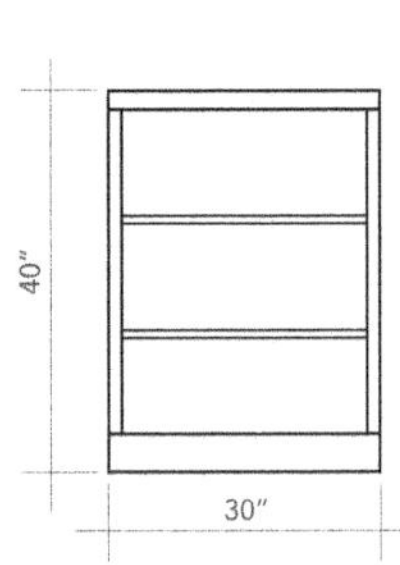

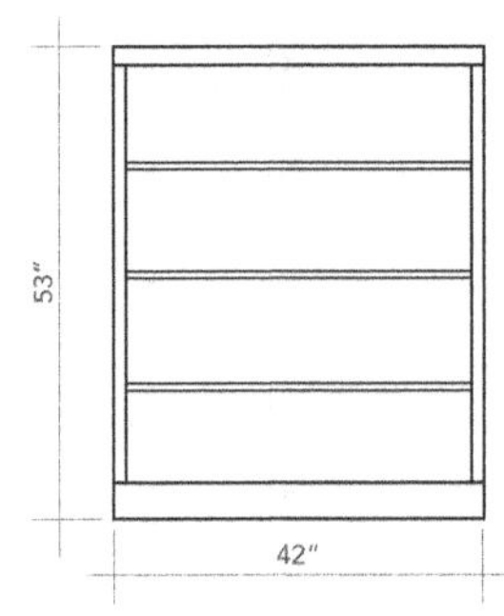

Imperial	Metric
40″	1,009 mm
24″	660 mm
30″ or 36″	690 or 800 mm
53″	1,252 mm
42″ or 48″	1,000 or 1,070 mm

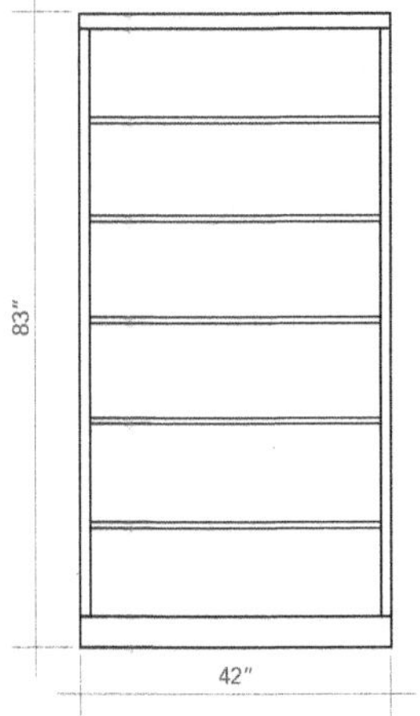

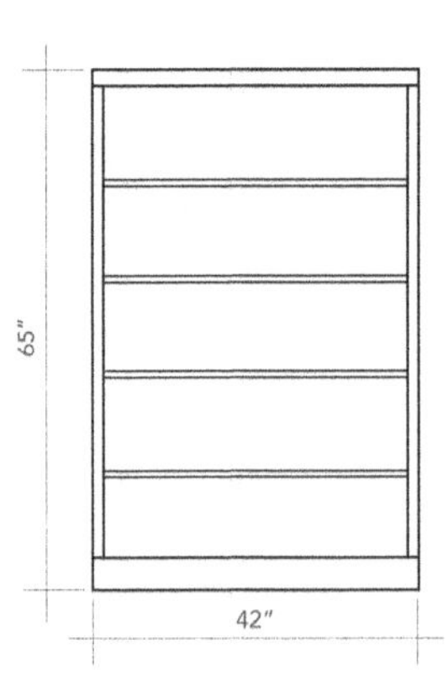

Imperial	Metric
83″	2,062 mm
42″	1,000 mm
42″	1,000 mm
65″	1,657 mm

F4

FILES AND BOOKCASES

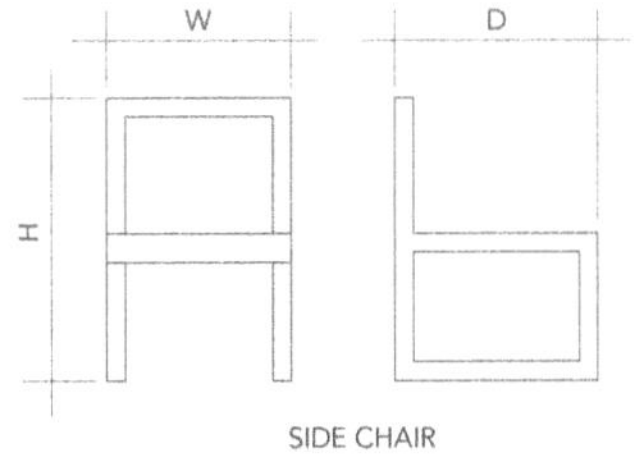

SIDE CHAIR

H 2′ 6″
W 1′ 8″
D 1′ 10″
SEAT HEIGHT RANGE:
1′5″to1′7″

Imperial	Metric
2′-6″	76 cm
1′-8″	51 cm
1′-10″	56 cm
1′-5″–1′-7″	432–483 mm

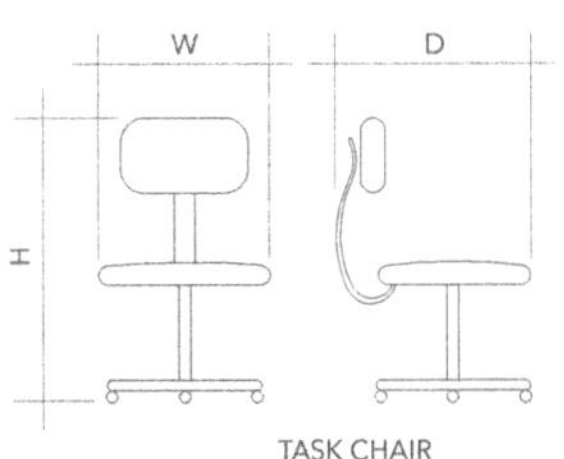

TASK CHAIR

H 2′ 6″
W 1′ 5″
D 1′ 7 1/2″
SEAT HEIGHT RANGE:
1′4″to1′8″

Imperial	Metric
1′-4″–1′-8″	406–508 mm
1′-5″	43 cm
1′-7-1/2″	50 cm
2′-6″	76 cm

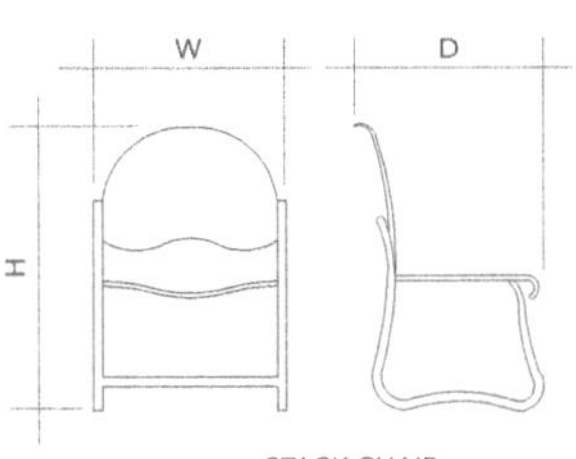

STACK CHAIR

H 2′ 6″
W 1′ 9″
D 1′ 9″
SEAT HEIGHT RANGE:
1′5″to1′6″

Imperial	Metric
1′-5″–1′-6″	432–457 mm
1′-9″	53 cm
1′-9″	53 cm
2′-6″	76 cm

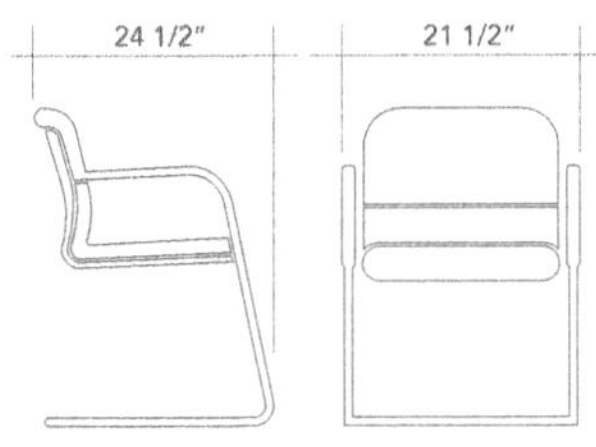

SLED BASE

HEIGHT RANGE:
33″
ARM HEIGHT RANGE:
25 1/2″
SEAT HEIGHT RANGE:
18″

Imperial	Metric
18″	46 cm
21-1/2″	55 cm
24-1/2″	62 cm
25-1/2″	65 cm
33″	84 cm

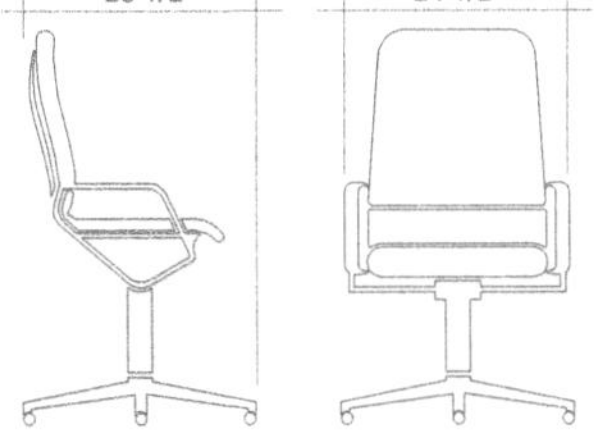

HIGH BACK MID-MANAGER

HEIGHT RANGE:
39 1/2″–43″ PNEUMATIC
39 1/2″–43″ VECMATIC
ARM HEIGHT RANGE:
25 1/2″–29″ PNEUMATIC
25 1/2″–29 1/2″ VECMATIC
SEAT HEIGHT RANGE:
17″–21″ PNEUMATIC
17″–21″ VECMATIC

FURNITURE ELEVATIONS—CHAIRS

F5a

Imperial	Metric
39-1/2″–43″	1003–1092 mm
39-1/2″–43″	1003–1092 mm
25-1/2″–29″	648–737 mm
25-1/2″–29-1/2″	648–750 mm
26-1/2″	67 cm
24-1/2″	62 cm
17″–21″	432–533 mm
17″–21″	432–533 mm

Imperial	Metric	Imperial	Metric	Imperial	Metric
30″	762 mm	26″	660 mm	46″, 75″, 100″	117, 190.5, 254 mm
30″	762 mm	23-1/2″	597 mm	35″	890 mm
30″	762 mm	32″	813 mm	25″	635 mm
17″	432 mm	18-1/2″	470 mm	16″	405 mm

W 30″
D 30″
H 30″
SH 17″

W 26″
D 23 1/2″
H 32″
SH 18 1/2″

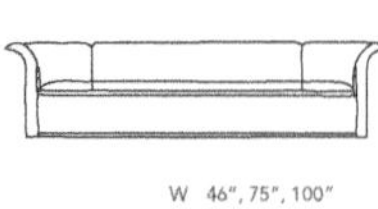

W 46″, 75″, 100″
D 35″
H 25″
SH 16″

Imperial	Metric	Imperial	Metric	Imperial	Metric
32-1/2″	825.5 mm	32″	813 mm	21-3/4″	552 mm
32-1/4″	819 mm	31-1/2″	800 mm	32-1/4″	819
33-3/8″	848 mm	30″	762 mm	32-1/4″	819 mm
15″	381 mm			17-1/2″	445 mm

W 32 1/2″
D 32 1/4″
H 33 3/8″
SH 15″

W 32″
D 31 1/2″
H 30″

W 21 3/4″
D 32 1/4″
H 32 1/4″
SH 17 1/2″

Imperial	Metric	Imperial	Metric	Imperial	Metric
19-1/2″	495 mm				
21-1/2″	546 mm	40″	1016 mm	16″	410 mm
29-1/4″	743 mm	34″	864 mm	20″	510 mm
18″	457 mm	35-1/2″	902 mm	35″	890 mm
		25-1/2″	648 mm		
		20″	508 mm		
		16″	406 mm		

W 19 1/2″
D 21 1/2″
H 29 1/4″
SH 18″

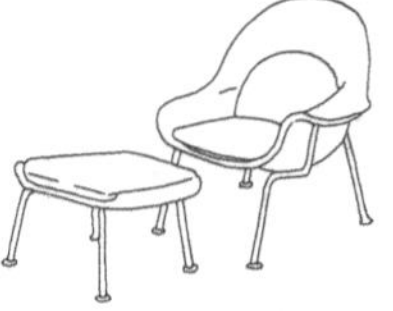

W 40″
D 34″
H 35 1/2″

OTTOMAN: W 25 1/2″
D 20″
H 16″

W 16″
D 20″
H 35″

F5b

DESIGNER CHAIRS

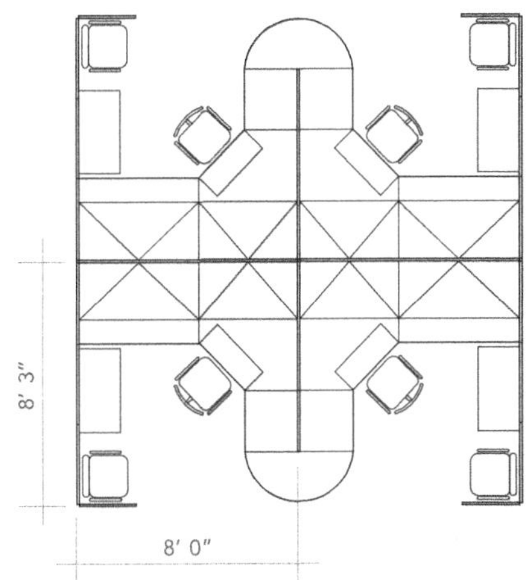

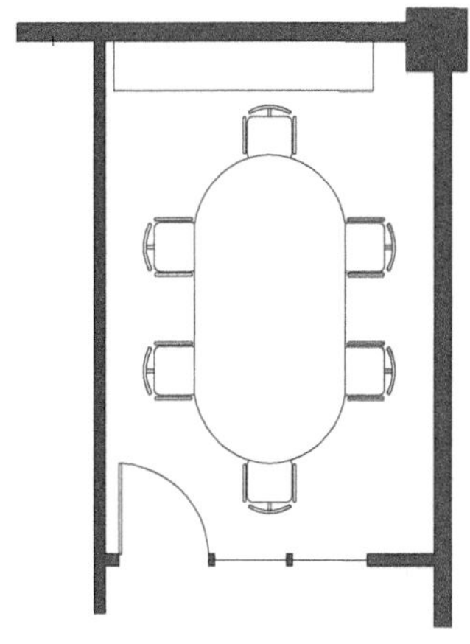

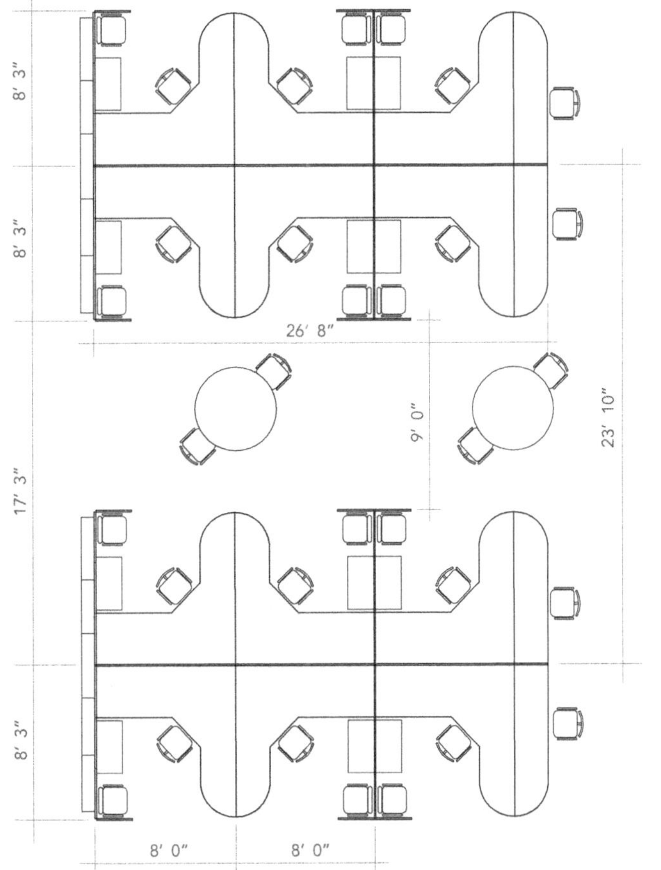

Imperial	Metric
8'-3"	2.51 m
8'	2.44 m

Imperial	Metric
8'-3"	2.51 m
8'-3"	2.51 m
26'-8"	8.13 m
9'-0"	2.74 m
23'-10"	7.26 m
17'-3"	5.26 m
8'-3"	2.51 m
8'-0"	2.44 m
8'-0"	2.44 m

F6

WORKSTATION LAYOUTS

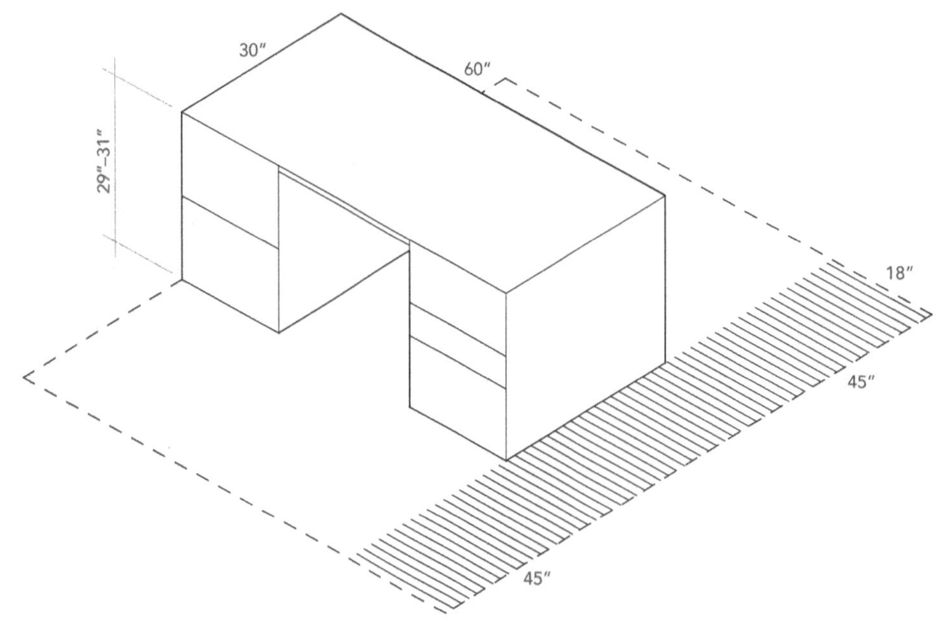

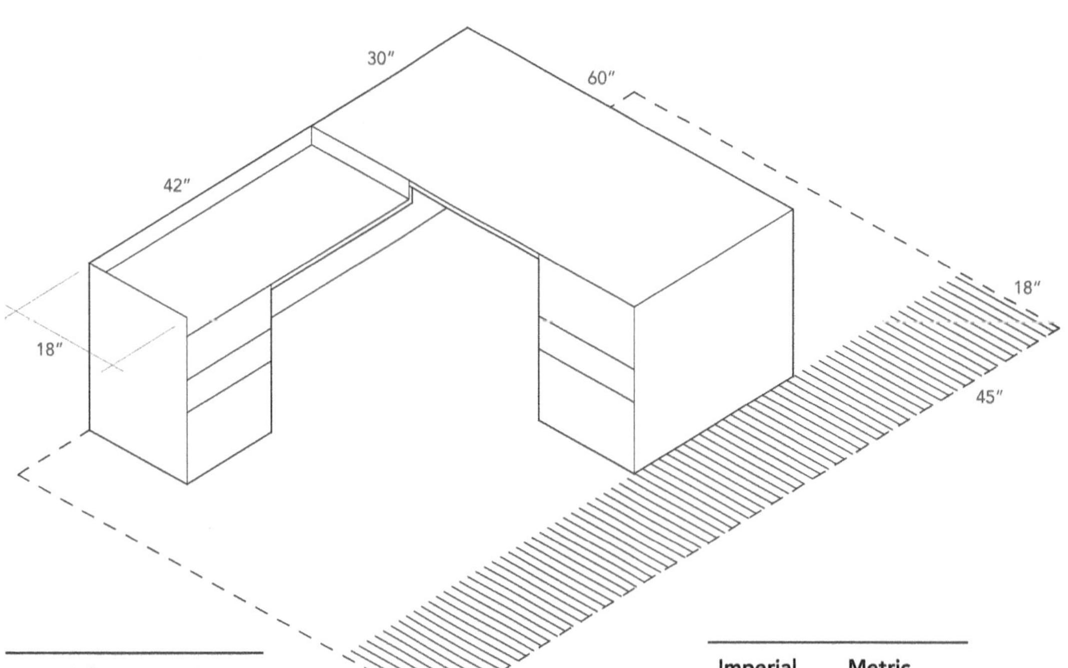

Imperial	Metric
29″–31″	737–787 cm
30″	762 cm
60″	1,524 cm
18″	457 cm
45″	1,143 cm

OFFICE WORKSTATIONS

Imperial	Metric
18″	457 mm
42″	1,067 mm
30″	762 mm
60″	1,524 mm
18″	457 mm
45″	1,143 mm

F7

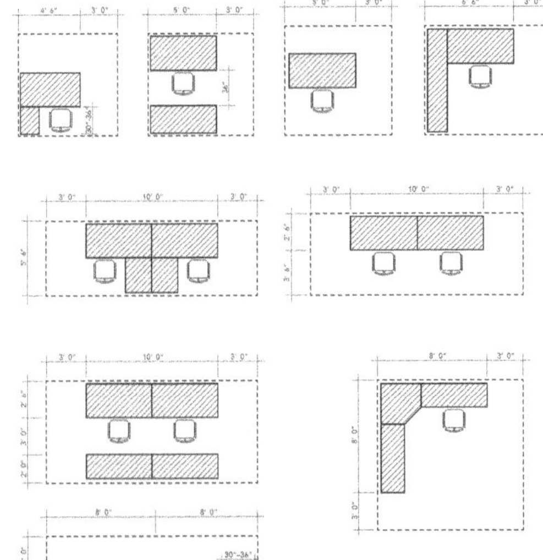

F8

OFFICE WORKSTATIONS

Imperial	Metric	Imperial	Metric	Imperial	Metric	Imperial	Metric
4′-6″	137 cm	5′-0″	152 cm	5′-0″	152 cm	6′-6″	198 cm
3′-0″	91 cm	3′-0″	91 cm	3′-0″	91 cm	3′-0″	91 cm
30″–36″	76–91cm	36″	91 cm				

Imperial	Metric	Imperial	Metric
5′-6″	168 cm	3′-6″	107 cm
3′-0″	91 cm	2′-6″	76 cm
10′-0″	305 cm	3′-0″	91 cm
		10′-0″	305 cm

Imperial	Metric
2′-0″	61 cm
3′-0″	91 cm
2′-6″	76 cm
10′-0″	305 cm

Imperial	Metric
3′-0″	91 cm
8′-0″	244 cm
3′-0″	91.5

Imperial	Metric
7′-0″	213 cm
3′-0″	91 cm
8′-0″	244 cm
30″–36″	76–91 cm

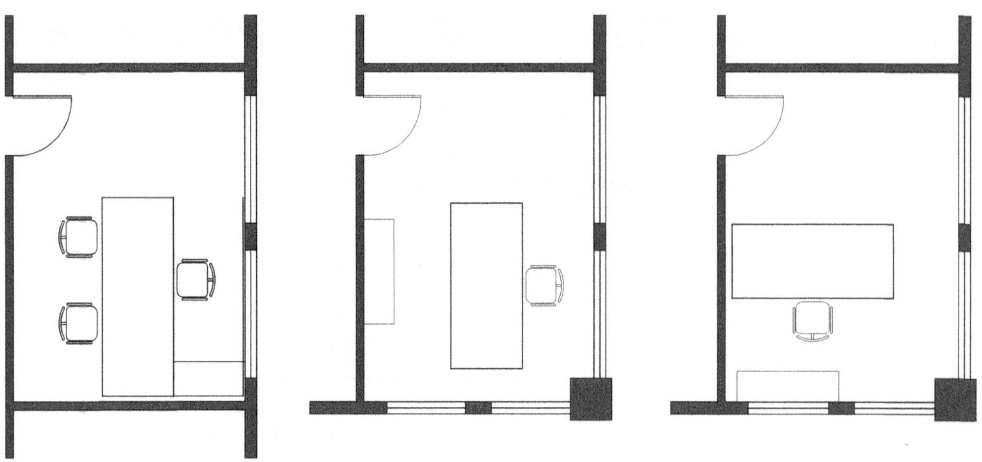

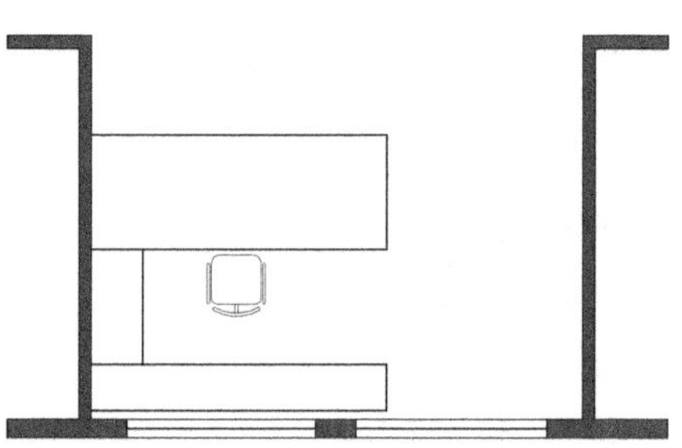

Imperial	Metric
10′ × 15′	3 m × 4.6 m

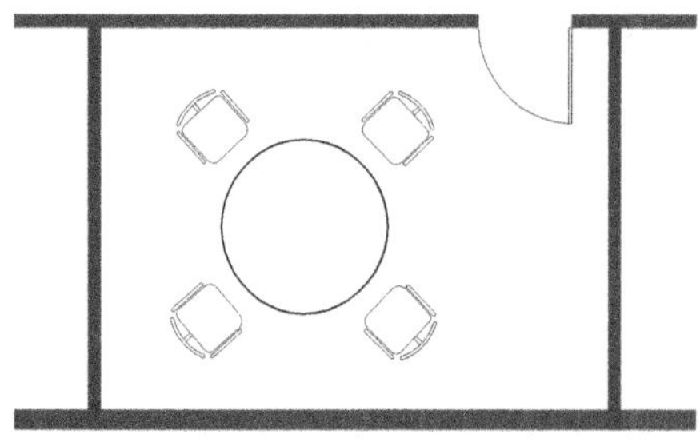

10′ × 15′ OFFICE OPTIONS

F9

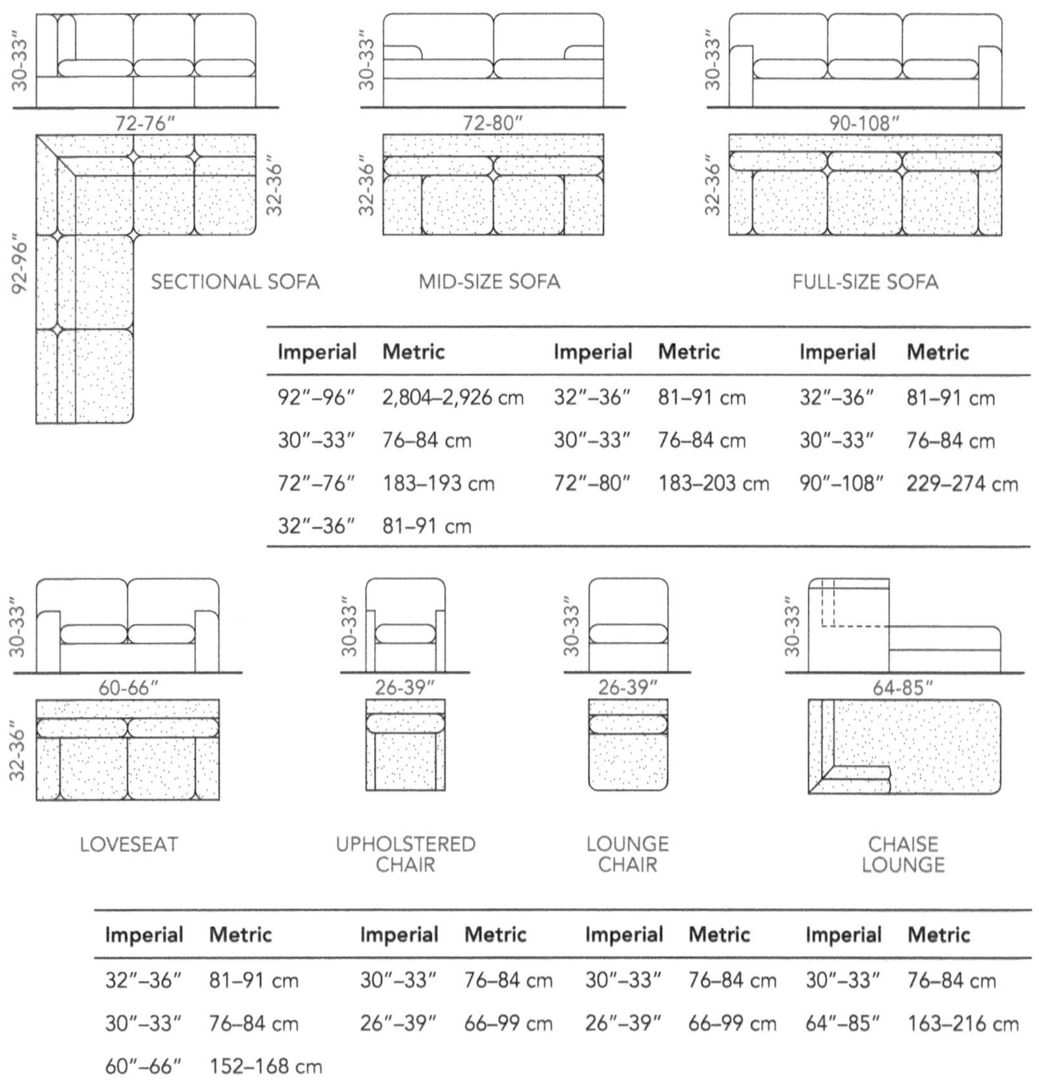

Imperial	Metric	Imperial	Metric	Imperial	Metric
92"–96"	2,804–2,926 cm	32"–36"	81–91 cm	32"–36"	81–91 cm
30"–33"	76–84 cm	30"–33"	76–84 cm	30"–33"	76–84 cm
72"–76"	183–193 cm	72"–80"	183–203 cm	90"–108"	229–274 cm
32"–36"	81–91 cm				

Imperial	Metric	Imperial	Metric	Imperial	Metric	Imperial	Metric
32"–36"	81–91 cm	30"–33"	76–84 cm	30"–33"	76–84 cm	30"–33"	76–84 cm
30"–33"	76–84 cm	26"–39"	66–99 cm	26"–39"	66–99 cm	64"–85"	163–216 cm
60"–66"	152–168 cm						

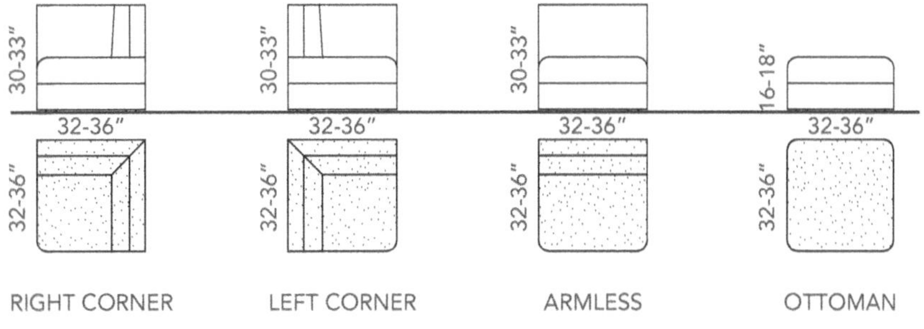

F10

SECTIONAL PIECES

Imperial	Metric	Imperial	Metric	Imperial	Metric	Imperial	Metric
32"–36"	81–91 cm	30"–33"	76–84 cm	30"–33"	76–84 cm	16"–18"	41–46 cm
30"–33"	76–84 cm	32"–36"	81–91 cm	32"–36"	81–91 cm	32"–36"	81–91 cm
32"–36"	81–91 cm	32"–36"	81–91 cm	32"–36"	81–91 cm	32"–36"	81–91 cm

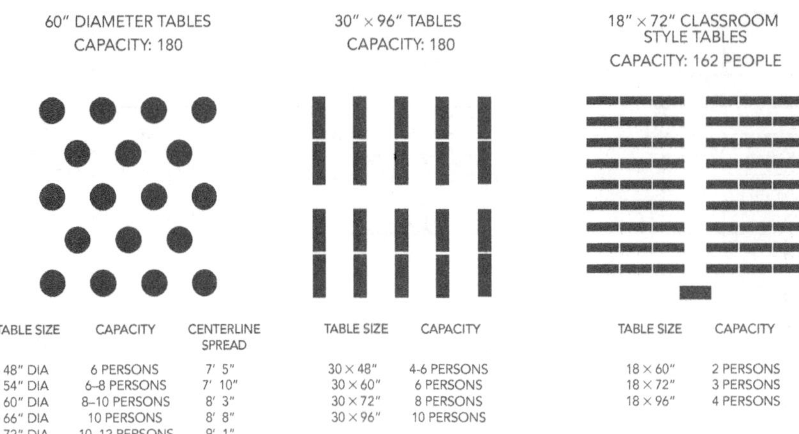

AUDITORIUM AND CONFERENCE ROOM SEATING ARRANGEMENTS

F11a

Imperial	Metric	Imperial	Metric	Imperial	Metric
60"	152 cm	30" × 96"	76 × 244 cm	18" × 72"	46 × 183 cm
48"	122 cm				
54"	137 cm	30" × 48"	76 × 122 cm	18" × 60"	46 × 152 cm
60"	152 cm	30" × 60"	76 × 152 cm	18" × 72"	46 × 183 cm
66"	168 cm	30" × 72"	76 × 183 cm	18" × 96"	46 × 244 cm
72"	183 cm	30" × 96"	76 × 244 cm		
7'-5"	226 cm				
7'-10"	239 cm				
8'-3"	251 cm				
8'-8"	264 cm				
9'-1"	277 cm				

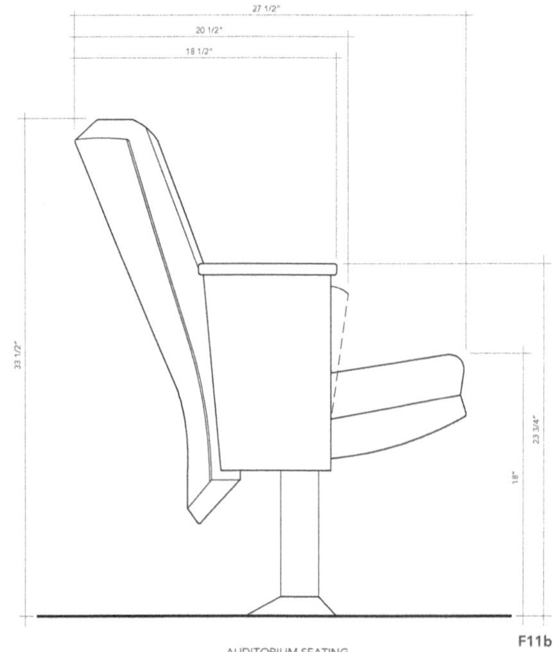

AUDITORIUM SEATING

F11b

Imperial	Metric
33-1/2"	85 cm
18-1/2"	47 cm
20-1/2"	52 cm
27-1/2"	70 cm
18"	46 cm
23-3/4"	60.5 cm

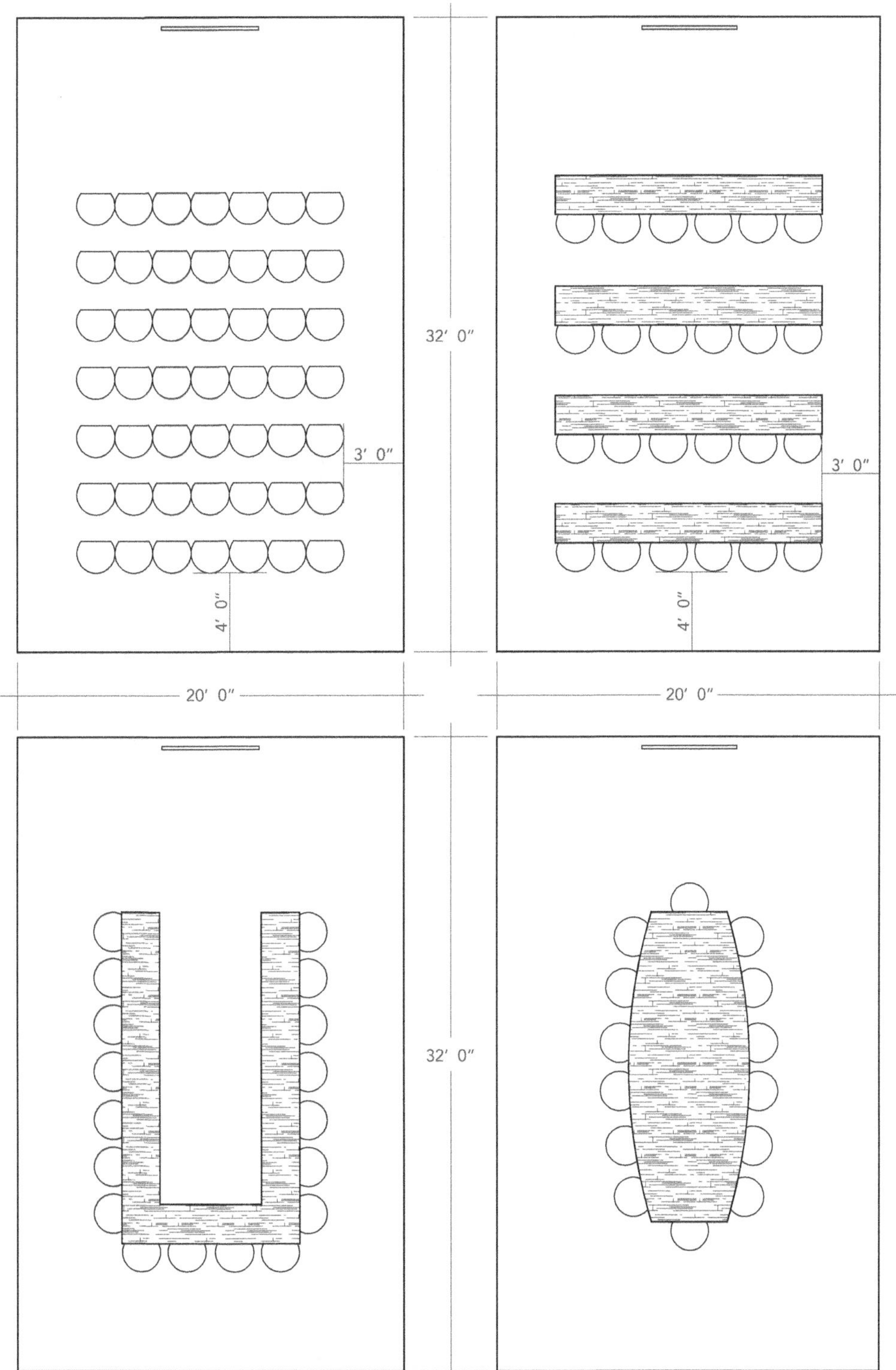

Imperial	Metric
4′	122 cm
3′	76 cm
32′	9.75 m
20′	6.1 m
32′	9.75 m

F12

AUDITORIUMS AND CONFERENCE ROOMS

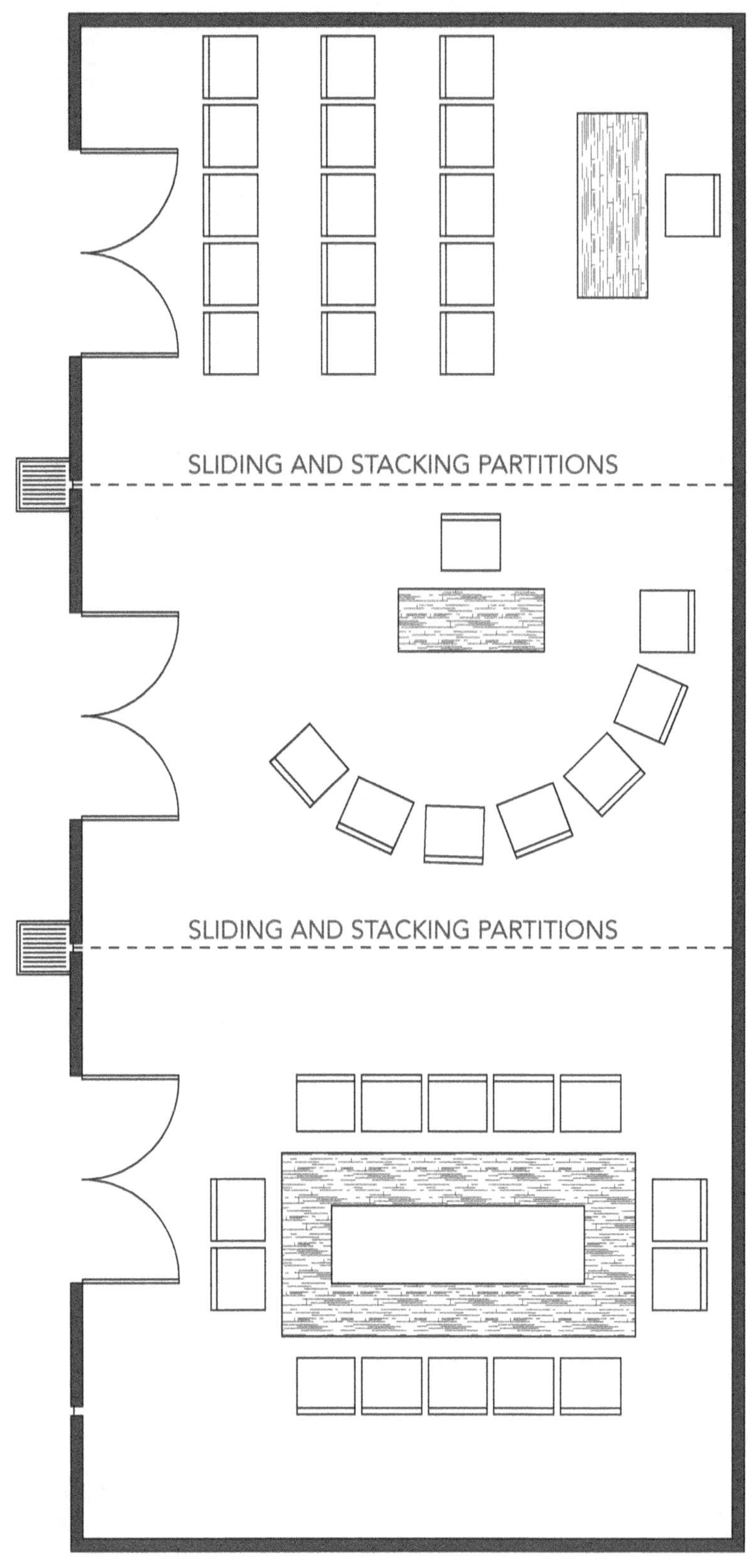

F13

CONFERENCE SPACE

Imperial	Metric
15′ × 17′	4.57 × 5.18 m

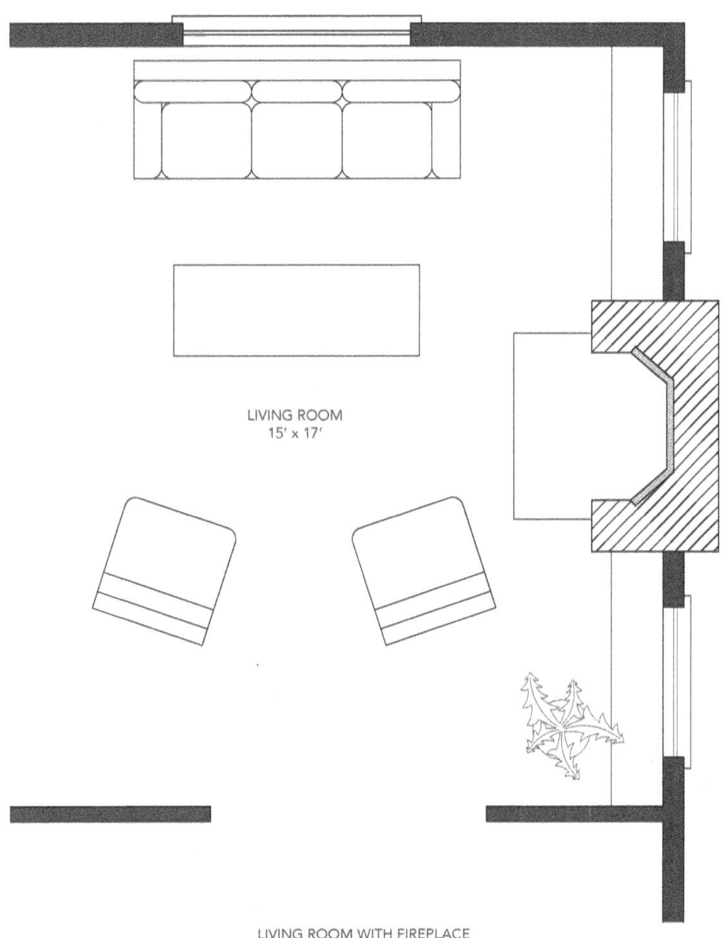

LIVING ROOM WITH FIREPLACE

F14a

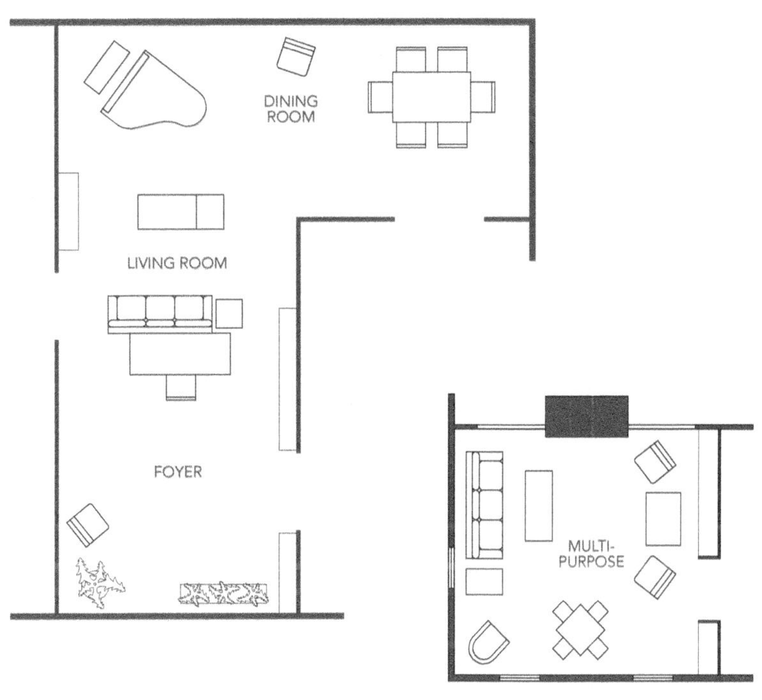

RESIDENTIAL LIVING ROOM FURNITURE PLANS

F14b

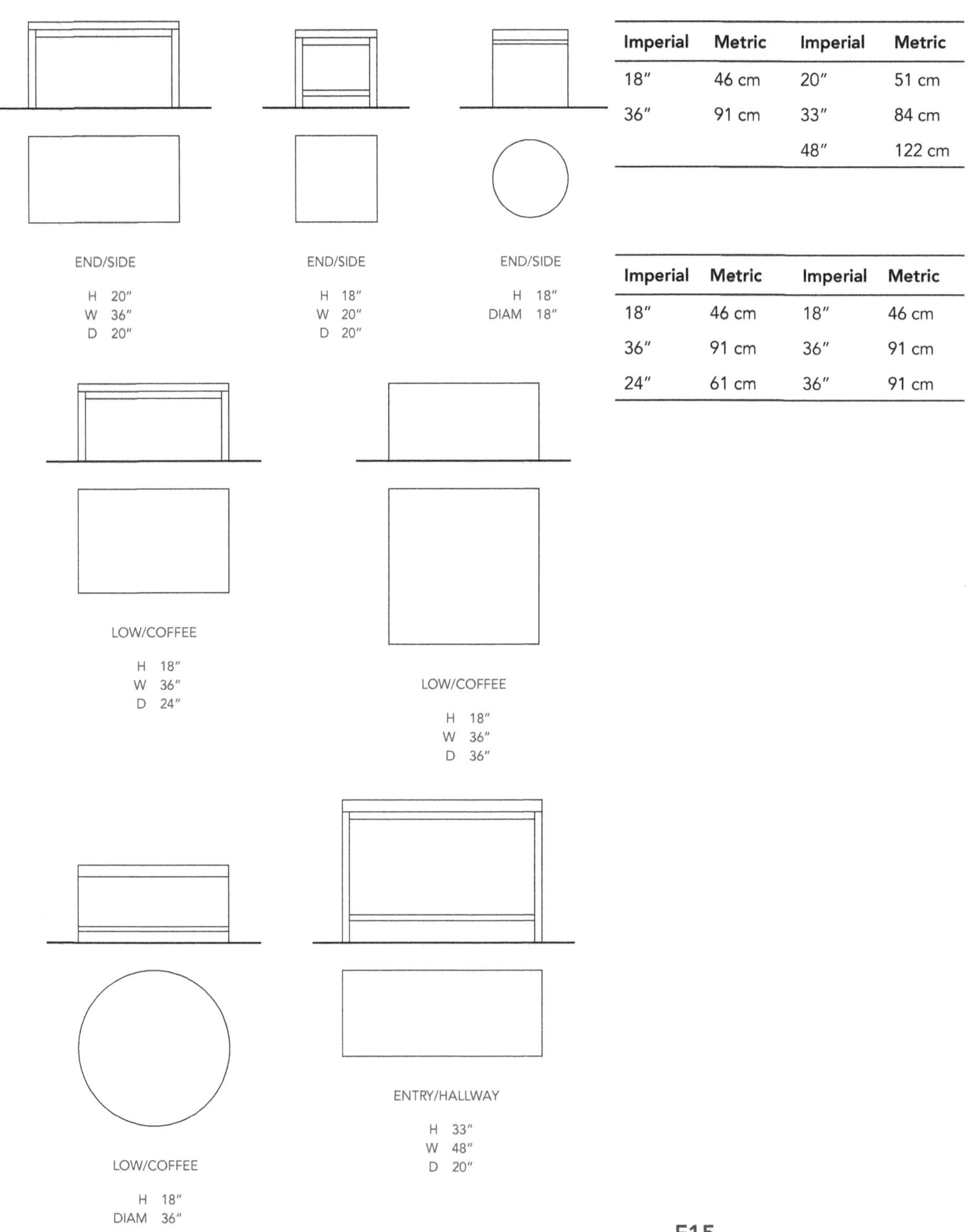

Imperial	Metric	Imperial	Metric
18″	46 cm	20″	51 cm
36″	91 cm	33″	84 cm
		48″	122 cm

Imperial	Metric	Imperial	Metric
18″	46 cm	18″	46 cm
36″	91 cm	36″	91 cm
24″	61 cm	36″	91 cm

TABLES

F15

Imperial	Metric	Imperial	Metric	Imperial	Metric
20″	51 cm	18″	46 cm	18″	46 cm
36″	91 cm	20″	51 cm	18″	46 cm
20″	51 cm	20″	51 cm		

	Imperial	Metric	Imperial	Metric	Imperial	Metric	Imperial	Metric
	Depth		Width		Height		Ht. w/lid	
CONCERT GRAND TO THE LEFT OF 9′ 8″	9′-8″	295 cm	5′-4″	162.5 cm	3′-3″	99 cm	4′-9″	145 cm
MUSIC ROOM GRAND TO THE LEFT OF 7′	7′	213 cm	5′	152 cm	3′-4″	102 cm	4′-10″	148 cm
PARLOR GRAND TO THE LEFT OF 6′ 3″	6′-3″	190 cm	4′-10″	147 cm	3′-4″	102 cm	4′-10″	148 cm
BABY GRAND TO THE LEFT OF 4′ 5″	4′-5″	135 cm	4′-7″	140 cm	3′	91.5 cm	4′-3″	129.5
SPINET TO THE LEFT OF 2′ 1″	2′-1″	64 cm	4′-10″	147 cm	3′-4″	102 cm	4′-2″	127cm
STUDIO TO THE LEFT OF 2′ 1″	2′-1″	64 cm	4′-9″	145 cm	3′-10″	117 cm	4′-2″	127 cm

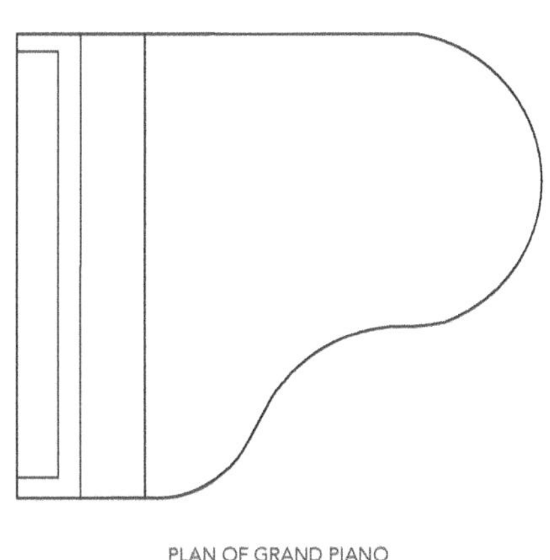

PLAN OF GRAND PIANO

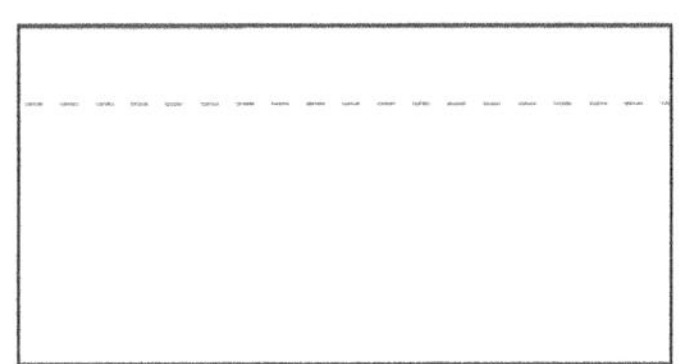

PLAN OF SPINET PIANO

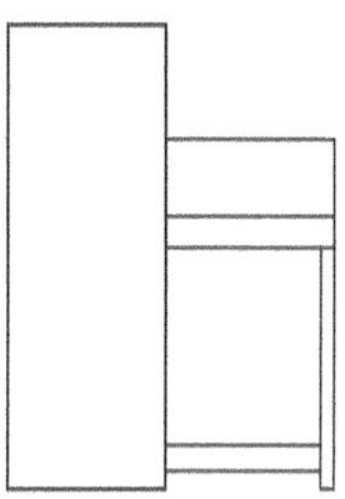

ELEVATION OF SPINET PIANO

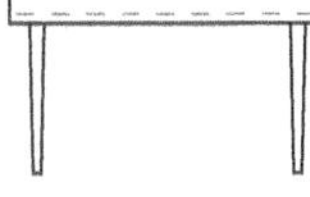

BENCH
H 20″
W 36″
D 16″

Imperial	Metric
20″	51 cm
36″	91.5 cm
16″	41 cm

F16

PIANOS

Imperial	Metric
2-3/4″	70 mm
3-1/4″	83 mm

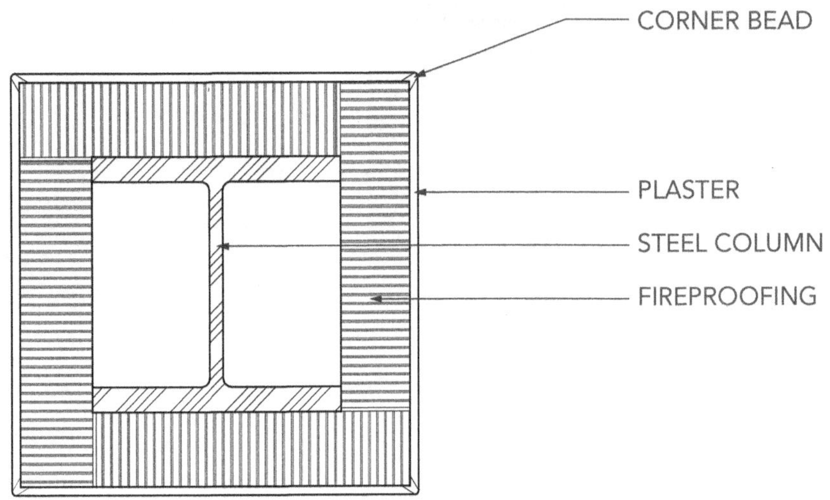

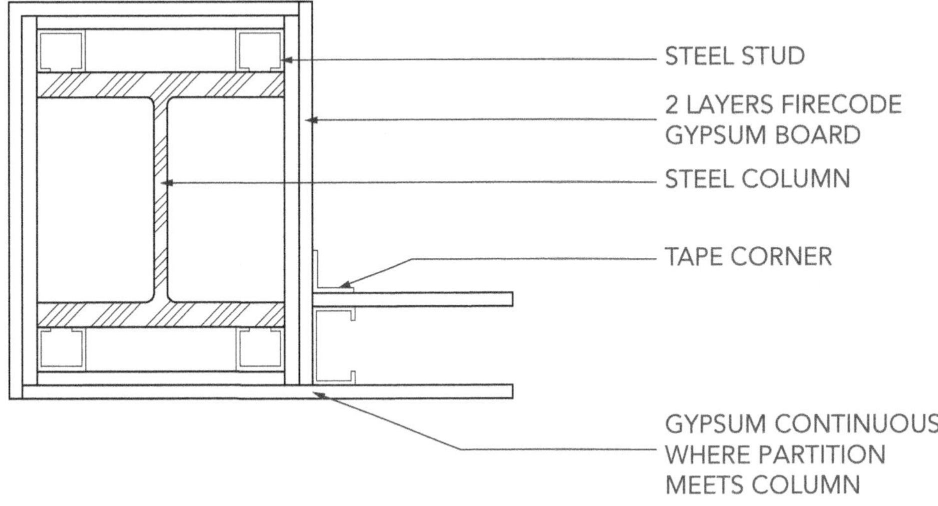

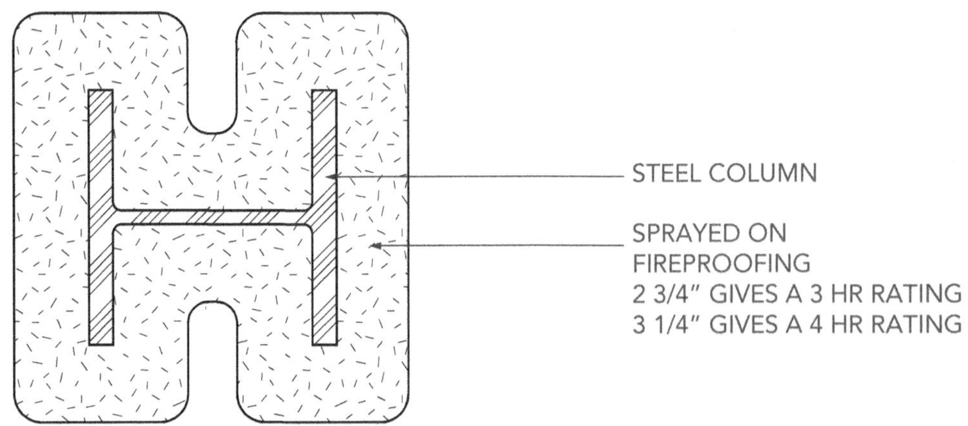

C1

COLUMN FIREPROOFING DETAILS

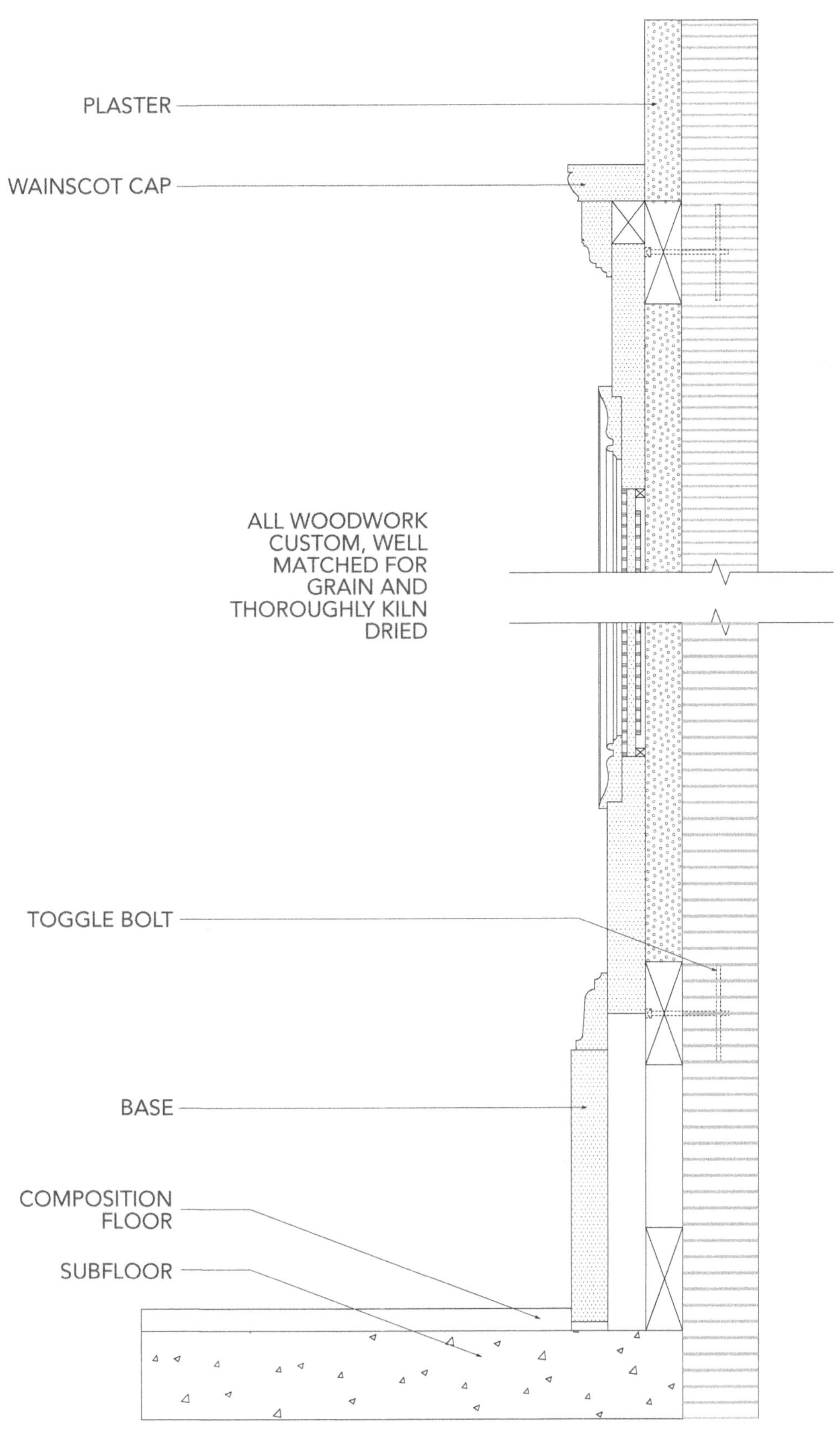

C2

WOOD WALL PANELING AND WAINSCOTING DETAILS

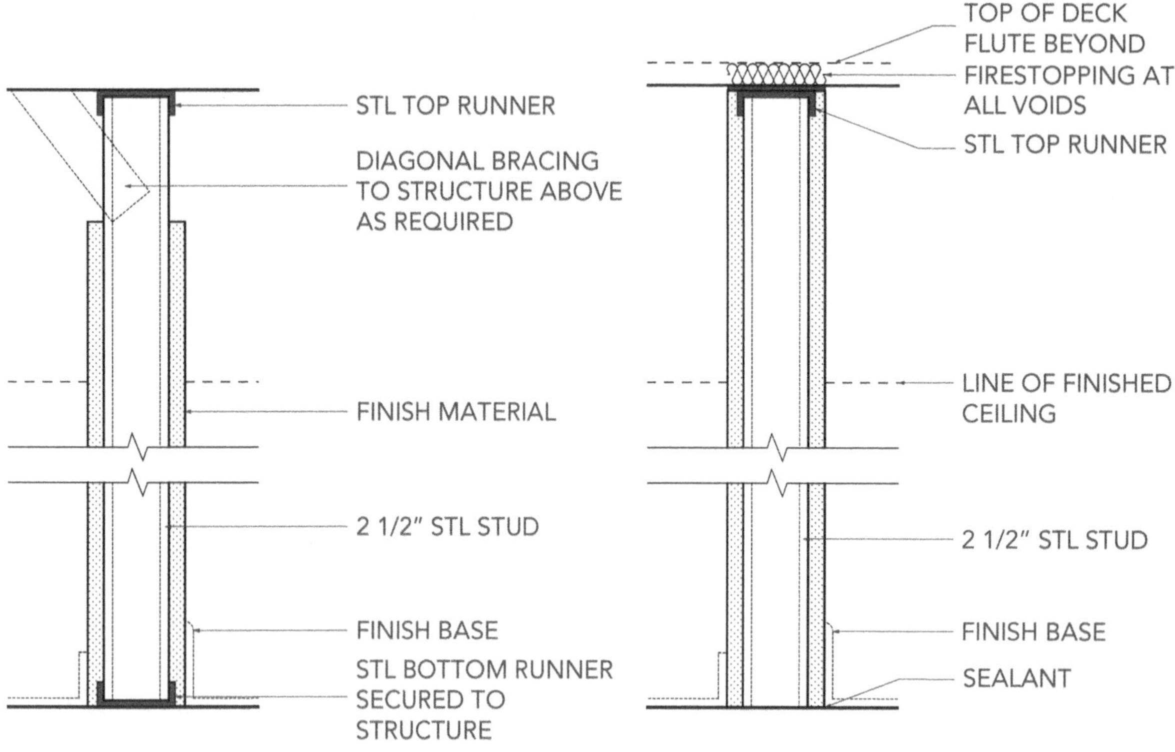

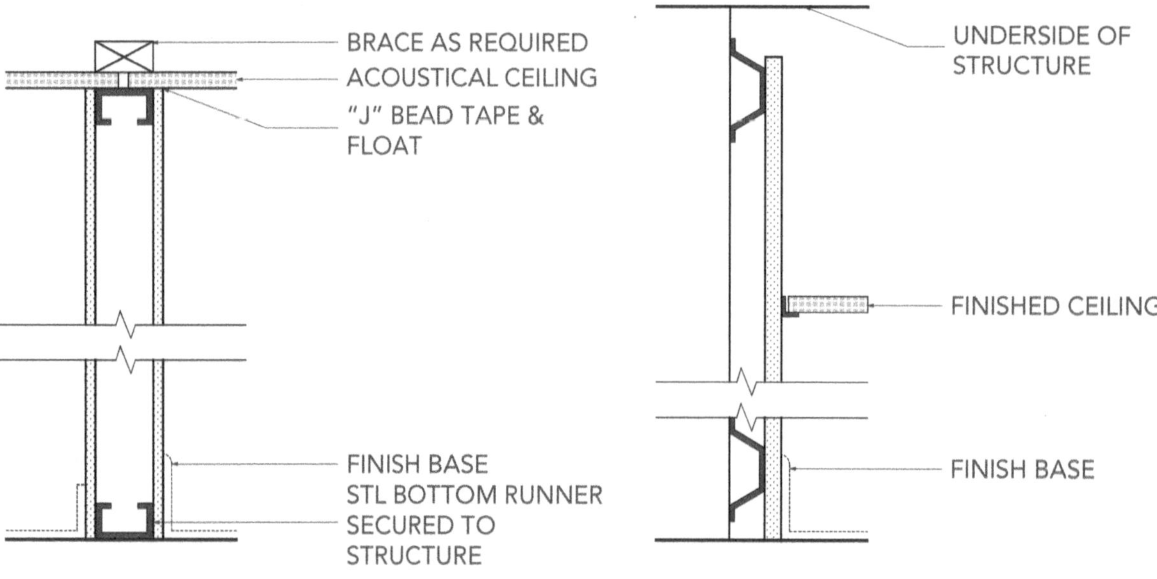

C3

Imperial	**Metric**
2-1/2"	63 mm

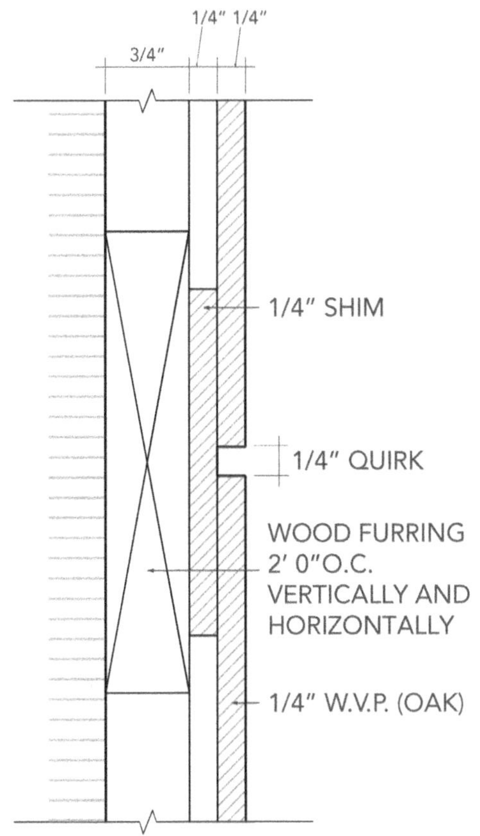

TYPICAL JOINT FOR WOOD VENEER
PANELED WALLS - PLAN

4 3/4"
2' 5 3/4"
1 1/2"
3/4"
3/4"
7' 3"
1/4" W.V.P. (OAK)
7' 8"
4"
CARPET

WALL/CEILING/FASCIA

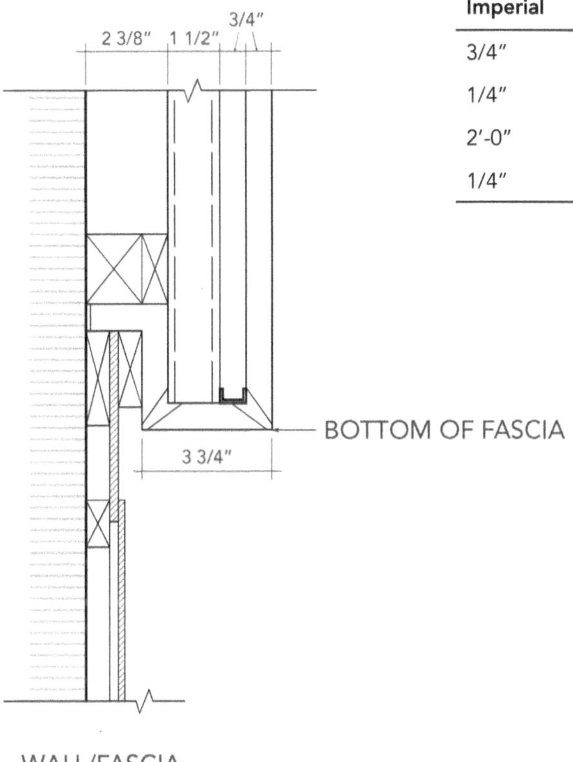

WALL/FASCIA

Imperial	Metric
3/4"	19 mm
1/4"	6 mm
2'-0"	61 cm
1/4"	6 mm

Imperial	Metric
4-3/4"	121 cm
2'-5-3/4"	75.5 cm
1-1/2"	38 mm
3/4"	19 mm
7'-3"	2.21 m
1/4"	6 mm
4"	10 mm
7'-8"	2.34 m

Imperial	Metric
2-3/8"	60 mm
1-1/2"	38 mm
3/4"	19 mm
3-3/4"	95 mm

C4

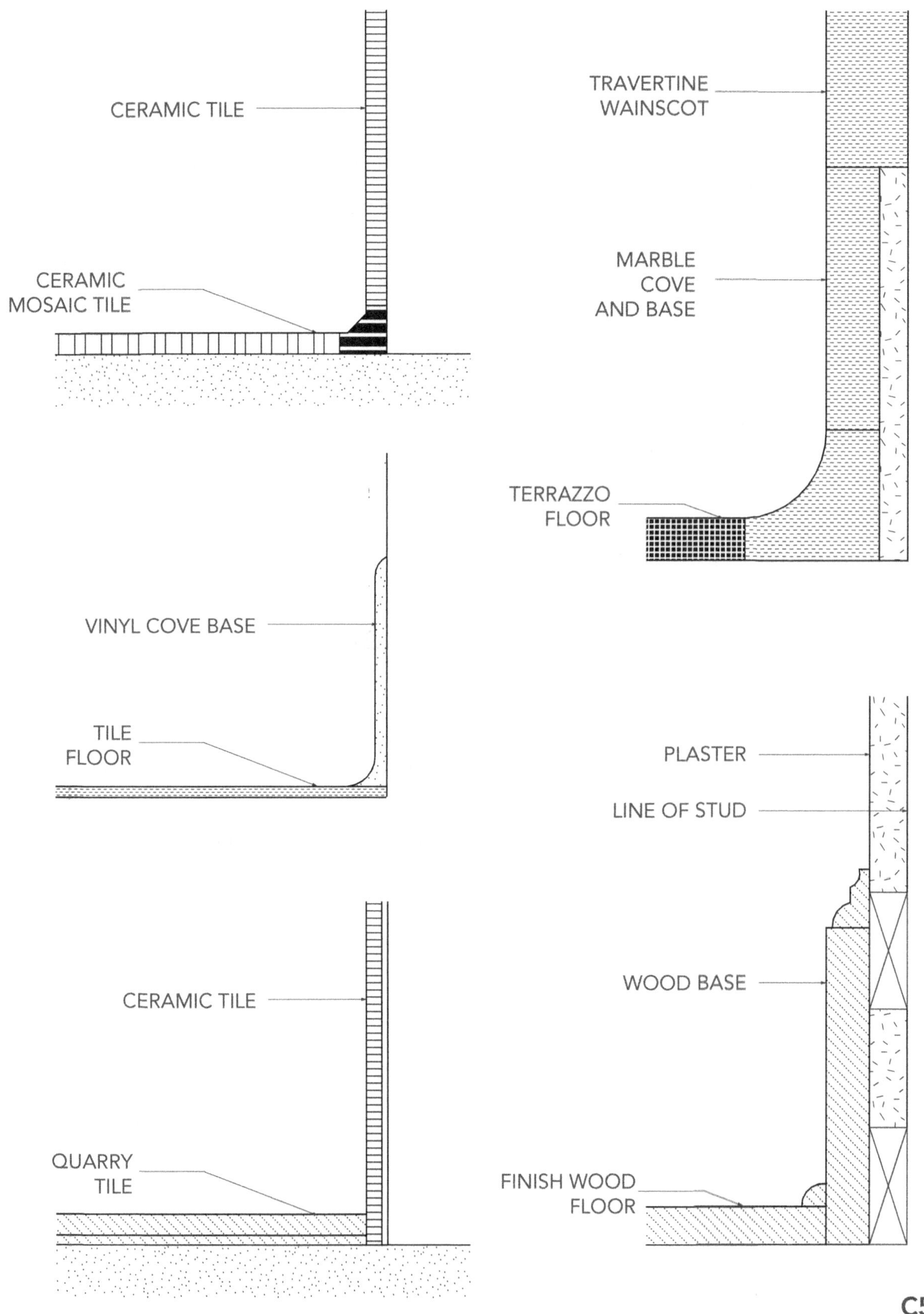

FLOORS AND FLOOR FINISHES

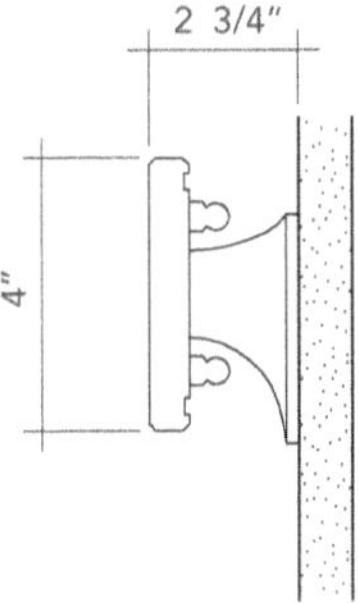

Imperial	Metric
4"	102 mm
2-3/4"	70 mm

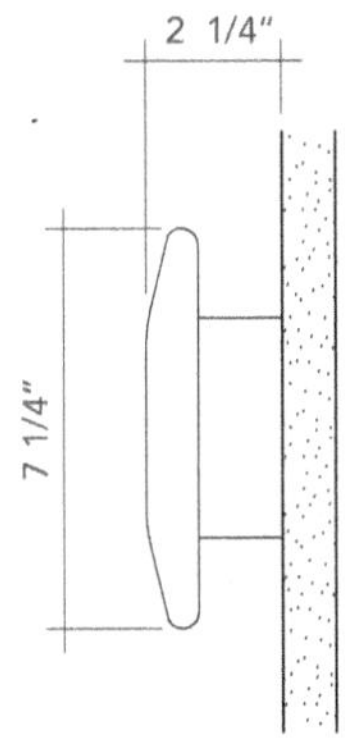

Imperial	Metric
7-1/4"	184 mm
2-1/4"	57 mm

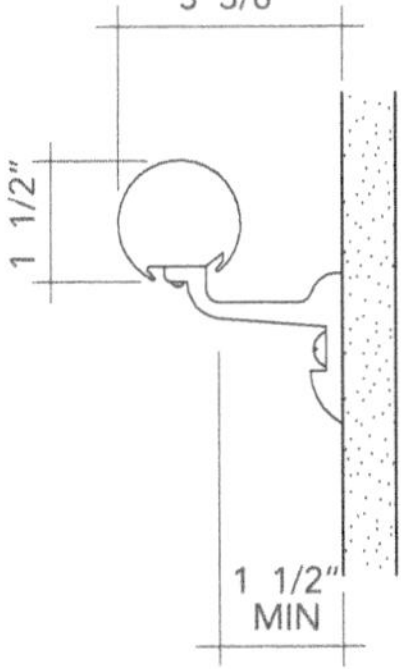

Imperial	Metric
1-1/2"	38 mm
3-3/8"	86 mm
1-1/2"	38 mm

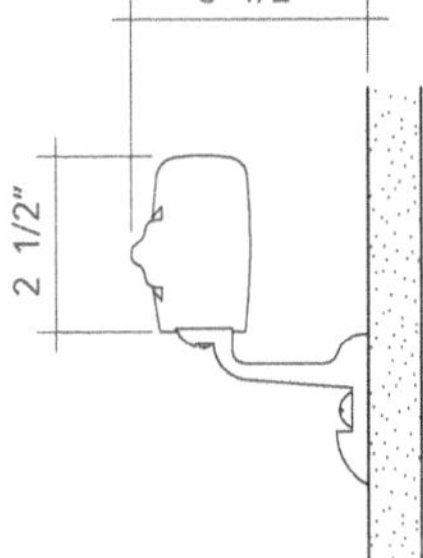

Imperial	Metric
2-1/2"	63.5 mm
3-1/2"	89 mm

C6

HANDRAIL DETAILS

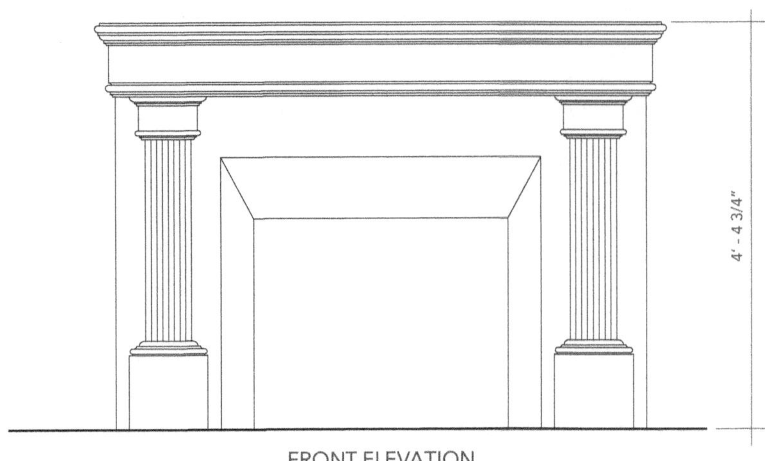

FRONT ELEVATION

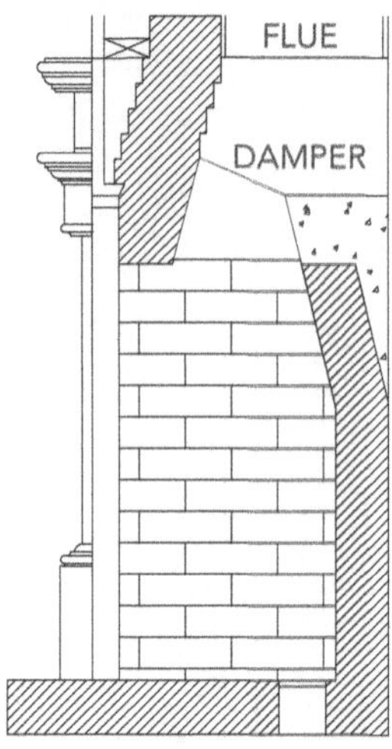

SECTION

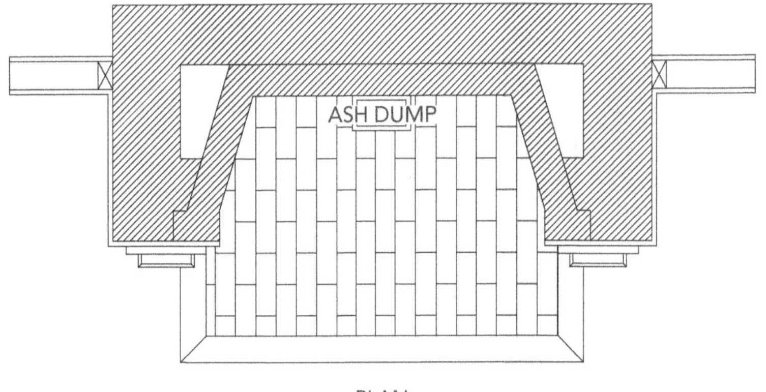

PLAN

Imperial	Metric
4′-4–3/4″	134 cm

C7

FIREPLACES

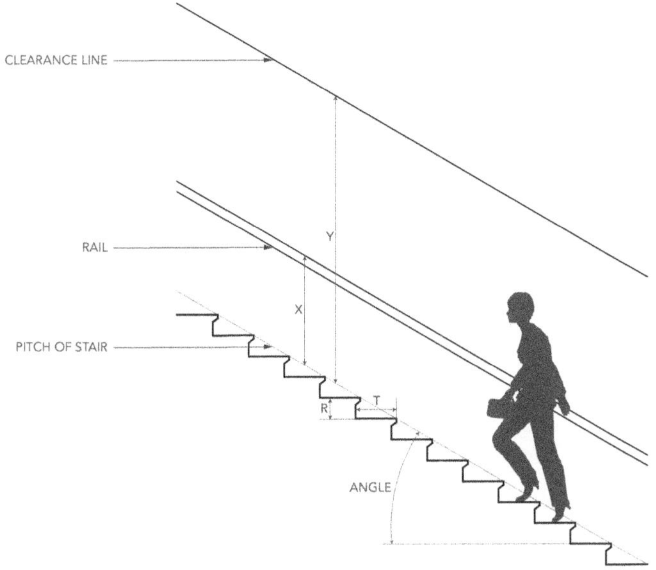

C8

HANDRAIL HEIGHT X IN INCHES	STEP DIMENSIONS RISER R IMPERIAL	RISER R METRIC	TREAD T IMPERIAL	TREAD T METRIC	GRADIENT DESIGNATIONS ANGLE IN DEGREES, MINUTES	PERCENT GRADE
33" - 34"	5"	12.7 cm	16"	41 cm	17 21	31.25
	5-1/4"	13 cm	15-1/2"	39 cm	18 43	33.87
	5-1/2"	14 cm	14-3/4"	37.5 cm	20 27	37.28
	5-3/4"	15 cm	14"	36 cm	22 20	41.07
33	6"	15.25 cm	13"	34 cm	23 58	44.44
	6-1/4"	16 cm	13-1/2"	33 cm	25 40	48.07
	6-1/2"	16.5 cm	12-1/4"	31 cm	27 57	53.06
	6-3/4"	17 cm	11-3/4"	30 cm	29 52	57.44
	7"	18 cm	11"	28 cm	32 28	63.63
	7-1/4"	18.5 cm	10-1/2"	27 cm	34 37	69.04
	7-1/2"	19 cm	10"	25.5 cm	36 52	75
33 1/2	7-3/4"	20 cm	9-1/2"	24	39 12	81.57
	8"	20.25 cm	9"	23	41 38	88.88
	8-1/4"	21 cm	8-1/2"	22	44 9	97.05
	8-1/2"	22 cm	8-1/4"	21	45 51	103.02
34	8-3/4"	22.25 cm	8-1/8"	20.5	46 57	107.07
	9"	23 cm	8"	20	48 22	112.5

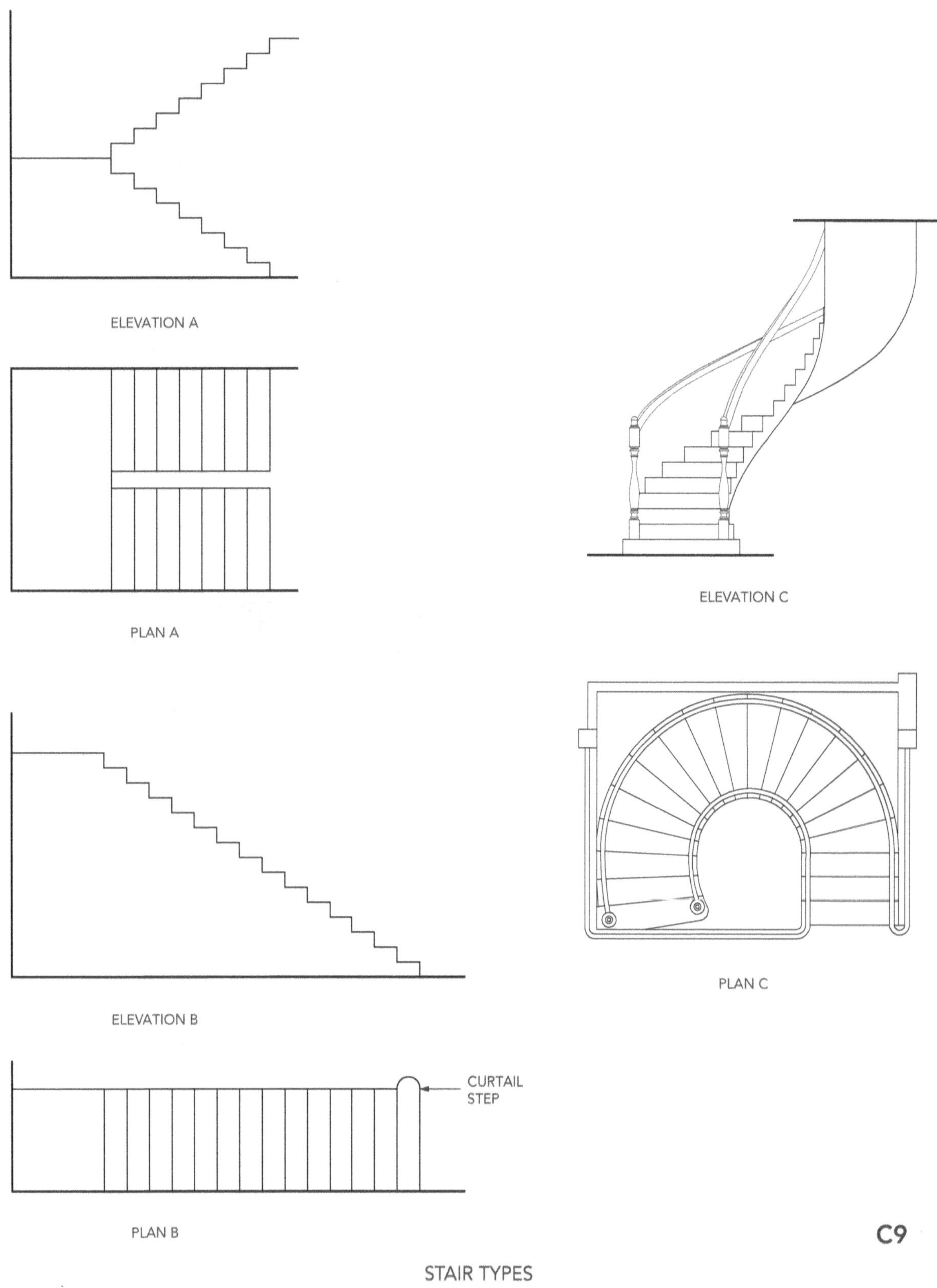

C9

STAIR TYPES

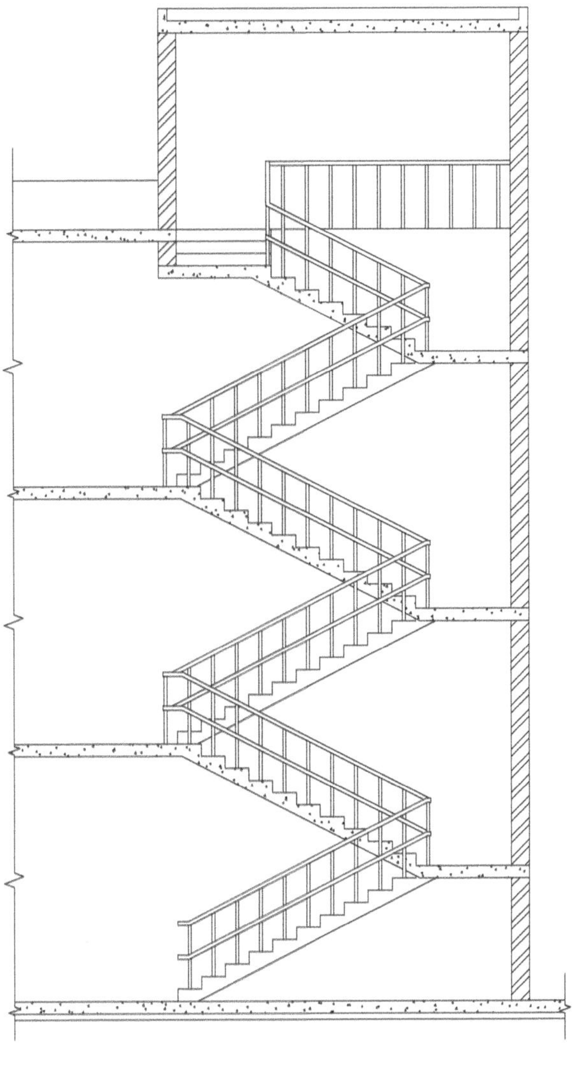

STAIR 1

STAIR WIDTH: 4′ 0″
RISERS: 63
RISER: 6″
TREAD: 12″

STAIR 2

STAIR WIDTH: 4′ 0″
RISERS: 40
RISER: 6 1/2″
TREAD: 11 1/2″

C10

STAIR SECTIONS

Imperial	Metric
4′-0″	122 cm
6″	15 cm
12″	30 cm

Imperial	Metric
4′-0″	122 cm
6-1/2″	16 cm
29″	29 cm

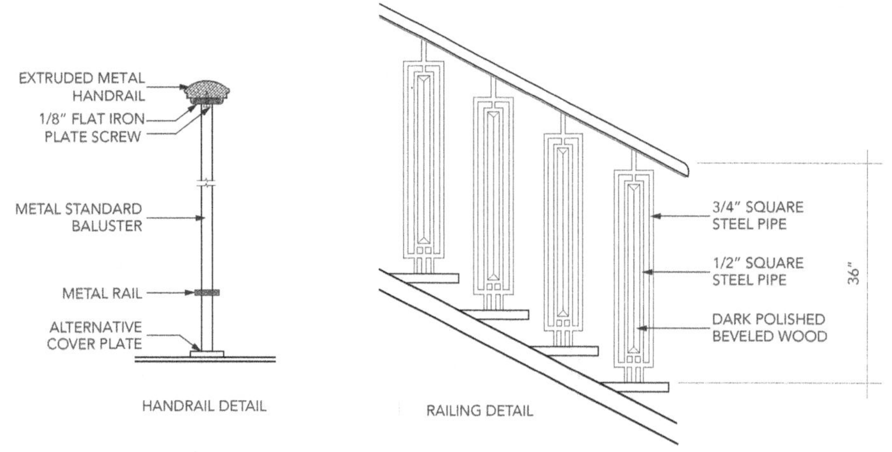

Imperial	Metric
1/8"	3.2 mm
3/4"	19 mm
1/2"	13 mm
36"	91.5 cm

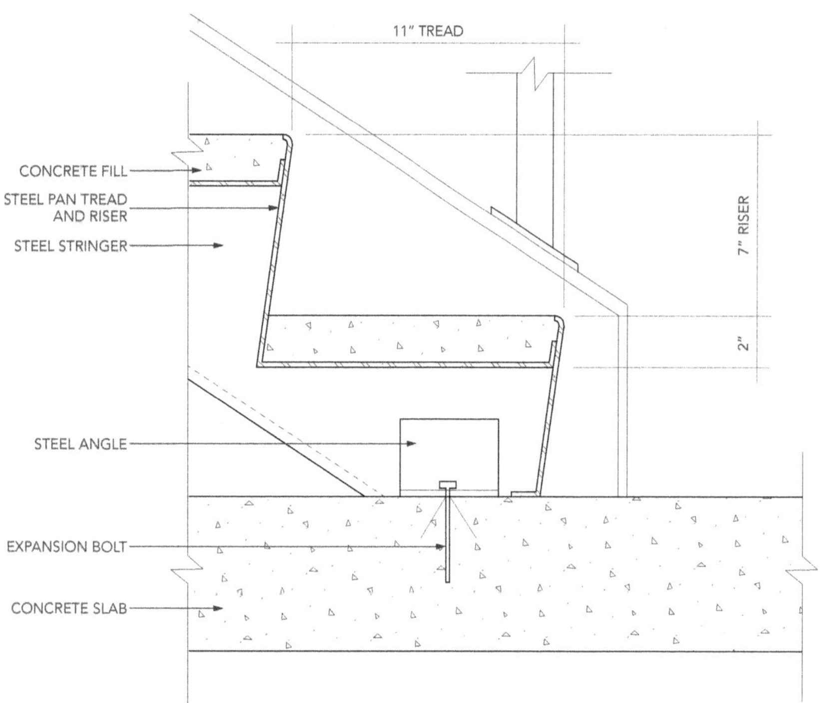

C11

STAIR DETAILS

Imperial	Metric
11"	28 cm
7"	18 cm
2"	5 cm

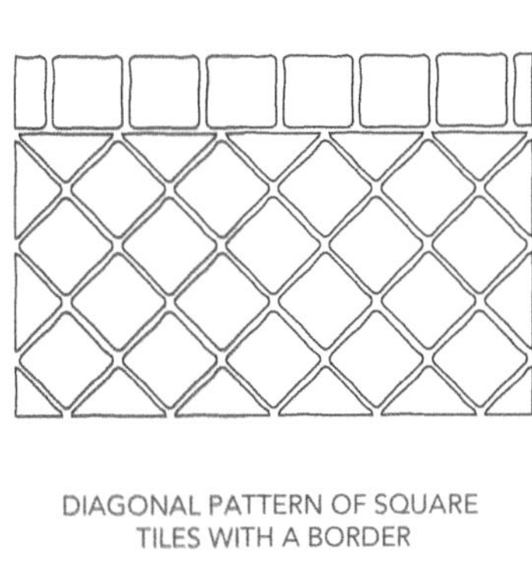

DIAGONAL PATTERN OF SQUARE TILES WITH A BORDER

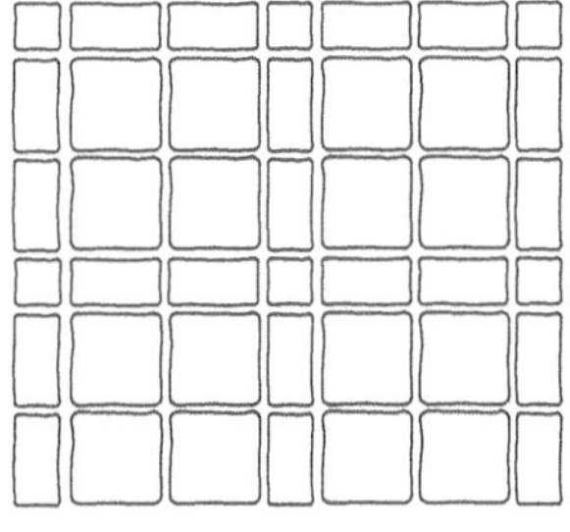

SUGGESTED PLAID PATTERN

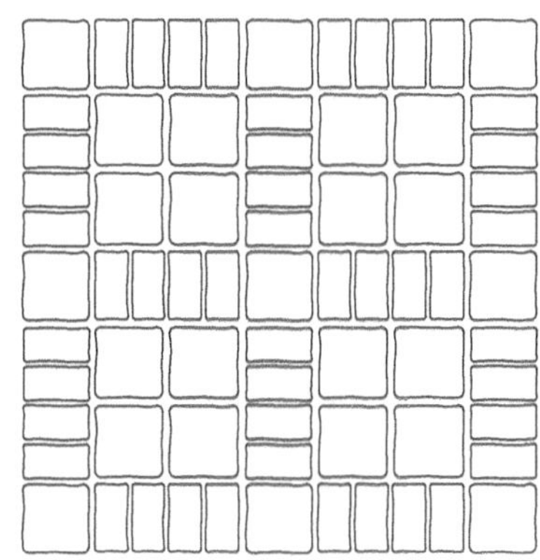

SIMPLE PATTERN FOR PANELLING OR A LARGE ROOM

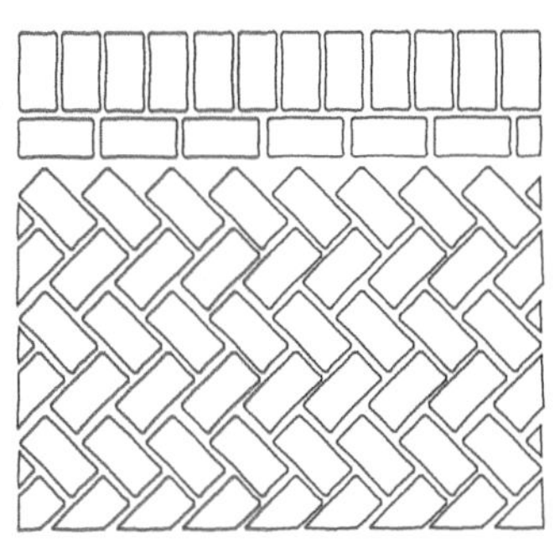

"HERRINGBONE"

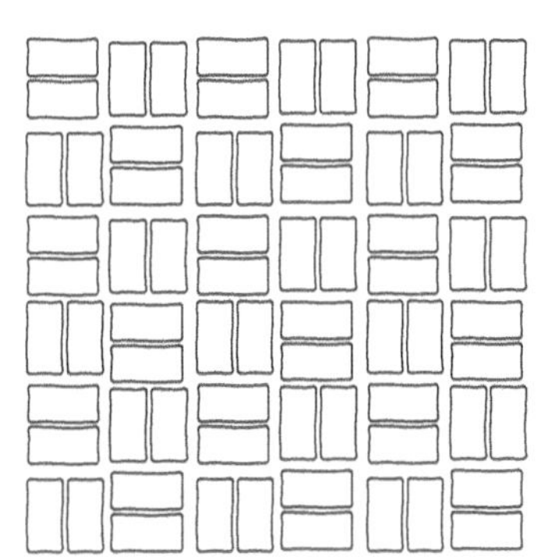

"BASKET PATTERN," NECESSARY ALLOWANCE FOR JOINTS ADDS INTEREST

SMALL SQUARES MUST BE MORE THAN ONE-QUARTER THE SIZE OF THE LARGE SO PATTERN DOES NOT RUN OFF AT SIDES

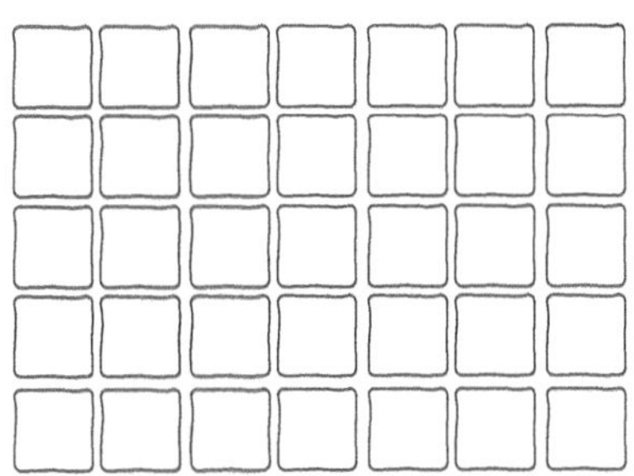

SIMPLE FLOOR OF SQUARE TILES, INTERESTING IF JOINTS ARE IN SCALE

GOOD PATTERN FOR CORRIDORS

C12

BRICK, STONE, AND TILE PATTERNS

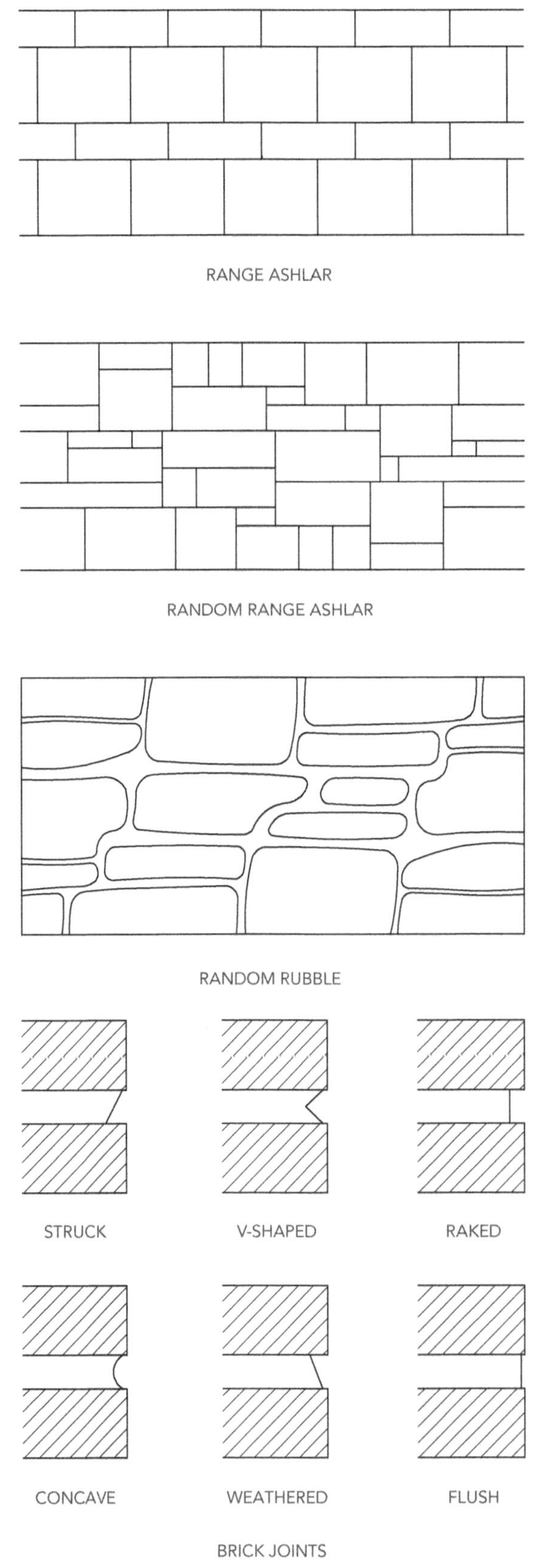

C13

PARTITIONS AND WALL FINISHES

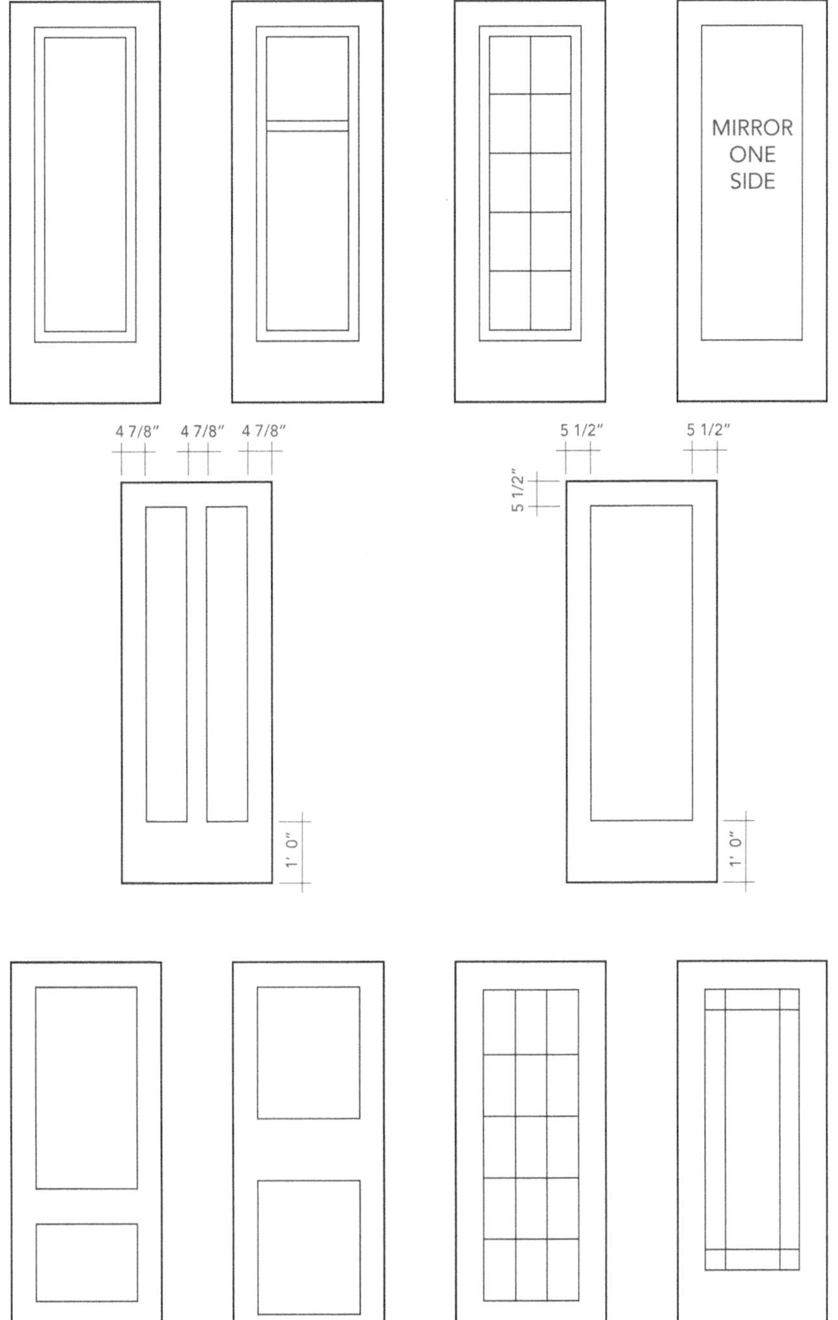

Imperial	Metric
4-7/8"	12.5 cm
1'	30 cm

Imperial	Metric
5-1/2"	14 cm
1'	30 cm

DOOR TYPES

DW1

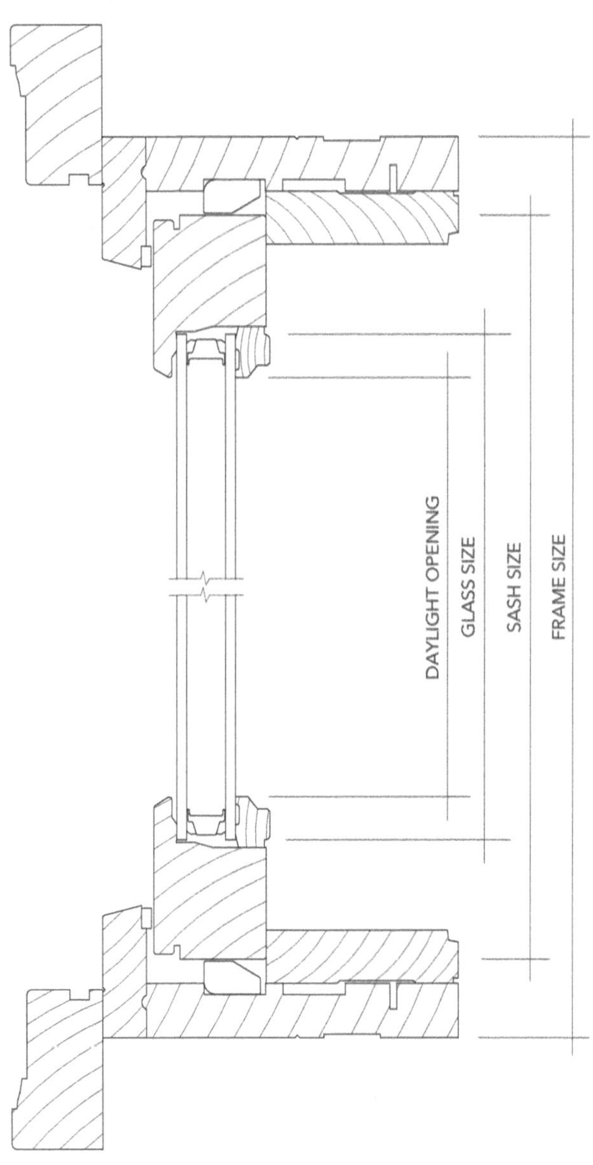

WOOD DOUBLE HUNG SECTION

HEAD

CHECKRAIL

SILL

DW2

WINDOW TREATMENTS

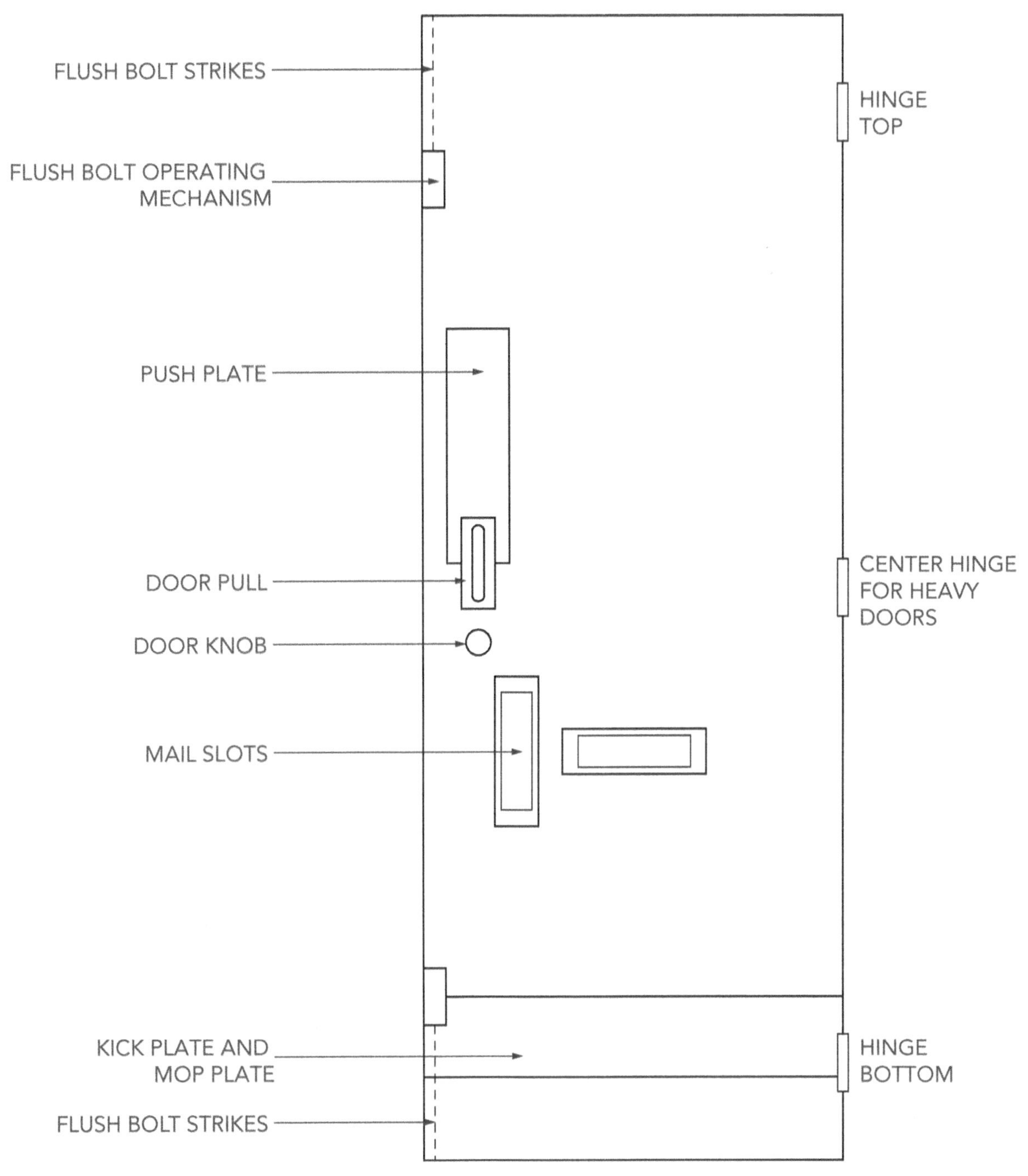

DW3

FINISH HARDWARE LOCATION
FOR ALL TYPES OF DOORS

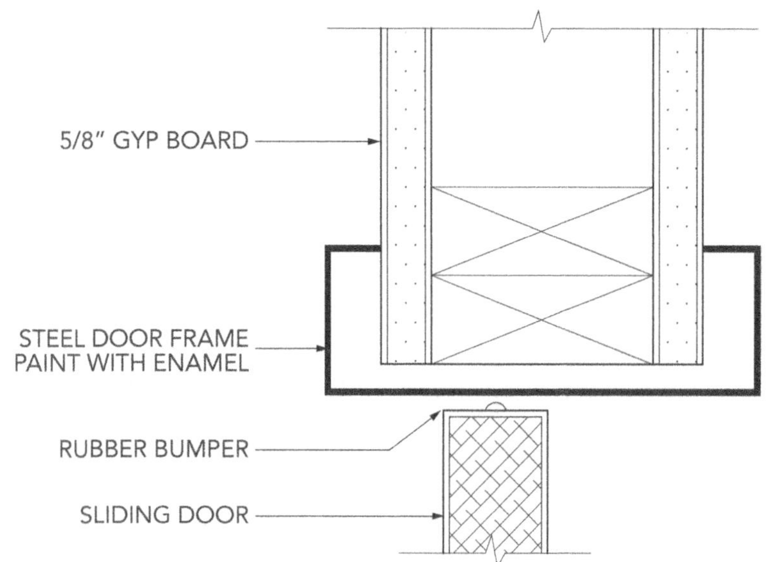

Imperial	Metric
5/8"	16 mm
1-3/8"	35 mm
5"	13 cm
2"	5 cm
6"	15 cm
1-5/8"	41 mm
1-3/8"	35 mm

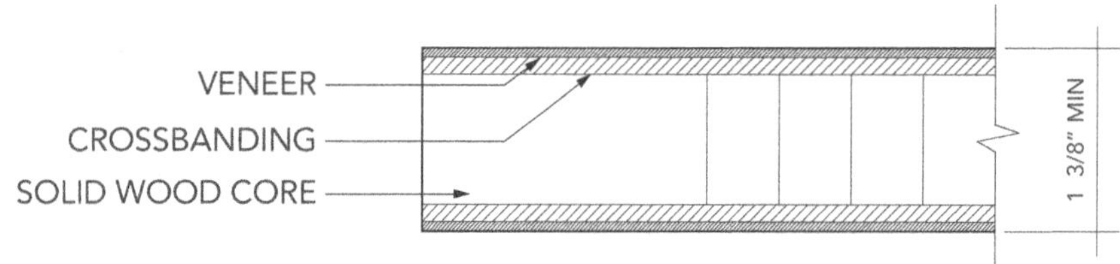

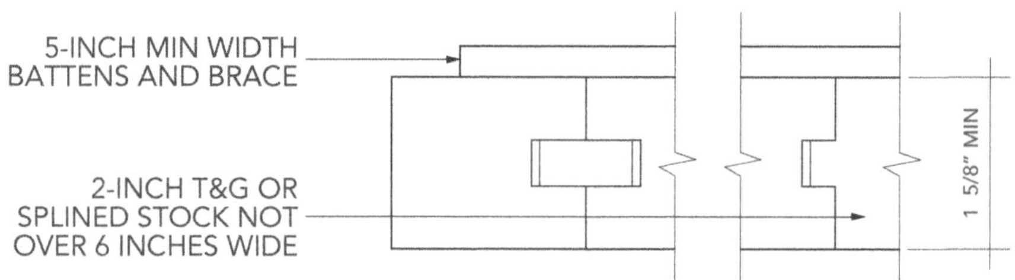

SOLID WOOD CORE FLUSH DOORS

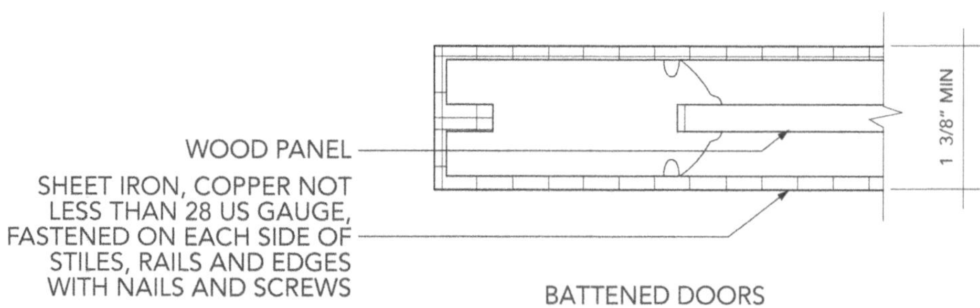

BATTENED DOORS

DW4

DOOR DETAILS

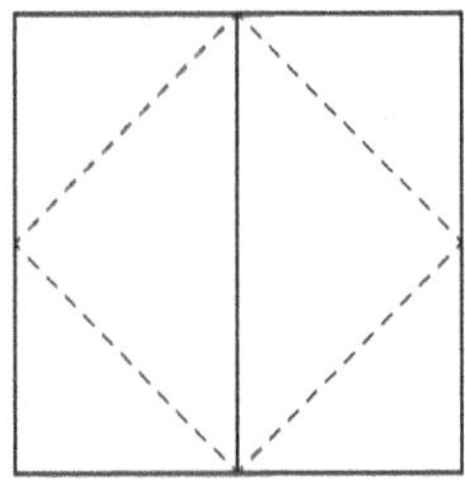

CASEMENT

Imperial	Metric
60″ × 84″	152 × 213 cm
72″ × 60″	183 × 152 cm
36″ × 24″	91 × 61 cm
60″ × 36″	152 × 91 cm

60″ X 84″ ALUMINUM

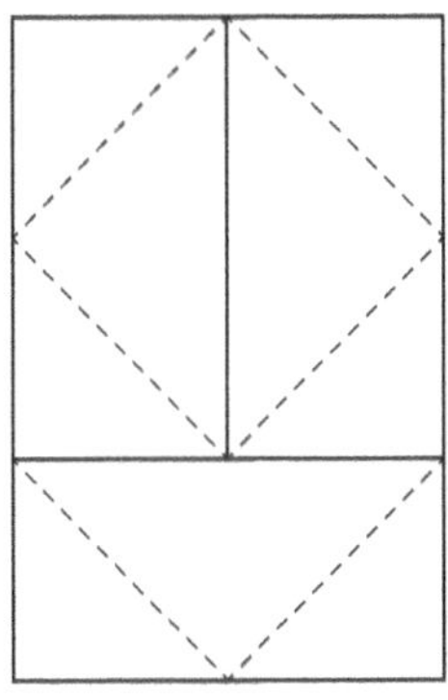

CASEMENT - COMBINATION

60″ X 84″ WOOD

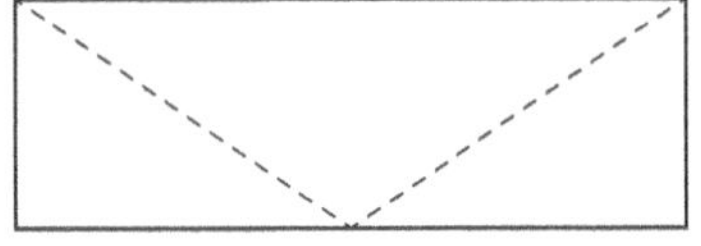

HOPPER - BOTTOM HINGED

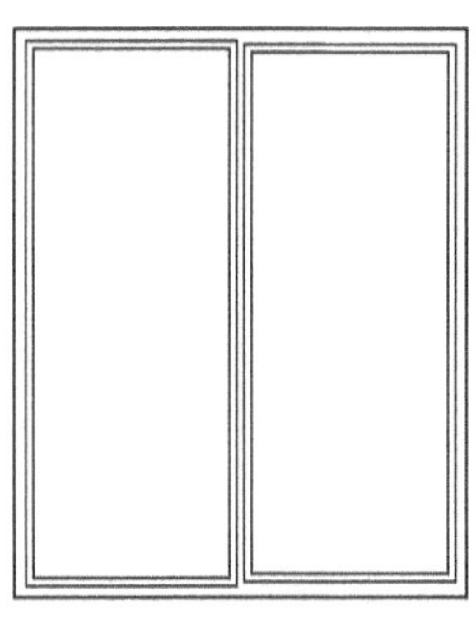

72″ X 60″ WOOD

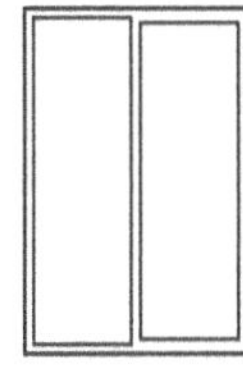

36″ X 24″ ALUMINUM

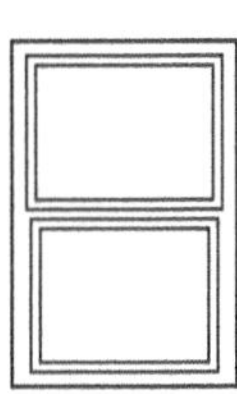

36″ X 24″ WOOD

60″ X 36″ WOOD

DW5

WINDOW OPERATION CATEGORIES

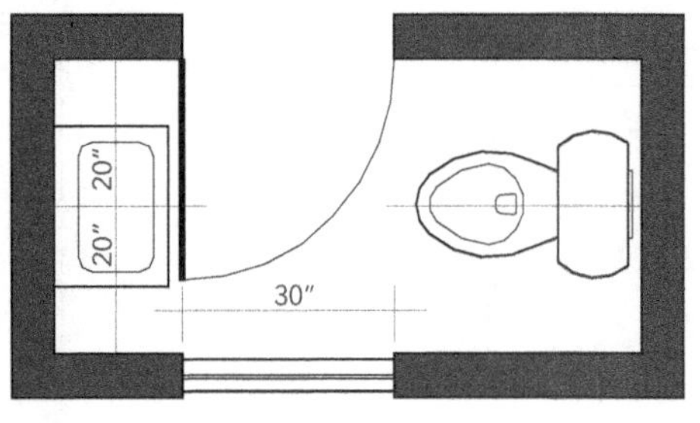

Imperial	Metric
20″	51 cm
30″	76 cm
18″	46 cm
16″	41 cm
20″	51 cm
42″	107 cm

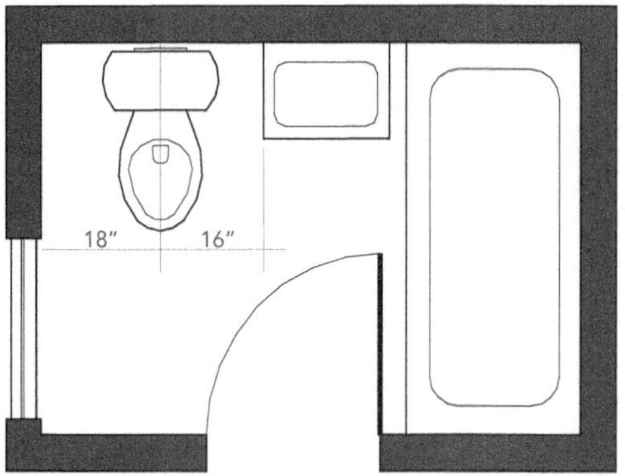

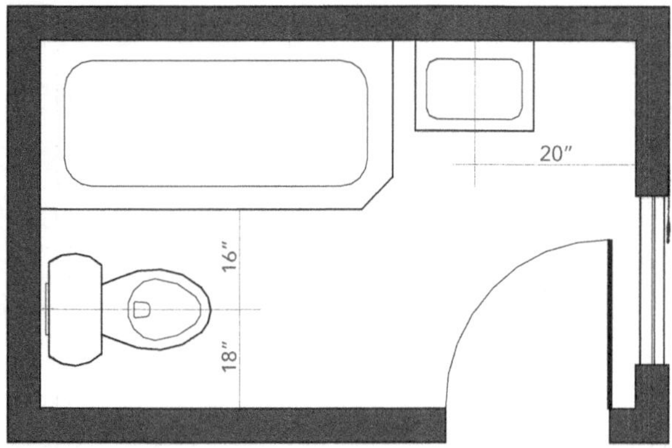

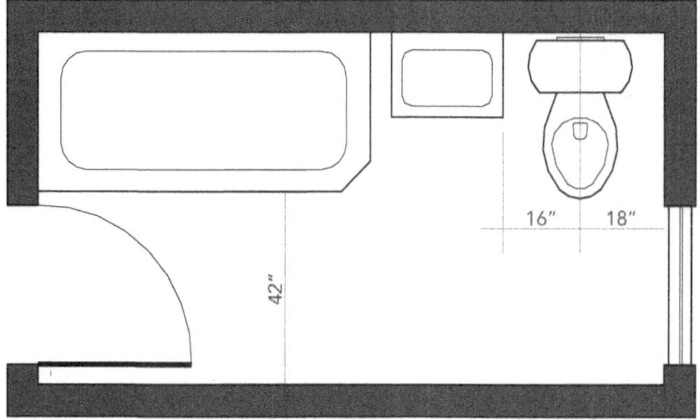

R1

NON ADA TYPICAL BATHROOM PLANS AND FIXTURE CONFIGURATIONS

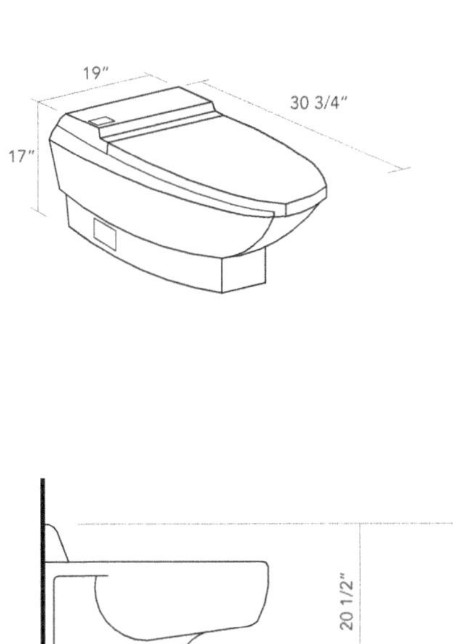

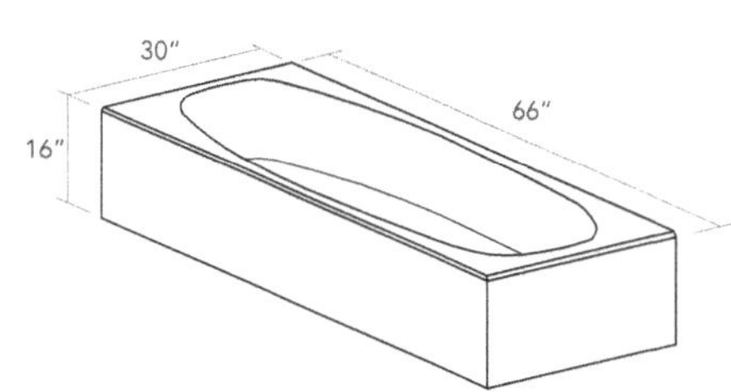

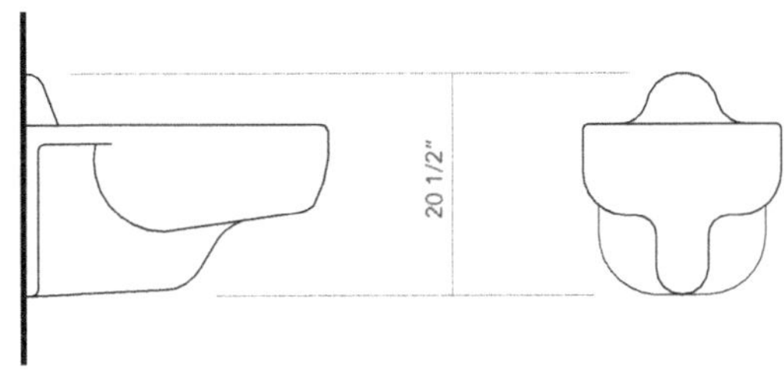

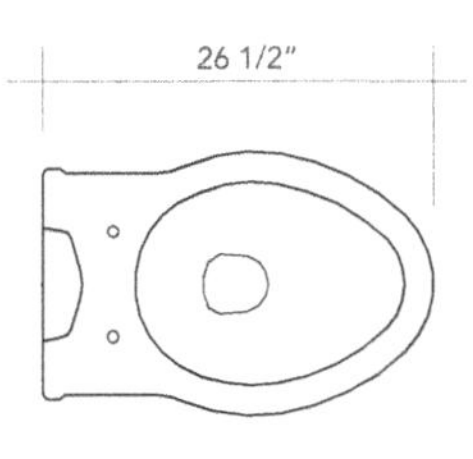

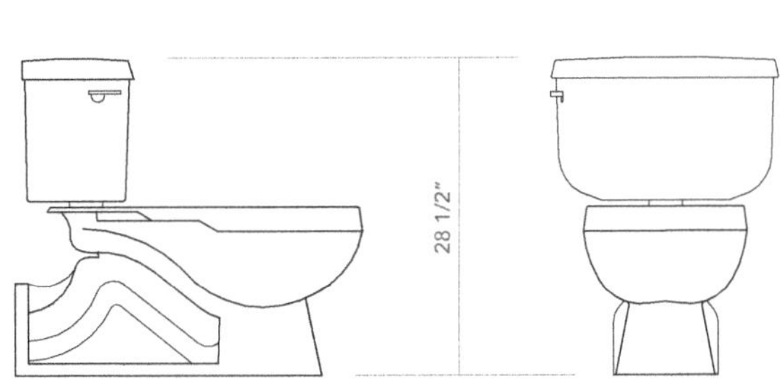

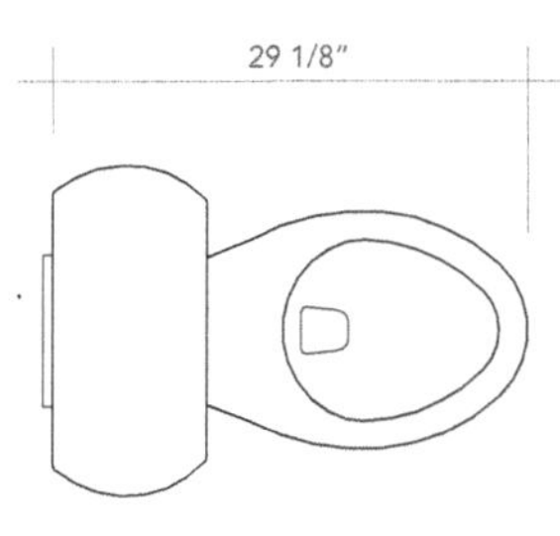

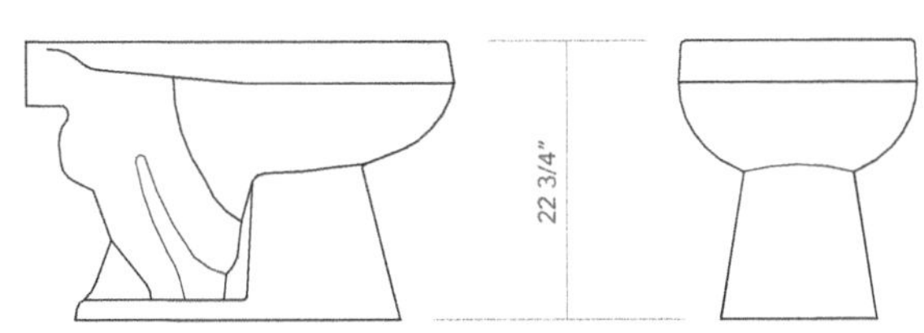

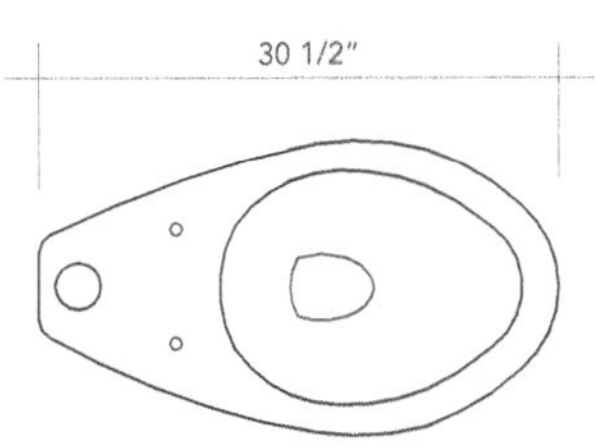

R2

BATHTUB AND TOILET DIMENSIONS

Imperial	Metric
17"	43 cm
19"	48 cm
30-3/4"	78 cm
16"	41 cm
30"	76 cm
66"	168 cm

Imperial	Metric
20-1/2"	52 cm
26-1/2"	67 cm
28-1/2"	72 cm
29-1/8"	74 cm
22-3/4"	58 cm
30-1/2"	77.5 cm

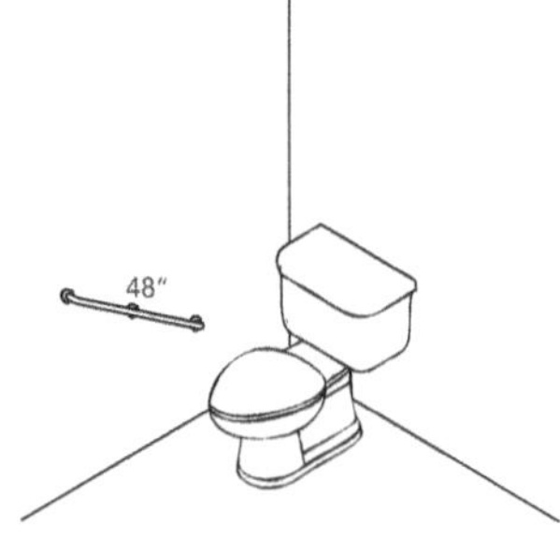

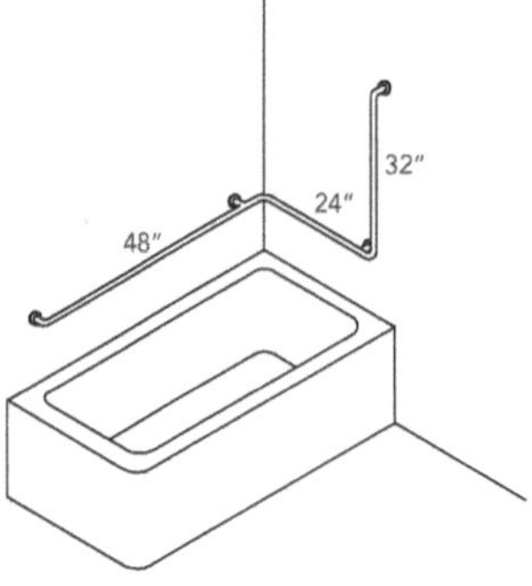

Imperial	Metric
48″	122 cm
24″	61 cm
32″	81 cm
30″	76 cm
33″	84 cm
48″	122 cm
24″	61 cm
32″	81 cm
16″	41 cm
30″	76 cm

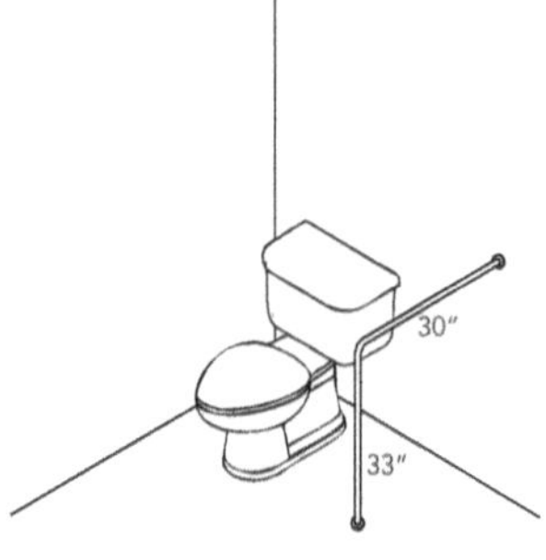

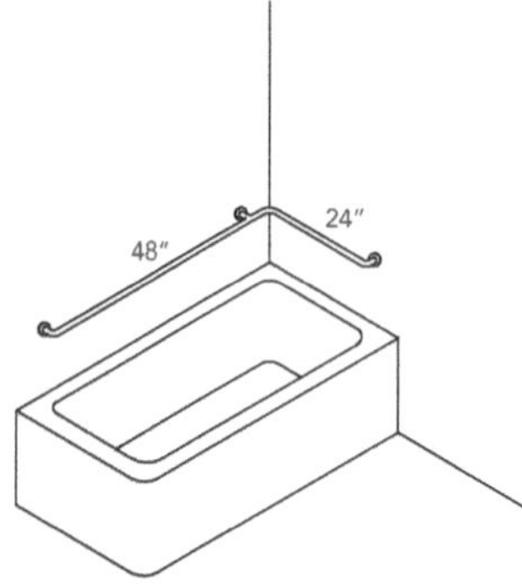

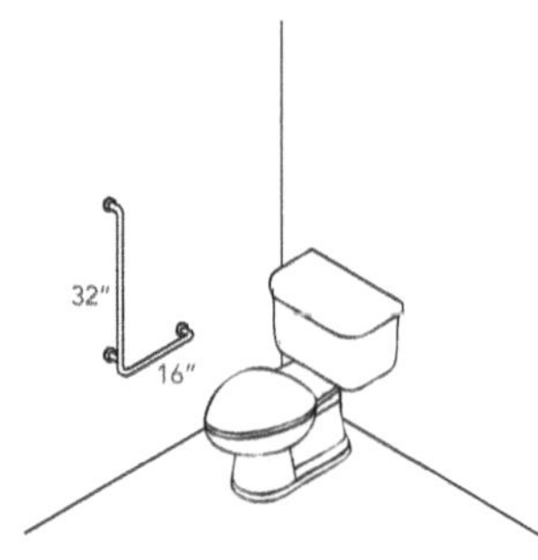

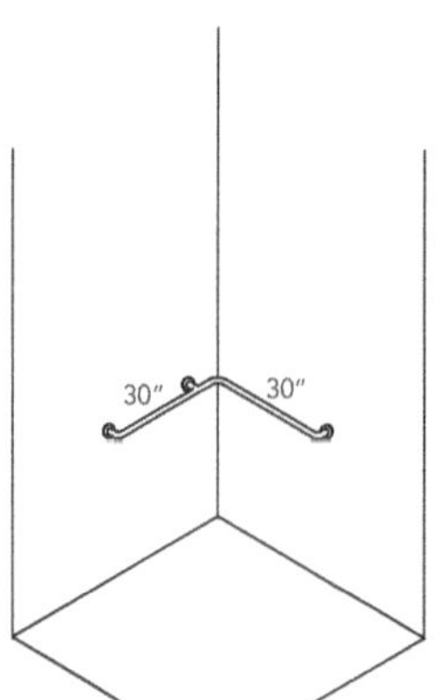

R3a

RESTROOM GRAB BAR CONFIGURATIONS

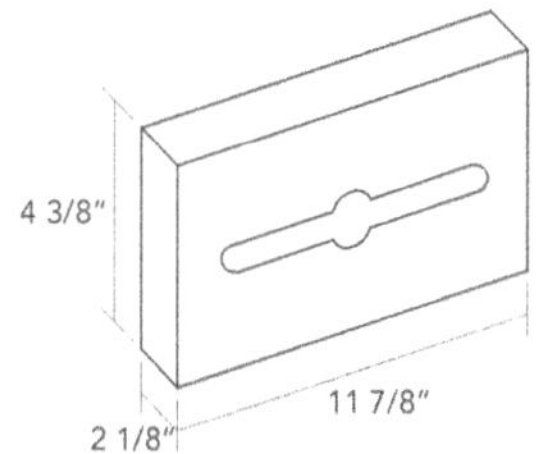

FACIAL TISSUE DISPENSER

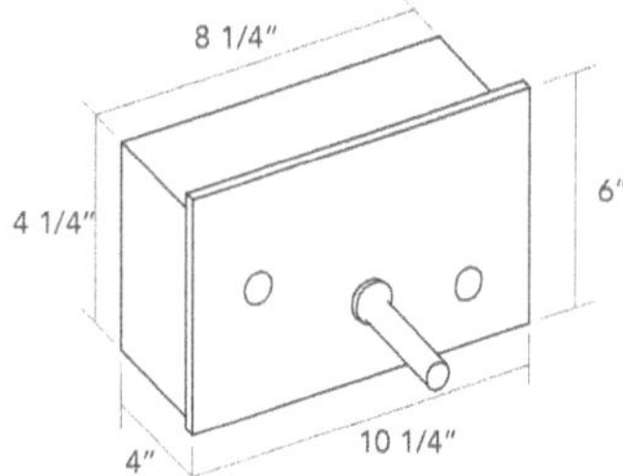

LIQUID SOAP DISPENSER

Imperial	Metric
4-3/8"	11 mm
2-1/8"	5.4 mm
11-7/8"	30 mm
4-1/4"	11 mm
8-1/4"	21 cm
6"	15 cm
10-1/4"	26 cm

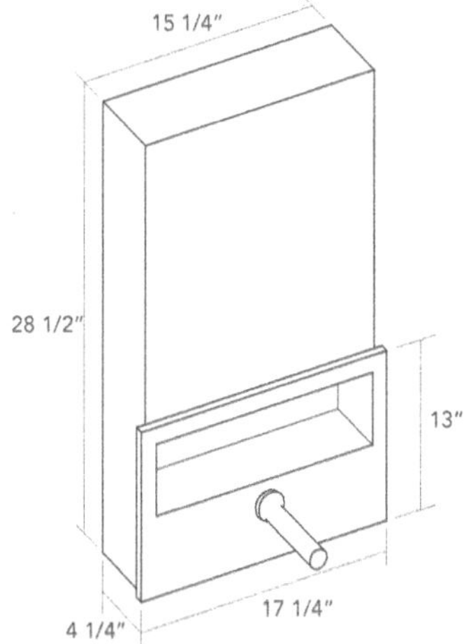

ALL-PURPOSE UNIT
W/ CONCEALED TOWEL CABINET

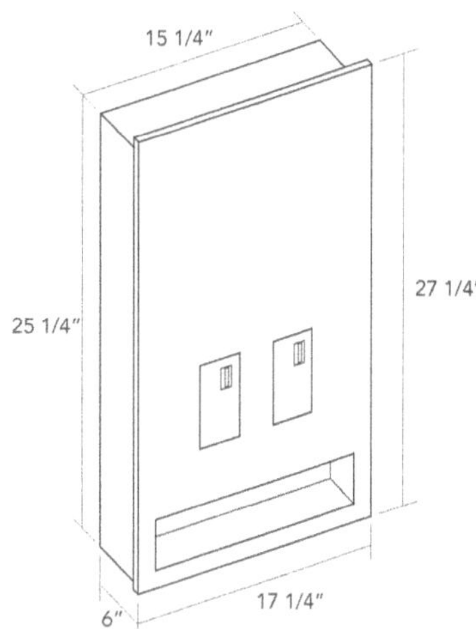

DUAL FEMININE
NAPKIN/TAMPON VENDOR

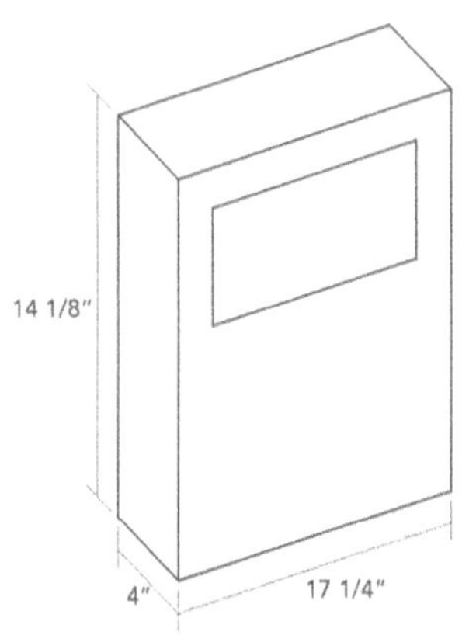

SANITARY NAPKIN DISPOSAL

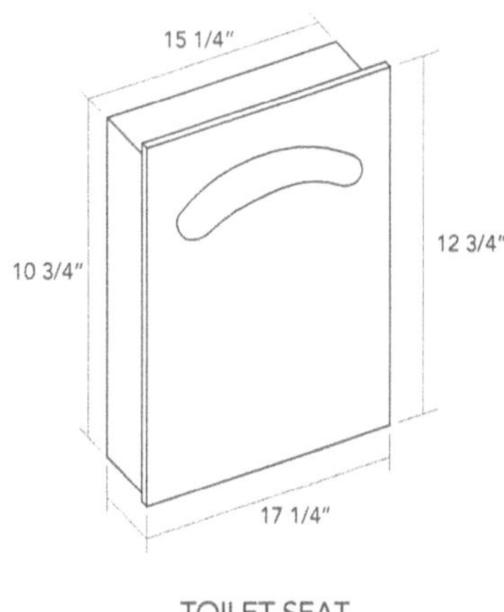

TOILET SEAT
COVER DISPENSER

R3b

Imperial	Metric
28-1/2"	72.5 cm
4-1/4"	11 cm
15-1/4"	39 cm
13"	33 cm
25-1/4"	64 cm
15-1/4"	39 cm
27-1/4"	69 cm
6"	15 cm
14-1/8"	36 cm
4"	10 cm
17-1/4"	44 cm
10-3/4"	27 cm
15-1/4"	39 cm
12-3/4"	32 cm
17-1/4"	44 cm

RESTROOM ACCESSORIES

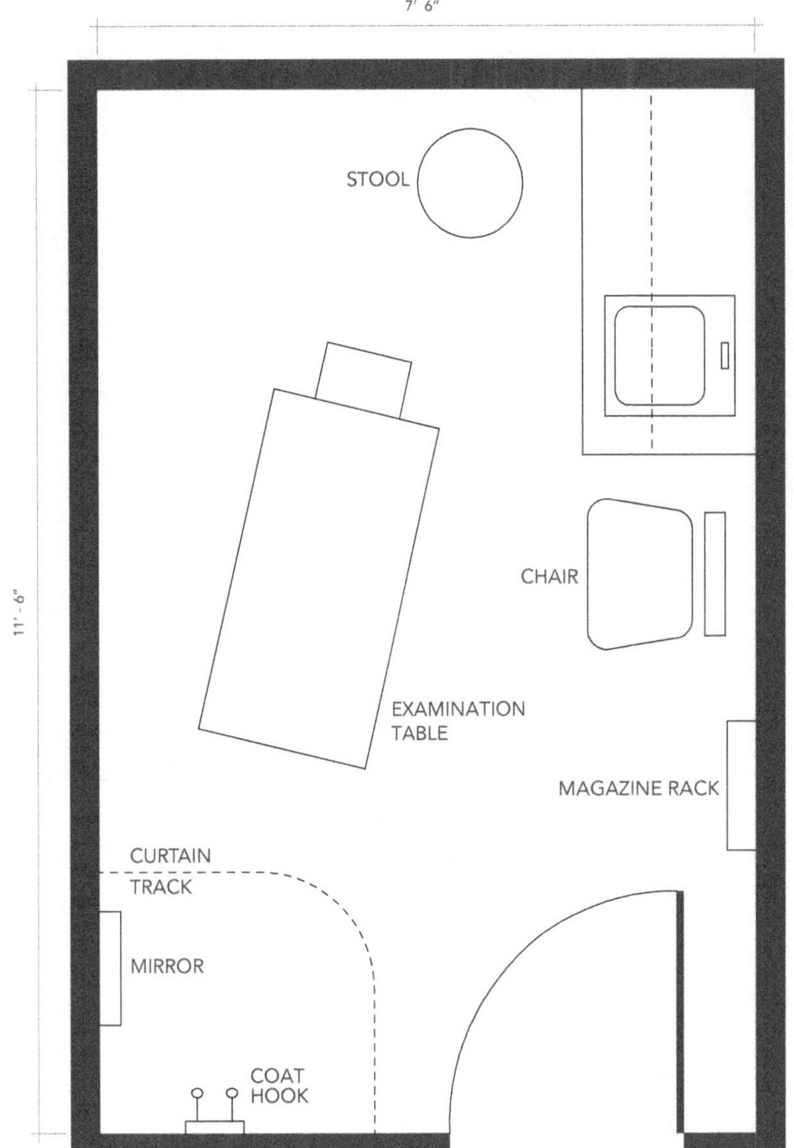

Imperial	Metric
7'-6"	2.29 m

HC1

DOCTOR'S OFFICE

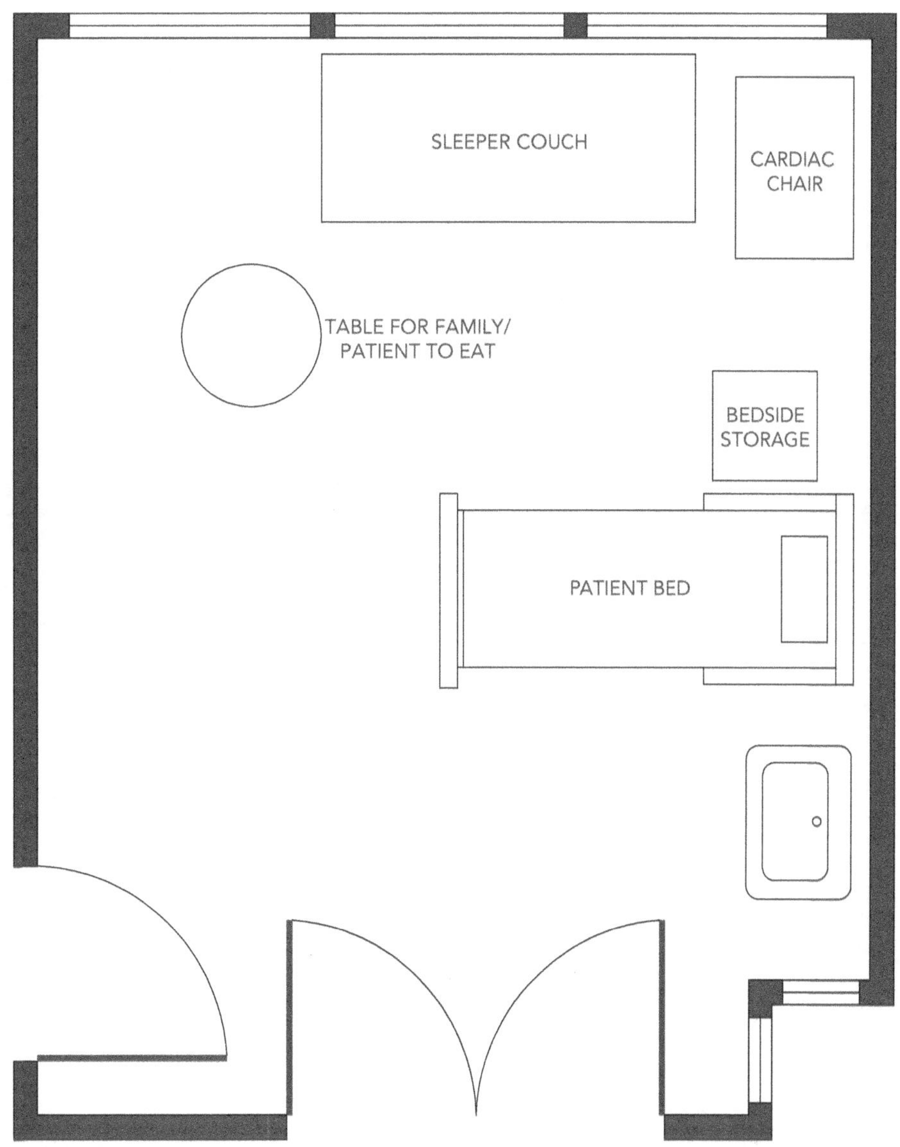

HC2

HOSPITAL PATIENT ROOM

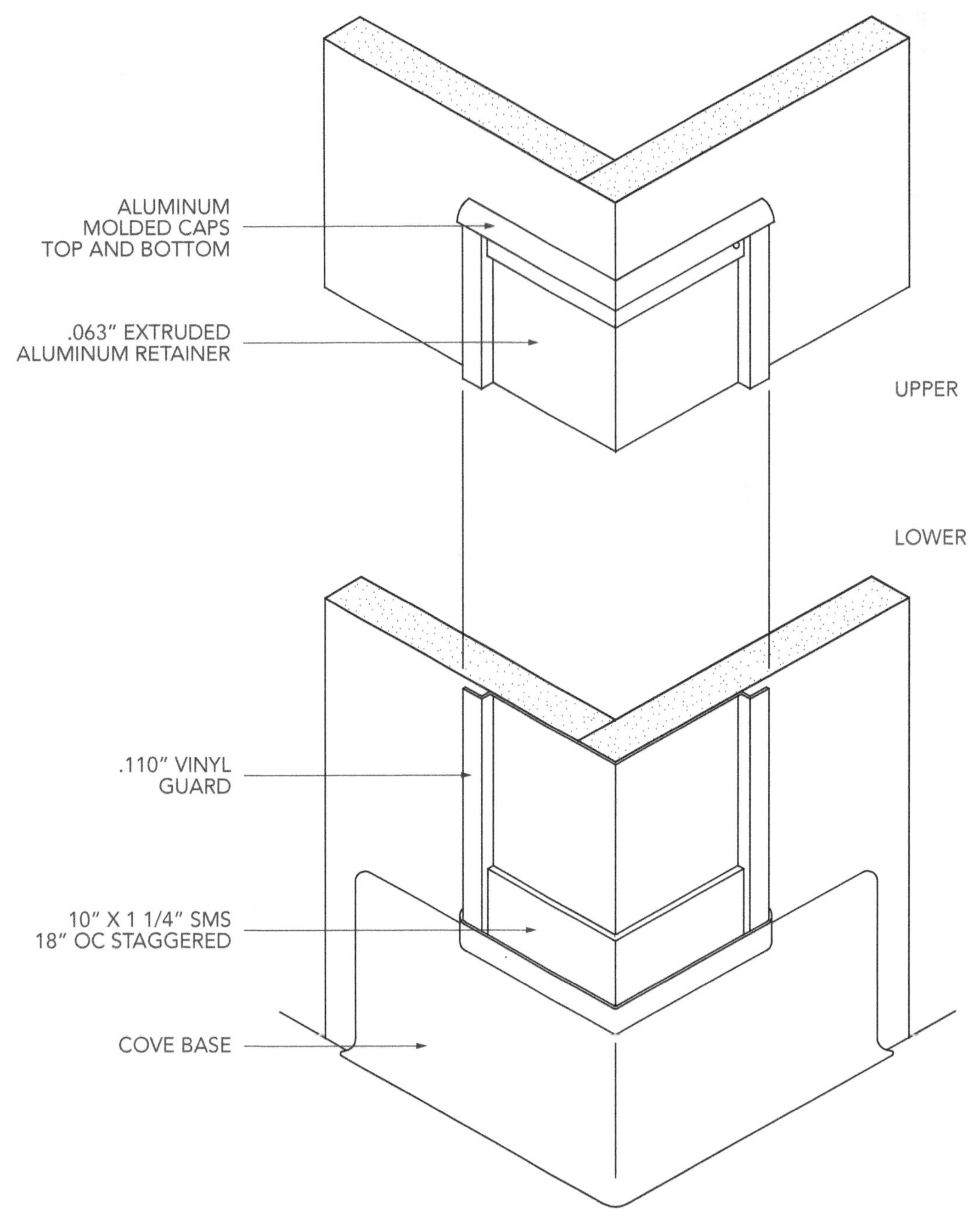

WAINSCOT INSTALLATION AND CORNER GUARD—SURFACE MOUNT **HC3**

Imperial	Metric
.063"	1.6 mm
.110"	2.8 mm
10"	25.4 cm
1-1/4"	3.175 cm
18"	46 cm

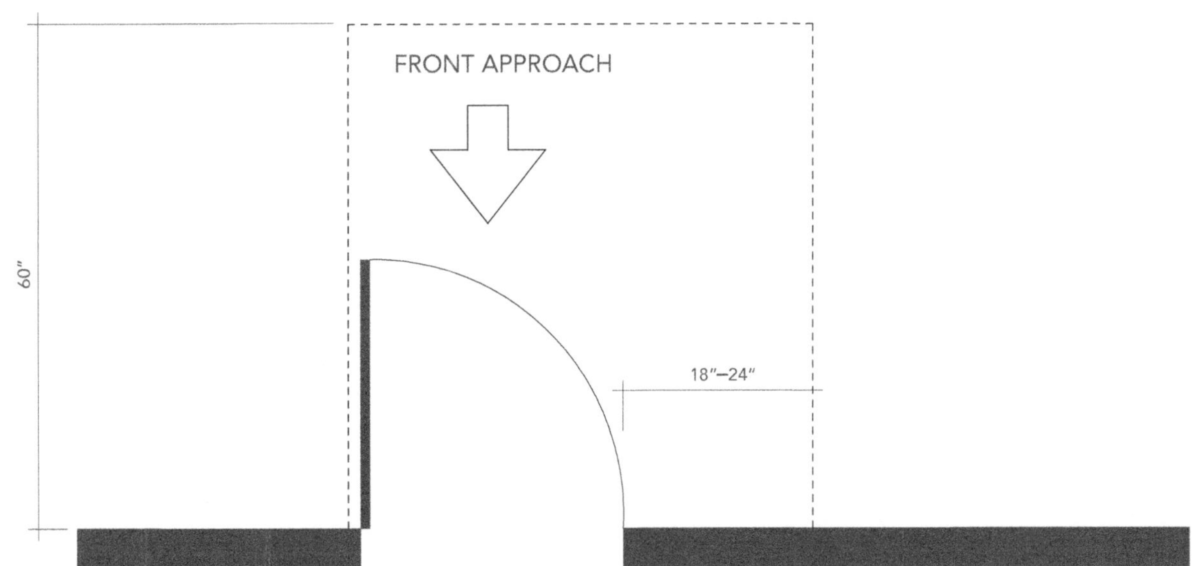

SWINGING DOOR—FRONT APPROACH

HC4

WHEELCHAIR CLEARANCE

Imperial	Metric
60"	153 cm
18"–24"	46–61 cm

Imperial	Metric
48″	122 cm
35″	89 cm

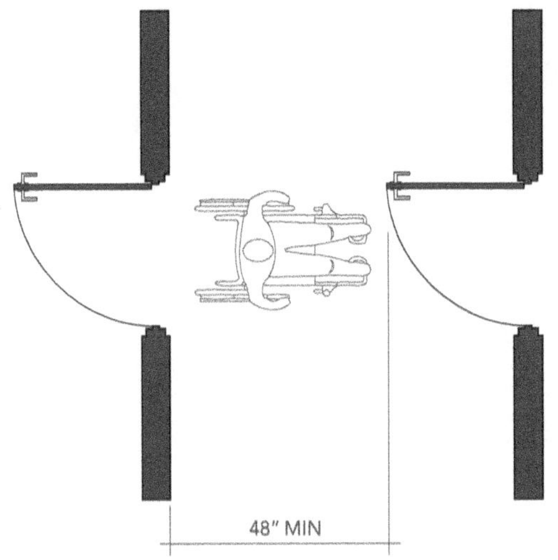

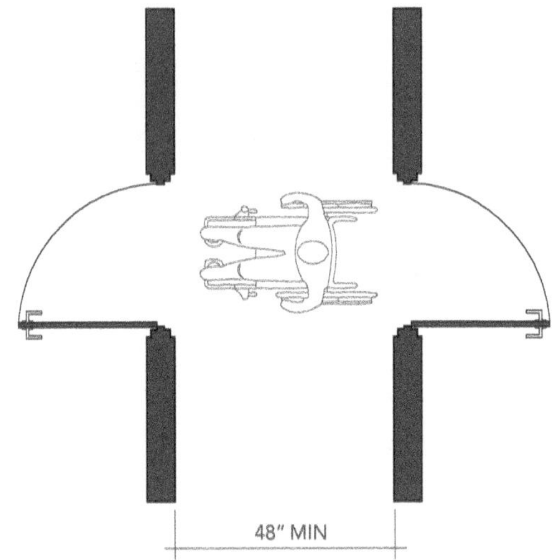

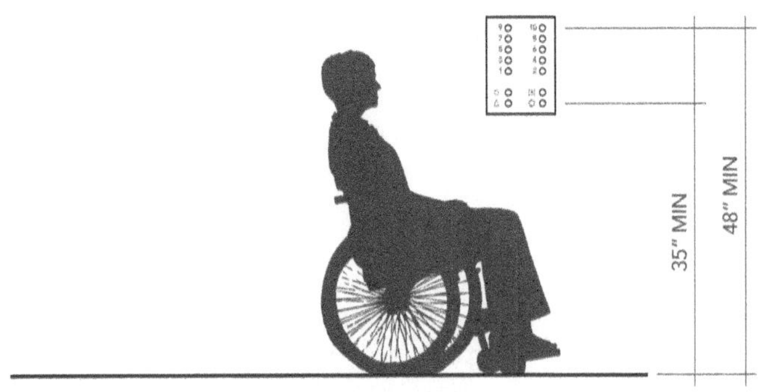

CONTROL HEIGHT

HC5

WHEELCHAIR CLEARANCES AND DIMENSIONS

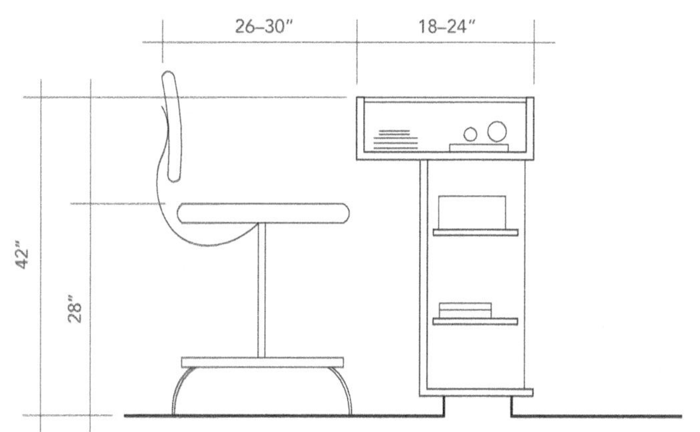

SEATED CUSTOMER / HIGH COUNTER

Imperial	Metric
42"	107 cm
28"	71 cm
26"–30"	66–76 cm
18"–24"	46–61 cm

Imperial	Metric
2'-0"	61 cm
25-1/2"	65 cm

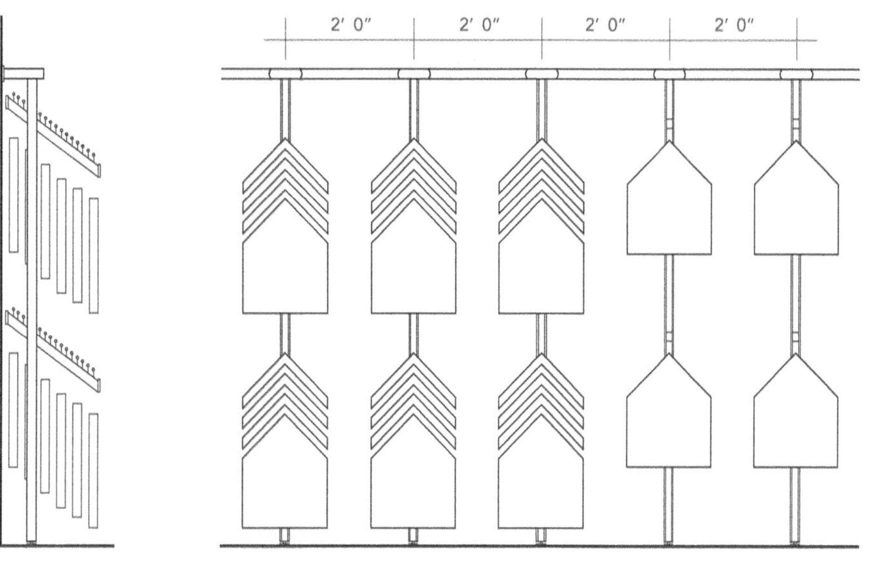

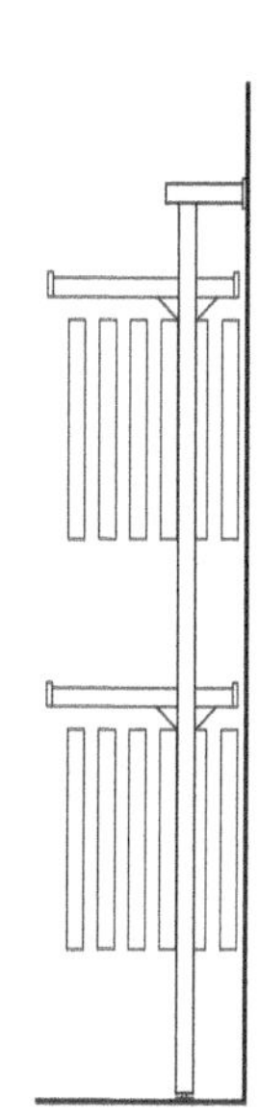

FACE OUT AND WATERFALL DISPLAY

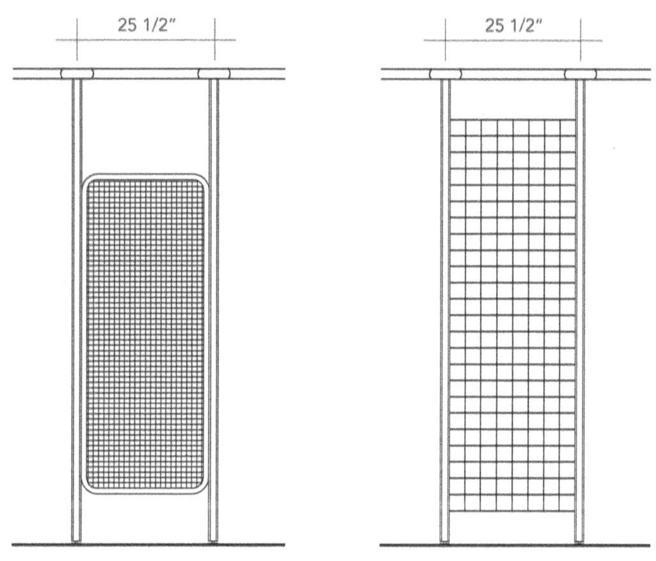

MESH PANEL DISPLAY SYSTEMS

RT1

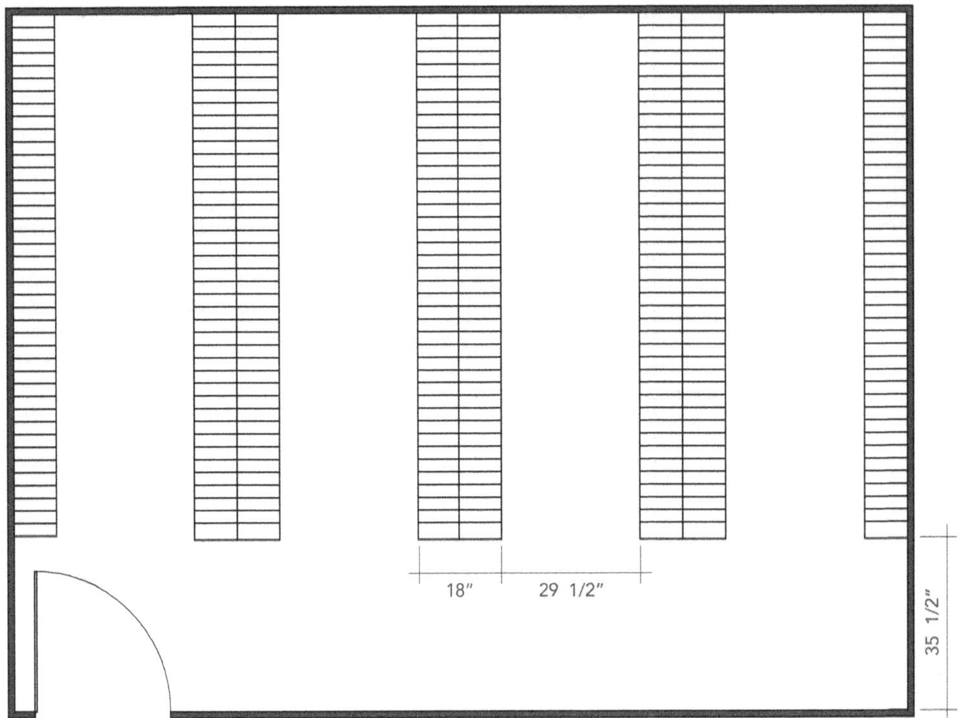

LARGE WINE STORAGE WITH METAL RACKS

Imperial	Metric
18"	46 cm
29-1/2"	75 cm
35-1/2"	90 cm
1'-6"	46 cm

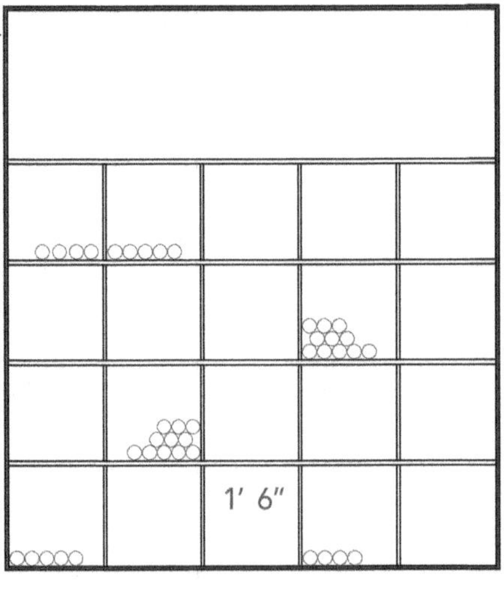

ELEVATION

RT2

WINE STORAGE

Imperial	Metric
4-1/4″	11 cm
2′-2″	66 cm
1′-5-3/4″	45 cm
3″	8 cm
2″	5 cm
3/4 ″	19 mm
2′-5″	74 cm
4″	10 cm
8″	20.3 cm

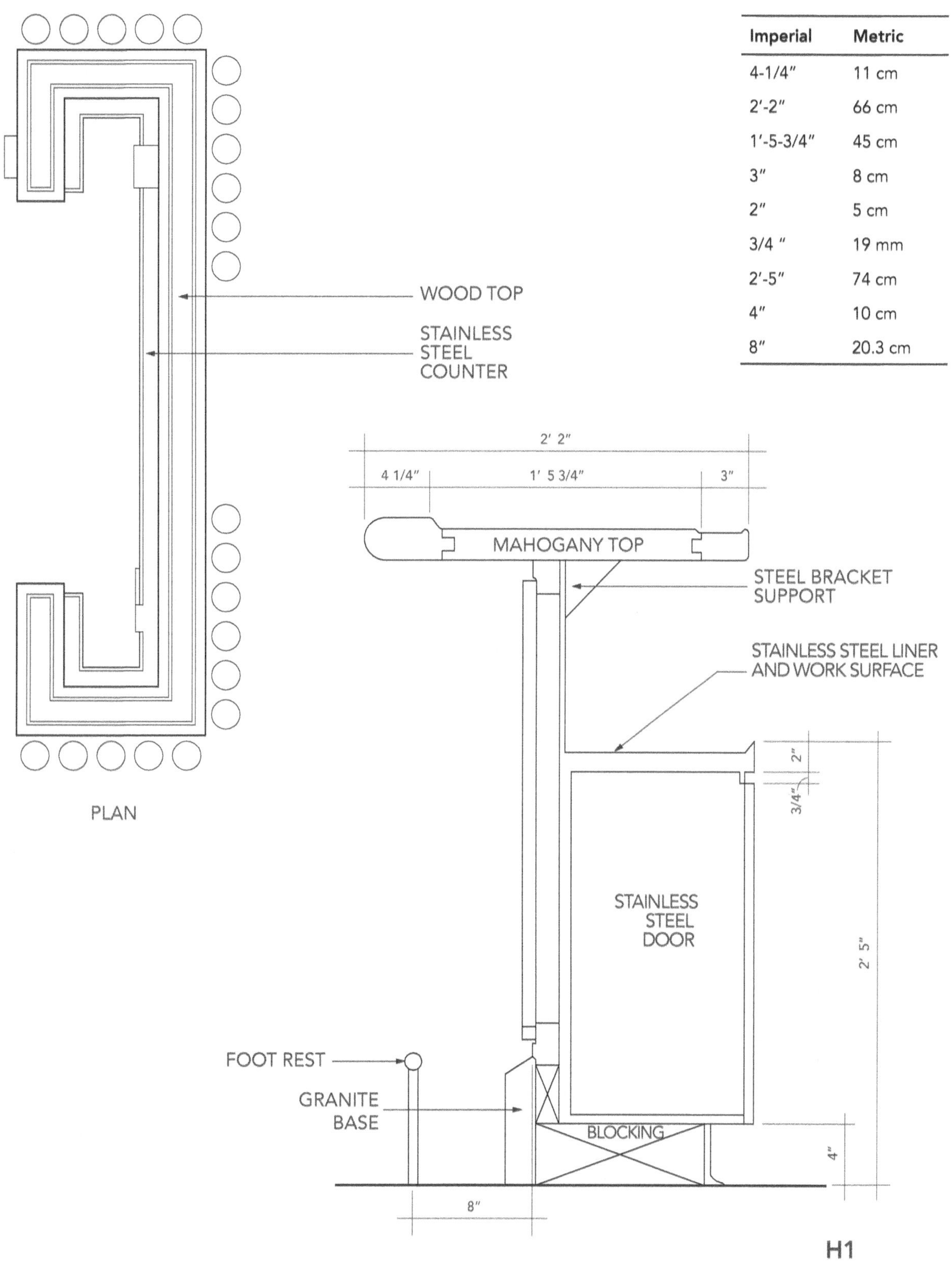

BAR LAYOUT AND VERTICAL SECTION

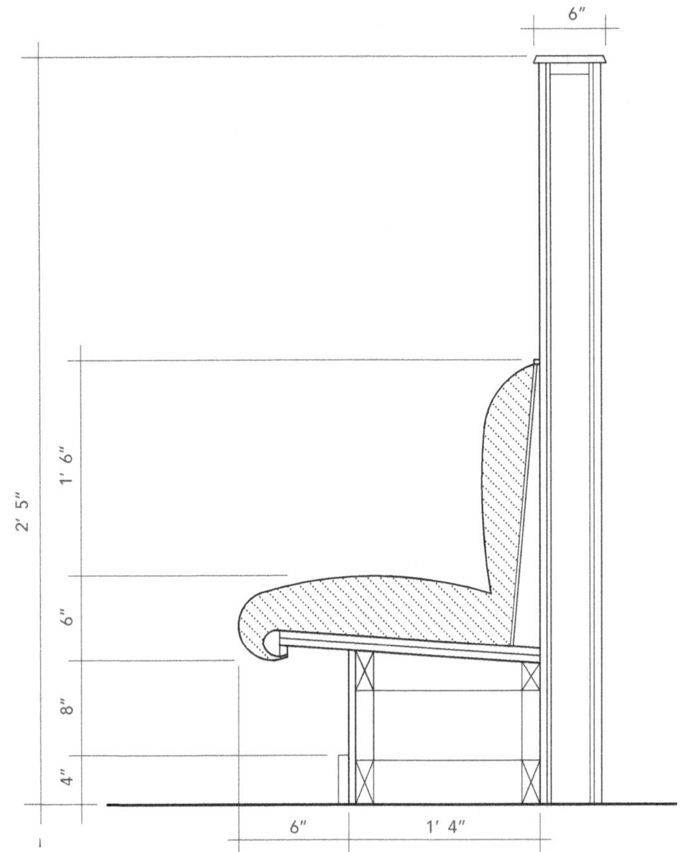

Imperial	Metric
2'-5"	74 cm
4"	10 cm
8"	20 cm
6"	15.25 cm
1'-6"	46 cm
1'-4"	41 cm

Imperial	Metric
18"–22"	46–56 cm
29"–42"	74–107 cm

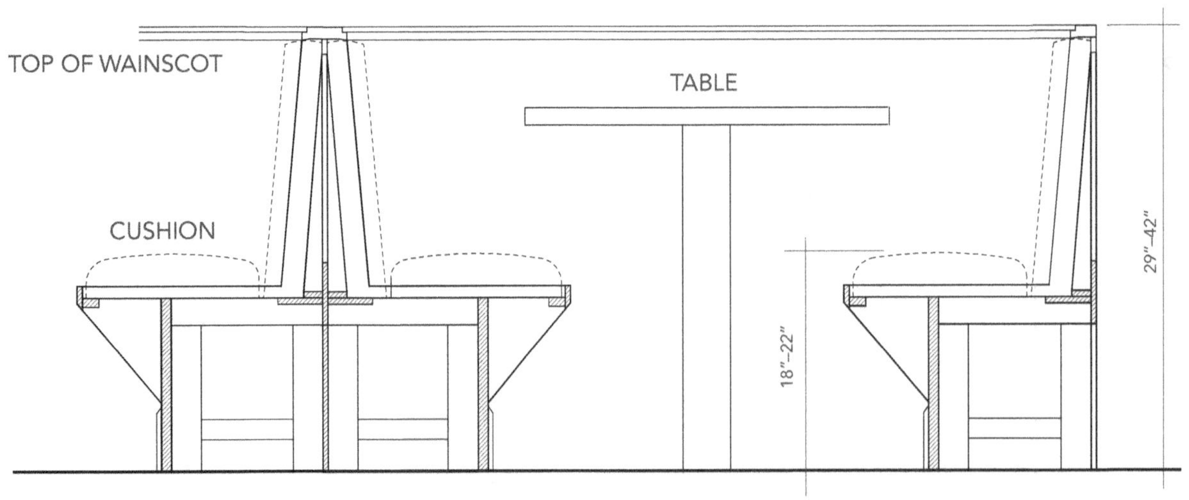

H2

RESTAURANT BOOTHS

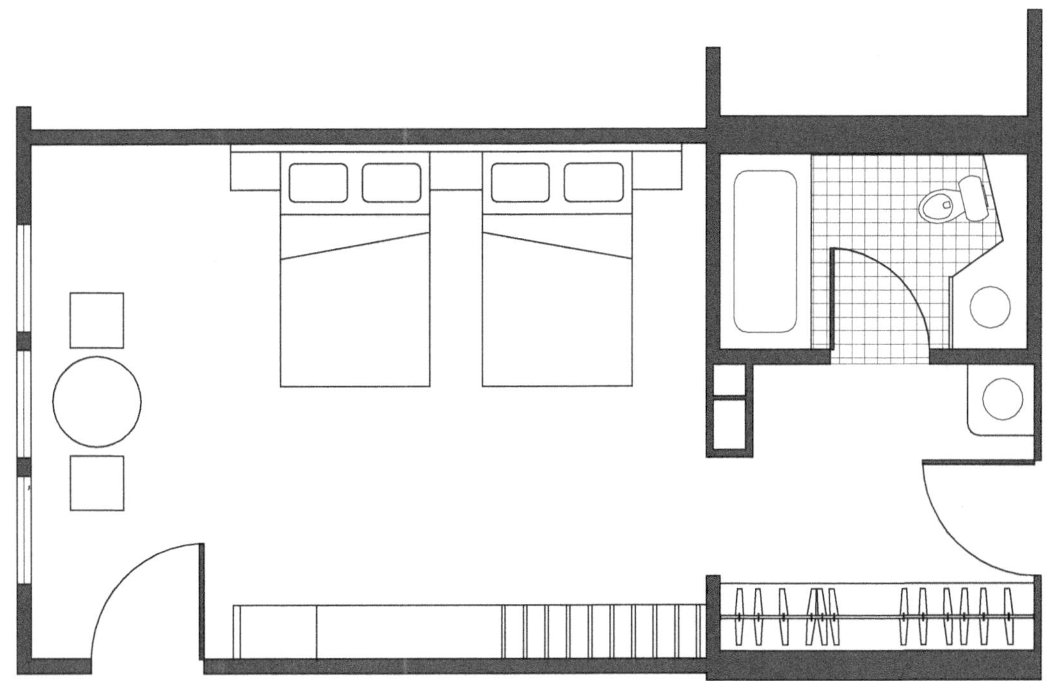

ROOM WITH 2 DOUBLE–BEDS

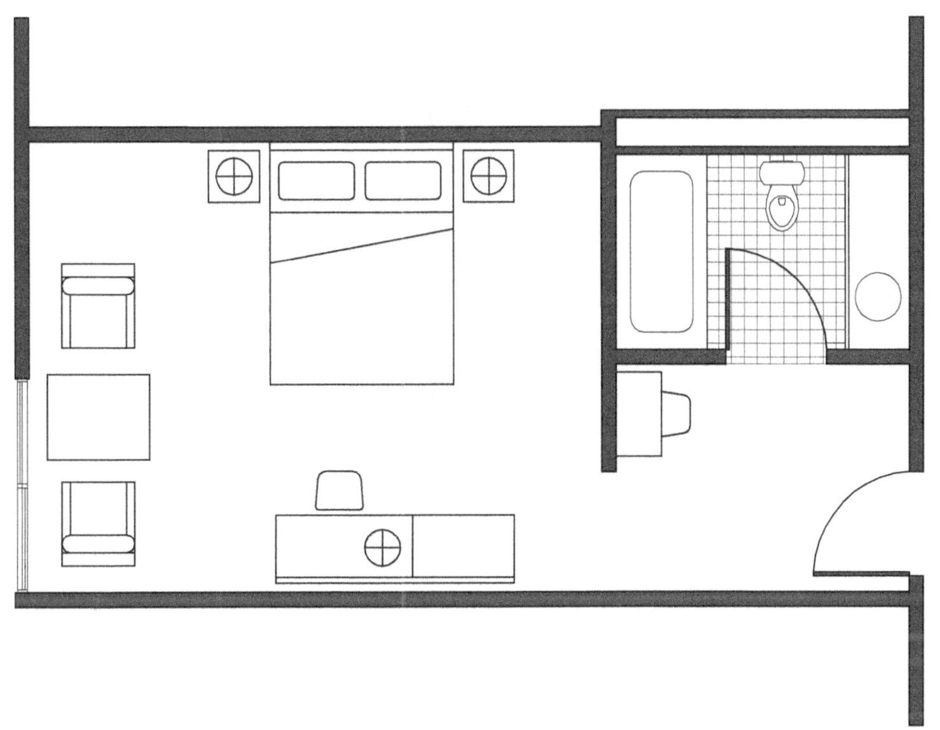

H3

HOTELS–ROOM WITH KING-SIZED BED

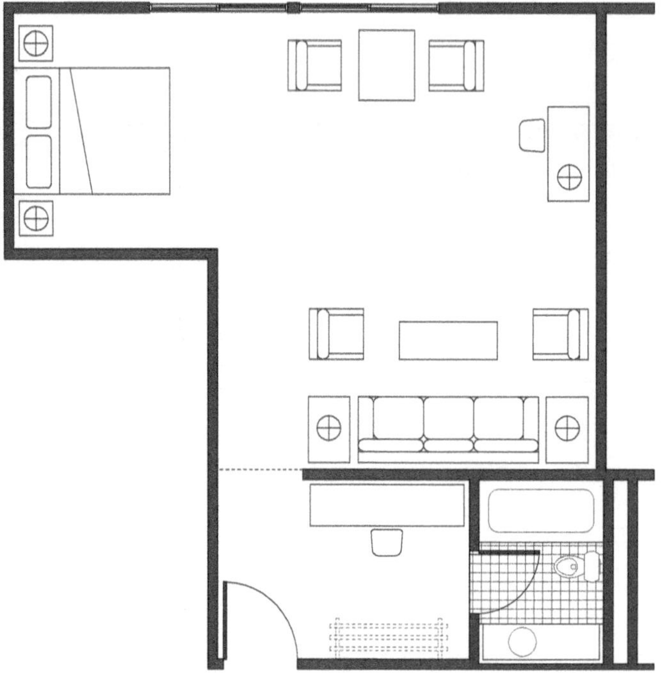

HOTELS–LARGE ROOM WITH KING-SIZED BED

H4

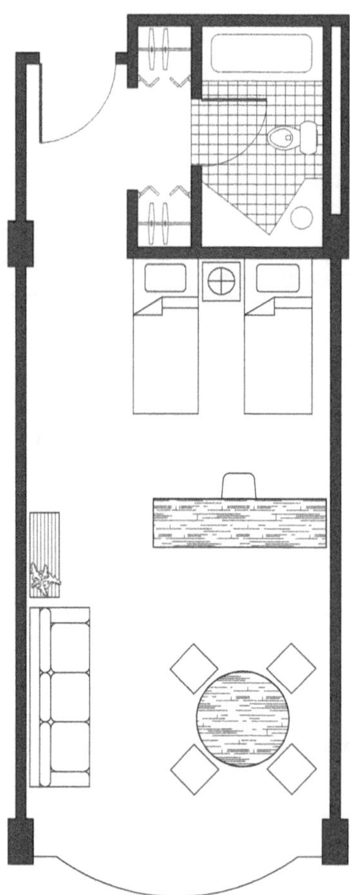

H5

HOTELS–GUEST ROOM WITH 2 TWIN BEDS–FLOOR PLAN

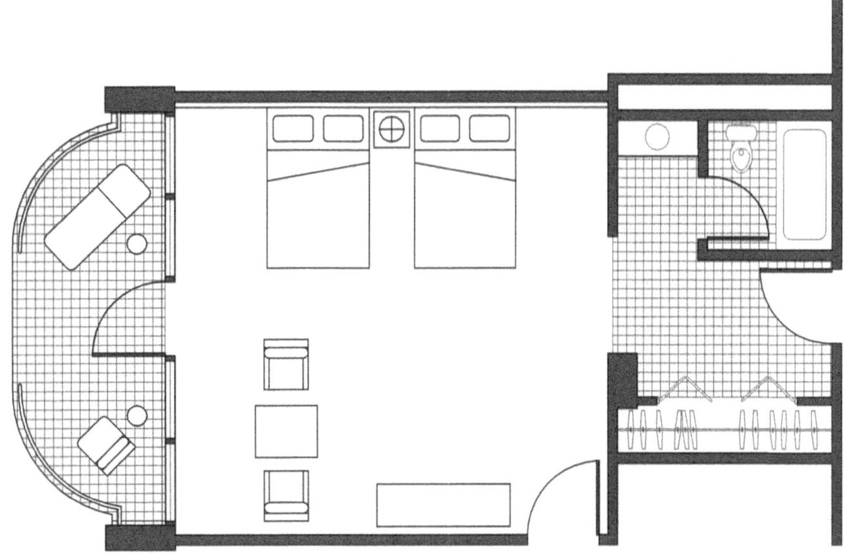

ROOM WITH 2 DOUBLE BEDS AND BALCONY

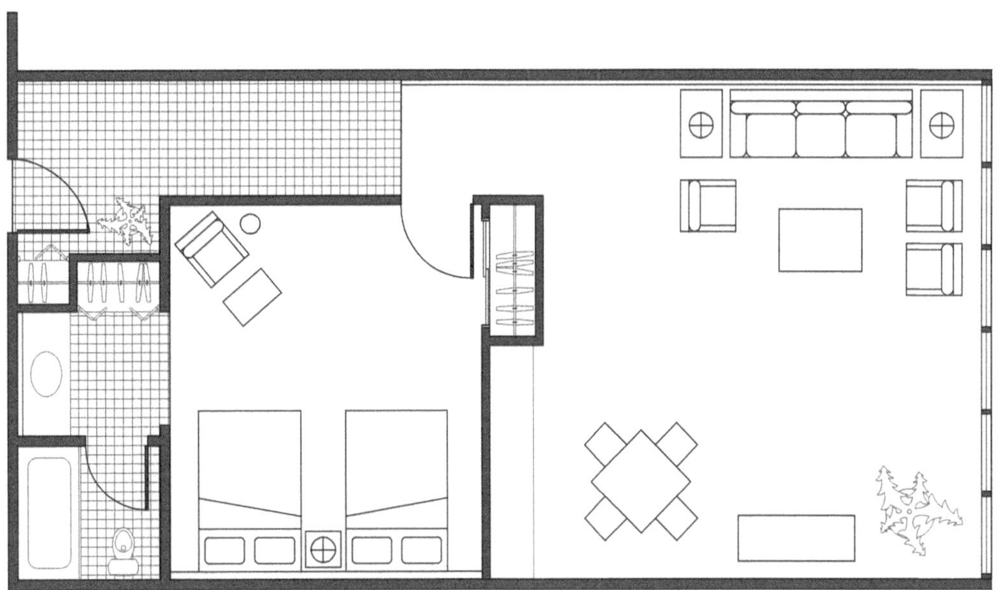

H6

HOTELS–HOSPITALITY OR INTERVIEW SUITE

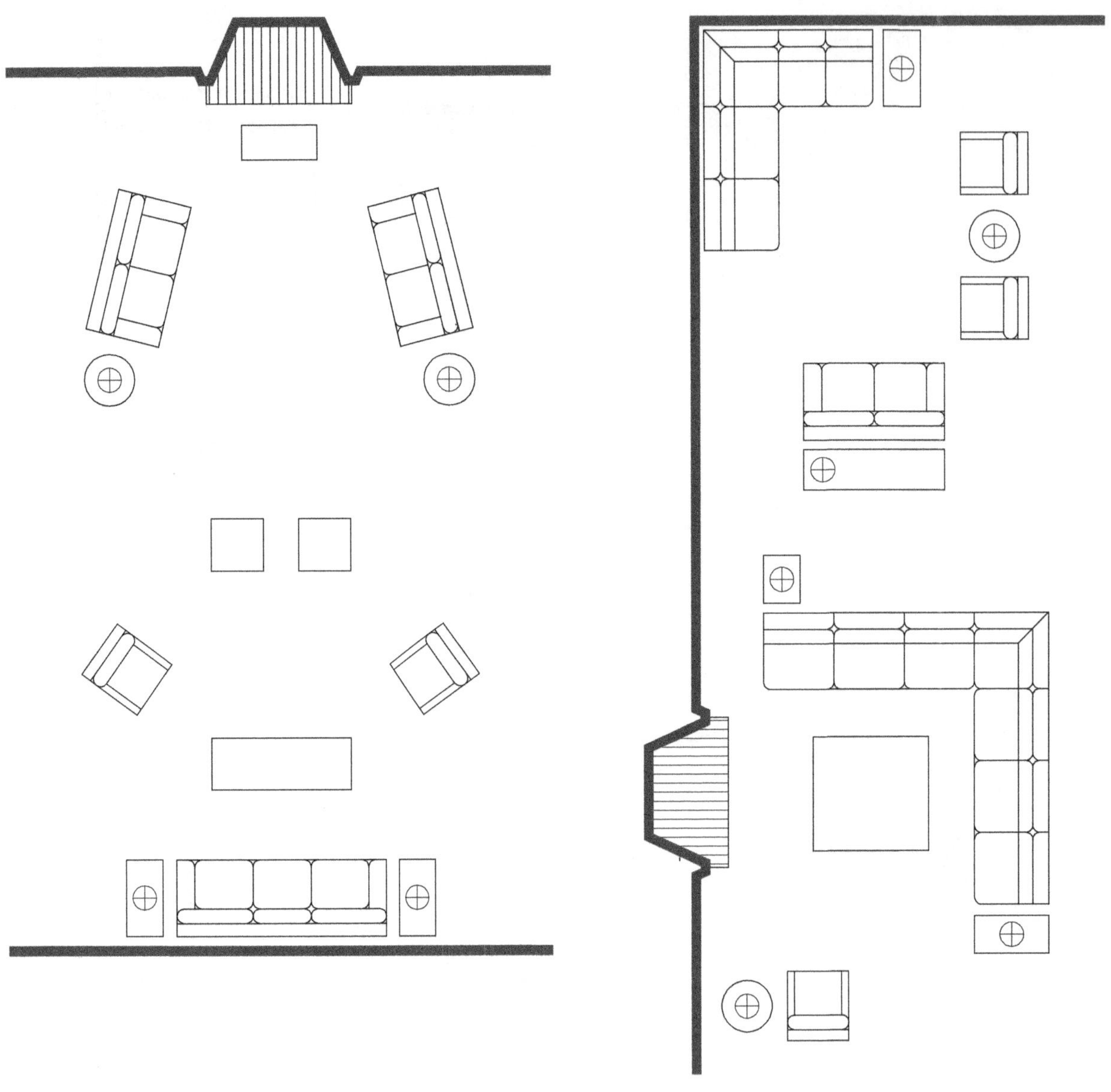

H7

HOTELS–LOBBY FURNITURE PLANS

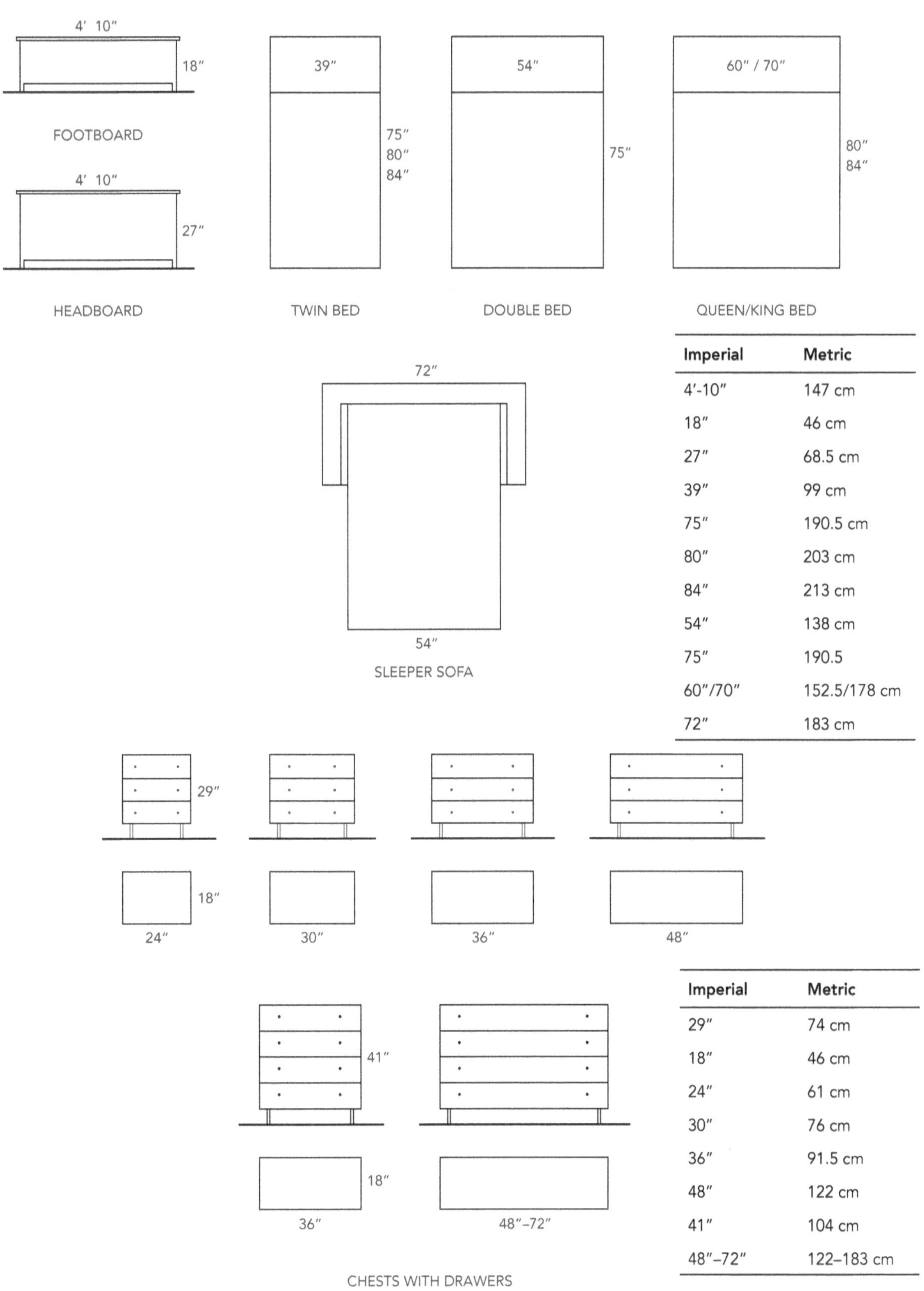

Imperial	Metric
4′-10″	147 cm
18″	46 cm
27″	68.5 cm
39″	99 cm
75″	190.5 cm
80″	203 cm
84″	213 cm
54″	138 cm
75″	190.5
60″/70″	152.5/178 cm
72″	183 cm

Imperial	Metric
29″	74 cm
18″	46 cm
24″	61 cm
30″	76 cm
36″	91.5 cm
48″	122 cm
41″	104 cm
48″–72″	122–183 cm

H8

BEDROOMS, BEDS, CHESTS

HOSPITALITY

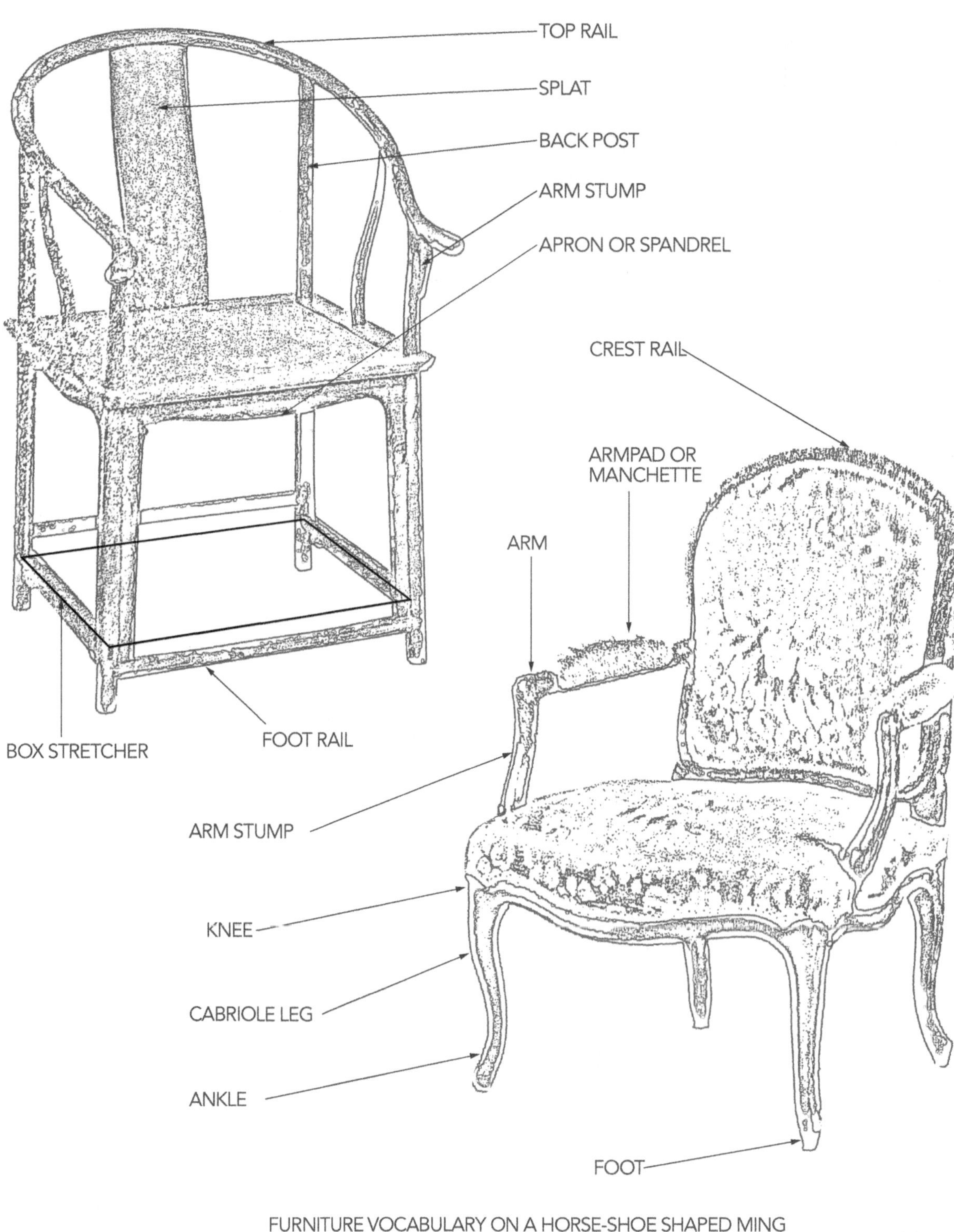

FURNITURE VOCABULARY ON A HORSE-SHOE SHAPED MING ARMCHAIR (LEFT) AND ON A LOUIS XVI FAUTEUIL (RIGHT)

H9

appendix 4: tables

Table 1 *Carpet Construction Categories*

		Characteristics	
Carpet Style/Texture	**Density**	**Height**	**Amount of Twist**
Cut Pile			
Frieze—High stability, long wear-life, very resilient; grainy appearance; hides dirt well	Medium	Medium	Very tightly twisted heat-set yarns
Plush—Also called velvet or velvet plush; a very smooth luxurious surface that may show footprints and shading	Very dense	Low (.625–.75 inch)	Relatively low
Saxony—Similar to plush but with higher twist; uneven surface with textured appearance; may show footprints and shading	Medium	Low (.625–.75 inch)	Medium to high (higher than plush, usually made with heat-set yarns)
Shag—May mat down; informal appearance	Lower than plush or Saxony	Over 1 inch	Low
Velour—Good wear resistance	Very dense	Low (.25 inch)	Tightly twisted
Loop Pile	Medium	Variable	Medium
Carved—Three-dimensional appearance, usually higher loops are cut and lower loops are uncut; formal in appearance			
Cut and Loop	Medium	Low-Medium	Medium
A combination of the two principal construction types to produce the appearance of pile with some of the durability of loop			
Loop	Low-Medium	Low	Medium
The knitted loops remain uncut. The intact structural unit of the knit makes it durable			

Conversions: .25″ = .635 cm; .625″ = 1.59 cm; .75″ = 1.9 cm; 1.0″ = 2.54 cm.

Table 2 ***Textile Fibers***

Natural Fibers		
Cellulosic Fibers	**Protein Fibers**	**Other Natural Fibers**
Seed Fibers Cotton Kapok Coir (coconut)	**Silk (silkworm)** **Wool (sheep)**	**Mineral Fibers** **Natural Rubber**
Bast Fibers Flax Ramie (China grass) Jute Bamboo	**Specialty Hair Fibers** Alpaca (alpaca) Cashmere (cashmere goat) Camel (Bactrian camel) Mohair (angora goat)	
Leaf Fibers Abaca (manila fiber) Sisal	**Fur Fibers** Angora (angora rabbit)	
Manufactured Fibers		
Manufactured Cellulosics		**Major Synthetic Fibers**
Regenerated Cellulosics Rayon **Derivative Cellulosics** Acetate Triacetate		Acrylic Modacrylic Nylon Olefin Polyester Saran

Table 3 ***Floor Coverings***

Hard Floor	Advantages	Disadvantages	Maintenance
Brick—Usually available in shades of buff, purple, blue, and a variety of browns; thickness ranges from 1/4 inch to 1 1/2 inches	Can be used inside and out; hard surface; suitable for radiant heating; can be rough or smooth; pre-sealed bricks are available for indoor use	Hard, cold, poor noise absorption	Sweep and wash; must be sealed to prevent absorption of spills
Concrete and Cement Floors—Generally used in commercial interiors or residential basements and garages	Durable, low cost; can be painted or sealed	Cracks and chips, difficult to repair; hard, cold; poor noise absorption; limited colors but can be waxed with colored wax	Sweep and wash with detergent; must be sealed to prevent absorption of spills
Flagstone—Thin slabs of stone; generally fine-grained sandstone, bluestone quartzite, or slate; irregularly shaped (1 to 4 square feet, 1/2 inch to 4 inches thick)	Durable	Uneven surface unsuitable for tables and chairs; hard, cold; poor noise absorption	Sweep and wash; sealing necessary to make impervious to staining and wear
Granite—An igneous rock having crystal grains of visible size; light to dark shades of white, gray, buff, beige, pink, red, blue, green, and black	Durable; may be polished	Hard, cold; poor noise absorption	Similar to marble
Marble—True marble is a metamorphic rock derived from limestone; all rocks that are capable of taking a polish are considered to be marble; dolomitic limestone (hard limestone) is known commercially as marble; available in a wide variety of colors; most marble today is 3/8 inch thick and backed with fiberglass, epoxy resins, or Styrofoam	Long-wearing natural material	Cold, hard, heavy, porous; scratches; slippery when wet; expensive	Must be sealed to prevent staining; can be swept and washed; do not use harsh abrasives or acid cleaners; worn marble can be sealed with a water-based sealer
Travertine (stone classified as marble)—Porous limestone; pores are filled with an epoxy resin	Long wearing	Cold, hard, dense, porous; scratches; slippery when wet	Must be sealed to prevent staining; can be swept and washed; do not use harsh abrasives or acid cleaners; worn travertine can be sealed with a water-based sealer
Slate—A dense fine-grained metamorphic rock; nonporous; available in blues, gray-green, purple-red, charcoal, and heather colors	Beautiful, easy to care for, exceptionally long wearing	Expensive; poor noise absorption; cold, hard, dense; can be slippery when wet	Sweep and wash; may be waxed but turns the stone a darker shade
Terrazzo—There are two types of terrazzo: 1. Marble chips set in cement 2. Marble chips set in polyester resin Also categorized by size of chips	Hard wearing and maintenance free; good in bathrooms; terrazzo made with polyester resin is less hard	Poor noise absorption and sometimes slippery; if set in cement, the floor must be sealed	Sweep and wash but do not polish; do not use acid or alkaline cleaners

(continued)

Conversions: 1/4″–1 1/2″ = .635–3.81 cm; 1-4 sq ft = 930–3,715 sq cm; 1/2″–4″ = 1.27–10 cm; 3/8″ = .9525 cm.

Table 3 ***Floor Coverings (continued)***

Fiber	Characteristics	
Acrylic	Durability:	Good
	Soil resistance:	Good
	Abrasion resistance:	Good
	Resilience:	Good
	Care requirements:	Easy care
	Additional comments:	Available in a wide range of colors; nonallergenic; resistant to mildew, moths, and insects; resists degradation from sunlight; may pill
Nylon	Durability:	Very good
	Soil resistance:	Very good
	Abrasion resistance:	Very good
	Resilience:	Very good
	Care requirements:	Easy care, hides dirt well
	Additional comments:	Available in a wide range of colors; good color retention; resistant to mildew, moths, and insects; nonallergenic; may cause static
Polyester	Durability:	Good
	Soil resistance:	Fair unless soil-resistant finish is added
	Abrasion resistance:	Good
	Resilience:	Good
	Care requirements:	Easy care; resists most soil; oil-based stains may be difficult to remove
	Additional comments:	Available in a wide range of colors; good color retention; resists moths, mildew, and insects; nonallergenic
Olefin	Durability:	Good
	Soil resistance:	Excellent
	Abrasion resistance:	Excellent
	Resilience:	Average, may flatten and crush
	Care requirements:	Very easy care, stain-resistant, resists almost all acids and chemicals
	Additional comments:	Nonabsorbent; can withstand weather and moisture
Wool	Durability:	Very good
	Soil resistance:	Very good
	Abrasion resistance:	Very good
	Resilience:	Very good
	Care requirements:	Resists soil well but cannot be cleaned as easily as synthetic fibers, may be damaged by alkaline detergents
	Additional comments:	Expensive, flame-resistant, attracts moths
Cotton	Durability:	Fair
	Soil resistance:	Fair unless soil-resistant finish is added
	Abrasion resistance:	Poor
	Resilience:	Poor
	Care requirements:	Easy care, small rugs can be washed and dried at home
	Additional comments:	Not appropriate for high-traffic areas
Rayon	Durability:	Poor
	Soil resistance:	Good
	Abrasion resistance:	Poor
	Resilience:	Poor
	Care requirements:	Easy care
	Additional comments:	Not appropriate for high-traffic areas

Table 4 *Wood Finishes*

Finish	Effect	Use
Bleach	Lightens wood, usually makes grain less conspicuous; wood loses some of its luster; may not be permanent	To make interior wood paneling and furniture pale, blond; give weathered look to outdoor furniture and siding
Enamel	Durable; hard; usually glossy but may be dull; wide range of colors	Primarily used for furniture, cabinets, and walls that get hard use and washing; may be used on floors
Lacquer	Hard, durable coating, resistant to heat, acids; may be glossy, satiny, or dull	Transparent lacquer on furniture, cabinetry, and walls; opaque lacquer on furniture
Oil	Protective but not conspicuous; very durable finish with soft luster; darkens and yellows wood; must be renewed	For indoor and outdoor furniture on siding
Paint	Opaque coating that hides the character of the wood; may be glossy to dull	Widely used on exterior and interior walls and furniture
Polyurethane	A synthetic. Durable; long lasting; resistant to abrasion, most chemicals, and water; may be clear or tinted, and dull to glossy	The most common type of finishing. Good when abrasion, moisture, or weathering is a problem; used on exterior and interior walls, floors, furniture. Has usurped the role once held by shellac and varnish
Shellac	Very little change to character of wood; soft, satiny finish to high-gloss finish; wears poorly; affected by heat and moisture; retains water spots	Primarily a quick-drying undercoat
Stain	Changes color of wood without covering the grain; often emphasizes the grain; usually darkens wood	To alter color of furniture woods; used outdoors to compensate for weathering
Varnish	Thin, durable brownish coating with little penetration; darkens the wood and emphasizes the grain; can be dull to high gloss	Usually used on furniture and interior walls and floors

Table 5 *Woods*

Hardwoods	Characteristics	Uses	Where Found
Apple	Highly variable grain patterns; low productive yield; color ranges from cream white to dark walnut	Furniture and smaller items	Central Asia, Europe, North America
Alder	Uniform grain; lightweight but not strong; resists denting, abrasion; shrinks little; stains well	Chairs and other furniture	North Temperate Zone
Ash	Straight grain; good strength; hard; firm; intermediate in warping; good bending qualities; moderate weight; white in color	Cutting blocks, cabinetwork, furniture frames, exposed parts of less expensive furniture	Europe, North America, Asia
Beech	Strong, dense, hard; warps, shrinks, subject to dry rot; reddish-brown in color; rag marks (small dark dashes); good for turning; polishes well	Cabinetmaking, furniture, flooring, woodware, handles and veneers (especially good for wooden food containers because it does not impart taste to the food)	North America and Europe
Birch (also known as yellow birch, silver birch, and sweet birch)	One of the strongest, hardest woods; little shrinkage or warping; yellow to reddish-brown in color; close-grained; durable; tends to warp; can be stained to imitate mahogany or walnut	Veneer for furniture and doors, flooring, upholstery frames, high-grade plywood, paneling, marquetry	North America, Europe, Asia
Ebony	Very dark brown (may have orange streaks); hard; heavy; very fine texture	Piano keys, ornaments, knife handles, parts of musical instruments, inlaid work, sometimes available as a veneer for repair of antiques	Japan, Philippines, India, Africa, Madagascar (North and South American ebony has little commercial value)
Fruitwoods (apple, cherry, olive, pear)	Fine, straight, close grain; cherry has natural luster; carves and polishes well; excellent for turning and carving	Ornaments, decorative veneers, furniture	Temperate Zone
Gumwood			
Red Gum	Medium strength, weight, or shrinkage; rosy in color with a smooth grain pattern; easily split and dented; susceptible to decay; finishes well	A leading wood for unexposed parts of high-end furniture and exposed parts of low-end furniture	Southern Hemisphere
Tupelo (also called black gum)	White-gray to gray-brown in color; heavier, harder, and has greater tendency to warp than red gum	Unexposed furniture parts	Southeastern United States
Hickory	Strong; tough; good resilience; coarse texture	Handles for hammers etc., sporting equipment	North America
Mahogany	Light reddish-brown in color; durable; strong; resists warping and shrinking; smooth surface; easy to work with; takes polish well	Paneling, ornaments, furniture	Latin America, Africa

Softwoods	Characteristics	Uses	Where Found
Cedar			
Western Red Cedar	Soft; weak; lightweight; close-grained; decay-resistant; pungent spicy odor; light brown in color; holds nails well; low stiffness; easy to work	Shingles and siding of houses, paneling; porch and trellis columns; cabinetwork; interior paneling; some outdoor furniture	True cedar trees grow in Africa and Asia. True cedars are the deodar tree (India), atlas cedar (North Africa), and cedar of Lebanon (Asia). The western red cedar and white cedar are actually juniper trees. They grow in North America
Aromatic or Eastern Red Cedar	Similar to western red cedar except that the wood contains an oil that kills moths	Especially useful in closets and chests to repel moths	North America
Cypress	Moderately strong; resists decay; lightweight	Doors, window sashes, siding, shingles, porch materials	North America, Europe, and Asia
Fir	Warp-resistant; light color; lightweight; easy to work; moderate strength; knots may loosen; tends to check and split; does not stand or paint well	Plywood for exterior and interior walls, doors, cabinetwork, trim, and interior finishing; flooring; low-cost furniture; top-quality fir for cabinets, bookcases	Cooler parts of the North Temperate Zone (North America, Europe, and Asia)
Pine			
Northern White Pine (also called western white pine and sugar pine)	Lightweight; soft; even-textured; relatively weak; easy to work; resistant to shrinkage, warping, and swelling; decays on contact with earth; pale color	Core for veneers; construction; unpainted furniture; interior trim	Subarctic zones to subtropic zones
Yellow Pine	Similar to northern pine, but harder; ideal for carving	Flooring, woodware, furniture, general carpentry	
Redwood	Moderately strong; fine-grained; light red to mahogany in color; resistant to insects; resistant to decay; soft; splinters easily	Outdoor furniture; longterm construction, such as farm structures, towers	Northern California and Oregon
Spruce	Even-textured; easy to use; creamy white in color; medium strength	Cabinetwork; scaffolding; fencing; papermaking	Northern Hemisphere

bibliography

Abercrombie, Stanley. *A Century of Interior Design 1900–2000: A Timetable of the Design, the Designers, the Products, and the Profession*. New York: Rizzoli, 2003.

Aronson, Joseph. *The Encyclopedia of Furniture*. New York: Crown, 1938.

Asensio, Oscar, ed. *Office Furniture Design*. Gloucester, MA: Rockport, 2006.

Auslander, Leora. *Taste and Power: Furnishing Modern France*. Berkeley: University of California Press, 1996.

Blakemore, Robbie. *History of Interior Design and Furniture: From Ancient Egypt to Nineteenth-Century Europe*. New York: Wiley, 1997.

Britton, John. *The Architectural Antiquities of Great Britain*. London: Longman, Hurst, Rees and Orme, 1807.

Caan, Shashi. *Rethinking Design and Interiors: Human Beings in the Built Environment*. London: Laurence King, 2011.

Coates, Michael, Graeme Brooker, and Sally Stone. *The Visual Dictionary of Interior Architecture and Design*. London: Thames & Hudson, 2009.

Crochet, Treena. *Designer's Guide to Furniture Styles*. Upper Saddle River, NJ: Pearson, 2013.

Crouch, Christopher, ed. *Contemporary Chinese Visual Culture: Tradition, Modernity, and Globalization*. Amherst, NY: Cambria Press, 2010.

de Haro, Fernando, and Omar Fuentes. *Mexican Interiors: Current Trends*. Mexico City: AM Editores, 2004.

Dickinson, Joan, et al. "The Design and Testing of a Student Prototyped Homeless Shelter." *Journal of Interior Design* 42(3) (2016): 53–70.

Elleh, Nnamdi. *African Architecture: Evolution and Transformation*. New York: McGraw Hill, 1997.

Farson, Richard. *The Power of Design: A Force for Transforming Everything*. Norcross, GA: Greenway Communications, 2008.

Fleming, John, Hugh Honour, and Nikolaus Pevsner. *The Penguin Dictionary of Architecture and Landscape Architecture*. London: Penguin, 1999.

Getty Research Institute. "Union List of Artist Names Online." http://www.getty.edu/research/tools/vocabularies/ulan. Accessed October 19, 2013.

Gilliatt, Mary. *Mary Gilliatt's Dictionary of Architecture and Interior Design*. New York: Watson-Guptill, 2004.

Ginzberg, Marc. *African Forms*. New York: Abbeville, 2000.

Gloag, John. *A Complete Dictionary of Furniture*. New York: Random House, 1992.

Gura, Judith. *The Abrams Guide to Period Styles for Interiors*. New York: Abrams, 2005.

Gura, Judith. *Design after Modernism: Furniture and Interiors 1970–2010*. New York: Norton, 2012.

Haggar, Reginald. *A Dictionary of Art Terms*. Berkeley: University of California Press, 1962.

Handler, Sarah. *Austere Luminosity of Chinese Classical Furniture*. Berkeley: University of California Press, 2001.

Harwood, Buie, Bridget May, and Curt Sherman. *Architecture and Interior Design through the 18th Century*. Upper Saddle River, NJ: Prentice Hall, 2002.

Hatner, Paul. "What is a Ballast?" https://www.youtube.com/watch?v=4IbjTFDZXBw. Accessed October 1, 2020.

Hinchman, Mark. *History of Furniture: A Global View*. New York: Fairchild, 2009.

Israel, Toby. *Some Place Like Home: Using Design Psychology to Create Ideal Places*. Hoboken, NJ: Wiley, 2003.

Johnson, Samuel. *A Dictionary of the English Language*. London: William Strahan, 1755.

Julier, Guy. *Thames & Hudson Dictionary of Design since 1900*. London: Thames & Hudson, 2004.

Kornfeld, Albert. *The Doubleday Book of Interior Decorating*. New York: Doubleday, 1965.

Kurtich, John, and Garret Eakin. *Interior Architecture*. New York: Van Nostrand Reinhold, 1993.

Lasc, Anca, ed. *Interior Provocation: History, Theory, and Practice of Autonomous Interiors*. New York: Routledge, 2020.

Lees-Maffei, Grace, and Rebecca Houze, eds. *The Design History Reader*. Oxford: Berg, 2010.

Leski, Kyna. *The Storm of Creativity*. Cambridge, MA: MIT Press, 2015.

Lewis, Adam. *The Great Lady Decorators: The Women Who Defined Interior Design, 1870-1955*. New York: Rizzoli, 2010.

Lovell, Sophie. *Furnish: Furniture, and Interior Design for the 21st Century*. Berlin: Die Gestalten Verlag, 2007.

Lucie-Smith, Edward. *Furniture: A Concise History*. London: Thames & Hudson, 1993.

Lupkin, Paula, and Penny Sparke, eds. *Shaping the American Interior: Structures, Contexts, and Practices*. New York: Routledge, 2018.

Massey, Anne. *Interior Design of the Twentieth Century*. London: Thames & Hudson, 1990.

Matthews, Carl, and Caroline Hill. "Niche Housing as Social Prosthetic for LGBT Seniors." *Journal of Interior Design* 42(6) (2016): 29–51.

Mitsuyuki, Hisashi. *Japanese Interiors*. Tokyo: Gakuyo Shobo, 1962.

Morley, John. *The History of Furniture: Twenty-Five Centuries of Style and Design in the Western Tradition*. New York: Little, Brown, 1999.

Móvel, Brasil. "O Móvel Brasil Feira de móveis e decorações, 2013." http://www.movelbrasil.com.br. Accessed October 8, 2013.

Nakamura, Katsuya. *Alcove, Ceiling, and Garden*. Tokyo: Johnan Shoin, 1966.

Nielson, Karla, and David Taylor. *Interiors: An Introduction*. New York: McGraw Hill, 2007.

Ormsbee, Thomas. *The Story of American Furniture*. New York: Macmillan, 1941.

Pile, John. *Drawings of Architectural Interiors*. New York: Whitney Library of Design, 1967.

Piña, Leslie. *Furniture in History: 3000 BC-2000 AD*. Upper Saddle River, NJ: Prentice Hall, 2003.

Piotrowski, Christine. *Designing Commercial Interiors*. New York: Wiley, 2007.

Rabun, Josette, and Catherine Kendall. *The Anglicized and Illustrated Dictionary of Interior Design*. Upper Saddle River, NJ: Pearson/Prentice Hall, 2013.

Roberts, Edna. *Oriental Rugs: The Way to Know and Judge Them*. New York: Dry Goods Economist, 1928.

Ruskin, John. *The Seven Lamps of Architecture*. London: Smith, Elder and Co., 1849.

Santos, Maria Cecilia dos. *Móvel Moderno no Brasil*. São Paulo: Studio Nobel, 1995.

Schreffler, Michael. *The Art of Allegiance: Visual Culture and Imperial Power in Baroque New Spain*. University Park: Pennsylvania State University Press, 2007.

Sheraton, Thomas. *Cabinet-Maker and Upholsterer's Drawing Book*. London: T. Bensley, 1793.

Sieber, Roy. *African Furniture and Household Objects*. Bloomington: Indiana University Press, 1980.

Souchal, Geneviève. *French Eighteenth-Century Furniture: Pleasures and Treasures*. New York: Putnam's Sons, 1961.

Sparke, Penny. *The Modern Interior*. London: Reaktion Books, 2008.

Sullivan, Edward. *The Language of Objects in the Art of the Americas*. New Haven, CT: Yale University Press, 2007.

Taschen, Angelika. *Interiors Now!* Cologne: Taschen, 2010.

Taylor, Mark, and Julieanna Preston. *Intimus: Interior Design Theory Reader*. Chichester, UK: Wiley, 2006.

Thailand Creative & Design Center. "TCDC." http://www.tcdc.or.th/home.php. Accessed May 9, 2013.

Tortora, Phyllis, and Ingrid Johnson. *Dictionary of Textiles*, 8th ed. New York: Fairchild, 2014.

Turner, Jane, ed. *Dictionary of Art*. New York: Grove's Dictionaries, 1996.

Tyler, Norman. *Historic Preservation: An Introduction*. New York: Norton, 2000.

U.S. Department of Agriculture. *The Encyclopedia of Wood*. New York: Skyhorse, 2007.

van Uffelen, Chris. *Performance Architecture + Design*. Salenstein: Braun, 2010.

Victoria and Albert Museum. "Search the Collections." http://collections.vam.ac.uk. Accessed October 8, 2013.

Waugh, Alice. *Interior Design: A Laboratory Manual for House Furnishing*. Minneapolis, MN: Burgess Publishing, 1958.

Wen, Zhu. *Chinese Motifs of Good Fortune*. New York: Better Link Press, 2011.

Wharton, Edith, and Ogden Codman, Jr. *The Decoration of Houses*. New York: Scribner's, 1898.

Whiton, Sherrill. *Interior Design and Decoration*. New York: Harper Collins, 1974.

Wilson, Henry. *India Contemporary*. London: Thames & Hudson, 2007.

Zinnkann, Heidrun. *Roentgenmöbel aus dem Bestand*. Frankfurt: Museum für Angewandte Kunst, 2005.